Investor Protection in Europe

Corporate Law Making, the MiFID and Beyond

Investor Protection in Europe

Corporate Law Making, the MiFID and Beyond

Edited by

Guido Ferrarini and Eddy Wymeersch

OXFORD
UNIVERSITY PRESS

This book has been printed digitally and produced in a standard specification in order to ensure its continuing availability

OXFORD
UNIVERSITY PRESS

Great Clarendon Street, Oxford OX2 6DP

Oxford University Press is a department of the University of Oxford.
It furthers the University's objective of excellence in research, scholarship,
and education by publishing worldwide in

Oxford New York

Auckland Cape Town Dar es Salaam Hong Kong Karachi
Kuala Lumpur Madrid Melbourne Mexico City Nairobi
New Delhi Shanghai Taipei Toronto

With offices in

Argentina Austria Brazil Chile Czech Republic France Greece
Guatemala Hungary Italy Japan South Korea Poland Portugal
Singapore Switzerland Thailand Turkey Ukraine Vietnam

Oxford is a registered trade mark of Oxford University Press
in the UK and in certain other countries

Published in the United States
by Oxford University Press Inc., New York

Reprinted 2007

ISBN 978-0-19-920291-1

Preface

The new century is witnessing a reorientation of EU policy in the area of corporate governance and capital markets. Harmonisation is less frequently a keyword for company law, regulatory competition is on the rise, and soft law is being experimented. Several Member States recently reformed their corporate laws, either as a reaction to financial scandals or in an effort to enhance investments. Convergence has increased as a result, particularly towards Anglo-American standards. Yet, differences still exist, profoundly rooted in national systems of corporate governance. Capital market law would appear to make an exception to it, by having undergone intense harmonisation in the last few years through the Lamfalussy regulatory architecture. Nonetheless, a European system of securities regulation is not yet in place. Regulation is predominantly domestic, each country having its own securities supervisor, while private laws affecting capital markets are still divergent. Cooperation between European securities regulators is on the rise through CESR, however a huge amount of work still needs to be done.

This volume tries to contribute to the on-going debate on corporate and financial law reform from an interdisciplinary perspective. Part 1 examines the political determinants of corporate governance, both in the EU and in the Member States, and asks questions such as the likelihood of convergence and the role of regulatory competition. It also explores the role of competition for investments and different regulatory strategies for harmonisation. Part 2 takes the Markets in Financial Instruments Directive (MiFID) into consideration, for its central role in the harmonisation of EU securities trading and for the intense debate that preceded its adoption. The MiFID represents an ideal case study for those interested in EU financial law making, while possibly accelerating the process of European (and transatlantic) exchange consolidation. Part 3 expands on the legal analysis of the MiFID and other core harmonisation measures, such the Prospectus and Transparency Directives. Part 4 takes this analysis one step further by examining future perspectives in the post-FSAP era, with particular reference to retail investing and investor education, minimum v. maximum harmonisation, post-trade activities, and the perspectives for regulatory structure reform.

Some of the papers included in this volume were presented, in draft form, at a Conference on 'EU Corporate Law Making: Institutional Structure, Regulatory Competition and Regulatory Strategies', held in Cambridge, Mass., on October 29-30, 2004, by initiative of Harvard Law School and ETH, Zurich. We are grateful to Professor Gerard Hertig of ETH and Professor Mark Roe of Harvard, for authorising publication of the relevant papers. Preliminary drafts of other papers were presented at a Conference on 'Capital Markets Integration and Investor Protection in Europe' held in Milan, on November 11-12, 2004, by initiative of Assosim, TLX S.p.A. and the University of Milan. We are grateful to Alessandro Zignani and Marta Cozzi of TLX, Franco Gherra of Assosim, Professors Alessandra Daccò and Andrea Vicari of the University of Milan, for making this Conference possible.

We express our gratitude to Enrica Cremonini and Andrea Zanoni of the Genoa Law School, and Justin Rainey for their assistance in editing this book. Many thanks to Gwen Booth for her encouragement throughout the project.

May 2006
Guido Ferrarini, Genoa
Eddy Wymeersch, Ghent

Contents

Abbreviations .... xiii-xvii

The Contributors .... xix-xxvi

Part 1: Institutional Structure, Regulatory Competition and Regulatory Strategies 1

Chapter1: The Economics and Politics of Corporate Governance in the European Union
by Dennis C. Mueller 3

A. Introduction *3*
B. Corporate Governance and Economic Performance *4*
C. Institutional Explanations for Differences in Performance *15*
D. Is There a Best Corporate Governance System? *20*
E. Are Corporate Governance Systems Converging? *21*
F. Will Corporate Governance Systems Achieve a Full Convergence? *22*

Chapter 2: Political Yardstick Competition and Corporate Governance in the European Union
by Pierre Salmon 31

A. Introduction *32*
B. Selected Features of Yardstick Competition Among Governments *33*
C. The Peculiar Path Borrowed by European Integration *37*
D. Corporate Law and Yardstick Competition Among EU Member Countries *41*
E. Is Yardstick Competition at a Higher Level Likely to Start a Centralizing Dynamic Akin to that of the Single Market? *50*
F. Conclusion *55*

Chapter 3: Using Corporate Law to Compete for Investments
by Ehud Kamar 59

A. Introduction *59*
B. Competition for Investments *64*
C. The Incentives to Compete *80*
D. Normative Implications *99*
E. Toward a General Theory of Regulatory Competition *113*
F. Conclusion *117*

Chapter 4: A Legal Options Approach to EC Company Law
by Gerard Hertig and Joseph A. McCahery 119

A. Introduction *120*
B. Toward a Flexible Approach to EU Company Law *123*

C. Impact on Regulatory Arbitrage and Competition *126*
D. The Benefits of a Pro-Choice Approach *128*
E. Step-by-Step Reform Recommendations *131*
F. Conclusion: The Future of the Pro-Choice Approach *138*

Chapter5: How Can Corporate Governance Codes Be Implemented?
by Eddy Wymeersch 143
A. Regulating Corporate Governance *144*
B. Enforcing Corporate Governance Codes *149*
C. Conclusion *158*

Part 2: The New European Regulation of Trading Venues 161

Chapter 6: The MiFID: Competition in a New European Equity Market Regulatory Structure
by Ryan Davies, Alfonso Dufour and Brian Scott-Quinn 163
A. Introduction *163*
B. Internalisation and Fragmentation *166*
C. U.S. Regulatory Experience *174*
D. European Landscape *179*
E. The MiFID *187*
F. Conclusion *191*

Chapter 7: The European Securities Industry. Further Evidence on the Roadmap to Integration
by Barbara Alemanni, Giuseppe Lusignani and Marco Onado 199
A. Foreword *199*
B. The Roadmap: the European Approach *200*
C. The Roadmap: Main Issues and Findings *211*
D. The Present Landscape *216*
E. The Trading Costs in European Exchanges: A Comparative Analysis *218*
F. Costs of Post-Trading in Europe: A Comparative Analysis *226*
G. Conclusions and Policy Implications *229*

Chapter 8: The MiFID and Internalisation
by Guido Ferrarini and Fabio Recine 235
A. General *236*
B. The ISD Review *241*
C. The MiFID and Internalisation *256*
D. Conclusions *267*

Chapter 9: Internalisation under the MiFID: Regulatory Overreaching or Landmark in Investor Protection?
by Johannes Köndgen and Erik Theissen 271

A. Breaking New Ground in European Securities Regulation *271*
B. The Case for Regulation: Some Economic Fundamentals *274*
C. The German Version of Internalisation: A View on Current (Pre-MiFID) Market Practice and Regulation *277*
D. A Critical Assessment of the Directive *283*
E. Xetra Best – A Blueprint for Other European Exchanges? *290*
F. Conclusions *294*

Part 3: Further Issues in Regulatory Harmonization 297

Chapter 10: The Eclipse of Contract Law in the Investment Firm-Client-Relationship: The Impact of the MiFID on the Law of Contract from a German Perspective
by Peter O. Mülbert 299

A. Introduction *299*
B. The Present Contractual Approach to Regulating the Firm-Client Relationship: The German Example *300*
C. The Contents of the Conduct of Business Obligations: Selected Issues *303*
D. Implications for the (German) Law of Contract Relating to Securities Transactions *316*
E. Concluding Remarks *320*

Chapter 11: Conflicts of Interest in Investment Services: The Price and Uncertain Impact of MiFID's Regulatory Framework
by Luca Enriques 321

A. Introduction *322*
B. Why Specific Rules on Conflicts of Interest? *324*
C. The MiFID and Prospective Level 2 Rules on Conflicts of Interest *325*
D. Too Much Scope for 'Honesty and Fair Dealing' to Achieve Uniformity? *331*
E. Same Rules for Different Investor Protection Needs: A Wise Choice? *334*
F. Conclusions *338*

Chapter 12: The 'Public Offering of Securities' Concept in the New Prospectus Directive
by Alain Pietrancosta 339

A. An Innovative but Evasive Definition of the 'Offer of Securities to the Public' *345*
B. The Clarifications Brought on by an A Contrario Interpretation of the Exemptions *351*

Chapter 13: Nonfinancial Disclosure between 'Shareholder Value' and 'Socially Responsible Investing'
by Francesco Denozza 365

A. Financial and Nonfinancial Disclosure *365*
B. The Notion of Nonfinancial Information *367*
C. The Interpretation of the Transparency Directive and its Relationship with the Market Abuse Directive *368*
D. The Notion of 'Inside Information' *369*
E. From the Interpretation of Law to the Analysis of Conflicts Amongst the Different Interests of the Individuals Involved: The 'Shareholder Value' Model *372*
F. Disclosure Duties: Not a Matter of Increasing Overall Welfare, but of Favouring One Out of Different, Conflicting, Interests *375*

Part 4: After the Financial Services Action Plan 379

Chapter 14: Effective Policy Design for the Retail Investment Services Market: Challenges and Choices Post FSAP
by Niamh Moloney 381

A. The EU Investment Services Market and Retail Investor Policy *381*
B. The Delivery of Retail Policy Through a Regulatory Strategy *386*
C. The Regulatory Strategy as Expressed Through the MiFID Conduct of Business Regime *391*
D. The Risks of a Regulatory Strategy *407*
E. A Multi-Stranded Strategy for the Retail Markets *422*
F. Conclusion *440*

Chapter 15: Financial Market Integration in the Post FSAP Era. In Search of Overall Conceptual Consistency in the Regulatory Framework
by Michel Tison 443

A. Introduction *443*
B. The Underlying Regulatory Concepts: From Minimum to Maximum Harmonisation or Something in Between? *445*
C. Division of Regulatory Powers Between Home and Host State *452*
D. Conclusions *463*

Chapter 16: Securities Clearing and Settlement:Regulatory Developments in Europe
by Eddy Wymeersch 465

A. A Short Introduction to Securities Clearing and Settlement *465*
B. The Legal and Regulatory Environment of Securities Clearing and Settlement *469*
C. Conclusion *483*
D. Later Developments *483*

Chapter 17: Structuring Securities Regulation in the European Union: Lessons from the U.S. Experience
by Donald C. Langevoort 485

A. The Primacy of Enforcement *488*
B. The Influences on SEC Enforcement Discretion *491*
C. The Potential for Home Bias in SEC Enforcement *496*
D. Lessons for the EU *501*
E. Conclusion *506*

Index 507

Abbreviations

ABI	Italian Banking Association
AFTI	Association Francaises des professionals des titres
AG	Aktiengesellshaft (German Stock Corporation)
AnSVG	Gesetz zur Verbesserung des Anlegerschutzes (Law for Improving Investor Protection)
APCIMS	Association of Private Client Investment Managers and Stockbrokers
ATSs	Alternative Trading Systems
Assosim	Associazione Italiana Intermediari Mobiliari (Italian Association of Financial Intermediaries)
AVO	Average Value of Orders
BaFin	Bundesanstalt für Finanzdienstleistungsaufsicht (German Federal Financial Supervisory Authority)
BAWe	Bundesaufsichtsamt für den Wertpapierhandel (German Federal Securities Supervisory Office)
BBA	British Bankers' Association
BGBl	Bundesgesetzblatt
BIS	Bank for International Settlement
BME	Bolsas y Mercados Españoles (Spanish Exchanges and Markets)
bp	basis point
BTDruks	Bundestagsdrucksache
CalPERS	California Public Employees' Retirement System
CBFA	Commission Bancaire, Financière et des Assurances (Belgian Banking, Finance and Insurance Commission)
CC&G	Cassa di Compensazione e Garanzia (Italian clearing house)
CCP	Central Counterparty
CEO	Chief Executive Officer
CEPS	Centre for European Policy Studies
CESAME	Clearing and Settlement Advisory and Monitoring Expert (Group)
CESR	Committee of European Securities Regulator
CFO	Chief Financial Officer
CFS	Center for Financial Studies
CLOB	Central Limit Order Book
COB	Commission des opérations de bourse (former French Echange Commission)
COD	Codified Banking Directive
Consob	Commissione Nazionale per le Società e la Borsa (Italian Financial Services Authority)

CPSS	Committee on Payment and Settlement Systems
CQS	Consolidated Quotation System
CSD	Central Securities Depository
CSX	Chicago Stock Exchange
Ct.	Court
CTA	Consolidated Tape Association
DB	Deutsche Börse
DMD	Distance Marketing Directive
DTCC	The Depository Trust & Clearing Corporation
DTI	Department of Trade and Industry (UK)
DVP	Delivery Versus Payment
EASDAQ	European Association of Securities Dealers Automatic Quotation
EC	European Commission
ECGF	European Corporate Governance Forum
ECGI	European Corporate Governance Institute
ECJ	European Court of Justice
ECMI	European Capital Market Institute
ECN	Electronic Communication Network
ECOFIN	Council of Economics and Finance Ministers of the European Union
ECON	Committee on Economic and Monetary Affairs
ECOSOC	European Economic and Social Committee
ECSDA	European Association of Central Securities Depositories
EIRIS	Ethical Investors Research Services
EMU	European Monetary Union
ERISA	Employee Retirement Income Security Act
ESC	European Securities Committee
ESCB	European System of Central Banks
ESF	European Securities Forum
ETF	Exchange Traded Fund
EU	European Union
FBE	European Banking Federation
FBF	French Banking Federation
FD	Fair Disclosure
FESCO	Forum of European Securities Commissions
FinDAG	Gesetz über die Bundesanstalt für Finanzdienstleistungsaufsicht (Law Establishing the Federal Financial Supervisory Authority)
FIN-NET	Consumer Complaints Network for Financial Services
FIN-USE	Forum of user experts in the area of financial services
FOA	The Futures and Options Association
FRC	Financial Reporting Council

FSA	Financial Services Authority
FSAP	Financial Services Action Plan
FSAPs	Financial Stability Assessment Programmes
FSE	Frankfurt Stock Exchange
FWB	Frankfurter Wertpapierbörse
GAAP	Generally Accepted Accounting Principles
Gazz. Uff. Supp. Ord.	Gazzetta Ufficiale Supplemento Ordinario (Italian Official Gazzette Ordinary Supplement)
GDP	Gross Domestic Product
GmbH	Gesellshaft mit beschränkter Haftung
IAS	International Accounting Standards
ICSDs	International Central Securities Depositories
IDA	Ireland Development Authority
IFRS	International Financial Reporting Standards
IIMG	Inter Institutional Monitoring Group
IMF	International Monetary Fund
IOSCO	International Organization of Securities Commissions
IPMA	International Project Management Association
IPO	Initial Public Offering
IRI	Istituto per la Ricostruzione Industriale (Italian Institute for Industrial Reconstruction)
ISD	Investment Services Directive
ISDA	International Swap and Derivative Association
ISMA	International Securities Market Association
ITS	Intermarket Trading System
KapAEG	Kapitalaufnahmeerleichterungsgesetz (Capital Raising Relief Law)
KapMuG	Gesetz über Musterverfahren in kapitalmarktrechtlichen Streitigkeiten (Law on Model Case Proceedings in Disputes under Capital Markets Law)
KonTraG	Gesetz zur Kontrolle und Transparenz im Unternehmensbereich (Law on Control and Transparency in Business Enterprises)
LCH	London Clearing House
LIBA	London Investment Banking Association
LIFFE	London International Financial Futures and Options Exchange
LLC	Limited Liability Corporation
LLP	Limited Liability Partnership
LSE	London Stock Exchange
MAD	Market Abuse Directive
MEFF	Mercado Español de Futuros Financieros (Futures and Options Spanish Official Market)
MiFID	Markets in Financial Instruments Directive

MTFs	Multilateral Trading Facilities
Murcef	Mesures urgentes de réformes à caractère économique et financier (Urgent Economic and Financial Reform Measures)
NAASA	North American Securities Administrators Association
NASDAQ	National Association of Securities Dealers Automatic Quotation
NBBO	National Best Bid and Offer
NCSD	Nordic Central Securities Depository
NMS	National Market System
NYSE	New York Stock Exchange
OECD	Organisation for Economic Co-operation and Development
OFT	Office of Fair Trading
OTC	Over-The-Counter
PIP	Price Improvement Platform
PLC	Public Limited Corporation
POSIT	Portfolio System for Institutional Trading
PSSS	Payment Systems and Securities Settlement Systems
RMs	Regulated Markets
RSP	Retail Service Provider
SE	Societas Europaea
SEC	Securities and Exchange Commission
SENAF	Sistema Electrónico de Negociación de Activos Financieros (Spanish Electronic Trading System of Financial Assets)
SIA	Securities Industry Association
SIBE	Sistema de Interconexión Bursátil Español (Spanish Central Electronic Trading Platform)
SMEs	Small and Medium Enterprises
SMS	Standard Market Size
SOES	Small Order Execution System
SOX/SOA	Sarbanes-Oxley Act
SRO	Self-Regulatory Organization
SSO	Sistema di Scambio Organizzato (Italian Alternative Trading System)
STP	Straight Through Processing
StSenkG	Gesetz zur Senkung der Steuersätze und zur Reform der Unternehmensbesteuerung (Law on Reduction of Tax Rates and Reform of Business Taxation)
TBMA	The Bond Market Association
TransPuG	Transparenz und Publizitätgesetz (Law for further Reform of Stock and Accounting Law to Achieve Transparency and Disclosure)

UCITS	Undertakings for Collective Investment in Transferable Securities
UKLA	United Kingdom Listing Authority
UMAG	Gesetz zur Unternehmensintegrität und Modernisierung des Anfechtungsrechts (Law on Corporate Integrity and Modernization of Rescission Proceedings)
wp	working paper
WpÜG	Wertpapiererwebs-und Übernahmegesetz (Securities Acquisition and Takeover Law)

The Contributors

Barbara Alemanni

Barbara Alemanni is Professor of financial markets and institutions at the University of Genoa. She is a research affiliate of the Bocconi University Financial Innovation Research Centre (NEWFIN) and is faculty member of SDA-Bocconi MBA programme. She received a master in finance from the CUBS in London. Her research interests are financial markets structure, securities market microstructure and behavioural finance.

Ryan Davies

Ryan J. Davies is an Assistant Professor and holder of the Lyle Howland Term Chair in Finance at Babson College. Previously, he was a lecturer at the ICMA Centre, University of Reading. He received a Ph.D. in economics from Queen's University in Canada. He is currently conducting research on methods to estimate trading costs; the role of stale limit orders in causing portfolio return patterns; mutual fund manager trading behaviour; and optimal fund of hedge funds portfolio allocation. His latest working papers can be found at: http://faculty.babson.edu/rdavies.

Francesco Denozza

Francesco Denozza graduated at the University of Milan on July 13, 1968; Professor of Industrial Law at the University of Ferrara and later at the University of Modena; Professor of Commercial Law at the University of Brescia; since 1986 to date, Professor of Commercial Law, Faculty of Law, University of Milan. From 1990 to 1992, Director of the Institute of Commercial Law, Faculty of Law, University of Milan; from May 2001 to November 2002, Director of the Milan University School of Specialization for the Legal Profession. He is Co-Editor of the legal review 'Giurisprudenza Commerciale'.
Researcher at the Juristisches Seminar of the Tuebingen University 1971-1972; Visiting Scholar at the University of California at Berkeley 1996. Since November 2001 member of the Board of Directors of Telecom Italia spa. Since March 2005 Presidente Collegio Sindacale Siemens spa. He is a member of the Milan Bar.

Alfonso Dufour

Alfonso Dufour is a lecturer in Finance at the ICMA Centre, University of Reading. He has conducted extensive research on market structures, intraday dynamics of asset prices and liquidity and has advised market regulators and exchange officials. He holds an MA and a PhD in Economics from the University of California, San Diego where he has collaborated with 2003 Nobel prize laureate Robert F. Engle.

Luca Enriques

Luca Enriques is Professor of Business Law at the University of Bologna Faculty of Law and ECGI Research Associate. He received a doctorate in business law at the Bocconi University (Milan) (1999), an LL.M. at Harvard Law School (1996) and a law degree at the University of Bologna (1993). He advises the Italian Ministry of the Economy on policy issues in banking, securities and corporate law and is a member of the Forum of market experts on auditors' liability set up by the European Commission in 2005. His research focuses on corporate law, corporate governance, takeovers and securities law.

Guido A. Ferrarini

Guido Ferrarini graduated from the Genoa Law School in 1972, and obtained an LL.M. from Yale Law School in 1978. He is Professor of Business Law at the University of Genoa and Director, Centre for Law and Finance. He is Lead Independent Director of Telecom Italia S.p.A.; Independent Director of Autostrade S.p.A., and Chairman of TLX (an Italian MTF and investment exchange). He is Vice-Chairman and Fellow of the European Corporate Governance Institute (ECGI), Brussels, and Independent Director of Assogestioni (the Italian Asset Managers Association). He was a member of the Board of Trustees of the International Accounting Standards Committee (IASC), London, from 2000 to 2004. He is the author of various books and articles in the fields of financial law, corporate law, and business law. He was a Visiting Professor at Bonn University, Columbia Law School, Hamburg University, NYU Law School and University College London. He was Commerzbankstiftung Visiting Professor at the Institute for Law and Finance, Frankfurt University, for the Spring Semester 2006.

Gerard Hertig

Gerard Hertig is Professor of Law and Economics at the Swiss Federal Institute of Technology (ETH Zurich), where he is responsible professor for the post-graduate program 'Intellectual Property'. He teaches intellectual property and specializes in corporate law and financial services. He was previously Professor of Administrative Law and Director of the Centre d'Etudes Juridiques Européennes at the University of Geneva Law School (1987-1995). He served as Visiting Professor at UCL (Louvain), ULB (Brussels), Collège of Europe, University of Tokyo and practiced law as a member of the Geneva bar. Recent publications include: 'On Going Board Reforms: One Size Fits All and Regulatory Capture', 21 Oxford Review of Economic Policy 269 (2005); 'Using Basel II to Facilitate Access to Finance: The Disclosure of Internal Credit Ratings', in Klaus J. Hopt et al. (eds.), Corporate Governance in Context, Corporations, States, and Markets in Europe, Japan, and the US 511 (Oxford University Press 2005); The Anatomy of Corporate Law, A Comparative and Functional Approach, with Reinier Kraakman et al (Oxford University Press 2004) .

Ehud Kamar

Ehud Kamar is a professor of law at the University of Southern California, specializing in corporate and securities law, mergers and acquisitions, and corporate governance. His work examines the interplay between law and economics, the balance between certainty and flexibility in the law, and regulatory competition. He was a visiting professor at New York University in 2005 and will be a visiting professor at Harvard University in 2006-07. He has practiced law in Israel and New York and was a J. William Fulbright Scholar. His publications include 'A Regulatory Competition Theory of Indeterminacy in Corporate Law' (Columbia Law Review, 1998); 'Shareholder Litigation Under Indeterminate Corporate Law' (University of Chicago Law Review, 1999); 'Price Discrimination in the Market for Corporate Law' (Cornell Law Review, 2001); and 'The Myth of State Competition in Corporate Law', Stanford Law Review, 2002).

Johannes Köndgen

Johannes Köndgen holds the Commercial and Comparative Law Chair at the Rheinische Friedrich-Wilhelms-Universität School of Law in Bonn, Germany. He is a graduate of the University of Tübingen (1969), where he also received his doctorate in law. Prior to joining the Bonn faculty Professor Köndgen held chairs at the Universities of Hannover, Hamburg, and St. Gallen (Switzerland). He has also been a visiting professor of law at Oxford, Strasbourg, London (University College) and Gainsville (University of Florida). Between 1984 and 1990 he served as a judge at the Hamburg Court of Appeals. Professor Köndgen is a managing editor of the Journal of Banking Law and Financial Economics (Zeitschrift für Bankrecht und Bankwirtschaft). His recent publications include topics from German and international banking regulation, stock markets law, European private law, and real estate financing (law of mortgage banks).

Donald C. Langevoort

Donald C. Langevoort is the Thomas Aquinas Reynolds Professor of Law at Georgetown University Law Center, Washington, D.C. He joined the Georgetown faculty in 1999 after eighteen years at Vanderbilt University School of Law, where he had been the Lee S. & Charles A. Speir Professor. He has also been a visiting professor at the University of Michigan, Harvard Law School, and the University of Sydney in Australia. Professor Langevoort graduated from the Harvard Law School in 1976, and went into private practice with the law firm of Wilmer, Cutler & Pickering in Washington. In 1978, he joined the staff of the U.S. Securities & Exchange Commission as Special Counsel in the Office of the General Counsel.

Since entering academia in 1981, Professor Langevoort has written a treatise on insider trading, co-authored a casebook on securities regulation, and produced numerous law review articles on topics such as insider trading, the impact of technology on securities regulation, investor behavior and the intersection between cognitive psychology and lawyers' professional responsibilities. He has served on the Legal Advisory Committee of the New York Stock Exchange, the Legal Advisory Board of the National Association of Securities Dealers, the SEC's Advisory Committee on Market Information (chairing its subcommittee on alternative models for data consolidation), and the Nominating Committee of the Municipal Securities Rulemaking Board, and has testified numerous times before Congressional committees on matters relating to securities regulation and litigation. Professor Langevoort is also a member of the American Law Institute.

Giuseppe Lusignani

Giuseppe Lusignani is Professor of Banking and Finance at the University of Bologna. After the degree in Economics at the University of Modena (1984), he studied Finance at the Graduate School of Business Administration, New York University (1986-87) and received a doctoral degree in Financial Markets and Institutions from the University of Bergamo (1989). His research focuses on financial markets structures, risk management, asset management and financial regulation. He has advised and carried out research projects for the Bank of Italy, Con-sob and the Italian Antitrust Authority. He is Chairman (independent) of CR Firenze Gestion Internationale S.A., member of the Board of Directors of Banca Popolare dell'Emilia Romagna, and of the 'Wise Men' Committee of TLX (an Italian MTF and investment exchange).

Joseph A. McCahery

Joseph A. McCahery is Professor of Corporate Governance and Innovation at the University of Amsterdam Faculty of Economics and Econometrics. He is also Professor of International Business Law at Tilburg University Faculty of Law, Research Fellow at the Tilburg Center of Law and Economics, and Research Associate at the European Corporate Governance Institute (Brussels). Previously, he held an appointment at Warwick University, where he also received a Ph.D. degree. He was also a law clerk for Judge Nathaniel R. Jones of the US Court of Appeals for the Sixth Circuit. He researches interests are corporate control, corporate finance, European corporate law, the political economy of federalism, and international banking and securities regulation. He has written extensively on corporate law, corporate governance, securities, and regulation.

Niamh Moloney

Niamh Moloney (LL.B, Trinity College Dublin (1992), LL.M., Harvard (1993)) is Professor of Capital Markets Law at the School of Law, University of Nottingham. She is the author of the first book on EC capital markets and investment services law (EC Securities Regulation, OUP (2002)) and has published numerous articles on this subject. She is a Research Associate of the European Corporate Governance Institute.

Dennis C. Mueller

Dennis C. Mueller is professor of economics at the University of Vienna. His main research interests are in public choice, industrial economics and constitutional political economy. He is the author of many articles and several books; among them being Public Choice III (Cambridge University Press, 2003), The Corporation (Routledge, 2003) and Constitutional Democracy (Oxford University Press, 1996). Dennis Mueller is a past president of the Public Choice Society, the Southern Economic Association, the Industrial Organization Society, E.A.R.I.E., the International Joseph A. Schumpeter Society and the European Public Choice Society.

Peter O. Mülbert

Peter O. Mülbert is Professor of Civil Law, Corporate Law and Securities Law, Banking Law and Director of the Institut für deutsches und internationales Recht des Spar,- Giro- und Kreditwesens. at Johannes Gutenberg University (Mainz). Previously, he was Professor of Law at Heidelberg University and Trier University. He is Director of the Bankrechtliche Vereinigung, Member of the German Takeover Council and Research Associate at the European Corporate Governance Institute (Brussels).

Marco Onado

Marco Onado is professor of Financial Intermediation in the Bocconi University of Milan and previously in the Universities of Modena (1972-1984) and Bologna (1984-2001). He has been a commissioner of Consob, the Italian financial regulator (1993-1998). He is author or co-author of many papers in the field of financial regulation, corporate governance, economics of financial markets, economics of asset management. He has coordinated an important research project of 'Ente Luigi Einaudi', Rome on 'Towards a European financial system' (2002-2005).
He is member (independent) of the board of directors of Telecom Italia (listed in Milan and New York) and chairman (independent) of Pioneer Global Asset Management (Unicredito group).

Alain Pietrancosta

Alain Pietrancosta is Professor of French and European business, company, financial and securities law at the University of Paris I Panthéon-Sorbonne. He also teaches in the joint masters degree program run by the University of Paris I Panthéon-Sorbonne, the Institute of Political Studies of Paris ('Sciences Po'), Columbia Law School, Cornell University School of Law. He is director of the newly created Masters of Securities Regulation program at the University of Paris I Panthéon-Sorbonne. Member of the European Corporate Governance Institute (ECGI), founding member of the Financial Law Research Center of the University of Paris I Panthéon-Sorbonne and a director of the Financial Law Association (ADFIN), Professor Pietrancosta is also the founder and director of the new 'Revue Trimestrielle de Droit Financier – Corporate Finance and Capital Markets Law Review'.

Fabio Recine

Fabio Recine is senior expert in the Financial Stability Directorate of the European Central Bank. He joined the ECB staff in 2000, and he was the ECB's representative in the EU Council Working Groups on: the review of the Investment Services Directive; the Transparency Directive; the Regulation on International Accounting Standards. Previously, he worked in a law firm in Genoa and in the Supervision Department of Banca d'Italia in Rome.
He graduated from the University of Genoa, School of Law with a thesis on 'Institutional and contractual aspects of merchant banking in Italy', for which he was awarded the Banca d'Italia Menichella Prize. He holds a doctorate in law in Banking Law and Regulation, University of Siena, and an LL.M. from the London School of Economics. He is a member of the Genoa Law Bar.

Pierre Salmon

Pierre Salmon is professor of economics emeritus at the Université de Bourgogne (Dijon, France) and remains an active member of one of its research centres (Laboratoire d'Economie et de Gestion -UMR CNRS 5118). After undergraduate studies in private law at the University of Paris and of public administration at the Institut d'Etudes Politiques de Paris ('Sciences Po'), he specialized in economics at the post-graduate level, both at the University of Rennes (France) and at the University of Paris (where he obtained his doctorate in 1965). He was professor of economics at the Université de Bourgogne and for a few years at the European University Institute in Florence (Italy). He also spent some time in the central administration in Paris, in particular as Counsellor for Social Science in the department for scientific research of the French government. He is a past president of the European Public Choice Society and vice-president of the Villa Colombella Group on the Economics of Institutions. Pierre Salmon's two main research interests are economic methodology and the economic approach to politics. He is the co-author of a book on economic methodology and the co-editor of several books in the second area. He has published articles and contributed chapters to volumes in both fields. Following 'Decentralisation as an Incentive Scheme', published in the *Oxford Review of Economic Policy* (1987), several of these articles and chapters concern yardstick competition among governments.

Brian Scott-Quinn

Professor Brian Scott-Quinn is Chairman of the International Capital Markets Association (ICMA) Centre – the business school for financial markets which he created as a new venture in 1991 at the University of Reading. It has since received donations from ICMA amounting to £5m for the construction of new facilities. It has also recently formed a joint venture with the National Association

of Securities Dealers (NASD), the regulator of the NASDAQ market, for the provision of regulation and compliance training outside the US. In 1981, he became finance director of Drexel Burnham Lambert Securities Ltd. In 1986, he became strategy advisor to the Chief Executive of Security Pacific Hoare Govett.
His research area is the functioning of securities exchanges and clearing, settlement & payments mechanisms. He has been a consultant to the chief executive of the London Stock Exchange (LSE) and was on the Market Advisory Panel of Tradepoint Investment Exchange (now Virt-X). He has been a consultant to the US Treasury and to a central bank as well as to a number of commercial/ investment banks. He was a monetary policy advisor to a former UK Chancellor of the Exchequer, Lord Howe of Aberavon (Sir Geoffrey Howe). As well as speaking at many industry conferences, he has published 'The New Euromarkets', 'The Eurodollar System', and 'Investment Banking' as well as many papers on trading systems, clearing and settlement, offshoring financial services (published by the Corporation of London in March 2005), the Single European Securities Trading Market, and European financial market regulation. He was the academic member of the Financial Services Authority (FSA) industry working group on Secondary Bond Market Transparency which examined issues relevant to the forthcoming EU, Markets in Financial Instruments, Directive (MiFID).

Erik Theissen

Erik Theissen is professor of Finance at the University of Bonn. He received his PhD from the University of Frankfurt in 1997. He was assistant Professor in Finance at the University of Frankfurt and visiting assistant professor at Groupe HEC, Jouy-en-Josas, before accepting an offer from the university of Bonn in 2000. The focus of his research is empirical finance with a special emphasis on the organization of and the price formation in securities markets.

Michel Tison

Michel Tison is professor at the Financial Law Institute, Ghent University (Belgium), where he graduated in law (1990) and obtained a Ph.D. degree in law with a thesis on the European internal market for banking and financial services (1997). He teaches courses in domestic and European banking and securities law, corporations and general commercial law. He has published on various issues of domestic, comparative and European banking and financial law, company law and insolvency law. He was visiting professor at the University of Pittsburgh in winter 2001, and at the University of Bonn in 2004. He was appointed assessor at the legislative section of the Council of State in 2005.

Eddy Wymeersch

At present, Chairman of the Banking Finance and Insurance Commission, Belgium; co-chair of the CESR-ECB, working on clearing and settlement; member of the Committee of European Securities Regulators (CESR); chairman of the

European Regional Committee of IOSCO; member of the European Corporate Governance Forum. Part-time Professor of Commercial Law, University of Ghent where he is teaching company law, securities regulation and banking law. Formerly Consultant to EC Commission, World Bank and IFC; member of the corporate governance commission of the Brussels stock exchange and chairman of the SLIM working party (Simpler Legislation for the Internal Market) on the 1st and 2nd directive. He also acted as adviser to the Belgian Government, inter alia as member of the Legislative Branch of the Council of State. He was a member of the Board of the National Bank of Belgium and the Belgian Corporate Governance Commission. He was Chairman of the Board of Brussels International Airport Company (BIAC) and adviser on governance issues to several listed Belgian companies. He has published extensively on securities regulation, company law, especially groups of companies, and corporate governance in the Belgian, European and comparative perspective.

Part 1:

Institutional Structure, Regulatory Competition and Regulatory Strategies

The Economics and Politics of Corporate Governance in the European Union

DENNIS C. MUELLER

Over the last 25 years the term 'corporate governance' has entered the lexicon of economists and other students of business. This development has been accompanied by growing interest in differences in institutional structures – like corporate governance systems – across countries. Among the many questions regarding the effects of corporate governance systems that have been examined, one of the most important has been to measure the effects of corporate governance systems on corporate performance somehow measured, or more broadly the economic performance of countries. This paper reviews some of this evidence and takes up the questions of which system is 'best', and whether this superiority is likely to lead to a convergence of corporate governance structures over time. With a few exceptions, most studies of the effects of corporate governance institutions treat them as exogenous. This paper also discusses the historical and political determinants of corporate governance institutions.

A. Introduction
B. Corporate Governance and Economic Performance
C. Institutional Explanations for Differences in Performance
D. Is There a Best Corporate Governance System?
E. Are Corporate Governance Systems Converging?
F. Will Corporate Governance Systems Achieve a Full Convergence?

A. Introduction

Over the last 25 years the term 'corporate governance' has entered the lexicon of economists and other students of business. This development has been accompanied by growing interest in differences in institutional structures – like corporate governance systems – across countries. A generation ago theoretical models of the firm (often implicitly) would have assumed an 'Anglo-Saxon' institutional environment, and empirical tests of various hypotheses would be made using data from the United States, or perhaps other Anglo-Saxon countries like the United Kingdom or Canada. Today economics and finance journals are filled with empirical investigations of corporate behavior and performance in countries with non-Anglo-Saxon institutions with Continental Europe, Asia, and the transition countries being popular choices for data samples. Although the literature is still dominated by researchers from Anglo-Saxon countries, their research is no longer confined to analyses of companies in these countries.

Among the many questions regarding the effects of corporate governance systems that have been examined, one of the most important has been to measure the effects of corporate governance systems on corporate performance somehow measured, or more broadly the economic performance of countries. As recently as a decade ago, some scholars saw 'insider corporate governance' systems in which banks play an important role monitoring managers and allocating capital as superior to the 'outsider systems' of the Anglo-Saxon countries.[1]

More recent research has tended to claim superiority for Anglo-Saxon institutions.[2] Some evidence regarding this question is summarized and discussed in the next section. We take up the questions of which system is 'best', and whether this superiority is likely to lead to a convergence of corporate governance structures over time in the final two sections of the paper.

Most studies of the effects of corporate governance institutions treat them as exogenous variables. Germany and France have insider-systems with large fractions of a company's shares or votes controlled by a single family or institution. The United States and United Kingdom have widely dispersed share distributions. A few studies have questioned why this is so, which is to say they have treated corporate governance institutions as *endogenous* variables. The historical and political determinants of corporate governance institutions are discussed in Section C. Knowledge of the determinants of corporate governance institutions is, of course, essential when making predictions about whether corporate governance systems can change or are likely to converge.

B. Corporate Governance and Economic Performance

I. The Effects of Legal Systems

The assumption that corporate governance institutions have important effects on corporate and economic performance rests on the assumption that there are potential principal-agent problems between managers and owners of a firm. A company's performance as judged by its shareholders suffers, if managers can use their positions to advance their interests instead of those of the shareholders. The most blatant examples of such conflicts of interest involve managers diverting the resources of the firm into their own pockets – as occurred at Enron. Less conspicuous conflicts can arise, however, over dividend and investment policies. Starting with Robin Marris (1964) a large literature has posited that managers are

[1] See, for example, RJ Gilson and MJ Roe (1993), and JP Charkham (1994).

[2] See, for example, R LaPorta, F Lopez-de-Silanes, A Shleifer and R Vishny (1997, 2000), and K Gugler, DC Mueller and BB Yurtoglu (2003, 2004b).

'empire builders' who pursue growth in excess of the levels which would maximize shareholder wealth.[3]

The pursuit of excessive growth by managers produces a conflict between them and their shareholders over dividend and investment policies. From the perspective of the shareholders, growth-maximizing managers invest too much and pay out too little in dividends. Here it is important to keep in mind that investment might not solely take the form of purchases of plant and equipment in a company's major line of economic activity, but may also consist of unprofitable diversification and wealth-destroying mergers.

The conflict between managers and shareholders over dividends and investment underlies LaPorta, Lopez-de-Silanes, Shleifer and Vishny's (2000) test of the importance of legal institutions in aligning shareholders' and managers' interests. They argue that Anglo-Saxon legal institutions are better at aligning shareholders' and managers' interests than civil law systems, and within the latter category that Scandinavian legal systems are better than Germanic-origin systems, with French-origin systems offering shareholders the least amount of protection. Column 3 of Table 1 reports the dividend payout ratios for large listed companies in a set of countries arranged in accordance with the LaPorta, Lopez-de-Silanes, Shleifer and Vishny legal system categorization. I have limited the set of countries to Europe and the highly developed Anglo-Saxon countries outside of Europe (Australia, Canada, New Zealand and the United States) to eliminate differences in stages of development that might affect cross-national comparisons. The mean dividend-to-sales payout ratios conform to the predictions of LaPorta, Lopez-de-Silanes, Shleifer and Vishny insofar as the mean ratio for the Anglo-Saxon countries substantially exceeds that for each of the three civil law groups. Within the civil law countries, however, the four Scandinavian countries have the lowest mean payout ratio, where LaPorta, Lopez-de-Silanes, Shleifer and Vishny would predict that they should have the highest ratio.

[3] Early contributions to this literature include DC Mueller (1969, 1972), WJ Baumol, P Heim, BG Malkiel and RE Quandt (1970), and H Grabowski and DC Mueller (1972, 1975). Two recent empirical tests of the hypothesis are RM Stulz (1990), and DJ Denis, DK Denis and A Sarin (1997).

Country	No. of firms	Dividend pay-out (% sales)	qm= r/i	Returns on equity	External Capital/ GDP	Domestic firms/ pop.	IPOs/ pop.	GDP growth
Anglo-Saxon								
Australia	346	0.048	0.94	0.082	0.49	63.55		3.06
Canada	1,478	0.027	1.16	0.097	0.39	40.86	4.93	3.36
Great Britain	1,331	0.035	0.85	0.129	1.00	35.68	2.01	2.27
Ireland	63	0.017	1.10	0.138	0.27	20.00	0.75	4.25
New Zealand	66	0.040	0.86	0.059	0.28	69.00	0.66	1.67
United States	8,591	0.026	1.05	0.118	0.58	30.11	3.11	2.74
Mean		**0.032**	**0.99**	**0.104**	**0.50**	**43.20**	**2.29**	**2.89**
Scandinavian								
Denmark	101	0.014	0.65	0.138	0.21	50.40	1.80	2.09
Finland	79	0.015	0.96	0.088	0.25	13.00	0.60	2.40
Norway	103	0.018	1.04	0.123	0.22	33.00	4.50	3.43
Sweden	156	0.019	0.65	0.152	0.51	12.66	1.66	1.79
Mean		**0.017**	**0.78**	**0.125**	**0.30**	**27.26**	**2.14**	**2.42**
Germanic								
Austria	82	0.031	0.71	0.105	0.06	13.87	0.25	2.74
Germany	425	0.015	0.57	0.117	0.13	5.14	0.08	2.60
Switzerland	160	0.022	0.64	0.136	0.62	33.85		1.18
Mean		**0.023**	**0.64**	**0.119**	**0.27**	**17.62**	**0.16**	**2.17**
French								
Belgium	79	0.026	0.51	0.144	0.17	15.50	0.30	2.46
France	495	0.020	0.57	0.116	0.23	8.05	0.17	2.54
Italy	150	0.014	0.64	0.067	0.08	3.91	0.31	2.82
Luxembourg	12	0.010	0.70					
Netherlands	174	0.034	0.69	0.155	0.52	21.13	0.66	2.55
Portugal	49	0.010	0.46	0.231	0.08	19.50	0.50	3.52
Spain	117	0.035	0.54	0.098	0.17	9.71	0.07	3.27
Mean		**0.021**	**0.59**	**0.135**	**0.21**	**12.97**	**0.34**	**2.86**

Table 1: Differences across countries in legal systems and various economic statistics.

If all companies have the same levels of investment opportunities relative to their cash flows, all will have the same optimal retention ratio for maximizing shareholder wealth, and all will have the same optimal dividend payout ratio. Lower dividend payout ratios will imply overinvestment and more significant agency problems. When investment opportunities differ across firms, however, so too will optimal retention and dividend ratios. For a company with very attractive investment opportunities, the optimal dividend payout for the shareholders may be zero. Indeed, for firms with very attractive investment opportunities, no conflict between managers and shareholders over investment and growth may exist. Both wish to see the firm raise as much capital and grow as fast as possible (Mueller 1972). Thus, a better test for the presence of agency problems would be to compare companies' returns on investment to their costs of capital. For companies which maximize shareholder wealth, returns on investment should equal their costs of capital. Firms with growth-maximizing managers will have returns on investment that are less than their costs of capital.

Column 4 of Table 1 reports estimates of the ratios of returns on investment to costs of capital for large companies listed on the stock exchanges of each country. (The number of firms in each country sample is presented in column 2). These figures constitute estimates of a *marginal* Tobin's q, and are thus designated as q_m.[4] The means of each set of estimates are in *exact* accordance with the LaPorta, Lopez-de-Silanes, Shleifer and Vishny predictions based on the country legal system categorization. Four of the six estimates are either insignificantly different from 1.0, or significantly greater than 1.0 (Australia, Canada, Ireland, and the United States), with the mean q_m for the Anglo-Saxon countries being just under 1.0. In contrast the mean q_m for *none* of the other three country groups comes close to 1.0, with the relative sizes of the means conforming exactly to the predictions of LaPorta, Lopez-de-Silanes, Shleifer and Vishny (Scandinavian $q_m = 0.78$ > Germanic-origin $q_m = 0.64$ > French-origin $q_m = 0.59$). *No* country with either a Germanic- or French-origin legal system had an estimated q_m equal to or greater than 1.0.

For testing for the existence of agency problems, marginal q is superior to both Tobin's q, which is often used as a measure of company investment performance, and dividend payout ratios. We have already commented on the difficulty with the latter, and this problem is nicely illustrated by the figure for Ireland. Ireland had the lowest dividend payout ratio of any Anglo-Saxon country (0.017), a figure that is also less than the mean values for both the German- and French-origin countries. Yet, the estimate of q_m for Ireland is above 1.0 indicating an absence of agency problems regarding investment for the average Irish firm. Apparently Irish firms had very attractive investment opportunities – as suggested

[4] The methodology for estimating these marginal qs was first presented in DC Mueller and E Reardon (1993).

by the very large mean growth rate of the economy reported in column 9 – and thus low dividend payouts were consistent with optimal dividend payout policies.

Tobin's q is a measure of a firm's *average* investment performance and equals the ratio of the returns on its total capital stock to its cost of capital. A company like Microsoft could have a very large Tobin's q because of large infra-marginal monopoly rents, and yet be wasting its shareholders' money through bad investments like mergers. To test for the presence of agency problems with respect to investment policies, it is the ratio of returns on investment to cost of capital that is relevant, and these ratios suggest significant agency problems in non-Anglo-Saxon countries with the severest problems being in the countries with Germanic- and French-origin legal systems.

After presenting estimates of marginal q like those in Table 1, I am often asked how it would be possible that firms in countries like Belgium and France can survive. Will shareholders not abandon them, and thus they will not be able to raise capital to finance investment? Here it is important to emphasize the difference between returns on the investments companies make, and returns on their shares. Once the market recognizes the existence and size of an agency problem, the share price of a company adjusts to reflect the magnitude of this problem and shareholders can expect to earn the same returns on this company's shares as on one whose managers maximize shareholder wealth. Abnormal returns on shares are a result of unexpected changes in company policies not of the policies themselves. This point is confirmed in column 5, where estimates of returns on common equities in each country are reported. The highest returns on equity were earned by shareholders in the French-origin countries, the lowest returns were earned in the Anglo-Saxon countries.

In countries with weak protections for minority shareholders, both the demand and supply of new shares will be lower. Individuals will be reluctant to purchase shares for fear of being exploited by the managers, founding owner-managers will be reluctant to issue shares because they will not be able to sell them at an attractive price. In countries with weak minority shareholder protection, the market for shares suffers from a form of the lemons' problem and can be expected to be very thin.[5] These predictions are by and large confirmed in columns 6-8 of Table 1, where three measures of the size of external capital markets are presented – the value of all equities listed on a country's stock exchange divided by GDP, the number of domestic firms divided by population, and the number of IPOs divided by population. All three measures are highest for the Anglo-Saxon countries and lowest for either the French-origin (first two), or German-origin countries (third). Additional evidence linking the size of external capital markets to the strength of corporate governance institutions has been presented by Modigliani and Perotti (1997) and Demirgüç-Kunt and Maksimovic (1998).

[5] See MC Jensen and W Meckling (1976), and F Modigliani and E Perotti (1997).

Levine and Zervos (1998) have presented evidence linking the size of a country's external capital market to its rate of economic growth, and Rajan and Zingales (1998) establish a link between investment rates and external capital market size. Thus, one can posit a causal chain running from the strength of corporate governance institutions to the size of external capital markets to economic growth. The last column of Table 1 presents average growth rates for the various countries. A clear link between corporate governance institutions and economic growth is not apparent as the average of the growth rates for the six French-origin countries is about the same as for the Anglo-Saxon countries. The average for the French-origin countries is clearly pulled up by the strong growth-performance of Portugal and Spain, which started the period with much lower average incomes than the other countries and were thus able to benefit from the 'catch-up' effect, as did Ireland in the Anglo-Saxon country sample. Macroeconomic growth rates depend on more than just the strength of corporate governance institutions.[6]

II. The Effects of Ownership Identities

The early literature dealing with managerial discretion and principal-agent problems assumed that an owner-manager would maximize profits, and thus deviations from profit maximization would arise only in the presence of a separation of ownership and control. The assumption that owner-managers are profit maximizers is questionable, however. An owner-manager may also get psychological rewards from commanding a large empire. Indeed, writing almost a century ago, Joseph Schumpeter characterized entrepreneurs as empire builders rather than profit maximizers.[7] The likelihood that an owner-manager pursues goals other than profit maximization becomes even greater when she is not the sole owner of the firm, but rather owns a controlling stake in it (see following subsection). Thus, one cannot unequivocally predict that a firm controlled by an individual or family will perform better than one with dispersed ownership.

When a dominant shareholder exists in the United States, it is usually a person or family. In other countries, dominant shareholders are often institutions, – other firms, financial institutions (banks, insurance companies), or the state. As when individuals own controlling stakes, it is not possible to make clear predictions about the effects of these institutional shareholders on the performance of companies. For example, it was once commonly believed that German banks improved

[6] When the Anglo-Saxon and French-origin samples are expanded to include countries in lower stages of development, the Anglo-Saxon sample does exhibit a much higher growth rate than the French-origin sample (4.30 versus 3.18 percent) (K Gugler, DC Mueller and BB Yurtoglu (2004a) Table 3).

[7] JA Schumpeter (1934) 93-94. The reference is to the 1934 translation of a book originally published in German in 1911.

the performance of German companies by performing the monitoring role that shareholders in Anglo-Saxon countries fail to carry out (Cable 1985). Through their direct ownership of shares and their authority to vote with those shares that are deposited with them, however, German banks essentially control themselves, and their managers are free to pursue their personal goals (Edwards and Fischer 1994). Why should bank managers not be empire builders? If they are, they are likely to encourage the companies that they control to pursue growth, for this will allow the banks to expand their loans and consulting services.[8] Similar ambiguities exist for the other two institutional ownership categories.[9] As so often happens, determining the effects of ownership identity on company performance turns out to be largely an empirical issue.

Table 2 presents estimates of marginal *q*s for companies divided into five ownership categories and the four legal-system country groups. The estimates for the Scandinavian and Germanic groups are for the same seven countries that appear in Table 1. The other two groups include developing countries with Anglo-Saxon- or French-origin legal systems. A company is classified as controlled by *X*, if *X* is the largest shareholder in the company and holds at least 10 percent of its outstanding shares. When no person or institution owns at least 10 percent of the outstanding shares, a company is placed into the dispersed ownership category. What stands out in the table is the importance of legal system origin relative to the identity of the control category. All five q_ms for the Anglo-Saxon countries are greater than 1.0, only two of the remaining 15 q_ms in the table are greater than 1.0.

Control Category	**Country Group**			
	Anglo-Saxon	Scandinavian	Germanic	French
Family	1.08	0.77	0.60	0.57
Non-Financial Company	1.06	0.72	0.63	0.57
Financial Corporation	1.00	0.56	0.56	0.69
State	1.01	0.80	0.37	0.95
Dispersed	1.00	1.15	1.36	0.54

Table 2: Estimates of marginal *q* for various control categories and country groups (Source: Gugler, Mueller, Yurtoglu 2004c).

The two q_ms that are greater than 1.0 are for firms with dispersed ownership in the Scandinavian and Germanic countries. These can be explained in the follow-

[8] E Boehmer (2001) claims that German banks are not interested in shareholder value.

[9] See discussion in DC Mueller (2003) 98-105.

ing way. We expect and observe very few firms with dispersed ownership structures in countries with weak corporate governance systems. When we do observe such a firm in these countries, one of two explanations is possible. Either the firm had such attractive investment opportunities that many individuals were enticed to purchase its shares despite the lack of protection afforded by the corporate governance institutions, or the managers were somehow able to bond themselves not to exploit minority shareholders, as for example by also listing their shares on the New York or London stock exchanges.

The lowest estimate of q_m in the table is for state-controlled firms in the three Germanic countries ($q_m = 0.37$). Agency problems appear to be particularly acute for these companies. On the other hand, the q_m for state-controlled firms in the French-origin countries is larger than for any other ownership category and insignificantly different from 1.0. This might be because the state in French-origin countries is a good monitor of the firms it controls, or because state-controlled companies in these countries are largely located in markets with limited competition and attractive investment opportunities.

The last observation to be made about Table 2 is that it provides little evidence of any positive effects from control by financial institutions. Only within the French-origin group was the q_m for financial-controlled firms significantly larger than for all other ownership categories, but this was not because financial-controlled firms performed so well ($q_m = 0.69$), but rather because all other firms in the French-origin countries performed so poorly ($q_m = 0.58$).

III. The Effects of Managerial Entrenchment and Financial Incentives

Morck, Shleifer and Vishny (1988, hereafter MSV) were the first to explore the relationship between firm performance and the fraction of shares held by managers using data for large U.S. corporations. They estimated an equation of the following form

$$q_a = \mathrm{aIS}_5 + \mathrm{bIS}_{25} + \mathrm{cIS}_{25+} \qquad (1)$$

where q_a is Tobin's q or *average q* as explained above, and IS_5, IS_{25} and IS_{25+} are the fractions of shares held by managers (insiders) over the ranges 0 to 5 percent, 5 to 25, and greater than 25. Their estimated coefficients exhibited the following pattern of signs, $a > 0$, $b < 0$, and $c > 0$. Tobin's q rose as insider ownership increased over the range 0 to 5 percent reaching a value of roughly 1.0 at a 5 percent ownership stake. Tobin's q than fell as insider ownership increased over the range 5 to 25 percent reaching roughly 0.7 at a value of 25 percent. From then on it rose. MSV attributed this zig-zag pattern of coefficients to two conflicting incentive effects of insider ownership – an entrenchment and a wealth effect. As insiders' shareholdings in their firm increase they become more entrenched as it is more difficult to remove them by launching a proxy contest or a hostile takeover. On the other hand, the larger their financial stake in their firm, the more insiders will identify with shareholders. These two conflicting effects were assumed to be of different strengths over different ownership ranges.

Several studies have reported the same up/down/up again relationship between performance and ownership concentration (Cho 1988; Short and Keasey 1999; Cosh, Guest and Hughes 2000; and Gugler, Mueller and Yurtoglu 2004b). McConnell and Servaes (1990, 1995) observed only the first part of the curve – an inverted parabola – in their U.S. data, as did Thomsen and Pedersen (2000) for European corporations.

In a recent paper, Gugler, Mueller and Yurtoglu (2004d) eliminate the awkward non-linear relationship between firm performance and ownership concentration by using two variables to capture the two effects of ownership concentration. They argue that the wealth effect of insider ownership is captured better by the value of the insiders' stake in the firm. A manager owning $10 million dollars of her company's shares has the same financial incentive to increase their value regardless of whether this stake amounts to 2 percent or 20 percent of the firm's outstanding shares. Gugler, Mueller and Yurtoglu estimated the following equation

$$q = \mathrm{aIS} + \mathrm{bVS} + \mathrm{cVS}^2 \qquad (2)$$

where *IS* is again the fraction of shares held by insiders and is assumed now to capture only the negative entrenchment effect of insider ownership, and *VS* is the total value of their shareholdings. As measures of firm performance Gugler, Mueller and Yurtoglu used both average and marginal q. For a sample of over 3,500 U.S. companies they estimated coefficients with the following pattern of signs, a > 0, b > 0, and c < 0. Both measures of q fall as insider ownership increases due to the entrenchment effect, and rise with increases in the value of the insiders' ownership stake, although at a diminishing rate.

Gugler, Mueller and Yurtoglu included firm size and a few other variables in the estimated equation, since firm size, and *IS* and *VS* are partially related to one another, one needs to take these relationships into account when determining the ultimate relationship between insider ownership and firm performance as measured by both average and marginal q. This ultimate relationship is depicted in Figure 1. An inverted U or parabola is observed for both measures of performance. At low levels of ownership concentration, the wealth effect of insider ownership dominates. At a level of ownership between 40 and 50 percent, however, the entrenchment effect begins to dominate. As economic theory predicts, marginal returns on capital as measured by q_m tend to lie below average returns.

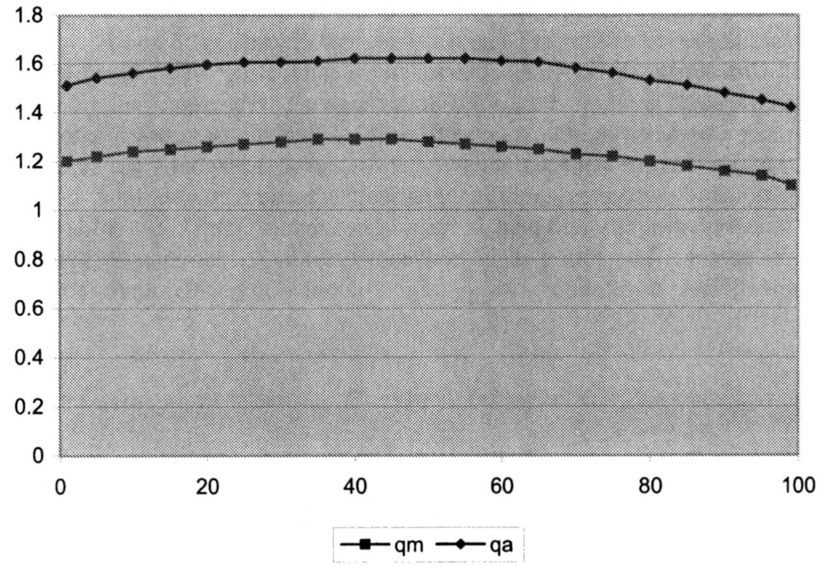

Figure 1 - The Relationship between *IS* and q_a, and *IS* and q_m in the U.S.

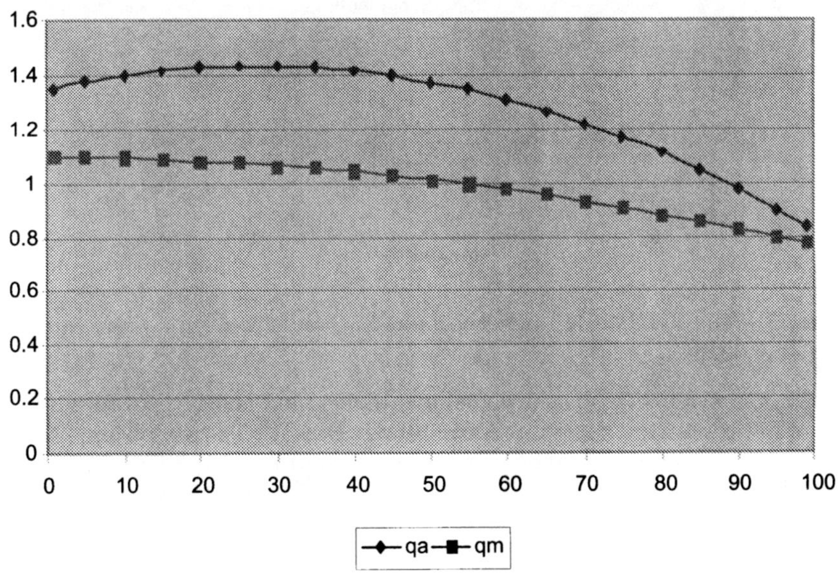

Figure 2 - The Relationship between *IS* and q_a, and *IS* and q_m in the English-origin non-U.S. sample.

The same exercise was repeated for samples of companies from Anglo Saxon countries other than the U.S., and for European, non-Anglo-Saxon countries. In both cases the same pattern of signs was observed on the key *IS* and *VS* variables. For the Continental European countries the wealth effect of insider ownership was much weaker than for the United States, however. Figures 2 and 3 depict the relationships between the two *q*s and *IS* for the other two samples of companies. For the Anglo-Saxon countries, the two curves start at essentially the same point. The relationship between q_a and *IS* is quadratic as for the United States, but the q_a curve rises only slightly and peaks much earlier than for the U.S. – at around an *IS* of 30 percent. The relationship between q_m and *IS* is dominated by the entrenchment effect throughout with q_m falling below 1.0 at an *IS* of around 25 percent.

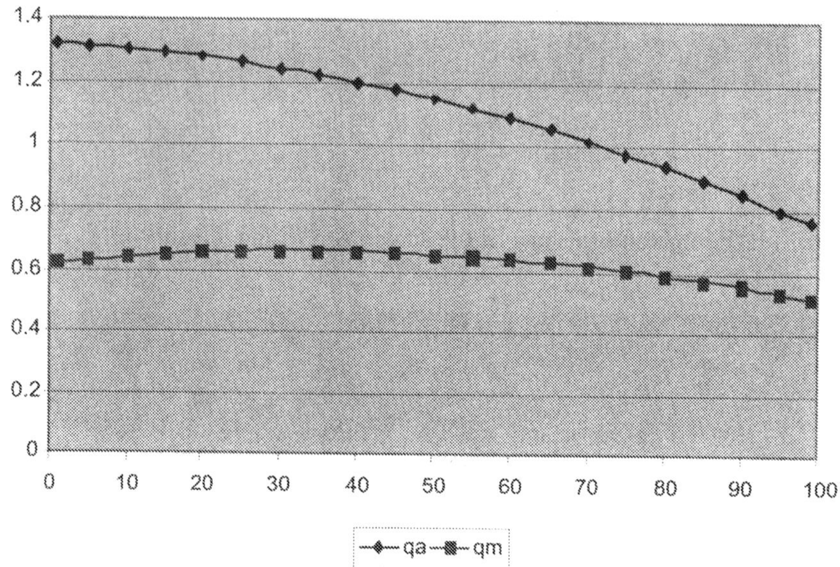

Figure 3 - The Relationship between *IS* and q_a, and *IS* and q_m in the European Civil Law sample.

The q_a-curve for the civil law countries slopes continuously downward dropping below 1.0 at an *IS* slightly above 70 percent. The q_m-curve begins significantly below 1.0, rises a bit and then gradually declines toward 0.5 as insider ownership increases. A comparison of the heights of the curves in the three figures again reveals the superior investment performance of firms in Anglo-Saxon countries relative to Continental European countries. In the latter, the negative entrenchment effects of insider shareholdings and firm size tend to dominate the positive wealth effects of ownership over the entire range of *IS* values.[10]

C. Institutional Explanations for Differences in Performance

I. Legal History

LaPorta, Lopez-de-Silanes, Shleifer and Vishny (1997, 1998) identify significant differences across legal systems in the protection they afford outside shareholders from exploitation by insiders, and minority shareholders from exploitation by majority shareholders. By better aligning the interests of all major actors in a firm, Anglo-Saxon and to some extent Scandinavian legal institutions produce better corporate performance as is evidenced in Tables 1 and 2 and Figures 1-3.

Paul Mahoney (2001) has offered a different explanation for why differences in legal institutions affect economic performance from that of LaPorta, Lopez-de-Silanes, Shleifer and Vishny. Mahoney argues that it is not the protection common law systems afford to *stockholders* that explains their superior economic performance in terms of things like growth, but rather the protection they offer to the *citizens* of these countries. By providing stronger protection of property rights, common law systems protect citizens from the arbitrary expropriations of property that can and do occur in civil law systems. This protection provides greater incentives to start businesses, enter into contracts, make investments and the like, and thus lead, according to Mahoney, to greater growth. This argument is somewhat related to that presented next.

II. Political History

Mark Roe (2000, 2003) also offers an alternative explanation for the differences in ownership and capital market structures between Europe and the United States to that of LaPorta, Lopez-de-Silanes, Shleifer and Vishny. Roe questions the legal institutions explanation, on the grounds that Europe's laws in other relevant areas like contract law are every bit as good as America's (Roe 2000). Moreover, constructing the institutions that would support large equity markets and protect minority shareholders is not 'rocket science', and thus one expects that countries like Germany and France would take this step to achieve the economic advantages claimed for the Anglo-Saxon model of corporate governance

[10] Managerial entrenchment is also assumed to increase with firm size, because it is more difficult to launch successful proxy fights or hostile takeovers against large firms.

(Roe 2000). The reason that they do not, according to Roe, lies in their politics and not in their legal systems.

'In social democracies – nations committed to private property but whose governments play a large role in the economy, emphasize distributional considerations, and favor employees over capital-owners when the two conflict – public policy emphasizes managers' natural agenda and demeans shareholders' agenda. The pressure on the firm for low-risk expansion is high, the pressure to avoid risky organizational change is substantial, and the tools that would induce managers to work in favor of invested capital – such as high incentive compensation, hostile takeovers, transparent accounting, and acculturation to shareholder-wealth maximization norms – are weak ...

Hence, managerial agency costs have been higher in social democracies than elsewhere, and we have ... a deeper, richer political explanation not only for the persistence of family ownership in France, Germany, Italy and Scandinavia, but also for the rise of the public firm in the United States. Social democracies do not strongly control public firm agency costs because they do *not* want unbridled shareholder wealth maximization, and, hence, by weakening shareholder-wealth maximization institutions, they widen the gap between managers and dispersed shareholders. When the gap is wide enough, the large American-style public firm is rendered unstable' (Roe 2000, footnote omitted, italics in original).

Thus, people who might become small shareholders, if they were afforded better protection from managerial agency costs, in social democracies opt for fixed income forms of investments over common equity. Those people who do own common equity in social democracies prefer large blocks, which offer them some protection against managers' opportunistic behavior.

Thus, Roe's political determinants theory of corporate governance provides an explanation for both the difference in ownership structure between the United States and Europe, and the difference in corporate performance. Large public companies in social democracies are essentially forced to behave like growth-maximizing firms. They invest too much and pay out too little dividends in part, perhaps, because such policies are to the advantage of the managers, but also because they are to the advantage of the workers in a firm who seek job security, and to the advantage of politicians who seek happy worker voters. Given the institutional and political bias in favor of workers over shareholders, the queue of people wishing to become shareholders is much shorter than in the United States.

Roe (2003) presents considerable evidence in support of his thesis in terms of both regression results and detailed political histories of individual countries. The thesis does not, however, fully account for the differences in investment performance presented in Table 1. It is not simply the United States which has a superior investment performance to the Continental European countries, *all six* Anglo-Saxon countries have higher q_ms than any of the ten countries with Germanic- or French-origin legal systems. The only two countries listed in Table 1 whose investment performance matches that of the six Anglo-Saxon countries are Finland and Norway, members of the highest ranked corporate governance systems by

LaPorta, Lopez-de-Silanes, Shleifer and Vishny among the civil law countries. Here too it is perhaps worth pointing out that the differences in investment performance are not simply between 'old Europe' and 'young new world'. Within Europe the four highest q_ms are for countries in the Anglo-Saxon and Scandinavian categories, while the seven lowest q_ms are for countries in the Germanic or French groups. Moreover, the superiority in investment performance between Anglo-Saxon- and French-origin countries holds up, once developing countries are added to the sample, as is evidenced in Table 2.

Thus, something needs to be added to Roe's political explanation for the differences between the United States and Continental Europe in terms of corporate governance institutions and corporate performance to extend the argument to other countries. Canada and the United Kingdom, for example, look very much like the social democracies of Continental Europe when one examines the size of their public sectors (roughly 50% of GDP), their health care systems, and other indexes of social democracy. Yet the performance of the corporate sectors is much different from that of the Continental European countries. Why the difference? What is it in the heritage of Anglo-Saxon countries, which makes them less receptive to the adoption of social democratic institutions governing business than other countries? As an economist, one would like to believe that a knowledge of the English language makes it more likely that one has read, *and understood,* the message of Adam Smith, whereas individuals with other mother tongues are more likely to have been exposed to the writings of Marx and other socialist writers from Continental Europe. But as an *institutional* economist, one seeks an explanation that is more directly linked to institutional differences across countries. An attempt at such an explanation is offered in the next subsection.

III. Political Institutions[11]

Money buys votes. It does so in two senses: (i) the more money a candidate spends in an election campaign, the higher his expected share of the vote is; (ii) contributions from an interest group to politicians increase the likelihood that they vote for legislation that benefits the interest group. Both of these propositions follow logically from the assumptions that politicians and interest groups are rational actors. Why would an interest group give money to a politician, if it would not affect the way that she is likely to vote on legislation of concern to the interest group? Why would the politician accept the money and spend it, if it did not increase the probability of her reelection? A large literature within public choice provides considerable empirical evidence for these two logical propositions.[12]

[11] This subsection draws heavily on DC Mueller (2002).

[12] See DC Mueller (2003) ch. 20.

If an interest group wants to buy a piece of legislation in the United States, it must purchase the votes of at least 223 members of the House of Representatives, 51 Senators, and if it does not want the legislation to be vetoed, it had better contribute something to the president's campaign. Although the empirical literature implies that an individual Congressman's vote can be bought relatively cheaply, the sum over all required representatives is likely to be quite large.

If an interest group wants to buy a piece of legislation in Austria, it must purchase the votes of only two parties. Although it is reasonable to assume that it costs more to buy the vote of a party than of an individual member of a party, it is also reasonable to assume that there are some economies of scale in buying votes from parties than from individuals. Thus, the cost of buying a piece of legislation in a multiparty parliamentary system of the type found in Continental Europe is cheaper than in the United States. Interest groups can be expected to buy more legislation in Continental Europe than in the United States, and thus to be politically more powerful than in the United States.

When a member of Congress is defeated, or retires, or dies, the past investments by an interest group in buying this Congressman's vote are wiped out. It must begin again to establish an exchange relationship with this Congressman's replacement or with some other member of Congress. Parties in parliamentary systems seldom die or are defeated in the sense that they fail to win any seats in an election. Thus, once an interest group has established an exchange relationship with a particular party in a parliamentary system, it can most likely maintain this relationship over time with relatively modest further investments. This feature of parliamentary systems again implies that interest groups are politically more powerful in Continental Europe than in the United States.

In a multiparty system parties take positions across the full ideological spectrum. Thus, an interest group can readily find a party whose ideological position comes reasonably close to its own. This proximity of ideological positions should make it easier for an interest group to establish an exchange relationship with a party, and reinforces the prediction that interest groups are more powerful in Continental Europe than in the United States.

A fourth reason to expect interest groups to be more powerful in Continental Europe exists in countries like Austria and Germany with corporatist histories. Interest groups in corporatist countries are formally part of political decision process. In Austria, for example, the leaders of some unions are also members of parliament. Legislation, which materially affects the welfare of a particular interest group, often formally or tacitly requires its approval. Since virtually all groups of workers are represented by well-organized unions, and no or at best weak interest groups exist to represent stockholders, it is not surprising that the latter fare poorly in any political battles involving the two groups.

When the British colonized large parts of the world in the 18th and 19th centuries, they brought with them not only their common law legal institutions, but also their political institutions. The salient characteristic of these political institutions relative to those of the Continental European multiparty systems is that in

Anglo-Saxon countries voters are allowed to elect only one representative from the particular electoral district in which they reside, whereas in the Continental European multiparty systems voters elect several representatives from much larger electoral districts, with the Netherlands being the extreme case of the entire country being defined as a single electoral district. Within any district the seats are divided among the parties in rough proportion to the votes each party receives.[13] Thus, in multiparty systems, the voter's attention is drawn more toward the characteristics and platforms of the various parties competing for votes than to those of individual candidates. In single-member-district systems, voters can be expected to consider both the characteristics of the individual candidates and of the parties to which they belong.

Thus, the reasoning presented above for why interest groups should be politically weaker in the United States than in Continental Europe can be extended to predict less political influence for interest groups in other countries with single-member-district electoral systems, i.e., other Anglo-Saxon countries.[14] Within the family of Anglo-Saxon countries, however, the United States is unique in having a presidential system, which grants the president strong veto power. Because of this strong veto power, a party cannot implement particular policies merely by obtaining a majority of seats in one House of Congress or even in both Houses. This being the case, U.S. voters have less reason to vote for particular parties in Congressional elections to obtain what they want. Parties become weaker and the personal characteristics and promises of individual candidates become more important. In British-style parliamentary systems there is no president with veto powers, and a party can implement particular policies if it obtains a majority of seats in the parliament. Thus, in British-style parliamentary systems voters can be expected to give more weight to the party identifications of the candidates than in the United States. These considerations lead us to expect that in general interest groups will be more powerful in the other Anglo-Saxon countries than in the United States, although less powerful than in countries with multiparty systems.

Persson and Tabellini (1999, 2000, 2003) have developed a somewhat different, but complementary, argument to the one just presented. They predict that the state sector will be smaller in majoritarian systems of the British type than in proportional representation, multiparty systems, because the competition for votes focuses on the marginal districts rather than the entire nation, and thus politicians

[13] France is the major exception to this rule. It is also divided into single-member-electoral districts, but uses a two-stage, 'majority system' to elect representatives rather than the one-stage, plurality system common in the Anglo-Saxon countries. For further discussion and references, see DC Mueller (2003) ch. 13.

[14] New Zealand had an Anglo-Saxon, plurality system up until the election of 1996, when it adopted electoral rules to produce a proportional representation system. The reasoning of this section predicts ceteris paribus an increase in interest group power in New Zealand after 1996, although presumably with some time lag.

tend to make more targeted and in the aggregate smaller commitments in majoritarian systems. Although the emphasis of Persson and Tabellini is more on the supply than on the demand side of providing legislation, if we think of the demanders of legislation as being interest groups rather than individual voters, then their thesis also implies that interest groups in aggregate get more of what they want and thus can be said to be more effective at getting what they want in multiparty systems.

D. Is There a Best Corporate Governance System?[15]

In a recent symposium on globalization, Dowrick and Golley (2004) point out that levels of national income can be regarded as very long-run measures of economic growth under the assumption that all countries essentially started off at the same low level of income. Using this measure of performance, all of the main forms of corporate governance systems described above must be deemed to be good, since the countries which typify each – the United States, Sweden, Germany and France, and, if we add in an Asian category, Japan – have all become very rich. This is essentially the conclusion Shleifer and Vishny (1997) reached in their comprehensive survey of the corporate governance literature. Each system has its particular strengths and weaknesses.[16]

Although I agree that each system has its strengths and weaknesses, I do not draw the same conclusion that no system is superior to the others. For much of the 20th century, companies in the major industrial countries did not face domestically the intense international competition that they do today. Japan still has a fairly closed economy. The *relatively* weaker competitive environment in the domestic economy over the first three quarters of the 20th century may have concealed weaknesses in corporate governance institutions that have only become apparent in the last couple of decades. The evidence reviewed in section B, which comes from this most recent period, clearly implies that institutions in Anglo-Saxon countries – and these presumably include corporate governance systems if they are not exclusively confined to them – are better at protecting shareholders than institutions in non-Anglo-Saxon countries, and there is some evidence that they lead to better macroeconomic performance. This suggests that countries which do not possess Anglo-Saxon institutions might achieve better economic performance by adopting them. Have political leaders realized this? Have corporate governance systems begun to converge? We now briefly look at some evidence.

[15] The last two sections of the paper draw heavily from K Gugler, DC Mueller and BB Yurtoglu (2004b).

[16] WC Kester (1992) takes a similarly equivocal position.

E. Are Corporate Governance Systems Converging?

I. The United States

Even before the Enron and WorldCom scandals at the beginning of the 21st century, several changes had taken place in the United States that tended to strengthen the hands of shareholders vis-á-vis managers. Some of these were precipitated by the increasingly important role of institutional investors, some by the results of Securities and Exchange Commission rulings and court decisions (see, Bradley, Schipani, Sundaram, and Walsh 1999, hereafter BSSW). The Enron scandals sped these changes along and brought the U.S. Congress into the picture. Thus, the Anglo-Saxon corporate governance model, as it is embodied in U.S. institutions has, if anything, become more Anglo-Saxon.

II. Continental Europe

Several countries have introduced new corporate governance codes in the last few years, and these generally entail a movement towards the Anglo-Saxon institutions.[17] Often the movement is only partial, however. In the recently issued corporate governance codes of Austria and Germany, for example, it is only *recommended* that managers report their compensation. Nevertheless, the direction of change is unmistakable. Prohibitions against insider trading are on the increase, and companies are being forced to make their financial statements more transparent. Indeed, a large majority of the world's leading countries has adopted accounting standards that are either identical to or come close to those formulated by the International Accounting Standards Committee. The necessity to raise large amounts of capital to finance cross-border acquisitions has also led many Continental European firms to list their securities on the London or New York stock exchanges, thereby subjecting them to Anglo-Saxon corporate governance constraints even though their main headquarters remains outside of one of these countries.[18] Within the last year the Commission of the European Union has put forward a corporate governance code, which it *recommends* that all member countries adopt. *If* they were to do so, corporate governance systems in Europe – at least on paper – would have reached full convergence.

[17] For the codes of nearly 40 countries, see <http://www.ecgi.org/codes/all_codes.htm>.

[18] For further discussion of these developments and references to the literature, see M Bradley, CA Shipani, AK Sundaram and JP Walsh (1999) 69-74.

F. Will Corporate Governance Systems Achieve a Full Convergence?

I. No

Ownership structures change very slowly over time. The best predictor of the identity of a firm's largest shareholder and the size of her/its shareholding today are the identity and size of the largest shareholder's shareholding last year. Bebchuk and Roe (1999) identify two causes for this path dependence. One they label *structure-driven* and the other *rule-driven path dependence*. Structure-driven path dependence can arise either because an organization has adapted to a particular ownership structure and thus would sacrifice efficiency by changing, or because certain stakeholders – like the managers or the dominant shareholder – would lose from a shift to a more efficient structure, and thus resist such a change. Rule-driven path dependence can arise for similar reasons. A country may adopt laws and regulations that are designed to make companies with the existing ownership structures most efficient, and/or influential managers and shareholders may be able to induce the political system to maintain a set of rules, which, although inefficient, is to their advantage.

Barca and Trento (1997) give an account for why banks in Italy play such a modest role in its corporate governance structure, which illustrates the importance of path dependence.[19] During the first part of the 20th century, banks in Italy played much the same role in financing and monitoring firms as they did in Germany. The stock market crash at the end of the 1920s produced a crisis for the banks, however. The state rescued the banks by buying out their industrial holdings and placed them into a newly corrected state-owned company – the Institute for Industrial Reconstruction (IRI). At the same time the government passed legislation resembling the Glass-Steagall Act in the United States limiting banks' involvement in the industrial sector. Thus, the weak role played by banks in corporate governance in both the United States and Italy can be traced to essentially the same event at the same point in time.

II. Yes

If the best practice technology in an industry is characterized by a U-shaped average cost function, then perfect competition will ensure that every firm in the industry adopts the best practice technology, *and* that every firm is of the size defined by the bottom of the U. If globalization is increasing competitive forces in every country, then the obvious implication would seem to be that countries should converge on the 'best practice' corporate governance system. In an article

[19] Mediobanca has been an exception to this generalization, however.

that has received much attention, Hansmann and Kraakman (2001) have made such a prediction. They see the efficiency enhancing aspect of competition in capital markets driving convergence on the Anglo-Saxon system.[20]

III. Maybe

Although one cannot rule out the possibility of a full convergence of corporate governance institutions on a single, Anglo-Saxon model, the analogy between competition within industry leading to convergence among firms and competition across countries leading to convergence of countries' institutions is somewhat problematic. In a competitive environment inefficient firms go bankrupt and disappear. Countries seldom go bankrupt and only disappear if they are defeated in war. The greater efficiency and faster growth that are likely to follow reforms in corporate governance should tempt politicians to introduce these reforms, but there will be counter pressures resisting such reforms, and it is by no means clear that all countries' governments will resist these pressures.

In the first study in which I estimated marginal *q*s, I used a sample of nearly 700 U.S. corporations and data for the period 1969-88 (Mueller and Reardon 1993). The results for the U.S. over that period were much the same as those reported in Tables 1 and 2 *for the civil law countries.* Eight out of ten large U.S. corporations had a marginal *q* less than one, with the mean being just over 0.7. The estimated marginal *q*s for U.S. firms were much higher in the late 1980s and 1990s. I attribute this improvement in performance to an important degree to the hostile merger wave of the 1980s. The poor performance of U.S. managers was recognized by the market, and *for the first time* was corrected by 'the market for corporate control' as Marris (1964) and Manne (1965) had predicted 20 years earlier. That wave of hostile takeovers made managers more attentive to shareholder interests, led to 'downsizing', returns to 'core competencies', share buy backs, and the like, all to the benefit of corporate shareholders. The hostile merger wave had a second, important consequence, however, it drove managers to approach state legislatures and demand legal protection from hostile takeovers, and to threaten them with migration if they did not comply. Naturally, almost all complied (Romano 1987; Roe 1993; Bebchuk and Ferrell 1999).

Good corporate governance structures benefit shareholders by reducing managers' discretion to pursue their own goals. Both managers and workers have an interest in seeing their firms grow, or at least survive. If national governments are

[20] K Palepu, T Khanna and J Kogan (2002) find evidence of *de jure* convergence at the country level. This convergence is, however, not on U.S. standards. Rather, pairs of economically interdependent countries appear to adopt common corporate governance standards, especially if the pairs of countries are in the same geographic region and are relatively developed countries.

more sensitive to the interests of corporate managers and workers than to shareholders, reforms in corporate governance system may not take place, or be implemented. A recent EU Commission proposal to make takeovers easier has been significantly weakened by pressures from member countries' governments, which in turn were presumably responding to pressures from their largest companies (Economist 2003). Recent state interventions in France to save national champions Alstom from bankruptcy, and Aventis from the clutches of a foreign company give one a certain sense of *déjà vu*, to a time when no European common market existed and national governments were totally free to respond to domestic political pressures and pursue their industrial policies oblivious to their impacts on other countries. The policy implications of the work of LaPorta, Lopez-de-Silanes, Shleifer and Vishny (1997, 2000), Mahoney (2001), and myself and my colleagues (Gugler, Mueller and Yurtoglu 2003, 2004b) would appear to be that if France and Italy wish to have a better economic performance over the next 20 years than they have shown over the last 20, they had better adopt Anglo-Saxon legal institutions, install a common law, adversarial legal system and scrap their civil law systems. If this is the bottom policy line of these studies, then it is discouraging news for all civil-law system countries, since institutional changes of this order of magnitude are virtually impossible to achieve. The civil law countries would appear to be doomed to second class economic citizenship in the globalized world of the 21st century.

Fortunately for the civil law countries, legal reforms to improve corporate governance should be possible without having to revamp the entire legal system. We have observed significantly better investment performance in civil law countries, if they have strong accounting standards and strong contract enforcement (Gugler, Mueller and Yurtoglu 2003, 2004b). Reforms such as these should be within the reach of every country, *if* it has the political will to introduce them. The main obstacle to institutional reforms in Europe must be seen as political.

Mark Roe (2003) is certainly correct in stressing the importance of ideological differences between the United States and Continental Europe in explaining differences in their corporate governance systems. In Austria, France, Sweden and I would guess most if not all Continental European countries, anyone who is favorably disposed to market institutions or globalization is automatically labelled a *neoliberal,* and the term 'neoliberalism' invariably carries with it a negative connotation. Neoliberalism is also generally identified as an American ideology. Thus, there is an underlying ideological aversion to American economic institutions in Continental Europe that stands in the way of a full adoption of the American or Anglo-Saxon model of corporate governance.

I have argued, however, that more stands between Anglo-Saxon and Continental European countries than just ideology. Politicians in all countries seek to win public office, and once elected to be reelected. Politicians like everyone else respond to incentives. Political institutions, like electoral rules, give politicians different incentives – and they respond to them. The political institutions of Continental Europe make interest groups like labor unions much more powerful than in the Anglo-Saxon countries, and this difference helps to explain the differences in economic institutions and outcomes in these two sets of countries. If I am right about this, then this conclusion is even more discouraging than attributing these differences to legal institutions, for laws, and by implication, legal institutions are easy to change compared to political institutions. Changes in laws that affect corporate governance do not affect politicians directly, but only through their indirect effects on voters' preferences. Changes in laws that govern elections, on the other hand, will generally affect politicians and parties directly, even if they have no effects on voters' preferences. Any fundamental change in electoral rules is almost certain to be strongly opposed by one group of parties. Since the parties themselves generally must introduce such changes, it is not surprising that they seldom occur. Fundamental changes in political institutions are seldom observed save following a revolution or defeat in war.

On this sombre note I shall bring this essay to a close. If fundamental improvements in economic outcomes do require fundamental changes in political institutions, they are unlikely to come about. Change must come about in the preferences and ideologies of individual voters and interest groups. An optimist can see such changes in Europe today. Germany's largest labor union has just agreed to a new contract *increasing* the number of hours per work week. French labor unions seem willing to move away from their beloved 35 hour work week. Such instances of economic enlightenment, or perhaps more accurately pragmatism, are indeed encouraging. But such reforms are fragile, and even a partial victory for economic liberalism seems still a long way off. A global economic crisis, as say following terrorist attacks on the oil fields of Middle East, could easily rekindle the antimarket, anti-liberal ideological fires in Europe.

References

Barca, F and S Trento 'State Ownership and the Evolution of Italian Corporate Governance' (1997) 6 Ind Corp Change 533-559.

Baumol, WJ, P Heim, BG Malkiel and RE Quandt 'Earnings Retention, New Capital and the Growth of the Firm' (1970) 52 Rev Econ Statistics 345-355.

Bebchuk, LA and A Ferrell 'Federalism and Corporate Law: The Race to Protect Managers from Takeovers' (1999) 99 Colum L Rev 1168-1199.

Bebchuk, L and MJ Roe 'A Theory of Path Dependence in Corporate Governance and Ownership' (1999) 52 Stan L Rev 127-170.

Boehmer, E 'Germany' in K Gugler (ed) *Corporate Governance and Economic Performance* (Oxford University Press 2001).

Bradley, M, CA Shipani, AK Sundaram and JP Walsh 'The Purposes and Accountability of the Corporation in Contemporary Society: Corporate Governance at a Crossroads' (1999) 62 Law & Contemp Probs 9-86.

Cable, J 'Capital Market Information and Industrial Performance: The Role of West German Banks' (1985) 95 Econ J 118-132.

Charkham, JP *Keeping Good Company* (Clarendon Press 1994).

Cho, MH 'Ownership Structure, Investment, and the Corporate Value: An Empirical Analysis' (1998) 47 J Finan Econ 103-121.

Cosh, AD, PM Guest and A Hughes 'Managerial Discretion and Takeover Performance' (Centre for Business Research, Cambridge University wp, 2000).

Demirgüç-Kunt, A and V Maksimovic 'Law, Finance, and Firm Growth' (1998) 53 J Finance 2107-2137.

Denis, DJ, DK Denis and A Sarin 'Agency Problems, Equity Ownership, and Corporate Diversification' (1997) 52 J Finance 135-160.

Dowrick, S and J Golley 'Trade, Openness and Growth' (2004) 20 Oxford Rev Econ Pol 38-56.

Economist 'Takeovers in Europe: Lowest Common Denominator' (29 November 2003).

Edwards, JSS and K Fischer *Banks, Finance and Investment in Germany* (Cambridge University Press 1994).

Gilson, RJ and MJ Roe 'Understanding the Japanese Keiretsu: Overlaps between Corporate Governance and Industrial Organization' (1993) 102 Yale L J 871-906.

Grabowski, H and DC Mueller 'Managerial and Stockholder Welfare Models of Firm Expenditures' (1972) 54 Rev Econ Statist 9-24.

Grabowski, H and DC Mueller 'Life-Cycle Effects on Corporate Returns on Retentions' (1975) 57 Rev Econ Statist 400-409.

Gugler, K, DC Mueller and BB Yurtoglu 'The Impact of Corporate Governance on Investment Returns in Developed and Developing Countries' (2003) 113 Econ J F511-F539.

Gugler, K, DC Mueller and BB Yurtoglu 'Marginal q, Tobin's q, Cash Flow and Investment' (2004a) 70 Southern Econ J 512-531.

Gugler, K, DC Mueller and BB Yurtoglu 'Corporate Governance and Globalization' (2004b) 20 Oxford Rev Econ Pol 129-156.

Gugler, K, DC Mueller and BB Yurtoglu 'Corporate Governance and the Returns on Investment' (2004c) 47 J Law Econ 598-633.

Gugler, K, DC Mueller and BB Yurtoglu 'Separating the Wealth and Entrenchment Effects of Insider Ownership on Investment Performance' (2004d) (SSRN wp http://www.ssrn.com/abstract=514702, 2004).

Hansmann, H and R Kraakman 'The End of History for Corporate Law' (2001) 89 Geo L J 439-468.

Jensen, CM and W Meckling 'Theory of the Firm: Managerial Behavior, Agency Cost, and Capital Structure' (1976) 3 J Finan Econ 305-360.

Kester, WC 'Industrial Groups as Systems of Contractual Governance' (1992) 8 Oxford Rev Econ Pol 422-442.

LaPorta, R, F Lopez-de-Silanes, A Shleifer and R Vishny 'Legal Determinants of External Finance' (1997) 52 J Finance 1131-1150.

LaPorta, R, F Lopez-de-Silanes, A Shleifer and R Vishny 'Law and Finance' (1998) 106 J Polit Economy 1113-1155.

LaPorta, R, F Lopez-de-Silanes, A Shleifer and R Vishny 'Agency Problems and Dividend Policies around the World' (2000) 55 J Finance 1-33.

Levine, R and S Zervos 'Stock Markets, Banks and Economic Growth' (1998) 88 Amer Econ Rev 537-558.

Mahoney, PG 'The Common Law and Economic Growth: Hayek Might Be Right' (2001) 30 J Legal Stud 503-525.

Manne, HG 'Mergers and the Market for Corporate Control' (1965) 73 J Polit Economy 110-120.

Marris, R *The Economic Theory of Managerial Capitalism* (Free Press 1964).

McConnell, J and H Servaes 'Additional Evidence on Equity Ownership and Corporate Value' (1990) 27 J Finan Econ 595-612.

McConnell, J and H Servaes 'Equity Ownership and the Two Faces of Debt' (1995) 39 J Finan Econ 131-157.

Modigliani, F and E Perotti 'Protection of Minority Interest and the Development of Security Markets' (1997) 18 Managerial Dec Econ 519-528.

Morck, R, A Shleifer and RW Vishny 'Management Ownership and Market Valuation: An Empirical Analysis' (1988) 20 J Finan Econ 293-315.

Mueller, DC 'A Theory of Conglomerate Mergers' (1969) 83 Quart J Econ 643-59; reprinted in G Marchildon (ed) *Mergers and Acquisitions* (Edward Elgar 1991).

Mueller, DC 'A Life Cycle Theory of the Firm' (1972) 20 J Ind Econ 199-219.

Mueller, DC 'Interest Groups, Redistribution and the Size of Government' in SL Winer and H Shibata (eds) *Political Economy and Public Finance* (Edward Elgar 2002) 123-144.

Mueller, DC *The Corporation – Investment, Mergers, and Growth* (Routledge 2003).

Mueller, DC and E Reardon 'Rates of Return on Investment' (1993) 60 Southern Econ J 430-453.

Palepu, K, T Khanna and J Kogan 'Globalization and Similarities in Corporate Governance: A Cross-Country Analysis' (Harvard University, Negotiation, Organization and Markets wp No. 02-31, 2002)

Persson T and G Tabellini 'The Size and Scope of Government: Comparative Politics with Rational Politicians' (1999) 43 Europ Econ Rev 699-735.

Persson T and G Tabellini *Political Economics – Explaining Economic Policy* (MIT Press 2000).

Persson, T and G Tabellini *The Economic Effects of Constitutions* (MIT Press 2003).

Rajan, RG and L Zingales 'Financial Dependence and Growth' (1998) 88 Amer Econ Rev 559-586.

Roe, MJ 'Takeover Politics' in MM Blair (ed) *The Deal Decade* (Brookings Institution 1993) 321-353.

Roe, MJ 'Political Preconditions to Separating Ownership from Corporate Control' (2000) 53 Stan L Rev 539-606.

Roe, MJ *Political Determinants of Corporate Governance* (Oxford University Press 2003)

Romano, R 'The Political Economy of Takeover Statutes' (1987) 73 Va L Rev 111-199.

Schumpeter, JA *The Theory of Economic Development* (Harvard University Press 1934).

Shleifer, A and RW Vishny 'A Survey of Corporate Governance' (1997) 52 J Finance 737-783.

Short, H and K Keasey 'Managerial Ownership and the Performance of Firms: Evidence from the UK' (1999) 5 J Corp Finan 79-101.

Stulz, RM 'Managerial Discretion and Optimal Financing Policies' (1990) 26 J Finan Econ 3-27.

Thomsen, S and T Pedersen 'Ownership Structure and Economic Performance in the Largest European Companies' (2000) 21 Strategic Management Journal 689-705.

Political Yardstick Competition and Corporate Governance in the European Union

PIERRE SALMON*

The question whether regulatory competition in the area of company law could take place in the European Union (EU) in a way similar to that in the United States (the Delaware phenomenon) is topical in the light of some recent judgments of the European Court of Justice as well as various documents and projects produced by the European Commission. The discussion, however, typically ignores the importance of voters and tends to view competition among governments as if it was exclusively based on the mobility of firms across jurisdictions. But intergovernmental competition can also take the form of yardstick, or relative performance, competition. Voters and democratic politics then become essential. Voters assess the performance of incumbents by comparing results in their own and in other jurisdictions. The first part of the paper is devoted to spelling out some characteristics of the mechanism. It notes in particular that, depending on circumstances, yardstick competition may provide office-holders with the wrong incentives. This result is important in the EU context. The second part stresses some aspects of the path followed by European integration. One factor is that Europe is under construction, with integration tending to be monotonous. The process of integration can slow down or stall but seldom if ever does it regress. Another feature is the enduring reliance on internal market commitments and their legal implications. Structural characteristics of the integration process such as these have consequences on yardstick competition as well as on the kind of policies to be expected from the EU. The third and fourth parts of the paper are devoted to corporate governance and law making in the EU context, also in the light of the foregoing analysis of yardstick competition. Two points are stressed. The nature of yardstick competition among the governments of the Member States may provide insights into the fact that differences in company law and corporate governance can subsist without preventing a strong convergence of economic outcomes. Yardstick competition between the EU as a whole and other parts of the world, however, is likely to start a dynamic process that could lead to the centralization of a large part of company lawmaking at the EU level and the emergence of a distinctive legal environment for firms doing business in Europe.

* I am grateful for remarks and suggestions to Gérard Charreaux and to participants in the conference on *EU Corporate Law Making: Institutional Structure, Regulatory Competition, and Regulatory Strategies*, Harvard Law School, Cambridge (Mass.), and in the meetings of the European Public Choice Society, Durham (UK), especially Josse Delfgaauw, Jeffrey Gordon, Ehud Kamar and Roland Vaubel. The usual disclaimer applies.

A. Introduction
B. Selected Features of Yardstick Competition Among Governments
C. The Peculiar Path Borrowed by European Integration
D. Corporate Law and Yardstick Competition Among EU Member Countries
E. Is Yardstick Competition at a Higher Level Likely to Start a Centralizing Dynamic Akin to that of the Single Market?
F. Conclusion

A. Introduction

Competition among governments is generally treated in a way that leaves no room for voters and democratic elections. This is as true of regulatory competition in the area of corporate law as it is of tax competition and, more generally, of all forms of competition among governments striving to attract or keep households, firms or capital. Indeed, were governments, instead of being elected and accountable to voters, dictatorships or purely private institutions, this would entail very little change in the major strands of the literature on intergovernmental competition.

In contrast, this paper is based on a perspective under which voters and elections are central. Competition is assumed to take place in different arenas. Within each jurisdiction, candidates or political parties compete to win elections. Or, to put it more effectively for our purposes: because of electoral competition, incumbents do their best to be reelected. The problem is that voters encounter serious information problems, especially in a rapidly and irregularly changing world. Hence the utility for voters of comparisons of how results in their own jurisdiction compare with those in others. As we will see, this can stimulate a form of competition, currently called yardstick competition, in which the governments of the different jurisdictions vie for a good place in terms of relative performance – a purely informational and intangible good, but, because of competition in the first arena, a most valuable one. Then, of course, there is also intergovernmental competition of the more conventional type, in which agents (households, firms, capital) respond to differences in what the governments offer them by exit (and entry) rather then by voice (and support), to use Hirschman's well-known distinction (1970). This form of competition must also be taken into account in most concrete situations. In fact, by its strength, it often pre-empts yardstick competition.

Has this approach anything to contribute to the understanding of regulatory competition in the area of corporate law and governance? I will address the question not as such but in one of its specifications. Does yardstick competition play a role in the way regulatory competition and harmonization or centralization interact in the area of corporate law and governance and in the setting of the European Union (EU)? In a most exploratory and tentative way, I will try to show that this is the case – a positive answer that logically extends, with the same caveat, to the larger question. My tentative demonstration is based on an interpretation of the way policies are decided and implemented in the EU. One implication of that interpretation is that EU policy-making in one area – corporate law and governance being an instance – cannot really be understood or predicted independently of what the EU does in other areas. Issue linkages, especially over time, are a major feature of the way integration proceeds in Europe.

Sections B and C summarize important aspects of yardstick competition among governments and of decision-making in the EU, respectively. I turn then to corporate governance and lawmaking in the EU context. In Section D, I try to demonstrate that yardstick competition among the governments of the Member States may explain the fact that differences in corporate law and governance can subsist without preventing a strong convergence of economic outcomes. The point made in Section E is that yardstick competition between the EU as a whole and other parts of the world may well start a dynamic process leading eventually to the centralization of a large part of corporate lawmaking (in a broad sense) at the EU level and the emergence of a distinctive legal environment for firms doing business in Europe. Section F is a brief conclusion.

B. Selected Features of Yardstick Competition Among Governments

The basic mechanism can be summarized as follows (Salmon 1987).[1] The main problem encountered by voters, especially in a world marked by considerable change and uncertainty, is information asymmetry. Given circumstances that they do not know, or whose impact they cannot assess, the voters of a jurisdiction J cannot say whether the performance of their government – or a set of its decisions and policies – is good or bad. If disturbances are not wholly idiosyncratic to J but, to a sufficient degree, correlated across different jurisdictions, the observation of what obtains in some other jurisdictions may help voters in J to form an opinion. Thus, if a voter of J, in domains of interest to her, considers that it makes sense to compare the services delivered or the decisions made by the government of J to those offered or decided in some other jurisdictions, and if the result of these comparisons is that the said voter considers the relative performance of the government of J on the said matters to be bad, this may decrease the probability that she will vote for the incumbents on the next occasion.

Incumbents do not know exactly the domains which count most for that voter or for others, nor with what other jurisdictions she or others will compare results obtained in J. They know that exerting themselves as much and in as many areas

[1] In microeconomics or organization theory, yardstick competition can be traced back at least to Baiman and Demski (1980) even though it is usually associated with Shleifer (1985). In Salmon (1987), whose topic was political decentralization in a governmental system, the analysis was inspired not by yardstick competition but by the then recent literature on tournaments, in particular Lazear and Rosen (1981). Differences between the two mechanisms can be disregarded for our purpose. The title of Besley and Case (1995), the most influential work in that area, refers to 'yardstick competition' and, as everybody else now, I will use that expression.

as possible enhances the chance that their performance will be judged comparatively good by the voters of their own jurisdiction, and thus increases the probability that they will win the next election. If this is their main concern, this may produce in incumbents an incentive toward good performance, and moreover performance of a kind that tends to be aligned with the way voters themselves perceive their interests. The mechanism, however, either may not work or have perverse effects.

To complete the summary, let me introduce here an important distinction. If the jurisdictions with which comparisons are made are on the same level as J (as was perhaps implied by the formulation used so far), yardstick competition is horizontal. It takes place among the governments of cities, or of regions, or of countries or, as we will see, at the level of the EU as a whole. If jurisdictions are not on the same level, yardstick competition is vertical (I simplify somewhat). If C is a country and J a region of that country, voters in J may compare the performance of J's government with that of C's. If, as a consequence, they are pleased with the performance of J's government more than with the performance of C's government, this makes them on average more likely to vote for the incumbents in the next *regional* election and less likely to vote for the incumbents in the next *national* one. The incentives of elected office-holders generated or strengthened in this way are more or less the same as previously.

The following seven features of the mechanism are particularly relevant for our purpose in this paper.

(1) Even though voters have idiosyncratic interests, some variables are a concern common to many. Thus, rather than the very general formulation above, it is often both more convenient and productive for certain purposes to assume that yardstick competition takes place mainly over one or a few salient variables. The one I will stress in the remainder of this paper is simply economic performance as measured by GDP growth and/or GDP per capita.

(2) The strength of the mechanism, measured by the degree to which incumbents feel constrained by voters' interjurisdictional comparisons, is determined by two sets of factors. The first is related to the availability of the relevant information and the attention given to it by the population or subsets thereof. The second is the nature of the political, and *at the limit* electoral, system. In other words, the strength of the constraint introduced by comparisons will depend, first, on how much discontent a given performance gap generates in the population, and, second, to what degree that discontent translates into genuine pressure on incumbents.

One's view about the nature of electoral competition has a very important bearing on the way both sets of factors can be assessed. A probabilistic view of voting (see Hillman 2003, e.g.) makes the mechanism much more plausible than it will be under the median voter assumption. Under the probabilistic approach, individual candidates and political parties consider *all* voters, or categories of voters, as having a positive, even if often tiny, probability of voting for them, and this probability is endogenous in the sense that it depends in part on the policies candidates implement or promise to implement. Thus the opinion of even relatively small constituencies might count, and consequently deserves some attention. If electoral competition is sufficiently tight, politicians will be attentive to interjurisdictional comparisons even if they know that only a minority of voters makes them. Moreover, if some features of the situation cause the mechanism to be relatively weak, that only means, regarding a potentially widespread concern such as economic performance, that a larger gap along that dimension will be necessary for the political constraint to become significant. A quasi-philosophical problem is that the observation of zero performance gaps and no visible comparative activities on the part of voters may be the result of office-holders having made sure, because of their awareness of the potential effect of yardstick competition, that no gap develops.

(3) As stressed by Breton (1996), voting is only one of the ways for the population or subsets thereof to award or withdraw support. Even in democratic settings, incumbents may be attentive to public opinion independently of elections, or, in specialized domains, to the judgment and support of groups that have no or little electoral power. This possibility gives these specialized domains a second chance – the first resulting, albeit weakly by definition, from the probabilistic view just mentioned – to be host directly to yardstick competition.

(4) In any case, many areas that are not concerned directly by yardstick competition may be involved indirectly as a consequence of governments being engaged in yardstick competition along other dimensions. To illustrate, environmental concerns may be sacrificed as a result of a concentration on economic growth imposed by yardstick competition. Combinations of direct and indirect involvement may emerge as yardstick competition over a salient variable disturbs a second variable in a way that makes the latter also a salient issue in the public debate. As a consequence, that second variable may become also a politically significant object of voters' comparisons across jurisdictions and thus of yardstick competition. The actual working of this mechanism as well as awareness by office-holders of its potential activity may affect their current decisions.

(5) The relationship between yardstick competition and the better known form of competition based on the mobility of individuals, firms and capital is, in general, very complex. I will make only two remarks. Mobility-based competition often pre-empts yardstick competition. This seems to be clearly the case of the Delaware-type of interstate competition for incorporation in the United States. Yardstick competition plays little or no role in that competition as far as I know. One reason is that the mobility costs incurred by firms are particularly small. Another is that, except in Delaware, the consequences for constituencies other than managers and shareholders of the choice made by firms are also small (or perceived as such). Mobility-based regulatory competition in the European context is or would be a completely different matter.

The second remark, related to the first, is that the agents most likely to respond by mobility to differences in policies across jurisdictions may not belong to the same categories as the agents most likely to respond to these differences by their votes. To illustrate, if it is the case, as often claimed in the European context, that the mobility of labour across Member States is much smaller than that of capital, mobility-based competition may be above all something for the latter, whereas yardstick competition may be the only possibility available to the former. Voters should of course take mobility-based competition, actual or potential, into account but this does not mean that, influenced by interjurisdictional comparisons, they will never decide collectively in a way that runs against what is induced by mobility-based competition. A policy more in favour of labour in country A than in country B may elicit a movement of capital from A to B but give the edge to A in terms of relative performance as gauged by labour-oriented voters in A and B – possibly inducing the government of B to emulate the government of A and adopt the same labour policy.[2]

(6) I indicated at the outset that yardstick competition may provide office-holders with wrong incentives. This may happen in various ways (Bordignon, Cerniglia and Revelli 2004). One important case for our purpose is when yardstick competition causes a convergence of policies and policy-outcomes toward a low-effort and low-performance equilibrium. This phenomenon is more likely to arise when the number of compared jurisdictions is small or when comparisons are asymmetric, one jurisdiction serving as a benchmark for the performance of all others. If, in absolute terms, for some reason, that benchmark jurisdiction performs badly, this may induce the governments of the others to reduce the intensity of their efforts.

(7) Vertical yardstick competition can also be important (Breton 1996). In particular, it is in the essence of federalism, as conceived by its American inventors, that governments situated on two different levels 'compete for the people's affection' (Pettys 2003). That type of competition is possible inasmuch as the governments operate to some degree in the same policy areas. In turn, this may result from the two levels officially sharing some powers or responsibilities, from the assignment of powers being ambiguous or flexible, or, most importantly, from the governments using different powers to intervene in the same policy area.[3]

Merely potential entry in a policy area may be enough to generate incentives. Suppose that only regional governments deal with some important issues in a given policy area and that the office-holders at the central level of government decide that they could do better than the regional governments to deal with the said issues. If the office-holders on the regional level think that the danger of invasion is serious, that the invader would be efficient, and that enough voters would notice the difference in performance, their concern over the chances of winning the next election will generate amongst them an incentive to improve their own performance, and this even if, in fact, the invasion does not take place

[2] Of course, assessments are likely to be biased according to party lines or in relation with internal debates – which raises a number of problems. See Heyndels and Ashworth (2003).

[3] For another, more general, possibility, see Breton and Fraschini (2003).

(Breton and Salmon 2001). The same mechanism of invasion can work in the other direction. Policies by subcentral governments may crowd out, or threaten to crowd out, inefficient policies by the central government in a domain that seemed to be its exclusive responsibility.

An important matter in this context is whether the rights of the different governments are entrenched. In federal systems, 'regional' governments enjoy, almost by definition, some constitutional protection against the deeds of the central government. Otherwise – in unitary states – the competitive character of the vertical relation may be more fragile, the central government being tempted to change the rules (even if only over funding) when in danger of losing the race. I will return to the case of vertical competition in the EU.

C. The Peculiar Path Borrowed by European Integration

Sticking to a strategy devised by the founders, European integration is a roundabout and somewhat conspiratorial process.[4] Its *raison d'être* is mainly political – such as forging ties and constructing a political unit – but the concerns driving it at any point in time are largely economic – or, when not, of a practical and utilitarian character that makes them similar to economic concerns. The strategy has allowed integration to proceed without being burdened by the need to agree on its final destination. It has worked well so far in particular because new Member States have been socialized over time into an understanding and acceptance of its nature. There is no reason to think that, eventually, that socialization will not operate also with regard to the ten countries that joined the EU in 2004. A number of features of integration ensue. After listing them, I will consider the sequence associated with the Single European Act. As discussed later (in Section E), this sequence suggests one way corporate governance could evolve in the EU context.

I. Features of European Integration Related to the Underlying Strategy

The EU set-up is designed or contrived to be biased towards integration (Salmon 2003). One factor is the presence of expansionary incentives in institutions such as the Commission, the European Parliament and the European Court of Justice (ECJ). These incentives, natural in themselves, are strengthened by the duties assigned to the institutions. The Commission and the ECJ are 'guardians of the treaties', and thus of the *acquis communautaire* entrenched in the accession treaties.

[4] It is argued in Salmon (1995) that no conspiracy by elites need be assumed to account for these features.

In spite of the diversification of EU competences, the main legal basis used by EU institutions (the Commission and the ECJ in particular) to foster integration remains the same as in the 1950s and the 1960s: establishing a competitive and integrated internal market. Drawing all the implications of this goal has been and still is the main engine of integration and centralization in the EU (Salmon 2003).

Unanimity is still required for many decisions (despite several rounds of extension of qualified majority-voting). The consequences of the unanimity rule, however, should not be misunderstood. It does not systematically reduce decisions, as often claimed, to a 'lowest common denominator'. Many arrangements are adopted unanimously in spite of a majority being hostile to them. What makes this possible is that issues are linked and positions over them are exchanged. Especially under a perspective of repeated interaction, this allows many policies favoured by only a majority, or even a minority, to be adopted unanimously. Thus the difference between (qualified) majority-voting and unanimous decision-making is more one of degree than of nature.

Thus, whether the rule is unanimity or majority-voting, what will count is the intensity of preferences of all the members on all the issues over which linkages have been established. To make things even more complex, preferences include, or are biased by, a preference for (*europhily*) or against (*euroscepticism*) integration in general. An example is the agreement that yielded in 1986 the Single European Act. How could the British and the French governments, under Margaret Thatcher and François Mitterrand respectively, both acquiesce to the Single European Act? The Act was a major step in the sense of more integration. This was valued negatively by eurosceptical Thatcher and positively by europhile Mitterrand. But these negative and positive values were integrated in calculations that included also the British rebate, enlargement, and subjective expectations of increased competition, deregulation, and centralization.

Integration has often slowed down or even stalled but seldom if ever significantly turned backwards or regressed. Reversals are not precluded but, in fact, their occurrence is rarely plausible (Salmon 2004). The most important effect of this 'monotonocity' is policy spillover or '*engrenage*'. This mechanism, stressed in the earlier literature on integration and almost forgotten today, should be analysed now under the perspective of what the recent literature on the economics of transition calls 'strong aggregate uncertainty' (Roland 2000). In a complicated aggregate process such as integration, decisions can have completely unforeseen consequences, escaping any probability calculus. However, contrary to the prescriptions of the said literature, in the EU context reversals are rarely an option. This affects the way the problem raised by aggregate uncertainty may be coped with. Suppose that it turns out that an integrative step decided or carried out earlier creates serious, unforeseen, problems and suppose that the solution consisting in reversing the integrative step is unavailable. The choice then is either to do nothing or to embark on a second integrative step in the hope that it will solve or mitigate the problems caused by the first. In turn, this second step may have unforeseen consequences, whose mitigation will be sought in further integration, and so on. Of course, the knowledge that an integrative step might start dynamics of that kind, even if it might make the first step attractive to some governments, justifies in most an attitude of extreme caution. Such caution manifests itself in the form of both a reluctance to decide integrative steps and in a propensity to limit the size of the steps undertaken.

The overall bias towards integration finds its best and most important illustration in the vast, macroscopic, process of *engrenage* entailed by the commitment to implement a common market, as was agreed in 1957, or to 'complete the single market', as was repeated in different words thirty years later. I turn to that dynamic now. It is highly relevant for our purpose in two ways. First, it is closely related to yardstick competition. Second, something akin to it may be emerging again from the current EU situation, this time involving corporate lawmaking more directly than it did in the 1980s. I will discuss these two points in Section E.

II. The Dynamic Generated by the Single Market Commitment

Let me start the story with the famous *Cassis de Dijon* ruling of 1979, by which the ECJ interpreted the Treaty of Rome of 1957 as obliging, with exceptions, each Member State to accept on its own market the products imported from any other Member State provided these products satisfied the domestic regulations of that 'home' country. This principle of mutual recognition, confirmed by other judgments, was a powerful way to fight impediments to the internal trade of products. It inspired the 'new approach' to the harmonization of standards adopted by the Commission, and, as a consequence, together with an increased role for qualified majority voting (instead of unanimity) in the Council of Ministers, it became a major piece of the mechanism set by the Single European Act of 1987 and its '1992 programme' to 'complete the single market'. One remark at this stage: without the ECJ jurisprudence imposing mutual recognition, it is not all certain that governments would have agreed to it as they did in the Single Act.

With the Single Act, the Member States undertook the elimination of all remaining barriers and impediments to trade within the Union and of the establishment of a 'level-playing field' so as to eliminate all distortions to competition among firms. This has had consequences whose significance was probably not foreseen by many of those who acquiesced to the undertaking (Salmon 2003). Some politicians and commentators apparently thought at the time that the result would be a decentralized market-oriented system of governance – something like the transposition to the EU setting of the system that Weingast (1993) defends under the name of 'market-preserving federalism'. Its characteristics, according to that author, are 'first, that the authority to regulate markets is not vested with the highest political government in the hierarchy; and, second, that the lower governments are prevented from using their regulatory authority to erect trade barriers against the goods and services from other political units'.

The Single Act did not produce this kind of system. Three facts explain why the outcome was different. First, in the Single European Act itself, as noted, the principle of mutual recognition was accompanied by a change in decision rules that allowed increased recourse to qualified majority voting for measures concerning the single market. The two ways in which the programme could be realized were deregulation and/or regulation centralization. The extension of qualified majority voting increased the feasibility of the second.

The second reason is related to the nature of the impediments to trade and distortions of competition that the Single Act purported to eliminate. Most manifestations of overt protectionism between Member States, such as tariffs and quotas, had been eliminated for some time. Thus the objectives of the single market programme implied contesting aspects of domestic policies that were possibly motivated by protectionism but could as well be claimed to pursue non-protectionist objectives. One aim of the programme was to bring to an end the fragmentation or segmentation of the market. Most if not all regulations by Member States, however, do fragment or segment the market in some regard. A second aim, labelled 'fair competition' or the establishment of a 'level-playing field', consisted of preventing or eliminating distortions of competition. Many regulations again, but also subsidies (and other forms of aid) to firms, as well as privileges granted to the public sector, distort competition. To a large extent, however, all three categories are also unavoidable side-effects of policies that pursue 'domestic', not *a priori* illegitimate, objectives (Breton and Salmon 2001).

Thus a purely negative process of elimination of all sources of fragmentation of the market and distortions of competition meant doing away with the domestic policies themselves, by ruling them out and/or by letting regulatory competition and mutual recognition do the job. This brings us to our third reason why the single market programme did not have the consequence that some expected. Doing away with the said policies was incompatible with the entrenchment of many of them in a social fabric common to all contemporary Western societies.[5] Getting rid of them would have involved drastically down-sized government. On the contrary, a positive process of centralization of policies at the Brussels level was compatible both with the aims of the single market programme and with the preservation of the main responsibilities of government in general.

In the domains in which the programme has been implemented, EU directives, typically on the basis of a claimed need to deal with a source of fragmentation of the market or a distortion of competition, have often intruded into matters that are left to junior governments in most existing federations – the examples of Canada and Switzerland being particularly telling in that respect. In the current EU set-up, reversing the process where it is clearly excessive, however, might seem to signal a renunciation to, or a dilution of, the single market commitment and would encounter the obstacles to reversals in general mentioned earlier. In a sense, un-

[5] Including the United States under Reagan; see Rodden and Rose-Ackerman (1997).

founded centralization is the price to pay for constructing Europe in the way chosen.

D. Corporate Law and Yardstick Competition Among EU Member Countries

The influence of yardstick competition among governments on corporate lawmaking may be direct or indirect. A government may be directly influenced in its decisions regarding corporate law by the thought that some of its voters will compare what it does, or what the situation is in that policy area, to what is done or is the case elsewhere. The influence of yardstick competition is indirect when it has to do with variables unrelated to corporate law but having nonetheless an effect on the policies directly concerned with it. To complicate matters, policy sequences may increase the salience of some aspects of the social system in such a way that they become possible objects of yardstick competition. I will also return in this section to the possibility that yardstick competition leads to an unsatisfactory equilibrium and argue that, indeed, this has been the case in Europe for more than a decade.

I. Direct Influence

A direct influence is less implausible in the EU than in the American context. The reason, as noted earlier, is that, in the United States, the costs of mobility from one jurisdiction to another are very low when that mobility concerns only incorporation. And there is not much harm in assuming that it concerns only incorporation because the characteristics of the legal environment of firms that are outside corporate law are more or less uniform across states. Two features of the European situation make the matter quite different. One is the 'real seat' doctrine. Where that doctrine is enforced, mobility is more costly, imposing a displacement of substantial real activities. The other feature is that the part of the legal environments of firms which is not governed by corporate law but by various other legal and regulatory blocks is more diverse across EU countries than it is across states in America. Inasmuch as a part of these other regulatory blocks is related to the country of incorporation and/or of real seat, changing that country is a more consequential decision than if only corporate law proper was concerned. Thus it is less the case in Europe than it is in the United States that mobility-based competition over features of corporate law pre-empts yardstick competition over the same variables.

For direct yardstick competition over characteristics of corporate law to be significant, however, a precondition is that their salience is sufficient for politicians to think that the way they deal with them might have an electoral impact. Admittedly, if we accept the probabilistic insights, it is not necessary that a concern be shared by a majority of voters for it to become relevant in electoral terms and generate incentives among incumbents. Corporate law affects large numbers of wage-earners and shareholders. It must be enough that only a subset of these large categories pays attention to it and makes use of comparisons with what occurs abroad for that to have a policy impact which we can consider a manifestation of direct yardstick competition. Yet casual observation does not suggest that this is very much the case, except with regard to some hot issues such as executive officers' and directors' pay or, in the wake of scandals, the need for more reliable accounts. Regarding wage-earners, one could argue that, in continental Europe, corporate law and other parts of the legal environment of firms protect them sufficiently and perhaps even a bit too much. This may explain why they are not strongly dissatisfied with the status quo.

What about small shareholders, a category which the literature generally considers as insufficiently protected by corporate law in continental Europe? It is true that gauging corporate law by way of comparisons is a particularly complex exercise, notably because differences across countries often compensate each other, and different provisions or practices may be functionally equivalent (Kraakman et al 2004). Thus it may be difficult for small shareholders to engage in comparisons across countries. But this informational obstacle could be overcome by the agency of intermediaries such as specialized media, associations, and politicians. In reality, the reason why shareholder's electoral pressure remains inexistent or modest should perhaps be sought not mainly in the obvious informational problems just mentioned but in the fact that current shareholders, after all, are not badly treated given the price they paid for their shares. The return expected by the marginal shareholder is comparable to what its brethren expect on the other side of the Ocean or the Channel. Otherwise, why for instance would American pension and mutual funds hold such a large proportion of the shares of the main European firms (30% on average in France)? Inasmuch as there is some difference between the United States and the United Kingdom, on the one hand, and continental Europe, on the other, with regard to the protection of minority shareholders, this is reflected in the size of the stock-markets or the extension of shareholding (100 and 150% of GDP in France and in the United States, respectively; a larger difference with the United States in the case of Germany and Italy).[6] Improvements in small shareholders' protection would constitute for them a sort of windfall. It is understandable that they are less likely to respond to the uncertain prospect of a windfall, their present position being fair, than they would if they had grounds to perceive themselves as victims of mismanagement or exploitation.

The fact that direct effects in this area will as a rule tend to be weak does not mean, however, that they cannot acquire some significance when, for example, scandals, or the remuneration of top managers, make it to the front pages of the press, as has happened recently. In addition, as noted, incumbents may seek sup-

[6] The difference may also be reflected in the cost of capital.

port, independently of elections, from various constituencies (academics, lawyers, accountants, bankers, etc.) and these constituencies, even though they do not face the information asymmetry obstacles encountered by voters, may nonetheless seek in international comparisons a way to evaluate the laws and regulations in force in their own country, stimulate the public debate about them, and, possibly, induce some change. The incentives provided in this manner to office-holders may not be very different from those provided to them by the main form of yardstick competition, that which involves voters.

II. Indirect Influence

Yardstick competition among European countries over macroeconomic performance may account for some of the findings about corporate governance associated with the recent 'Law and Finance' literature.[7] That literature uses a typology of four 'legal families' or 'origins' – English, French, Germanic and Scandinavian – to explain differences observable across countries in several sets of variables. Two variables are of interest to us here. One is the average performance of business firms or, related to that, the degree to which corporate law protects investors. The other is macroeconomic performance, as measured in particular by income per head or economic growth.

In Table 1, I have extracted some figures pertaining to European countries from Table 3 of Gugler, Mueller and Yurtoglu (2004) and recalculated the averages for the four legal families.[8] A look at Table 1 will confirm that there is something in the relationship between legal families and an indicator of the financial performance of firms, marginal q (defined as return on investment over cost of capital, and supposedly required to be at least equal to 1 if the interests of shareholders are to be maximized). By contrast (a formal procedure to establish that is not really needed), GDP long-run growth (32 years) shows little variation among the core European countries (the founding EU members in particular) – and even within the whole group once two outliers, Ireland and Switzerland, are (for reasons easy to provide) excluded.[9]

[7] In this discussion, I will disregard the ten countries that joined in 2004.

[8] Although all the countries selected, except Norway and Switzerland, are members of the EU now, only six were members over the whole period (1960-1992) to which the figures for GDP growth apply. Thus, including Norway and Switzerland raises no particular problem.

[9] In fact, it was conceded from the start by the promoters of the approach which came to be called the Law and Finance approach that the relationship between legal origins and economic growth could not plausibly concern developed countries (see La Porta et al 1998).

	Marginal q	GDP growth 1960-92
Britain	0.85	2.27
Ireland	1.10	4.25
English-origin average	**0.98**	**3.26**
Denmark	0.65	2.09
Finland	0.96	2.40
Norway	1.04	3.43
Sweden	0.65	1.79
Scandinavian-origin average	**0.83**	**2.43**
Austria	0.71	2.74
Germany	0.57	2.60
Switzerland	0.64	1.18
Germanic-origin average	**0.64**	**2.17**
Belgium	0.51	2.46
France	0.57	2.54
Greece	0.54	2.46
Italy	0.64	2.82
Netherlands	0.69	2.55
Portugal	0.46	3.52
Spain	0.54	3.27
French-origin average	**0.56**	**2.80**
General average 16 countries*	**0.70**	**2.65**
(United States)	**(1.05)**	**(2.74)**
* Luxembourg is excluded because its GDP growth rate is not indicated in the original table.		

Table 1: Legal origins and performance (European countries extracted from Gugler, Mueller and Yurtoglu 2004, Table 3).

I will discuss differences over shorter periods, but, for the moment, I take as fact the existence, within the EU, of significant differences in the average financial performance of firms but not in (long-term) macroeconomic growth. The combination of these two observations is in need of some explanation. I suggest that yardstick competition over macroeconomic performance among the Member States of the European Union may contribute something to that explanation. To justify that proposition, I will argue, first, that yardstick competition precludes enduring differences in growth rates (never mind other possible sufficient causes for their absence), and then that the observed convergence of growth rates can be the outcome of very different arrangements regarding in particular corporate governance.

As noted in Section B, intergovernmental competition of the yardstick variety will be more effective when the political systems are themselves competitive, when information about what happens in other jurisdictions is readily available to the public at large, and when that public or a significant subset of it pays attention to that information. These conditions are fulfilled to a particularly large degree by yardstick competition among the governments of the Member States of the EU. In each of them, electoral competition is generally intense and incumbents are typically far from sure of being reelected. This makes them attentive to the state of all sectors of opinion. Moreover, information about what obtains in other Member States is abundant and widely commented on. This can cover particular domains, of interest to single-issue categories of voters, but comparisons are more likely to constrain governments when they are focused on broad macroeconomic indicators such as unemployment and economic growth (or income per head).

Given this responsiveness of the political system and this high degree of information availability and awareness, an enduring or increasing negative performance gap in a country, as measured in particular by comparisons of economic growth with other countries, is likely to induce in that country a powerful reaction against the policies followed by the incumbents, and against the incumbents themselves if they prove unable to change policies in time. As far at least as the countries that have been members of the EU for a long time are concerned, a substantial and enduring divergence in income levels or rates of growth is thus unlikely.

The word 'enduring' above is important, especially given the widespread perception that, in Europe, Britain is now doing better than the other countries in a kind of permanent or structural way. It must be recalled that Britain had a high level of income per head just after World War II, as compared to other European countries. Then, it had a negative performance gap in terms of economic growth but still not in terms of income per head over a relatively long period of time. This could be interpreted as reflecting a process of catching up by the other European countries. When income per head in the UK did fall below that of several other Member States of the EU (first Germany, then France, then Italy), it needed some time for public opinion in Britain to react, but eventually, the reaction took place. The policy change was radical and, one may assume, it did cause the British economy to catch up. Currently, income per head in Britain is more or less equal to, when not slightly above, that of Germany, France, Italy and the Benelux countries (the differences are statistically insignificant). So far, thus, there is not much ground to assume an 'enduring' difference in terms of macroeconomic performance between Britain and countries such as France, Germany and Italy. This does not imply however, that the recent success of the British economy does not inspire some interest among various constituencies and even among voters in these countries. Some pressure on politicians towards reforms ensues, but this phenomenon is embedded in a larger one, to which I will turn shortly.

Given the inferior record regarding financial performance of some of the countries included in Table 1, together with the absence of any ensuing gap in macroeconomic performance, either the first kind of performance has no impact on the second, or it is compensated somehow by the positive impact of other variables. Because of the difference in financial performance, functional equivalence limited to corporate law, even understood liberally as in Kraakman et al (2004), will not yield the kind of equivalence required here. What we need is a functional equivalence between the policies and arrangements that allow different countries to achieve comparable levels of GDP per head or rates of GDP growth. Corporate law plays an important role, undoubtedly. But it is only one element of the legal environment of firms, other bodies of law – concerned with financial markets, labour, competition, bankruptcy, taxation, and the environment – being also important. And the legal environment of firms is itself only one the factors of macroeconomic performance over which governments may exert some influence. Other factors include transportation and communication, public services, aggregate levels of saving and investment, and education.

It is understandable and even unavoidable that the broader picture is often neglected in discussions focused on corporate law and governance. I will give a single example. Hertig and McCahery (2003) suggest a number of measures, to be taken at the EU level, that would facilitate litigation by minority shareholders – a mode of protection of their interests relatively underdeveloped in continental Europe as compared to the United States. One of these measures would be to allow, or to recognize, contingent fees. But do we really want to legitimise contingent fees in Europe? There are certainly advantages and drawbacks to such a decision, in both cases necessarily transcending the limits of corporate governance. Regarding the negative side, the main problem is not frivolous litigation, as discussed in their very interesting paper, but the aggregate level of litigation in general, and with it the number of people engaged in legal professions (lawyers, judges, law professors, etc). Several well-known economists – Gordon Tullock and Jack Hirshleifer in particular – have long argued that the aggregate cost of litigation is increased in excess of any additional benefit by features typical of the American system – adversarial procedure, use of juries in civil matters, and practice of contingent fees, for example. I do not know whether they are right. The point is only that, both from a policy-oriented perspective and from a purely positive wish to understand economic growth differentials, the main issues of corporate governance should not be discussed in isolation.[10]

This brings me to the idea defended by Charreaux (2004): we should move from the idea of national systems of corporate governance to that of governance of national systems. An analysis that does concentrate on the characteristics of the national systems and treats differences in corporate law as relatively secondary is that of Roe (2003a, e.g.). In continental Europe, according to him, the agency problem central to corporate governance is not the risk of malfeasance, self-dealings, etc. on which most of the literature concentrates but the tendency among

[10] A frequently met difficulty is that the incidence of a feature of the legal system cannot easily be restricted to a particular domain, such as corporate law. This is a general phenomenon. In early January 2005, on the occasion of the ceremonies in which French presidents speak at that time of the year, the incumbent president was understood to announce that something like class action would or should be introduced in France to improve the protection of consumers. This started a controversy in which it was clear that any reform was bound to involve domains other than that of consumers' protection. Along the same line, it must also be noted that different factors of macroeconomic performance may not be treated as independent explanatory variables in a separable function, as often assumed. More effect from one factor may entail getting less from another.

managers to follow policies that are not fully aligned on the interests of shareholders. The reason is the influence of the social democratic tradition that is a characteristic of these countries. Given this nature of the agency problem, concentrated ownership of the firms is a way to monitor managers' decisions – blockholders having both the capacity and the incentives to ensure that managers follow policies that suit them or shareholders in general.

One can fully agree with the general approach adopted by Roe without subscribing, at least as far as France is concerned, to all his interpretations. The main traits of corporate governance in France are certainly in part related to social-democratic tendencies, as in the rest of continental Europe, and as Roe shows very well. This is particularly true and important with regard to lay-offs and to the downsizing of firms. However, perhaps as relevant, corporate governance is also related in France to the fact that nationalism or patriotism is a motivation shared, across the private-public divide, by CEOs, higher civil servants, and even private founders or owners of large industrial and financial firms (many members of the three groups being graduates of the same schools anyhow). This explains that the discretionary power of CEOs tends to be regarded in that country as something highly valuable, to be preserved at all costs, rather than the troublesome manifestation of an agency problem (which it is also, of course).

A concern with safeguarding this discretionary power, threatened potentially from three directions by shareholders, employees and some parts of the public administration or government, may explain much of the strategy the French managers have followed, with the acquiescence and help of the government, since the early 1980s (Hancké 2001). They have found in the international stock markets not only a source of finance and a convenient mean to absorb other firms in France or abroad, but also an essential counterweight to pressures from employees or ministerial departments. Thanks to block- or cross-holdings and to government regulation (in particular with regard to lay-offs), they have protected themselves against pressure from shareholders and threats of takeovers from abroad. And CEOs have used this discretion to enhance the growth of the firms they managed - probably (going back to the values of q in Table 1) above the rate of growth that would have maximized the interest of shareholders. In a sense, the old managerial model of maximization of the size (or growth rate) of the firm under a minimal profit constraint (Baumol 1959, 1962) applies fairly well to contemporary French managers, albeit with the motivations underlying the growth objective partly different from that assumed in that model.

Interestingly, the large French firms that are family-held – Peugeot-Citroen, Michelin and many others – do not seem less growth-oriented than those which are not family-held and, in particular, those which have a diffused ownership. Is this surprising? In a recent issue of the *Financial Times*, the 'willingness to take risk' observed on the part of Dassault Aviation was ascribed to 'the company's lack of exposure to the stock market'.[11] The views defended by Albert (1991), among others, in the late 1980s and early 1990s might be, after all, dormant rather than obsolete.

To sum up, for France at least, I think that it is not surprising that a system of corporate governance different from the one deemed optimal, and a low level of financial performance as measured by q in Table 1, prove compatible in the long run with a level of macroeconomic performance quite normal or average, as the same Table 1 indicates. This does not mean that characteristics of corporate governance that lead to some misallocation of capital (as measured here by q being less than 1) do not reflect *ceteris paribus* some kind of inefficiency. But the *ceteris paribus* clause here is dubious. The misallocation of capital may be compensated by many things – by more efforts or loyalty on the part of employees, for example. More importantly, let me recall that the whole normative discussion of the 1960s and 1970s about the merits of takeovers, the optimal level of investment, misallocation of capital, and so on, was concerned with efficiency and optimality, by no means with macroeconomic growth. It is the Law and Finance literature which has confused the two criteria.[12] From the standpoint of efficiency or optimality, growth can be excessive. Thus it is quite possible that the arrangements in place in a given country produce a high rate of growth and at the same time deserve to be deemed inefficient. For this to be the case, it is enough, for instance, that these arrangements cause capital to be misallocated and at the same time, through a higher level of aggregate saving, the total quantity of it to be larger.

III. Direct Entailed by Indirect

I have argued that, with some exceptions, yardstick competition has little direct effect on corporate law and works mainly at the level of macroeconomic performance. This is true in the absence of change, actual or potential. Competition to ensure a sufficient level of macroeconomic performance, however, may endow some issues, closer to corporate governance, with such a level of salience that they become objects of direct relationships.

[11] M Odell 'Technology puts group in front' *Fin Times* (12 October 2004). The statement in the text is formulated by a consultant cited in the article. It is elaborated as follows: 'Unlike their US competitors, Dassault does not have to worry about its stock price .... Less than 5 per cent of Dassault shares are freely available to trade on stock markets with just over 50 per cent owned by Serge Dassault, the son of founder Marcel.'

[12] Perhaps rightly so, one must admit. It can be argued that in a world in which most if not all countries grow, it would be unsustainable and inefficient for a single country not to grow also, even in the case where zero growth would be optimal according to the conventional social welfare criteria.

The foregoing discussion on France suggests that, sometimes at least, what counts most for corporate governance may be the relative weight the government of a country and, in a sense, the country itself give to various concerns and issues. These may be the interest of shareholders as weighted against that of other categories, the degree of intolerance of lay-offs, working conditions, attitudes toward inequality and competition, the credibility of claims to serve a collective interest, or attention paid to the national identity of firms. For each country, if we add to these concerns other relevant national traits – such as the nature and status of the public administration – we get a distinctive blend of characteristics that typically proves to be relatively robust or entrenched.

Entrenched characteristics may or may not be embodied or reflected in corporate law, this depending to a large extent on the availability of substitutes outside it. A case in point is the treatment of takeovers. Inasmuch as one of their functions is to 'rationalize' production and reduce its cost by laying off personnel, a country in which lay-offs are considered a major nuisance will not be inclined to facilitate takeovers. This reluctance may be reflected in corporate law and securities regulations. Alternatively, it may have no direct incidence on corporate law or the legal treatment of takeovers but be reflected instead directly in labour law, employment protection and the regulation of layoffs.

To maintain macroeconomic performance, some deep-seated concerns and entrenched characteristics may have to give way or lose their priority. This is usually difficult. The fact that one country accepts to give up some well anchored principle, reflecting a major concern, may help the government of another country to persuade various constituencies and voters in general that similar sacrifices are unavoidable if the economy is to remain 'in the race'. So far, for the reason to which I turn now, this mechanism has not been working very much in Europe and, in any case, the incidence on corporate governance, if any, has been relatively modest.

IV. Perverse Effects

A very important fact, in my view, is that yardstick competition among the governments of the EU Member States has been a major influence over the last decade albeit, on the whole, a negative one. The mechanism has worked perversely. The macroeconomic performance of Germany has been relatively weak, largely for understandable reasons such as the economic burden of unification and the relative disadvantage entailed by European monetary union. Because Germany, and definitely not Britain, is the traditional benchmark used by all to gauge relative performance, the governments of countries such as France and

Italy have felt able to relax and accept that their economies are also doing badly without arising too much concern among voters.[13]

This perverse mechanism has affected domains other than the macroeconomy. The adjournment of reforms considered almost unanimously as necessary in one country is easily mimicked in others under the political pressure of potential losers or of sufficiently influential sectors of public opinion. The reasoning is: if other countries can afford to wait, why can't we? Lately, however, in the press and, to some extent, in public opinion in general, comparisons have turned, within the EU, to countries such as Britain and, outside the EU, to the United States and other continents. The reforms perceived to have enabled the satisfactory performance of the British economy – even though, as noted, that performance is overestimated (because largely due to catching up) – as well as various features of the American economy are becoming inputs in the political debate in Germany itself. In turn, the start of reforms in that country has now a significant impact on the political debates in several other Member States and in Switzerland. This change already has important political consequences, observable in particular in the relative popularity of the various leaders and in governments' agenda. Perhaps even more important for our purpose, there is a growing awareness of the need to do something at the European Union level. This also can be interpreted as a manifestation of yardstick competition.

E. Is Yardstick Competition at a Higher Level Likely to Start a Centralizing Dynamic Akin to that of the Single Market?

If, notably in the light of a comparison with the American economy, competition among Member States seems unable to generate sufficient economic growth in the EU as a whole, is it possible that a dynamic akin to that started by the Single Act of 1987 would do the job? This is a serious possibility, I think, even though I will not claim that it is also highly probable. I will present the argument in a schematic way.

Europessimism is back. The performance of the European economy over the last decade has not been satisfactory. Some European countries have done better than others but mainly because they were catching up. Overall, growth has been weak and, in spite of its size, Europe has remained mostly passive, largely dependent in particular on impulsions from outside (mainly the United States) to move out of recessions. These failures – as well as other dimensions of an actual

[13] The text suggests the presence, to a degree, of an asymmetry in the comparisons. Indeed, there is some empirical evidence that differentials in macroeconomic performance between France and Germany have an effect on votes in the former country but not in the second (Lewis-Beck, Jérôme and Jérôme-Speziari 2001). As noted, a low-performance equilibrium may, however, obtain even in the absence of such asymmetry.

or looming relative decline such as the emergence of China, possibly followed by that of India – are increasingly perceived by public opinion, or influential sectors thereof. They are discussed, indeed *ad nauseam*, in the media, in popular books, and in public debates.

The mood today is akin to the widespread feeling of 'europessimism' and the related perception of 'eurosclerosis' that played a large role in the design and acceptance of the Single Act of 1986 and its '1992' programme. The 2004 elections to the European Parliament reflect in several ways that sentiment.[14]

Europessimism illustrates one ingredient of horizontal yardstick competition, i.e., popular discontent caused by comparisons that reveal the existence of a negative performance gap. The comparisons are first of all with the United States, even though, as noted, accelerated growth on other continents also plays a role. In other words, public opinion, say in France and Italy, is less prone than in the past to look at Germany and more inclined to look (as does public opinion in Germany itself) at the United States and then, with the encouragement of the national governments, to put the blame for the relatively low performance of the European economy on the EU as such.

What may seem lacking at the EU level is the second ingredient of yardstick competition: political pressure on office-holders to act and eliminate the gap. The problem, of course, is the structure of the EU and, in particular, the absence in it of any electoral contest comparable to the elections that influence policy-makers in democratic countries. It is not clear who the policy-makers are at the EU level, anyhow. But widespread discontent may have an impact on policy-making nonetheless. The way discontent translates into incentives and from there into policy measures is certainly not as transparent in the EU setting as it may be in democratic nation states, but I suggest that to a degree, somehow, and eventually, such translation normally takes place. If this is the case, the inexistence of our second ingredient is more apparent than real. It may not bear, after all, the main responsibility for what looks, so far, like a weak response of the EU to discontent.

Vertical competition cannot play a large role. Popular dissatisfaction with the EU is not of the same order as discontent with the Member States or some of them. In a sense what is expected from the EU is that it makes up for failures of the Member States. If the EU were a federation, the fact that discontent is largely

[14] As demonstrated by Blanchard (2004), the performance gap between the EU and the United States, in terms of productivity and growth, arose only in the mid-1990s. It is thus quite normal that awareness of the gap is a recent phenomenon. It must also be noted that the performance of Japan has been as weak as that of Europe and that it is only recently that countries such as China, India and Brazil have stopped being considered exclusively as third-world countries and started being perceived by public opinion as major potential competitors. See also in Blanchard (2004) an explanation of the differences this time not in growth rates but in levels of income per capita between the EU and France, on the one hand, and the United States, on the other. One thing suggested by his analysis, I think, is that differences in income levels tend not to become objects of yardstick competition; the difference in income per head between Europe and the United States is about the same today as it was in 1970.

addressed to the subcentral level of government – that is, here, to the Member States – would offer the EU level a marvellous opportunity to extend its responsibilities and invade policy domains heretofore exploited by the Member States alone. Something like the phenomena analysed by Breton (1996) in general and by Roe (2003b) in a particular setting would happen. One might argue that, sometimes, manifestations of vertical yardstick competition of that kind do have an analogue in the EU. In some areas, including corporate law and the regulation of financial markets, the Commission does offer to substitute itself in part to Member States. It is not clear, however, that these initiatives reflect a desire to compete. Vertical competition in the European Union is necessarily limited because decision-making in Brussels is not really independent or autonomous vis-à-vis the Member States, and also because 'Europe is under construction'. It is of the essence of the integration process that increasing powers be progressively reallocated to the EU level, not only with the agreement but as the result of the deliberate long-term strategy of the Member States' governments referred to earlier. As a rule, thus, policy-making at the EU level cannot be in a significantly competitive relation with that of the Member States. A major exception is the ECJ – and the Commission itself when it has a quasi-judicial function, as is the case with regard to competition.

The comparative advantage of the EU level. To invigorate the European economy, it can be argued that the most important necessary reforms fall into the competences of the Member States rather than in those of 'Brussels'. This explains why the so-called Lisbon Agenda – adopted by a European Council in 2000 and aiming at improving Europe's global competitiveness so that the EU would 'achieve a very high level of growth and employment in 2010', to use its phrasing – is above all an exercise in exhortation and has had little effect so far.[15] The new Commission contemplates stronger devices to induce each country individually to play its part in the implementation of the programme, but I doubt that much can be done along that line.

Almost fifty years after the Treaty of Rome, the strength of EU activism remains the same: its *raison d'être* is in establishing a competitive and integrated internal market, including whatever implications can be drawn from that objective. Thus if something is to be done at the EU level to foster economic growth, as is perhaps genuinely on the European agenda, the most reliable path to follow remains, as in the mid-1980s, relating all initiatives to the completion and deepening of the common or single market. Fortunately in a sense, the task is far from being fully realized. Fostering more competition in markets that remain segmented (finance, services, etc.), more specialization among Member States, and the emergence of larger transnational European firms so as to benefit from

[15] To a degree, the implementation of the Lisbon agenda was intended to work through something like yardstick competition, or at least reform emulation, among member states. For reasons that could be spelled out, this was more or less doomed to fail.

economies of scale remains the set of policies that matches most closely the economic *raison d'être* of the EU and is also the most likely to make a distinctive impact on long-term growth.

Application to corporate governance. The doubts expressed above about the Lisbon approach have some implications for corporate governance in the EU. Many suggestions and projects, some of them endorsed by the Commission, are defended as means to improve corporate governance. This is the case, for instance, of proposals regarding auditor rotation, off-balance sheet financing, mandatory statements, and the profile of non-executive directors. The motivation underlying these suggestions and projects is typically that their implementation will make the economy more efficient and will contribute, even if only modestly, to enhancing economic growth. Let us assume that better corporate governance will have the latter effect – even though, as argued in Section D, this is far from obvious. It remains that the efficiency or growth objective is in the spirit of the Lisbon approach and raises the same queries. Inasmuch as lawmaking can improve corporate governance, and then enhance growth, the Member States can undertake severally to reform corporate law. If they do not introduce the necessary reforms at their own level, it is an illusion akin to those that inspired the Lisbon agenda to think that, as a rule and in a significant way, this introduction will be achieved by decision-making at the EU level.

In other words, if reform proposals are defended only as a means to improve corporate governance (admitting that the claim is warranted), they are unlikely to make much headway. European integration does not function in this way, as we saw. Or, rather, it does so only at the margin or in appearance. In contrast, endeavours aiming at eliminating or mitigating features of company law or corporate governance that can be characterized as obstacles to the realization of a competitive and integrated market have a much better chance.

Admittedly, one could argue that diversity across countries with regard to corporate law, auditing, securities regulation and so on, has many advantages. To mention one, now that in the wake of Enron and Parmalat it is difficult to deny that all regulatory systems may fail, and moreover fail in a way which is largely idiosyncratic, diversification across these systems, reducing in this way the 'regulatory failure risk', may seem a good idea, in particular from the standpoint of shareholders and fund managers. But, as shown by previous episodes of integration, some of which I alluded to earlier, this kind of argument is not really likely to be deemed relevant in the EU setting. There, what counts is that differences across Member States, whatever their rationale or merits, should be treated above all as impediments to trade and a source of additional transaction costs. They should also be suspected of distorting fair competition among firms and preventing the establishment of a perfect 'level-playing field' (Breton and Salmon 2001).

Thus, as in the early 1980s, europessimism (related, as we saw, to a yardstick competition in which the EU as a whole has become engaged) and the perception of an urgent need to do something at the EU level may justify and push through a new programme of elimination of barriers to trade and distortions of competition, this time possibly in the area we are concerned with – that of commercial law, mergers and financial services. This line is, I think, the most promising that the Commission can use to increase substantially its involvement in these domains.

Beginnings. There are several signs that a first stage of this development is underway. An early indicator is – as was the *Cassis de Dijon* ruling of 1979 that imposed mutual recognition – the recent bold jurisprudence of the ECJ. The *Centros* and subsequent judgments open possibilities for firms to incorporate in Member States other than the one in which they have their main activities. This is explicitly authorized by the Court as an implication of the internal market. How far will jurisprudence bring us in the direction of regulatory competition? This is still a matter of controversy, but the signal and the direction are clear. Then there is the *Societas Europea* – the European company statute – which is currently entering in use and which also offers a means, with some restrictions, to choose one's rules among those in force in different countries. Again, it is difficult to predict the implications of that legal instrument but there is a possibility that the consequences will be important. The remaining signs include the Action Plan of the Commission and other recent initiatives, actions and proposed directives on its part.

Regulatory competition or centralization? Many aspects of the national systems of governance discussed or alluded to earlier, those of France, Germany and Italy in particular, are quite suspect from a perspective focusing on the elimination of all barriers and distortions of competition. Patriotism or nationalism and its implications on the behaviour of government, management and large owners, as in France, or cosy and informal relations within various kinds of national groups and networks, as in Germany and Italy, constitute an obstacle to the full integration of the internal market. In addition, they hinder the process of mergers among firms (including banks) across the borders of Member States, and thus the emergence of a sufficient number of really trans-European large firms. The Anglo-Saxon model of corporate governance, with public firms and diffuse ownership, seems more transparent and, for that reason and others, more compatible with the rules governing in principle the internal market than are the continental models (Gordon 2004). One might be tempted, thus, to imagine that the beginnings just mentioned announce a vast movement of regulatory competition, the generalized adoption of home rather than host regulation, the dismantling of most barriers, the elimination of most distortions, and a convergence towards the Anglo-Saxon model of corporate governance – not because that model is better in some sense but, as Gordon stresses, simply because of the said greater compatibility.

The experience of the Single Act and of the 1992 programme suggests that such an outcome is unlikely. Countries such as France, Germany and Italy will probably build up a coalition that will impose a compromise between the safeguard of many of the principles entrenched in their societies on the one hand, and the need to facilitate mergers across their borders and to allow more competition and integration in those sectors of activity that have remained relatively segmented, on the other. An example is takeover law, or more generally the regulation of mergers. Most of the governments in continental Europe will be wary of letting takeovers and mergers entail unprotected or non-negotiated lay-offs, involving large numbers. These governments will make sure that transformations in the legal framework will not lead to such a result. If the said transformations were to be expected as an effect of regulatory competition, and if – for instance because of ECJ judgements – governments could not block or limit that competition by the use of their own regulatory or lawmaking power, then they would seek a solution in the form of centralization at the EU level.

As with the implementation of the Single Act, the most comfortable way to eliminate impediments to an integrated market while safeguarding regulation is to accept substantial centralization at the EU level – if necessary with some possibility of opting-out. Because many of the concerns dominant in France, Germany and Italy are shared by some of the other Member States, and because these three countries have a weight which renders their priorities influential in the processes of issue-linkage and position-trading that precede any major decision in the EU, it is probable that the rules that will emerge at the EU level will not converge towards those in force in the United States or Britain but will present a distinctive European or 'continental European' character. As many other outcomes of the usually tortuous processes that lead to decisions in the EU, these rules will not necessarily be those that optimal design or scholarly discussion would have recommended.

F. Conclusion

Regulatory competition in the area of corporate law is becoming a topical issue in the context of the European Union as it has been for some time in that of the United States. The approach underlying our discussion of the matter has been based on the presupposition that, in democracies, voters count. Their influence is felt in all sectors of public policies. This applies to corporate lawmaking as to other domains. Voters, however, are in a situation of information asymmetry. The possibility of comparing the performance of their own government with that of others mitigates the informational difficulties they face. These comparisons have an effect on office-holders' incentives and decisions and generate a situation of yardstick competition among governments – a form of competition that must be taken into account together with the better known form based on the cross-border mobility of individuals, firms and capital. In the case of corporate law, however, the role played by yardstick competition will typically be indirect.

I have tried to show that the particular intensity, among Member States of the EU, of yardstick competition over macroeconomic variables may account for economic growth in these countries converging in the long run in spite of their systems of corporate governance being quite diverse and, under some criteria, of uneven quality. I have also argued that, over the last decade or so, yardstick competition within the EU has had a perverse effect, leading to a low-performance equilibrium.

In contrast, yardstick competition between the EU as a whole and other parts of the world, the United States in particular, seems able to have a positive effect on the rate of economic growth in Europe. That possibility, however, must be discussed in the context of the peculiar path followed by European integration and the idiosyncrasies of EU decision-making. One feature of the EU system, as it works in practice, is a pervasive recourse to issue-linkages and intergovernmental bargaining. This entails that entrenched preferences of Member States are seldom bypassed, even when formal decision-making rules could allow it. Another characteristic is that the comparative advantage of decision-making at the EU level rather than at the level of each Member State still lies, as it has always done, in the task of drawing up and implementing all the implications of the internal market commitment.

Some of these implications concern us directly. Differences in corporate law and governance across Member States will typically be interpreted as a source of additional costs for transactions across borders as well as an obstacle to perfectly fair competition among firms. In other words, they will be interpreted as not fully consonant with a fully integrated and competitive internal market. If the EU as such is to play a role in the effort (induced by yardstick competition with the outside world and involving first of all the Member States) to enhance economic growth in Europe, and if, for this role to be credible, the EU concentrates on the internal market, this may justify EU policies aiming at reducing differences in corporate law or, more generally, in the legal environment of business firms. These policies will be constrained, however, by the entrenchment of voters' preferences. I have tried to show, consequently, that the dynamic entailed is more likely to lead to centralized regulation than to deregulation or enduring regulatory competition, and may well end up in a distinctive legal environment for firms doing business in Europe. This outcome will have to be sustainable, notably in its ability to allow macroeconomic performance at the level required by competition with the outside world. But, as is usual with EU arrangements, judging it in terms of efficiency or optimality will be largely irrelevant.

References

Albert, M *Capitalisme contre capitalisme* (Editions du Seuil 1991).

Baiman, S and JS Demski 'Economically Optimal Performance Evaluation and Control Systems' (1980) 1 J Acc Res (Suppl) 184-220.

Baumol, WJ *Business Behavior, Value and Growth* (Macmillan 1959).

Baumol, WJ 'On the Theory of Expansion of the Firm' (1962) 52 Amer Econ Rev 1078-1087.

Besley, T and A Case 'Incumbent Behavior: Vote-seeking, Tax-setting, and Yardstick Competition' (1995) 85 Amer Econ Rev 25-45.

Blanchard, O 'The Economic Future of Europe' (2004) 18 (4) J Econ Perspect 3-26.

Bordignon, M, F Cerniglia and F Revelli 'Yardstick Competition in Intergovernmental Relationships: Theory and Empirical Predictions' (2004) 83 Economics Letters 325-333.

Breton, A *Competitive Governments: An Economic Theory of Politics and Public Finance* (Cambridge University Press 1996).

Breton, A and A Fraschini 'Vertical Competition in Unitary States: the Case of Italy' (2003) 114 Public Choice 55-77.

Breton, A and P Salmon 'External Effects of Domestic Regulations: Comparing Internal and International Barriers to Trade' (2001) 21 Int Rev Law Econ 135-155.

Charreaux, G 'Corporate Governance Theories: from Micro Theories to National Systems Theories' (Université de Bourgogne, Fargo wp No. 10401202, 2004).

Gordon, JN 'The International Relations Wedge in the Corporate Convergence Debate' in JF Gordon and MJ Roe (eds) *Convergence and Persistence in Corporate Governance* (Cambridge University Press 2004) 161-209.

Gugler, K, DC Mueller and BB Yurtoglu 'Corporate Governance and Globalization' (2004) 20 Oxford Rev Econ Pol 129-156.

Hancké, B 'Revisiting the French Model: Coordination and Restructuring in French Industry' in PA Hall and D Soskice (eds) *Varieties of Capitalism: The Institutional Foundations of Comparative Advantage* (Oxford University Press 2001) 307-334

Hertig, G and JA McCahery 'Company Takeover Law Reforms in Europe: Misguided Harmonization Efforts or Regulatory Competition?' (ECGI Law wp No. 12/2003 <http://www.ssrn.com/abstract=438421>, 2003).

Heyndels, B and J Ashworth 'Self-serving Bias in Tax Perceptions: Federalism as a Source of Political Instability' (2003) 56 Kyklos 47-68.

Hillman, AL *Public Finance and Public Policy: Responsibilities and Limitations of Government* (Cambridge University Press 2003).

Hirschman, AO *Exit, Voice and Loyalty* (Harvard University Press 1970).

Kraakman, RR et al *The Anatomy of Corporate Law: A Comparative and Functional Approach* (Oxford University Press 2004).

La Porta, R, F Lopez de Silanes, A Shleifer and R Vishny 'Law and Finance' (1998) 106 J Polit Economy 1113-55.

Lazear, EP, and S Rosen 'Rank Order Tournaments as Optimal Labor Contracts' (1981) 89 J Polit Economy 841-864.

Lewis-Beck, M, B Jérôme and V Jérôme-Speziari 'Evaluation économique et vote en France et en Allemagne' in D Rénié and B Cautrès (eds) *L'opinion européenne 2001* (Presses de Sciences Po 2001) 101-122.

Pettys, TE 'Competing for the People's Affection: Federalism's Forgotten Marketplace' (2003) 56 Vand L Rev 329-391.

Roe, MJ *Political Determinants of Corporate Governance: Political Context, Corporate Impact* (Oxford University Press 2003a).

Roe, MJ 'Delaware's Competition' (2003b) 117 Harv L Rev 588-646.

Rodden, J and S Rose-Ackerman 'Does Federalism Preserve Markets?' (1997) 83 Va L Rev 1521-72.

Roland, G *Transition and Economics: Politics, Markets, and Firms* (The MIT Press 2000).

Salmon, P 'Decentralisation as an Incentive Scheme' (1987) 3 (2) Oxford Rev Econ Pol 24-43.

Salmon, P 'Nations Conspiring Against Themselves: an Interpretation of European Integration' in A Breton, G Galeotti, P Salmon and R Wintrobe (eds) *Nationalism and Rationality* (Cambridge University Press 1995) 290-311.

Salmon, P 'Accounting for Centralization in the European Union: Niskanen, Monnet or Thatcher?' in JM Josselin and A Marciano (eds) *From Economic to Legal Competition: New Perspectives on Law and Institutions in Europe* (Edward Elgar 2003) 165-191.

Salmon, P 'The Assignment of Powers in an Open-ended European Union' in CB Blankart and DC Mueller (eds) *A Constitution for the European Union* (The MIT Press 2004) 37-60.

Shleifer, A 'A Theory of Yardstick Competition' (1985) 16 RAND J Econ 319-327.

Weingast, BR 'Constitutions as Governance Structures: the Political Foundations of Secure Markets' (1993) 149 J Inst Theoretical Econ 286-311.

Using Corporate Law to Compete for Investments

EHUD KAMAR*

This Chapter documents and analyzes a powerful form of regulatory competition – competition for investments – that has transformed national corporate laws in the European Union in recent years. Unlike competition for incorporations, competition for investments shapes corporate law when firms cannot easily incorporate outside the jurisdiction in which they operate. These dynamics are not special to the European Union. They characterized state lawmaking in the United States in the early nineteenth century, and may well characterize lawmaking outside the European Union today. The high political payoffs that await successful participants in the competition for investments enable them to overcome opposition that could stifle competition for incorporations. Together with the fact that no single jurisdiction can monopolize the market for investments, these payoffs drive multiple jurisdictions, including large ones, to compete. Allowing firms to incorporate abroad, as recent European Court of Justice rulings require, may or may not breed competition for incorporations. Either way, as long as the existing competition for investments does not lose its steam, the effect on firms will be the same. Judging from the reforms that the competition for investments has produced so far, it will be positive.

A. Introduction
B. Competition for Investments
C. The Incentives to Compete
D. Normative Implications
E. Toward a General Theory of Regulatory Competition
F. Conclusion

A. Introduction

The notion that jurisdictions may compete for incorporations by tailoring their corporate laws to the preferences of corporate decisionmakers has long fascinated legal commentators. It is easy to see why. The competition paradigm provides a powerful analytical tool for evaluating the entire body of corporate law without pondering the merits of every detail. All one must do is examine the preferences of those who make incorporation decisions. As long as corporate decisionmakers prefer laws that maximize the value of the firm, jurisdictions will offer such laws.

* This Chapter is based on E Kamar 'Beyond Competition for Incorporations' (2006) 94 Geo L J (forthcoming).

Nearly half a century of legal scholarship has produced scores of articles explaining state corporate laws in the United States as products of just such competition. The basic facts are undisputed. First, firms in the United States are free to incorporate in any one of fifty states and the District of Columbia regardless of where they conduct their business. Second, states introduce and copy legal innovations from each other. Finally, the state that innovates and copies more than any other – Delaware – prospers by attracting the most incorporations. These facts leave no doubt that Delaware competes for incorporations. Commentators only disagree over whether other states also compete,[1] and whether corporate decisionmakers pull the competition in a desirable direction.[2]

It could be tempting to apply the same analysis to other parts of the world, with the European Union as a natural place to start.[3] However, the European Union does not meet a necessary condition for a market of incorporations to evolve. Unlike American states, most Member States in the European Union follow the so-called real-seat rule, which prevents companies operating in these Member States from incorporating abroad.[4] If this rule were to change, commentators have argued, intense competition for incorporations would immediately follow.[5]

[1] Compare M Kahan and E Kamar 'The Myth of State Competition in Corporate Law' (2002) 55 Stan L Rev 679, 684 (arguing that no American state but Delaware is actively pursuing incorporations); LA Bebchuk and A Hamdani 'Vigorous Race or Leisurely Walk: Reconsidering the Competition over Corporate Charters' (2002) 112 Yale L J 553, 580 (same); MJ Roe 'Delaware's Competition' (2003) 117 Harv L Rev 588, 607 (arguing that Delaware's real competition is the federal regulator), with R Romano 'Is Regulatory Competition Irrelevant for Corporate Governance?' (2005) 21 Oxford Rev Econ Pol'y 212, 217-223 (arguing that all American states pursue incorporations).

[2] Compare R Romano 'Law as a Product: Some Pieces of the Incorporation Puzzle' (1985) 1 J L Econ and Org 225, 279-281 (arguing that competition produces efficient law); DR Fischel 'The "Race to the Bottom" Revisited: Reflections on Recent Developments in Delaware's Corporation Law' (1982) 76 Nw U L Rev 913, 921 (same); and RK Winter Jr 'State Law Shareholder Protection, and the Theory of the Corporation'(1977) 6 J Legal Stud 251, 290 (same), with LA Bebchuk 'Federalism and the Corporation: The Desirable Limits on State Competition in Corporate Law' (1992) 105 Harv L Rev 1435, 1509 (arguing that state competition can produce undesirable results for public shareholders) and WL Cary 'Federalism and Corporate Law: Reflections upon Delaware' (1974) 83 Yale L J 663, 705 (arguing that the 'race to the bottom' results in deteriorating standards).

[3] For example, the theory of competition for incorporations has also been applied to Canadian provinces. See generally DJ Cumming and JG MacIntosh 'The Role of Interjurisdictional Competition in Shaping Canadian Corporate Law' (2000) 20 Int'l Rev L and Econ 141; RJ Daniels 'Should Provinces Compete? The Case for a Competitive Corporate Law Market' (1990) 36 McGill L J 130, 188.

[4] See E Wymeersch 'The Transfer of the Company's Seat in European Company Law' (2003) 40 Common Mkt L Rev 661, 666-673 (reviewing legal barriers to incorporation abroad).

[5] See BR Cheffins *Company Law: Theory, Structure, and Operation* (Clarendon Press 1997) 443 (arguing that the English judiciary has attributes that would help the United Kingdom succeed if it chose to compete for incorporations); S Deakin 'Regulatory Competition versus

cont. ...

This moment of truth has arrived. In fact, it arrived several years ago, when the first in a series of decisions by the European Court of Justice required Member States to recognize companies incorporated in other Member States and to refrain from imposing local corporate law on them.[6] Will the new freedom to choose where to incorporate unleash a wild race among Member States to win incorporations? Probably not. There is no reason to believe that European countries will be any more interested in incorporations than most American states, which make virtually no visible efforts to compete with Delaware.[7] The European Union may indeed remain without a single Member State motivated to compete like Delaware because the Member State that corporate decisionmakers favor for incorporation – the United Kingdom – does not compete for incorporations and is unlikely to begin doing so in the future.

This does not mean that corporate law in the European Union will stand still. It certainly has not done so for the last fifteen years. These years have seen a surge in corporate legislation sweeping the largest and most industrialized Member States. These reforms, however, have had nothing to do with competition for

Harmonization in European Company Law' in DC Esty and D Geradin (eds) *Regulatory Competition and Economic Integration: Comparative Perspectives* (Oxford University Press 2001) 190, 204-205 (arguing that lawyers and accountants may drive Member States to compete for incorporations); G Hertig and JA McCahery 'Company and Takeover Law Reforms in Europe: Misguided Harmonization Efforts or Regulatory Competition?' (2003) 4 Eur Bus Org L Rev 179, 187 (arguing that small Member States may compete for incorporations to obtain chartering revenue); JC Dammann 'Freedom of Choice in European Corporate Law' (2004) 29 Yale J Int'l L 477 (arguing that Member States are likely to compete for incorporations once firms are free to incorporate abroad); L Enriques 'EC Company Law and the Fears of a European Delaware' (2004) 15 Eur Bus L Rev 1259, 1273 (arguing that a freedom to choose where to incorporate may pressure national legislators in the European Union to emulate other jurisdictions' rules in order to retain existing corporations, though not in order to attract incorporations from abroad); E Wymeersch 'Company Law in the Twenty-First Century' (1999) 1 Int'l and Comp Corp L J 331, 339 (arguing that a freedom to choose where to incorporate is certain to stimulate competition between Member States); but see M Baudisch 'From Status to Contract? An American Perspective on Recent Developments in European Company Law' in F Snyder (ed) *The European Union and Governance* (2003) 23, 54 (arguing that sufficient incentives to compete for incorporations exist in the United States but not in the European Union).

[6] See Case C-212/97 *Centros Ltd v Erhvervs-og Selskabsstyrelsen* (1999) ECR I-1459 (requiring the Danish authorities to recognize a British company operating in Denmark); Case C-208/00 *Überseering BV v Nordic Construction Company Baumanagement GmbH (NCC)* (2002) ECR I-9919 (requiring the German authorities to recognize a Dutch company operating in Germany); Case C-167/01 *Kamer van Koophandel en Fabrieken voor Amsterdam v Inspire Art Ltd* (2003) ECR I-10155 (requiring the Dutch authorities to recognize a British company operating in the Netherlands). While these three decisions are most commonly cited in describing the trend, earlier decisions with similar holdings exist. See Case 79/85 *DHM Segers v Bestuur van de Bedrijfsvereniging voor Bank- en Verzekeringswezen Groothandel en Vrije Beroepen* (1986) ECR 2375 (requiring the Dutch authorities to recognize the right of access to a Dutch national sickness insurance scheme for the director of a British company operating in the Netherlands).

[7] See (n 1) and accompanying text.

incorporations. Instead, they have been prompted by mounting pressure on member governments to instill trust in their securities markets, which were becoming important drivers of economic growth during a time of mass privatizations, capital mobility, and corporate scandals. The reforms have taken place without any Member State relaxing the restrictions on incorporating abroad, and they have applied only to companies operating locally.

This renaissance of corporate legislation within the European Union is not merely extraneous to any market for incorporations. It actually *draws* on the fact that no such market exists. If companies could easily incorporate abroad, companies operating in Member States with inferior corporate laws would be less disadvantaged in their quest for investments, and their home Member States would see less urgency in reforming their corporate laws than today. But without the ability to incorporate abroad, these companies are hamstrung by the corporate laws where they are based. Ironically, precisely because firms *cannot* incorporate elsewhere, Member State legislatures have needed to ensure that local corporate law meets the expectations of the international investor community. This is certainly competition, and an intense one at that, but it owes its very existence to the fact that a market for incorporations does not exist. Indeed, the same type of competition existed in the United States in the nineteenth century, when American firms lacked the mobility they currently enjoy, and it likely exists today outside the European Union as well.

Competition for investments is different from competition for incorporations, not only in its origin, but also in its potency. The incentives for lawmakers to stimulate economic growth and address public concerns about corporate mismanagement are much stronger than the incentives to attract incorporations by foreign firms. Competition for investments can therefore overcome political and economic obstacles that competition for incorporation cannot. In the European Union, competition for investments has overcome opposition from labor and management lobbies, and has resulted not only in the copying of foreign law but also in the formation of regulatory agencies with real powers and considerable costs of operation. In terms of political and financial commitment, this is more than any American state has done in a century.

The policy implications of this analysis depart significantly from the conventional wisdom about the likely outcome of giving companies the freedom to choose where to incorporate. Allowing firms to incorporate abroad may not only fail to foster new competition, but may also *weaken* the competition that already exists. To be sure, the outcome will be different if enough local companies remain incorporated in their home Member States. The lack of regulatory interest in companies that incorporate abroad would then be offset by the drive to continue developing law that benefits local companies. This drive may persist especially if the reforms of the last fifteen years have sufficiently transformed national economies and politics to create a momentum that can perpetuate itself. But all this will not be competition for incorporations; it will still be competition for investments.[8]

This analysis contributes to the growing scholarship on convergence of corporate governance and path dependence. One strand in the literature, associated with Lucian Bebchuk and Mark Roe, focuses on limits of the power of globalization to pull corporate laws around the world towards greater efficiency.[9] The other strand, associated with Henry Hansmann and Reinier Kraakman, holds that these limits will yield over time to the forces pushing for change.[10] This Article complements the discussion by documenting the forces of convergence at play and relating them to the debate on regulatory competition.[11] In particular, it recasts legal convergence as a form of regulatory competition that is not only more powerful than competition for incorporations, but indeed dependent on the very absence of a necessary condition for competition for incorporations to exist.[12]

[8] This outcome is not guaranteed. If too many companies incorporate abroad, or if the momentum created by previous reforms is not stable, corporate laws in Member States whose firms exit in droves will atrophy. The result may well be a correlation between the retention of local incorporations on the one hand, and the quality of corporate law on the other. But it will reflect a softening of the competition for investments, rather than the emergence of competition for incorporations.

[9] See LA Bebchuk and MJ Roe 'A Theory of Path Dependence in Corporate Ownership and Governance' (1999) 52 Stan L Rev 127, 170 (noting that important differences exist despite the influence of globalization); see also WW Bratton and JA McCahery 'Comparative Corporate Governance and the Theory of the Firm' (1999) 38 Colum J Transnat'l L 213, 213-214.

[10] See H Hansmann and R Kraakman 'The End of History for Corporate Law' (2001) 89 Geo L J 439 (arguing that 'the deeper tendency is toward convergence'); see also RJ Gilson 'Globalizing Corporate Governance: Convergence of Form or Function' (2001) 49 Am J Comp L 329, 331-332.

[11] Previous commentators have anedoctally mentioned changes in corporate laws in the European Union driven by competition for investments as part of their analysis of competition for incorporations. See JA McCahery and EPM Vermuelen 'Limited Partnership Reform in the United Kingdom: A Competitive, Venture Capital Oriented Business Form' (2004) 5 Eur Bus Org L Rev 61, 75 (suggesting different corporate law and tax treatment may lead to competition for investments within the European Union); WW Bratton and JA McCahery 'The New Economics of Jurisdictional Competition: Devolutionary Federalism in a Second-Best World' (1997) 86 Geo L J 201, 256-259. This Article reverses the focus. It argues that competition for investments is far more important than competition for incorporations as an explanation of corporate lawmaking in the European Union. It also analyzes the fundamental differences between the two types of competition.

[12] Competition for investments is different from yardstick competition (or benchmark competition) by involving efforts of regulators for a share of a limited pool of mobile capital. Yardstick competition – efforts by suppliers serving different consumer markets to match each other's performance – was originally suggested as a way of ensuring that regulated monopolies do not overcharge customers. See A Shleifer 'A Theory of Yardstick Competition' (1985) 16 Rand J Econ 319, 319-320 (explaining that regulators rely on the costs of comparable firms to set prices at the social optimum). Subsequently, yardstick competition was said to be the method voters use to evaluate local lawmakers. See P Salmon 'Decentralisation as an Incentive Scheme'

cont. ...

Moreover, this analysis argues that, in a departure from the predictions of the convergence literature, recent history shows that competition for investments may push lawmakers to lead the way to convergence more rapidly than firms. The reason for this is twofold. First, lawmakers can transform the legal system as a whole and thus overcome complementarities that have developed between its parts. Second, in a twist of logic, lawmakers can create value by ignoring the transition costs that reform imposes on existing firms and focus instead on their own political capital, which is tied to the success of new firms that result from privatizations.

B. Competition for Investments

Until recently, firms in most Member States of the European Union were unable to incorporate abroad. Competition for incorporations was therefore impossible. But this lack of legal domicile mobility did not prevent the emergence of another type of regulatory competition. This competition is hardly hidden. It is very visible and seems to motivate Member States to do everything they would do if they competed for incorporations. They reform their laws. They imitate each other. They protect shareholders. Only they are not competing for incorporations. They are competing for investments.

The pursuit of investments involves the creation of a hospitable business environment. In part, this is achieved through financial incentives in the form of tax breaks, subsidies, loans, monopoly rights, and other direct transfers. It also involves offering the necessary physical and legal infrastructure on which businesses rely for their development. For many years, corporate taxation was the main dimension on which states competed for investments. But the globalization of capital, products, and labor markets generally, coupled with the economic integration of the European Union particularly, intensified the competition for investments among Member States of the European Union and rendered tax competition insufficient. In addition, the need to shore up budget deficits pushed some Member States towards mass privatization, which in turn increased the extent of public stock ownership and the dependence on equity markets. All these changes – together with a prolonged economic stagnation, the collapse of major domestic corporations, and a growing awareness of the link between law and finance – led lawmakers to turn their attention to corporate law reform as an additional way to

(1987) 3 Oxford Rev Econ Pol 24, 34-38. Corporate lawmaking in the European Union can also be shaped by yardstick competition, whereby national governments satisfy voters by matching corporate laws available abroad. See P Salmon 'Political Yardstick Competition and Corporate Governance in the European Union' in this volume 31-58. For the distinction between yardstick competition and mobility-based competition generally, see P Salmon 'Horizontal Competition among Governments' in E Ahmad and G Brosio (eds) *Handbook of Fiscal Federalism* (Edward Elgar Publishing 2006).

attract investments, resulting in waves of reforms aimed at modernizing corporate law and increasing shareholder protection.

I. The Old Way: Tax Incentives

A time-honored method of stimulating the economy is offering tax incentives. In the European Union, the Member States most often mentioned in this regard are Ireland and the Netherlands.[13] Ireland is known for charging a low corporate tax on revenue earned within its borders.[14] As recently explained by Ireland's then-finance minister in rejecting a call from France and Germany to establish a minimum corporate tax rate: 'Ireland had successfully and determinedly pursued a policy of low personal and business taxation, including our 12.5 per cent rate of Corporation Tax, with spectacular success. We have created a dynamic employment and investment-friendly environment in which over 300,000 new jobs have been created and countless tens of thousands of existing jobs maintained over the past 7 years'.[15]

The Netherlands is known for its favorable taxation of holding companies' revenues.[16] Here too the goal is to stimulate the economy.[17] Accordingly, holding companies must establish physical presence in the Netherlands to enjoy the tax breaks.[18] Ireland and the Netherlands are not the only Member States that use tax incentives to attract business; other Member States do the same.[19]

[13] See WW Bratton and JA McCahery 'Tax Coordination and Tax Competition in the European Union: Evaluating the Code of Conduct on Business Taxation' (2001) 38 C M L Rev 677, 701 (noting that Ireland and the Netherlands are known for their hospitable tax regimes); 'Gimme Shelter: Is Tax Competition among Countries a Good or a Bad Thing?' *The Economist* (29 January 2000) Special Section 5-17 (reporting widespread tax competition around the world and naming Ireland, the Netherlands, and Luxembourg as the Member States of the European Union engaged in tax competition).

[14] See e-mail from G Miccoli (Associate), Janni, Magnocavallo, Fauda, Brescia e associati (Milan) to E Kamar (19 August 2004) (noting that certain Italian pharmaceutical companies have their production plants in Ireland because taxation on production there is low).

[15] Press Release 'McCreevy Rejects Corporation Tax Harmonisation Proposals' (Ireland Department of Finance 8 June 2004) <http://www.finance.gov.ie/Viewtxt.asp?DocID=2187&CatID=1&m=n&StartDate=01+January+2004&m>.

[16] See AR Sorkin 'Is the Dutch Advantage Unsettling Europe?' *NY Times* (2 April 2000) Money and Business 4 (explaining that the Netherlands' 'ultraflexible tax policies' have made it the 'Delaware for Europe').

[17] See e-mail from E Barten (Associate), Stibbe, Amsterdam to E Kamar (22 September 2004) (noting that the purpose of offering tax incentives to Dutch holding companies is to make the Netherlands attractive as a business location).

[18] See E Barten (n 17) (noting that a Dutch holding company must be managed and controlled in the Netherlands to be exempt from tax in the Netherlands on gains arising from holding or selling shares of a qualifying subsidiary and to be able claim a tax deduction for interest

cont. ...

But offering tax incentives is very different from using corporate law to attract incorporations. Delaware, the paragon of competition for incorporations, relies on its corporate legal regime, rather than on tax breaks, to attract incorporations, and its goal is to have companies choose Delaware as their legal domicile, rather than as their physical home. In fact, the so-called franchise tax Delaware charges to companies incorporated in it (which is different from the tax it charges to companies on revenue they earn in it regardless of where they are incorporated) is higher than the franchise tax other American states charge – not the other way around.[20] By contrast, Ireland and the Netherlands strive to build their manufacturing and services sectors, rather than the list of foreign businesses using their laws. Accordingly, they rely on tax incentives, rather than their corporate legal regimes, to achieve this goal.[21]

II. The New Way: Corporate Law

Tax breaks are not the only way to stimulate the economy. Many other inducements can be offered to encourage growth under the label of business-friendly legislation. The globalization of capital markets, together with the economic integration of the European Union, has made corporate law reforms an important component of the probusiness legislation that lawmakers in the various Members States are expected to provide. The reason, ironically, is that firms currently do not have the freedom to incorporate abroad. They are trapped within their home states. If Member States are to attract investments in local companies, they must therefore see to it that the legal protection they afford to investors does not fall behind.

This pressure did not exist several decades ago, when capital markets were segmented and investments were local. But the globalization of capital markets and the economic integration of the European Union in recent years have created

paid to purchase these shares).

[19] For discussion by corporate lawyers of tax advantages their Member States offer to companies, see generally M Kyprianou 'Cyprus as a Venue for the Establishment of a Holding Company' (2004) 32 Int'l Bus Law 66; BM Pedersen and M Hertz 'Legal Aspects of Acquiring a Publicly Traded Danish Company' (2000) 28 Int'l Bus Law 365, 368.

[20] See M Kahan and E Kamar (n 1) 690 (comparing marginal revenues from annual taxes for incorporation in the fifty states and the District of Columbia).

[21] See Industrial Development Agency of Ireland <http://www.idaireland.com> (website of the Ireland Development Authority, which bills itself as an 'Irish Government agency with responsibility for securing new investment from overseas in manufacturing and internationally traded services sectors' and advertises Ireland's 'skilled and flexible workforce', '[o]ne of the lowest corporate tax rates in the world', '[y]oungest and one of the best educated populations in Europe', and a 'positive political and economic environment' – without mentioning Ireland's corporate law).

a new reality in which Member States cannot take investors for granted, and cannot afford to lose investments – including those by their own citizens – by keeping on their books unattractive corporate laws that apply to any company conducting business within their borders. Between 1987 and 1996, for example, American investors nearly tripled the portion of foreign investments in their stock portfolios, from 3.8% to 10%, adding an important consideration to the political calculus of lawmakers in the European Union.[22] Between 1995 and 1999, the share of foreign investments by European investment funds increased from approximately 40% to close to 70%.[23] Their investments too could no longer be taken for granted.[24]

This transformation intensified competition for investments in a number of ways. First, it pressured firms to grow while depleting their internal cash reserves and forcing them to raise new capital or use their stock as acquisition currency.[25] Second, it motivated firms to move production abroad to reduce costs, including costs associated with operating under the law of their home Member State. Third, it shrank the profits into which managers could dip to extract private benefits, weakening their resistance to change.[26] Fourth, it prompted massive privatizations, which depended on the quality of local corporate law.[27]

[22] See LL Tesar and IM Werner 'The Internationalization of Securities Markets Since the 1987 Crash' in RE Litan and AM Santomero (eds) Brookings-Wharton Papers on Financial Services (Brookings Institution Press 1998) 281, 296.

[23] See L Baele et al 'Measuring European Financial Integration' (2004) 20 Oxford Rev Econ Pol'y 509, 528. The share of foreign investments by these funds within Europe increased over that period from about 18% to about 30%. See L Baele et al (supra) 529. The integration of European equity markets is also manifested in a tripling of the part of the variance of European stock returns explained by news common to all Europe from about 8% in 1973-86 to about 23% in 1999-2003. See L Baele et al (supra) 527. The part of the variance of European stock returns explained by American news doubled over that period from about 11% to about 20%, suggesting that European equity markets integration proceeded faster than global equity markets integration. See L Baele et al (supra) 527 fig 12. See also G Bekaert, CR Harvey and Angela Ng 'Market Integration and Contagion' (2005) 78 J Bus 39 (reporting evidence of global integration of equity markets).

[24] See FESE 'Share Ownership Structure' (2002) 3 Europe <http://www.fese.org/statistics/studies/share_ownership.pdf> (hereinafter Share Ownership Survey) 3 (reporting that globalization and the introduction of the euro have resulted in the emergence of foreign institutional investors as the driving force of European markets and in the increase of foreign holdings by domestic institutional investors).

[25] A well-known example is the acquisition of United States carmaker Chrysler by German carmaker Daimler Benz in 1998, which required the acquiring company to register its stock in the United States and subject itself to United States accounting principles prior to the acquisition.

[26] See MJ Roe 'Rents and Their Corporate Consequences' 53 Stan L Rev (2001) 1463 (arguing that the availability of monopoly rents helps to explains the persistence of weak shareholder protection in European corporate law); A Dyck and L Zingales 'Private Benefits of Control: An International Comparison' (2004) 59 J Finance 537 (arguing that product market com-

cont. ...

The agents of legal change varied across Member States according to their institutional and political settings. In some Member States, interest groups that would benefit from the change openly demanded it. This was the case in Germany, where a new breed of investment banks emerged that depended for their survival on the existence of a vibrant stock market and lobbied for reform.[28] In other Member States, government officials acted as political entrepreneurs by personally pushing for change.[29] This was the case in Italy, where corporate reform has been advanced by individuals such as Prime Ministers Giuliano Amato (who at other times served as Treasury Minister and head of the antitrust authority) and Romano Prodi (who later headed the state corporate holding apparatus that led the privatization process); Treasury Director, commissioner of privatization, and drafter of the new corporate law, Mario Draghi (who had received his doctorate in economics in the United States); and Bank of Italy governors Carlo Azeglio Ciampi (who later became Treasury and Economics Minister and President) and Antonio Fazio.[30] Thus, for example, in a 1998 article titled 'Corporate Governance and Competitiveness,' Mario Draghi described his vision of corporate law and financial regulation as drivers of national economic growth through 'increasingly competitive market rules and standards of company law' where 'the ability of national enterprises to raise funds will depend to an ever greater extent on the efficiency of Italy's "financial centre" and the "quality" of the products, representing administrative as well as property rights, that are traded'.[31] In all

petition lowers monopoly rents and leaves less room for extracting private benefits of control).

[27] The active interest taken by governments in corporate law in countries undergoing extensive privatization take in corporate law is illustrated by the frustration in the Italian government with the 1997 ouster of the chairman of recently privatized Telecom Italia by directors averse to reform. See P Betts and J Blitz 'At the Head of Italy's Table' *Fin Times* (22 December 1997) 14 (quoting the Italian Prime Minister saying: 'We are carrying out privatisations but we still have not done enough to create a proper financial market .... We do not have guarantees for small shareholders, no rules for public companies').

[28] See R Deeg *Finance Capitalism Unveiled: Banks and the German Political Economy* (University of Michigan Press 1999) 90-93 (describing the transition of major German banks from lending to investment banking, the penetration of the German banking industry by foreign investment banks, and the lobbying by both groups of banks for corporate reform). Perhaps no German bank has changed more than Deutsche Bank, which has filled its top posts with U.S.-trained investment bankers and reduced corporate lending. See J Guyon 'The Trials of Josef Ackermann' *Fortune* (26 January 2004) 111. Recently, the chairman of its supervisory board of directors joined the growing criticism of employee representation on supervisory boards. See 'Deutsche Bank Sichtet Fusionskandidaten' [Deutsche Bank Looks for Merger Candidates], Frankfurter Allgemeine Zeitung (5 June 2004) 11.

[29] See R Hardin *Collective Action* (John Hopkins University Press 1993) 35-37 (discussing political entrepreneurs as public figures who advance their own careers by promoting a certain public or group interest).

[30] See R Deeg 'Remaking Italian Capitalism? The Politics of Corporate Governance Reform' (2005) 28 W Eur Pol 521, 529.

Member States, pressure was applied by institutional investors, who relied on growing equity holdings to voice their concerns to corporate managers and lawmakers.[32]

The competition for investments has had a very noticeable impact on Member State legislation.[33] Consider the following examples.

Germany began its journey to shareholder capitalism in the second half of the 1980s as part of a campaign to make the country a desirable place for production ('*Wirtschaftsstandort Deutschland*'),[34] which later mutated into a campaign to strengthen the country's position as a finance center ('*Finanzplatz Deutschland*').[35] Early reforms were designed to modernize the existing platforms for securities trading. These reforms included the introduction of electronic trading on the national stock exchange in 1986,[36] amendments to the stock exchange law in

[31] See M Draghi 'Corporate Governance and Competitiveness' (1998) 3 Rev Econ Conditions in Italy 341, 344.

[32] At the end of July 2004, American pension fund CalPERS (California Public Employees' Retirement System) had at the end of July 2004 assets worth $163.5 billion – $34.2 billion of which were shares of companies outside the United States. It dedicates a section of its website to its corporate governance philosophy in general and international investments in particular, with tailored corporate governance principles for investment in the United Kingdom, Germany, and France. See CalPERS 'International Corporate Governance' <http://www.calpers-governance.org/principles/international/>. Similarly, at the end of June 2004, British fund manager Hermes managed at the end of June 2004 assets worth $82 billion, $23 billion of which were shares of companies outside the United Kingdom. Like CalPERS, it dedicates a section of its website to corporate governance both domestically and internationally, with translations to French and Italian. See Hermes 'Publications: Corporate Governance' <http://www.hermes.co.uk/publications/publications_corporate_governance.htm>. Institutional investors even travel abroad to clarify their expectations. See e.g. JA Fanto 'The Transformation of French Corporate Governance and United States Institutional Investors' (1995) 21 Brook J Int'l L 1 70 (noting that the general counsel of CalPERS and the head of Global Proxy Services traveled to France before the privatizations began to discuss corporate governance with government officials). Most importantly, institutional investors vote with their feet against countries with inadequate law. See K Chan, V Covrig and L Ng 'What Determines the Domestic Bias and Foreign Bias? Evidence from Mutual Fund Equity Allocations Worldwide' (2005) 60 J Finance 1495; C Leuz, KV Lins and FE Warnock 'Do Foreigners Invest Less in Poorly Governed Firms?' (ECGI Finance No. 43/2004 wp <http://ssrn.com/abstract=512042>, 2005); M Giannetti and Y Koskinen, 'Investor Protection and the Demand for Equity' (ECGI Finance wp No. 64/2004 <http://ssrn.com/abstract=554522>, 2004).

[33] See e.g. M Valencia 'Good Heavens, Good Governance' *The Economist* (29 April 2000) S13 (quoting the editor of a corporate governance newsletter referring to an 'enormous uptick' in both legislation and practice in continental Europe during the previous year).

[34] See M Höpner 'European Corporate Governance Reform and the German Party Paradox' (Max-Planck-Institut für Gesellschaftsforschung Discussion Paper, March 2003) <http://www.mpi-fg-koeln.mpg.de/pu/mpifg_dp/dp03-4.pdf>.

[35] See J Beyer and Martin Höpner 'The Disintegration of Organised Capitalism: German Corporate Governance in the 1990s' (2003) 26 W Eur Pol 179, 191.

[36] See R Deeg 'Change from Within: German and Italian Finance in the 1990s' in W

cont. ...

1989,[37] the elimination of taxes on stock trading in 1989,[38] and the opening of a futures exchange in 1990.[39]

A series of laws to liberalize securities trading while tightening investor protection followed. They included a 1990 law requiring corporate issuers to prepare an offering prospectus;[40] a 1994 law banning insider trading, introducing disclosure obligations, and establishing a new securities agency charged with regulation and enforcement;[41] a 1998 law allowing companies to use American or international accounting standards;[42] a 1998 law deregulating investment funds;[43] a 1998 law broadening disclosure obligations, authorizing stock option compensation, expanding the responsibilities of supervisory boards, limiting voting by banks, requiring shares to have equal voting rights, and strengthening auditor independ-

Streeck and K Thelen (eds) *Beyond Continuity: Institutional Change in Advanced Political Economies* (Oxford University Press 2005) 169, 180.

[37] See R Deeg (n 36) 180.

[38] See Gesetz zur Stärkung des Finanzplatzes Deutschland [Law Bolsterning the Finance Center Germany], also known as Erstes Finanzmarktförderungsgesetz [First Financial Market Promotion Law] BGBl I (1989) 1412; E Nowak 'Investor Protection and Capital Market Regulation in Germany' in JP Krahnen and RH Schmidt (eds) *The German Financial System* (Oxford University Press 2004) 425, 429.

[39] See R Deeg (n 36) 180.

[40] See generally R Deeg (n 36) 180; Gesetz über Wertpapier-Verkaufsprospekte und zur Änderung von Vorschriften über Wertpapiere [Law Governing Sales Prospectuses for Securities and Revising Securities Regulation] BGBl I (1990) 2749.

[41] See Zweites Finanzmarktförderungsgesetz [Second Financial Market Promotion Law] BGBl I (1994) 1749; E Nowak (n 38) 429-433. The agency began to operate in 1995 with 96 staff members and a budget of DM 14.9 million. See E Nowak (n 38) 429-433. The agency began to operate in 1995 with ninety-six staff members and a budget of DM 14.9 million. See E Nowak (n 38) 430; Bundesaufsichtsamt für den Wertpapierhandel (BAWe) 'Annual Report' (1996) 6 <http://www.bafin.de/jahresbericht/jb96_e_wa.pdf>. By the end of 2000, the agency had a staff of 138 and a budget of DM 18.07 million. See BAWe 'Annual Report' (2000) 39-40 <http://www.bafin.de/jahresbericht/jb00_e_wa.pdf>. In 2002, the agency was combined with the banking and insurance agencies to form a single financial services agency, the Federal Financial Supervisory Authority (Bundesanstalt für Finanzdiensleistungsaufsicht, or BaFin). See Gesetz über die Bundesanstalt für Finanzdienstleistungsaufsicht (FinDAG) [Law Establishing the Federal Financial Supervisory Authority] BGBl I (2002) 1310.

[42] See Gesetz zur Verbesserung der Wettbewerbsfähigkeit deutscher Konzerne an Kapitalmärkten und zur Erleichterung der Aufnahme von Gesellschafterdarlehen [Law for Improving the Competitiveness of German Companies in Capital Markets and Facilitating the Taking of Loans by Shareholders], also known as Kapitalaufnahmeerleichterungsgesetz (KapAEG) [Capital Raising Relief Law] BGBl I (1998) 707; E Nowak (n 38) 435. For the positive response to the law in business circles, see generally M Glaum 'Bridging the GAAP: The Changing Attitude of German Managers towards Anglo-American Accounting and Accounting Harmonization' (2000) 11 J Int'l Fin Mgm't & Acct 1.

[43] See Drittes Finanzmarktförderungsgesetz [Third Financial Market Promotion Law] BGBl I (1998) 529; E Nowak (n 38) 434-435.

ence;[44] a 2000 law using a capital gains tax exemption to encourage banks to liquidate their stock holdings;[45] a 2001 law regulating takeovers;[46] a 2002 law criminalizing market manipulation, requiring disclosure of director trading, and creating a private right of action for securities fraud;[47] a 2002 law requiring public companies to follow a code of corporate governance or disclose their failure to do so;[48] and a 2004 law modifying various areas of securities law.[49] The list of reforms continues to grow. Recent government actions include, for example, a 2005 law on shareholder class actions[50] and a 2005 law on shareholder derivative lawsuits.[51]

The British and American influence on these reforms is evident. Yet their goal was to boost economic growth, not to attract incorporations.[52] Apart from aiming

[44] See Gesetz zur Kontrolle und Transparenz im Unternehmensbereich (KonTraG) [Law on Control and Transparency in Business Enterprises] BGBl I (1998) 786; E Nowak (n 38) 435-437.

[45] See Gesetz zur Senkung der Steuersaetze und zur Reform der Unternehmensbesteuerung (StSenkG) [Law on Reduction of Tax Rates and Reform of Business Taxation], BGBl I (2000) 1433; E Nowak (n 38) 437-438.

[46] See Wertpapiererwebs-und Übernahmegesetz (WpÜG) [Securities Acquisition and Takeover Law] BGBI I (2001) 3822. Responding to management concerns raised by a recent takeover of German telephone company Mannesmann by British rival Vodafone, the law authorized supervisory boards to resist takeovers without shareholder permission. See JN Gordon 'An American Perspective on Anti-Takeover Laws in the EU: The German Example' in G Ferrarini, KJ Hopt, J Winter and Eddy Wymeersch (eds) *Reforming Company and Takeover Law in Europe* (Oxford University Press 2004) 541-549 (criticizing the law). Many other aspects of the law, however, such as the mechanism for cashing out minority shareholders, streamlined takeovers, prompting legal practitioners to describe the law as 'a critical step toward a fairer, more open environment for potential acquirors of German public companies', which 'appears to signal foreign investors that German capital markets are now ready to treat unsolicited tender offers, sophisticated LBOs and other going-private transactions as routine'. See 'New German Takeover Scheme: Shaping Germany's Market for Corporate Control' (Skadden Arps Slate Meagher & Flom Memorandum to Clients, April 2002) <http://www.skadden.com/content/publications/809library.pdf>.

[47] See Viertes Finanzmarktförderungsgesetz [Fourth Financial Market Promotion Law] BGBl I (2002) 2010; E Nowak (n 38) 439-440.

[48] See Transparenz und Publizitätgesetz (TransPuG) [Law for further Reform of Stock and Accounting Law to Achieve Transparency and Disclosure] BGBl I (2002) 2681.

[49] See Gesetz zur Verbesserung des Anlegerschutzes (AnSVG) [Law for Improving Investor Protection] BGBl I (2004) 2630.

[50] See Gesetz über Musterverfahren in kapitalmarktrechtlichen Streitigkeiten (KapMuG) [Law on Model Case Proceedings in Disputes under Capital Markets Law] BGBl I (2005) 2437.

[51] See Gesetz zur Unternehmensintegrität und Modernisierung des Anfechtungsrechts (UMAG) [Law on Corporate Integrity and Modernization of Rescission Proceedings] BGBl I (2005) 2802.

[52] See generally T Baums 'Company Law Reform in Germany' (2003) 3 J Corp Legal Stud 181-182 (noting that the reasons for Germany's corporate law reform were corporate scandals

cont. ...

to make Germany a finance center, the reforms responded to corporate failures that were blamed on bank-dominated corporate boards asleep at the switch.[53] The reforms also were part of a transition to shareholder capitalism signaled by the ambitious privatization of Deutsche Telekom in 1996.[54] And, with the German government's effort to overhaul the country's ailing pension system in 2001 by encouraging private saving for retirement, the reforms raised the profile of the stock market as a viable avenue for investment.[55] All of these objectives pushed lawmakers to meet shareholder demands.

Consider, for example, the corporate governance code that public companies were required to follow.[56] The code was the work of a commission formed by the German government to propose how to modernize corporate law in light of the globalization of capital markets.[57] The commission did not disband after handing over its report. It continues to monitor and periodically update the corporate gov-

involving German companies, the need to reconcile the law with foreign law that applies to cross-listed German companies, the need to meet the expectations of foreign institutional investors who buy shares of German companies, the transformation of the German pension system into one partly based on institutional investors managing privately invested capital, competition among regulators to offer corporate law that meets the need of the market, and the need to offer flexibility to German companies financed by venture capital); J Guyon (n 28) 111 (noting that Germany is 'struggling to liberalize its labor laws, overhaul its pension system, cut unemployment benefits, and reform its corporate governance rules in order to boost growth, which was flat in 2003').

[53] See JN Gordon 'Pathways to Corporate Governance? Two Steps on the Road to Shareholder Capitalism in Germany' (1999) 5 Colum J Eur L 219 220-221 (describing the board failures at Daimler-Benz, Metallgesellschaft, Schneider, and Klöckner-Humboldt-Deutz that precipitated the 1998 reform); E Nowak (n 38) 433-434, 438-439 (noting that the 2002 reform was partly a response to the 2001 scandals that brought down the four-year-old stock exchange for technology firms known as Neuer Markt).

[54] See JN Gordon 'An International Relations Perspective on the Convergence of Corporate Governance: German Shareholder Capitalism and the European Union 1990-2000' (ECGI Law wp No. 6/2003 <http://ssrn.com/abstract=374620>, 2003) (linking the expansion of stock ownership in public companies, the launch of a stock trading platform for young companies, the tightening of legal protection of shareholders, and the growing acceptance of a market for corporate control to the privatization of Deutsche Telekom in 1996).

[55] See S Vitols 'Changes in Germany's Bank-Based Financial System: Implications for Corporate Governance' (2005) 13 Corp Gov Int'l Rev 386, 390 (noting that the overhaul sought to increase investment in Germany's capital markets).

[56] See (n 48) and accompanying text.

[57] According to a government bill based on the commission's recommendations, the commission 'was asked to consider changes in [Germany's] corporate and market structures caused by globalization and internationalization of capital markets in order to submit proposals on how to modernize [Germany's] law'. See BTDruks 14/8769 (11 April 2002) 10 <http://dip.bundestag.de/btd/14/087/1408769.pdf> ('[S]ollte sie im Hinblick auf den durch Globalisierung und Internationalisierung der Kapitalmärkte sich vollziehenden Wandel unserer Unternehmens- und Marktstrukturen Vorschläge für eine Modernisierung unseres rechtlichen Regelwerkes unterbreiten').

ernance code and maintains an informative website in German, English, French, Italian, and Spanish on corporate governance in Germany.[58] The multilingual site fits the purpose of the code. 'The aim of the German Corporate Governance Code', the site explains, 'is to make Germany's corporate governance rules transparent for both national and international investors, thus strengthening confidence in the management of German corporations'.[59] The same objective underlies the law on derivative suits.[60] Here too, according to the financial press, there is no doubt about the motivation for reform: '[A]s corporate Germany opens its shareholder registers to the world, the government has realised the old order has to change. It is rushing a vast package of reforms through parliament to overhaul companies' relations with investors'.[61]

The transformation of Italian corporate law began in 1990 with the Amato Law, named after the Treasury Minister who sponsored it, which incorporated all state-controlled banks in preparation for their privatization.[62] It was followed in 1992 by the conversion of other state-controlled businesses to corporations.[63] The privatization plan had two objectives, both related to the economic integration of the European Union. The first objective was to facilitate the consolidation of the Italian industry to compete with foreign businesses.[64] The second objective was to lower the national deficit to qualify for admission into the euro system pursuant to the Treaty of Maastricht.[65] The privatizations started in 1993 and peeked in

[58] See Government Commission in the German Corporate Governance Code <http://www.corporate-governance-code.de/index-e.html>. The corporate governance code has thus far been amended thrice. See <http://www.corporate-governance-code.de/eng/archiv/index.html> (displaying previous versions).

[59] See <http://www.corporate-governance-code.de/index-e.html>. This is consistent with the government bill that introduced the 2002 law, which noted that, 'especially for informing foreign investors, it appeared inevitable to adopt a corporate governance code for Germany'. See BTDruks 14/8769 (n 57) 21 ('Gerade im Hinblick auf die Information ausländischer Anleger erschien es unvermeidlich, einen maßgebenden Corporate-Governance-Kodex für Deutschland zu initiieren').

[60] See (n 51).

[61] B Benoit and P Jenkins 'Germany Looks to Call Time on Its Business War Games' *Fin Times* (30 December 2004) 32.

[62] See Law No. 218/90 of 30 July 1990 'Disposizioni in materia di ristrutturazione e integrazione patrimoniale degli istituti di credito di diritto pubblico' [Provisions Related to Restructuring and Integration of Credit Institutions under Public Law] Gazz. Uff. 182 (6 August 1990) (Italy).

[63] See R Deeg (n 36) 187. The need to compete with foreign banks resulted from the European Union Investment Services Directive, which required Member States to allow foreign banks to operate inside their borders. See again R Deeg (n 36) 187.

[64] See R Deeg (n 36) 187.

[65] See e.g. R Prodi 'Italy's Would-Be Record-Breaker' *The Economist* (10 October 1998) 58 (noting that Italian Prime Minister Prodi, formerly an economics professor, 'pushed ahead with privatisation ... liberalised shopping hours and licences, tried to shake the fat out of the

cont. ...

1997 with the public offering of Telecom Italia and Borsa Italiana.[66] In the same year, the government formed a committee to draft a new public company law and appointed the Commissioner of Privatizations, Mario Draghi, as its chair. The resulting legislation, enacted in 1998, revamped the law governing public companies. Coming at the heels of a recent tax reform to encourage public equity offerings,[67] it introduced new disclosure obligations, strengthened shareholder rights, facilitated voting by proxy, and expanded the enforcement power of the securities authority.[68] The following years saw further legislation – in the form of a 2001 law and four decrees to implement it – vastly expanding the flexibility that both public and private companies have in financing and structuring their operations.[69] Among other things, the legislation allowed for different board structures, limited the ability of shareholders to bring strike suits, authorized the issuance of preferred stock, redeemable stock, tracking stock, bonds of any kind, and hybrid securities; and facilitated shareholder voting.[70] To Italian commentators it is obvious that all these changes were 'expressly inspired by comparative analysis in that a number of new governance and financing options for Italian companies were borrowed or "transplanted" from other systems'.[71] But the changes were not

economy, made bureaucrats jump' to meet the euro qualification criteria); N d'Aquino 'Italy Prepares for EMU' (1997) 368 Europe 14 (noting that Italy's ability to meet the euro qualification criteria is 'repeated everyday in the newspapers', that the prime minister and his coalition members 'are betting all their international – and a great deal of their national – credibility on whether or not they can do it', and that 'what counts most is the first and most important parameter: the percentage of the public deficit with regard to the gross national product').

[66] See R Deeg (n 36) 188. In addition to adding the public float on the market, the privatization of Borsa Italiana created a powerful new supporter of corporate reform. See again R Deeg (n 36) 188.

[67] See P Betts 'Market Half the Size It Should Be' *Fin Times* (10 December 1997) 2.

[68] See R Deeg (n 36) 188; G Ferrarini 'Corporate Governance Changes in the 20th Century: A View from Italy' in KJ Hopt, E Wymeersch, H Kanda and H Baum (eds) *Corporate Governance in Context: Corporations, States, and Markets in Europe, Japan, and the U.S.* (Oxford University Press 2005) 31; A Aganin and P Volpin 'The History of Corporate Ownership in Italy' in R Morck (ed) *The History of Corporate Ownership Around the World: Family Business Groups to Professional Managers* (The University of Chicago Press 2005) 325.

[69] See Law No. 366/01 of 3 October 2001, Gazz. Uff. 234 (8 October 2001); Legislative Decree No. 61/02 of 11 April 2002, Gazz. Uff. 88 (15 April 2002); Legislative Decree No. 5/03 of 17 January 2003, Gazz. Uff. 17, Supp. Ord. 8 (22 January 2003); Legislative Decree No. 6/03 of 17 January 2003, Gazz. Uff. 17, Supp. Ord. 8 (22 January 2003); Legislative Decree No. 37/04 of 6 February 2004, Gazz. Uff. 37, Supp. Ord. 24 (14 February 2004).

[70] For a detailed discussion of the reforms, see generally G Ferrarini, P Giudici and M Stella Richter 'Company Law Reform in Italy: Real Progress?' (2005) 69 Rabels Zeitschrift fuer auslaendisches und internationales Privatrecht 658; P Montalenti 'The New Italian Corporate Law: An Outline' (2004) 1 Eur Co & Fin L Rev 368.

[71] See M Ventoruzzo 'Experiments in Comparative Corporate Law: The Recent Italian Reform and the Dubious Virtues of a Market for Rules in the Absence of Effective Regulatory Competition' (2004) 40 Tex Int'l L J 113; G Ferrarini, P Giudici and M Stella Richter (n 70)

cont. ...

meant to attract incorporations. Rather, in the words of one Italian Treasury official, their objective was 'to enhance the competitiveness of Italian companies and enhance their efficiency and their ability to grow in an increasingly competitive environment, working on the assumption that global competition not only involves a country's economic conditions, but also the legal system in which companies operate. For when investors decide how to allocate the resources they manage, they assess both the economic factors and the reliability and accountability of the legal system, as well as the management of individual companies'.[72]

These words are echoed in the law authorizing the decrees itself, which states its goal 'to pursue the foremost objective of promoting the birth, the growth, and the competitiveness of enterprises through access to domestic and international capital markets.'[73] With this purpose in mind, it is not surprising to find a summary of the new rules by the Italian Ministry of Economy and Finance on a website linked to the website of the Italian embassy in the United States under the heading 'Doing Business in Italy: Regulations and Incentives'.[74]

In 2005, the Italian parliament adopted an investor protection law prompted by the collapse of dairy producer Parmalat in 2003.[75] The conceptual framework of the law is reminiscent of legislation introduced in the United States in the wake of the Enron debacle two years earlier. However, Italy's lawmakers have different motives. Whereas, the American legislation has been viewed as a political reflex to placate domestic citizens with little concern for how foreign issuers would re-

(analyzing the Italian company law reform and its influences).

[72] R Ulissi 'Company Law Reform in Italy: An Overview of Current Initiatives' unpublished manuscript presente at the Conference on Company Law Reform in OECD Countries: Comparative Outlook of Current Trends <http://www.oecd.org/dataoecd/21/32/1857507.pdf>. Elsewhere, that author reiterates: 'Making Italy a more attractive environment for investors can be considered the idea lying behind the reform initiatives: this has meant revising securities, company and bankruptcy law. The judicial mechanism for enforcing shareholders' and creditors' rights also need to be improved'. Italian commentators agree. See G Ferrarini, P Giudici and M Stella Richter (n 70) 661 (describing the reforms as '[d]irected at enhancing the creation of new business firms and the competitiveness of the same both with regards to product and capital markets').

[73] See Law No. 366/01, Article 2 (1) (a) (n 69) ('La riforma del sistema delle società di capitali ... è ispirata a ... perseguire l'obiettivo prioritario di favorire la nascita, la crescita e la competitività delle imprese, anche attraverso il loro accesso ai mercati interni e internazionali dei capitali').

[74] See Embassy of Italy in Washington 'Doing Business in Italy: Regulations and Incentives' <http://www.ambwashingtondc.esteri.it/Ambasciata_Washington/Menu/Informazioni_e_servizi/Fare_affari_in_Italia/Norme_ed_incentivi/>; Ministry of Economy and Finance 'Business Italia' <http://businessitalia.finanze.it/inglese/company_law/company_law1.htm>.

[75] See Law No. 262/05 of 28 December 2005, Gazz. Uff. 301 (28 December 2005); 'Reform of Italian Corporate and Securities Law: The Investor Protection Act' (Cleary, Gottlieb, Steen & Hamilton Memorandum to Clients, 6 March 2006) <http://www.cgsh.com/files/tbl_s5096AlertMemoranda/FileUpload5741/355/19-2006.pdf>.

act to the changes,[76] the Italian law has been seen as an attempt to repair the country's reputation among investors.[77]

The development of French corporate law is also linked to the massive privatizations that started in 1986 and increased the dependence of the economy on equity markets. The reform's opening shot was fired in 1984 with a law enhancing the independence of corporate auditors.[78] Drawing political force from two financial scandals involving state-owned aluminum company Pechiney and recently privatized bank Société Générale, the reform continued with a 1988 law that expanded the enforcement powers of the country's securities agency; created two additional securities agencies; and imposed new disclosure, manipulation, and insider-trading rules. A 1989 law further strengthened the enforcement powers of the primary securities agency.[79] The next step was a 2001 law which improved corporate disclosure, facilitated shareholder litigation, enhanced shareholder protection in takeovers, and allowed companies to separate the roles of chief executive officer and chair of the board.[80] The government-commissioned report on which the reform was based was clear about its motivation. As translated from French to English: 'Economic competition also puts in competition legal systems. From this perspective, the heavy-handedness and rigidities of French corporate law are a handicap. Among the considerations taken into account in the choice of the host country for a commercial company, the adaptability of the law to the specific needs of the company and to changes in the economic and social environment is undoubtedly an important factor'.[81]

[76] See R Romano 'The Sarbanes-Oxley Act and the Making of Quack Corporate Governance' (2005) 114 Yale L J 1521 (presenting Gallup poll that reflects public opinion of confidence in Big Business).

[77] See 'Turning Sour' *The Economist* (3 January 2004) 8 (discussing effects of Parmalat scandal); 'Not So Super Consob' *The Economist* (7 February 2004) 78 (reporting that the government 'is keen to rush through a new law to reform financial regulation in Italy because of the collapse of Parmalat', which 'destabilised Italy's fragile banking sector and left the reputation of the country as a wise place in which to invest more than a little dented').

[78] See JA Fanto 'The Role of Corporate Law in the Adaptation of French Enterprises' (1998) 97 Colum Bus L Rev 112 ('French legal policy-makers substantially modified the law in 1984 to increase the verification responsibilities of the *commissaire* and to ensure his or her independence from management').

[79] See LA Goldman 'The Modernization of the French Securities Markets: Making the EEC Connection' (1992) 60 Fordham L Rev 227, 238-240 ('This law broadened the COB's oversight responsibilities by rendering the Commission responsible for the proper functioning of the Bourse and the Matif ... and expanded the definition of insider trading to include transactions involving futures contracts. The 1998 law also modified the structure of the regulatory system by establishing the CBV and SBF').

[80] See Law No. 2001-420 of 15 May 2001, JO 7776 (16 May 2001).

[81] See P Marini 'La Modernisation du Droit des Sociétés' (La documentation Française Rapport au Premier Minister 13 July 1996) [Report to the Prime Minister on the Modernization of Corporate Law] 20 ('[L]a compétition économique met également en concurrence les systè-

cont. ...

In 2003, another law came into effect in France which transformed three corporate regulatory agencies with shared responsibilities into a single body.[82] According to French lawyers, one of the goals of the change was to 'help restore investors' confidence in the financial markets in the wake of recent U.S. and European financial scandals'.[83] Confidence in the market, however, was not all that mattered, if the goal was to attract investments rather than merely to appease the public. Investments required flexibility alongside shareholder protection. And flexibility is what the legislature sought to provide in an ordinance signed by the French President in 2004.[84] That ordinance, which has the force of law, removes procedural constraints on seasoned stock offerings, enables issuers to define the terms of preferred stock, and simplifies the treatment of convertible stock.[85] It is neither driven by scandal nor designed to reign in renegade managers; but it is nevertheless what investors want.

In 1998, the British Department of Trade and Industry commissioned a comprehensive review of the country's corporate law. In 2005, the British government introduced a company law reform bill based on this review.[86] Some commentators argue that this initiative is evidence of competition for incorporations.[87]

mes juridiques. De ce point de vue, la lourdeur et les rigidités du droit français des sociétés constituent un handicap. Parmi les éléments pris en considération dans le choix du pays d'accueil d'une société commerciale, nul doute que la faculté d'adaptation de l'instrument juridique aux besoins spécifiques de l'entreprise et aux modifications de l'environment économique et social soit un factuer important'.); see also P Marini (supra) 6 ('[I]l faut à présent envisager d'assurer la compétitivité juridique de la France par rapport aux systèmes d'inspiration anglo-saxonne d'un côté et germanique de l'autre, dans le contexte de marchés financiers totalement interconnectés et d'une liberté de plus en plus large de localisation des activités économiques'. ['It is now necessary to plan to ensure the legal competitiveness of France relative to Anglo-American systems on the one hand and German systems on the other hand, in the context of completely inter-connected financial markets and increasingly broad freedom where to place economic activity'].); P Marini (supra) 9 ('Aujourd'hui, les impératifs de l'ouverture internationale et la nécessité pour nos enterprises d'évoluer dans un cadre juridique compétitif semblent appeler une remise en cause de ce modèle afin de laisser plus de place à la liberté contractuelle'. ['Today, the requirements of the international opening and the need for our enterprises to evolve in a competitive legal environment seem to call into question [the rigid structure of the existing French corporate law] in order to leave more room for contractual freedom']).

[82] See Law No. 2003-706 of 1 August 2003, JO 13220 (2 August 2003).

[83] See N Bombrun and F Mary 'France' in The International Financial Law Review Guide to Mergers and Acquisitions (2004) <http://www.iflr.com/?Page=17&ISS=16378&SID=515244>.

[84] See Ordinance No. 2004-604 of 24 June 2004, JO 11612 (26 June 2004).

[85] See 'France Adopts New Legislation to Modernize its Securities Laws' (Cleary Gottlieb Steen and Hamilton Memorandum to Clients 8 July 2004) <http://www.cgsh.com/files/tbl_s5096AlertMemoranda%5CFileUpload5741%5C188%5C55-2004.pdf>.

[86] See Company Law Reform Bill, 2005, HL Bill [34].

[87] See e.g. G Hertig and JA McCahery (n 5) 186; JA McCahery and EPM Vermeulen 'The Evolution of Closely Held Business Forms in Europe' (2001) 26 J Corp L 855, 864; Deakin (n

cont. ...

It is not. It is evidence of competition for investments. Its self-proclaimed aim is 'to develop a simple, modern, efficient and cost effective framework for carrying out business activity in Britain for the twenty-first century'.[88] And while the initiative originally highlighted 'small private companies' that constitute the majority of the '1.5 million companies in Great Britain',[89] the reforms that the government has adopted since the beginning of the process target public companies, which are more relevant to internationally mobile capital.[90] These reforms include regulations from 2002 requiring public companies to disclose executive compensation and have shareholders approve it,[91] an act from 2004 strengthening the audit of public companies while expanding the power of companies to indemnify directors for liability,[92] and regulations from 2005 (which have since been re-

5) 205.

[88] See <http://www.dti.gov.uk/cld/review.htm>. The reform was presented as part of a broader policy of economic development, which in an earlier stage included steps to '[create] the conditions for macro-economic stability' by '[ensuring the country's] public finances were put in order' and '[giving] independence to the Bank of England so that decisions on interest rates were taken for economic rather than political reasons', thereby 'providing business with the foundations for growth and consumers with low prices and competitive markets', and setting the stage for 'promoting enterprise and raising productivity' by fitting corporate law 'for the twenty-first century and beyond'. See P Hewitt 'Preface by the Secretary of State to DTI Modernising Company Law' (DTI Command Paper 5553) (July 2002) 3 <http://www.dti.gov.uk/companiesbill/prelims.pdf>. See also K Brown and M Peel 'Blueprint to Help Bring Business Into the 21st Century' *Fin Times* (27 July 2001) 4 (reporting that the trade and industry Secretary explained the need for the reform by saying that 'UK company law, once regarded as the best in the world, has fallen well behind that of other countries' and that '[y]ears of neglect have left us with an archaic Victorian system that is holding British business back'). Consistently, the reform project received strong support from industry group. See again K Brown and M Peel (supra) (reporting that supporters of the reform included the Institute of Directors and the Trade Union Congress).

[89] See DTI 'Modernising Company Law – The Government Policy' (DTI Command Paper 5553) (July 2002) 15-16 <http://www.dti.gov.uk/companiesbill/part2.pdf>.

[90] See E Ferran 'Company Law Reform in the UK: A Progress Report' (2005) 69 Rabels Zeitschrift fuer auslaendisches und internationales Privatrecht 629, 641-652 (discussing recent legislative developments and proposals). The delay of other parts of the reform was criticized by representatives of the local industry. See A Parker 'Delay on Company Law Reform Attacked' *Fin Times* (11 July 2003) 4 (noting that industry organizations such as the Confederation of British Industry and the Federation of Small Businesses attacked the government for delaying the corporate law reform, and that the member of the opposition party serving as shadow trade and industry said that 'the government's failure to proceed with a swift overhaul of company law undermined its pro-business stance').

[91] See Directors' Remuneration Report Regulations 2002 S.I. 2002/1986 Article 3.

[92] See Companies (Audit, Investigations and Community Enterprise) Act 2004. According to the official notes to the act, it 'forms part of the Government's strategy to help restore investor confidence in companies and financial markets following recent major corporate failures'. See DTI 'Explanatory Notes to Companies (Audit, Investigations and Community Enterprise) Act 2004' 4 <http://www.opsi.gov.uk/acts/en2004/2004en27.htm>.

pealed) requiring public companies to disclose more fully their performance and business risks.[93]

Examples from other Member States abound.[94] In 1999, for example, a takeover law modeled after the British City Code on Takeovers came into effect in Austria. The law was not meant to attract incorporations. Accordingly, it applies only to target companies located and listed in Austria.[95] Similarly, in 2004, the Dutch parliament enacted a law setting forth new requirements regarding the election of directors, shareholder approval for major corporate changes, shareholder proposals, and voting by holders of share depository receipts. The impetus for the reform was not a government plan to attract foreign incorporations, but rather a series of major domestic bankruptcies, financial scandals, and lavish executive compensation packages that resulted in a public uproar.[96] The reform was nonetheless informed by solutions given elsewhere in the world to similar problems. In particular, the reforms seemed to reflect increasing sensitivity in the accountancy profession to the need for independence in conducting corporate audits 'due to international developments (the Sarbanes-Oxley Act, IAS/IFRS, and various financial scandals such as Enron, Parmalat and Ahold)'.[97]

Finally consider voluntary codes of corporate governance. By the end of 2001, there were no less than thirty-five codes setting similar best practices of corporate governance in the various Member States of the European Union; twenty-five of these codes were issued after 1997.[98] Subsequent years saw the introduction of additional voluntary codes. They too resembled each other in their handling of executive compensation, financial auditing, and public disclosure.[99]

The legal innovation and diffusion in these examples is not the product of competition for incorporations. Even commentators who predict such competition

[93] See Companies Act 1985 (Operating and Financial Review and Directors' Report) Regulations 2005 S.I. 2005/1011; Companies Act 1985 (Operating and Financial Review) (Repeal) Regulations 2005 S.I. 2005/3442.

[94] For a survey of corporate reforms in 21 European countries prepared for the British DTI, see Centre for Law and Business, Faculty of Law, University of Manchester 'Company Law in Europe: Recent Developments' (February 1999) <http://www.dti.gov.uk/cld/milman.pdf>.

[95] See N Callister-Radcliffe et al 'Rejection of the EU Takeover Directive – The Implications' (2001) 29 Int'l Bus Law 337, 339-340; see also PM Polak 'Austria' in *The International Financial Law Review Guide to Mergers and Acquisitions 2004* <http://www.iflr.com/?Page=17&ISS=16378&SID=515234>.

[96] See JL Burggraff and J Winnubst 'The Netherlands' in *The International Financial Law Review Guide to Mergers and Acquisitions 2004* <http://www.iflr.com/?Page=17&ISS=16378&SID=515251>.

[97] See JL Burggraff and J Winnubst (n 96).

[98] See Weil, Gotshal and Manges 'Comparative Study of Corporate Governance Codes Relevant to the European Union and Its Member States' (January 2002) <http://europa.eu.int/comm/internal_market/company/docs/corpgov/corp-gov-codes-rpt-part1_en.pdf>.

[99] See Weil, Gotshal and Manges (n 98).

in the European Union acknowledge its absence today and regard large industrialized Member States as unlikely candidates for spearheading it. Yet it is these Member States that seem to have adopted the most sweeping legal reforms. Far from trying to win new incorporations, or trying not to lose existing ones (neither of which can motivate laws applicable only to local businesses) Member States modified their laws so as to attract investments into their economies. Sometimes they innovated. Often they borrowed from others.[100]

C. The Incentives to Compete

The ability and willingness of corporate decisionmakers to shop for laws is not enough of a driver for regulatory competition to develop. Another key condition is a desire by lawmakers to respond. But this condition is not easily met. In the United States, birthplace of the competition-for-incorporations theory, only Delaware pursues incorporations by foreign firms. Other states, by some accounts, make far weaker efforts to retain incorporations by local firms. By other accounts, they compete at all. In contrast, the incentives to compete for investments can be strong because the rewards of such competition are high and because these rewards accrue to all competitors rather than to only one. The integration of the markets for capital, products, and labor in recent years has set the stage for this competition to develop in the European Union. The resulting dramatic response by Member States leaves no doubt about the high potential of competition for investments to shape corporate law.

I. Benefits

An important reason why competition for investments thrives where competition for incorporation might fail to get the attention of lawmakers is that its stakes

[100] In some cases, Member States copied foreign law specifically at the request of local companies. Germany, for example, passed a law in 1998 (*Kapitalaufnahmeerleichterungsgesetz*, or KapAEG) that allows companies to balance their books using international or American accounting standards in order to enable them to list their stock overseas without having to prepare two sets of financial statements. See E Nowak 'Recent Developments in German Capital Markets and Corporate Governance' (2001) 14 J Applied Corp Fin 35, 44 (linking the legislation to the listing of Daimler Benz in the United States as part of its merger with Chrysler). For illustration of the two sets of financial statements that used to be filed by German companies listed in the United States prior to the change, see 'Deutsche Telekom Consolidated Financial Statements for 1996' (1997) 61-62 <http://download-dtag.t-online.de/englisch/investor-relations/4-financial-reports/annual-reports/1996/abschluss.pdf>. Germany also changed its law in 1998 under pressure from corporate managers and investment banks to allow the use of stock option compensation as in the United States. See Telephone Interview with Joachim von Falkenhausen (Partner), Latham & Watkins LLP Hamburg (28 June 2004) (hereafter von Falkenhausen Interview).

are higher and its rewards are more suitable to becoming part of a political platform.[101]

1. Competition for Incorporations

Much has been said about the lure of the fiscal gains that a jurisdiction can earn from incorporations by foreign companies and about the profits its legal community can reap from providing services to these companies. In reality, however, only jurisdictions with limited financial means can be moved by the possible fiscal gains from incorporations. And the legal community, as enthusiastic as it may be about attracting incorporations, must point to significant gains accruing to the entire polity in order to motivate lawmakers to adopt corporate legislation that could face significant opposition.

It is difficult to estimate the potential of incorporations as a source of tax revenue. Any such estimate depends on the number of incorporated firms, their need of corporate law, and the alternatives available to them elsewhere.[102] It is easy, however, to observe the experience that Delaware has had in this regard. Delaware is a success story. It stands in the enviable position of attracting half the public companies in the United States,[103] and almost all public companies that incorporate outside their home state[104] – with virtually no political costs and only

[101] Another difference between competition for incorporations and competition for investments is that only the former can theoretically be replicated by private actors. The politics involved in any public lawmaking have led commentators to conclude that private actors competing for incorporations would produce better corporate law than elected officials. See G Hadfield and E Talley 'On Public versus Private Provision of Corporate Law' (2006) 22 J L Econ & Org (forthcoming). Private actors, however, cannot capture the gains from economic development, and thus they cannot replicate the competition for investments.

[102] Member States do not have to tax incorporations directly. They can also, for example, tax the use of their courts or legal services by chartered firms. But these indirect taxes may not yield higher revenues. Court fees, which are meaningful only in legal regimes that rely on litigation, are borne by shareholder plaintiffs, rather than chartered companies. Indeed, Delaware, which relies heavily on courts in the administration of corporate law, imposes no such fees. Similarly, legal services taxes are borne only by firms that use local legal services, and can easily be avoided by using foreign legal services. More generally, it is fair to assume that decades of experimentation have brought Delaware close to optimizing its incorporation tax subject to political constraints. A new competing Member State in the European Union is unlikely to derive significantly higher gains from a similar market.

[103] See G Subramanian 'The Influence of Antitakeover Statutes on Incorporation Choice: Evidence on the "Race" Debate and Antitakeover Overreaching' (2002) 150 U Pa L Rev 1795, 1813 (examining Delaware's share of American public companies in 2000). Delaware public companies also tend to be bigger than other public companies. While constituting half the public companies in the sample, they account for 59% of net sales. See again G Subramanian (supra).

[104] See R Daines 'The Incorporation Choices of IPO Firms' (2002) 77 NY U L Rev 1159, 1562 (examining Delaware's share of initial public offerings in the United States between 1978 and 2000); LA Becbchuk and A Cohen 'Firms' Decisions Where to Incorporate' (2003) 46 J L

cont. ...

minimal financial costs. The result? A respectable tax revenue of $523 million forecasted for 2005 on budgeted outlays of $15 million, constituting a fifth of the state's revenue.[105]

But this American dream may remain out of reach for Member States of the European Union even as the freedom to choose where to incorporate reaches their shores. Taxing incorporated firms more than the cost of servicing them is simply not allowed under European Union law.[106] Not that such a tax would make a big difference anyhow. In 2004, gross domestic product in the United States was $11.7 trillion. The equivalent figure for the European Union was $9.6 trillion.[107] Domestic stock market capitalization in the United States in that year was $16.3 trillion. The equivalent figure for the European Union was $9.6 trillion.[108] Even if a single Member State assumed overnight a position similar to the one enjoyed by Delaware, its tax revenue from incorporations would probably be lower because it would command a smaller market.[109] This revenue might be significant for some of the smallest Member States. But, as the following Section will explain, these Member States lack the necessary legal infrastructure to attract the sort of large public companies that can generate such revenue.[110]

The benefit to lawyers in providing services to incorporating companies is another force that is said to drive jurisdictions to compete for incorporations. However the obvious interest of lawyers in incorporations does not mean that lawmakers will cooperate. Lawmakers will need a better reason to spend political capital before they will push any legislation that might encounter significant opposition.

Two factors explain the ease with which the Delaware corporate bar routinely pushes its proposals through the state legislative process. The first is the absence of any interest group in the state that might object to these proposals. The second is the state's reliance on the fiscal gains from incorporations.[111] Delaware law-

& Econ 383, 386 (arguing that Delaware's 'dominance of this market is greater than is commonly recognized').

105 See 'An Act Making Appropriations for the Expense of the State Government for the Fiscal Year Ending June 30, 2005' Delaware State Senate 142nd Gen Assem Bill 320 (2004) <http://www.state.de.us/budget/budget/fy2005/fy2005-sb320-budget-bill.pdf>.

106 See M Baudisch (n 5) 51-52 (arguing that such a tax might violate Council Directive 69/335/EEC, raise constitutional concerns in many Member States, and be resisted by business).

107 See World Bank 'Data & Statistics' <http://www.worldbank.org/data/countrydata/countrydata.html>.

108 See World Federation of Exchanges 'Domestic Equity Markets' <http://www.world-exchanges.org/WFE/home.asp?menu=315&document=2490> (reporting stock market capitalization of domestic companies by stock exchange).

109 See G Miccoli (n 14) describing as unrealistic the possibility that Member States would compete for incorporations by companies that operate and pay income tax elsewhere.

110 See infra Section C.II.1..

111 See R Romano *The Genius of American Corporate Law* (American Enterprise Institute

cont. ...

yers, to be sure, gain handsomely from their state's thriving incorporations business[112] – but so does the state. It reaps fiscal gains from incorporations that pay for a fifth of its public consumption at minimal political and economic costs, placing it second nationally in revenue per capita.[113] With this symbiotic relationship between local lawyers, politicians, and the state government, it is no wonder that corporate lawyers in Delaware get their way.

By comparison, corporate lawyers in other states have a much tougher time pushing legislation to attract incorporations – precisely because interest groups exist in these states that resist these initiatives. It was politics, not the lack of support from corporate lawyers, that derailed a Pennsylvania effort to form a juryless corporate tribunal with judges appointed based on merit.[114] Politics also derailed an effort to form a Nevada corporate tribunal without juries and with nonrotating judges.[115] The lesson from these experiences is clear: It is not enough that corporate lawyers want the legislation to pass; if they are to overcome political objections, the public benefits to the state and the political benefits to lawmakers must at least appear significant.

2. Competition for Investments

Capital investments fuel economic development. The direct effect of capital investments on growth is obvious. Indirectly, however, capital investments stimulate growth also by deepening domestic stock markets,[116] which serve as an outlet

Press 1993) 60 (arguing that Delaware corporate law is minimally affected by an individual firm's lobbying because of the large number of Delaware incorporated companies and because most Delaware companies operate outside the state).

[112] See M Kahan and E Kamar (n 1) 694-698 (estimating the additional income per Delaware lawyer from incorporations at roughly $35,000 per year in 2000).

[113] See U.S. Census Bureau 'State Rankings – Statistical Abstract of the United States: State Government General Revenue Per Capita 2003' <http://www.census.gov/statab/ranks/rank24.html>.

[114] See JL Kennedy 'Chancery Ct. Plan Sent to Senate' *Legal Intelligencer* (17 May 1993) 1 (stating that 'powerful labor unions ... will likely fight to have that provisions quashed').

[115] See Minutes of the Nevada Legis. Commission's Subcomm. to Encourage Corporations and Other Business Entities to Organize and Conduct Business in This State: Sub-Subcomm. for the Examination of the Business Court and Business Laws, 1999 Leg. 1999-2000 Interim Session (30 May 2000) (testimony of A William Maupin, Associate J., Nevada Supreme Court) <http://www.leg.state.nv.us/70th/Interim/Studies/Business/Minutes/IM-Business-20000530-2367.html>.

[116] See PL Rousseau and P Wachtel 'Equity Markets and Growth: Cross-Country Evidence on Timing and Outcomes 1980-1995' (2000) 24 J Banking & Fin 1933, 1955 (finding that liquid stock markets promote economic growth); A Demigrüç-Kunt and V Maksimovic 'Law, Finance, and Firm Growth' (1998) 53 J Finance 2107, 2134 (finding that active stock markets are associated with externally financed firm growth); R Levine and S Zervos 'Stock Markets, Banks, and Economic Growth' (1998) 88 Am Econ Rev 537, 537 (finding that stock market

cont. ...

for selling startup companies,[117] allocate funds to well-performing firms,[118] and facilitate corporate restructuring through mergers.[119] This insight has not been lost on policymakers. Italian policymakers, for example, have acknowledged that 'the growth of national industries does not depend only on their capacity for independent growth but also on the search for combinations with Italian or foreign partners, by means of mergers or stock swaps', and accordingly have endorsed '[l]egislation that facilitates such consolidation by reducing the reorganization costs that integration between different company structures inevitably entails'.[120]

The sheer magnitude and visibility of these gains make them a much stronger political incentive to act than the gains from incorporations. After all, the difference between winning and losing in the competition for international capital is the difference between having billions of euros invested in local businesses and not having them. The mounting economic pressures on many Member States in recent years, however, have raised the stakes of competition for investments, making it almost a political necessity.

One way these pressures have manifested themselves is in privatizations aimed at balancing the national budget and facilitating industry consolidation.[121]

liquidity predicts growth, capital accumulation, and productivity improvements). For the link between corporate law and stock markets, see R La Porta, F Lopez-de-Silanes, A Shleifer and RW Vishny 'Legal Determinants of External Finance' (1997) 52 J Finance 1131 (finding that countries that protect shareholders have more valuable stock markets, larger numbers of listed securities per capita, and a higher ratio of initial public offerings than other countries).

[117] See W Carlin and C Meyer 'How Do Financial Systems Affect Economic Perfomance?' in X Vives (ed) *Corporate Governance: Theoretical and Empirical Perspectives* (Cambridge University Press 2000) 137 (finding that equity markets are associated with national economic growth through research and development).

[118] See J Wurgler 'Financial Markets and the Allocation of Capital' (2000) 58 J Finan Econ 187, 188-189 (finding that investor protection and developed stock markets improve capital allocation).

[119] See S Rossi and PF Volpin 'Cross-Country Determinants of Mergers and Acquisitions' (2004) 74 J Finan Econ 277 (finding that acquirers are based in countries with better corporate governance); M Baker, CF Foley and J Wurgler 'Stock Market Valuations and Foreign Direct Investment' (SSRN wp <http://ssrn.com/abstract=556127>, 2004) (finding that cross-border acquisitions increase with the current aggregate market-to-book ratio of the acquirer's stock market and decrease with subsequent returns on that market).

[120] See M Draghi (n 31) 356.

[121] The privatization of Deutsche Telekom stock in 1997 illustrates the international dimension of privatizations driven by budgetary needs. See G Steinmetz and MR Sesit 'Bigger Bang: Rising U.S. Investment in European Equities Galvanizes Old World' *Wall St J* (4 August 1999) A1 ('When Germany privatized Deutsche Telekom AG two years ago in one of the largest initial public offerings in history, it marketed the stock to American investors, as well as Europeans. It did the same earlier this year when it carried out a secondary offering. By plugging the stock to Americans, it increased demand and so boosted the value of Telekom shares. Deutsche Telekom is now worth three times what it was two years ago. And when Berlin begins selling the rest of its stake, the proceeds will give a much-needed boost to the government's finances').

Privatizations motivate state officials to pay attention to the quality of corporate law for two reasons. First, during the privatization, quality law and liquid markets increase the revenue from selling shares of state-owned firms.[122] Second, after the privatization, maintaining the value of privatized firms is vital to the public trust in the government and the politicians associated with the privatization.

In fact, a major corporate scandal can shake up the government even if it involves a company that was never state owned.[123] This too has been a common occurrence in recent years, as can be expected during an economic downswing. To be sure, corporate scandals can precipitate reform independently of competition for investments. Indeed, much of federal securities legislation in the United States – including the Securities Act of 1933, the Securities Exchange Act of 1934, the Williams Act of 1968, and the Sarbanes-Oxley Act of 2002 – responded to perceived abuses that affected domestic investors. But corporate scandals carry with them an added penalty for countries that depend on mobile capital.[124] The knowledge that a scandal involving a single domestic company can taint the entire economy creates a strong incentive for lawmakers to adopt legislation that will prevent a scandal before it happens and, if it has already happened, to adopt legislation to prevent a reoccurrence.[125] If lawmakers have any doubt about their re-

[122] A telling example is the success that American mutual fund Fidelity had in 1997 dissuading the French government from using its control over mining company Eramet to placate New Caledonian separatists by swapping one of the company's mines for an inferior one controlled by the separatists. It helped that the skirmish took place less than three months before a $7 billion initial public offering of France Telecom. All Fidelity had to do was to remind the French government that American investors would shun French privatizations if it did not back down. See G Steinmetz and MR Sesit (n 121).

[123] This scenario is rather common even in an era of global capital markets because investors tend to invest locally to exploit information advantages. See H Hau 'Location Matters: An Examination of Trading Profits' (2001) 56 J Finance 1959; LL Tesar and IM Werner 'Home Bias and High Turnover' (1995) 14 J Int'l Money & Fin 467; I Coopers and E Kaplanis 'Home Bias in Equity Portfolios, Inflation Hedging, and International Capital Market Equilibrium' (1994) 7 Rev Fin Stud 45; T Gehrig 'An Information Based Explanation of the Domestic Bias in International Equity Investment' (1993) 95 Scandinavian J Econ 97; KR French and JM Poterba 'Investor Diversification and International Equity Markets' (1991) 81 Am Econ Rev 222; see generally A Karolyi and R Stulz 'Are Financial Assets Priced Locally or Globally?' in GM Constantinides, M Harris and RM Stulz (eds) *The Handbook of the Economics of Finance* (JAI Press 2003).

[124] See R Evans 'Applying Pressure: European Funds Increasing Corporate Activism' *Pensions & Investments* (23 February 2004) 14 (reporting growing activism by British pension fund manager Hermes, Dutch pension fund managers ABP and PGGM, and French pension fund manager Caisse des Dépôts at Consignations following a string of corporate governance scandals); see also C Karmin and J Hookway 'Calpers to Reverse Position on Investing in Philippine Market' *Wall St J* (13 May 2002) C1 (reporting a widespread belief among stock market participants that the decision by CalPERS to liquidate its stock investments in the Philippines in 2002 had a more negative impact on the Manila stock exchange because it came at the heels of a stock manipulation scandal one year earlier).

[125] See e.g. N George 'Sweden in Business Law Move' *Fin Times* (19 January 2004) 24

cont. ...

sponsibility, the financial press will quickly erase it, as the following article published after the collapse of Parmalat illustrates:

'Now, in Parmalat, an Italian food and milk-products company, Europe has a corporate scandal of truly Enronesque proportions. If the integrity of European business is to be restored, and public confidence in the continent's capital markets is to be sustained, Europe's response will have to be as determined and sweeping as America's ….

It has been tempting for international investors to think of Europe as a single investment space. The reality is that harmonisation of Europe's industrial and financial markets still has a long way to go. Local practices matter, never more so than when things go wrong ….

The danger to honest Italian business could not be clearer: their cost of capital will rise if investors begin to discriminate against a country that had been trying to shake off a reputation for dark dealings. In fact, this is precisely what international investors should now do. The sheer scale of the Parmalat scandal raises serious questions about Italian business practices which only a thorough, and very un-Italian, clean-up can now dispel'.[126]

The link between legislation triggered by corporate scandals and competition for investments is evident when the scandals involve foreign companies and cannot be blamed on the local law. Unlike legislation triggered by local corporate scandals, which can be explained both as a response to public outcry and as an effort to shore up investor confidence in local companies, legislation triggered by foreign corporate scandals can only be explained by the latter. Foreign scandals have played a significant role in catalyzing reform in a number of European Member States, sometimes even more than local events. One such scandal was the 2002 collapse of giant American corporation Enron amid accounting irregularities. The Enron scandal was followed closely in the European Union. In the United Kingdom, for example, the debacle prompted the government to accelerate and expand a preexisting plan for corporate reform, labeling its actions 'post-Enron initiatives'.[127] In Italy, it similarly fueled calls for accounting reform.[128]

(reporting that the Swedish Minister for financial markets expressed disappointment with the failure of business leaders to take effective measures to restore the confidence in Swedish business, which 'has been rocked by several corporate scandals, the most high-profile domestic example involving huge bonus payments and management perks at Skandia, the financial services group' and expressed resolve to address the crisis in legislation if this failure continued).

126 'Turning Sour' (n 77); see also R Heller 'Parmalat: A Particularly Italian Scandal' Forbs.come (30 December 2004) <http://www.forbes.com/2003/12/30/cz_rh_1230parmalat-print.html> ('Parmalat is reminiscent of several other florid Italian scandals, especially the Banco Ambrosiano affair …. The Parmalat story simply does not fit into a global corporate-governance argument. It's beyond the pale; it's very Italian').

127 See P Davies 'Post-Enron Developments in the United Kingdom' in G Ferrarini, KJ Hopt, J Winter and E Wymeersch (eds) *Reforming Company and Takeover Law in Europe* (Oxford University Press 2004) 185 (documenting the legislative response in the United Kingdom to Enron); DTI 'Corporate Law and Governance: Post Enron Initiatives' <http://www.dti.gov.uk

cont. ...

Enron did not anger British or Italian voters; rather, it was a focusing event that reminded British and Italian lawmakers that their countries too could be hit by a similar scandal and lose their appeal to investors.[129] In the case of Italy, this fear took only two years to become a reality.

Last, capital investments strengthen the local financial services industry and solidify local financial centers which – in addition to being drivers of the national economy[130] – can be rather influential. The keen interest in helping the local financial industry compete internationally is a recurring motif in the legislative agenda of more than one Member State. It has played an important role, for instance, in Italy, where reformers emphasized, under the heading 'The Prospects of the Italian and European Stock Exchanges': 'The future of the European financial industry will see savings channeled towards the financial centres where they are most efficiently managed. Those centers will unfailingly become the places of greatest concentration of financial structures and infrastructure. An intensive planning effort will be necessary to avert the marginalization of the Italian financial industry and prevent it from being reduced merely to managing local monopoly positions'.[131]

Building a strong financial center has been an important legislative goal also in Germany, where the government went in 1992 as far as branding its legislative

/cld/post_enron.htm>.

[128] See R Galbraith 'Disappointment and Dissatisfaction in Italy' *The Accountant* (25 September 2002) 16 (reporting on stories of accounting scandals in the United States are fueling calls for accounting reforms in Italy).

[129] See JW Kingdon *Agendas, Alternatives, and Public Policies* (HarperCollins 1995) 94 ('Problems are often not self-evident by the indicators. They need a little push to get the attention of people in an around government. That push is sometimes provided by a focusing event like a crisis or disaster that comes along to call attention to the problem, a powerful symbol that catches on, or the personal experience of a policy maker'); TA Birkland *An Introduction to the Policy Process: Theories, Concepts, and Models of Public Policy Making* (ME Sharpe 2001) 116 ('Focusing events are sudden, relatively rare events that spark intense media and public attention because of their sheer magnitude or, sometimes, because of the harm they reveal. Focusing events thus attract attention to issues that may have been relatively dormant .... Focusing events can lead groups, government leaders, policy entrepreneurs, the news media, or members of the public to pay attention to new problems or pay greater attention to existing but dormant (in terms of their standing on the agenda) problems, and, potentially, can lead to a search for solutions in the wake of perceived policy failure').

[130] The contribution of strong financial institutions to growth is well established. For recent studies, see T Beck, R Levine and N Loayza 'Finance and the Sources of Growth' (2000) 58 J Finan Econ 261 (finding that financial intermediaries increase factor productivity and gross domestic product growth); RG Rajan and L Zingales 'Financial Dependence and Growth' (1998) 88 Am Econ Rev 559 (finding that industrial sectors in need of external financing develop faster in countries with more developed financial markets); K Neusser and M Kugler 'Manufacturing Growth and Financial Development: Evidence from OECD Countries' (1998) 80 Rev Econ Stat 638 (finding that financial intermediaries increase factor productivity).

[131] M Draghi (n 31).

campaign 'Finance Center Germany' ('*Finanzplatz Deutchland*').[132] Accordingly, the proposal for one of the recently adopted omnibus laws to modernize corporate law states that its objective is to 'strengthen Germany's ability to compete as a financial centre and enhance the function of the capital market as a force promoting growth and employment'.[133] Similarly, the website of the recently created securities agency explains: 'Securities supervision is the youngest discipline within Germany's regulatory framework. It was created as a result of the Second Financial Market Promotion Act, which was adopted on 26 July 1994. This legislation prompted a far-reaching reform of Germany's regulatory system for securities markets. The principal objective was to bolster the efficiency of Germany's financial sector, thus enhancing its ability to compete within the international arena'.[134]

The same has been the case in France,[135] and in the United Kingdom, where a 1995 government white paper titled 'Competitiveness' concluded that, while London was still 'the leading international financial centre in Europe', it would 'continue to face competitive pressures from elsewhere', noting in particular 'initiatives to promote the attractions of established rival centres, such as Europlace for Paris and Finanzplatz Deutschland for Frankfurt'.[136]

The market for investments is different from the market for incorporations not only in its higher stakes but also in its ability to sustain vigorous participation by multiple jurisdictions. There are two related reasons for this. The first is the difference in stakes. Delaware, the leading state of incorporation in the United States, currently earns about $500 million a year by taxing incorporations. If Delaware were to split this amount with an equal rival, each would collect no more than half. This is not a lot of revenue for a state, and certainly not a lot for a

[132] See R Deeg (n 36) 180; see also Federal Ministry of Finance 'A Clear Strategic Vision: Preparing German Financial Markets for the European Future' (30 September 2005) <http://www.bundesfinanzministerium.de/cln_02/nn_12996/EN/Investment__and__Capital/001.html>; H Eichel (Federal Minister of Finance) Speech on 'Exchanges and their Customers' at the 8th European Financial Markets Convention in Frankfurt (2 June 2004) <http://www.fese.be/initiatives/speeches/2004/eichel_1jun2004.htm>.

[133] See Federal Ministry of Finance 'Draft of a Fourth Financial Market Promotion Act' (14 November 2001) <http://www.bundesfinanzministerium.de/nn_13044/EN/10420.html>. The proposal further explains that to achieve this objective the government intends 'to improve investor protection by enhancing market integrity and transparency, to afford market participants extended and more flexible scope for action, and to close gaps in the defences against money laundering'. See again Federal Ministry of Finance (supra).

[134] Federal Financial Supervisory Authority 'History of Securities Supervision' <http://www.bafin.de/bafin/historie_wa_en.htm>.

[135] See generally C Gordon 'The Business Culture in France' in C Randlesome et al (eds) *Business Cultures in Europe* (Butterworth-Heinemann 1993) 86.

[136] See Department of the Environment, Transport and the Regions 'Competitiveness: Forging Ahead' (May 1995 Cm 2867) 3.3 <http://www.archive.official-documents.co.uk/document/dti/dti-comp/tchap3.htm#t3-25>.

country. By contrast, the stock capitalization of public companies alone in the European Union was $8 trillion in 2003. A conservative estimate of the foreign investments in these companies in that year exceeds $2 trillion.[137] Splitting this amount and the economic development it can generate between several jurisdictions still leaves enough worth fighting for.

Secondly, unlike the market for incorporations, the market for investments is not one in which the winner takes all. Delaware dominates the market for incorporations in the United States. It is the legal domicile of half of the public companies, and virtually all of the companies that incorporate outside their home state when they go public. But it carries this burden in stride. Indeed, judging from the modest outlays for its chartering business,[138] as well as from its efforts to attract additional business to its division of corporations and five-judge chancery court,[139] Delaware could easily handle the chartering of all public companies in the United States if only given the chance. The market for capital is different from the market for incorporations because it channels investments into physical businesses. There is a limit to the amount of capital that investor-friendly legislation can attract to a jurisdiction because, as production increases, so does the cost of local labor and other means of production that are less mobile than capital.[140] This limit gives hope to other jurisdictions that, with proper legislation, they too can attract capital.[141]

[137] In the years 2000 and 2001, foreign institutional investors held between 30% and 40% of publicly traded stock in the United Kingdom, Spain, Norway, France, Sweden, and Poland, between 20% and 30% in Germany, Greece, Portugal, and Denmark; 15% in Italy; and 5% in Estonia. See Share Ownership Survey (n 24) 40.

[138] See (n 105) and accompanying text (stating that the 2005 budget forecasted outlays of $15 million).

[139] See e.g. LE Strine Jr '"Mediation-Only" Filings in the Delaware Court of Chancery: Can New Value Be Added by One America's Business Courts?' (2003) 53 Duke L J 585.

[140] See CM Tiebout 'A Pure Theory of Local Expenditures' (1956) 64 J Pol Econ 416. Previous analyses of corporate lawmaking in federal systems, including my own, have analogized the competition for incorporations to the regulatory competition described by Tiebout. See e.g. E Kamar 'A Regulatory Competition Theory of Indeterminacy in Corporate Law' (1998) 98 Colum L Rev 1908, 1948; R Romano 'The Future of Hostile Takeovers: Legislation and Public Opinion' (1988) 57 U Cin L Rev 457, 466 and note 21 (same); JC Coffee Jr 'Competition Versus Consolidation: The Significance of Organizational Structure in Financial and Securities Regulation' (1995) 50 Bus Law 447, 453 and note 27; FH Easterbrook and DR Fischel 'Mandatory Disclosure and the Protection of Investors' (1984) 70 Va L Rev 669, 691 and note 29. Competition for investments, however, is closer to the Tiebout model because, in both, jurisdictions face increasing costs of providing services to businesses. While in theory jurisdictions should also face increasing costs of providing incorporation services, in practice these costs are small.

[141] In 2002, when Indonesia, Malaysia, the Philippines, and Thailand went out of favor as worthy places for investment, CalPERS decided to reallocate some of its investments in the four Southeast Asian countries to Hungary and Poland. See C Karmin and K Scannell 'Calpers's Withdrawal Hits Markets in Asia, but Fallout May Be Brief' *Wall St J* (25 February 2002) C12.

cont. ...

II. Costs

Competing for incorporations is costly. It differs from competition in the private sector only in that it involves political costs in addition to economic ones.[142] The costs that stand out in the European Union are the cost of building legal infrastructure and the cost of overcoming resistance from interest groups. The former cost inhibits competition by small Member States; the latter inhibits competition by large ones. The combination of the two leaves precious little ground for competition to develop. While these costs do not disappear in competition for investments, they can be offset by the higher stakes involved, which can induce even large jurisdictions with developed legal infrastructure to compete and can mollify even strong interest groups by forcing them to bear the cost of their resistance.

1. Competition for Incorporations

Impressed by tiny Delaware's successful pursuit of incorporations, some commentators have suggested that the smallest Member States in the European Union might compete for incorporations on the theory that they alone would value the modest gains to be had.[143] But these Member States lack the necessary legal infrastructure to attract incorporations. Consider, for example, Estonia, Latvia, and Malta, the Member States with the smallest budgets in the European Union and with total government revenues in 2004 of less than €4 billion each.[144] It is true that these Member States might be interested in incorporations, but their interest is not enough.[145] Corporate laws in these Member States are antiquated versions of German or French corporate law that have been in hibernation for

CalPERS presumably did not reallocate the freed up funds to jurisdictions with stronger records of investor protection because the quality of investor protection was only one of its investment criteria.

142 See M Kahan and E Kamar (n 1) 730-735.

143 See J Dammann (n 5) 528-530 (listing Estonia, Hungary, Cyprus, the Czech Republic, Latvia, Lithuania, Malta, Poland, and Slovakia as potential competitors).

144 See I Jablonska 'General Government Expenditure and Revenue in the EU in 2004' (30 May 2005) <http://epp.eurostat.cec.eu.int/cache/ITY_OFFPUB/KS-NJ-05-024/EN/KS-NJ-05-024-EN.PDF>.

145 While corporate law is not their strongest point, all of the new Member States have historically offered foreign businesses an array of tax incentives regarded by the European Commission as harmful. See D Dombey 'New EU Entrants Fail to Cut Tax Breaks' *Fin Times* (22 July 2003) 6. Malta, for example, has been better known for its advantageous taxation of offshore holding companies than for its corporate law. See 'Good Havens' *The Economist* (30 September 1995) 90 (noting tax exemptions for offshore holding companies); G Grima 'Malta Aspires to Become a Leading Financial Centre' *Fin Times* (9 December 2003) 3 (noting displeasure of the European Commission with taxation of offshore holding companies in Malta).

several decades and only recently received a facelift to meet the minimum requirements of the European Union.[146] These Member States also generally rank low in the European Union in terms of political stability, rule of law, and control of corruption.[147] It is hard to believe that any of them would attract the sort of large public companies that generate the bulk of Delaware's profits.[148]

Recognizing the disadvantages of these Member States, some commentators look to Luxembourg, the smallest developed Member State in the European Union, to carry the torch of competition.[149] Perhaps. But Luxembourg is not really that small. In 2003, its revenue totaled €6.35 billion – three times higher than Delaware's.[150] Accordingly, Luxembourg has done absolutely nothing to signal any intention to compete for incorporations despite much academic speculation that it should.[151] It did not rush to amend its law to allow foreign companies to

[146] See MA Arlt, C Bervoets, K Grechenig and S Kalss 'The Status of the Law on Stock Companies in Central and Eastern-Europe: Facing the Challenge to Enter the European Union and Implement European Company Law' (2003) 4 Eur Bus Org L Rev 245, 247 (describing the corporate laws of Bulgaria, the Czech Republic, Estonia, Hungary, Latvia, Lithuania, Poland, Romania, Slovakia, and Slovenia, and stating that '[m]ost Central and Eastern European company law can be traced back to the German … or French legal tradition').

[147] See World Bank Institute 'Governance Indicators: 1996-2004 – Global Comparative Charts' <http://www.worldbank.org/wbi/governance/govdata/> (ranking Estonia and Latvia in the bottom half of the European Union for political stability, rule of law, and control of corruption; ranking Malta in the bottom half for rule of law and control of corruption but in the top half for political stability); see also Transparency International 'Corruption Perceptions Index 2005' <http:// www.transparency.org/policy_and_research/surveys_indices/cpi/2005> (ranking these Member States in the bottom half of the European Union in perceived corruption).

[148] Experience shows that it is large public companies that can generate for a popular incorporation state the bulk of its benefits. Without their active involvement in incorporations, lawmakers have little reason to compete. Cfr M Kahan and E Kamar 'Price Discrimination in the Market for Corporate Law' (2001) 86 Cornell L Rev 1205, 1251 (reporting that about 1,600 large public companies out of more than 200,000 Delaware companies on average generated for the state more than half of its franchise tax revenue over the 1997-1999 period).

[149] See J Dammann (n 5) 528-530 (mentioning Luxembourg, along with Ireland, Portugal, and Greece as potential candidates); G Hertig and JA McCahery (n 5) 187 (mentioning Luxembourg and Ireland as potential candidates).

[150] See State of Delaware, Office of the Governor 'Financial Overview Fiscal Year 2004' (2003) 23 <http://www.state.de.us/budget/budget/fy2004/operating/04FinancialOverview.pdf> (noting a budget of $2.3 billion in 2003). The exchange rate in 2003 ranged between 0.94 and 0.81 euro for one U.S. dollar. Some commentators argue that the relevant figure for a state's incentive to compete for incorporations is its gross domestic product, rather than its budget, because it reflects the extent of economic activity that could be taxed should the need arise in the future. These commentators also note that Luxembourg's gross domestic product is one-half of Delaware's. See J Dammann (n 5) 528. As a practical matter, however, state policymakers tend to consider existing budgetary needs, rather than hypothetical ones, and value any revenue source according to its relative contribution to that budget.

[151] While Luxembourg used to attract some incorporations by protecting investor privacy, international pressure to combat money laundering has narrowed this tax loophole in its law.

cont. ...

incorporate in it, nor did it respond to the call for comments on a proposed European Union directive that would enable companies to reincorporate.[152] Although Luxembourg may begin to show interest in incorporations as the ability to incorporate abroad becomes established in the European Union, there are reasons to doubt that it will.[153]

The backbone of Luxembourg's economy is private banking.[154] Corporate law, by contrast, is not the country's strong point. In fact, along with other corporate laws in the French tradition, Luxembourg corporate law receives low marks in international comparisons,[155] few lawyers outside Luxembourg are familiar with this law, and many would find the fact that English is not an official language in Luxembourg to be a deterrent.[156] That Luxembourg will compete for incorporations by the sort of public companies that can generate significant profits is not impossible, but it is unlikely.

This lack of legal infrastructure is particularly problematic because of the need to offer an alternative to incorporation in the United Kingdom. Unlike Luxembourg, or any other Member State for that matter, the United Kingdom does

See Telephone Interview with G Fauda (Partner) and G Miccoli (Associate), Janni Magnocavallo Fauda Brescia e associati, Milan (28 July 2004).

[152] Of 127 responses to the call by the European Commission in 2004 for comments on the proposal, 52 responses came from Germany; 21 from France; 9 from the Netherlands; 7 from Belgium; 6 from Spain; 5 from the United Kingdom; 4 from Finland and Portugal; 3 from Austria, Greece, and Italy; 2 from the Czech Republic and Estonia; 2 from undisclosed countries; and 1 from Denmark, Ireland, and Sweden. No responses came from Luxembourg, Cyprus, Hungary, Lithuania, Latvia, Malta, Poland, Slovakia, or Slovenia. See Public Consultation on the Outline of the Planned Proposal for a European Parliament and Council Directive on the Cross-Border Transfer of the Registered Office of a Company <http://europa.eu.int/yourvoice/results/transfer/index_en.htm>.

[153] Note that a market in which only one state attempts to attract incorporations is quite different from a market in which many states compete. See M Kahan and E Kamar (n 1) 736-747 (comparing a market with a single competing state among many inactive ones with a market in which several states compete).

[154] In 1998, Luxembourg and Switzerland refused to be bound by the Organization for Economic Co-operation and Development's (OECD) guidelines for combating harmful tax competition because these guidelines called for sharing information about the income of individuals and businesses with foreign tax authorities. See OECD 'Harmful Tax Competition: An Emerging Global Issue' (1998) 73, annex II <http://www.oecd.org/dataoecd/33/0/1904176.pdf>. Luxembourg maintains its refusal to exchange this information today. See OECD 'Project on Harmful Tax Practices: The 2004 Progress Report' (2004) 10 <http://www.oecd.org/dataoecd/60/33/30901115.pdf>.

[155] See R La Porta, F Lopez-de-Silanes, A Shleifer and RW Vishny 'Law and Finance' (1998) 106 J Pol Econ 1113, 1139 (noting that 'French-civil-law countries protect [investors] the least').

[156] See 'The Galling Rise of English' *The Economist* (1 March 2003) (noting that English has become the language of business in the European Union). It is irrelevant that many Luxembourgian speak English because this language is not used in courts.

not need to build legal infrastructure from scratch to attract incorporations. Its law already offers both flexibility and shareholder protection,[157] and legions of legal and financial professionals both inside and outside its borders are already familiar with it.[158] This track record is important. In the early twentieth century, when New Jersey drove away its chartered companies with tough antitrust laws, incorporators looked no further than Delaware because it already had the law they wanted. The United Kingdom appears to be the instinctive choice for incorporators in the European Union for similar reasons.[159]

The United Kingdom, however, is not competing for incorporations and is not likely to do so in the future.[160] It is too big to care about the modest incorporation fees it can hope to collect, and it does not even bother to charge such fees.[161] Its corporate law is liberal because of its common law tradition, not because of any government plan to attract incorporations. Indeed, what some regard as the centerpiece of British corporate law, The City Code on Takeovers and Mergers, applies only to companies headquartered in the United Kingdom,[162] and was introduced in the 1960s – long before incorporations abroad were thought possible in the European Union – in response to a public uproar against abuses in the domes-

[157] British corporate law does contain a duty to consider employee interests. See Company Act 1985, ch. 6 s. 309. However, in reality, this duty is used by management to justify actions not favored by shareholders, rather than being used by employees to claim protection of their interest. See Company Law Review Steering Group 'Modern Company Law for a Competitive Economy – The Strategic Framework' (February 1999) 41, 5.1.21 <http://www.dti.gov.uk/cld/comlawfw/framewrk.pdf>.

[158] Unlike most other Member States, the United Kingdom already allows local businesses to incorporate abroad. That virtually none of them ever incorporates in other Member States or, for that matter, in the United States, suggests that the British law appeals to their managers and shareholders more than the alternatives.

[159] See DF Hickok and T Schürrle 'The "Inspire Art" Judgment of the European Court of Justice: New Ways to Structure Acquisitions in the European Union?' Debevoise & Plimpton Memorandum to Clients (20 January 2004) <http://www.debevoise.com/newseventspubs/publications>; '*Inspire Art:* New Opportunities for Corporate and Private Equity Structuring' Latham & Watkins Corporate Department Client Alert No. 372 (26 February 2004) <http://www.lw.com/resource/Publications/_pdf/pub931_1.pdf>; H Halbhuber 'National Doctrinal Structures and European Company Law' (2001) 38 Common Mkt L Rev 1385, 1403 ('England is widely perceived as the most likely candidate for a European Delaware'); see also 'UK Governance Is the Best in Europe' *Accountancy* (3 April 2004) 113 (citing a report by Brussels research firm Deminor that concluded that 'Britain has Europe's best corporate governance while Germany, Spain and the Netherlands have among the worst').

[160] Some commentators argue that the legal and accountancy professions in the United Kingdom have both the desire and power to cause the United Kingdom to compete for incorporations. See (n 87) and accompanying text. I understand the motivation behind the British proactiveness differently.

[161] See B Cheffins (n 5) 435.

[162] See The Panel on Takeovers & Mergers *The City Code on Takeovers and Mergers* (7th ed 2002) A8 <http://www.thetakeoverpanel.org.uk>.

tic takeover market.[163] Similarly, the corporate governance requirements of the state-sponsored listing rules apply only to companies that use the London Stock Exchange for primary listing.[164] These important parts of the law were designed with local businesses in mind, and given the difficulty of forcing foreign businesses to comply, the law will probably continue to apply only locally in the future.[165]

The costs of building legal infrastructure are only part of the burden involved in competing for incorporations. Other barriers result from the need to overcome political opposition. Lawmakers will not spend political capital to attract incorporations just because doing so might benefit the state. They will first consider the effects of such an effort on their careers, taking into account the magnitude of the benefits to the state, the time and likelihood involved in achieving results, the ability to claim personal credit for success, the repercussions of failing, the availability of alternative legislative projects, and the likely opposition.[166]

It is beyond the scope of this Article to catalogue all the political costs that could stand in the way of competition for incorporations. Suffice it to say that these costs can be substantial because an intricate web of interest group politics shapes corporate law in many Member States, especially ones possessing the necessary legal infrastructure to attract incorporations. Developed Member States tend to carry significant political baggage that can be crippling in a market for incorporations. One such political hurdle is strong labor. If there is one matter on which managers and shareholders agree it is limiting employee influence over

[163] See S Kenyon-Slade *Mergers and Takeovers in the U.S. and UK Law and Practice* (Oxford University Press 2004) 506-507 (noting that the impetus for establishing the code and the panel was widespread criticism of the issuance of a large block of shares by Metal Industries to white squire Thorn Electrical to ward off an attempted takeover by Aberdare Holdings' in 1967).

[164] See UKLA Listing Rules 17.12 <http://www.fsa.gov.uk/pubs/ukla/chapt17-3.pdf>. Of 142 foreign European Union firms listed on the London Stock Exchange on 17 March 2006, only 15 firms had their primary listing there. Of these, 11 firms were Irish, 3 were German, 1 was Danish, 2 were Italian, 1 was Belgian, 4 were from Luxembourg, and 2 were from the Netherlands. The total number of Irish companies listed on the London Stock Exchange was 70. See London Stock Exchange List of Companies <http://www.londonstockexchange.com/en-gb/pricesnews/statistics/listcompanies>.

[165] Corporate lawyers bemoan the refusal of the British City Panel on Takeovers to apply the City Code on Takeovers and Mergers to companies incorporated and listed in the United Kingdom but operating abroad. See 'Public Takeovers in Europe' (Freshfields Bruckhaus Deringer Memorandum to Clients, 2004) 17 <http://www.freshfields.com/practice/corporate/publications/pdfs/publictakeovers/Europe2004.pdf> (noting that these so-called 'orphan' companies currently 'have to include certain takeover precautions in their articles of association to reassure investors').

[166] See M Kahan and E Kamar (n 1) 727-735; cfr RD Arnold *The Logic of Congressional Action* (Yale University Press 1990) 68-71 (decribing the difficulty of mobilizing an inattentive electorate).

corporate strategy.[167] Yet this is also among the most sensitive political issues in these Member States. A related hurdle is protectionism. Efficient corporate law allocates corporate assets to their best use. Yet it requires neutrality that politicians tend to lack when it implies the transfer of local businesses to foreign hands.[168] This protectionist impulse has so far stymied efforts in most developed Member States to pass legislation that might expose domestic manufacturers to foreign acquisitions.[169]

[167] See M Pagano and P Volpin 'The Political Economy of Corporate Governance' (2005) 95 Am Econ Rev 1005 (finding that employee protection tends to be stronger, and shareholder protection tends to be weaker, in proportional, as opposed to majoritarian, electoral systems); MJ Roe 'Political Preconditions to Separating Ownership from Corporate Control' (2000) 53 Stan L Rev 539, 541 (arguing and presenting evidence that social democracies tend to have weaker shareholder protection).

[168] The desire to protect local industry has many a time driven elected officials in developed Member States of the European Union to weigh in when major domestic manufacturers were about to be sold to foreign buyers. See e.g. P Betts and V Mallet 'A French Solution' *Fin Times* (3 July 2002) P18 (describing the political opposition that blocked the acquisition of French oil company Elf Aquitaine by Italian group Eni in 1999 and the acquisition of Belgian company Société Générale de Belgique by Italian financier Carlo De Benedetti in 1988); A Bulkeley and R Tieman 'Fighting the Inevitable in France' (2004) Corp Control Alert 20 (describing the intervention by the French government to stir French pharmaceutical Aventis away from Swiss acquirer Novartis and into the hands of its domestic rival Sanofi-Synthelabo in 2004); P Jenkins 'Ackermann's Agenda: Deutsche Bank Grapples With Divisions Over Strategy' *Fin Times* (16 September 2004) 19 (describing the lobbying by German powerhouses Siemens, Deutsche Telekom, and SAP to prevent foreigners from buying Deutsche Bank). European governments have been particularly persistent in using so-called golden shares to block the acquisition of privatized companies by foreign buyers. See C Vitzthum 'Madrid Exercises Its "Golden Shares" on Foreign Deals' *Wall St J* (18 May 2000) A23 (describing the government blocking of an acquisition of the Spanish company Telefonica by Dutch company KPN, an acquisition of the Spanish company Hidroelectrica del Cantabrico by Electricité de France, and an acquisition of Telecom Italia by Deutsche Telekom). In 2003, the European Court of Justice declared this practice illegal. See J Kanter 'EU's Top Court Further Curbs Use of Golden Shares' *Wall St J* (14 May 2003) A12. But the motivation to avert acquisitions of major local companies by foreign buyers persists. See 'Banco Bilbao Vizcaya Argentaria: Italian Bank Endorses Offer, Moving Closer to a Final Deal' W*all St J* (11 April 2005) 1 (noting that the Bank of Italy 'stymied previous attempts at foreign takeovers'); D Dombey and H Williamson 'Germany Tells Brussels It Will Not Alter VW Law' *Fin Times* (3 July 2004) 11 (describing a showdown between Germany and the European Commission over a law specifically designed to protect carmaker Volkswagen from foreign acquisitions).

[169] See 'The Takeover Directive' (Freshfields Brukhaus Deringer Memorandum to Clients, July 2005) 3 <http://www.freshfields.com/practice/corporate/publications/pdfs/12218.pdf> (explaining that what ended the 14-year debate over the takeover directive was a comprise allowing Member States to permit antitakeover defenses); JW Cioffi '"Germany, Inc.": The Politics of Company and Takeover Law Reform in Germany and the European Union' (2002) 24 L Pol 355 (describing opposition in Germany to legislation that would expose German firms to takeovers by British and Dutch firms); SV Simpson 'The Effect of the 13th Directive on U.S. Bidders' in *The International Financial Law Review Guide to Mergers and Acquisitions 2004* <http://www.iflr.com/?Page=17&ISS=16378&SID=515275> (explaining that the permission granted in the

cont. ...

All of these political hurdles can easily retard legislation that would attract incorporations at the expense of local workers. This hindrance can be significant. Laws mandating labor representation on the board of directors or requiring consultation with employees in mergers are hardly the way to go if Member States are to attract incorporations, because neither managers nor shareholders gain from these requirements. And while commentators still disagree on the effect of antitakeover laws on incorporations,[170] they agree that American states that adopted them in the past were motivated solely by a desire to shelter local businesses from foreign acquisitions and did not consider their effect on incorporations.[171] If these states were to follow Delaware, whose law is driven by the pursuit of incorporations, they would have adopted much milder antitakeover statutes – if any at all.[172]

2. Competition for Investments

It is hard to compare the costs of harnessing corporate law for the purpose of competing for investments to the costs of harnessing corporate law for the purpose of competing for incorporations. Some of the costs are higher in the case of

Takeover Directive to Member States banning antitakeover defenses to exempt defenses against bidders not subject to a similar ban protects European firms from takeovers by American firms).

[170] Compare LA Bebchuk, A Cohen and A Ferrell 'Does the Evidence Favor State Competition in Corporate Law' (2002) 90 Cal L Rev 1775 (arguing that corporate decisionmakers favor states with antitakeover statutes), and G Subramanian (n 103) (same) with M Kahan 'The Demand for Corporate Law: Statutory Flexibility, Judicial Quality, or Takeover Protection?' (2006) 22 J L Econ & Org (forthcoming) (finding no evidence that antitakeover laws affect incorporation decisions) and R Daines (n 104) (same).

[171] See HN Butler 'Corporate-Specific Antitakeover Statutes and the Market for Corporate Charters' (1988) Wis L Rev 365 (describing state antitakeover statutes as an effort to shelter local businesses from takeovers); WJ Carney 'The Production of Corporate Law' (1998) 71 S Cal L Rev 715, 750-751 (same); R Romano (n 140) 461 and note 11 (same).

[172] Some commentators argue that Delaware makes up with case law upholding the use of poison pills for what it misses in antitakeover legislation. See LA Bebchuk, A Cohen and A Ferrell (n 170) 1803-1804. However, Delaware adopted its mild antitakeover statute in early 1988. See 'An Act to Amend Chapter 1 Title 8 Delaware Code Relating to the General Corporation Law' 66 Del Laws ch. 204 s. 1 (2 February 1988) (codified at Del Code Ann, tit. 8 s. 203 (2001)). The Delaware Chancery Court at that time did not allow the use of poison pills against takeover bids deemed inadequate by the board of directors. See *AC Acquisitions Corp v Andreson, Clayton & Co* 519 A2d 103, 114 (Del Ch 1986) (prohibiting the use of a self tender offer against an inadequate bid). This judicial approach persisted after the enactment of the antitakeover statute. See *Grand Metropolitan, PLC v Pillsbury Co* 558 A2d 1049, 1060 (Del Ch 1988) (prohibiting the use of a poison pill against an inadequate bid); *City Capital Associates Ltd Partnership v Interco Inc* 551 A2d 787, 798 (Del Ch 1988) (same). It was not until 1989 that the Delaware Supreme Court replaced this approach with greater deference to the board of directors. See *Paramount Communications Inc v Time Inc* 571 A2d 1140, 1152-1153 (Del 1989) (upholding the use of a poison pill against an inadequate bid).

the former type of competition, other costs are higher in the latter, and still other costs are the same. This Section, therefore, does not argue that competition for investments will always be present where competition for incorporations is not, only that it can be. In the European Union, this is already the case.

Consider first the cost of building legal infrastructure. This cost is the same whether Member States compete for investments or for incorporations. In either case, only Member States that provide quality legislation, adjudication, and legal services can compete. But in the case of competition for investments, the Member States that possess the necessary legal infrastructure (which tend to be the larger and more developed ones) are not precluded from competing. The Member States that have been the most active in the wave of corporate law reforms of recent years are not the smallest in the European Union. Indeed, they may well be the largest. Whether large states use corporate law to lure investments more than other states, size is evidently not an impediment.

Member States with underdeveloped legal infrastructure would find the pursuit of incorporations particularly challenging because they would need to match the solid legal infrastructure of the United Kingdom. It does not matter that the United Kingdom is not competing for incorporations; any Member State wishing to attract incorporations must still offer a viable alternative. Competition for investments is different. Such competition does not lend itself to only one winning jurisdiction because the product for sale is a package that contains more than corporate law. Even if all corporate decisionmakers agree that the combination of legal infrastructure and substantive corporate law in the United Kingdom is superior to that in any other Member States, not all firms will choose the United Kingdom as their home, and not all capital investments will flow into the United Kingdom. Both businesses and investments will be spread among Member States in accordance with the distribution of means of production, both physical and legal. It should be entirely possible for a Member State offering, for example, cheap labor, low taxes, or rich natural resources, to use corporate law to stimulate economic development even if its legal infrastructure falls short of the United Kingdom's.

In contrast, consider the political costs of overcoming opposition to corporate law reform. Some of these costs are present in both the competition for investments and the competition for incorporations because they stem from opposition by interest groups that are not directly affected by production activity. In the 1990s, for example, Nevada abandoned a plan that would have designated certain judges to hear only business disputes because the change would have required a protracted constitutional amendment and would have reopened an earlier debate about designating judges to hear only family disputes.[173] Around the same time, Pennsylvania scrapped an initiative to form a jury-less business court partly due to opposition from public interest lawyers who were concerned that low income

[173] See Minutes (n 115).

individuals might find themselves in that court.[174] Because the opposition in both instances did not come from corporate constituencies, it would likely have been the same regardless of whether the reform had affected mostly local firms (as in competition for investments), or firms operating in other states (as in competition for incorporations).

But opposition to corporate law reform can also come from corporate constituencies, such as employees, consumers, or residents in areas where production takes place. These groups show greater resistance to corporate law reform when it affects local firms. The failed Pennsylvania chancery court initiative serves again as a useful example because it was opposed not only by the public interest bar but also by labor unions.[175] These unions presumably would have been less resistant to the reform had the initiative affected mostly corporations operating in other states. They cared about the reform and had the clout to block it because it would have affected a great number of local employees. By contrast, consider the restraint that Delaware has shown in not adopting strong antitakeover statutes despite their popularity with labor unions. Few local employees were affected by that policy because most Delaware firms are based in other states.[176]

Because competition for investments mainly affects local businesses, it will normally encounter stronger opposition than competition for incorporations. But this opposition can be muted if competitive pressures in the markets for products, capital, and labor compel local corporate constituencies to internalize the cost of inefficient corporate law and to accept reform. This is forcefully illustrated by the recent push in Germany to relax the so-called codetermination right entitling employee representatives to half of the supervisory board seats in large companies.[177] Such a reform was unthinkable only a decade ago. Today, it is endorsed

[174] See MA Tarasiewicz 'Chancery Ct. Opposed By Bar Assn., Resolution Is Withdrawn' *Legal Intelligencer* (1 June 1992) 1 (reporting that the Philadelphia Bar Association Board of Governors opposed a joint resolution seeking to create the business court).

[175] See JL Kennedy 'Chancery Ct. Plan Sent To Senate' *Legal Intelligencer* (17 May 1993) 1.

[176] See R Romano (n 111) 59-60.

[177] See M Karnitschnig 'German Board Law Targeted; Industry Seeks to Cut Seats of Workers to Reduce Unions' Power' *Wall St J* (28 October 2004) A13 (reporting a 'declaration of war' by the German Industry Association and the German Employers Association on a 'pillar of the German workers' movement that has defined labor relations for a generation' – the rights of employees to half of the seats on supervisory boards of big corporations – 'as companies increasingly shift factories and jobs from Germany to cheaper, less regulated markets'); G Edmondson 'Cut Labor's Clout on German Boards; The "Co-determination" System is Hobbling the Nation's Economy' *Bus Wk* (15 November 2004) 84 (noting that relaxing the decades old co-determination rules 'could be a secret bullet against outsourcing and high unemployment'); D Gow 'Chill Enters Cosy German Boardrooms; Industry Chiefs Want to Consign to History British-Inspired Era of Co-determiantion' *Guardian* (25 October 2004) 22 (noting the President of Kiel's Institute for the World Economy opining that Germany's co-determination 'must be adapted to meet modern demands for entrepreneurial flexibility, especially among for-

cont. ...

by employer organizations, large banks, and state officials as essential to prevent business from fleeing Germany in an increasingly integrated and competitive economic environment.[178] Thus, a recent report by the two largest employer organizations in Germany complains that codetermination inhibits the growth of German companies by making them unattractive merger partners abroad.[179] Similarly, according to the chair of the German government's standing committee on corporate governance, who also chairs the supervisory board of ThyssenKrupp, the country's fifth-largest industrial company, '[o]ther countries do not regard German codetermination practices in their current form as a plus point for Germany as a business location'.[180] Reforming codetermination would no doubt adversely affect German employees. But losing jobs to employees abroad is worse.[181]

D. Normative Implications

Standard accounts of corporate lawmaking in federal systems explain both the rate at which jurisdictions innovate and the degree to which these innovations ac-

eign investors' and adding '[t]hat the most telling business argument for change is that codetermination is an obstacle to cross-border mergers or, as in the case of Hoechst and Rhone-Poulenc (now Aventis), forces the transfer of the company headquarters outside Germany').

178 'Workers Cut Back: Germany's Codetermination Law Must Adapt to New Times' *Fin Times* (1 November 2004) 18 (noting that 'global competition and European integration are finally putting pressure on ... the 28-year-old law that gives employees equal representation on the supervisory boards of large companies').

179 For the claim by Germany's largest employer organizations that labor representation on the board deters foreign investors and makes German companies unattractive merger partners, see Bundesvereinigung der Deutschen Arbeitgeberverbände & Bundesverband der Deutschen Industrie, Mitbestimmung Modernisieren [Union of the German Employers' Associations & Association of the German Industry, Modernizing Codetermination] (2004) 7-8, 19 <http://www.bdi-online.de/dokumente/berichtbdabdikommissionmodernisierungmitbestimmung.pdf>. For a similar claim by a leading German commentator, see M Lutter 'Perspektiven des Gesellschaftsrechts in Deutschland und Europa' [Perspectives on Corporate Laws in Germany and Europe] (2004) 59 Betriebs Berater I.

180 See G Cromme 'Status and Development of Corporate Governance in Germany' at the 3rd German Corporate Governance Code Conference (24 June 2004) <http://www.corporate-governance-code.com/eng/download/CGC_Conference_Berlin_2004_D r_Cromme.pdf> 17.

181 The danger of job loss was illustrated vividly in the threats made by the large German microprocessor maker Infineon to relocate into Switzerland to cut taxes and labor costs associated with Germany's codetermination. See M Karnitschnig 'Infineon May Shift Base from Germany' *Wall St J Eur* (29 April 2003) A1; 'A Warning Shot' *Wall St J Eur* (30 April 2003) A8. The pressure on German labor unions to accept a cutback on their co-determination rights is part of a general pressure on them and on labor unions in other Member States to share the burden of economic recovery under threats of layoffs. See M Karnitschnig and M Walker 'Firms in Germany Pressure Unions to Accept Change' *Wall St J* (21 December 2004) A14.

commodate corporate decisionmakers as a product of competition for incorporations.[182] This does not mean, however, that the law must stagnate when this type of competition is absent. Competition for investments has powerful and quite different effects of its own. It affects companies based on their physical location rather than their choice of legal domicile, and can readily spread over many jurisdictions, including large and developed ones, without any one jurisdiction dominating the market. This explains why corporate legal reforms marshaling shareholder rights have been spreading in the European Union notwithstanding the absence of freedom to incorporate abroad and, as will be explained further below, why introducing such freedom may undermine this trend. The choice to incorporate abroad may thus be a mixed blessing. On the one hand, it frees firms from having to wait for their home jurisdiction to bring the quality of local corporate law up to the level available elsewhere. On the other hand, to the extent that the freedom to incorporate abroad weakens the pressure on jurisdictions with inferior corporate law to improve, it also deprives firms locked in these jurisdictions of the improvements that more intense competition for investments would produce.

I. Competition for Investments and Competition for Incorporations Compared

In order to understand how the introduction of a freedom to incorporate abroad will affect corporate lawmaking in the European Union, it is helpful to first compare current regulatory dynamics in which this freedom is missing and Member States compete only for investments, to a world in which this freedom exists and Member States compete only for incorporations. This comparison is not meant to suggest that the introduction of the freedom to incorporate abroad will replace the existing competition for investments with competition for incorporations. It will probably not. Rather, the comparison here situates the current regulatory dynamics of the European Union against those postulated in traditional analyses of corporate lawmaking in federal systems, and marks the two as extreme points along a continuum of possible regulatory dynamics that later Sections will explore.

1. Who Competes and How

Perhaps the most apparent distinction between competition for investments and competition for incorporations is in the type and the number of jurisdictions

[182] The definitive work in this area is R Romano (n 2). For updated empirical findings, see R Romano 'The States as a Laboratory: State Competition for Corporate Charters' in A Gerber and E Patashnik (eds) *Promoting the General Welfare: American Democracy and the Political Economy of Government Performance* (Brookings Institution Press 2006 forthcoming); see also WJ Carney (n 171) 760-777.

likely to compete. Competition for incorporations naturally involves only a handful of small jurisdictions, or a single small jurisdiction, because the benefits from attracting incorporations are modest and because firms gravitate towards the jurisdiction with the largest number of incorporations. In the United States, that jurisdiction is Delaware, a state that ranks forty-fifth in population and thirty-eighth in gross product.[183] A similar pattern in the European Union would mean a clustering of incorporations in a single small Member State and a lack of attention by larger Member States to incorporations.

Competition for investments is different. The higher stakes involved, and the inability of firms to cluster in a single jurisdiction, enable any number of jurisdictions of any size to compete. These are the dynamics of corporate lawmaking in the European Union today, where competition for investments has been fueling corporate law reforms even – and perhaps especially – in the largest and most developed Member States. It is beyond the scope of this Article to empirically test whether large and developed jurisdictions use corporate law to compete for investments more than other jurisdictions. Such a finding would certainly be consistent with the major corporate law reforms in such Member States as Germany, Italy, and France in recent years. It could be explained by the pressure for regulatory reform that a developed industry can apply to lawmakers, as well as by the likelihood that a developed jurisdiction will possess the necessary legal infrastructure to compete.[184] But it is not necessary to resolve this question here. Regardless of whether large and developed jurisdictions use corporate law to compete for investments more than other jurisdictions, they certainly do not appear to fall behind.

While competition for investments and competition for incorporations attract different sets of jurisdictions, the incentives they create are similar. In both cases, competing jurisdictions produce the law most likely to win the approval of both managers, who must initiate corporate decisions, and shareholders, who must consent to them. In the European Union, competition for investments has thus far resulted in a trend towards shareholder protection, a reassuring sign for the view that regulatory competition results in a race to the top.[185] Thus, between 1993 and

[183] See U.S. Census Bureau 'State Rankings – Statistical Abstract of the United States: Resident Population – July 2005' <http://www.census.gov/statab/ranks/rank01.html>; U.S. Census Bureau 'State Rankings – Statistical Abstract of the United States: Gross State Product in Current Dollars' (2004) <http://www.census.gov/statab/ranks/rank28.html>.

[184] Other factors that may affect the propensity to compete for investments through corporate law reform include government budget deficit, privatizations, exposure of local industry to foreign competition, and demand by local industry for additional capital.

[185] See M Pagano and P Volpin (n 167) (finding that over the 1990s shareholder protection improved on average in forty-five countries despite the absence of changes in electoral systems or legal origin, and concluding that in that decade there was international convergence in shareholder protection); 'UK Governance Is the Best in Europe' (n 159) 113 (citing a report by Brussels research firm Deminor that concludes that corporate governance standards are improving in continental Europe as a whole).

2002 alone – before several important reforms took place – a widely-used country score for shareholder protection either increased or remained unchanged in each of fourteen European Member States surveyed in a study of corporate laws around the world.[186]

More specifically, however, the trend has been towards adopting rules and practices similar to those in the United Kingdom and the United States.[187] The use of Anglo-American corporate law as a reference point is noteworthy. While there are many ways to appease shareholders, the Anglo-American way is a particularly effective one because British and American investors have been the ones to spread shareholder activism globally,[188] and because – with the advent of international law firms, investment banks, and accounting firms – the legal template these investors endorse has become the gold standard in shareholder protection worldwide.[189]

[186] The shareholder protection score is the so-called 'antidirector rights' indicator constructed in La Porta, Lopez-de-Silanes, Shleifer and Vishny (n 155). It is tracked for every year from 1993 to 2002 in Pagano and Volpin (n 167). The Member States in the study are Austria, Belgium, Denmark, Finland, France, Germany, Greece, Ireland, Italy, the Netherlands, Portugal, Spain, Sweden, and the United Kingdom. The unweighted average increase for the fourteen Member States was 24%, compared to an unweighted average increase of 10% for the other thirty-three countries in the study. The increase was the highest for Italy, which received a score of 1 in 1990 and 5 in 2002; this was consistent with the fact that Italian government officials had publicly cited that score as a benchmark for Italy's corporate reform. See R Ulissi (n 72).

[187] While British corporate law and American corporate law are similar, important differences between them do exist. An example of a British rule without an American equivalent that has spread across the European Union is the rule mandating a buyer of a substantial equity stake in a company to offer to buy the remaining shares on the same terms. For the British rule, see S Kenyon-Slade (n 163) 676. For its adoption in other Member States between 1990 and 2004, see M Goergen, M Marynova and L Renneboog 'Takeover Regulation Reforms in Europe and Corporate Governance Convergence' (2005) 21 Oxford Rev Econ Pol 243, 257-262.

[188] See S Targett 'Custodians Are Casting Votes as They Take On a More Active Role' *Fin Times* (6 July 2001) 8 (noting that investors are becoming increasingly active in corporate governance). Continental European investors have gradually adopted Anglo-American shareholder activism and expectations themselves. See S Pfeifer 'Shell Investors Demand Royal Dutch Meeting' *Sunday Telegraph* (28 March 2004) 2 (reporting that institutional investors from the United States, the United Kingdom, the Netherlands, and Germany requested a meeting with the chairman of Royal Dutch to discuss accounting irregularities); R Evans (n 124) (reporting shareholder activism to improve voting rights and broader governance by ABP and PGGM in the Netherlands, Caisse des Dépôts et Consignations in France, and DWS, Union, and SEB in Germany); P Garrido 'Shareholders Want Their Voices Heard' *Fin Times Mandate* (8 March 2004) (describing the European Corporate Governance Service, an umbrella organization that comprises eight regional corporate governance organizations representing France, Germany, Italy, the Netherlands, Switzerland, the United Kingdom, and the Nordic Region); S Calian 'Making Union Investment's List Isn't Pleasing to European Firms' *Wall St J* (15 February 2002) C10 (reporting the German pension fund Union's use of public shaming to pressure underperforming companies).

[189] Cfr M Klausner 'Corporations, Corporate Law, and Networks of Contracts' (1995) 81

cont. ...

2. Firms Whose Costs of Incorporating Abroad Are Low

Thus far we have identified two key differences between the existing competition for investments and the potential competition for incorporations among Member States of the European Union. First, the competition for investments involves large industrialized jurisdictions across the continent rather than a single or a few small jurisdictions. Second, the beneficiaries of this competition are local corporations in competing jurisdictions rather than foreign corporations that incorporate in these jurisdictions. It is now a simple matter to describe the effects of the two types of competition on social welfare.

The beneficiaries of competition for incorporations are likely to be firms that are currently located in Member States that do not offer the best corporate law in the European Union and that given the choice would incorporate abroad. Italian firms, for example, may well benefit from the efforts of Italian lawmakers to improve local corporate law. But these efforts do not mean that Italian corporate law is the best in the European Union today or, more importantly, the best that would be found in the European Union if Member States competed for incorporations. From the perspective of Italian firms that would incorporate abroad, competition for incorporations would be preferable to the current competition for investments because it would grant them access to the leading corporate law in the European Union.

These Italian firms would also reap the benefits of higher scale economies in the production and the consumption of corporate law than available to them today. The current inability of companies in the European Union to incorporate abroad creates balkanization. It is impractical for all, or even most, firms to operate in one Member State. They must spread geographically and be governed by different legal regimes. While these regimes may over time come to resemble each other, they do not offer the full benefits that a single regime governing all firms would offer in administrative and judicial expertise, access to legal services, comprehensive case law, and comparability among firms. All of these benefits would be available to European firms if they incorporated in a single jurisdiction as many American firms do.

3. Firms Whose Costs of Incorporating Abroad Are High

Not all firms would rush to incorporate abroad even if they were free to do so.

Va L Rev 757, 841-847 (arguing that Delaware's dominance in attracting corporations will continue in part because of the presence of network externalities arising from legal precedents and services). For standardization in the contracts governing investments other than in stock, see S Choi and M Gulati 'Innovation in Boilerplate Contracts: An Empirical Examination of Sovereign Bonds' (2005) 53 Emory L J 929 (addressing sovereign bonds); M Kahan and M Klausner 'Standardization and Innovation in Corporate Contracting (Or "The Economics of Boilerplate")' (1997) 83 Va L Rev 713 (addressing corporate bonds).

Many small companies – mostly private, but also public – would consider the cost of incorporating abroad to be too high, especially if it entails changing lawyers. In the United States – where there are no language or culture barriers to incorporating in Delaware while conducting business in another state, and where legal advice on Delaware law is readily available nationwide – the vast majority of private companies incorporate in their home state. In 1999, for example, Delaware was the legal domicile of only 230,000 companies out of roughly five million companies in the country.[190] Even public companies do not necessarily incorporate in Delaware. Only half of them do so (typically the larger ones).[191] Many companies in the European Union would find themselves in a similar position if they could choose where to incorporate. It is hard to tell whether their attachment to their home jurisdictions would be higher or lower than that of companies in the United States because the greater diversity of corporate laws in the European Union compared to the United States would raise both the costs and the benefits of incorporating abroad. But the nature of the barriers to incorporating abroad should be similar in both cases.

Companies whose employees, creditors, or managers would oppose a move would also find incorporation abroad costly.[192] Shareholders and managers would probably support incorporation in a Member State with minimal employee or creditor protection.[193] But while their agreement would be enough for incorporating new companies,[194] existing companies would need to negotiate with employ-

[190] Compare M Kahan and E Kamar (n 148) 1251 (reporting that 229,249 companies paid franchise tax in Delaware in 1999), with U.S. Census Bureau 'Statistical Abstract of the United States' (2002) 471 <http://www.census.gov/prod/2003pubs/02statab/business.pdf> (reporting that 4,936,000 companies filed tax returns in the United States in 1999).

[191] See R Daines 'Does Delaware Law Improve Firm Value?' (2001) 62 J Finan Econ 525, 526-527 (noting that public companies that incorporate in Delaware tend to have higher total assets than companies that incorporate in other states).

[192] See LA Bebchuk and MJ Roe (n 9) 143-147 (arguing that entrenched participants in firms may block even efficient structural changes if these changes would harm them). Note that not all companies will be deadlocked by such divergence of preferences because some could buy the consent of the participant blocking the reincorporation. There will probably be firms, however, for which the cost will be too high. Only time will tell how many firms will fall under this category. Compare LA Bebchuk and MJ Roe (n 9) 147-148 (suggesting that many efficient changes can be expected to be blocked) with H Hansmann and R Kraakman (n 10) 460-464 (suggesting that few efficient changes can be expected to be blocked).

[193] See Debevoise and Plimpton (n 159); Latham and Watkins (n 159) 2.

[194] Much like the protagonists of the famous European Court of Justice decisions requiring Member States to recognize foreign incorporations – Centros, Überseering, and Inspire Art – the only companies attempting to incorporate outside their home Member State thus far have been startup companies aiming to avoid minimum capital requirements. See von Falkenhausen Interview (n 100); Telephone Interview with RH Haas (Partner), Latham & Watkins, Frankfurt, (29 June 2004).

ees and creditors with vested rights.[195] Moreover, managers themselves could be reluctant to reincorporate if they believed the foreign law overly limited their discretion.[196] They would not even need to sue to block the reincorporation. They would simply not initiate it.[197]

These immobile firms would benefit from the competition for incorporations only if they happen to be located in Member States that would compete for incorporations more than they compete today for investments. But since, unlike competition for investments, competition for incorporations would likely involve mainly small jurisdictions, few firms would fall under this category.[198] Other immobile firms would fare worse than they do now because mobile firms in their Member States would incorporate abroad, leaving behind them smaller networks of domestic incorporations and legislatures with fewer reasons to maintain the quality of local corporate law.

While it is easy to identify the advantages and disadvantages of the current competition for investments in the European Union compared to competition for incorporations – the gain to immobile firms from the wider spread of competition,

[195] Both existing and proposed European Union legislation protect vested rights of creditors and employees of companies that merge with foreign companies or reincorporate abroad. See Council Regulation 2157/2001/EC on the Statute for a European Company (SE), OJ L294 10.11.2001 1-21, Articles 1, 8 (7), 24 (1), and 34; Council Directive Supplementing the Statute on the European Company with Regard to the Involvement of Employees, OJ L294 10.11.2001 22, paragraph 7; Directive 2005/56/EC of the European Parliament and of the Council on Cross-Border Mergers of Limited Liability Companies, OJ L310 25.11.2005 1, Articles 4 and 16; Press Release, European Commission 'Company Law: Commission Consults on the Cross Border Transfer of Companies' Registered Offices' IP/04/270 <http://europa.eu.int/rapid/pressReleasesAction.do?reference=IP/04/270&format=HTML&aged=0&language=EN&guiLanguage=en>.

[196] The Sarbanes-Oxley Act of 2002, which has been criticized in the United States on precisely these grounds, is commonly viewed as the main reason for the decline in the popularity of American stock listing among foreign issuers. See e.g. R Romano (n 76) 1589, 1597-1599; see also S Ascarelli 'Citing Sarbanes, Foreign Companies Flee U.S. Exchanges' *Wall St J* (20 September 2004) C1; C Karmin and K Kelly 'For Stock Listings, the U.S. Pull Gets Weaker' *Wall St J* (12 November 2002) C1; A Parker and T Tassell 'Rank Could Look at U.S. Delisting' *Fin Times* (1 December 2004) 19; B Sherwood 'Long Arm of the U.S. Regulator' *Fin Times* (10 March 2005) 14.

[197] This should be contrasted with the ease with which New Jersey and its successor Delaware attracted reincorporations by promising minimal antitrust regulation. See J Seligman 'Brief History of Delaware's General Corporation Law of 1899' (1976) 1 Del J Corp L 249, 269-270. There is little doubt that, in the absence of effective federal antitrust enforcement, reincorporation into New Jersey or Delaware could have significantly harmed consumers – only consumers could not have stopped it.

[198] See U.S. Bureau of Census 'Statistical Abstract of the United States 2004-2005' 21 <http://www.census.gov/www/statistical-abstract-2001_2005.html> (ranking Delaware as the sixth smallest jurisdiction in population), 213 (ranking Delaware as the third smallest jurisdiction in area), 428 (ranking Delaware as the ninth smallest jurisdiction in gross state product).

and the loss to mobile firms from the ban on incorporation abroad – it is hard to assess which effect dominates. On the one hand, there are probably many more immobile firms than mobile firms. That only a fraction of American firms incorporate in Delaware while operating in other states suggests as much. On the other hand, immobile firms tend to need corporate law less than mobile firms, and indeed low willingness to pay for corporate law can account for their immobility. This explains why Delaware attracts less than five percent of incorporations by private firms but roughly half of the incorporations by public firms, and why it charges the latter much higher taxes.[199] The inability to determine which type of competition is socially more desirable, however, leaves open a more practical comparison between the current competition for investments, in which firms cannot incorporate abroad, and the regulatory dynamics that will develop once this freedom is introduced. The insights acquired above will inform this inquiry. We shall turn to it next.

II. The Effects of Firm Choice on the Competition for Investments

Comparing the social welfare implications of the current competition for investments in the European Union with those of competition for incorporations is only the first step towards informing the debate about the desirability of firm choice in the European Union or, indeed, anywhere else. To be sure, with the European Court of Justice expressing growing impatience with Member States that do not recognize foreign corporations, and with the European Commission appearing poised to pass a directive that would lift existing barriers to cross-border mergers, the freedom to pick any Member State as a place to incorporate seems to be just around the corner for European Union companies. But allowing firms to incorporate abroad will not necessarily replace the current competition for investments by competition for incorporations. It may just as well weaken the competition for investments without introducing any new competition for incorporations or, if it does introduce such competition, it may result in the coexistence of the two types of competition. This Section outlines the social welfare implications of each of these scenarios.

1. The Incentives to Compete

While the ability to incorporate abroad may or may not accelerate the development of national corporate laws or make them more favorable to shareholders by fostering competition for incorporations, it may lead to the opposite result by discouraging Member States from using their corporate laws to compete for investments. Member States will have fewer reasons to worry about the quality of

[199] See M Kahan and E Kamar (n 148) 1251.

their corporate law once firms become free to choose where to incorporate because local corporate law will matter less than it does now to their prosperity. This appears to be the case in the United States. New York corporate law, for example, imposes personal liability on the ten largest shareholders of a company for unpaid salaries and wages.[200] Investors consider this rule highly unattractive.[201] But this does not prevent New York from being one of the most prosperous states and home to numerous companies; many of these companies simply incorporate in Delaware instead of New York.

Thus, while the freedom to choose where to incorporate will make the regulatory dynamics in the European Union more like those in the United States, ironically this may weaken, rather than strengthen, the incentives that Member States have to develop their corporate laws. The reason is that these Member States will be left with fewer local firms incorporated domestically, and these firms will tend to depend on the law less than the firms that reveal their dependence by incorporating abroad.[202] Unless the firms that incorporate domestically need a different kind of corporate law from that needed by firms incorporating abroad – which will often not be the case[203] – their needs will likely receive less attention from lawmakers than they did prior to the departure of their peers.[204]

[200] See NY Bus Corp Law, s. 630 (a) (McKinney 2003) ('The ten largest shareholders ... shall jointly and severally be personally liable for all debts, wages, and salaries due ...').

[201] See F Attea 'State Has Hard Time Following a Lead' *Bus First of Buffalo* (17 April 2000) 30 (noting that shareholder liability for wages and salaries is the main reason why many New York businesses incorporate in Delaware); MM Membrado and CJ Gulotta 'Navigating the Formation of Start-Up Companies' *New York Law Journal* (1 September 2000) S6 (same).

[202] In theory, even the competitive drive of the United Kingdom, which will likely experience an inflow of incorporations, may dwindle because – like any other provider of a public good – it will share the returns to its lawmaking efforts with other Member States whose firms will piggyback its corporate law. In practice, however, any weakening of the incentives of British lawmakers as a result of incorporations by foreign firms will likely be negligible. To be sure, the desire to stimulate the economy is, by the British government's own account, a source of motivation to develop corporate law. But this motivation is only one of many reasons that account for the present state of British corporate law, and not necessarily the most important reason. Indeed, the United Kingdom does not appear to be the most active Member State in using corporate law to compete for investments, and most of the features of its corporate law that appeal to incorporators date long before this competition assumed the proportions it has today. To expect that corporate lawmaking in the United Kingdom will stall as a result of incorporations by foreign firms is just not realistic.

[203] It is possible that private firms need different corporate law than public ones. See e.g. RC Clark *Corporate Law* (Aspen Publishers 1986) 234-238 (advocating greater tolerance towards usurpation of corporate opportunities by insiders in private firms than by insiders in public firms). The American experience shows, however, that while it is mainly public firms that incorporate outside the state which they operate, half of public firms remain incorporated in-state. Cfr (n 103) and accompanying text (reporting that half of all public companies in the United States are incorporated in Delaware).

[204] It is a real possibility that legislators will be glad to be relieved of the pressure to reform

cont. ...

The analysis above outlines one possible outcome of the introduction of firm ability to incorporate abroad. It does not purport to predict the only possible outcome. The outcome may be different, for example, if the last decade of intense competition for investments has created new institutional dynamics that will perpetuate the current pace and direction of corporate lawmaking. The outcome may also be different if a substantial number of companies face practical hurdles to incorporating abroad despite the freedom to do so. Nevertheless, to the extent that the present momentum of corporate law reforms persists, it will do so despite the new mobility, not because of it.

One mechanism that could sustain the existing momentum is adaptation of the market to the changed legal environment.[205] The intense competition for investments that economic integration has fostered in the European Union may have altered the existing institutional and political map, and introduced new actors who would want to see the current legal trend continued. In Italy, for example, many new business leaders, and more than one leader of the old business aristocracy, have jumped on the corporate governance bandwagon;[206] foreign investment banks have entered the securities and mergers and acquisitions markets;[207] local banks have converted to the new gospel of shareholder capitalism;[208] and the newly privatized stock exchange has become a proponent of reform.[209] Similarly, in Germany, formerly creditor-oriented banks have embraced the corporate governance movement by shifting much of their operations from corporate lending to investment banking;[210] formerly corporatist managers have become more attuned to shareholder value as a result of the growing popularity of stock option com-

local law and take the blame when it fails. To a certain extent it has already been demonstrated in the changes that Germany made to its corporate accounting rules in 1998 to enable German firms to list their securities in the United States and become subject to American securities law and listing rules. See (n 100). For the argument that jurisdictions with less developed markets and corporate law can benefit from allowing local firms to piggyback more developed markets and corporate law abroad, see BS Black and RJ Gilson 'Venture Capital and the Structure of Capital Markets: Banks versus Stock Markets' (1998) 47 J Finan Econ 243, 273; EB Rock 'Greenhorns, Yankees, and Cosmopolitans: Venture Capital, IPOs, Foreign Firms, and U.S. Markets' (2001) 2 Theoretical Inquiries L 711, 712.

[205] See generally R Deeg (n 36).

[206] See F Kapner 'An Emerging Generation of Business Leaders Is Promising to Sweep Away Secrecy and Cronyism' *Fin Times* (7 April 2003) 19. The internalization of shareholder values by corporate managers, even if widespread, does not obviate the need for corporate law because the law helps managers to commit to these values.

[207] See 'Mediobanca on the Back Foot' *The Economist* (23 June 2001) 70 (stating that 'international investment banks, and not the Italian banking aristocracy, now dominate business in Italy').

[208] See H O'Brien 'IntesaBCI, Lazard Link in Italy' *Daily Deal* (10 September 2002).

[209] See R Deeg (n 36) 188.

[210] See (n 28).

pensation;[211] and formerly insular employees have started to invest their own pension money in stock.[212] To be sure, the interests of these groups continue to diverge, but the gap between them is narrower than it used to be.[213]

The momentum can also be fueled by companies that will remain practically locked in their home Member States notwithstanding the freedom to incorporate abroad. Numerous companies may find themselves in this position.[214] They will probably include, among others, small and midsize companies for which the cost of incorporating abroad will not be justified; companies whose managers, employees, or creditors resist reincorporation; large companies that wish to use their local political clout for shaping corporate law; and companies intent on avoiding the jurisdiction of foreign courts and regulators, which may extend to matters unrelated to corporate internal affairs.

All of these companies will be captives of their home Member States' corporate laws. As the freedom to choose where to incorporate will be of little relevance to them, they will continue to pressure their home Member States for modern law. Much of the resulting legislation will be uncontroversial. It will involve making the law more flexible, adapting it to technological and economic developments, and improving the effectiveness of the institutions supporting it.[215] These uncontroversial attributes of corporate law are important. In the relatively uniform landscape of state corporate laws in the United States, they appear to tip

[211] See JW Cioffi 'Building Finance Capitalism: The Regulatory Politics of Corporate Governance Reform in the United States and Germany' in JD Levy (ed) *The State after Statism: New State Activities in the Age of Globalization and Liberalization* (Harvard University Press 2006 forthcoming) (describing the growing acceptance in the 1990s of shareholder primacy by managers of corporations with global operations, such as Daimler Benz and Siemens).

[212] See JW Cioffi and M Höpner 'Left-Wing Support for Shareholder Capitalism?' (2005) 51 Die Mitbestimmung 58.

[213] For a recent account of the persistence of old traditions in German corporate boards, see P Jenkins 'The Clubby World of German Business Refuses to Accept New Membership Rules' *Fin Times* (28 August 2004) 20 (reporting that 'corporate governance reformers are failing in Germany'). In reality, the spread of the corporate governance movement has been uneven across firms. Thus, while it was pressure from the corporate sector that drove Germany and the Scandinavian countries to block the inclusion of a ban on the use of dual-class stock as antitakeover defense (see infra (n 218) and (n 219)), some companies in these same countries have recently decided to declassify their stock voluntarily. See P Betts 'Companies Start to See the Case for Fairer Votes' *Fin Times* (17 February 2004) 20 (reporting voluntary decisions by L'Oréal in France, ABN Amro in the Netherlands, Nokia in Finland, and SAP and Metro in Germany to scrap dual-class stock capitalization).

[214] See Section D.I.3..

[215] Flexibility-increasing rules range from technical issues like using electronic communication to hold virtual shareholder meetings to substantive issues like designing hybrid securities. A recent example is the ordinance signed by the French President in 2004 to modernize the country's securities law by removing procedural constraints on secondary stock offerings, enabling issuers to define the terms of preferred stock, and simplifying the treatment of convertible stock. See (n 84) and (n 85) and accompanying text.

the scales for incorporation decisions.[216] And in the European Union, these attributes already figure prominently in corporate counsel's discussions of the possibilities that incorporation abroad presents.[217]

Legislation promoting the interests of shareholders at the expense of managers, employees, or creditors will meet with greater resistance. The persistence of employee board representation and antitakeover defenses in various Member States demonstrates as much. But this does not mean that Member States that have traditionally guarded the interests of managers, employees, or creditors will continue to do so in an unqualified way. At the urging of local managers, for example, Germany fought the inclusion of a ban on antitakeover defenses in the European Union Takeover Directive,[218] and passed a law expressly making antitakeover defenses legal. This did not stop Germany from adopting corporate governance reforms of which managers were less critical. Sweden, under pressure from local industry, also campaigned against banning antitakeover defenses in the Takeover Directive.[219] This did not stop the Swedish financial markets minister from publicly chastising local industry for not responding to corporate scandals and threatening to address the problem with legislation if this failure persisted.[220]

More generally, the quest for investments may well continue to lead Member States to keep updating their laws and replicating shareholder protection available elsewhere. But it is local companies that will provide the impetus for doing so, not companies that operate abroad.[221]

[216] See M Kahan (n 170) (presenting evidence consistent with the claim that American firms tend to incorporate in states with flexible corporate statutes and effective courts).

[217] See Debevoise & Plimpton (n 159) (discussing the benefits for bilateral joint ventures of avoiding supermajority voting requirement for issuing new stock, and the benefits for private equity investors of avoiding restrictions on the issuance of redeemable or convertible preferred stock); 'A New Vehicle for European Cross-Border Transactions' Jones Day Memorandum to Clients (April 2004) <http://www.jonesday.com/pubs/pubs_detail.aspx?pubID=S1502> 1-4 (same).

[218] See D Dombey 'European Parliament Backs Takeover Directive Compromise' *Fin Times* (17 December 2003) 4 (reporting that Germany blocked the inclusion in the Takeover Directive of a ban on antitakeover defenses at the behest of large manufacturers like BASF and Volkswagen).

[219] See C Brown-Humes and C MacCarthy 'Family Fortunes Face Brussels Power Shift' *Fin Times* (15 May 2003) (reporting that Sweden, Finland, and Denmark blocked the inclusion in the takeover directive of a ban on dual-class stock capitalization under pressure from industrial barons such as the Walenberg family).

[220] See N George (n 125).

[221] In principle, firms locked in their home Member States may pressure lawmakers to reform local corporate law to help them compete for capital with local firms that are incorporated abroad. But the pressure on lawmakers is likely to be stronger when no local firm can incorporate abroad and all firms rely on local corporate law for attracting foreign capital.

2. The Effects on Firms

The freedom to incorporate abroad will be good news for companies whose costs of incorporating abroad are low and that are located anywhere other than the Member State with the most attractive corporate law. These mobile firms will see their options expand and will be able to choose between incorporating in their home Member States and incorporating in any other Member State in which the law fulfills their needs. Since these firms will incur only low costs if they incorporate abroad, they could gain, but not lose, from their freedom. They will forgo the opportunity to incorporate abroad only if they do not really need it.

The effect of the freedom to incorporate on firms that do not take advantage of this freedom because doing so would be costly to them is more ambiguous. They will neither lose nor gain to the extent that lawmakers in their home Member States maintain the quality of corporate law despite the outflow of incorporations by other local companies. But they will lose – up to their cost of incorporating abroad – to the extent that the incentives of lawmakers in their home Member States suffer as a result of such corporate migration.

It is hard to tell which of these two possible outcomes will materialize. One can reasonably predict, however, that even if the latter outcome occurs, the cost it will impose on firms that do not incorporate abroad will be smaller than the benefit it will confer on firms that do incorporate abroad. The reason is twofold. On the one hand, lawmakers driven by the desire to stimulate the local economy will have a strong interest in maintaining the quality of corporate law if a significant number of local firms with a pressing need for it cannot incorporate abroad. On the other hand, as both logic and experience in the United States suggest, firms that do incorporate abroad tend to have a greater need for corporate law than firms that incorporate locally.

Viewed from this perspective, the introduction of firm choice to the current competition for investments comes close to achieving the benefits of both competition for investments and competition for incorporations while avoiding the associated costs. Competition for investments without firm choice benefits companies that would face high costs of incorporating abroad. Competition for incorporations benefits companies that face low costs of incorporating abroad. Competition for investments combined with freedom to incorporate abroad, assuming this freedom does not significantly weaken the competition, benefits both types of firms.

3. Competition for Incorporations as a Complement

Ever since the possibility that firms in the European Union would be free to incorporate outside the jurisdiction in which they operate was first considered, one of the most debated questions among commentators has been whether the competition for incorporations, which to most commentators appeared inevitable, would advance or harm social welfare. Today, since a recent series of decisions by the European Court of Justice has made the possibility of freedom to incorporate abroad a near reality, this question is more relevant than ever.

However, it is far from obvious that any Member States will decide to compete for incorporations, given the high costs and low benefits of doing so. Rather telling in this regard is the fact that none of the Member States regarded as potential competitors have positioned themselves to compete or have stated an intention of doing so. No Member State has even bothered to abandon the real-seat rule to compete for incorporations. This inaction is notable considering the time that has passed since Member States were put on notice that the days of the real-seat rule across the European Union were numbered following the recent decisions of the European Court of Justice.

In 1986, the European Court of Justice ordered the Dutch authorities to recognize a British company operating in the Netherlands.[222] The court reiterated its position to the Danish authorities, to the German authorities, and again to the Dutch authorities in subsequent decisions in 1999,[223] 2002,[224] and 2003.[225] The decisions stirred a storm among academics. A flurry of commentary examining the new reality from all possible angles quickly filled the pages of legal journals. Since the rewards of early entry are a lesson from Delaware's experience, one would have expected a mad rush to scrap the real-seat rule and bid for foreign incorporations.[226] But Member States showed no interest in competing. There was no mad rush, not even a lazy stroll. There was no reaction at all. Soon Member States will have no choice but to delete the real-seat rule from their books. The European Commission is already drafting a directive requiring them to do just that. However, compliance with this requirement should not be mistaken for competition for incorporations. European capitals may have already revealed their lack of interest in this regard during two decades of apathy.

But would competition for incorporations make a difference? Perhaps less than most would think. From the standpoint of migrating firms, the specific identity of the jurisdiction in which they incorporate is secondary to the quality of its law. With or without competition for incorporations, the freedom to incorporate abroad would allow firms to incorporate in any Member State they choose. Whether it is a Member State that competes for incorporations or one that competes for investments, by and large, its law will be the same.

[222] See *Segers* (n 6). A subsequent decision upholding British restrictions on the relocation to the Netherlands of the corporate headquarters of a company incorporated and headquartered in the United Kingdom caused temporary uncertainty about the direction that the court was taking. See *The* Case 81/87 *Queen v HM Treasury and Commissioner of Inland Revenue, ex parte Daily Mail and General Trust PLC* (1988) ECR 5483.

[223] See *Centros* (n 6).

[224] See *Überseering* (n 6).

[225] See *Inspire Art* (n 6).

[226] See M Klausner (n 189) 841-847; R Romano (n 111) 37-44.

E. Toward a General Theory of Regulatory Competition

The European Union is a case study of using corporate law to compete for investments. But there is nothing uniquely European about this competition. Given the right circumstances, it could develop elsewhere. In fact, it already has, in the United States. Earlier I noted that the ease with which American firms nowadays incorporate outside their home state reduces the importance of local corporate law for a state's economy.[227] But what if American firms did not enjoy this freedom? Would states then adopt corporate laws to attract capital? History shows that this is precisely what happened.

Most modern accounts of state competition in corporate law begin the analysis in the late nineteenth century.[228] They recount how firms that had originally incorporated in New Jersey, the first state to commercialize its chartering business, reincorporated into Delaware to avoid New Jersey legislation preventing them from owning stock in other firms.[229] As New Jersey became more industrialized, the story goes, it no longer needed the fees these firms paid, and so it passed the legislation with little regard for its effect on incorporations. Delaware, by contrast, was eager to increase its tax revenue and accepted the reincorporated firms with open arms.[230]

This description does not say what had happened before this episode. Had it always been easy for firms to reincorporate in another state without moving their business? Had New Jersey always been the incorporation state of choice? To both questions, the answer is no. In the beginning of the nineteenth century, firms used to incorporate where they operated.[231] New Jersey was by no means the most popular incorporation state at that time. It was only with the shift to out-of-state incorporation during the nineteenth century that New Jersey assumed dominance.

Both practical and legal reasons explained why firms incorporated in their home state in the early years of the nineteenth century. The practical reason was the lack of modern transportation and communication.[232] The legal reason was the

[227] See (n 200) and (n 201) and accompanying text.

[228] An important exception is HN Butler 'Nineteenth-Century Jurisdictional Competition in the Granting of Corporate Privileges' (1985) 14 J Legal Stud 129. This Section draws on that article and the sources cited in it.

[229] See R Romano (n 111) 42-43; C Grandy 'New Jersey Corporate Chartermongering, 1875-1929' (1989) 49 J Econ Hist 677, 685; WE Kirk III 'A Case Study in Legislative Opportunism: How Delaware Used the Federal-State System to Attain Corporate Pre-Eminence' (1984) 10 J Corp L 233, 246-258; J Seligman (n 197) 265-276.

[230] See R Romano (n 111) 42-43; C Grandy (n 229) 689-691.

[231] See EM Dodd *American Business Corporations Until 1860 With Special Reference to Massachusetts* (Harvard University Press 1954) 179, 400 and note 29.

[232] See HN Butler (n 228) 154; see generally GR Taylor *The Transportation Revolution, 1815–1860* (ME Sharpe 1962); RB Du Boff 'Business Demand and the Development of the Telegraph in the United States, 1844–1860' (1980) 54 Bus Hist Rev 459.

common demand by states that chartered firms operate locally,[233] and the absence of federal law recognizing out-of-state incorporations.[234]

In this environment, states that wished to lure business had to offer attractive corporate law. And they did. Competition for investments was instrumental in the advent of general corporation statutes,[235] the spreading of limited liability,[236] and the liberalization of corporate laws.[237]

Thus, in 1826, Massachusetts governor Levi Lincoln called on the legislature to limit shareholder liability for corporate debt, citing the large sums of money Massachusetts citizens had recently invested in factories in Maine and New Hampshire, where shareholders enjoyed limited liability.[238] A year later, the legislature passed a law exempting from liability shareholders who transferred their shares and entitling shareholders who paid a corporate debt for reimbursement by other shareholders.[239]

[233] See EM Dodd (n 231) 178-180; EQ Keasbey 'New Jersey and the Great Corporations' (1899) 13 Harv L Rev 198, 204; HW Stoke 'Economic Influences upon the Corporation Laws of New Jersey' (1930) 38 J Pol Econ 551, 561. The Central American Transit Company, for example, secured a New Jersey charter on condition that its principal depot is in Jersey City. See 'An Act to Recognize and Authorize the Organization of, and to Incorporate the Central American Transit Company' ch. 187, s. 2, 1862 NJ Laws 328, 329-330. This was required under a general law from 1849. See 'An Act to Authorize the Establishment, and to Prescribe the Duties of Companies for Manufacturing and Other Purposes' 1849 NJ Laws 300.

[234] The watershed decision requiring states to allow foreign corporations to do interstate business was *Paul v Virginia*, 75 U.S. (8 Wall) 168 (1869). See EM Dodd (n 231) 152, 179-181 (describing the effect of the decision); GC Henderson *The Position of Foreign Corporations in American Constitutional Law* (Harvard University Press 1918) 116 (same); HG Henn *Handbook of the Law of Corporations and Other Business Enterprises* (West Publishing Company 1970) 19; HN Butler (n 228) 154-156 (same).

[235] See JW Cadman Jr *The Corporation in New Jersey: Business and Politics, 1791–1875* (Harvard University Press 1949) 18-23, 35, 422-423 (attributing New Jersey's enactment of a general incorporation law for manufacturing companies in 1816, duplicating New York's law of 1811, to the intention 'to encourage manufacturing in the midst of depression as the New York legislators had seemingly hoped to encourage it in anticipation of war').

[236] See EM Dodd (n 231) 378-381; CF Ware *The Early New England Cotton Manufacture: A Study in Industrial Beginnings* (Houghton Mifflin Company 1931) 148. Proponents of limited liability claimed a hundred years later that limited liability was essential for attracting capital to California. The claim was no longer credible, however, given the freedom to incorporate California businesses in another state, and the fact that the proponents were lawyers who stood to lose clients as a result of such incorporations, rather than industrialists. See MI Weinstein 'Limited Liability in California 1928–31: It's the Lawyers' (2005) 7 Am L & Econ Rev 439, 452-454.

[237] See JW Cadman (n 235) 36-38, 174-177, 440; HW Stoke (n 233) 553-555.

[238] See Governor's Speech (6 June 1826), Mass. Resolves 1824–28, pp. 377, 383-384.

[239] See 'An Act in Addition to the Several Acts Respecting the General Powers and Duties of Manufacturing Corporations' (10 March 1827), Mass. Laws May Session 1825 – March Session 1828, ch. 137, p. 547.

These changes were not enough given the large number of business failures in New England's textile industry in 1829.[240] In 1830, owners of the Lowell cotton mill companies warned the Massachusetts legislature in a widely-circulated petition: 'Responsible people would part with their stock rather than hold it [without limited liability] and the control of manufacturing was in danger of passing into the hands of speculators, while Massachusetts money sought safe investment in other states'.[241]

A similar concern was voiced in an unsigned article published in a legal magazine that year: '[Unlimited liability] has heretofore been introduced in the grant of charters for manufacturing purposes in Massachusetts. The effect has been to drive millions of capital into the neighboring states for investment. And there it will remain. It is questionable whether the recent alleviating act is an adequate remedy'.[242]

Another unsigned article published a year earlier acknowledged there was no proof that unlimited liability alone drove away investments, but suggested it was a contributing factor, saying: 'But what is the tendency of the system which has been pursued in Massachusetts? In other states the laws are less severe against stockholders. This must tend to attract capital from that state into others where it can be more safely invested. That this personal responsibility has, in fact, drawn manufacturing capital from Massachusetts, we do not affirm; for other causes may have operated to prevent this result. But the tendency is obvious, and it has been frequently asserted that the injurious consequences resulting from it are very great. It is sufficient, however, for us to show the tendency, since it is not to be taken for granted that Massachusetts will, in spite of these laws, always offer attractions for manufacturing capital superior to those of any of the surrounding territories'.[243]

Governor Lincoln highlighted a related evil of unlimited liability. Not only did it deter investments by citizens of other states, he asserted in a message to legislators, but it also deterred investments by local citizens, creating a risk that 'the manufacturing interest, to a great extent, must be abandoned in Massachusetts'.[244]

The pressure produced its desired results with the enactment of the Manufac-

[240] See CF Ware (n 236) 91-92.

[241] Massachusetts State Archives, Committee Reports for Massachusetts Laws, 1830, Chapter LIII, quoted in CF Ware (n 236) 148. The petition is probably the one referred to by EM Dodd (n 231) 378, as a November 1829 petition 'presented to the legislature by a large number of Massachusetts industrialists urging the complete abandonment of the individual liability principle' and claiming that 'the existence of that liability was drawing industrial capital into other states whose legislatures were willing to grant limited-liability charters.'

[242] 'Corporations' (1830) 4 Am Jurist 298, 307.

[243] 'Manufacturing Corporations' (1829) 2 Am Jurist 92, 104.

[244] See Governor's Message (6 January 1830), Mass. Resolves 1828-31, pp. 212, 228-230.

turing Corporations Act in 1830, which greatly restricted shareholder liability.[245] In the legislative debate, Representative Lowell backed the capital flight argument with figures. More than $7 million of Massachusetts money, he maintained, was invested in New Hampshire, where limited liability charters had been available for several years, and large Massachusetts investments were in Connecticut and New York, which also offered limited liability.[246]

Later in the century, proponents of granting New Jersey charters to firms owned by citizens of other states emphasized that 'it is our policy to offer every facility to persons out of our state to come and work our mines for our benefit',[247] and noted the large amount of New York and Pennsylvania capital that had been 'attracted' to New Jersey 'by liberal charters'.[248] This claim was repeated by New Jersey governor Theodore Randolph, who reminded lawmakers in 1869: 'The community that invites labor and capital within its borders by liberal legislation, adds to its own stability and enriches its citizens .... I feel assured you will fully appreciate the propriety of continuing that policy which heretofore induced manufacturing enterprise and capital to seek our protection'.[249]

The shareholder-friendly approach proved effective.[250] So effective, indeed, as to bring a member of the 1867 New York constitutional convention to observe with envy: 'One of the smallest States of the Union, with not more than two-thirds of her area susceptible of being devoted to agriculture, [New Jersey] has placed herself, by the aid of her location and corporations, as a power in the Union. Strip her of what her corporations have made her, the wealth and position she has obtained through them, and where would New Jersey be today?'.[251]

The above glimpse into history supports the general applicability of the analysis in this Article. Other examples from different times and different places surely exist. The ongoing corporate reform in Japan, for instance, resembles in many ways the developments in the European Union. Here too, recent laws tighten shareholder protection while deregulating other aspects of corporate law expressly to stimulate the economy and attract capital.[252] And, as in the European

[245] See 'An Act Defining the General Powers and Duties of Manufacturing Corporations' Mass. Laws May Session 1828 – March Session 1831, ch. 53, p. 325.

[246] See EM Dodd (n 231) 380.

[247] See Newark Daily Advertiser (29 January 1847), quoted in JW Cadman (n 235) 175.

[248] See Newark Daily Advertiser (3 February 1864), quoted in JW Cadman (n 235) 175.

[249] New Jersey Legislative Documents, 1869, pp. 185-186.

[250] See JW Cadman (n 235) 37, 177.

[251] See EF Underhill, reporter, Proceedings and Debates of the Constitutional Convention of the State of New York, Held in 1867 and 1868, II, 1075.

[252] See CJ Milhaupt 'A Lost Decade for Japanese Corporate Governance Reform?: What's Changed, What Hasn't, and Why' in M Blomström and SJ La Croix (eds) *Institutional Change in Japan* (Routledge 2006 forthcoming); RJ Gilson and C Milhaupt 'Choice as Regulatory Reform: The Case of Japanese Corporate Governance' (2005) 53 Am J Comp L 343; T Fujita cont. ...

Union, it is firms in need of additional capital, and firms that rely on foreign investment, that take advantage of the change.[253] Far from being an isolated case, the regulatory dynamics in the European Union, it seems, follow a pattern that is old, perhaps even universal. Exploring the presence and nature of these dynamics in other times and places is a promising area for future research.

F. Conclusion

How different will Member State laws be with freedom to incorporate but no competition for incorporations from what they could be with such competition? Perhaps not much.

Normally, the rate of legal innovation and diffusion – and the degree to which the law serves shareholders – can be expected to be higher in jurisdictions that pursue incorporations. In the United States, for example, Delaware appears to be consistently faster than other states in innovating and copying innovations from others. Other states are slower because they do not pay as much attention to their laws. Delaware also appears to be more careful in balancing shareholders' preferences against managers', as evidenced by its decision not to match the potent antitakeover statutes that some other states adopted with a similarly potent statute of its own.[254] Other states have more powerful antitakeover statutes because local managers lobby for their enactment while out-of-state shareholders are largely ignored.

Competition for international capital currently provides Member States with a stronger reason to update their laws and accommodate shareholders than the hope of attracting incorporations does. This motivation may weaken if incorporation abroad becomes an easy alternative for all firms to use. But to the extent that many firms find this option impractical – which is more likely to be the case in the European Union than it is in the United States – the need to support economic development by attracting foreign investment may continue the momentum of corporate innovation close to its present pace. This may compensate, and perhaps more than compensate, for the absence of competition for incorporations as a motivation to develop the law.

While the current regulatory dynamics in the European Union provide a particularly vivid illustration of the power of competition for investments to shape

'Modernising Japanese Corporate Law: Ongoing Corporate Law Reform in Japan' (2004) 16 Singapore Academy of Law J 321; T Seki 'Legal Reform and Shareholder Activism by Institutional Investors in Japan' (2005) 13 Corporate Governance: An International Review 377.

[253] See R Gilson and C Milhaupt (n 252) 357, 363 (reporting that foreign ownership and financial distress is common to the firms that have adopted an optional governance structure introduced in 2002).

[254] See M Kahan and E Kamar (n 1) 740; WJ Carney (n 171) 328; R Romano (n 111) 59.

corporate law, these dynamics appear universal. They shaped corporate law in the United States in the nineteenth century, when firm mobility was limited, and likely shape corporate law in other parts of the world today.

A Legal Options Approach to EC Company Law

GERARD HERTIG* and JOSEPH A. McCAHERY**

In recent years, legal options have gained acceptance in the European Union. Legal options refer to the ex ante and ex post choices that are created by law. Not surprisingly, legislators have tended to introduce choice for Member States or private parties when they have found it difficult to make headway with resolving a conflict. This approach made a difference when the European Commission (EC), for example, resolved the conflict between Member States over the Takeover Directive by creating legal provisions that give jurisdictions the option not to implement the board neutrality and the breakthrough provisions.

Even though it is debatable whether the new legislation will have dramatic efficiency or distributional effects, the decision to provide freedom of choice can, under the circumstances, be considered a credible approach to law reform. It has been suggested that the EC's widespread use of mandatory rules has been costly for many firms, imposed considerable delay in the development of a comprehensive company law regime, resulting in gaps of coverage, and has ultimately led to the implementation of legislation that does not match the needs of a substantial number of firms. It is clear, moreover, that the problems associated with the EC's reliance on directives was the rationale for the EC's Company Law Modernization and Corporate Governance Action Plan. Under the Action Plan, the EC has proposed non-binding recommendations.

Notwithstanding the move toward soft law measures, the EC's appetite for options or pro-choice company law provisions remains unclear. There are significant barriers to the EC's ability to promote efficient regulatory choice due to interest group pressures, diffuse control over the agenda-setting process, and a limited capacity to anticipate and meet a wide range of Member State demands.

This article contends that allowing firms the choice of different legal rules would be beneficial and would respond to industry demands for low-cost regulatory choices. We explore the different sorts of legal options, and assess whether they offer a cost advantage over the Commission's earlier approaches to company law reform. We show that bringing options to the forefront of company law reform can reduce costs for small and medium-sized firms and provide clear benefits to com-

* Professor of Law, ETH Zurich.

** Professor of Corporate Governance and Business Entrepreneurship, University of Amsterdam Faculty of Economics and Econometrics. He is also Goldschmidt Visiting Professor of Corporate Governance at the Solvay Business School (Brussels), and Professor of International Business Law, Tilburg University Faculty of Law. The authors thank Richard Buxbaum, Aaron Edlin, Luca Enriques, Jesse Fried, Amir Licht, Erik Vermeulen and seminar participants at the Law and Economics workshop at the University of California at Berkeley Law School and conference participants at the Tilburg University Conference on Real Seat Transfers and Reincorporations in the EU for helpful comments.

panies that differ in their ownership and control structure from most large public corporations. Switching to a company law regime with different sorts of options can have a good effect on stakeholders as well. As a regulatory strategy, we advocate a step-by-step change, beginning with the adoption of a limited number of opt-in provisions. For many, switching to even a restricted set of menu choices would undoubtedly represent a major shift in EC company law policy reflecting a new approach to the legal system, the freedom of contract and the cost of legislation.

A. Introduction
B. Toward a Flexible Approach to EU Company Law
C. Impact on Regulatory Arbitrage and Competition
D. The Benefits of a Pro-Choice Approach
E. Step-by-Step Reform Recommendations
F. Conclusion: The Future of the Pro-Choice Approach

A. Introduction

Legal options are not a new thing. For many years, default rules and a variety of option techniques have been used in a wide range of contexts. More recently, default rules have been used in the U.S., for example, to accommodate the diversity in organization, capital structure, and lines of business. They clearly are a dominant strategy for governments that want to facilitate innovation and supply a set of rules that appeal to different business parties' preferences. Perhaps more importantly, a default approach can supply small and medium-sized firms with rules that can provide value by lowering formation and operation costs. Unlike mandatory rules, which are necessary under certain conditions to ensure financial disclosure, limit collective action problems and protect shareholders' and creditors' interests, the terms specified in a default rule are not immutable. With default rules, parties are free to opt out and choose among different rules.

Economic theory has emphasized that, where contracts are silent or incomplete, options provide firms with an array of contractual terms on particular subjects (such as capital contributions, dividend rate, management remuneration and tenure) that encourages efficient contracting. Options provide a framework that allows parties to reduce information problems and lower the cost of contracting that they otherwise would have to pay. Default rules, in particular, can enable shareholders to protect themselves from managerial opportunism by simply relying upon rules that presumptively are biased in their favor.

There is some debate as to whether options provide a promising alternative to corporate law regimes based on mandatory rules. On the one hand, there are a number of situations where a mandatory rule would benefit shareholders against the self-interested conduct of insiders. There can also be some circumstances where a mandatory rule may be desirable to protect third parties. Further, a switch to an enabling regime may impose excessive costs for firms that cannot simply opt out and into a legal regime that is consistent with their own interests. On the other hand, an options approach can ensure that companies are able to select arrangements that may cause fewer difficulties, can allow for reductions in transaction costs and promotes the institutional environment that could facilitate choice between regulatory regimes. Some scholars, moreover, argue that a policy of facilitating choice is likely to enhance individual options pricing and may well, in certain circumstances, give rise to welfare effects.

However, regardless of the extent to which options may inflict damages on some parties or may be more costly than the benefits created, there is sufficient evidence that their value can be considerable and that expanded choice over corporate law rules is desirable given the high costs of mandates that govern the affairs of companies in the EU. In the United States, the state law's enabling structure supplies firms with few mandates and provides a menu of default rules that help firms economize on transaction costs such as drafting, information and enforcement costs. The enabling approach does not prevent firms from defining the relationship between the participants inside the firm and the representation of the firm in its dealings with outside participants, particularly creditors.

To be sure, there are areas where mandates are required. U.S. state law addresses managerial opportunism ex post, imposing fiduciary constraints against self-dealing transactions and oppression of minority shareholders. However, although the fiduciary regime imposes a duty of care, the standard of care is minimal. Mandates can also significantly facilitate the freedom of choice. U.S. states meet the diverse requirements of close corporations, for example, by offering a menu of distinct legal business forms which act as off-the-rack default packages which parties can use to structure a firm. If a particular state has sufficient incentives, its lawmakers may innovate and tailor the state's legal business forms to match market preferences.

While state corporate law generates many options in the U.S., lawmakers in Europe correspondingly have few incentives to allow companies to choose between legal rules. On the one hand, several prominent scholars have argued that the absence of state competition in the EU may explain why lawmakers, on both the EU and national level, have for so long advocated the use of mandatory rules over an enabling regime. To the extent that corporations have been unable to opt into a different corporate law regime, lawmakers face few pressures from organized interest groups to provide default rules that would allow firms to contract into their preferred legal arrangement. Under this view, the promise of regulatory competition will provide incentives for governments to give credible assurance to firms that lawmakers can be relied on to supply optimal legal rules which are attractive to many different types of firms.

While the choice-enhancing role of regulatory competition is well established, the empirical evidence is less unified on the question of whether the threat of competition induces governments to promulgate value-enhancing default rules (Bratton and McCahery 1997; Bar-Gil, Barzuza and Bebchuk 2001; Bebchuk and Cohen 2005). In this paper, we contribute to the literature by focusing on a related question: If the EC's company law reform program has not yielded regulation that firms require, will the options approach proposed here help?

A central issue in the debate has been whether the EC's reliance on a narrow range of legal mechanisms has been the main factor constraining the move toward choice. This is important because existing theory and practices suggests that the process of providing for more flexible law, such as those provisions introduced by best practice recommendations, fails to control for the distinctively mandatory characteristics of its 'comply or explain' features (Wymeersch 2005).

In this context, the EC has sought to introduce wide-spread reforms (Communication on Modernizing Company Law and Enhancing Corporate Governance in the EU – A Plan to Move Forward, 'Action Plan', European Commission 2003). While many of the reforms address the need to align principal-agent interests, particularly in the wake of the Enron and Parmalat scandals, by providing more shareholder oriented rules, there is a sense that the reforms are also designed to move the EU toward delivering more cost-effective regulation.

Thus, the EU legislative agenda has been designed to deal with cross-border mobility, board structure, financial and non-financial disclosure, director and management remuneration, appointment of auditors, managers' and directors' conflicts of interests, and shareholder voting rights. To accommodate these wide-ranging regulatory reforms, the prevailing EU regulatory strategy is to rely on a combination of directives, recommendations and self-regulation. The conventional wisdom is that the EC Action Plan will succeed in creating the type of legal framework needed to enable firms to compete more effectively in a dynamic and changing business environment. While few question the potential benefit of the reforms, several commentators wonder whether alternative legal strategies could be used to deliver more effective results (Hopt 2005; Davies 2006).

In the absence of evidence to the contrary, we are also less than sanguine about the EC's capacity to create a more flexible set of legal strategies which is sufficiently responsive to the need for better regulation and is likely to have a positive impact on economic growth, employment and productivity. We argue that pro-choice measures offer an alternative to mandatory harmonization when abstaining from regulating is not an alternative. Indeed, an options system is preferable to a mandatory regime since it favors shareholder welfare as the basis for assessing regulatory reforms. Regulatory intervention though legal options, moreover, poses a more limited threat of regulatory mistake and also address the very real cost problems caused by a single regulatory strategy.

This article develops various justifications for a EC company law reform strategy that uses opt-in and opt-out rules. It can be expected that opt-ins and opt-outs will make a difference by providing firms with a set of rules allowing them to respond better to market needs and other risks. In addition, the regulation of EC company law through legal options has two political economy advantages over the present approach. First, the use of options permits the EC and Member States to limit the risk of disruptive intrusions by the European Court of Justice (ECJ) in the company lawmaking process. Second, to the extent that options are preferred by interest groups and companies, they will have strong incentives to support the approach through increased demand for their use in most corporate law areas.

Naturally there is concern that optional arrangements may be subject to behavioral shortcomings. Some studies suggest that default rules can induce cognitive distortions that can have significant effects when people treat them like endowments. On this view, even if a default rule is biased in favor of a group of individuals, it will have no positive impact on these people. Moreover, there is evidence that also points to the stickiness of default rules making it more difficult for firms to opt out of legal provisions. On the other hand, many commentators have observed that these results are at odds with the widely accepted intuition that default rules may have little impact on distribution. Moreover, even if cognitive defects are sometimes difficult to overcome, it is argued that switching to default rules may have desirable effects by improving welfare (Sunstein 2002). Finally, since we think the possible cognitive problems associated with defaults rule are not substantial in a corporate environment (see also Arlen, Spitzer and Talley 2002), it makes great sense to provide for options so as to achieve the benefits that cannot be accomplished by harmonized mandates.

That said, there are good reasons for recommending a cautious, piece-meal approach to the introduction of options into the lawmaking process at this stage. First, putting too many reform items on the agenda may create the very same implementation delay and complexity issue than under the mandatory harmonization approach. Second, it is always preferable to adopt a step-by-step approach when introducing new regulatory mechanisms, especially when there is a risk of legal diversity becoming excessive.

This article will proceed as follows. Part B summarizes the flexible elements of EU company law. Part C will assess the impact of the evolution of EU company law policy changes on regulatory arbitrage and competition. Part D evaluates the benefits of a pro-choice approach. In Part E, we advocate a step-by-step approach focusing on a limited number of options to allow for the advantages of choice without the welfare reductions associated with too many choices. Part F concludes by discussing the future of the pro-choice approach in Europe.

B. Toward a Flexible Approach to EU Company Law

This part considers the implications of the significant change of EC company law policy in favor of a flexible approach that relies on soft law measures.

I. The Evolution of EU Company Law

The EC has built a record of company law reform that enjoys a mixed reputation. Early legislation has been praised for quickly developing a company law infrastructure that was in some important respects similar to the corporate law structures in most Member States. Second, the Commission was successful in implementing laws that facilitated cross-border trading by minimizing the risk of companies or their transactions being considered void in other Member States. Third, the adoption of accounting and capital maintenance rules aimed at protecting minority shareholders and creditors secured some enthusiasm for Commission efforts in devising mechanisms dealing with financial assistance and disclosure.

In the past two decades, however, the situation has changed. A series of high profile legislative efforts by the European Commission, ranging from the regulation of takeover bids to establishing new business entities, ran into conflict with the European Parliament. What explains the shift in legislative policymaking authority encountered by EC? Influential theories of EU lawmaking emphasize that the policy-making space became very limited due to the mixed motives of Member States (Pollack 2003). The presumption that Member States should want to weaken, not strengthen the Commission's company law agenda, has led some scholars to entertain the possibility that major company law reforms are not considered important enough for member governments to mobilize resources to achieve legislative compromises (Wouters 2000).

In order to regain significant agenda-setting powers and the ability to conclude agreements, the EC eventually reversed its legislative strategy in this area. Standard public choice theory would explain the shift in terms of organized special interest groups persuading Commission policymakers that the group's preferences would serve the policymakers' own political interests and become useful in putting together a winning coalition (Dixit and Londregan 1998). Naturally there are numerous other explanations to consider. It is surely no coincidence that the Commission sought to counter the moves of member governments that seek to block reforms by placing the Lisbon Council's objectives as a top priority.[1] Similarly, the EC may have had an incentive to take an early position on the U.S. corporate scandals in order to shift expectations of domestic voters, which could be expected to guide member governments' subsequent behavior. This is clearly represented by the efforts of the Internal Market Commissioner to have the High Level Group of Company Law Experts reach beyond their original mandate to recommend certain audit and accounting rules regarding publication of annual accounts.[2]

Perhaps more fundamentally, the EC has responded to the direct political influence of the European Court of Justice' (ECJ) decisions on freedom of establishment.[3] These ECJ decisions have challenged the core elements of the *siège*

[1] See Lisbon European Council 'Presidency Conclusions' (23-24 June 2000) (<http://ue.eu.int/en/Info/eurocouncil/index.htm>).

[2] See <http://europa.eu.int/comm/internalmarket/en/company/company/news/01-1237.htm>

[3] Cases C-212/97 *Centros Ltd.. v Erthvers-og Selskabbsstyrelsen* (1999) ECR I-1459 (Centros); Case C-208/00 *Überseering BV v Nordic Construction Company Baumanagement GmbH (NCC)* (2002) ECR I-9919 (Überseering); and Case C-167/01 *Kamer van Koophandel en*

cont. ...

réel (real seat) doctrine, thus questioning some of the main principles enshrined in the company law frameworks in the majority of Member States. A growing number of studies have demonstrated the direct effect of the ECJ's judgments on cross-border mobility of start-up companies (Becht, Mayer and Wagner 2005). With regard to established companies, the impact of the ECJ case law is subject to debate, as it remains costly for them to switch from one Member State regime to another. Nonetheless, these decisions have increased the attractiveness of regulatory arbitrage which may make it easier for corporations to select among legal rules from diverse company law codes.

These disruptive features have induced the EC policymakers to adopt a less constraining legislative approach. For example, the Commission proposed – in a radical departure from its previous policy –, that Member States be allowed to opt-out of Articles 9 (board neutrality) and 11 (break-through rule) of the Takeover Bids Directive. The proposal was received favorably by Member States, ending a regulatory deadlock that had lasted for more than a decade.[4] The Commission has subsequently created a large and growing number of soft law initiatives that link together national governments' and EU policymakers' concerns to succeed in transforming their relationship concerning agenda setting and implementation of corporate law.

The provision of flexible corporate law rules has many advantages. In particular, the greater range of choice in policy-making instruments makes it easier to avoid the costs of relying on rigid instruments alone. The Commission can choose to: 1) enact mandatory EU provisions (as was generally done in the past); 2) offer Member States a choice among a finite number of EU-defined options (an approach originally adopted in the Accounting Directives); 3) enact harmonized provisions, but empower Member States to opt-out of them (an approach adopted by the Takeover Bids Directive); 4) enable firms to opt out of applicable Member State provisions by providing substitutable EU provisions (as was also done in the Takeover Bids Directive); 5) adopt a EU regime that firms can opt-out of (which has not been tried yet, but is in line with the flexible approach adopted by the Takeover Bids Directive); and 6) and abstain from legislating.[5]

Fabrieken voor Amsterdam v Inspire Art Ltd (NL) (2003) ECR 1-10155 (Inspire Art). These judgments are available at <http://europa.eu.int/cj/en/content/juris/index.htm>.

[4] Directive 2004/25/EC of the European Parliament and of the Council of 21 April 2004 on Takeover Bids, OJ L142 30.04.2004 12-23.

[5] Furthermore, reformers can combine approaches. For example, the Takeover Bids Directive allows Member States to opt-out of its board neutrality and prohibition of defensive measures provisions, while enabling firms incorporated in Member States that do so to opt into the EU regime. Or, to take another example, firms could be allowed to opt-out of their domestic regime not only to escape mandatory provision, but also when EU law has a standardization advantage over Member State default provisions.

C. Impact on Regulatory Arbitrage and Competition

Overall it is intuitive that while many of the policy changes discussed above can have some impact on regulatory arbitrage, their practical effect on cross-border mobility, charter competition and freedom of choice is so far quite limited. Exit taxes or workers' protection and other social constraints are more important to more choice than the Commission's new soft law approach to company law-making.

It is well know that tax constraints are a significant barrier to mid-stream re-incorporations. The ECJ's ruling in Daily Mail shows clearly that re-incorporations will trigger exit taxes on hidden reserves, effectively restricting the demand for chartering.[6] Conversely, there is evidence that corporate law does not significantly constrain tax-driven firm mobility.[7] The same is true for social constraints. The attractiveness of incorporation or reincorporation is often seriously reduced by having no effect on applicable labor law – a situation that is likely to persist over the longer run, given unwavering opposition to the adoption of EU corporate governance provisions that would affect the scope of German co-determination requirements. Note also that corporate law considerations are unlikely to significantly affect labor-driven firm mobility.

On the other hand, the ECJ recent rulings on freedom of establishment can and do challenge the existing EC tax landscape. Since 2000, the ECJ has repeatedly ruled that tax provisions were precluded by the freedom of establishment principle if they discriminated between domestic and foreign subsidiaries, and more generally between domestic and international groups. More importantly, Member States have generally proven unsuccessful in trying to justify such discrimination by arguing that they are necessary to ensure the coherence of the national tax system or the need to preserve the tax base.[8] This is both in sharp contrast with the ECJ's previous reluctance to challenge tax barriers to cross-border activities (as exemplified by Daily Mail and Bachmann[9]) and in line with the recent ECJ's pro-freedom of incorporation and reincorporation cases.

[6] Case 81/1987 *Regina v H.M. Treasury and Comm'rs of Inland Revenue, ex parte Daily Mail and General Trust Plc* (1988) ECR 5483.

[7] See GR Simpson 'EU's Tax Changes Scatter Corporations' *Wall St J (European ed)* (9 October 2003) A6.

[8] See e.g. Case C-324/00 *Lankhorst-Hohorst GmbH v Finanzamt Steinfurt* (2002) ECR I-1179 – a German tax case; Case C-168/01 *Bosal Holding BV v Staatsscretaris van Financien* (2003) ECR I-9409 – a Dutch tax case; Case C-446/03 *Marks & Spencer plc v David Hasley (HM Inspector of Taxes)*, not yet reported – a UK tax case. These judgments are available at <http://europa.eu.int/cj/en/content/juris/index.htm>.

[9] Case C-204/90 *Bachmann* (1992) ECR I-249.

As a consequence of these tax cases and the implementation of the amendments to the Merger Directive,[10] commentators are confident that the current tax barriers to cross-border reincorporation will be removed shortly by the ECJ (Schön 2003). Such optimism finds support in the de Lasteyrie du Saillant judgment.[11] The ECJ ruled in favor of an individual who moved to France from Belgium and objected to having to provide a guarantee in respect of a tax bill on the future sale of a shareholding. The Court indicated that the principle of freedom of establishment precluded a Member State keen to prevent a risk of tax avoidance from taxing latent increases in value when a taxpayer transfers his residence outside that State.

While the pattern in ECJ case law suggests that the Court is likely to rule in favor of restricting Member States from levying corporate exit taxes on foregone claims and hidden reserves, this is by no mean certain. Moreover, should the ECJ eventually do so, the main beneficiaries (larger established companies) may be worse off from changes in the *status quo*. Pro-taxpayer case law is likely to trigger tax measures at the domestic and international level that could prove more costly than the gains from greater freedom of movement (Hertig 2004). Hence, there is some evidence that Member States, in particular the UK, systematically adjust their tax laws to minimize the impact of ECJ judgments and that freedom of establishment case law is driven by smaller rather than larger firms – an indication that the latter generally do not expect to significantly gain from it.

This does not mean that only those firms that can afford reincorporation will benefit from regulatory arbitrage and regulatory competition in the corporate law area. The trend set in train by the Centros, Überseering and Inspire Art judgments has directly influenced the policy space of the European Commission. Hence, the introduction of the new Directive on Cross-Border Mergers,[12] and announced plans for a directive on the cross-border transfer of the administrative office of firms can be considered as initiatives that evidence the shift toward a mobility-oriented lawmaking agenda. In addition, various Member States have responded to demands of domestic firms for innovative company law terms. An ever-wider array of Member States, such as Ireland, UK, Luxembourg and the Netherlands, have prioritized the creation of corporate law rules that directly benefit footloose foreign companies operating in other jurisdictions. But others, France and Germany in particular, have the more specific objective to make reincorporation in the UK less economically attractive (see also Heine 2003; Vermeulen 2003).

[10] See the Council Directive 2005/19/EC, amending Council Directive 90/434/EEC of 230 July 1990 on the common system of taxation applicable to mergers, divisions, transfer of assets and exchanges of shares concerning companies of different Member States, OJ L58 2005 19.

[11] Case C-9/02 *Hughes de Lasteyrie du Saillant v Ministère de l'Economie, des Finances et de l'Industrie* (2004) ECR I-2409.

[12] Directive 2005/56/EC of the European Parliament and of the Council of 26 October 2005 on cross-border mergers of limited liability companies, OJ L310 25.11.2005 1-9.

Given these pressures, it now becomes easier to understand why EC policymakers – with fixed positions – have agreed to adopt a new legislative model that fosters diversity and allows (some) choice.

D. The Benefits of a Pro-Choice Approach

This section examines the advantages of a pro-choice approach as applied to corporate law, taking into account the economic theory of incomplete contracts, the risk of opportunistic behavior and endowment effects.

I. Economic Theory of Incomplete Contracts and Default Rules

As many corporate contracts are incomplete, the economic theory of incomplete contracts can play an important role in deciding how to resolve conflicts when there is a missing term or a contract is opaque (Bratton, Hviid and McCahery 1996). A contract is complete only if all relevant contingencies and corresponding control rights are specified unambiguously. Still, parties may deliberatively choose non-contingent contract or be unable to design a contract that deals with all contingencies ex ante (Hart and Moore 1998).

The literature predicts that a particular type of agreement may be incomplete due to informational asymmetries and limitations in contractual language. The intuition behind this approach is that the parties could most likely write a complete contract if they could focus on a breach and through backward induction develop a full set of governing optional terms. Whether parties can depend on backward induction to deal with their long-term contracting problems is, however, questionable (Posner 2003).

Law and economics theory has produced an impressive variety of gap-filling alternatives to deal with the incompleteness of corporate contracts. Prominent scholars have argued that corporate law should provide a single set of gap-filling rules that hypothetical parties would have bargained for (Easterbrook and Fischel 1991). The adoption of an efficient set of default rules provides firms with opportunities and solutions that otherwise would not be available and reduces transaction costs of opting into specific terms. Naturally, business parties who find the default rule undesirable would remain free to opt out and contract into a term they prefer.

In recent years, scholars have challenged whether market-mimicking rules encourage efficiency, positing that under other circumstances the majoritarian default rule does not have any efficient effects at all, and that courts presumably will find it more complex to apply such defaults to all types of firms (Posner 2003; Ben-Shahar 2004). A contrasting approach is offered by scholars who endorse the penalty default doctrine. In this view, suppletory rules that parties would not have chosen for themselves, called 'penalty defaults', may prove more efficient than majoritarian defaults because they force parties to share information with third parties who might be affected by the contract (Ayres and Gertner 1989). However, even if penalty defaults could limit negative externalities, it is not clear at all whether the doctrine could become effective generally (Posner 2003).

A more straightforward alternative approach to a single set of state-supplied defaults is to encourage lawmakers to supply a wide-range menu of corporate law options. We argue that, given the dire experience of so many European countries with mandatory corporate law regimes, passing reforms that allow corporations to select from a menu of contractual provisions is likely to result in significant benefits. More specifically, the next section will show how a corporate law regime using both opt-in and opt-out rules can yield benefits to business parties and shareholders.

II. Opt-In and Opt-Out Rules in EC Company Law

It follows from the above discussion, that if the European Commission were to introduce reforms designed to provide a menu of optional substantive rules, the resulting legislation could increase the incentives to reduce transaction costs, thereby increasing shareholder value. Given the ever-changing nature of the business environment, an effective enabling approach ideally should also include both opt-in and opt-out procedures (Joll and Sunstein 2005). To illustrate this point, lawmakers could draft an opt-in provision that allows shareholders a choice in favor of a rule that will give them the right to sue directors (a procedural option) or to benefit from appraisal rights (a substantive option) in case of a squeeze-out.

The shift toward an opt-in/opt-out approach could also diminish member government conflicts and regulatory deadlocks and thus increase the value of the EC company law regime. The beneficial effects are likely to include the development of a richer regulatory menu and allow for alternative contractual arrangements when abstaining from lawmaking is not an alternative. In the past, such situations may have led to the adoption of mandatory corporate law arrangements that where biased in favor of one set of contracting parties or another (O'Hara 2000; Rachlinski and Farina 2002; Korobkin 2003). By giving business parties the opportunity to opt-in alternative to biased and costly rules or to opt-out of them through internal bargaining, their interests can be protected against regulatory interventions that they deem inefficient. Another potential benefit of this approach is that firms can benefit directly from the choice of a-la-carte legal rules without having to re-incorporate into a friendlier Member State company law regime.

Conversely, the uncertainly surrounding a policy permitting business parties to decide among options may create some skepticism about the wealth effects of this approach. There are a number of reasons. First, allowing shareholders to opt into or out of EU or Member State's rules could undermine, given heterogeneous preferences of Member States, the incentives of the Commission to propose and implement legislation. In particular, moving from a mandatory harmonization regime or an 'abstain or comply' approach to a clear choice regime with multiple alternatives may increase (albeit probably only slightly) the chances of deadlock by preventing the emergence of clear majorities. Second, the process of introducing enhanced contractual choice could significantly increase the number of legal options available thereby making it more difficult and costly for business parties to ascertain and select the most appropriate rule.

Finally, while the presumption is that parties tend toward efficient outcomes, it may be necessary for regulators who care about efficiency to introduce the conditions which enable the parties to achieve the result. In some cases, this will require the creation of stringent mandatory provisions, rather than defaults, in order to constrain opportunistic behavior. Economic theory indicates that costly opportunism typically occurs at the entry or exit stages. This means that minority investors could be better off with a mandatory provision, such as a fair value squeeze out rule, as a protection against opportunism by controlling shareholders and managers. Some commentators argue, moreover, that stringent mandatory rules can protect entrepreneurs from early stage hold-up problems, which is likely to promote social welfare by facilitating the absolute number of start-ups (Hyytinen and Takalo 2005). What emerges from these arguments is the observation that policymakers must, when designing mandatory rules and legal options, find the proper balance between the different interests and ensure that parties reach efficient agreements.

III. The Endowment Effect and Legal Options

It is well know that cognitive distortions, such as the endowment effect, can explain why economic actors do not always reach efficient outcomes. The endowment effect, which is reflected in people's preferences for the status quo, can be observed in laboratory experiments. To be sure, the cost of the endowment effect for markets remains uncertain (Glaeser 2004; Plott and Zeiler 2005) and the regulatory implications are not yet well understood (Korobkin 2003). Yet the behavioral analysis of legal options is a robust literature that takes seriously the implications of cognitive biases for legal rules and economic welfare (see Bar-Gill 2005; Jolls and Sunstein 2005).

From a behavioral perspective, corporate law reformers considering a switch to a legal options approach should pay special attention to stickiness issues. We know that lawmakers can reduce the cost of contracting by providing off-the-shelf provisions that permit parties to avoid the costs of negotiating and drafting a customized term. What remains unclear is the extent to which the benefits resulting from economic actors taking advantage of such provisions are reduced by the costs imposed by the existence of default rules on firms for which it would be efficient to opt-out. In particular, opting-out may prove expensive or even overly costly because of stakeholders' preference for the standardized norm provided by the default rule.

Conversely, offering firms a set of opt-in provisions that depart from 'comply or explain' corporate governance codes may prove efficient. It could make it less costly for firms to exit inefficient one-size-fits-all rules by reducing the transaction and reputation costs of justifying to investors why they are not in compliance with a good practice recommendation. But opt-ins may have their drawbacks too. For example, investors may resist the opting into a more favorable EU regime because a status quo bias makes them prefer the existing national corporate law regime or because they do not want the firm to adopt an approach that deviates from the mean (Sunstein 2002).

More generally, it could also be argued that default rules can deter the opportunistic conduct of majority shareholders and managers more effectively than the current mandatory regime. For example, adopting an unlimited liability default rule for corporate tortfeasors could have significant redistributive consequences for contract creditors (Hansmann and Kraakman 1991). On the other hand, such a default rule does not necessarily benefit the intended group (Sunstein 2002).

It is difficult to compare these advantages and disadvantages in the abstract, even more so considering that cognitive biases are context specific. On the other hand, it appears that there is no indication that legal options should be avoided provided some attention is given to their efficiency in terms of status quo or other bias, such as excessive optimism.

Overall, we argue that adopting pro-choice provisions will prove advantageous to the interests of firms and investors. The opportunity to select rules that firms prefer without having to reincorporate in another Member State is likely to lead to significant cost-savings. These advantages are unlikely to be offset due to capture by interest groups, excessive diversity, and cognitive uncertainties. First, adopting entry/exit voting rules should prevent one constituency (managers controlling shareholders, minorities) from acting opportunistically. Second, any increase in legal diversity should benefit most European firms as their needs tend to differ across classes. Some firms may suffer higher costs because of reduced standardization, but this should not prove sufficient to outweigh the benefits for other firms (Berglöf and Burkart 2003). Third, and most importantly, adopting a step-by-step approach, under which a limited number of legal options are tested during an introductory phase, should limit the risk of regulatory inefficiencies or distortions.

E. Step-by-Step Reform Recommendations

In this section, we develop a set of reform suggestions based on the investigations above. It is crucial to note that most studies suggest that a new regulatory approach cannot be expected to be incorporated within the existing framework without proper consideration and assessment regarding the impact on other rules and regulations as well as the effect of such an approach for investors, creditors and other stakeholders (European Policy Forum 2004a; 2004b).

A law reform proposal based on our regulatory choice model may prove complex and thus place a burden on EU policymakers and regulators. Moreover, a legal options approach is likely to create significant market and regulatory uncertainties. In this respect, we propose that implementation should occur initially in only a handful of areas. Adopting a simpler, unbundled approach makes it possible to pay closer inspection to the respective merits of the default measures and their effectiveness in practice.

In the next sections, we examine the company and governance law areas that are best suited to mandates and the areas that would benefit, in principle, from legal options. This will permit us to propose a step-by-step approach allowing for early adoption of a limited number of opt-ins and opt-outs. A trial introductory phase would permit benchmarking and testing of their use and potential impact.

I. Mandatory Requirements

As noted above, the introduction of default rules does not eliminate the need for mandatory requirements to address contracting problems of firms. A good example is corporate disclosure, an area in which regulatory mandates have significant coordination and standardization advantages. It is worth noting also that legal options may have to be complemented by mandatory procedural rules (Hertig and McCahery 2004). In the next section, for example, we will show that EU opt-in or opt-out provisions would make little sense as a governance mechanism in controlling shareholders environments, unless reinforced by mandatory approval requirements such as minority shareholder or judicial ratification.

In recent years, the EU has adopted a fair number of transparency requirements. Despite the demand for more disclosure and the importance of such information for asset allocations, scholars have questioned the effectiveness of these reforms without the creation of an agency, such as a European SEC, to induce firms to make reliable and accurate disclosure of financial and nonfinancial information (Hertig and Lee 2003). Since none of the crucial enforcement mechanisms or institutions are likely to be introduced in the short term, it may not make much sense to propose new corporate disclosure requirements that will end up increasing the cost to firms and provide little additional information to investors.

Still, it appears that the mechanism of disclosure is particularly crucial for investors, especially in light of the sequence of increasingly blatant misinformation by public companies (culminating with the Parmalat scandal), and the emphasis given by policymakers to it, despite the absence of effective enforcement bodies, is understandable. Hence, the EU has recently adopted new auditing standards as well as requirements to rotate auditors on a regular basis and to designate a single, fully responsible auditor for groups of companies.

Various commentators question the efficiency of some of these new reforms for protecting the interests of investors. For example, even though Italy has been the first (and only) Member State to introduce auditor rotation requirements, it seems that this measure did little to prevent the Parmalat scandal – and may even have contributed to it. On the other hand, imposing some level of gatekeeper supervision could reinforce investor confidence (Jain, Kim and Rezaee 2004) and prevent auditor liability from becoming prohibitive (Coffee 2002). A case can thus be made for new auditing firm regulation that addresses some of the perceived technical shortcomings and the conflicts of interest problems that have contributed to costly governance failures.

Restoring investor confidence has particular appeal in the EU context and has led to calls for EU lawmakers to liberalize the barriers to private enforcement (Hertig and McCahery 2003). Given the importance of ensuring effective financial reporting and limiting opportunism, lawmakers could simply mandate that all shareholders of firms incorporated in the EU have the right to sue for breaches of shareholder voting rules and for violations of managerial or controlling shareholder fiduciary duties. At the same time, Member States could also be required to establish courts specialized in shareholder litigation, with the French *Tribunal de Commerce*, the German *Handelsgericht* or the Delaware Chancery Court as possible models. Finally, the EU could further introduce reforms that lead to the adoption of pre-trial discovery procedures and mass litigation devices such as class actions and contingent fees. Such a shift would build on mechanisms that already exist (in law or in fact) in several Member States and therefore appear to reinforce and extend upon the institutions that exist in these countries.

Yet there are a number of objections that could be advanced against such proposals. First, there is the view that EU policymakers should address only substantive law issues, leaving the enforcement of company law and securities regulation to member governments. While the case can be made for such a delegation, it is not very persuasive particularly in light of the level of harmful activity and the complexity of the regulatory task. In any event, EU policymakers and the Commission naturally assume that the need for effective enforcement is a high priority of the EU. Moreover, given the large number of Member State enforcement systems that clash with the fundamental objective of providing equivalent levels of substantive protection across the internal market, EU intervention could be considered compatible with the principle of subsidiarity.[13]

Another, more fundamental, objection is that facilitating private litigation is not necessarily effective or efficient means to curb internal governance abuses. This is a difficult topic to tackle, not least because the evidence is murky. For ex-

[13] See Directive 2004/48/EC of the European Parliament and of the Council of 29 April 2004 on the enforcement of intellectual property rights, OJ L157 30.4.2004 45-86; Directive 2003/6/EC of the European Parliament and of the Council of 28 January 2003 on insider dealing and market manipulation (market abuse), OJ L96 12.04.2003 16-25.

ample, U.S. class actions were much criticized in the early 1990s as the source of abusive law suits against auditors and civil procedure reforms were passed to curtail their effectiveness. Today, these type of reforms are listed among the top reasons why auditors undertook the more risky and conflicted activities that facilitated the occurrence of corporate scandals in recent years (Coffee 2002). Or, to take another example, the jury system is often considered crucial for damage awards to be larger (and litigation level higher) in the U.S. than in Europe. The empirical evidence, however, is mixed (compare Eisenberg et al 2002; Hersch and Viscusi 2004). The effect of fees reforms on enforcement levels is still another area where there is no clear direction which could give guidance in the debate. For many years, the law and economics literature has suggested that contingent fees are the fuel that has powered U.S.-type litigation. Conversely, an apparently innocuous reduction of filing fees was apparently sufficient to cause an impressive increase in shareholder litigation in Japan (West 2001).

It would seem that these studies make it difficult to summarily dismiss the efficiency of an EU imposed reduction in enforcement barriers. On the other hand, it cannot be disputed that such a reform presupposes a sophisticated economic analysis of the costs and benefits of the proposed measures and their effect on other rules and procedures as well. More importantly, mandatory enforcement reforms would face fierce opposition by Member States who challenge the introduction of litigation on political, cultural or even protectionist grounds. In other words, any attempt to impose a reduction in enforcement barriers is likely to face considerable delay or even certain defeat. In short, it would make little sense to propose mandatory requirements in this area at this stage. As far as further steps are concerned, the ease with which the UK has sought to introduce new regulation on auditing and shareholder litigation suggests that some countries would certainly benefit from EU enhanced enforcement through private litigation in order to shore up weak institutions.

II. Finite Set of Competing Legal Options

A competing options approach of the kind previously adopted by the EC in the case of the accounting directives, permits Member States to choose among a finite set of more or less conservative standards as well as to exempt small to medium-size firms (SMEs) from specific requirements deemed to be too costly. Our analysis suggests that this approach has important beneficial effects. It makes it easier for firms to identify variations in the Member States' rules. There is some evidence, moreover, that enhanced choice will lead Member States to switch to a less demanding regime for SMEs and hence reduce the regulatory burden for this class of firms.

It is worth pointing out, however, that the experience with the Accounting Directives has been far from successful. To be sure, whilst there are a number of factors responsible, we suspect that the problems may be due to the options being designed to deal with other regulatory concerns than efficiency. More generally, the experience tends to confirm that it is generally a mistake to impose a fixed menu of options from the top. On the one hand, standardization benefits are significantly reduced, as there is no single set of EU provisions that firms and investors can rely upon. On the other hand, harmonization costs are likely to increase.

An additional key point is that adopting a finite set of competing legal options approach will reduce Member States willingness to compromise, as they have good reasons to hope that a hard stance will insure the adoption of an option that is close to their own preferences. Unfortunately, the likely result will be a set of options which has few benefits and thus all the more difficult to justify. In addition, the existence of multiple options should increase the petrifaction effect, as amendments would have to be coordinated and should thus be more difficult to pass than when there is only one mandate or one legal option. The potential weakness of the finite set of competing legal options approach suggest that it is not ideally suited to the current institutional and political environment and hence should not be considered as a mechanisms for first step company law reforms.

III. Opting-Out of EU Provisions

It was argued earlier that an opting-out approach is more efficient than mandates, particularly where there are significant variations in corporate governance and company law regimes across Member States. In such a situation, a single mandatory set of EU provisions would have a different impact in each Member State, with many firms incurring costs far in excess of standardization and other benefits. For example, differences in the use of the open corporate form by smaller firm and shareholder structure (dispersed or concentrated) can considerably affect the efficiency of director independence mandates.

By contrast, permitting Member States or firms to opt out of EU provisions should eliminate most of the costs due to legal diversity. Unsurprisingly, this is particularly relevant in light of the debate on one-share-one-vote. The EC has recently announced plans to introduce legislation that would mandate one-share-one-vote. Most studies indicate that, within the EU, there are voting systems in which blockholders enjoy all or most of the private benefits as a consequence of their use of dual-class stock, non-voting ownership certificates, trust companies, and other cash flow rights (McCahery et al 2003). However, there are significant differences in voting systems and impact across EU Member States (Deminor 2005).

Given this diversity, the question is whether shareholders would support a EU proposal where there is some uncertainty about its potential outcome. Indeed, there are complex economic arguments in respect of the efficiency of the one-share-one-vote rule. On the one hand, deviations form the one-share-one-vote rule may decrease controlling shareholders' cost of capital (Hart and Moore 1988) and possibly increase takeover efficiency (but see Coates 2001; McCahery et al

2003). On the other hand, the issuance of dual class voting shares may facilitate the transfer of resources from the company to a large shareholder and lead to the oppression of minority shareholders. Thus shareholders, in balancing these considerations, will have to take account of a large number of factors in determining what capital structure can be expected to produce the highest value. This is a complex firm-specific undertaking, and shareholders may prefer having a one-share-one vote regime that they can opt out of rather than having it imposed upon them.

This one-share-one-vote example is not meant to imply that opt-outs are costless. First, as indicated, stickiness may prevent firms from opting out of all but the most costly EU provisions. Stickiness costs may, however, be reduced by adopting EU provisions that are tilted in favor of shareholders (Bebchuck and Hamdani 2002). Secondly, allowing opt-outs reduces the standardization advantage of EU lawmaking, especially when domestic corporate law regimes vary significantly. This is, however, precisely the situation where Member States are likely to oppose or delay mandatory harmonization, but agree on opt-out provisions. Indeed, member government opposition to EU lawmaking should remain relatively light when they themselves are allowed to opt-out.[14] Naturally, opposition could be more significant when firms also have the right to opt-out, but that can be mitigated by combining Member State opt-out powers and firms' right to opt back into EU law.

That said, most studies indicate that it would be efficient for the EU to adopt legal provisions with opting-out possibilities in many areas of company law and corporate governance. Such an approach would have a number of advantages. First, it could enable Member States to also opt-out of controversial provisions such as the Takeover Directive's equitable price, squeeze-out and sell-out provisions. Second, new firms could be subject to one share/one vote, no staggered boards, no voting caps, no pyramid structures requirements, but allowed to opt-out in favor of the regime of the Member State they are incorporated in – the latter limitation aiming at insuring some degree of uniformity and transparency. Third, shareholders of both new firms and firms established in new Member States could be recognized standing to sue for breaches of shareholder voting rules and violations of fiduciary duties, but allowed to opt-out in favor of the regime of the Member State they are incorporated in. (By contrast, established firms in pre-2004 Member States could be recognized to opt into such a regime.)

At this stage, however, there are several reasons to caution against the adoption of opt-out provisions in such a large array of corporate law areas. In practice, such a reform could place too many items on the reform agenda, thereby creating the very same delay in implementation that has arisen under the Commission's mandatory company law harmonization program. At the same time, as indicated,

[14] Opposition will not necessarily be inexistent, as some Member States may fear that the adoption of EU provisions may make opt-outs unsustainable in the long-term.

it is preferable to adopt a step-by-step approach when introducing new regulatory mechanisms. Finally, the shift to opt-out provisions must remain limited to avoid excessive legal diversity.

IV. Opting into EU Law

As argued above, EU intervention could also increase firms' choice while avoiding reincorporation issues by supplying firms with selective opt-in provisions that allow them to opt-out of *specific* Member State level company law arrangements – as opposed to the full opt-out brought by reincorporation.

The opt-in approach can be cost effective since it provides firms with a small menu of EU provisions that lower transaction costs and increases the degree of standardization and, therefore, legal certainty. Firms may also be better served by opt-ins that credibly signal a commitment to comply with state-of-the-art regulation. Another important factor is that opt-in provisions can be useful for companies that must address legal difficulties, such as workers' participation requirements.

The opt-in approach, however, may also be compelled by political expediency. Subjecting an EU opt-in proposal on related party transactions, for instance, to a shareholder vote would have no impact on constraining controlling shareholder opportunism – but still looks better than forgoing any intervention. Member States may also favor opt-in provisions to prevent the adoption of more efficient opting-out provisions. A potential example is a proposal on dividend rights for minority shareholders. Likewise, Member States could support opt-in provisions because they are likely to increase legal diversity and either make it more difficult for investors to ascertain the costs of their domestic regime or increase their own corporate law's stickiness.

Thus, under certain conditions, the adoption of opt-in provisions, could prove to be less cost effective than expected. In such circumstances, caution is welcome, particularly when there are hard opt-in choices. In our view, the benefits of an opt-in approach should generally exceed its costs in areas where Member States have adopted costly mandatory provisions that cannot be dismantled through mandatory or opt-out EU intervention. In addition, the opt-in approach should be an appropriate one in areas where Member State law is diverse, but standardization or 'best practice' signaling is important for investors or stakeholders.

Opt-ins seem particularly suited for dealing with Member State mandatory provisions on employee participation structures, multiple voting and dividend rights, as well as on various takeover issues (board neutrality, mandatory bid thresholds and exit prices). However, EU mandatory requirements might, in some cases, be required to complement such opt-in arrangements, both to prevent Member States from opposing their adoption and minimize managerial and shareholder opportunism. Thus, opting into EU employee participation provisions could, for instance, be made subject to court ratification. Similarly, the opting into EU multiple voting and dividend rights provisions or into EU mandatory bid thresholds and exit prices might be made subject to qualified majority or minority shareholder approval.

As far as standardization and signalization are concerned, new firms or firms incorporated in new Member States should benefit from opt-in provisions that establish simple and transparent procedures for the disclosure and approval of related party transactions (be it self-dealing, compensation agreements, or the appropriation of corporate opportunities).

Finally, the opt-in approach could serve a pro-enforcement function. Under this approach, existing firms in 'old' Member States would be encouraged to choose litigation arrangement. To be sure, managers or controlling shareholders may resist such a move, fearing a reduction of their private benefits due to minority shareholder litigation. However, it may not even be necessary to give the majority of minority shareholders the power to exercise the opt-in option for it to be effective. As recent events of shown, managers or controlling shareholders may endorse an opt-in measure, to the extent it provides a civil enforcement alternative to criminal investigations and sanctions.

F. Conclusion: The Future of the Pro-Choice Approach

Our review suggests that it might be feasible in the near term for the EU to adopt a legal options approach. However, the EU's experience could prove short lived if it cannot quickly develop a feasible role for this mechanism. Should options not play the role promised, the Commission could easily slip back into anti-choice mode if it perceives there are better ways to maximize its role in the legislative process. In this respect, the Commission could be expected to revert to a mandatory approach should this secure the support of a lawmaking majority comprising Member States and members of the European Parliament opposed to regulatory arbitrage and competition.

That said, it may be difficult for policymakers to limit the momentum of the pro-freedom movement that has been opened-up by the ECJ's freedom of establishment judgments. First, it is well established that legislative attempts to counter major case law developments are usually unsuccessful (Cooter and Ginsburg 1996). Even if it is not unusual to see diverging positions gradually erode toward a common middle ground, this process is time-consuming and firms are unlikely to remain idle throughout the convergence process. Second, access to the pro-freedom path is now substantially controlled by the judiciary and pro-choice Member States, and therefore largely outside the reach of a political alliance comprising the European Commission and anti-choice constituencies.

Moreover, we suspect that Member States and interest groups opposed to regulatory arbitrage and competition may find it preferable to 'guide' firms' legal regime strategies through pro-choice EU legislation rather than engage less effective mandatory harmonization exercises. Indeed, given the mentioned history of slow legislative reaction to major case law developments and continued diversity of national governance regimes, one should expect years of intergovernmental negotiations on the possible terms the new mandatory measures. While generally accepted by parties in the past, this cumbersome process is unlikely to prove sustainable in the face of continuing regulatory arbitrage and competition.

By contrast, a pro-choice approach could serve to significantly accelerate the lawmaking process. More importantly, the approach is likely to permit EU lawmakers to set the framework within which regulatory arbitrage and competition take place. Indeed, EU legal options have two major advantages. First, their standardization value automatically extends to the EU as a whole. Second, they allow for selective choices. Firms will be able to opt into those EU provisions they prefer, whereas Member States can only offer full opt-ins (incorporation or reincorporation results in the applicability of the corporate law regime as a whole).

While it is difficult to predict with certainty, we foresee the Commission moving toward the adoption of a pro-choice approach as it provides the best mechanism for successfully adopting and implementing 'essential' legislation. This prediction is reinforced by a variety of other considerations. A review of the legislative history of the Takeover Bids Directive suggest that the key institutional actors within the EU have already recognized there is no longer one approach to regulatory design in corporate law. Moreover, pro-choice arrangements are becoming a favored mechanism to secure benefits in unrelated areas (e.g. trading temporary workers legislation against takeover provisions), to target regulatory beneficiaries (e.g. by allowing sophisticated capital market players to opt-out of investor protection provisions) or to facilitate the EU enlargement process (e.g. by permitting firms in new Member States to signal their commitment to 'best practice' by opting into EU corporate law provisions). Thus, while options may not in themselves create efficiency, they are crucial for parties to bargain to such conclusions and can play an important role in promoting the goals of economic integration.

References

Arlen, J, M Spitzer and E Talley 'Endowment Effects Within Corporate Agency Relationships' (2002) 31 J Legal Stud 1-37.

Ayres, I *Optional Law: Real Options in the Structure of Legal Entilements* (University of Chicago Press 2005).

Ayres, I, and R Gertner 'Filling Gaps in Incomplete Contracts: An Economic Theory of Default Rules' (1989) 99 Yale L J 87-130.

Bar-Gill, O 'Pricing Legal Options: A Behavioral Perspective' (New York University Law and Economics wp No. 04-05, 2005).

Bar-Gill, O, M Barzuza and LA Bebchuk 'The Market for Corporate Law' (SSRN wp <http://www.ssrn.com/abstract_id=275452>, 2002).

Bebchuk, LA and A Cohen 'Firms' Decisions Where to Incorporate' (2005) 46 J L & Econ 383-435.

Bebchuk, LA and A Hamdani 'Optimal Defaults for Corporate Law Evolution' (2002) 96 Nw U L Rev 489-519.

Becht, M, C Mayer and H Wagner 'Mobility Comes to Europe: The Evidence' (Oxford University wp 2005).

Ben-Shahar, O 'Agreeing to Disagree': Filling Gaps in Deliberately Incomplete Contracts' (SSRN wp <http://www.ssrn.com/abstract_id=496183>, 2004).

Berglöf, E and M Burkart 'European Takeover Regulation' (2003) 36 Economic Policy 171-213.

Bratton, WW, M Hviid and JA McCahery 'Repeated Games, Social Norms and Incomplete Contracts' in C Willett (ed) *Aspects of Fairness in Contract* (Blackstone Press 1996) 161-193.

Bratton, WW and JA McCahery 'New Economics of Jurisdictional Competition: Devolutionary Federalism in a Second-Best World' (1997) 86 Geo L J 201-278.

Coates, JC 'Explaining Variations in Takeover Defences: Blame the Lawyers' (2001) 89 Cal L Rev 1301-1422.

Coffee, JC 'Understanding Enron: 'It's About the Gatekeepers, Stupid' (2002) 57 Bus Law 1403-1420.

Cooter, RD and T Ginsburg 'Comparative Judicial Discretion' (1996) 16 Int'l Rev L & Econ 295-313.

Davies, P 'Enron and Corporate Governance Reforms in the UK and European Community' in J Armour and JA McCahery (eds) *After Enron: Improving Corporate Law and Modernising Securities Regulation in Europe and the US* (Hart Publishing 2006).

Deminor Ratings 'Application of the One-Share-One-Vote Principle in Europe' (2005).

Dixit, A and J Londregan 'Ideology, Tactics, and Efficiency in Redistributive Politics' (1998) 113 Quart J Econ 497-529.

Easterbrook, F and DR Fischel *The Economic Structure of Corporate Law* (Harvard University Press 1991).

Eisenberg, T, N LaFountain, B Ostrom, D Rottman and MT Wells 'Juries, Judges, and Punitive Damages: An Empirical Study' (2002) 87 Cornell Law Review 743-782.

European Policy Forum 'Reducing the Regulatory Burden: The Arrival of Meaningful Regulatory Impact Analysis' (2004a).

European Policy Forum 'Implementing EU Directives: A Least Cost Working Model' (2004b).

Glaeser, EL 'Psychology and the Market' (2004) 94 Amer Econ Rev 408-23.

Hansmann, H and R Kraakman 'Toward Unlimited Shareholder Liability for Corporate Torts' (1991) 100 Yale L J 1879-934.

Hart, O and J Moore 'The Governance of Exchanges: Members' Cooperatives vs. Outside Ownership' (1996) 12 Oxford Rev Econ Pol 53-69.

Heine, K 'Regulatory Competition Between Company Laws in the European Union: the Überseering Case' (2003) 38 Intereconomics 102-108.

Hersch, J and WK Viscusi 'Punitive Damages: How Judges and Juries Perform' (2004) 33 J Leg Stud 1-36.

Hertig, G 'Efficient Fostering of EU Regulatory Competition' (2004) 76 Swiss Review of Business Law 360-371.

Hertig, G and R Lee 'Four Predictions about the Future of Securities Regulation' (2003) 3 J Corp L Stud 359-377.

Hertig, G and JA McCahery 'Company and Takeover Law Reforms in Europe: Misguided Harmonization Efforts or Regulatory Competition' (2003) 4 Eur Bus Org L Rev 179-212.

Hertig, G and JA McCahery 'An Agenda for Reform: Company and Takeover Law in Europe' in G Ferrarini, KJ Hopt, J Winter and E Wymeersch (eds) *Reforming Company and Takeover Law in Europe* (Oxford University Press 2004) 21-49.

Hopt, KJ 'European Company Law and Corporate Governance: Where Does the Action Plan of the European Commission Lead?' (ECGI Law wp No. 52/2005 <http://www.ssrn.com/abstract_id=863527>, 2005).

Hyytinen, A and T Takalo 'Corporate Law and Small Business Finance: Mandatory v. Enabling Rules' (2005) 6 Eur Bus Org L Rev 449-468.

Jain, P, JC Kim and Z Rezaee 'The Effect of The Sarbanes-Oxley Act of 2002 on Market Liquidity' (SSRN wp <http://www.ssrn.com/abstract_id=488142>, 2004).

Jensen, MC and WH Meckling 'Theory of the Firm: Managerial Behavior, Agency Costs and Ownership Structure' (1976) 3 J Finan Econ 305-60.

Jolls, C and CR Sunstein 'Debiasing Through Law' (SSRN wp <http://www.ssrn.com/abstract_id=590929>, 2005).

Korobkin, R 'The Endowment Effect and Legal Analysis' (2003) 97 Nw U Rev 1227-1293.

Lo, AW 'Reconciling Efficient Markets with Behavioral Finance: The Adaptive Market Hypothesis' (SSRN wp <http://www.ssrn.com/abstract_id=728864>).

McCahery, JA, L Renneboog, P Ritter and S Haller 'The Economics of the Proposed Takeover Bids Directive' in G Ferrarini, KJ Hopt, J Winter and E Wymeersch (eds) *Reforming Company and Takeover Law in Europe* (Oxford University Press 2004) 575-646.

O'Hara, EA 'Opting Out of Regulation: A Public Choice Analysis of Contractual Choice of Law' (2000) 53 Vand L Rev 1551-1575.

Plott, CR and K Zeiler 'The Willingness to Pay – Willingness to Accept Gap, the "Endowment Effect", Subject Misconceptions, and Experimental Procedures for Eliciting Valuations' (2005) 95 Amer Econ Rev 530-545.

Pollack, M *The Engines of European Integration, Delegation, Agency, and Agenda Setting in the EU* (Oxford University Press 2003).

Posner, E 'Economic Analysis of Contract Law After Three Decades: Success or Failure' (2003) 112 Yale L J 829-880.

Rachlinski, JJ and CR Farina 'Cognitive Psychology and Optimal Government Design' (2002) 87 Cornell L Rev 549-615.

Schön, W 'EC Company Statute and Taxation: Tax Issues and Constraints to Reorganizations and Reincorporations in the EU' (Max Planck Institute wp 2003).

Sunstein, CR 'Switching the Default Rule' (2002) 77 NY U L Rev 106-134.

Vermeulen, EP *The Evolution of Legal Business Forms in Europe and the United States* (Kluwer Law International 2003).

West MD (2001) 'Why Shareholder Sue: The Evidence from Japan' 30 J Legal Stud 351-382.

Wouters, J 'European Company Law: Quo Vadis' (2000) 37 Common Market Law Review 257-307.

Wymeersch, E 'Enforcement of Corporate Governance Codes' (ECGI wp No. 46/2005 <http://www.ssrn.com/abstract_id=759364>, 2005).

How Can Corporate Governance Codes Be Implemented?

EDDY WYMEERSCH*

In most European States, corporate governance rules are laid down in self regulatory instruments, drawn up by different types of specialists or practitioners (academic, stock exchanges, business associations). Legislators have most of the time refrained from intervening in this matter. However, a great variety of factual situations exist: in some States, the corporate governance code is a mere recommendation, without any enforcement mechanism, in others the code is part of the listing conditions. In Germany and the Netherlands, the companies act makes express reference to the governance code, without incorporating it. It is understood that outside monitors (such as auditors, securities commission and the like) would only check whether the company has acknowledged the code, but would not verify substantive compliance. The different enforcement instruments are reviewed, going from market-led enforcement, enforcement by civil law instruments, or by name and shame techniques. Most systems are based on the 'comply and explain' technique, which is also recommended by the European Corporate Governance Forum. In some States, the securities commission has recently been charged with an unclear mandate for supervising compliance.

A. Regulating Corporate Governance
B. Enforcing Corporate Governance Codes
C. Conclusion

Corporate governance has become a central subject in numerous economic policies all over the world. Good governance – both by public institutions and by private business – is considered one of the building blocks upon which economic success is based. Hence the efforts undertaken by many international[1] and national organisations and bodies to improve governance, especially by enacting rules, standards or recommendations that have to be respected, or which can serve as conduct models for directors of these institutions and businesses alike.

* Professor at the University of Ghent Law School, Member of the European Corporate Governance Forum, Chairman of the Belgian Banking, Securities and Insurance Supervisor. The paper expresses only personal opinions.

[1] OECD 'Corporate Governance Principles' (2004) <http://www.oecd.org/dataoecd/32/18/31557724.pdf>. The OECD principles have served as a direct and explicitly mentioned source for some of the national codes, e.g. the Czech Corporate Governance Code (2004) <http://www.sec.cz/export/EN/Publications/get_dms_file.do?FileId=1253>.

Corporate governance is a subject that is notoriously difficult to define in one sentence. Some view corporate governance in the narrow sense, as dealing with the structure and functioning of the boards of directors, and their relationship to management. This narrow definition is the one often found in corporate governance codes. A broader definition includes relationships with shareholders, especially in firms with concentrated ownership. Finally academic studies dealing with governance broaden the angle to all internal relationships within the firm, including the issues raised by the conduct of shareholders, especially institutional investors, the functioning of the general meeting and the relationship with the financial markets. As the subject of the present study relates to the implementation of the corporate governance codes and not to their substance, the narrow definition will be followed.[2]

A. Regulating Corporate Governance

I. Companies Acts v. Governance Codes

Rules relating to corporate governance are usually of a mixed nature: the basic rules are laid down in statutory instruments, usually the companies' act. This act determines e.g. whether there should be a one or a two tier board, whether management is part of the board, and how conflicts of interest are dealt with. More complex topics like the rules on takeover bids also contain often crucially important elements of corporate governance.[3] Apart from the companies act, securities regulation should be mentioned, especially as it contains the basis for the disclosure rules, which are the usual vectors for enforcing corporate governance codes.

In addition to the statutory rules, governance rules and practices are often imposed by the stock exchange on which the shares of the company are traded. The articles of association of the company as well as internal rules of the board of directors may also contain governance provisions. Traditions and good practice in a given jurisdiction should not remain unmentioned.

Recently, a need has been felt to streamline and coordinate these more informal sources of corporate governance into 'codes', a somewhat ambitious terminology for what is essentially rules of good practice, or 'conduct of business rules', as these were referred to in the Cadbury Code, the first authoritative in-

[2] See also E Wymeersch 'Enforcing Corporate Governance Codes' (ECGI Law wp No. 46/2005 <http://ssrn.com/abstract=759364>, 2005) and (2006) 1 JCLS forthcoming.

[3] One could refer here to Articles 9 and 11 of the Directive 2004/25/EC of the European Parliament and of the Council of 21 April 2004 on Takeover Bids, OJ L142 30.04.2004 12-23.

strument in this field.[4] These codes should not be considered as being equivalent to law, or to contractual provisions relating to governance.

II. A Short Typology of Corporate Governance Codes

Looking at the different 'codes' that have been drawn up in Europe, one will find that these are of sometimes considerably varying content, legal status, origin, while their implementation may be founded on different techniques. Although the subject of this paper relates to the implementation and enforcement of the codes, these are directly related to their origin and their legal status. As to their ambit, corporate governance codes most of the time only relate to listed companies, although one also finds codes addressed to unlisted ones, especially family owned companies.[5] Governance by – fully or partially – state owned firms is another subject.[6] The latter will not be included in this survey.

As to the origin and legal status of the codes, several models can be distinguished.

In a first series of cases the code was the result of a private initiative, often originating either from academia,[7] or from the leading association of business firms.[8] These 'recommendations', as they sometimes are referred to, would have a mainly moral value, being presented as the way governance should be dealt with but without a clear technically binding force. This does not mean however that these instruments have no value: they serve as an example to the business community, and violation of its precepts will often be stigmatised as a violation of rules of good behaviour. Sometimes, external sources – academia, newspapers

[4] Most of the codes that have been released worldwide can be found on the website of the European Corporate Governance Institute (<http://www.ecgi.org/codes/all_codes.php>).

[5] Reference is made to unlisted companies to which the principles of the code is declared of use: see the Czech Code <http://www.sec.cz/export/EN/Publications/get_dms_file.do?FileId=1253>.

[6] See OECD 'OECD Guidelines on Corporate Governance of State-Owned Enterprises' (13 October 2005) <http://www.oecd.org/dataoecd/46/51/34803211.pdf>.

[7] This was the case in Germany where a group of academics published a first corporate governance code: Corporate Governance Grundssätze, a Frankfurt Initiative, Der Betrieb 2000, 238 and Berliner Initiativkreis, Der Betrieb, 2000, 1573. See M Lutter 'Deutscher Corporate Governance Codex' in P Hommelhoff, KJ Hopt and A von Werder (eds) *Handbuch Corporate Governance* (Otto Schmidt 2003) s. 737.

[8] See M Lutter (n 7). See e.g. for France 'The Principles for Corporate Governance' (October 2003) amalgamating the 1995 and 1999 Viénot and 2002 Bouton Reports; compare 'Code sur le gouvernement d'entreprise d'Economie Suisse' published by Fédération des enterprises suisses. See the comparative study by K Hofstetter 'Le gouvernement d'entreprise en Suisse – Rapport final du groupe d'experts sur le gouvernement d'entreprise' (July 2002) <http://www.economiesuisse.ch/f/content.cfm?upid=8F83D036-FABC-4C77-99CBC0C5536D0D8C&type=pdf&filety pe =pdf>.

– would publish lists identifying to what extent the code has been followed and identify shortcomings by specific companies, using some form of public pillory technique. Strikingly, the 'comply or explain' technique is usually not found in this type of governance recommendation. One could qualify this model as 'voluntary' regulation.

A second series of cases relates to governance codes that have a direct link with the securities markets. In a mild form, the code has been drawn up under the aegis of the stock exchange,[9] or by a committee mandated by the exchange.[10] In the stronger form, the code is mentioned as a listing condition, enabling the exchange to refuse non-complying companies, but not necessarily allowing it to impose the code on already listed companies. Here one will find that non-compliant companies have to explain the reasons for non-compliance.

According to a third type, the code will have some link with the public authorities. This link is very diverse: in some cases the initiative to draw up a code was made by the Ministry of Finance or of Justice, or the drafting committee appointed by the Ministry,[11] or with the participation of the ministry, or sometimes also with the participation of the market supervisor. Although this type of code has no legal standing in itself, it draws its authority from the support of the public authorities and the quality of its draftsmen. Publication in the Official Journal contributes to the authority of the code, but does not change its legal standing as a non mandatory instrument.[12] A monitoring committee may ensure compliance with the code, not on a company by company basis, but in overall terms.[13]

In a further model, a more explicit link is established with the legislation. In Germany and in the Netherlands the companies' act contains an express reference to the governance code. Listed companies are legally obliged to adhere to the code, and can only derogate by stating their reasons. This type of incorporation of the code into the companies' act raises difficult questions of enforcement, to which we will turn later.

The business community, especially institutional investors, will attach importance to these codes which, even if not fully binding, will be part of investors' as-

[9] See the Budapest Stock Exchange 'Corporate Governance Recommendation 2004' <http: //www.bse.hu/gfx/download.arg?ptype=FILE&id=10013558&uio=4LONG1GAN3B42006801J 127Z20I31326KBX6SEZ05guest>; in Slovakia, the 2002 Code is the product of a cooperation of the Stock Exchange and the Associations of Company Directors and Managers <http://www. cecga.org/core.php?sid=0&lang=2&f=pages&p=showpage&s=docs>.

[10] This was the case for the original Belgian code, named after its chairman Code Cardon.

[11] This was the case for the Netherlands Tabaksblat Code <http://www.commissiecorporate governance.nl/Nieuws#Nieuws_526>. Also in Spain: see infra (n 48).

[12] This is the case for the Slovenian Code (see <http://www.ljse.si/cgi-bin/jve.cgi?att=3313 &sid=>). Also the German Code was published in the official Gazette of the German Republic, but the reference is part of the German Companies Act.

[13] See the Dutch Frijns Committee, which has published its first report: <http://corpgov.nl/ Rapport%20Monitoring%20Commissie>.

sessment of the issuer's shares, and hence influence their willingness to invest in these shares. These codes are sometimes referred to as 'self-regulatory', but the term is rather ambiguous, as the degree of voluntary involvement of the regulated firms is extremely variable.

A final case would be the one in which the code would be referred to in the law and is supervised by a government body, more specifically the securities market supervisor. Although the practice is not clear, this seems to be the approach followed in Spain.[14] Depending on the way the supervision is exercised, one may come close to traditional company law.

The full statutory approach is the one followed in the US with the Sarbanes-Oxley Act. The rigidity of this regulation has often been regretted. In the U.S. too, there still is room for self regulatory instruments in this field.[15]

The dividing line between soft regulation and hard law is a shifting one. From a comparative review of the codes published in most EU Member States, one can see a relatively large variety: in the old Member States, codes focus on the functioning of the board, leaving company law questions aside. In the new Member States the codes broaden to issues of company law in general.[16] In one case the code is even composed of three columns, one relating to the 'corresponding' company law provision, one being the code, and the third commentary.[17]

Most of the time one sees 'advancing juridification', whereby at least the principle is laid down in the law, while the detailed rules of functioning would be left to internal, soft law rules. Independent directors and audit committees are recommended in most codes: the former have been the subject of an EU recommendation, while the principle of having an audit committee or a similar function is laid down in the amended 4th company law Directive. Further details will be left to the companies themselves.[18] Similar other cases of 'mutation' of soft law rules are known, in which case law may also play a role.

[14] This seems to be the case in Spain, where the securities supervisors seems to verify also the conformity of certain substantive requirements with the clearly stated provisions of the code. Adde: the 2006 Italian Codice di Autodisciplina and Articles 123-bis and 123-ter of the Legisltative Decree 58/1998 (Testo Unico della Finanza).

[15] See the NYSE 'Corporate Governance Rules' (November 2003).

[16] So e.g. are elements of group law, or on auditing mentioned in the Slovak Code, while the Czech Code includes in its addressees the rating agencies, custodians, auditors and institutional investors.

[17] See the code of the Budapest Stock Exchange (n 9). As to the effectiveness of the codes in the Central European States, see N Cankar 'Transition Economies and Corporate Governance Codes: Can Self-regulation of Corporate Governance Really Work?' (2005) 5 JCLS 285, who raises doubts as to the outcome on the basis of the existing concentrated share ownership structure.

[18] Following a political compromise however the rule has been formulated in a much broader wording.

III. 'Comply or Explain'

One of the essential differences between corporate governance codes and traditional company law is the fact that even though it is binding as a requirement – which is but rarely the case[19] – it is not binding in substance. This feature lies at the basis of the famous 'comply or explain' principle.[20] Firms subject to the code are invited or obliged to adhere to the code: in practice, they cannot 'just say no'. However, they are not bound to follow the provisions of the code on any given item. If the firms deem it preferable to set aside a specific provision of the code, they may do so provided they state reasons. This is the 'explain' alternative. According to the 'comply' principle, by stating the objectives that firms have to reach, codes introduce significant flexibility in the system, and allow taking account of the myriad of individual situations. Codes are an incentive for companies to grow towards better governance practices without having to revolutionise their internal structures and procedures. This dynamic function should not be underestimated: often it is said that 'corporate governance' is more about method, than about substance.

'Comply or explain' has one obvious drawback: if companies are free to set aside the provisions of the code, provided they publish some sort of explanation, will this explanation be true and reliable, and can companies subtract themselves from the detailed requirements of the code by giving general, boilerplate explanations? In other words, should codes not be made legally mandatory, and who will verify whether the explanation is true and meaningful?

IV. The Role of Disclosure

In most corporate governance 'codes', disclosure plays a central role: companies disclose, in their annual report, how they deal with corporate governance issues. If requirements have been 'codified', this information will have to conform to the code's provisions.

Third parties will be able to assess the company's position v.à.v. the applicable governance regime, and to identify its shortcomings. More generally, markets attach increasing importance to corporate governance disclosures, while companies are more and more aware of the effect their governance may have on their market evaluation. Disclosure therefore is a key element in all code driven governance systems, while conversely markets will strongly influence the governance practices.

[19] As mentioned further this is the case in Germany and in the Netherlands.

[20] The principle is expressly mentioned in the Belgian, Hungarian, Spanish and Polish codes. It is part of the companies act in Germany and in the Netherlands.

B. Enforcing Corporate Governance Codes

As almost all existing corporate governance codes are of a non-statutory nature, their binding force cannot be based on the usual legal techniques for enforcing the law, i.e. liabilities, injunctions, fines, imprisonment, or any other coercitive technique found in national law. Generally soft law rules have to rely on the voluntary behaviour of their addressees. Although voluntary in essence, this does not mean that there are no strong incentives for companies to comply with the codes. The sanctions will then essentially be economical or financial, not legal. To what extent these incentives will suffice to ensure effective implementation of the codes is often doubted, but difficult to affirm or deny for lack of empirical data. At present in many jurisdictions there are very sophisticated comparative data – some even on a cross-border basis – analysing the formal implementation of the code's provisions, e.g. by indicating how many companies have designated independent directors, or have appointed audit committees.[21] Whether these directors are effectively independent, or whether the audit committee adequately performs its tasks is much more difficult to assess. This is the debate between 'formal' and 'substantive' implementation of the codes, which is currently in progress in Europe. The debate has taken a political turn: in some states, the legislator has intervened by requiring that at least formal adoption of the code should be ensured. In other jurisdictions, the law maker would like to go further: should the securities supervisor not be involved, and check substantive compliance with the code, as seems to be the case in Spain, or should legal remedies – such as director's liability – not be attached to violations of the code?

There are numerous instruments and techniques that support the voluntary implementation of corporate governance rules. Most of these create incentives for companies to abide by the codes' provisions. Market pressure and the fear of reputation damage will often suffice for business leaders to adhere to the code. But some of these techniques present a harder face: although not part of the law as such, corporate governance codes do not function in a legal vacuum: the relationship with the existing legal system should be clarified. Finally, in some states, a formal link with the companies act has been introduced. This has also raised the

[21] See A von Werder 'Kodex Report 2005: Die Akzeptanz der Empfehlungen und Anregungen des Deutschen Corporate Governance Kodex' (2005) Der Betrieb 841; Assonime 'Analisi delle stato di attuazione del Codice di Autodisciplina delle società quotate (Anno 2005)' (Note e Studi No. 68) (December 2005) <http://www2.assonime.it:81/assonime/corpgov/ca.nsf/103/FF407677E7692B89C12571400031DC15/$File/testo_e_appendice_analisi_2005.pdf?OpenElement>; for France: 'Rapport de l'AMF sur le gouvernement d'entreprise et les procedures de contrôle interne' (13 January 2005) Revue AMF; see on the Belgian code <http://www.corporategovernancecommittee.be/en/corporate_governance_code/final_code/default.aspx> and subsequent comparative studies by the CBFA <http://www.cbfa.be/nl/publications/stu/stu.asp>. Deminor, a consultancy firm specialising in the protection of minority shareholders, also has established comparative tables covering several European jurisdictions <http://www.deminor.be/articles.do?id=3491>.

question to what extent these obligations can be supervised by the securities supervisors.

I. Incentives for Complying with the Corporate Governance Codes

Under this heading, a certain number of techniques are regrouped that create incentives for implementing the code. They have in common that these are not legal instruments while their effectiveness may greatly vary with the specific circumstances in which they are put to work. A director's concern for his reputation for instance may differ considerably not only from state to state, but also over time. Many of the techniques are put to work simultaneously, but not in all given cases.

The starting point is the initial responsibility of the board of directors to ensure that – within the applicable legal framework – the company's corporate governance is well balanced and in accordance with the applicable code. Hence the board should be paying sufficient attention to its own functioning, look into the contribution of each of its members, and evaluate its governance from time to time. Mechanisms should be introduced that ensure these objectives, e.g. by proceeding to self assessment, appointing a separate corporate governance committee within the board or call on external expertise.

The board should report on its governance and on the attention it has paid to it. This is the 'governance statement', which will become mandatory pursuant to a European directive.[22] Disclosing the report brings with it external responsibility, whether to shareholders, or to markets in general: apart from reputation risk, directors may become liable towards the company and towards third parties if the statement contains untrue facts, or is likely to mislead them. It may also trigger the intervention of the securities supervisor.

To what extent shareholders should be involved in this process differs considerably: in most codes, they are informed about the governance statement, but do not approve it, at least not formally.[23] In two tier board systems, the supervisory board – but not the general meeting – usually approves the statement. With respect to certain items, for example the designation of an independent director, the shareholders would be more directly involved: his election by the general meeting would give credibility to his qualification as an independent director. However, involvement of the shareholders will usually be considered as interference in the functioning of the board, and hence incompatible with the structural model of the company. Rather exceptionally, shareholders may have some say in developing

[22] See further Section C.III..

[23] If it is part of the annual report, the approval of the latter would cover the corporate governance statement. One could discuss whether this approval includes agreement with the governance statement contained therein.

specific governance, i.e. in cases where governance rules would be laid down in the articles of incorporation. In public companies, this is seldom if ever the case. Although no cases are known, boards may be fired if the statement – differently from the actual governance practices – is deemed utterly unsatisfactory by the general meeting, as this may have a negative influence on the share price, and undermine market confidence.

Should the auditor not be involved in verifying the corporate governance statement? In many jurisdictions he is an organ of the company and has intimate knowledge of its functioning. The responses found in the different systems vary considerably: in some states his intervention is considered part of the verification process leading to the annual accounts and report, of which the governance statement is part. In others it is stated that he should limit himself to verifying the figures that are mentioned in the report. But in any case, his intervention can only cover whether in accordance with the provisions of the code the required disclosures are made, but not whether the information is true or accurate. Here too, his intervention is merely formal, and does not cover substance.[24]

One of the strongest enforcement devices is the appreciation of a company's governance by the outside world. This underlines the importance of the disclosure obligation, whether of the governance statement or of other any other disclosures that are relevant from a governance point of view. By imposing disclosure, the codes expose the company and its board to justification, outside criticism and most importantly to market evaluation. In general, board members can be expected to protect their reputational capital and will voluntary adhere to good governance practices, even in the absence of formal codes. The media have become more alert to these issues and regularly expose blatant shortcomings. Pressure from peers should not be underestimated, as weak governance practices on one board may spill over to damage the reputation of other boards. More important is the pressure of the 'markets', with this notion being understood here in its broadest sense, including as it does all actors intervening in the capital markets: stock exchanges, rating agencies, investment bankers, proxy organisations, activist investors and their advisors, the media, public opinion and so on.[25] The most direct effect will be on the company's rating: rating agencies have recently begun to include governance in their rating criteria, with some developing specialised ratings that specifically address a company's governance. Investment bankers in charge of placing securities may also take a close look at governance, while consultants and lawyers in general will advocate compliance with the applicable governance code. These professionals will not bet their highly valued reputation on deficient governance of a company they are financially engaged with.

The effect of good governance on price formation is controversial in the sense that it is empirically very difficult to prove that good governance has a positive

[24] For further details, see E Wymeersch (n 2).

[25] This is the case for the Italian, French, Belgian, Swedish and Swiss codes.

impact on price formation, whereas it is far clearer that 'bad' governance has a negative impact as it undermines the market's confidence in the company.[26] In the same sense, the publication of incomplete, or worse, untrue facts in the governance report, is likely to severely damage company reputation, and affect its stock price.

Among investors, institutional investors should especially be mentioned as often they are obliged to vote at the general meeting and hence take a public stand on governance issues. They will hesitate to acquire shares in issuers whose practices do not adhere to usual governance standards. When these issues are voted on – e.g. introducing a poison pill, or other techniques allowing management to entrench itself – these investors will generally instruct a proxy organisation to vote against the proposals. In Europe we have not yet seen the abrasive techniques practised by U.S. institutionals putting the worst governed companies on a black list, thereby exercising considerable pressure on the board. But one sees that in Europe too, institutionals – and more recently hedge funds – are putting boards under increasing pressure also on governance issues.

Often corporate governance codes are linked to stock exchanges: the exchange has a clear interest that the companies it admits to trading are complying with good governance standards and hence deserve a high quality label. Therefore governance conditions are often found in listing rules.[27] Upon access, the exchange will usually be able to enforce its rules. To maintain abidance to the rules, or to impose them on already listed companies will be more difficult. Apart from 'name and shame', the exchange could delist its shares. In practice delisting is not an option, due to the damage that it will inflict to investors. Therefore some exchanges follow a softer approach and motivate companies to adhere to its code.

[26] A positive correlation was stated by P Coombes and M Watson 'Three Surveys on Corporate Governance' (2000) 4 The McKinsey Quarterly 74, which allegedly showed a positive correlation. Compare E Nowak, R Rott and TG Mahr 'Wer den Kodex nicht einhält, den bestraft der Kapitalmarkt?' (2005) Zeitschrift für Unternehmens und Gesellschaftsrecht ZGR 252. However, Roberta Romano carried out a substantial investigation into the effects of the Sarbanes-Oxley Act and its relative inefficiency. See R Romano 'The Sarbanes-Oxley Act and the Making of Quack Corporate Governance' (ECGI Finance wp No. 52/2004 <http://ssrn.com/abstract=596101>, 2004).

[27] This is the case with the Governance Code of the Budapest Stock Exchange, 2004. The UK case is different as the governance codes are part of the listing conditions, including important governance rules dealing e.g. with significant and controlling shareholders and conflicts of interest. These were self regulatory before but the competence has been transferred to the UK Listing Authority, exercised by the FSA. The consequences of this change of standing of the rules is unclear. The Euronext Amsterdam has decided that the Tabaksblat Code would take precedence over its own rules within the securities listing procedure <http://www.euronext.com/file/view/0,4245,1626_53424_607848262,00.pdf>.

Some even organise education and training of directors and investor relations specialists.[28] Here the carrot will win over the stick.

External monitoring may document the degree of implementation by the listed companies taken as a group. Reports on monitoring illustrate good practice and will stimulate other companies to adopt similar conduct. Here again peer pressure and pressure from the media will be important. This monitoring is sometimes done spontaneously for example by academics,[29] by associations of listed companies,[30] by consultancy firms[31] or even by the securities supervisor.[32] In a couple of cases, the monitoring committee was the direct continuation of the committee that drew up the governance rules.[33] The role of these committees is not to verify the compliance by individual companies, but to screen the overall practice in a given jurisdiction. The committee will publish its assessment, usually on an aggregate basis. It could also recommend changes to the code. This type of monitoring committee has been introduced in the Netherlands, in France, in Switzerland and in a different form in the UK.[34] One may wonder whether a monitoring committee could use the 'name and shame' technique with respect to companies that refuse to conform to its orders to comply with the code. The rules on libel or slander would most of the time prevent this approach. Official review panels could take a stronger stand, as the law would authorise them to publish the names of the recalcitrant companies.

Little analysis has been undertaken on the use of governance criteria in connection with loan conditions. Sometimes the loan documentation will contain explicit clauses that can be classified under the governance heading, such as the need to have a sufficient number of independent directors on the board, the requirement for a formal audit committee, and rules on transfer pricing or on substantial transactions. Well known are conditions on the change of control, as this

[28] This aspect is mentioned in the Polish Code (<http://www.gpw.com.pl/zrodla/gpw/pdf/Best2005.pdf>).

[29] A von Werder (n 21) reporting annually on the implementation of the German Code by listed companies and illustrating the continuous adaptation of issuers to the new standards.

[30] Assonime (n 21).

[31] See Deminor (n 21) and Deminor 'Trends and Ratings 2003' <http://www.deminor.org/articles.do?id=1326>. See the report of Ethical Investors Research Services (EIRIS) 'How Good is Global Corporate Governance' (August 2005) <http://corpgov.nl/page/downloads/corpgov05.pdf>.

[32] For France and Belgium (n 21).

[33] This was the case for the Dutch Frijns Committee.

[34] The Financial Reporting Council, an independent regulator for corporate reporting and governance, from 1 April 2004 is in charge of setting, monitoring and enforcing accounting and auditing standards. Its task has been widened to include the promotion of high corporate governance standards by monitoring and maintaining the Combined Code and associated guidance. The FRC acts without an explicit statutory base, although reference is made to the rules on listing on the exchange, which require compliance with the Code.

may lead to accelerating the loan. Also state contracts, or subsidies may be made contingent upon respecting a certain number of good governance rules. One could imagine that large creditors would be interested to know that the company is run according to the prevailing governance concepts and more specifically in accordance with the applicable code. These covenants may therefore be considered as another monitoring device.

The substantive effectiveness of the aforementioned enforcement instruments cannot be clearly established: the empirical studies, although containing very valuable information, indicate whether the separate provisions of the codes have been addressed, but do not yield reliable information as to the substance of implementation.[35] If implementation has been formally compliant, but is substantively unsatisfactory, ultimately only the board of directors would be able to identify the shortcomings and to impose corrective action. Therefore the question arises whether the legal order should not step in and prescribe stronger medicines: a short overview of present thinking in this matter follows.

II. Legal Rules Specifically Ensuring Compliance with the Corporate Governance Codes

Although corporate governances codes generally are not legally binding, being either voluntary or self-regulatory, there is little doubt that they have legal relevance. In case law, judges are likely to make reference to the codes when looking for guidance in matters that have not been dealt with in the law. They are likely to make reference to the code rather than determining themselves what is widely accepted business behaviour or 'good practice'. In order to determine whether directors have behaved with adequate care, this would be the usual standard. But also outside the field of directors' liability, the same criterion might be used, for instance in deciding whether to apply remedies related to wrongful trading, or according to some state laws, opting for a judicial enquiry.[36] This phenomenon of absorption of soft law rules by the legal system has been witnessed in several soft law fields, and is nothing else than a technique for filling in blank

[35] The assessment made by the Frijns Committee in the Netherlands was considered in the press too optimistic: see comment reproduced on <http://www.ey.nl/?pag=788&nieuws_id=2488>.

[36] On the basis of Article 2 (345) of the Dutch civil code, the court can mandate an investigation ('enquête') about the 'management and state of affairs' ('beleid en gang van zaken') of any company, allowing the court to take measures in case of 'mismanagement' ('wanbeleid'). One cannot exclude that grave violations of important principles or provisions of the corporate governance code be interpreted as constituting 'mismanagement'. This notion would include acting against the 'elementary principles of responsible entrepreneurship': 'elementaire beginselen van verantwoord ondernemerschap'. OK, 21 June 1979, NJ, 1980, 71 (Batco) and HR 10 January 1990, NJ, 1990, 446 (Ogem).

norms in the legal system. 'Good faith', liability for violating the duty of care, general principles like the Dutch 'reasonable and equitable conduct' ('redelijkheid en billijkheid') are the usual entry points through which the legal order absorbs elements drawn from soft law, such as professional conduct of business rules, 'state of the art' techniques, model contracts, and other rules grown out of business practice. Now that the corporate governance rules have been written down, 'codified' and supported by leading businessmen, by the stock exchanges or with the support of the securities commission, it is obvious that the judge will refer to them rather than apply rules of his own reasoning.

Although there are not many cases known where a reference to corporate governance principles have been mentioned, one should mention a Dutch Supreme Court case, in which the court considered that the obligation to consult shareholders in support of the company's decision on a takeover or other private reorganisation[37] has 'no legal basis in present law, nor in views accepted on corporate governance in the Netherlands'. A rule of that kind could not be accepted in the absence of a provision in the companies act or in the articles of association; and hence subscribing to such an obligation would lead to unacceptable uncertainty about the applicable law.[38] There is controversy in legal writing as to whether the Court's ruling allows taking into account generally accepted corporate governance rules,[39] or whether it should be considered as an insufficient basis for absorbing corporate governance rules into the law.[40]

The link with the legal system has been made explicit in the German and Dutch companies acts.[41] In both cases the companies act contains an express provision according to which listed companies have to publish an annual declaration, making express reference to the corporate governance code and declaring that it is respected while indicating which recommendations have not been followed.[42] The Dutch provision calls for an express motivation in case of non compliance. There is no doubt however that both systems adhere to the 'comply or explain' philosophy, but do not declare the substantive rules of the code applicable at law. Companies that did not formally adhere to the codes would hence violate the compa-

[37] This is not a widely accepted principle of corporate governance. It is part of the law in certain jurisdictions (e.g. the UK and the Netherlands).

[38] Hoge Raad, 21 February 2003, NJ, 2003, 182, nt.Ma (HBG case). Non literal translation.

[39] MC Schouten 'Toegang tot cassatie wegens schending van de Corporate Governance Code' (2004) 9 Vennootschap & Onderneming 142; also S Bartman 'De Code Tabaksblat: een juridisch lichtgewich' (2004) Ondernemingsrecht 125, referring to the Erdal decision. HR, 24 September 1976, NJ, 1978, 135, nt.BW.

[40] WJ Slagter 'De invloed van de voorstellen van de Commissie – Tabaksblat op de rechtspleging' (2004) NJB 976.

[41] Many commentaries and studies on the German and Dutch Acts have been published: for references see E Wymeersch (n 2).

[42] For a translated version of these two provisions, see E Wymeersch (n 2).

nies act, incurring the sanctions provided in that act.[43] Companies might also simply state that they adhere to the code without giving any further information. Usually companies are willing to explain in great detail their internal governance. The information so disclosed has to be approved by the board of directors and, where applicable, by the supervisory board. Should the information be untrue or false, this would trigger the liability of the members of these bodies, according to the general rules governing director's liability. However with respect to the substance of the information, the companies act contains no express provision: this is the sole responsibility of the board. Whether shareholders are allowed to have the board ordered to comply with the code will largely depend on the applicable company law: in many systems the shareholders are not entitled to intervene in the board's functioning and hence would not be entitled to impose a compliance order. Indirectly of course shareholders could threaten to dismiss the board. The Dutch corporate governance code – but not the companies act – states that the governance statement should be submitted to the general meeting and that significant changes should be discussed.

A difficult question relates to the consequences of deficient corporate governance statements. In this case, the board adheres to the code, and where applicable has published reasons for not complying with specific provisions. However, the motivation disclosed may be deficient in several respects: it may be futile, or boilerplate, it may state untrue or incomplete reasons, or finally the information may be misleading or even false.[44]

If the company publishes information it considers as a formal explanation, but which is intrinsically insufficient in justifying its non compliance with the code, there is no direct sanction applicable. Is it up to the general meeting to decide whether the board's statement is insufficient, and if so censure the board? The answer is likely to be no. But if the information is mandated by other provisions, for example, of company law, or should be published according to securities regulation, there might be a violation of these provisions. In this context, one should recall the obligation to publish price-sensitive information.[45]

In the case of untrue, or incomplete or even misleading information, basically the rules on board liability for disclosure would apply.[46] Untrue or misleading statements would expose directors to liability both towards the legal entity and towards third parties on the basis of the general rules on negligence. Whether

[43] It runs contrary to the law if the board 'just said no'.

[44] Once more this is the difference between formal and substantive compliance with the code.

[45] See Article 6 of the Directive 2003/6/EC of the European Parliament and of the Council of 28 January 2003 on Insider Dealing and Market Manipulation (market abuse), OJ L96 12.04.2003 16-25.

[46] For a very extensive study of these subjects, see KJ Hopt and HC Voigt (eds) *Prospekt- und Kapitalmarktinformationshaftung* (Mohr Siebeck 2005).

these would be effectively applicable, and what the consequences might be, depends on national law. In some legal systems, if the violated rules belong to the companies act, a stricter liability regime would apply: this would not be the case with a violation of the corporate governance code, as it is not part of company law. In other systems, only gross negligence or an intentional violation would lead to liability.[47]

In some jurisdictions, the question has been debated to what extent the securities supervisor should not be involved in monitoring the implementation of the corporate governance codes. Indeed securities supervisors have a privileged contact with listed companies. They already review some of the company's disclosures. As the governance statements often are part of the annual reports, it seems logical to charge the securities supervisors with this competence. This seems to be the approach followed in Spain, where the securities supervisor checks whether some of the substantive requirements of the code are met, e.g. whether directors meet the provisions on independence as precisely spelled out in the code, or whether the age limit – if any – is respected.[48]

According to the debate in some jurisdictions, especially in the Netherlands, the securities supervisor could only be involved in checking the formal conformity of the corporate governance statement with the code, but not its content. The content should be entirely left to the board of directors who are in charge and take responsibility for running the company. It should be avoided that indirectly the governance codes becomes part of the law, eliminating any flexibility that was originally aimed for. The role of the external monitors – securities commissions, review panels, etc – should remain defined within the limits of 'external review'. This would not prevent the securities supervisor from exercising its other legal competences, such as verifying whether the factual elements in the annual report – e.g. on directors' remuneration – are true, irrespective of whether these elements are part of the corporate governance statement or not.

Finally some opinions prefer to confer express legal status to the governance codes. By writing the governance rules into the law, they destroy the typical advantages of the soft law codes: adaptability, flexibility and the search for better solutions. However, with respect to specific items, if it has become apparent that the code provisions have not been effective, and that the business community refuses to abide, the law has to step in. This is the lesson that can be drawn from the German experience: the refusal by a large part of the business community to publish data on director's remuneration has led to a formal law, imposing such a dis-

[47] KJ Hopt and HC Voigt (n 46) 127. P Hommelhoff and M Schwab 'Regelungsquellen und Regelungsebenen der Corporate Governance: Gesetz, Satzung, Codices, unternehmensinterne Grundsätze' in P Hommelhoff, KJ Hopt and A von Werder (n 7) 69.

[48] A new Spanish Code has been published for consultation: 'Proyecto de Codigo Unificado de Recomendaciones sobre buen Gobierno de las sociédades cotizadas' (18 January 2006) <http://www.cnmv.es/index.htm>.

closure. One can hope that enlightened business leaders elsewhere will not follow such a path.

III. The Amendments to the 4th and 7th Directive.

Recently the EU adopted a Commission Proposal for a Directive amending the 4th and 7th company law Directives, and providing that listed companies should publish a 'corporate governance statement', whether as part of their annual reports, or in a separate report.[49] The content of the statement is defined in the directive as follows:

(i) reference to the mandatory corporate governance code; however a reference to a voluntary code may be allowed by company law. In addition, the statement should contain 'all necessary information about the corporate governance practices applied beyond the requirements under national law'.[50]

(ii) the 'comply or explain rule' for departures from a corporate governance code: this relates not only to specific provisions but to the code as a whole;

(iii) further information on internal controls and risk management systems; information about anti-takeover protections and on the way shareholders can exercise their voting rights.

The directive further calls for liability of the members of the boards for the corporate governance statement and by calling for penalties applicable to infringements of the implementing national provisions. Administrative sanctioning is not mentioned, but it is likely to constitute an effective enforcement instrument, provided it is clarified who is entitled to impose the fines.[51]

C. Conclusion

The enforcement of corporate governance codes is a complex matter. It creates a very special, and in many respects new relationship within the legal system,

[49] See proposed Article 46a of Proposal for a Directive of the European Parliament and of the Council amending Council Directives 78/660/EEC and 83/349/EEC concerning the Annual Accounts of Certain Types of Companies and Consolidated Accounts – New Revised Presidency Compromise' (22 April 2005) <http://www.focusifrs.com/content/FichiersFocusIfrs/ACTUALITE/actu_divers/Propos_modif_4-7_directive_04-2005.pdf>.

[50] This requirement seems rather unfortunate as it obliges companies to disclose what is voluntary practice thereby possibly triggering liability.

[51] See Article 60a of Compromise Proposal dated 2 June 2005. The final text of the directive, as adopted by Council and Parliament at the moment of writing still awaits publication.

whereby in some jurisdictions the code can be analysed as akin to a default rule:[52] the code and all its provisions are applicable, but the company can derogate if it wants to. In many jurisdictions the interplay between private and public law rules also constitutes a *novum* attracting intense academic interest.

Enforcement of corporate governance rules is a broader subject than enforcing the corporate governance codes: as there are many interconnections between the two, there will often be a certain mix of enforcement instruments applicable. Enforcing the codes will rely on these other instruments such as liability rules. These different levels of regulation – voluntary, charter provisions, legal backing, and express statutory provisions – coexist with unclear and shifting dividing lines.

In many jurisdictions the codes are voluntary, although not necessarily self regulatory: flexibility, adaptability, allowing experimentation and innovation are most of the time mentioned as the reasons for preferring voluntary instruments. Compliance is insured first and foremost by internal mechanisms: the board of directors and the management have to take responsibility for applying the code, under the guidance of the shareholders, acting individually or in the general meeting.

These codes are essentially market led: effectiveness of their external monitoring will depend on the overall efficiency of these 'markets' and on the leverage the markets can exercise. An active, investigative press can do wonders in enforcing a code provision. And active shareholders along with the increasing attention paid to governance ratings are powerful drivers for better governance.

Outside monitoring may be considered: first one should determine what is to be monitored? Here it is useful to distinguish formal from substantive compliance. It is widely admitted and practised that external monitors – be it the auditor, the supervisor, the regulated market, a review panel – could verify whether the company has formally declared to adhere to a code, or has published its statement declaring which provisions it has not followed. A substantive review, this is whether the provisions have in fact been followed and whether the explanation for not complying is a credible one, is generally considered impossible, and creates unjustified expectations, while leading to a formalistic attitude. Where it appears that specific options should be imposed, they should be laid down in the law, and the price for the rigidity should be paid.

Is a legal backing of the code, as is the case in Germany and in the Netherlands a useful model? In order to avoid a flat refusal to apply the code, it certainly would be. Even in the two mentioned cases, the same external monitoring remains necessary. It also adds very little with respect to the internal functioning of the board, which is the core of the corporate governance codes.

[52] S Berg and M Stöcker '(Haftungsfragen): Anwendungs- und Haftungsfragen zum Deutschen Corporate Governance Kodex' in W*ertpapier Mitteilungen (WM)*: *Zeitschrift für Wirtschafts- und Bankrecht*, s. 1571.

The law could step in and provide for appropriate sanctions. This is already the case for many specific governance rules that are part of the company laws. Should it be extended to the full range of governance codes? The American experience illustrates the burden and costs that a formal legal approach would create. But judicial enforcement is not necessarily stronger, as one can witness with existing statutory governance rules. However, for specific items, the law is sometimes needed to convince recalcitrant firms.

As choices have to be made between several conflicting objectives, the preference goes to market led enforcement, but alongside with the strengthening of the internal company monitoring mechanisms. The role of the shareholders and of the general meeting deserve to be strengthened: the minority shareholders' right of action, a better voting system, with proxy or remote voting, better disclosure obligations are company law instruments that will contribute to better surveillance of the company's management and to the accountability of the board. By establishing a stronger link between market led enforcement and these internal governance instruments the overall governance system is likely to be strengthened more than by imposing formal legal or administrative requirements. Inspiration can be sought in the recent initiatives of the European Commission on shareholder rights.[53]

On 22 February 2006, the European Corporate Governance Forum[54] published a statement on the 'comply and explain' technique, qualifying it as best suited for supporting good governance, for taking account of the differences that exist within the EU and allowing national governance systems to converge in practice, an aim that would be very difficult to achieve with statutory provisions.

The Forum stressed the board's role in insuring compliance with the codes: the board should review the governance statement and discuss with the shareholders the comply and explain applications. On the other hand the shareholders should take into account the governance statement upon casting their votes.

The external monitoring of the codes is addressed in the following terms: generally, states should support monitoring mechanisms, such as special commissions as the one that has been set up in the Netherlands. The regulators should only check the existence of the statement, and react to blatant misrepresentations of facts, but not engage in second-guessing of board decisions.

[53] See European Commission Internal Market and Services Directorate General 'Fostering an Appropriate Regime for Shareholders – Second Consultation' (13 May 2005) <http://europa.eu.int/comm/internal_market/company/docs/shareholders/consultation2_en.pdf>.

[54] See 'Statement of the European Corporate Governance Forum on the Comply-or-Explain Principle' (22 February 2006) <http://europa.eu.int/comm/internal_market/company/docs/ecg-forum/ecgf-comply-explain_en.pdf>.

Part 2:

The New European Regulation of Trading Venues

The MiFID: Competition in a New European Equity Market Regulatory Structure

RYAN DAVIES
ALFONSO DUFOUR
BRIAN SCOTT-QUINN*

In 2004, the European Council and Parliament adopted a new Directive on Markets in Financial Instruments (the 'MiFID'). The implementation of the Directive in EU Member States is still ongoing. We provide a framework for understanding some of the main features of this new regulatory structure. We summarize the economics of fragmentation and internalisation – issues that have been at the forefront of discussion throughout the MiFID consultation, approval and implementation process. We also provide lessons from the U.S. regulatory experience, with a special focus on U.S. trade reporting rules. We highlight relevant features of the largest European equity markets, describe the main features of the MiFID and provide recommendations on its implementation.

A. Introduction
B. Internalisation and Fragmentation
C. U.S. Regulatory Experience
D. European Landscape
E. The MiFID
F. Conclusion

A. Introduction

On 21 April 2004 the European Parliament and Council adopted the new Directive on Markets in Financial Instruments[1] (the 'MiFID'), which repeals the

* Davies is at Babson College; Dufour and Scott-Quinn are at the ICMA Centre, University of Reading.

Corresponding author: Alfonso Dufour, <a.dufour@icmacentre.rdg.ac.uk.> The authors are grateful to the European Capital Market Institute (ECMI) for supporting the original research conducted for this paper. This paper substantially updates material contained in an earlier ECMI short paper 'Building a competitive and efficient European financial market', published in 2003. We are grateful for discussions with Robert Schwartz, Jaime Aguilar, Luisella Bosetti, Luca Filippa, Luigi Spaventa, Joshi Dixit, Peter Gomber, Kai-Oliver Maurer, Olivier Lefebvre, Santiago Ximenez, Ramon Adarraga, Paul Arlman, Verena Ross, Matthew Elderfield, Jim Angel, Jeffrey Bacidore, John Minderides, Alasdair Haynes, Ian Domowitz, Timothy Baker, John Serocold, Nick Dutton, Hugh Brown, Adam Kinsley, Niki Beattie, Tim McCormick, Paul Bennett,
cont. ...

1993 Investment Services Directive (ISD). The MiFID provides high-level principles designed to foster a fair, competitive, transparent, efficient and integrated European financial market. It aims to create a regulatory environment capable of insuring investor protection while still being flexible enough to allow for the introduction of new markets and services. An important aspect of this new directive is the repeal of the so-called 'concentration rule' (Article 14 (3)) of the 1993 ISD. This rule had allowed national authorities to stipulate that retail investor orders be executed only on a 'regulated market'. In the absence of a concentration rule, trades may be executed away from the main market centre on alternative trading systems or by investment firms. This has caused a heated debate among stakeholders and policy makers about issues related to market fragmentation and internalization. Many of the actual issues involved have become clouded in a vapour of self-interested rhetoric. This paper provides a solid academic foundation to the current discussion, by summarizing past research; describing the current state of the major European markets; and drawing parallels to the U.S. regulatory experience.

We begin by defining the terms involved. Fragmentation occurs if there is no mechanism to ensure (i) interaction between orders submitted for the same security on multiple venues; and (ii) interaction between orders and the best quotes posted on multiple venues. Order flow fragmentation is often the consequence of competition from innovative market structures but also the result of preferencing arrangements and in-house matching practices. Internalisation of order flow is a specific type of preferencing and refers to the situation in which broker-dealers execute retail client orders in-house against their own positions or against another client order.

There are potential problems linked with the internalisation of order flow. Specifically, internalisation inhibits aggressive quoting and diverts away orders from the primary market. This may affect the quality of price discovery and lead to higher spreads. It also produces a conflict of interest between the broker/dealer's own profit maximizing goals and the broker/dealer's obligation to provide the best price to the client.

Ekkehart Boehmer, Li Wei, Ruben Lee, Marco Mazzucchelli, Gideon Saar, Joel Hasbrouck, Alessandro Zignani, Adrea Crovetto, Lee Hodgkinson, Charles Goodhart, John Board, John Spencer, Erik Sirri, and Michael Goldstein. We are also grateful for comments received from seminar participants at the London School of Economics, the Ontario Securities Commission, and the Capital Markets Integration and Investor Protection in Europe conference in Milan. All remaining errors are our own. The views expressed here do not necessarily reflect those of ECMI or the International Capital Market Association.

[1] Directive 2004/39/EC of the European Parliament and of the Council of 21 April 2004 on Markets in Financial Instruments amending Council Directives 85/611/EEC and 93/6/EEC and Directive 2000/12/EC of the European Parliament and of the Council and repealing Council Directive 93/22/EEC, OJ L 145 30.04.2004 1-44.

As financial markets become more fragmented, these issues become more and more important. To illustrate, consider an investor in the UK. This investor can trade domestic equities either on SETS (the electronic order book of the London Stock Exchange (LSE)), on the over-the-counter market through dealers, on virt-x (the pan-European blue chip electronic exchange) or on an international exchange. An institutional investor can also trade through investor-to-investor mechanisms such as POSIT and Liquidnet. As well, a retail investor using a retail broker is likely to trade through a Retail Service Provider (RSP), rather than directly with the 'central' market. Hence, the once clear distinction between the services offered by exchanges and those offered by broker/dealers is becoming blurred.

The challenge is to create a regulatory environment that is not too prescriptive and is flexible enough to adapt rapidly to change and to encourage innovation, while at the same time provides an appropriate level of investor protection and minimises systemic risk. The ultimate goal is to set conditions which will facilitate the development of a competitive, integrated and efficient European financial market – a market where traders can trade and settle securities of other European countries just as easily as domestic ones and where issuers can more easily raise capital in a *European* rather than *domestic* market.

This paper examines the extent to which MiFID accomplishes this goal. We examine the MiFID's provisions for the protection of investors and for the identification and removal of conflicts of interest rules. We also examine the MiFID's provisions on best execution, order handling and trade reporting rules as well as provisions on pre-trade and post-trade transparency. These provisions are designed to create a level playing field where alternative market structures and trading systems can compete for trade execution with no detrimental effect on market quality.

The remainder of the paper is organized as follows. Section B begins by providing an economic definition of internalisation, and explores the effects of fragmentation and internalisation on market quality. It then offers a summary of theoretical and empirical findings regarding market fragmentation with particular attention to preferencing and internalisation. It also introduces market quality concepts, such as best execution, price discovery, market efficiency, liquidity, and transaction costs. Section C provides a brief survey of recent developments in U.S. markets and regulations.

Section D examines the rules and trading environment of each of the major European financial markets. We consider the extent to which European financial markets are fragmented and how internalisation practices differ across major European financial centres. This is a major contribution, since surprisingly little is known about actual off-exchange execution practices in Europe. Next, in the context of our previous analysis, Section E outlines the main features of the MiFID and offers some recommendations for its implementation. Section F concludes.

B. Internalisation and Fragmentation

I. Definition of Internalisation

There is little agreement about the precise definition of internalisation.

Often the term internalisation is used synonymously with the practice of in-house matching. In this broad sense, such a definition refers to two types of trades:

(i) It may refer to direct executions of client orders against the broker-dealer's own account. This includes retail orders that are executed by UK-based RSPs in a principal capacity (for example, the orders of retail customers of Merrill Lynch that are executed on the RSP operated by Merrill Lynch). It also includes institutional orders executed by broker-dealers against the broker-dealer's own positions.[2]

(ii) It may also refer to agency crosses in which customer orders are matched against each other. This includes crosses of customer orders on proprietary order books and matches of (institutional) client orders at a reference price on crossing networks.

For the most part, in this paper we focus on a narrower definition of internalisation. We will refer to internalisation as the situation in which an investment firm (a bank or a broker) executes retail client orders in-house.

Specifically, our definition focuses on an investment firm that either acts as a principal and executes the retail orders against the firm's own position or sends the retail orders to an affiliated market maker. Typically, internalised retail orders must be executed at prices no worse than the current official quotes.

II. Formal Framework

Markets have a natural tendency to consolidate because they require a critical mass of liquidity (Pagano 1989a). At the same time, new markets continue to emerge more rapidly and frequently, often threatening the position of the dominant market. Inevitably, there is tension between those in favour of consolidation of order flow on a single market and those demanding competition.

A market is fragmented when the same security trades on multiple trading venues.[3] Market fragmentation results from different market mechanisms competing to provide low-cost and tailored services to different traders. This beneficial effect of fragmentation is offset by the impact on market quality. If quotes and orders are not given the opportunity to interact, market fragmentation can have a

[2] Note that although these trades are executed off SETS, they are still classified as on market trades being executed by LSE broker-dealers.

[3] For a discussion of market fragmentation in the U.S. context, see HR Stoll (2001).

negative effect on the production of price information and, consequently, on market and price efficiency. Also, fragmentation can reduce the speed and likelihood of limit order execution. In most circumstances, competition amongst traders to obtain the best price is best achieved in consolidated markets.

Prices and markets are efficient when prices are highly informative. Prices are close to 'efficient' values when all buy and sell orders can interact to 'discover' the 'true' price. In efficient markets, prices make only small and transitory deviations from these values. Short-term deviations between transaction prices and true prices may arise because of frictions reflecting order-handling costs or, more generally, illiquidity, information asymmetries and strategic behaviour of market participants. Market efficiency corresponds to lower volatility and greater economies of scale, probability of order execution and market depth (Hamilton 1979).

Special attention has been given to those cases in which market fragmentation is caused by preferencing and internalisation. These cases have raised a debate about their overall effect on market welfare and hence on the potential need for regulatory intervention.

Market fragmentation is often associated with preferencing practices. Order preferencing is the routing of order flow by a broker to a preferred market maker. Preferenced orders are not exposed to the whole market but executed by dealers at the prevailing best bid and offer quotes (often from the primary market).[4] Hence, order routing is based more on special relations between brokers and dealers than on prices and market conditions. Brokers route order flow to dealers because they receive a service, data, a payment for small retail orders or a liquidity fee for limit orders. Traders, in turn, may benefit from lower commissions if brokers engage in price competition to attract order flow.

Internalisation is a form of preferencing. If a large fraction of the order flow is internalised, dealers have little incentive to compete by narrowing the spread because this would reduce overall dealer rents (i.e. supernormal profit) and would not attract the order flow already allocated to other dealers, i.e. internalisation may reduce the level of competition. Although externalities give order flow a natural tendency to consolidate, multiple and fragmented markets might persist in equilibrium.

With internalisation, while current market prices are used as a reference, investment firms are executing their clients' orders away from the market. These orders are neither able to interact with other pools of liquidity (and possibly receive improved execution) nor participate directly in the price discovery process. As a result, opponents of internalisation believe that it leads to a lower degree of

[4] In the context of NYSE-listed stocks, the best bid and ask quotes are normally, but *not always* found on the primary market. H Bessembinder (2003) finds that, on average, the NYSE posts the most competitive quotes. But, he also finds that off-NYSE quotes also provide non-trivial displayed liquidity, as they almost always (95.4% of the time) match at least one side of the NYSE quotes, and establish one side of the best quotes without NYSE participation about 11% of the time. Similar results are found by ME Blume and MA Goldstein (1997).

pre-trade transparency and has a negative impact on the price discovery process. It may amplify potential principal-agent problems (especially when brokers trade for their own account as dealers) in which the interests of brokers conflict with those of their clients. This conflict is particularly important with internalised *retail* trades, since retail traders have limited market knowledge and limited means of auditing their broker's performance. Also, when internalising market orders (and at best orders), investment firms violate time priority by front-running limit orders standing on the central order book in the supply of liquidity. Finally, the internalisation of limit orders may increase short-term price volatility, and make prices less resilient. That is, prices may more easily, and for a longer time, diverge from the 'true' price.

Proponents of internalisation of order flow believe that, just like payment for order flow, internalisation may create positive competition for traditional market centres. Banks internalise the order flow to avoid the costs of executing orders on the order book (exchange and, in some cases, clearing and settlement fees) and to earn bid-ask spreads. If a bank rebates a portion of these savings to its (favourite) clients, they may provide a better overall total cost. Furthermore, the internalisation of market orders may decrease short-term price volatility.

Order crossing is another form of preferencing arrangement. It refers to the situation when brokers arrange internal matches of their clients' orders. Crossing systems are often used to reduce market impact of large orders by allowing institutional orders to be matched at pre-specified times and traded anonymously off-market, typically at the reference market's mid-quote. Crossing facilities address the needs of a certain type of trader, who is ready to sacrifice immediacy and execution guarantees so as to obtain anonymous execution, price improvement and lower trading costs. However, this practice gives rise to several concerns. First, orders are not exposed to the whole market. This may create information asymmetries and affect the price discovery process. Second, because orders are matched at reference prices (derivative pricing), brokers free ride on the price discovery of other markets. Third, if the execution of the cross is not transparent, brokers may favour some clients over other clients.

There are three main regulatory remedies to confront these problems:

(i) Best execution rules for brokers can be established.[5]

(ii) Concentration Rules: the regulator could prohibit preferencing and internalisation by enforcing order flow concentration on the primary market. This may be possible in a local market but may be difficult to enforce in a global market.[6]

(iii) Mandate Market Linkage: the regulator could try to foster order flow competition by imposing some form of market linkage.[7]

[5] For a survey of the issues concerning the definition of best execution rules see JR Macey and M O'Hara (1997).

[6] At one time, for some European countries, such a rigid approach meant (at least temporarily) losing market share to the London SEAQ-I market.

Best execution is a consumer protection measure. The problem addressed by the best execution obligations is the information asymmetry that exists between customers and firms in relation to the prices at which execution can occur. Customers do not have the same degree of access to price information as have firms. Often best execution requirements are too narrowly focused on the price dimension only and ignore other dimensions, such as execution speed. For instance, ideal best execution requirements may require firms to consider also client order characteristics and market conditions. Defining best execution precisely is not a simple task. In fact, best execution means different things to different people: in simple terms, market order traders demand fast execution and expect to obtain the current best price available whereas limit order traders generally expect to obtain fast execution only once the limit price is reached. At a higher level, to provide execution quality, brokers have to employ costly resources: time, effort, skill and systems. Harris (2002) comments that in 'a competitive brokerage market, brokers provide superior execution as long as traders can measure such quality and are willing to pay for it'.

U.S. experience shows that regulators can allow preferencing and internalisation if at the same time appropriate best execution and pre- and post-trade transparency requirements are introduced. Transparency refers to the disclosure of quote and trade related information. The benefits of transparency are two-fold. First, transparency means greater availability of information and so faster price discovery and enhanced market efficiency. Second, transparency helps customers monitor brokers. Consequently, brokers will compete and deplete their rents to attract order flow. Higher levels of transparency, however, may introduce other costs, such as greater difficulty executing large transactions and less incentive to post limit orders.

III. Past Research

A special study by the U.S. Securities and Exchange Commission (SEC, 1963) was the first to discuss the contrasting effects of fragmentation on market quality, namely the trade-off between competition and market efficiency. The SEC wanted to know whether market quality would be improved by imposing consolidation or by fostering competition and, hence, tolerating the resulting fragmentation.

[7] In the U.S., this led to the creation of the Intermarket Trading System (ITS) and the National Market System (NMS) with consolidated trade and quotation systems. Some commentators, however, argue that this system has impeded competition and the adoption of new technology (ME Blume 2002).

1. Theoretical Predictions

Alternative market structures and the effects of market fragmentation are often analysed with reference to the auction literature.[8] Academics have shown that, under certain conditions, the differences in spreads produced by alternative market structures should fade away. Despite this, the behaviour of trade prices and therefore the orderliness of the trading process may be intrinsically dependent on the structure of the market (Biais 1993). Theoretical studies of the competition between markets have produced opposite predictions. For instance, Biais et al (2000) point out the benefits of competition among liquidity suppliers in reducing spread, increasing depth and volume and eroding marker makers' rents. In contrast, Foucault and Parlour (2004) fail to find a clearly dominant market structure that provides greater overall welfare than a monopolistic liquidity supplier. When competing markets have liquidity costs differentials and/or brokers use preferencing practices, alternative market structures can become dominant markets or multiple market equilibria can emerge (Foucault and Parlour (2004) and Battalio and Holden (2001)).

Fragmentation. Pagano (1989a, 1989b), Chowdhry and Nanda (1991), Mendelson (1987), and Admati and Pfleiderer (1991) predict that, because of order flow externalities, trading has a natural tendency to concentrate on the market that is already the largest. As a consequence, all else equal, consolidated markets have greater order flow and lower spreads (Arnold et al 1999 and Jain 2001). If traders or orders are not homogeneous, however, they will seek alternative systems that better satisfy their needs.

When there is no mandatory disclosure of information, strategic liquidity suppliers may find it optimal to provide liquidity on market structures alternative to the primary market, leading to fragmentation (Harris 1995 and Madhavan 1995). Fragmentation can also occur if dealers decide to attract orders with certain characteristics (cream skimming). For example, Easley et al (1996) find that regional dealers attract order flow with lower information content than NYSE executed orders. Harris (1995, 2002) and Battalio and Holden (2001) argue that fragmentation may cause poor price formation and higher transaction costs. This will occur if limited transparency and market access impede arbitrage across alternative markets and hamper competition for order flow among.

Preferencing. Dutta and Madhavan (1997) and Kandel and Marx (1999) provide models which argue that preferencing reduces the incentives for liquidity suppliers to aggressively compete by cutting prices. As preferencing increases, markets show higher average bid-ask spreads, lower average execution quality and greater dealer profits. Chakravarty and Sarkar (2001) develop a model for a quote-driven market with multiple liquidity suppliers and informed traders. The

[8] For surveys of theoretical approaches to the fragmentation issue see M O'Hara (1995), A Madhavan (1995, 2000), B Biais et al (2002) and CMC Lee (2002).

presence of internalising dealers reduces market depth and price informativeness. Parlour and Seppi (2001) study the competition between alternative market structures (a pure limit order system versus a hybrid specialist/limit order system) in the presence of preferencing practices. Their model produces the following results: (i) different preferencing arrangements may lead to multiple equilibria; (ii) greater competition between exchanges, hence greater market fragmentation, does not have a clear effect on aggregate liquidity; and (iii) the establishment of a best price benchmark by the regulator may negatively affect exchange competition.

2. Experimental Results and Empirical Findings

With the provocative papers by Christie and Schultz (1994) and Christie et al (1994) attention is drawn to the effects of institutional practices on execution quality. Shapiro (1995) notes that increasing volumes of trading in NYSE-listed stocks have gradually moved away from the NYSE. Some orders have moved to other market centres such as the regional exchanges and NASDAQ, some have been matched in-house by brokers, and some have been executed through the so-called 'fourth-market' (which includes those trades not facilitated by a broker but crossed by a system such as POSIT).

It is relatively easy to construct 'hypothetical' numerical examples that demonstrate that certain investors would benefit or be hurt through the process of internalisation. These simplistic examples, however, implicitly make an 'all else equal' assumption which fails to fully account for changes in market participant behaviour in response to different market structures. A true measure of who wins and who loses in this process must come through a careful empirical examination of markets that have different policies with regard to internalisation.

Researchers have employed a range of alternative indicators to evaluate the effects of fragmentation on market quality. Some of these include:

(i) *Liquidity, bid-ask spreads and trading costs.* 'Liquidity is the ability to trade large size quickly, at low cost, when you want to trade' (Harris (2002)). Spread is only one of the dimensions of liquidity. Transaction costs include all costs linked with trading, including explicit costs (commissions, fees and taxes), implicit costs (bid/ask spreads and price impacts) and missed trade opportunity costs.

(ii) *Price and return volatility.* Hamilton (1979) considers the effects of fragmentation on market volatility in addition to spread. He finds that the positive effects of competition tend, albeit just marginally, to prevail over the negative effects of fragmentation. Hence, multi-market trading lowers trading costs in the form of narrower spreads and lower price volatility.

(iii) *Information share.* Price discovery refers to the process through which new (public and private) information gets impounded into prices. It is relatively 'expensive' for a market to provide a price discovery mechanism. In contrast, once a price has been determined and disseminated, it is relatively 'cheap' to provide order matching or crossing services that simply pair off buyers and sellers at that price. When the same security trades on multiple markets, it is useful to measure the information share of each market, that is, how the trading on each individual market contributes to the price discovery process. Hasbrouck (1995) and Harris et al (1995) provide alternative methods for computing the information share of individual markets.

We now summarise the significant research on fragmentation of markets.

Causes of market fragmentation. Fragmentation is often caused by traders searching for mechanisms that better satisfy their needs. For instance, Fong, Madhavan and Swan (2004) analyze data from the Australian Stock Exchange and find that the magnitude of trading on ECNs and other off-market trading venues in Australia is driven by institutional trading interest (trading volume, indexation) and liquidity (bid-ask spreads, market depth). Conrad, Johnson and Wahal (2003) examine trading strategies and execution costs of institutional traders in the presence of ATSs. They find clustering in the characteristics of orders sent to different systems – for example, small trades of NYSE stocks are often sent to crossing networks. Thus, different systems satisfy different trader needs.

Experimental and empirical studies that do not find negative effects of greater fragmentation and competition on market quality and price efficiency. Hasbrouck (1995) studies the thirty stocks in the Dow Jones Index. He shows that although most of the price discovery takes place on the NYSE, a small, but significant, amount of price discovery also occurs on the regional exchanges. Similar results are obtained by Dridi et al (2000) for a group of stocks which traded on both NASDAQ and EASDAQ.[9]

Battalio et al (1997) study how the practice of preferencing order flow to regional exchanges affects the quoted and effective spread of the U.S. national market. Their results indicate that fragmentation does not reduce market quality of the primary market.[10] Actually, spreads on the NYSE declined after a substantial part of order flow was diverted away toward regional exchanges. Battalio et al (2002) study whether orders routed to regional exchanges might have enjoyed an even higher fill rate if they had been routed to the NYSE. They conclude that the routing decision is unlikely to have a significant impact on retail limit orders.

Huang (2002) shows that greater pre-trade transparency provided by ECNs' open order books contributes to improving quote quality. The increased level of competition resulting from the introduction of ECN trading has significantly contributed to improving the efficiency of the price discovery process on NASDAQ. Boehmer and Boehmer (2002) consider the launch of ETFs trading on the NYSE

[9] EASDAQ later became NASDAQ Europe, which subsequently shut down operations in 2003. In 2005, Capricorn Venture Partners announced plans to reintroduce the EASDAQ stock exchange.

[10] A similar conclusion on the beneficial effect of competition is reached by R Battalio (1997), K Fong et al (2004), JS Conrad et al (2003), Y Amihud et al (2002) and S Mayhew (2002).

in direct competition with the American Stock Exchange, the dominant market for this type of security. The NYSE has managed to attract a significant market share of ETFs traded volume and this has led to a significant decline in quoted, effective and realized spread and a substantial increase in quoted depth across all market centres.

Blume and Goldstein (1997) find that non-NYSE markets obtain a substantial proportion of their total trading volume when both sides of their quotes are inferior to the best displayed bid or offer. They argue, however, that there is still scope for quote competition, since they find that when a market posts the very best bid or offer across all markets, that market does receive increased order flow. In support of this finding, Bessembinder (2003) finds that there is substantial quote-based competition for order flow. He finds that quotation strategies are shown to vary systematically with market conditions, and order routing is found to respond systematically to quote placement. This is inconsistent with order location being driven solely by preferencing agreements. He concludes that 'improved disclosure of trading costs would likely stimulate increased competition and improve the efficiency of order routing, without the need for extensive new regulation'. Re-visiting this analysis in the context of decimalization, Goldstein et al (2005) find that the tick size reduction to one penny has increased the ability of the regional markets to compete with the NYSE.

Studies showing negative effects of fragmentation. Davis and Lightfoot (1998) compare bid-ask spreads and return variances for two groups of NYSE stocks that trade under different competition regimes. Their results show that the introduction of greater competition does not lead to a significant reduction, but rather more often to an increase in bid-ask spreads. Also, the two groups of stocks have similar variances of returns.

Conrad et al (2001) analyse a proprietary dataset of institutional equity trades which identified trades preferenced to soft-dollar brokers. They find that, controlling for differences in order characteristics, preferenced orders generally pay higher implicit costs. Peterson and Sirri (2003) find that the effective spreads of market orders trading on preferencing regional exchanges tend to be lower than the effective spreads of market orders trading on nonpreferencing regional exchanges. They also find that limit orders have a greater probability of executing on preferencing regional exchanges than on nonpreferencing regional exchanges. Lee (1993) finds that the NYSE generally provides better effective spreads and points out how price execution of comparable orders differs systematically by location.

Chung et al (2004) find dealer quote aggressiveness is negatively related to the proportion of internalized volume during both the pre- and post-decimalization periods. Chung et al (2006) show that although internalisation does not reduce the impact of price aggressiveness on dealer market share, it mitigates the impact of size aggressiveness. They interpret this result as suggesting that although internalization may not affect the dealer's incentive to post aggressive prices, it may reduce the incentive to post large depths.

For a sample of LSE stocks, Hansch et al (1999) find that preferenced trades pay higher spreads whilst internalised trades pay lower spreads. Also, about 62% of trades for the constituent stocks of the FTSE-100 index during August 1994 are internalised (i.e. the market maker and the broker belong to the same firm). The average trade size for internalised trades is about £280,000, which suggests that a large proportion of these trades is from institutional investors who prefer to deal directly with the market makers. Moreover, the extent of preferencing and internalisation has no significant cross-sectional relationship with a stock's average inside and effective spreads.

Cai and Dufour (2002) study trading on and off the electronic limit order book on the London Stock Exchange. They find that in the UK the main price discovery mechanism is the SETS order book even though most of the retail business is executed off-SETS through RSPs (internalised business). Moreover, very few of the trades executed on SETS are matches of investors' orders, and dealers participate in most SETS trades. They conclude that the quality of the UK market could be improved by fostering greater direct access for private and institutional traders to order book liquidity.

C. U.S. Regulatory Experience

Debate in the U.S. has focused on the apparent choice between the consolidation and fragmentation of trading venues. The following quote from the introduction of the recently adopted SEC Regulation NMS summarizes this choice: 'The NMS [...] incorporates two distinct types of competition – competition among individual markets and competition among individual orders – that together contribute to efficient markets. Vigorous competition among markets promotes more efficient and innovative trading services, while integrated competition among orders promotes more efficient pricing of individual stocks for all types of orders, large and small. Together, they produce markets that offer the greatest benefits for investors and listed companies.

Accordingly, the Commission's primary challenge in facilitating the establishment of an NMS has been to maintain an appropriate balance between these two vital forms of competition. It particularly has sought to avoid the extremes of (i) isolated markets that trade an NMS stock without regard to trading in other markets and thereby fragment the competition among buyers and sellers in that stock; and (ii) a totally centralized system that loses the benefits of vigorous competition and innovation among individual markets. Achieving this objective and striking the proper balance clearly can be a difficult task'.[11]

In establishing its careful balance, the SEC believes that the key principles to uphold are: access, best execution, and transparency. We briefly comment on

[11] SEC (2005) 12-13.

some of the main regulatory developments here. It is worth noting upfront that many SEC rules have explicitly distinguished between the NYSE and NASDAQ markets – explaining, in part, why these markets developed so differently over time.

In response to the 1994 investigation into whether NASDAQ market makers had implicitly colluded by avoiding odd-eighth quotes, the SEC introduced the so-called 'Display Rule' (SEC Rule 11Ac1-4). This rule requires the display of customer limit orders that are priced better than a specialist/marketmaker quote or that add to the size associated with such a quote.

In combination with the display rule, best execution in U.S. markets is aided by the so-called 'Quote Rule' (SEC Rule 11Ac1-1). This rule requires a market maker, who is responsible for more than one percent of the aggregate trading volume for a given listed security, to publish quotations for that security and to make publicly available any superior quotes posted privately through certain ECNs.

In other words, these rules first require market participants to give the market data they generate to the exchanges and then require them to buy that information back from the exchanges in consolidated form if they distribute any quotation information to investors.

In a 1997 report, the SEC studied how the practice of preferencing affects the quality of markets (see SEC 1997). The study indicates that some form of preferencing practice has always existed on all of the U.S. exchanges since the Securities Exchange Act of 1934. The SEC concluded that, if appropriate protections were in place to prevent principal-agent types of conflicts of interest, preferencing can stimulate competition for order flow.

In particular, in 1996, before providing permanent approval of the Chicago Stock Exchange (CSX) preferencing program, the SEC had analysed thoroughly the potential effects of preferencing on the execution of customer orders, competition among markets and CSX market quality. The results of the investigation showed that market makers have incentives to provide fast execution to marketable (aggressively priced) limit orders and also that market orders are provided the opportunity for price improvement. Furthermore, the SEC has verified that preferencing has had no significant detrimental effect on quotes, depth and liquidity.

In the 2001 Report of the Advisory Committee on Market Information (commonly referred to as the Seligman Commission Report), the majority recommended a model under which multiple consolidators could compete to collect and resell market data from the exchanges.[12] Under this proposed 'multiple consolidator' model, the exchanges would retain exclusive control over access to, and fees for, market data and would face no competitive pressure to provide data on a

[12] A minority of the committee members did not believe that the economic benefits of implementing a new model outweigh the technological and economic risks of the new competing consolidator model.

more efficient and useful basis at more affordable rates. Exchanges would have the rights over data, but must be willing to distribute transaction prices and inside quotes at low cost. Notably, the committee recommended a further, much more detailed study that has yet to be commissioned. The 'multiple consolidator' model has not been implemented.

In addition to real-time trade data publication, the SEC has introduced rules that require market centers to distribute data on order execution.

According to SEC Rule 11Ac1-5 (Disclosure of Order Execution Information), market centres are required to prepare and make available to the public monthly reports in electronic form that categorize their order executions and include statistical measures of execution quality.

In effect, this rule requires all market centres to post statistics (commonly referred to as 'Dash 5 Statistics') on the execution of orders according to order size. A closely related SEC rule is SEC Rule 11Ac1-6 (Disclosure of Order Routing Information) which provides that a broker-dealer that routes orders on behalf of customers is required to prepare quarterly reports that disclose the identity of the venues to which it routed orders for execution. The reports must disclose the nature of the broker-dealer's relationship with those venues, including the existence of any internalisation or payment for order flow arrangements. Finally, broker-dealers are required to disclose, on customer request, where they routed a customer's individual orders for execution.

When these rules were introduced, the goal was to provide a standardised set of statistics that allowed market participants to compare broker performances and alternative execution venues. In practice, two vendors, Transaction Auditing Group and Market Systems, Inc., have been contracted by a large number of market centres to provide Rule 11Ac11-5 and Rule 11Ac11-6 reports. In part, because of the complexity and quantity of data involved, these reports often contain errors and are not normally subject to an independent audit.

The implementation of these rules has exposed vast differences in the reporting and interpretation of trade data. Boehmer (2005) and Boehmer, Jennings and Wei (2005) explain some of these differences. Despite these data quality issues, Boehmer, Jennings and Wei (2005) obtain evidence which suggests that the reports are informative to broker-dealers. They find that routing decisions depend significantly on execution quality and that market centers reporting low execution costs and fast fills subsequently receive more order flow. Thus, mandating public disclosure of order execution information can lead to greater market center competition.

The U.S. experience also highlights potential conflicts that can arise from poorly applied best execution guidelines. It is common practice for brokerages to send orders to the best bid/offer currently posted – normally taken to be the national best bid and offer (NBBO). The best price, however, is complicated by the possibility of trade rebates and access fees. Early on, Island ECN (now Inet ATS, Inc.) began to provide rebates to limit orders that added to the system's liquidity. While this was initially designed to be a marketing tool, many ECNs began offering rebates to customers that submitted aggressive limit orders to their systems, thereby ensuring that they had the NBBO. At the same time, however, the ECNs charged high access fees for using their systems. Thus, even though customer orders were being routed to the system that appeared to have the best bid/offer, they effectively were receiving a worse price after including access fees.

In response to this, NASDAQ's new SuperMontage system allows market participants to request that their order be handled by price/time priority with access fee consideration.[13] This made several ECNs concerned – so much so that SuperMontage had to go through nine stages of amendments to satisfy these concerns. The effect of these amendments was to ensure that niches remained in which the ECNs could operate – this highlights that the details of securities regulation clearly matter. Small rule changes can have large, and possibly unintended, consequences. In the context of the European debate, it is highly relevant that SuperMontage still allows for preferencing of order flow and automatically internalises order flow from the same member firm if it is at or within the current bid-ask spread.

The large number of execution options for NASDAQ-listed securities might suggest that the U.S. market is highly fragmented. In practice, however, an adequate combination of order handling and transparency requirements and private sector commercial solutions produces consolidated quotes and provides order routing mechanisms that search for the best prices across numerous pools of liquidity. This allows investors to have a menu of choice – for instance, some market participants on the NYSE want exposure to the floor auction whereas others want immediate trade execution. To facilitate these different needs, the NYSE introduced 'NYSE Direct+' which provides automatic execution of limit orders up to 1,099 shares against the published bid or offer. In return for automatic execution, customers give up the possibility for price improvement by the trading floor. Thus, orders sent via Direct+ and orders sent to the trading floor have little or no effective interaction, even though it is the same exchange! In the opinion of the NYSE, this multi-platform structure is optimal – it is not an interim stage towards the implementation of a fully electronic CLOB model.

The prevailing view in the U.S. is that there are benefits from the segmentation of the market. There is no reason why different traders should not face different prices and/or receive payment for order flow. In fact, one reason that retail commissions in the U.S. are lower (often as low as $8) than institutional commis-

[13] SuperMontage is designed to provide fully integrated order display and execution systems that will ensure better links between the NASDAQ dealer market and ECNs. SuperMontage gives market participants three options as to how their orders will interact with the quotes/orders in NASDAQ: (i) Price/Time; (ii) Price/Size; (iii) Price/Time with Access Fee Consideration. Price/Time with access fee considerations would cause a fee-charging ECN to be hit after all other market participants that do not charge a fee. Also, if an ECN charges a fee but flags their bid/offer as providing price improvement (their price plus the fee is equal to or better than the price in their bid/offer), they will be hit in strict Price/Time priority.

sions is because nobody is willing to pay for institutional (possibly information-based) order flow.

To make this fragmented system work, the ownership of trade records is key. After a trade occurs, the Consolidated Tape Association (CTA) sells the trade report to various market data providers such as Reuters and Bloomberg. The revenues from the CTA are divided among market centres according to how many trades occur at the market centre. This formula became complicated when Island started reporting Island NMS trades that do not involve NASDAQ's SelectNet to the National (former Cincinnati) Stock Exchange in February 2002. By reporting these internal Island trades to the NSE, Island was able to eliminate certain NASDAQ ACT and NASD-R related fees.

Since then, the SEC has adopted Regulation NMS, which in part, introduces amendments to the 'Market Data Rules' that 'update the requirements for consolidating, distributing, and displaying market information, as well as amendments to the joint industry plans for disseminating market information that modify the formulas for allocating plan revenues and broaden participation in plan governance'.[14] The new rules will allocate market data revenue based more closely on the market centre's contribution to the best displayed quotation, thereby removing an excessive focus on the number of trades executed, regardless of trade size.

A wealth of insights regarding the internalization of order flow in the U.S. can be found within the SEC documents relating to the rescission of NYSE Rule 390.[15] This rule had operated to preclude, among other matters, NYSE member firms from internalising their agency order flow by trading as dealer or principal against it. Its rescission allows NYSE members to act as over-the-counter market makers or dealers in all NYSE-listed securities. Prior to its rescission, some market observers believed that a significant amount of order flow previously routed to the NYSE may be subsequently divided among a number of different dealers in the over-the-counter market, where there may be a reduced opportunity for order interaction. In practice, the repeal of Rule 390 has had little effect on NYSE market share.

In 2002 the NYSE introduced OpenBook. This new service allows traders off the floor to observe the aggregated size available at all bid and offer prices in the specialist's book. These prices are updated every 5 seconds (and soon will be available in real-time). A recent study of the NYSE OpenBook data shows that increased pre-trade transparency can lead to improved market quality in terms of increased displayed liquidity and lower impact of trades on prices (Boehmer, Saar, and Yu 2005).

The reputation of the U.S. securities industry has been hard hit by recent corporate governance scandals. Despite the apparent imperfections of the U.S. sys-

[14] SEC (2005) 2.

[15] <www.sec.gov/rules/sro/ny9948o.htm>

tem, we believe that following the ongoing debate about exchange competition in the U.S., and gaining empirical evidence from it, is a vital input into successful European regulation.

D. European Landscape

The adoption of the ISD in 1993 started the process for the development of a more integrated European financial market. More recently, the adoption of a common currency and the emergence of an equity culture across Europe have generated greater interest in cross-border trading (McAndrews and Stefanadis 2002). These developments, in turn, have created the conditions for greater consolidation within the European financial markets. In the past few years, we have witnessed several consolidation initiatives. Whilst some of these attempts failed at the early stages, others led to the creation of multi-market stock exchanges[16] and to the adoption of more homogeneous trading structures.

One such initiative was the European Market Model – an ambitious 1998 plan by the European Equity Alliance for the creation of a new pan-European market for blue-chips stocks. In September 1999, this model was effectively dropped and replaced by an agreement by the eight stock exchanges which form the alliance (Amsterdam, Brussels, Frankfurt, London, Madrid, Milan, Paris and Zurich) to adopt common key market model principles with the goal of laying the foundations for an efficient, integrated, electronic cross border market for European blue chips.

Consolidation of trading in European securities could deliver greater economies of scale both within the exchanges and in broker/dealer offices through the adoption of common and efficient trading platforms, which could translate into lower trading costs. McAndrews and Stefanadis (2002) believe that although various impediments to consolidation persist (e.g. clearing and settlement inefficiencies, regulatory disparities, differences in listing requirements, etc.), these are mainly regulatory and financial and could be overcome faster than the technological impediments that slowed down the consolidation process for U.S. exchanges over the last century (see Arnold et al 1999).

Until now, European equity trading has had a domestic focus. This is changing as assets are increasingly managed on a sector basis, through the growth of index related products, pan-European and sector index products, futures, and exchange-traded funds. It has also been influenced by the growth in new trading strategies such as arbitrage and portfolio strategies, by the introduction of the Euro, and through the emergence of large blue-chip European companies that operate in multiple jurisdictions (e.g. Nokia and Vodafone plc).

[16] For an updated list, please refer to the Federation of European Securities Exchanges website <http://www.fese.be/statistics/exchange_landscape/index.htm>

The potential value of a true pan-European market in blue chip stocks has become increasingly apparent, as investors have shifted from diversification across stocks within one European country to diversification across market sectors, regardless of country. However, such a market need not be in the form of a single dominant exchange. Instead, competition between exchanges can be promoted while encouraging the development of one (or more) pan-European cross-border clearing and settlement system(s) in order to reduce cross-border clearing and settlement costs to be no higher than domestic.

The development of financial markets in Spain, Italy, and France has been heavily influenced by the concentration rule. The concentration provision in the 1993 ISD (Article 14) was an attempt to prevent nationals of a country which implemented the provision from transacting in domestic securities away from a regulated market. The concentration principle is based on the argument that a market in a security can only be fair if all transactions in it are undertaken on a single marketplace where every order can interact with every other order. Proponents of this view argue that a concentrated market ensures price and time priority. Thus all investors, whether large or small, transacting at the same time are ensured a fair deal in that they can transact at the same price. However, all of these markets allow for exceptions to the concentration rule. Large and special orders do not have to satisfy the time priority rule and often do not have to interact with orders on the central market. Hence, none of these markets is entirely concentrated with strict time and price priority.

Competition for trading services through multiple trading venues and internalisation of order flow by investment firms characterises trading in Germany and the UK. The difference in market structure between countries with a 'central market' mentality and those with a 'competitive market' mentality (though virtually all markets now exhibit features of both) is that in the former there is normally a higher proportion of retail business while in the latter (as in London) a higher proportion of wholesale business.

Traditional exchanges must adapt to meet evolving investor needs in the face of greater integration of European markets. For example, shortcomings in existing market mechanisms will soon become apparent as money management in Europe becomes more institutionalised and fund transaction sizes increase.

Traditional exchanges have already tried to diversify their services by introducing market segments tailored to the needs of particular types of traders: systems designed for crossing large institutional orders were recently introduced by the LSE and the Borsa Italiana. The introduction of after-hours trading segments, such as those found on the Borsa Italiana, the Deutsche Börse, and the Stockholmsbörsen, were designed to encourage retail direct trading. However, it is much more likely that the needs of different classes of investor would be better met by allowing, or even encouraging, competition in offering a more diverse range of market mechanisms which do not require dealers or regulated markets as intermediaries. Several of such mechanisms are already available in the UK: for example investors-to-investors trading services such as Liquidnet and crossing networks run by ITG Europe.[17]

We now provide specific details about the trading environment in the major European financial markets.

Germany. Deutsche-Börse AG operates the Frankfurt Exchange (FWB), the largest of the eight German stock exchanges.[18] Most of the shares traded on FWB can be traded on the Deutsche-Börse's electronic trading platform, known as Xetra. In 2004, Xetra had an 80% market share by turnover value of domestic equities, the FWB had a 15% share, and the remaining 5% was traded on other German exchanges (source: Deutche-Börse, Factbook 2004).

On 3 September 2002, the Deutsche-Börse introduced Xetra Best, which allows a bank's private clients to trade directly over Xetra via the bank's internal systems.[19] Xetra Best is designed to offer private investors benefits such as the possibility of immediate and full execution at a price better than those he/she could have obtained in the open Xetra order book for the same transaction at the same point in time. Xetra Best is designed to allow investors to preference a specific market maker and for the possibility of self-preferencing. The motivation behind the introduction of Xetra Best was to provide an attractive and cheaper alternative to firms that were considering developing their own in-house trading and matching systems.

There is no publishing obligation for off-exchange trades. Thus, the percentage of trades executed off-exchange is not known. Some private estimates suggest about 30-40% of trades (more by volume). Although these trades are not published, they are reported to BAFin, the Federal Financial Supervisory Authority of Germany, in order to uncover breaches of insider trading prohibition or ad hoc disclosure requirements. The majority of block trading occurs off-market. The next largest portion of block trading is executed using the exchange's floor trading facility. The remainder of block trading occurs on Xetra's crossing facility – but this does not attract much order flow.

In addition to the Frankfurt exchange, there are seven regional exchanges in Germany: Berlin, Bremen, Dusseldorf, Hamburg, Hannover, Munchen, and Stuttgart. These exchanges operate in a competitive relationship with the Frankfurt exchange. It is important to emphasize that there is no German equivalent of the U.S. National Market System (NMS) linking the regional exchanges to Frankfurt. The German Securities Trading Act does not require firms to send their customer orders to the exchange with the best price – the order simply needs to be sent to a recognized exchange.

[17] See C Gresse (2006) for a detailed empirical analysis of ITG Europe's crossing network.

[18] E Theissen (2003) provides a description of the German equity markets.

[19] J Grammig and E Theissen (2005) describe how the Xetra Best system allows banks and brokers to internalize retail customer orders.

The regional exchanges have strong political backing from regional governments. Traditionally, they have had strong relationships with locally oriented banks. The regional exchanges, however, no longer specialize solely in listing local companies. They are redefining themselves and beginning to compete with Frankfurt directly on the basis of trading technology – offering extended trading hours, special guaranteed trading conditions and alternative electronic trading systems. For example, the Dusseldorf Stock Exchange has a 40% ownership stake in Quotrix AG, which operates Quotrix, a quote-driven exchange trading system for private investors, and TradeLink, an ECN for over-the-counter securities trading.

Euronext (France, Belgium, The Netherlands, Portugal). Euronext was formed in March 2000 through the merger of the Paris Bourse, the Amsterdam Exchange and the Brussels Stock Exchange. In October 2001, Euronext outbid the LSE for the London International Financial Futures and Options Exchange (LIFFE). In 2002, the Lisbon Stock Exchange also joined Euronext and an alliance was formed with the Warsaw Stock Exchange. All of the Euronext operations for cash securities now have a fully integrated trading and clearing processes, thereby allowing them to act effectively as a single market.

Euronext markets share a common order-driven electronic trading system. Whilst there is a common set of rules for all Euronext markets, local differences still remain regarding listing requirements and enforcement procedures. Euronext uses Euroclear as its preferred settlement agent and collaborates closely with Clearnet and Euroclear to implement straight through processing on a cross-border basis. Trade reports are sent to the national securities regulator in France and the Netherlands and are sent to the market in Belgium. While block trade reporting to the exchange in Belgium must be immediate it is possible to ask for delayed disclosure.

French concentration rules require crosses involving a French-based counterparty to be undertaken on the exchange at prices between the current bid and offer spread. In addition, crosses can be executed at the touch (thereby by-passing normal time priority) if there is insufficient size to execute the trade on the book.[20]

Italy. The Italian concentration rule requires that trades are executed on regulated markets (Borsa Italiana and TLX are currently the only two regulated equity markets), except when broker/dealers obtain explicit authorization from the trader and are able to provide price improvement. In general, the concentration rule does

[20] While having the benefit of ensuring best execution, this rule has effectively prevented crossing networks such as POSIT from executing trades involving French counterparties. Because these crossing networks do not have a direct link to the central limit order book, they cannot guarantee that prices will not move between the time the trade is executed on their system and when they attempt to report it to the exchange. If they executed a trade involving French counterparties, they would be responsible for absorbing any difference in price.

not apply to: (a) foreign investors; (b) government bonds; (c) block trades; (d) odd lots; and (e) after-hours trading.

Authorised intermediaries satisfy best execution requirements when they carry out trades at the best possible conditions with reference to time, size and type of transaction. Best conditions refer to the total cost of trading, which includes not only transaction price but also any other explicit and/or implicit execution cost born by the trader. During official trading hours, best execution requirements are automatically satisfied for all trades executed on regulated markets; for all other times, best execution requirements are automatically satisfied for all trades executed on either regulated markets and/or Sistemi di Scambi Organizzati (SSOs) – recognised ATSs. Soft-commissions are allowed, but the intermediaries' code of conduct requires the terms of such arrangements to be clearly stated in the contract with the client (ASSOSIM 1998). About 98% of trades and 95% of traded value are executed on market at the Borsa Italiana.[21] Block trades accounts for most of the remainder, with off-market trading accounting for less than one percent.

All trades in instruments admitted to trading on a regulated market have to be reported to the regulated market within 15 minutes of execution and published within one hour. Trades executed after-hours must be reported to a regulated market before 9am of the following trading day. A stricter transparency regime applies to those SSOs that allow retail trading (admit trades with value lower than €150,000). These SSOs must publish the rules that govern the price discovery process. During trading hours, pre-trade transparency requires posting of best bid and ask prices and their respective sizes, whilst, post-trade transparency requires publication of time, price and quantity for the most recent transaction. At least once a month, SSOs with retail trading must publish trading summaries specifying monthly traded volume, maximum, minimum and weighted average prices for each traded instrument. SSOs that allow dealers to trade for their own account must report separately average buy and sell prices.[22]

Even if Italy is a country where order flow has been traditionally consolidated on the main exchange market forces are gradually pushing in the direction of multiple venues or segments for different investors. In this sense, order flow is becoming more fragmented not only in space but also in time.

The online trading platform TLX was launched in January 2000 as the first Italian ECN to exploit the non-applicability of the concentration rule to after-hours trading. TLX was recognised as a regulated market by Consob in 2003. It makes markets in domestic equities and thereby competes directly with the Borsa Italiana. By offering market-making services TLX, aims to increase liquidity, provide more flexible trading hours and offer a greater range of products. TLX is

[21] Figures obtained through private communication with Borsa Italiana.

[22] See Consob (1998a, b, c) and Legislative Decree 58/98; G Sabatini and I Tarola (2002).

a hybrid market where dealers and limit orders interact in the price discovery process and characterised by real-time pre- and post-trade transparency.

Spain. In contrast to the trend in the U.S., and to a lesser extent in the UK, the trading of financial instruments in Spain has become increasingly consolidated in fewer, more closely linked trading venues and the associated order flow concentrated on the central limit order book.

The consolidation and integration of Spanish financial markets was promoted by the laying of the legal groundwork in 2001 to allow the formation of a holding company which would acquire, directly or indirectly, the entire capital of some or all the entities running the secondary markets as well as the Spanish securities registration, clearing and settlement systems. This goal was advanced on 15 February 2002 with the creation of the Bolsas y Mercados Espanoles (Sociedad Holding de Mercadoes y Sistems Financieros S.A.). In 2003, this company integrated the markets for Spanish equities (Bolsa de Madrid, Bolsa de Barcelona, Bolsa de Bilbao, and Bolsa de Valencia), derivatives (MEFF) and fixed income products (the electronic trading platform for Spanish government debt, SENAF, and the private fixed income market, AIAF); along with the securities registration, clearing and settlement systems (Iberclear).

Regarding equities, almost all trading occurs on the central electronic trading platform (SIBE), which facilitates direct, real time communication among the four Spanish stock exchanges, allowing for a single price and order book per share. By law, during official trading hours, trading activity must be concentrated on the regulated market. Orders can be placed outside the central book where special regimes apply (i.e. in the case of large orders, off-exchange and extraordinary transactions).[23]

Some foreign market participants complain that it is difficult to enter the Spanish financial markets. The Spanish exchanges require members to have a 'technical and physical presence' in Spain. In general, having a subsidiary or a branch operating in Spain could satisfy this membership requirement. The MiFID addresses these concerns by giving investment firms an effective single passport, which allows them to operate throughout the EU on the basis of the authorisation by the authority of their home Member State.

United Kingdom. Best execution rules in the UK are mainly focused on achieving the best price for the customer and clearly identify a specific price benchmark as a minimum execution standard. Changes to best execution practices for transactions have been proposed in a recent FSA consultation paper (FSA 2002). The FSA recognises that best execution is more than the achievement of 'the best price' and the execution decision should take account of other factors, such as order type, size, settlement arrangements and timing, together with any other conditions set by the customer. Although setting the price of a

[23] Details of the SIBE block-trading regime can be found in RJ Davies, A Dufour and B Scott-Quinn (2003).

specific market as the benchmark simplifies the enforcement of best execution rules it also reduces the incentive for firms to actively seek price improvement for their customers across alternative trading venues. Essentially, this recognizes that best execution may be available on other venues, such as virt-x or POSIT.

While the FSA accepts that the quality of execution that a firm can achieve depends in part on its access to execution venues, the FSA does not believe that there is a case for prescribing mandatory minimum market access arrangements. The FSA also recognizes that overall trading costs (explicit and implicit) play a role in determining the net result for the customer.

The competitive environment for the provision of trading services in the UK is exemplified by the development of cross border trading services (e.g. virt-x and the Dutch Trading segment of LSE) and in-house trading and internalisation of order flow by investment banks.

Cross-border trading. For many years, the UK market has dominated European institutional trading. More recently innovative services have been introduced to promote European cross border trading. The virt-x exchange, now fully owned by the Swiss Stock Exchange, operates an electronic limit order book for trading in European blue-chip stocks. Some traders have been attracted by the 'virtual' single-settlement system formed by virt-x with Crest, Euroclear and SegaInterSettle (SIS), which allows virt-x to offer close to domestic settlement rates. In May 2004 the LSE launched the Dutch Trading Service, which enables LSE members to trade in the most liquid Dutch securities via the SETS order book. Hence, the LSE has entered in direct competition with Euronext.

Internalisation. When the LSE introduced the electronic order book SETS, it feared that the new trading system would not be able to handle large numbers of small retail orders. Thus, it promoted the internalisation of retail order flow by RSPs. RSPs offer an execution service for small- to medium-size trades aimed primarily, but not exclusively, at the private client broking market. RSPs provide a firm two-sided quote – typically held for 30 to 60 seconds. Some advocates of the RSP model emphasize that the investor's time 'option' to execute at the quote constitutes a service that is not available on a standard electronic limit order book. This service can be priced (in theory) using a variant of the Black-Scholes option pricing formula.

Services offered by RSPs provide both the advantage of immediacy and single executions at prices equal to or better than published SETS prices. They also provide a degree of flexibility over the settlement period to allow private clients still holding certificated stocks to deliver their paper for settlement. For settlement periods longer than five days, RSPs normally charge an additional fee. With the exception of the international market, RSPs do not have any specific status on the LSE. Like other market makers providing quotes for SETS stocks, RSPs are not obligated to quote in all market conditions.

There is a post-trade transparency obligation: each *individual* order that is traded with the RSP is reported to the exchange. Typically, RSPs manage incoming orders as follows: first, they attempt to match the order with other orders that are 'simultaneously' received by the RSP (this is very rare). Next, if the RSP is sufficiently large, they may pass the order imbalance onto their parent company's proprietary trading book. Finally, if the imbalance grows sufficiently large, they will trade against the SETS limit order book.

When SETS was originally introduced, the LSE discouraged retail trades by establishing a size threshold on SETS. But now there is no size limit and all orders with standard settlement conditions can be placed on the central limit order book. Most retail investors, however, are still either unwilling or unable to participate directly on the order book. There appear to be four main reasons why retail investors do not trade directly on SETS:

(i) Heuristic evidence suggests that RSPs offer retail brokers, and their clients, better prices than SETS for as much as 90% of all trades.[24] This is possible, in part, because of a finer price grid on RSPs than on SETS. SETS ticks are only 2 decimal places, in defined increments (e.g. 0.50 pence for stocks valued between 500p and 999p). RSP trades are usually in 3 decimal places and are in non-SETS increments (e.g. a price of, say, 513.117p, or even of 513.10p, is not currently possible on SETS).[25]

(ii) Historical inertia and preferencing arrangements: brokers always traded directly with dealers (and often do not present all the available execution options to the trader).

(iii) A large proportion of retail traders, often holding paper-based stock certificates, still require non-standard settlement.

(iv) Market orders are more common than limit orders. To some extent, the lack of limit orders may be caused by a lack of knowledge among UK retail investors about the available order types and the fact that all orders are entered as market orders by brokers into the RSP's automatic execution system.

Many of the major RSPs are partially (or fully) owned by a large retail brokerage. Thus, these brokerages have the incentive to send their customer orders to their own RSP. Brokerages that are not directly tied to an RSP are often enticed to give one RSP preferential treatment through 'soft money' incentives (e.g. free terminals). Despite these practices, there have been several recent initiatives driven by different categories of market participants (the LSE, investment firms and data vendors) to consolidate quotes from multiple RSPs. As a consequence, many retail brokers have now begun polling more than one RSP for prices (although not necessarily *all* available RSPs). Polling multiple RSPs promotes com-

[24] For instance, Barclays Stockbrokers, a large retail broker, reports that in January 2005 their "Price Improver" service improved 90% of deals over the SETS price, saving clients £890,000 or £7.17 per deal. This service scans multiple RSPs for the best price.

[25] Notably, in December 2004, the LSE was forced to shelve a plan narrow tick sizes for a trial group of stocks, in the face of fierce opposition from brokers (especially RSPs) who feared they would lose some of their lucrative retail business to the central limit order book. Details of the LSE proposal and 'customer' response are available here: <http://www.londonstockexchange.com>

petition among market makers and improves the price discovery process. In effect, it enhances the degree of pre-trade transparency.

E. The MiFID

The adoption of the 1993 ISD was a significant early attempt to create a legislative framework for a fully harmonised European market.[26] The ISD provides 'high level' principles for national securities regulations. The goal is the 'mutual recognition' of regulations across the EU. The ISD focuses on equity markets in the first instance. It creates the concept of a single 'passport' for investment firms, allowing them to be authorised and supervised by domestic authorities but still provide specified investment services in other EU states. It is modelled after the passport given to banks in the Second Banking Directive.

Soon after the introduction of ISD, it was clear that revisions were needed. Technological innovation has blurred the strict distinction between 'regulated markets' and 'investment firms'. This process has accelerated with the development of alternative trading systems (ATSs) and ECNs. New regulations have to be flexible enough to accommodate and foster future innovations in trading.

In 1998, the Cardiff European Council explicitly recognised the necessity for a revision of the ISD in order to create the infrastructure necessary for a stronger and more integrated European financial market. The Cardiff European Council set two deadlines, the year 2003 for an integrated European security market and the year 2005 for a fully integrated European capital market. The European Commission adopted a 'Financial Services Action Plan' (FSAP), in May 1999. The FSAP consists of 42 measures aimed at creating an appropriate legislative apparatus, building sound supervisory structures and consolidating retail and wholesale markets.

Because the implementation of the FSAP measures had been greatly delayed by burdensome bureaucratic processes, the European Council for Economic and Financial Affairs (commonly known as ECOFIN) commissioned Professor Lamfalussy and the 'Committee of Wise Men' to assess the situation and make recommendations to speed up the implementation process. Professor Lamfalussy recommended the adoption of a four level approach; the EU legislator should establish high-level principles and leave implementation details to the European Commission, assisted by two newly formed committees – the European Securities Committee (ESC) and the Committee of European Securities Regulators (CESR).

These committees soon began the process of revising the ISD, which later became renamed the MiFID. Herbst (2003) and Knight (2003) examine features of this revision process in the context of the FSAP. Table 1 provides the current

[26] G Ferrarini (2002) and M Levin (2003) provide a good overview of some of the legal aspects of the original ISD and subsequent European securities markets regulations.

timeline of the MiFID approval process. Transposition refers to the process by which each EU Member State brings into force the laws, regulations, and administrative processes necessary to comply with the Directive.

November 2000	The commission urges ISD updating.
July – October 2001	First round of consultation on ISD revisions.
March – May 2002	Second round of consultation on ISD revisions.
July 2002	CESR reaches agreement on new European guidelines for the implementation of legislation on ATSs within their respective jurisdictions.
September 2002	Private revised draft Directive distributed between national regulators for discussion.
November 2002	Revised draft publicly distributed to European Parliament and to European Council.
June 2003	European Parliament votes on amendments.
July 2003	First reading by European Parliament.
October 2003	Political agreement reached by European Council.
March 2004	European Parliament approves the Directive on Markets in Financial Instruments.
30 April 2004	Entry into force of MiFID.
2004-2005	ESC negotiation about 'Level 2' MiFID details, with advice provided by CESR.
2005	FSAP Target Deadline.
30 April 2006	Original deadline for MiFID transposition in the Member States.
30 April 2007	New extended deadline for MiFID transposition in the Member States.

Table 1: Timeline of ISD revision and MiFID approval.

The MiFID contains a set of high-level principles that govern the authorization and operation of alternative providers of trading services in financial instruments. The goal is to allow regulated markets to compete for order flow and liquidity with other regulated markets and with trading systems provided by alternative market centres and by investment firms without jeopardising the orderly and efficient operation of the European securities market system, or the interests of issuers and investors.

The MiFID identifies three categories of trading services to which it attributes a decreasing level of regulatory requirements: (i) regulated markets, (ii) multilateral trading facilities (MTFs), and (iii) systematic internalisers. Regulated markets and MTFs are defined as 'multilateral systems which bring together multiple third-party buying and selling interests in financial instruments in accordance with non-discretionary rules'.[27] These systems may have similar trading functionalities and differ only in the fact that regulated markets have to be authorised by the competent authority. Systematic internalisers are defined as investment firms 'which, on an organised, frequent and systematic basis, deal on own account by executing client orders outside a regulated market or an MTF'.[28]

[27] Article 4 (14) and (15) MiFID.

[28] Article 4 (7) MiFID.

The new regulatory principles of the MiFID apply not only to equity trading but also to trading in many other financial instruments such as fixed-income and derivatives securities. The European legislator recognises that trading in various financial instruments is becoming progressively similar and understands the importance of fostering competition and integration across markets for all financial instruments.

We identify three main themes of the new regulatory structure: investor protection, market access, and transparency.

Investor protection. The MiFID is particularly concerned with the protection of investors in potentially fragmented markets. It mandates the adoption by investment firms of adequate procedures for conducting their business as well as procedures for identifying and removing conflicts of interests (Articles 13, 18 and 19). This ensures that investors have adequate information about a firm's execution practices. The MiFID also includes provisions on best execution, order handling and trade reporting rules (Articles 21, 22 and 25) which ensure that (i) firms act in the best interest of the clients when executing their orders, (ii) orders are executed promptly and sequentially, (iii) there is no front-running of client's orders, and (iv) trades reports are standardised and sufficiently detailed so that execution performances across different trading systems can be measured and compared.

Market Access. Consistent with the previous ISD, the MiFID establishes a EU passport for investment firms. Precisely, investment firms authorised by a Member State may provide services in any other Member State (Article 31). Member States have to ensure that investment firms authorised from other Member States have access to regulated markets in their territory directly by setting up branches in the host state, by remote membership, or by having remote access (Article 33). Also, investment firms have the right of access to central counterparty, clearing and settlement systems in other Member States (Article 34).

Transparency. The MiFID attempts to create a level playing field where alternative market structures and trading systems can compete for trade execution with no detrimental effect on market quality (e.g. liquidity and price discovery). Hence, MiFID includes provisions on pre-trade (Articles 27, 29 and 44) and post-trade (Articles 28, 30 and 45) transparency. Note, however, that although the MiFID applies in general to trading in financial instruments, pre-trade transparency obligations apply only to trading in shares.

I. Comments and Recommendations

The MiFID has some clear implications. Obviously, the traditionally concentrated European markets, such as in Spain, Italy and France, will be exposed to greater order flow competition. And, the markets in Germany and the UK will need to adapt to allow for greater transparency.

These developments need to be carefully monitored. For instance, greater transparency may lead to increased preferencing and price matching practices, and thereby lead to less limit order submissions and hence *lower* liquidity and *less* price competition. Research on pre-trade transparency and disclosure has produced these *mixed* predictions and findings:

(i) On one hand, increased pre-trade transparency seems to decrease market liquidity because limit order traders are less willing to submit orders in transparent markets. Madhavan, Porter and Weaver (2005) supply empirical evidence from a natural experiment on the Toronto Stock Exchange.

(ii) On the other hand, greater transparency seems to lead to greater price efficiency. Baruch (2005) employs a stylised model of a specialist's single-price auction to study the welfare implications of making the limit-order book visible prior to market open. His model predicts that with an open order book the price impact of market orders is lower and prices reveal more information. In this model greater transparency leads to greater price efficiency. Boehmer, Saar and Yu (2005) finds evidence consistent with Baruch's model. They study the effects of the introduction of the NYSE's OpenBook, which allows traders off the NYSE floor to observe, in real-time, depth in the book at each price level for all securities.

Since there is no conclusive evidence on the effects of the new transparency rules, it is important to monitor and assess the effects of the new European transparency regime on market quality in order to implement procedures for timely introduction of any necessary adjustments.

The new order handling rules of MiFID impose strict price and time priority when executing orders within a specific trading venue. However, exchanges should carefully determine tick sizes that are sufficiently large; otherwise, intermediaries would easily gain trading priority by marginally improving the price and hence deter limit order traders from providing liquidity. Secondary priority rules become significant only if tick sizes are sufficiently large (Harris (2002)).

Investors are interested in net prices – that is, prices adjusted for commissions and fees. In order to ensure that adequate, reliable and comparable information is reported on executed trades, so that investors are able to monitor the performance of providers of trading services, it is desirable to require separate specification of trade price from commissions and venues' access fees. With such detailed data, consolidators of quote and trade information can provide fee adjusted comparisons (see the example of NASDAQ's SuperMontage which offers traders the choice of ranking quotes with or without commissions). Generally, retail investors can easily monitor commissions but cannot easily assess the execution of their orders. The separate specification of fees and prices promotes fair competition for order flow. As mentioned in Section B, the existence of preferencing arrangements does not have a detrimental effect on price competition and market quality if there is competition for retail order flow. When intermediaries compete for order flow, they lower commissions to attract retail orders and therefore rebate payments for order flow to their customers.

Furthermore, we believe trade reports, to be most useful, should identify the sign (buy or sell) of the trade. Without this vital information, practitioners and academics have to rely on approximation methods, possibly leading to inaccurate estimates of transaction costs. The sign of the trade corresponds to the position taken by the trade initiator, namely by the trader who demands liquidity. The trade initiator is clearly identifiable in pure dealership markets as the investor. In other markets the liquidity demander usually corresponds to the trade counterparty that submits the last order.

Finally, we believe that a common regulatory structure, greater integration, greater transparency, and the production of accurate, accessible, comparable data will foster much needed in-depth research on European markets.

F. Conclusion

The financial landscape has changed dramatically since the adoption of the original ISD in 1993. Political developments, technological innovations, changes in trading practices and increases in the sophistication of investors have made a revision of the ISD necessary to lay the foundations for a better integrated, more competitive and efficient European financial market.

The main theme in the development of the MiFID has been finding a balance between the occasionally conflicting goals of encouraging market competition and enhancing market quality. Under ISD countries could opt for 'concentration' in their equity market, whereas MiFID removes this option and explicitly allows 'internalisation' subject to best execution obligations and disclosure requirements.

Much of the debate that animated the consultation stage of the ISD revision process originated from a lack of focus on the core issues under discussion. To aid this process, in this paper we have carefully defined terms such as internalisation, fragmentation, and preferencing. We believe it is important to focus on the internalisation of *retail* trades because these are most susceptible to conflicts of interest between traders and intermediaries.

We then summarized previous empirical and theoretical research about the effect of fragmentation on market quality. This research shows that a careful balance must be struck between the gains in trade technology innovation resulting from competition and the costs of lower price efficiency caused by fragmentation.

Despite much discussion on the issue of internalisation within Europe, there has been little research on its extent in each Member State. To fill this void, this paper surveyed the off-exchange execution practices for the five largest European equity markets. We note that while it is well-known that internalisation (or in-house execution of retail trades) occurs frequently in the UK and Germany, it is not often recognized that off-exchange executions commonly occur in virtually all Member States. Our research also highlights that markets are becoming increasingly segmented. For example, new investor-to-investor trading systems such as Liquidnet are only available to buy-side institutional investors, Borsa Italiana has an after-hours segment only available to retail investors, and most crossing networks are only accessible to large traders.

Previous research has largely focused on U.S. markets. Unlike European markets, U.S. markets are governed by a common set of regulations, are characterised by better-educated retail investors, and have greater information linkage. Clearly, these differences demand differences in their regulatory frameworks. Nevertheless, lessons can be learned from how U.S. markets have dealt with issues of market fragmentation. We have highlighted some of the successes and potential pitfalls of the U.S. regulatory experience that regulators must strive to avoid (such as overly rigid rules).

Finally, we examine the new EU regulatory environment created by the MiFID. While much still needs to be done, the MiFID has made tremendous strides towards fostering greater competition and allowing internalisation in European financial markets. It ensures investors have: (i) access to alternative execution venues trading the same security; (ii) adequate information about a firm's execution practices and adequate post-trade information to measure execution performance; and (iii) assurances that their orders will be processed sequentially and provided best possible execution. As well, firms must make an order visible and accessible to the market if they cannot immediately execute the order. And, efficient price discovery will be promoted by the required dissemination of trade prices.

Regulators must remain *forward-looking*: the current revision process has taken almost a decade to complete. World financial markets continue to evolve in often unpredictable ways – the real danger is that the MiFID will be out-of-date before it is finished. Going forward, much more formal, sponsored research is needed on European financial markets. Positive steps must be taken to reduce the almost prohibitive cost of cross-border trade and thereby truly integrate European financial markets.

References

Admati, AR and P Pfleiderer 'Sunshine Trading and Financial Market Equilibrium' (1991) 4 Rev Finan Stud 443-481.

Amihud, Y, B Lauterbach and H Mendelson 'The value of trading consolidation: Evidence from the exercise of warrants' (2002) 38 J Finan Quant Anal 829-846.

Arnold, T, P Hersch, JH Mulherin and JM Netter 'Merging Markets' (1999) 54 J Finance 1083-1107.

ASSOSIM (Associazione Italiana Intermediari Mobiliari) Code of Conduct (1998).

Baruch, S 'Who Benefits from an Open Limit-Order Book?' (2005) 78 J Bus 1267-1306.

Battalio, R, J Greene, B Hatch and R Jennings 'Does the Limit Order Routing Decision Matter?' (2002) 15 Rev Finan Stud 159-194.

Battalio, R, J Greene and R Jennings 'Do Competing Specialists and Preferencing Dealers Affect Market Quality?' (1997) 10 Rev Finan Stud 969-993.

Battalio, RH 'Third Market Broker-Dealers: Cost Competitors or Cream Skimmers?' (1997) 52 J Finance 241-52.

Battalio, RH and CW Holden 'A Simple Model of Payment for Order Flow, Internalization, and Total Trading Cost' (2001) 4 J Finan Mark 33-71.

Bessembinder, H 'Quote-Based Competition and Trade Execution Costs in NYSE-Listed Stocks' (2003) 70 J Finan Econ 385-422.

Biais, B 'Price Formation and Equilibrium Liquidity in Fragmented and Centralized Markets' (1993) 48 J Finance 157-185.

Biais, B and D Davydoff 'Internalisation, Investor Protection and Market Quality' (OEE wp <http://www.oee.fr/pdf/oeefree_pdf/361_10.pdf>, 2002)

Biais, B, D Martimort and JC Rochet 'Competing Mechanisms in a Common Value Environment' (2000) 68 Econometrica 799-837.

Blume, ME 'The Structure of the U.S. Equity Markets' (Rodney White Center for Financial Research University of Pennsylvania wp 6-02).

Blume, ME and MA Goldstein 'Quotes, Order Flow, and Price Discovery' (1997) 52 J Finance 221-244.

Boehmer, B and E Boehmer 'Trading your Neighbor's ETFs: Competition or Fragmentation?' (2003) 27 J Banking Finance 1667-1703.

Boehmer, E 'Dimensions of Execution Quality: Recent Evidence for U.S. Equity Markets' (2005) 78 J Finan Econ 553-582.

Boehmer, E, R Jennings and L Wei 'Public Disclosure and Private Decisions: The Case of Equity Market Execution Quality' (2005) Rev Finan Stud forthcoming.

Boehmer, E, G Saar and L Yu 'Lifting the Veil: an Analysis of Pre-Trade Transparency at the NYSE' (2005) 60 J Finance 783-815.

Cai, C and A Dufour 'Market fragmentation and price discovery on the London Stock Exchange' (Unpublished manuscript ISMA Centre University of Reading 2002).

Chakravarty, S and A Sarkar 'A Model of Brokers' Trading, with Applications to Order Flow Internalization and Off-Exchange Block Sales' (2002) 11 Rev Finan Econ 19-36.

Chowdhry, B and V Nanda 'Multimarket Trading and Market Liquidity' (1991) 4 Rev Finan Stud 483-511.

Christie, WG, JH Harris and PH Schultz 'Why Did NASDAQ Market Makers Stop Avoiding Odd-Eighth Quotes?' (1994) 49 J Finance 1841-1860.

Christie, WG and PH Schultz 'Why Do NASDAQ Market Makers Avoid Odd-Eighth Quotes' (1994) 49 J Finance 1813-1840.

Chung, KH, C Chuwonganant and DT McCormick 'Order Preferencing and Market Quality on NASDAQ Before and After Decimalization' (2004) 71 J Finan Econ 581-612.

Chung, KH, C Chuwonganant and DT McCormick 'Does Internalization Diminish the Impact of Quote Aggressiveness on Dealer Market Share?' (2006) 15 J Finan Intermediation 108-131.

Conrad, JS, KM Johnson and S Wahal 'Institutional Trading and Soft Dollars' (2001) 55 J Finance 397-416.

Conrad, J, KM Johnson and S Wahal 'Institutional Trading and Alternative Trading Systems' (2003) 70 J Finan Econ 99-134.

Consob (1998a) Regulation No. 11768 of 23 December 1998 – Implementing the Provisions on Markets of Legislative Decree 58 of 24 February 1998.

Consob (1998b) Regulation No. 11522 of 1 July 1998 – Implementing the Provisions on Intermediaries of Legislative Decree 58 of 24 February 1998

Consob (1998c) Communication No. DM/98097747.

Davies, RJ, A Dufour and B Scott-Quinn 'Building a Competitive and Efficient European Financial Market' (ECMI wp <http://www.eurocapitalmarkets.org/ ?q=node/141>, 2003).

Davis, JL and LE Lightfoot 'Fragmentation Versus Consolidation of Securities Trading: Evidence from the Operation of Rule 19c-3' (1998) 41 J Law Econ 209-238.

Dridi, R, L Germain, B Kluger and D Stolin 'Quotation and Trading in Fragmented Markets' (Toulouse Business School wp, 2000).

Dutta, PK and A Madhavan 'Competition and Collusion in Dealership Markets' (1997) 52 J Finance 245-276.

Council Directive 93/22/EEC of 10 May 1993 on Investment Services in the Securities Field, OJ L 141 11.06.1993 27-46.

Directive 2004/39/EC of the European Parliament and of the Council of 21 April 2004 on Markets in Financial Instruments amending Council Directives 85/611/EEC and 93/6/EEC and Directive 2000/12/EC of the European Parliament and of the Council and repealing Council Directive 93/22/EEC, OJ L 145 30.04.2004 1-44.

Easley, D, NM Kiefer and M O'Hara 'Cream-Skimming or Profit Sharing? The Curious Role of Purchased Order Flow' (1996) 51 J Finance 811-833.

Ferrarini, G 'Pan-European Securities Markets: Policy Issues and Regulatory Responses' (2002) 3 Eur Bus Org L R 249-292.

Financial Services Authority 'Alternative Trading Systems' Consultation Paper No. 153, 2002.

Fong, K, A Madhavan and PL Swan 'Why Do Markets Fragment? A Panel-Data Analysis of Off-Exchange Trading' (University of New South Wales wp, 2004)

Foucault, T and CA Parlour 'Competition for Listings' (2004) 35 RAND J Econ 329-355.

Goldstein, MA, AV Shkilko, BF Van Ness and RA Van Ness 'Inter-Market Competition for NYSE-Listed Securities' (Babson College wp, 2005).

Gomber, P and KO Maurer 'Xetra BEST – Integration of Market Access Intermediaries' Requirements into Market Design' (2004) 14 Electronic Markets 214-222.

Grammig, J and E Theissen 'Is Best Really Better? Internalization in Xetra BEST' (University of Bonn wp, 2005).

Gresse, C 'The Effect of Crossing-Network Trading on Dealer Market's Bid-Ask Spreads' (2006) 12 Europ Finan Manage 143-160.

Hamilton, JH 'Marketplace Fragmentation, Competition, and the Efficiency of the Stock Exchange' (1979) 34 J Finance 171-187.

Hansch, O, NY Naik and S Viswanathan 'Preferencing, internalization, best execution, and dealer profits' (1999) 54 J Finance 1799-1828.

Harris, FH, TH McInish, G Shoesmith and RA Wood 'Cointegration, Error Correction, and Price Discovery on Informationally Linked Security Markets' (1995) 30 J Finan Quant Anal 563-579.

Harris, LE 'Consolidation, Fragmentation, Segmentation and Regulation' in RA Schwartz (ed) *Global Equity Markets: Technological, Competitive and Regulatory Challenges* (Irwin Professional Publishing Chicago IL 1995).

Harris, LE *Trading and exchanges: Market microstructure for practitioners* (Oxford University Press 2002).

Hasbrouck, J 'One Security, Many Markets: Determining the Contributions to Price Discovery' (1995) 50 J Finance 1175-1199.

Herbst, J 'Revision of the Investment Services Directive' (2003) 11 Journal of Financial Regulation and Compliance 211-218.

Huang, RD 'The Quality of ECN and NASDAQ Market Maker Quotes' (2002) 57 J Finance 1285-1319.

Jain, P 'Institutional Design and Liquidity on Stock Exchanges' (Indiana University wp, 2001).

Kandel, E and LM Marx 'Payments for Order Flow on NASDAQ' (1999) 54 J Finance 35-66.

Knight, A 'The Investment Services Directive – Routemap or Obstacle Course' (2003) 11 Journal of Financial Regulation and Compliance 219-224.

Lee, CMC 'Market Integration and Price Execution for NYSE-Listed Securities' (1993) 48 J Finance 1009-1038.

Lee, R *Capital Markets that Benefit Investors: a Survey of the Evidence on Fragmentation, Internalisation and Market Transparency* (Oxford Finance Group 2002).

Levin, M 'Competition, Fragmentation and Transparency: Providing the Regulatory Framework for Fair, Efficient and Dynamic European Securities Markets' (CEPS Task Force Report No. 46 2003).

Macey, JR and M O'Hara 'The Law and Economics of Best Execution' (1997) 6 J Finan Intermediation 188-223.

Madhavan, A 'Consolidation, Fragmentation, and the Disclosure of Trading Information' (1995) 8 Rev Finan Stud 579-603.

Madhavan, A 'Market Microstructure: A Survey' (2000) 3 J Finan Markets 205-258.

Madhavan, A, D Porter and D Weaver 'Should Securities Markets be Transparent?' (2005) 8 J Finan Markets 265-287.

Mayhew, S, 'Competition, Market Structure, and Bid-Ask Spreads in Stock Option Markets' (2002) 57 J Finance 931-958.

McAndrews, J and C Stefanadis 'The Consolidation of European Stock Exchanges' (2002) 8 Federal Reserve Bank of New York Current Issues in Economics and Finance 1-6.

Mendelson, H 'Consolidation, Fragmentation, and Market Performance' (1987) 22 J Finan Quant Anal 189-208.

Naik, NY and PK Yadav 'The Effects of Market Reform on Trading Costs of Public Investors: Evidence from the London Stock Exchange' (SSRN wp <http://www.ssrn.com/abstract_id=172328>).

O'Hara, M *Market Microstructure Theory* (Blackwell 1995).

Pagano, M 'Trading Volume and Asset Liquidity' (1989a) 104 Quart J Econ 25-74.

Pagano, M 'Endogenous Market Thinness and Stock Price Volatility' (1989b) 56 Rev Econ Stud 269-288.

Parlour, CA and DJ Seppi 'Liquidity-Based Competition for Order Flow' (2003) 16 Rev of Finan Stud 301-343.

Peterson, MA and ER Sirri 'Order Preferencing and Market Quality on U.S. Equity Exchanges' (2003) 16 Rev Finan Stud 385-415.

Sabatini, G and I Tarola 'Transparency on Secondary Markets: A Survey of Economic Literature and Current Regulation in Italy' (Consob Quaderni di Finanza <http://www.consob.it>, 2002).

Shapiro, JE 'U.S. Equity Markets: Recent Competitive Developments' in RA Schwartz (ed) *Global Equity Markets: Technological, Competitive, and Regulatory Challenges* (IRWIN 1995).

Stoll, HR 'Market Fragmentation' (2001) 57 Finan Analysts J 16-20.

Theissen, E 'Price Discovery in Floor and Screen Trading Systems' (2002) 9 J Empirical Finance 455-474.

Theissen, E 'Organized Equity Markets in Germany' (CFS wp No. 17, 2003).

U.S. Securities and Exchange Commission (1963) Report of Special Study of Securities Markets.

U.S. Securities and Exchange Commission (1997) Report on the Practice of Preferencing.

U.S. Securities and Exchange Commission (2001) Report of the Advisory Committee on Market Information: A Blueprint for Responsible Change (the 'Seligman Report').

U.S. Securities and Exchange Commission Regulation NMS (2005) Release No. 34-51808.

The European Securities Industry. Further Evidence on the Roadmap to Integration

BARBARA ALEMANNI
GIUSEPPE LUSIGNANI
MARCO ONADO

The integration of the European securities market is one of the most important and ambitious steps of the making of a unified financial system, particularly since the achievement of the monetary union. The paper contributes to the debate on the integration and shows why the issue of costs and competition between different trading and post-trading systems is the key point of future integration. In particular, the analysis starts with the roadmap set by the European Commission and the evolution of the regulatory approach towards the integration of the trading and post-trading sectors. After the roadmap, in the paper we review the results of the research on the main issues related to the integration of securities markets and we comment on the present situation, with particular reference to the alliances and mergers between the main actors of the trading and post-trading business. In addition we present some original measures of the explicit costs of trading for all main European exchanges, adopting a bottom-up approach, which allows to compare the prices paid by different investors for different sizes of trades. This comparison shows that the ranking of exchanges by level of prices varies, according to the trade size taken into account. This on the one hand makes more difficult the emergence of the most efficient and on the other hand has anti-competitive effects, in particular for non domestic traders. Integration becomes therefore more difficult. To complement the analysis on trading costs, we also briefly review the debate on fragmentation of different European post-trading systems. The paper concludes with some policy implications.

A. Foreword
B. The Roadmap: The European Approach
C. The Roadmap: Main Issues and Findings
D. The Present Landscape
E. The Trading Costs in European Exchanges: A Comparative Analysis
F. Costs of Post-Trading in Europe: A Comparative Analysis
G. Conclusions and Policy Implications

A. Foreword

The integration of the European securities market is one of the most important and ambitious steps in the making of a unified financial system, particularly since the achievement of the monetary union. This paper aims to examine the debate on

European integration and to show why the issue of costs and competition between different trading and post-trading systems is the key point of future integration. The paper is organised as follows. Section B follows the roadmap set by the European Commission and the evolution of the regulatory approach to the trading and post-trading sectors. Section C reviews the results of the research on the main issues related to the integration of securities markets. Section D comments the present situation, with particular reference to the alliances and mergers between the main actors of the trading and post-trading business. Section E measures the explicit costs of trading for all main European exchanges, adopting a bottom-up approach, which allows for a comparison of the prices paid by different investors for different sizes of trades. This comparison, made here for the first time, shows that the ranking of exchanges by level of prices varies according to the trade size taken into account. This, on the one hand, makes the emergence of the most efficient market more difficult and, on the other hand, has anti-competitive effects, in particular for non domestic traders. Integration becomes therefore more difficult. Section F briefly reviews the debate on fragmentation of different European post-trading systems. Section G summarises the results and draws the main policy implications.

B. The Roadmap: The European Approach

I. The Overall Strategy

The creation of a single financial system has always been one of the main objectives of the European Union. The first measures were directed to the banking sector and were mainly based on the principles of the European passport, which was expected to level the playing field, increase competition and eventually lead to the awaited integration. As the European financial systems were typically bank-oriented (particularly those of the founding countries) it was only too natural to start the strategy of integration with measures related to banking. This is why only in 1993 (16 years after the first Banking Directive) did the Investment Services Directive try to apply the principles of the European passport to the securities market. The underlying hypothesis was that financial markets were more and more important in all European countries. In particular, it was expected that integration would reduce trading costs, widen the range of opportunities and eventually bring benefits both to investors and issuers. Trading costs were expected to decrease; issuers to lower their cost of capital; investors to have a wider range of more competitively priced financial products. As a consequence, households could make more efficient decisions of consumption and investment. In other words, convergence of national financial systems began to be seen not only as a necessary condition for competitiveness of the securities industry of the Euro area, but as an achievement per se which was expected to bring important macroeconomic gains in terms of investment and growth.

The European Commission has sponsored a research[1] whose objective was to rigorously and independently assess and quantify the macroeconomic benefits that would flow from full integration of the European financial markets. More specifically, the study aimed to measure the effects of integration of the presently still regionally-fragmented exchanges on the cost of equity and bond financing and more generally on investment, consumption and production. The macroeconomic simulations pointed to important results; in particular, for the European Union as a whole: the level of total real GDP would be raised by 1.1%, or €130 billion in 2002 prices, in the long-run; total business investment would increase by 6.0% and private consumption by 0.8%; total employment would increase by 0.5%.

The growing awareness of these macroeconomic gains, together with the dismal results of cross-border competition in the securities markets, prompted at the end of the '90s a new wave of European measures, included in the Financial Services Action Plan (FSAP) which was approved in the same year of the introduction of the Euro.[2] The FSAP set 42 measures intended to provide a legal and regulatory environment that should support the integration of financial markets across the EU. In particular, the FSAP had the following objectives: a single wholesale market; an open and secure retail financial services market; state-of-the-art prudential rules and supervision.

While wholesale markets at that point were reasonably integrated, partial results were achieved both in the retail markets and the regulatory framework. It is therefore important to review European legislation in the field of the securities markets and the underlying theoretical assumptions. It is also worth looking separately at the trading and post-trading sector.

II. The Trading Sector

The trading side of the securities markets has for a long time been considered the most important, both by scholars and market participants. Not surprisingly, the ISD was mainly focused on trading. One of the objectives of this Directive was to remove the barriers of access to the European stock exchanges. This step was considered as a condition to enhance competition among different trading

[1] London Economics (in association with PricewaterhouseCoopers and Oxford Economic Forecasting) 'Quantification of the Macro-Economic Impact of Integration of EU Financial Markets, Executive Summary of the Final Report to the European Commission' (November 2002).

[2] The FSAP has been the legislative framework for developing the single market in financial services. In June 1998, the European Council in Cardiff invited the European Commission to prepare a framework for action to develop the Single Market in financial services. In May 1999, the Commission published a Communication containing the Plan, which was approved by the Lisbon European Council in March 2000.

venues. The condition proved to be necessary, but certainly not sufficient, for many reasons. First, there were striking differences among European exchanges in structural conditions such as size, trading architecture, ownership, regulation. The levelling of the playing field was therefore meaningless before a reasonable convergence of main structural conditions had taken place. Second, the ISD was based on a pure 'European passport' approach, i.e. on the idea that allowing intermediaries conditions of free access to each European market would automatically lead to the ideal conditions of pure competition among exchanges, ending up with the victory of the most efficient. Scarce importance, if any, was given to competition coming from alternative trading systems.

This cautious approach to competition was rooted on very practical reasons. The first worry of most European countries was to protect an infant regulated market and the interests of their respective securities industry. The provision of concentration rules in countries such as Italy, France or Spain is a good case in point. Both the European Commission and particularly the national regulators were mainly aiming at consolidating national markets; they were therefore only too ready to stress the dangers of fragmentation coming from competition among exchanges, at the expenses of possible gains in efficiency through lower trading costs.

From a theoretical point of view, it has been pointed out that fragmentation has dangerous side effects. Theoretical studies have traditionally predicted that order flows create externalities (liquidity attracts liquidity) which concentrate trading on the already largest market.[3] Alternative trading venues can be created only if traders have different needs and preferences.[4] In that case, quotes and orders may not be given the opportunity to interact completely, leading to a less efficient price discovery process and to a lower probability for investors (particularly retail investors) to get best execution conditions for their orders. In other words, competition among trading venues is not necessarily beneficial to investors.

Market fragmentation, i.e. the situation in which the same security trades on multiple venues,[5] became therefore the main issue from the point of view of competition between stock exchanges and financial institutions in particular.

At the end of the '90s European authorities, and particularly the new-born CESR (Committee of European Securities Regulators), began to look more favourably to competition between regulated markets[6] and alternative trading sys-

[3] M Pagano 'Trading Volume and Asset Liquidity' (1989) 104 The Quarterly Journal of Economics 255-274.

[4] L Harris *Trading and Exchanges* (Oxford University Press 2003) 530.

[5] IOSCO 'Transparency and Market Fragmentation' (Report from the Technical Committee) (2001).

[6] Since 2001 FESCO, (CESR's predecessor) had prompted the emergence of Alternative Trading Systems (also called Multilateral Trading Facilities, or ECN, Electronic Communica-

cont. ...

tems, defined by the CESR as 'a multilateral system, operated by an entity, which without being regulated as a regulated market, brings together multiple third party buying and selling interests in financial instruments – in the system and according to non-discretionary rules set by the system's operator – in a way that results in a contract'.[7]

In other words, the worries on competition between trading venues moved from the effect on price discovery towards the maintaining of results not only in terms of price, but on transparency, both pre- and post-trade. But as expressed by Levin, '[l]eaving the intermediary with discretion where to execute a particular order raises the question whether there is a conflict between the interest of clients – who wish best execution – and intermediaries – who have a self-interest in executing orders in own books or via a preferenced/paying agent. Broker-dealers may have an interest in executing orders in-house, as this could enable them not only to avoid paying exchange fees but also to time the execution of some of their clients' orders (e.g. retail) to fit their own proprietary trading interests or those of a large, favoured customer. This is not necessarily in the interest of those clients. This conflict, the argument goes, may be particularly pronounced when intermediaries are dealing with unsophisticated retail clients'.[8]

Although internalisation can have different meanings,[9] generally the term refers to the situation where 'a bank or a broker executes retail client orders in-

tion Network in U.S.) stating that 'competition and innovation in trading systems are to be welcomed' (FESCO 'The Regulation of Alternative Trading Systems' (September 2000)). At the same time, it stressed the importance of maintaining high standards in terms of market efficiency and investor protection. In the same vein, the UK authority remarked that 'these new platforms have been made possible by rapid advances in information technology. This has enabled the creation of new market places which have no need for physically trading floors. As such, they can be readily accessed from anywhere in the world, can handle large trading volumes in an orderly manner, and link seamlessly into back office and settlement process'. FSA 'Alternative Trading Systems' (Consultation Paper 152) (December 2002) 6 showed that around 25 ATS were active in the UK, in markets for equities, bonds, financial derivatives and commodities.

[7] CESR 'Standards for Alternative Trading Systems' (July 2002).

[8] M Levin 'Competition, Fragmentation and Transparency' (CEPS Task Force Review) (April 2003) 62.

[9] Often the term 'internalisation' is used in a broad sense to indicate the practice of order matching carried out by investment firms, also called in-house matching. Such a definition includes two types of trades: (a) Direct executions by broker/dealers of clients' orders for their own account. For example, in the UK, this includes retail trades executed by Retail Service Providers (RSPs) in a principal capacity (e.g. retail orders submitted by Merrill Lynch customers to the RSP operated by Merrill Lynch) as well as institutional orders executed by broker/dealers against own positions. (b) Agency crosses where customer orders are matched against each other. This includes crosses of customer orders on proprietary order books and matches of (institutional) client orders at a reference price on crossing networks. For the most part, we focus on a narrower definition of internalisation. Cfr R Davies, A Dufour and B Scott-Quinn 'Build-

cont. ...

house, either by acting as a principal and executing them against its own positions or by sending them to an affiliated market maker'.

The debate on fragmentation gradually proved that the advantages of competition overcome the negative side-effects, provided that both best execution and a certain level of pre- and post-trade transparency are guaranteed. The results were particularly favourable to competition among different trading venues, particularly in the United States, where 'the additional competition provided by ECNs, the structural diversity they offer and the attitude of regulators appear to have led to possible overall effects, even on price quality'.[10]

In Europe, the results are less clear-cut. While most market participants were sanguine on the importance of overcoming the monopoly power of regulated markets,[11] other studies – most of them coming from regulated markets – stressed the dangers of fragmentation and internalisation.[12] It has been also pointed out that present market arrangements and regulations provide a way of overcoming the side effects of fragmentation through pre- and post-trade transparency and best execution rules.[13] One research[14] measured the effects of fragmentation and particularly of internalisation on market quality. Using UK data for off central order book executions, the study finds that in the UK the main price discovery mechanism is the SETS order book, even though most retail business is executed off-SETS through retail service providers (internalised business). Moreover, very few of the trades executed on SETS are matches of investors' orders, and dealers participate in most SETS trades. This suggests that the quality of the UK market could be improved by fostering greater direct access for private and institutional traders to order book liquidity. At the same time, the study concluded that while internalisation should be allowed in European financial markets, there must also be regulatory provisions to ensure that: (i) investors have adequate information about a firm's execution practices, and adequate post-trade information to ensure best execution; (ii) investors are able to access alternative execution venues; and (iii) prices for trades executed at different trading venues are promptly disseminated so that competing data vendors can consolidate market information and thereby facilitate efficient price discovery.

ing a Competitive and Efficient European Financial Market' (European Capital Markets Institute Short Paper No. 4) (2003).

[10] M Levin (n 8) 58 who concludes: 'overall these studies dent the theoretical prediction that fragmentation of trading may decrease market quality'.

[11] International Primary Market Association et al 'Innovation, Competition Diversity Choice. A European Capital Market for 21st Century. A Position Paper' (May 2002).

[12] Euronext 'Internalisation' (2002).

[13] R Davies, A Dufour and B Scott-Quinn 'The MiFID: Competition in a New European Equity Market Regulatory Structure' in this volume 163-197.

[14] R Davis, A Dufour and B Scott-Quinn (n 9).

The debate on fragmentation gradually inspired the revision of the Investment Services Directive in favour of competition among all different trading venues. The final text approved in 2004 conceives a multi-facet world, made of regulated markets, alternative systems, defined as MTFs (Multilateral Trading Facilities) and internalisers. Concentration rules have therefore been phased out.

In this perspective, the protection of investors is based to a great extent on pre- and post-trade conditions. From this point of view the Directive had to make a difficult choice. Theory predicts that the maximum of pre-trade transparency optimises the price discovery process, but could have adverse effects on liquidity, as possible market participants could refrain from trading to avoid possible reactions from other traders. The problem is complicated in a scenario of competition between regulated markets and broker-dealers who internalise orders. The former (typically based on order-driven systems) gain from the maximum pre- and post-trade transparency. The latter (typically quote driven) need a certain degree of opacity.

These trade-offs have been reflected in the final version of the MiFID (Markets in Financial Instruments Directive), which allows investors to access alternative trading systems under a regime of internalisation. At the same time, under the new regulation:

(i) investors will have adequate information about a firm's execution practices and adequate post-trade information to measure execution performance;

(ii) orders will be processed sequentially and provided best possible execution. Should a firm not be able to execute immediately the order it has to make this information immediately visible and accessible to the market;

(iii) prices for trades executed at different trading venues will be promptly disseminated so that market information can be consolidated, thereby increasing the efficiency of price discovery.

Although important regulatory details are still to be worked out in the phase of implementation of the Directive into national legislations, it is evident that the MiFID completely reshapes the rules on trading, focusing on a new integrated concept of exchange, given by the sum of regulated markets, Multilateral Trading Facilities and internalisers.[15] In particular, the fundamental hypothesis underlying the Directive is that both regulated markets and MTFs perform essentially the same economic function.[16]

The MiFID solves the trade-off, requiring as a general rule the maximum pre-trade transparency from all possible trading venues. At the same time, it leaves the room to a variety of possible exceptions, according to the type of trades and/or intermediaries involved.

[15] C Salini 'La nuova regolamentazione comunitaria in materia di mercati finanziari' mimeo (2004).

[16] C Salini (n 15). The definition is the same for both markets, and the directive tries to design an equivalent framework.

Technically speaking this leads to three important provisions: (i) the identification of two different categories of internalisers (those that do it on a systematic way and those who do not), (ii) a threshold for the trades (the so-called SMS, standard market size) and (iii) a limitation of the rule to the most liquid stocks. The actual definition of these categories will be given by the CESR, leaving further flexibility to the whole regulation.

Although this pragmatic approach makes sense, it has lengthened the process of actual implementation of the Directive. Consultation is still under way[17] and, because of the many alternatives still open, the actual effects of this important part of the new Directive are not expected in the near term.

III. The Post-Trading Sector

In the debate on the optimal structure of a securities industry, the topic of post-trading did not until recently have the honour of the limelight.[18] Traditionally considered a backwater for failed book-keepers it now takes prime place, as market participants and regulators are becoming aware that clearing and settlement systems are of the outmost importance both for the overall efficiency of financial markets and for the integration of European exchanges.

Post-trading involves all activities required to finalise a securities transaction, in particular: (i) the confirmation of the terms of the trade; (ii) the calculation of the amounts due (clearing); (iii) the possible involvement of a central counter-

[17] See CESR's Technical Advice on Possible Implementing Measures of the Directive 2004/39/EC on Markets in Financial Instruments, April 2005 (CESR/05-290b) and the two draft Commission proposals for implementing measures published on 6 February 2006: the Draft Commission Regulation implementing Directive 2004/39/EC of the European Parliament and of the Council as regards record-keeping obligations for investment firms, transaction reporting, market transparency, admission of financial instruments to trading and defined terms for the purposes of that Directive (the Draft Commission Regulation); and the Draft Commission Directive implementing Directive 2004/39/EC of the European Parliament and of the Council as regards organisational requirements and operational conditions for investment firms, and defined terms for the purposes of that Directive Draft (the Draft Commission Directive). For a more detailed discussion of these level 2 measures, see G Ferrarini and F Recine 'The MiFID and Internalisation' in this volume 235-270.

[18] 'Settlement systems have been referred to as the "plumbing" infrastructure of financial markets, the "façade" being the trading systems provided by exchanges. As in a building, the plumbing represents an essential infrastructure; although invisibile at first glance, settlement systems in financial markets provide the infrastructure that plays a crucial role in order to ensure the performance of a contract once the terms of the trade have been agreed'. G Sabatini and I Tarola 'Is Governance an Issue for Plumbers? Remarks on Consolidation of Securities Settlement Systems' in G Ferrarini, KJ Hopt and E Wymeersch (eds) *Capital Markets in the Age of the Euro. Cross-border Transactions, Listed Companies and Regulation* (Kluwer Law International 2002) 217.

party; (iv) the delivery of securities against payment of cash (settlement); (v) the safekeeping of securities in custody; (vi) the registration of the change of ownership, if applicable. As for the trading component, the debate dealt with the problems of technical structure, comparative costs, and the trade-off between concentration and competition.

The attention at the EU level on European clearing and settlement services came from three sides: (i) the Giovannini group, an interdisciplinary group established by the European Commission's Directorate on Economic and Financial Affairs; (ii) the European Central Bank's scrutiny of CSDs compliance with its settlement procedures standards; (iii) the Commission Communications of 2002 and 2004.

The first Giovannini Report[19] identified three kinds of obstacles to an efficient working of clearing and settlement services: national differences in technical requirements and market practice; national differences in tax procedures; and issues relating to legal certainty. Whilst the first kind of obstacles can be solved by market forces, the second and the third raise public policy issues. The second report by the Giovannini group, issued in 2003,[20] brought proposals to deal with the barriers evidenced in the previous work.

In response to the Giovannini reports findings, the European Commission adopted two Communications setting out its strategy and priorities. In May 2002, a consultation paper[21] was prepared to gather the position of market participants. In April 2004, the Communication[22] was finally published. The Communication sets three objectives.

(i) The preparation of a Directive on Clearing and Settlement aiming to increase competition and efficiency and, as a result, to drive down costs. Such a Directive would introduce comprehensive rights of access for clearing and settlement providers to all EU markets. It would ensure choice for investment firms, banks, central counterparties (institutions that typically act as intermediaries between the counterparties to trades), Central Securities Depositories and markets. It would set up a common regulatory framework covering the functions performed by the various players in clearing and settlement, thus allowing the mutual recognition of clearing and settlement systems across the EU, protecting in-

[19] The Giovannini Group 'Cross-border Clearing and Settlement Arrangements in the European Union – First Report' (November 2001) <http://europa.eu.int/comm/economy_finance/publications/giovannini/clearing1101_en.pdf>.

[20] The Giovannini Group 'Second Report on EU Cross-border Clearing and Settlement Arrangements' (April 2003).

[21] Communication from the Commission to the Council and the European Parliament – Clearing and Settlement in the European Union – Main Policy Issues and Future Challenges, COM(2002) 257.

[22] Communication from the Commission to the Council and the European Parliament – Clearing and Settlement in the European Union – The Way Forward, COM(2004) 312.

vestors and further enhancing the integration of national systems. The Directive would also stipulate appropriate governance arrangements - disclosure requirements, accounting separation and unbundling of specific services - for entities who play a key role in the clearing and settlement process. This would address some regulators' concerns over competition and over the safety of systems.

(ii) The setting up of two expert groups: an advisory, and a monitoring group, composed of high-level representatives of various private and public bodies involved in this project, including the European System of Central Banks (ESCB) and the Committee of European Securities Regulators (CESR). These groups would advise on, promote and monitor the progress of market-led actions to bring down barriers and to promote the overall integration of EU securities clearing and settlement systems.

(iii) An enhancement of competition. In particular, the Commission advocates the careful and continuous implementation of competition policy in this sector, in close co-operation with national antitrust authorities, to address any current or emerging restrictive market practices and to monitor further industry consolidation.

A first step to implement the proposals was moved in July 2004 when the Clearing and Settlement Advisory and Monitoring Expert (CESAME) group expert was established. The expert group is chaired by the Commission and comprises approximately 20 high level representatives of entities involved in clearing and settlement, as well as four public authority observers. The group's purpose is to assist the Commission in the integration of EU securities clearing and settlement systems, to advise on both market-led and joint public and private sector initiatives towards breaking down the barriers to integration as identified in the Giovannini reports, and to keep industry participants informed of its progress. Two further expert groups were to be established to look at legal and tax barriers to integration.

The work of the Commission has been accompanied by other important contributions. Among others[23] a special mention goes to the 'Standards for Securities Clearing and Settlement in the EU' issued in September 2004 by a Committee joining the ECB and CESR. The so-called ESCB-CESR standards, while developed in independence, represent a good complement to the proposals included in the Commission's communication. The 19 standards have been developed with the following main set of objectives:

- to build confidence in the markets by providing clear and effective standards;
- to foster the protection of investors and, in particular, retail investors;

[23] See The Group of Thirty's (G30) 'Global Clearing and Settlement: A Plan of Action' (2003) (for an executive summary <http://www.group30.org/docs/executive_summary.pdf>) and IOSCO-CPSS 'Recommendations for Securities Settlement Systems' (November 2001) <http://www.bis.org/publ/cpss46.htm>.

- to limit and manage systemic risks;
- to promote and sustain the integration and competitiveness of European markets by encouraging efficient structures and market-led responses to developments;
- to ensure the efficient functioning of securities trading markets and the cost effective settlement of their transactions;
- to enhance the safety, soundness and efficiency of clearing and settlement of securities, and, where applicable, other financial instruments;
- to provide a consistent basis for the adequate regulation, supervision and oversight of securities clearing and settlement systems, and other relevant securities service providers in EU.

Issues related to market structure and to competition have not been tackled by the group, but are clear objectives in the Commission proposals.

These regulatory initiatives have been well accepted. With the second Giovannini report showing the priorities in the process to remove barriers, a regulatory reaction was required. In particular, the Commission communication helps to recreate momentum and to define the perimeters of regulatory guidelines and market-led initiatives. In addition, the creation of groups of experts may represent a very important aspect for the implementation of the whole process. The second Giovannini report is silent on who should lead the process, but these groups together with market organizations, such as the European Central Securities Depositories Association (ECSDA) and the European Securities Forum (ESF), seem perfectly equipped to orchestrate the overall course of action.

Some more specific comments spring from the contents of the framework directive and the way competition policy should be implemented. A first issue in the future framework directive should deal with free access right and choices. The first objective is to remove barriers to the finalisation of individual cross-border transactions in the form of national differences in technical requirements/market practice, tax procedures and laws applying to securities. The Commission considers that the removal of barriers related to technical requirements will be primarily in the hands of the private sector.

Nevertheless, national and EU authorities can play an important role in removing these barriers by encouraging harmonisation through the development of standards. The remaining barriers will require public intervention, as in the case of defining the legal system that is applicable to securities transactions and holdings in the EU.

The second objective is to remove competitive distortions or unequal treatment of entities performing similar clearing and settlement activities. A fully integrated EU clearing and settlement infrastructure would require that rights of access to systems be comprehensive, transparent, objective and, above all, effective. Market participants should not be constrained in making investment decisions by the location of counterparty, securities or infrastructure. There should be generalised access (i.e. by all markets, infrastructure providers and market participants) to all necessary systems.

This is for sure a topic worth including in a framework directive, however under current competitive circumstances all providers of infrastructure in the long run have a clear self interest to open their systems to as much business as they can attract. In spite of this, different degrees of access are possible. The range covers simple accounting relationships to complex links/bridges handling multiple batches together with a broad range of further services beyond simple book-keeping. This broad range implies that the commercial and technical aspects involved can be very different and must be taken into consideration when defining access right. For example, considering how important the interoperability issue is to market users, a level 2 and level 3 regulation must provide clear regulatory standards in such an area.

The Communication does not discuss the merits of different architectures or models for providing pan-EU clearing and settlement services. The choice of architecture should be determined by the market, subject to legitimate public-policy constraints (e.g. adequate competition, appropriate investor protection and minimised systemic risk). However, it is essential to create an environment in which market forces can deliver the most appropriate architecture for an efficient clearing and settlement infrastructure for the EU.

The second key topic in the proposed directive is 'a common regulatory framework' for clearing and settlement. In theory, this goal can be effectively achieved by a functional regulation, where the activities and not the institutions are central in defining the perimeters for regulation. In practice, a functional approach in clearing and settlement is not so straightforward. This would mean introducing definitions based on the appropriate value chain segments. Definitions have not a formal nature but they are an instrument to determine the field of application of certain provisions. This feature leads to the conclusion that, if not correctly drafted, definitions could hamper the development of the systems or forcing entities already performing some activities to abandon them. Unfortunately, the importance of definition seems to have been disregarded by the Commission who gives contradicting definitions.[24] A clear definition should also be given by bearing in mind which type of institutions are bundling together different parts of the value chain. This suggestion may seem a way to re-iterate an institutional approach, but this is not the case providing it serves to cluster more effectively the sources of risk (clearing risks vs settlement risk). A risk-based approach will indeed allow reaching the objectives of clarifying the level and types of risks undertaken by each of the institutions involved, and tailoring the prudential regulation accordingly. Clearly a lot of work must be done and a clear assessment of cost/benefit of different 'functional' approaches must be performed before an official position is put forward.

[24] See Communication (n 22) 4 in the text: 'all institutions performing pre-settlement, settlement and custody services' and 31 in the glossary (in which the definition of securities settlement systems excludes custodians).

The last point in the agenda refers to the governance and competition issues and it is where the battle is deemed to be more fierce. The European Commission has always been careful to state, also in the new communication, that it does not have a preference for one model of integration over another, provided that competition law is respected. However through governance rules it may indirectly discriminate in favour of one or the other model.

C. The Roadmap: Main Issues and Findings

It is generally agreed that European convergence of financial markets has been partial and lower than expected. From a macro-economic point of view, empirical research shows that the roadmap to integration has been less straightforward than expected, both in the banking and financial markets. The theoretical and empirical literature on integration of European financial markets can be divided into three fields:

(i) macro-analyses based on the convergence of rate of returns. Most of them[25] show that integration (i.e. the potential of diversifying across sectors thereby exploiting a decrease of country-specific factors) widened considerably in the late '90s. It has also been shown[26] that there is still a large 'country-bias' as investors tend to invest in domestic stocks more than an efficient asset allocation would suggest. In a nutshell, the glass is still half empty, to say the least.

(ii) Demand-side analyses on the financial portfolios held by European households. The results show that despite a general convergence in the allocation of portfolios, levels of equity investment are still very different in the Euro area, both for households[27] and institutional investors.[28]

(iii) Microanalyses of the characteristics of the exchange industry. This is the subject of the present section.

The recent debate on the integration of the European financial markets is intertwined with the structural changes of the industry determined worldwide by technological changes. The interest of scholars and market participants was mainly focused on how to optimise the following major points of the industry:

(I) ownership structure;

[25] K Adjaouté and JP Danthine 'European Financial Integration and Equity Returns: A Theory-based Assessment of the Transformation of the European Financial Systems' in V Gaspar, P Hartmann and O Sleijpen (eds) *The Transformation of the European Financial System* (ECB 2002).

[26] L Baele, A Ferrando, P Hördahl, E Krylova and C Monnet 'Measuring Financial Integration in the Euro Area' (ECB Occasional Paper No. 14) (2003).

[27] L Guiso, M Haliassos and T Japelli 'Household Stockholding in Europe: Where Do We Stand and Where Do We Go?' (2003) 36 Econ Pol 123-170.

[28] L Baele et al (n 26).

(II) trading mechanism and rules;
(III) best strategy of integration;
(IV) connection between trading and post-trading architectures;
(V) comparison of actual costs and efficiency of European (and American) exchanges, looking both at the trading and post-trading sector.

These points will be shortly reviewed in this section, which will end with a comment on the present European situation.

I. The Ownership Structure

As already noted, the ISD had the important effect of promoting the convergence of European regulated markets towards a private, for-profit model, thus overcoming both the public and co-operative model. This step, which took place for most exchanges in the second half of the '90s was not uncontroversial. The clearest evidence is given by the privatisation of Borsa Italiana which although priced at a bare 53 billion Lire, corresponding to € 27 million in 1997[29] received only lukewarm bids from Italian intermediaries. Oddly enough, the suspicions were not centered on the many conflicts of interest of a for-profit exchange owned by its clients (at least in the first stage), but on the profitability of the business and therefore on its economic value. The high profitability in the following years (thanks also to the stock exchange bubble) proved how wrong this position was and prompted a new structural change, i.e. the listing of the stock exchanges which became the new mantra worldwide: Australia first, then Europe and the United States.

Five exchanges are now listed in Europe: the London Stock Exchange, Deutsche Börse, Euronext, OM Group and Athens. Two others are eager to list: Madrid and Milan. The general favour towards the listing of the exchanges (also in this case notwithstanding the dramatic conflicts of interest involved) is explained by the wider opportunities of linkages between stock exchanges: participations, cross-participations, mergers, even hostile take-over bids. This contributed to changing the landscape, leading to the picture that will be discussed at the end of this section.

II. The Trading Mechanism and Rules

In this field, technological evolution proved to be stronger than vested interest (and theory, for that matter) as it led, on the one hand, to the superiority of screen-based systems and, on the other hand, to the co-existence of quote-driven and order-driven systems. It is interesting to note that Anglo-Saxon exchanges

[29] The most recent evaluation for Borsa Italiana is of around €800 million.

(burdened by the interests of intermediaries holding seats in their floor) were more reluctant to invest in the technology of screen-based systems and were handicapped (despite their greater size in terms of listed companies and volumes of trading) in the merger process.

III. The Strategy of Integration

Seminal papers on the integration among stock exchanges adopted the theory of network externalities to explore the issue of competition among stock exchanges. In particular, Di Noia[30] proved that implicit mergers (alliances) among stock exchanges together with remote access are always more efficient than actual competition. On the other hand, Di Noia's model proved that competition among stock exchanges may lead to a monopolist exchange, if no agreements are found.

IV. The Connection between the Trading and Post-Trading Organization

As market participants and regulators became more and more aware of the importance of the post-trading organisation, their interest moved towards the problems of the optimal forms of linkages and integration. Many solutions have been proposed. In general terms, the choice is between vertical solutions (i.e. the merger of exchanges with Central Securities Depositories – CSDs) and horizontal solutions (i.e. CSDs with other CSDs or International Central Securities Depositories – ICSDs – and Central counterparties with other CCPs).

Two recent theoretical studies[31] both using industrial economics perspective advocate that horizontal consolidation represents the best solution to enhance the benefits of integration (or reduce the costs of fragmentation) if some market conditions are met. From an economic welfare perspective, two goods that are substitutes should be supplied by different decision makers, while two complements should be supplied by a single decision maker. On the basis of this observation, the argument put forward is as follows. The link services of two CSDs are complements since each securities transfer from one to the other CSD requires both services. Furthermore, the link services of the one CSD and the settlement service of the other CSD are complements since transferring securities from one to the other country makes sense only if these securities are afterwards traded and thus

[30] C Di Noia 'Competition and Integration among Stock Exchanges in Europe: Implicit Mergers and Remote Access' (Wharton School wp No. 98-03) (1998).

[31] TV Koeppl and C Monnet 'Guess What: It's the Settlements!' (ECB wp No. 375) (2004); J Tapking and J Yang 'Horizontal and Vertical Integration and Securities Trading and Settlement' (ECB wp No. 387) (2004).

settled in the other country. The two CSDs should therefore be operated by the same decision maker (horizontal integration of CSDs). However, this argumentation is valid only if the operating costs of the link are low enough to allow the cross-border transfer of securities at a reasonable cost. If the link is too expensive, a horizontal integration of CSDs is desirable only if it reduces these costs significantly. If not, a vertical integration of the exchange and the CSD in each country is preferable. This is because trading and settlement in the given country are also complements. Furthermore, if there is no demand for foreign securities, there is also no demand for link transfers regardless of whether the link operating costs are high or low. However, in such a case, vertical integration is a better solution than complete separation. To expand this reasoning further, Takping and Yang analyze four different industry structures in a two-country model:

(i) complete separation (CS): all four services providers are operated by different independent firms and set their prices independently;

(ii) vertical integration (VI), the exchange and the CSD in both countries are operated by the same firm and thus coordinate their price setting;

(iii) horizontal integration of CSDs[32] at two different stages of development;

(iii)(a) purely legal integration (LHI), the CSDs are operated by the same firm, but still run different systems. This entails that the transfer of securities entails some costs, but link and on-exchange fees are set in a coordinated way.

(iii)(b) technical horizontal integration (THI), the CSDs are technologically merged into one system so as the operating cost of the link is zero.

Horizontal integration of CSDs should eventually lead to THI, however in several cases it stops at LHI. In complementary services, such as trading and post trading, both VI and LHI entail some competition effect as the transition from CS is always positive. If the link operating costs are high a transition from CS to VI entails a higher welfare than the one to LHI, the opposite stands true in case of low operating costs. In such an environment, the transition from LHI to THI represents the cost reduction effect in the merger. THI always entails the highest possible welfare. In other words, even if the competition effect of a transition from CS to VI is greater than the competition effect of a transition to THI, the overall effect is still greater in case of a transition to THI due to its cost reduction effect.

The policy implications of such a model are significant. Stakeholders are always better off if some degree of consolidation takes place and consequently authorities should help the process if market participants drag their feet. However, competition authorities should take a close look at the technological implications of different consolidation initiatives.

[32] In the model the exchanges are operated independently.

V. The Comparison of Actual Costs and Efficiency

From the point of view of the economics of the exchange, the fundamental questions, though thoroughly debated, are still open. How important are economies of scale in trading systems? Is there an optimal structure of a stock market and how can it be reached? Is this optimal structure identical for all market segments?[33]

European stock exchanges show fairly high standards of efficiency and integrity.[34] In an international comparison based on 25 exchanges (9 of which European) seven European exchanges were in the top ten rankings. It is also interesting to remember that the study also found little correlation between efficiency and integrity. This could be interpreted as evidence that exchanges had as a major objective the maximisation of revenues and profits. They were therefore focused too much on the building of trading (and settlement systems) rather than surveillance and other regulatory duties.

But how can one measure differentials in costs and efficiency?

A few years ago, Lusignani-Onado[35] pointed out that comparisons of explicit (and implicit) costs are difficult to make owing to significant differences across stock exchanges. The price paid for each transaction has three components: a one-off element (for instance, costs to be paid for access to the exchange); one fixed, i.e, costs independent of the size of the transaction; one variable, linked to the size of the transaction. A comparison therefore requires identifying a typical deal, with results strongly dependant on the assumptions made. The main results of this research, related to the 1999 data, can be summarised as follows:

(i) Frankfurt (with a flat pricing, inclusive of post-trading) and London had trading costs relatively independent of the number of trades made in a given span of time.

(ii) Other exchanges' prices (Milan, Paris, Stockholm) were negatively correlated with the number of trades and the size of the trades.

(iii) Looking at the average of the four typical dealers identified, Milan seemed to be the more competitive trading place (3.63 Euro per million traded) along with London (3.65).

(iv) The convenience of Milan was more pronounced with regards to large traders (and lowest in comparison to London and Frankfurt for small traders).

[33] ECB-CFS Research Network Report on 'Capital Market and Financial Integration in Europe. Result and Experiences after Two Years' (2004) <http://www.eu-financial-system.org/ecbcfs.html> 41.

[34] A Siow and M Aitken 'Ranking World Equity Markets on the Basis of Market Efficiency and Integrity' in H Skeete (ed) *The HP Handbook of World Stock, Derivatives & Commodities Exchanges 2003* (Mondo Visione 2003).

[35] G Lusignani and M Onado 'La *Securities Industry* italiana di fronte ai processi di integrazione europei' (Assosim 2001).

Further evidence of how difficult it is to reach clear-cut results comes from a more recent comparison between Euronext and London,[36] which shows that the cost of liquidity for a given security depends on the security's trading volume, free float and volatility. As a result, rigorous trading cost comparisons across different countries should be based on samples of comparable securities. Using this method, spreads are lower on Euronext than in London. The London market, however, records higher depth indicators. Another important result of the research is the difference of trading costs for different trading volumes: Euronext, for instance, is cheaper for small trades, whilst London offers lower immediacy costs for large trades.

While it is difficult to rank European exchanges by the level of trading costs, it is certain that they are higher than in an integrated structure. The already cited London Economics research suggests that trading costs could fall sharply as a result of full integration of European financial markets. Furthermore, as trading costs show a strong positive correlation with the cost of equity capital, the latter would fall across Europe by about 40 basis points on average. This estimate is close to the reduction in the cost of capital expected by a sample of market practitioners.

D. The Present Landscape

At the dawn of European monetary integration, the European Union had 15 national stock exchanges and several regional ones, more than 20 derivative markets and no natural centre for bond trading. Tommaso Padoa Schioppa remarked[37] that the Euro area had 18 large-value payment systems, 23 securities settlement systems and 13 retail payment systems. On the contrary, the United States had 2 large payment systems, 3 securities settlement systems and 3 retail payment systems.

Nowadays the landscape of the European Exchange industry appears as represented in Figure 1. The number of exchanges and post trading organisations has decreased, but we are still far from a consolidated pan-European exchange. With Euronext network and the Nordic alliance as the only remarkable exceptions, cross-border consolidation is lagging behind both in trading and in post trading. Three major exchange groups, (Euronext, LSE and DB) compete for European leadership, but so far their efforts to emerge as leader have been vain. Indeed, data released by FESE show that the cumulated market share of the top three has decreased in favour of second-tier competitors such as Madrid and Milan.

[36] JF Gajewski and C Gresse 'Trading Cost Analysis: A Comparison of Euronext Paris and London Stock Exchange' (OEE wp 2002) <http://www.efmaefm.org>.

[37] Speech by T Padoa-Schioppa on 'PSSS in EMU' to SIBOS (13 September 1999) <http://www.ecb.int>.

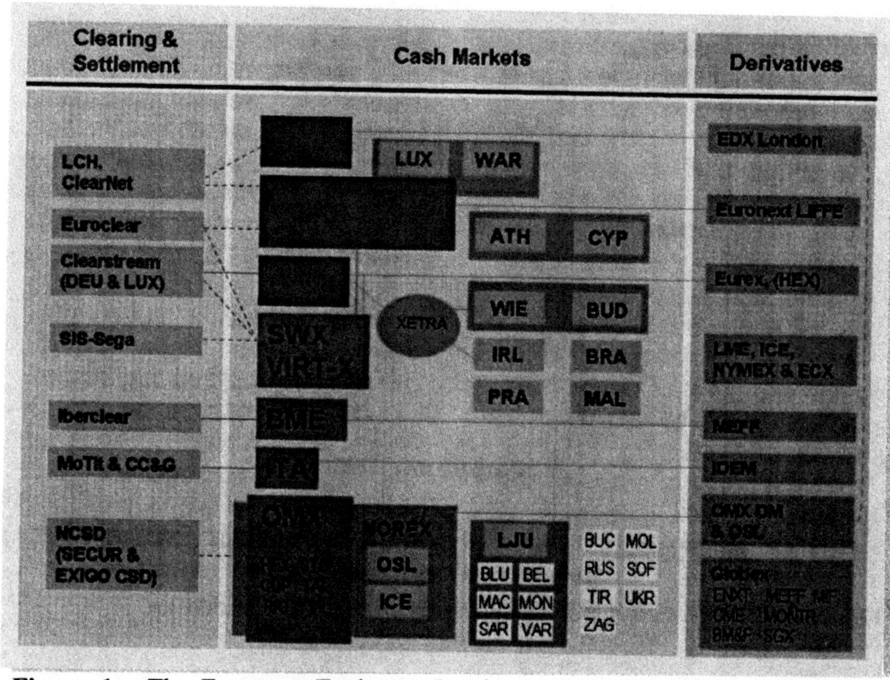

Figure 1 - The European Exchange Landscape (source: FESE, Federation of European Securities Exchanges).

As Figure 1 clearly shows, the fragmentation in the European exchange industry is not only testified by the number of competing national institutions, but also by the lack of a dominant business model. Figure 2 shows that in between the two extreme models with, on one side, LSE, specialising in the trading of cash instruments and, on the other, Deutsche Börse, with strong horizontal (i.e. cash and derivatives trading) and vertical (trading and post trading) diversification, lie several alternative business models where horizontal and vertical integration combine in different shapes. Take Euronext, horizontally as diversified as Deutsche Börse (i.e. Euronext-Liffe) but with a 'softer' vertical extension (participation in LCH. Clearnet and Euroclear are respectively around 25% and less than 4%). Another combination comes from the Nordic markets where OMX exchanges (Helsinki, Stockholm and the Baltic exchanges) share trading and post trading technology with other Norex members (Danish, Norwegian and Icelander markets) and where OMX group implements a Nordic CSD (NCSD) by merging the Swedish with the Finnish CSD (OMX owns around 20% of the new entity).

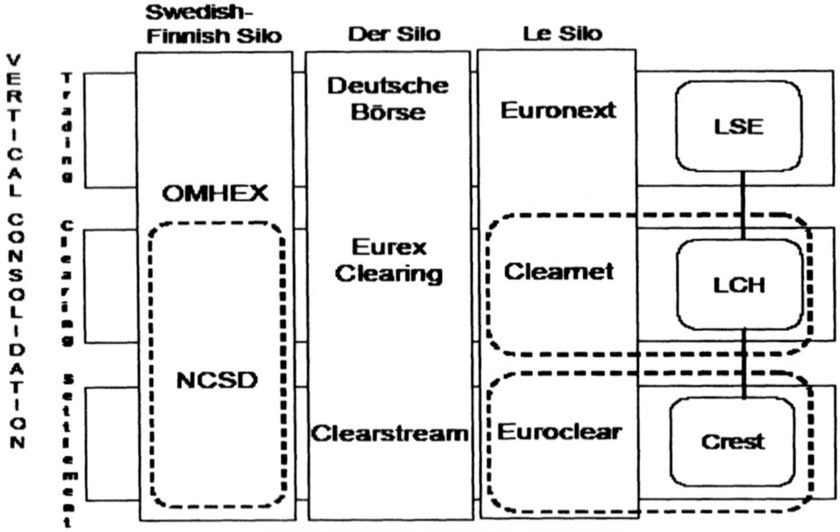

Figure 2 - Different business models in European exchange industry.

E. The Trading Costs in European Exchanges: A Comparative Analysis

In this section we compare the 'explicit' costs of trading in the main European exchanges: London, Frankfurt, Euronext, Stockholm and Milan. The aim of this analysis is to evaluate the effect of competition among European exchanges on the cost of trading services offered to brokers and whether there has been a convergence on costs for brokers that trade in the main European exchanges. For such an analysis different methodologies can be used. A first category groups top-down approaches, similar to those used by Financial News,[38] where total trading fees in each market have been divided by number of trades. This approach has the advantage of using objective and true data and does not require any assumption on model users; however it can be fundamentally flawed. Given the different fee scales, market structures, trading systems and ways of counting trading volumes, it is almost impossible to place an absolute value on the cost of an average trade and compare costs across markets. An alternative to top-down approaches comes from traditional and static bottom-up approaches. For example, a traditional bottom-up measure, developed by commercial entities such as Elkins/McSherry or Plexus, looks at trading costs from a microstructure perspective. In developing

[38] W Write 'Trading Fees Figures Support Claims from Deutsche Börse' *Fin News* (31 January 2005).

these comparisons, three cost components – commissions, fees and market impact (essentially a measure of how much the size of institutional orders affects the price at which they are filled) – are included. Other bottom-up approaches such as the one used by Lusignani-Onado[39] for trading and by NERA[40] for post trading are based upon price-lists. This approach requires a number of assumptions to generate results that are comparable across exchanges, notably about the model client characteristics and transaction type. The effort to measure both explicit and implicit costs leads to the difficulty of separating cost differences due to different trading models from those due to different competitive positions. The policy implications are therefore weak.

In order to make such a comparison and to overcome the shortcoming of both top-down and static bottom-up approaches we use the same bottom-up approach followed in Lusignani-Onado[41] based upon the price-list of each of the five selected stock exchanges, but differently from previous works we performed a dynamic estimate of the whole curve. First of all, one needs to identify a 'typical' (average) trader in order to make comparisons and this is the way followed by most analyses. In this way, all information on the position of remaining traders is lost. The first consequence is the need to identify at least an array of representative traders, reflecting different interests and needs. The second is to estimate the whole curve for each market, in order to have a complete picture of what happens to different investors. This is the criterion adopted in this section.

First, we analyse the information that is publicly available on the price list of each exchange in order to understand the main component of costs. As expected, the structure of the single price lists are very different in their components, as reported in table 1. For example some exchanges charge an annual membership fee, others have a membership fee only for high volume brokers, others do not charge any membership fee. The main differences in the price lists are due to different combinations of fixed and variable costs. On the one hand, exchanges use different methods to calculate fixed fees: all but London and Stockholm (and the program A of Euronext) charge a minimum fixed trading fee; on the other, a significant difference exists on the algorithm used to calculate the variable component of trading costs: Deutsche Börse calculates variable fees by charging a number of basis points (on average 0.6 bp) on the value of the transactions (with a cap and floor); the Stockholm stock exchange uses a method that includes both fees based on orders and on the value of the transactions. All other exchanges charge variable trading costs based upon the number of orders executed, but with significant differences on the algorithm used to calculate the discount tariff that applies for a

[39] G Lusignani and M Onado (n 35).

[40] E Linton and M Stark 'The Direct Costs of Clearing and Settlement. A EU-U.S. Comparison' (Corporation of London City Research Series No. 1) (2004).

[41] G Lusignani and M Onado (n 35).

growing number of executed contracts. All these methods result in decreasing unit costs per order executed as the number of such contracts increase.

	Offering	One Off Admission Fee	Annual Market Membership Fee	Minimum Annual Trading Fee	Fee per volume	Floor	Cap	Fee per order	Costs for linkups
London		No	Market Makers Only	No	No	No	No	Yes	Excluded
Frankfurt	High	No	Yes	Yes	Yes	Yes	Yes	No	Excluded
	Medium	No	Yes	Yes	Yes	Yes	Yes	No	Excluded
	Low	No	Yes	Yes	Yes	Yes	Yes	No	Excluded
Euronext	A	No	No	No	No	No	No	Yes	Not applicable
Euronext	B	No	No	Yes	No	No	No	Yes	Not applicable
Euronext	C	No	No	Yes	No	No	No	Yes	Not applicable
Euronext	D	No	No	Yes	No	No	No	Yes	Not applicable
Milan	A	No	No	Yes	No	No	No	Yes	Excluded
Milan	B	No	Yes	No	No	No	No	Yes	Minimum included
Stockholm		No	No	Yes	Yes	No	No	Yes	Excluded

Table 1: The main component of trading costs in European Exchanges.

With such differences in the price-list structure in terms of combinations of fixed and variable costs and of methods used to calculate both fixed and variable trading fees, the comparative analysis on trading costs among the five European exchanges requires assumptions on the annual activity of one or more representative brokers. The specification of a representative broker is important because, as we showed above, most European exchanges charge tariffs based on a sliding scale, with lower charges for high volume users. The type of broker can, therefore, have an impact on the resulting cost per transaction.

In this bottom-up analysis assumptions are made with respect to the total annual trading volume (number of executed contracts) and the total annual value of transactions. First, we assume four types (models) of representative brokers that have an annual trading activity of, respectively, 100 (large broker), 50 (medium-large broker), 25 (medium-small broker), 5 (small broker) billion Euro.[42] Second, we assume a range of value for single orders executed: from small orders of 500 Euro to the larger one of 600,000 Euro. The range of these values has been chosen in order to capture all the extremes of the price-curve of the exchanges. In figure 3, we report the iso-trading value curves of the four representative brokers that we use in the simulations of trading costs. Each iso-trading curve is obtained by the combination of the number of contracts and the value of each.

[42] The size of the 4-type brokers has been defined with respect to the distribution of the amount traded by Italian brokers.

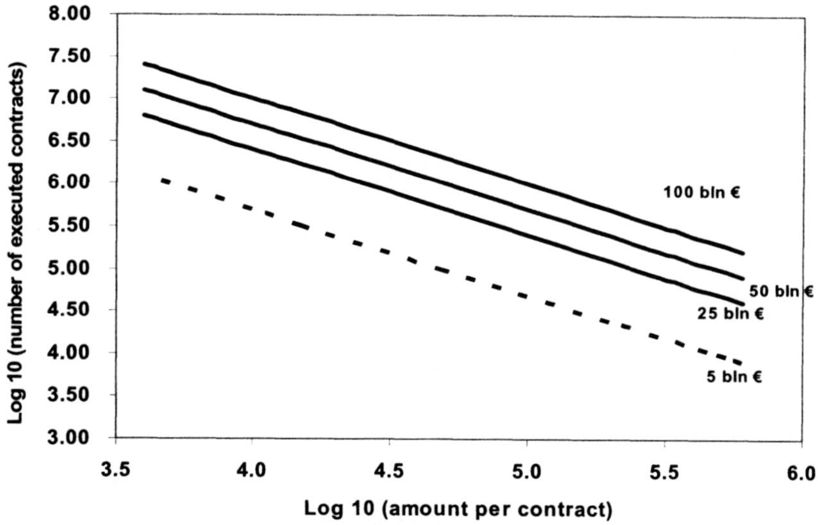

Figure 3 - Iso-trading value curves of 4 standard brokers.

In order to compare the trading costs among the five exchanges we run the simulations by moving along the 4 iso-trading value curves. In each simulation we calculate the cost of trading in terms of cost (in Euro) by single execution and the cost (bp, basis points) in terms of the value of the transaction. The results can be analysed in different ways: one is to compare the costs that the four different types of brokers face in each exchange; another is to compare the costs that the four representative brokers would sustain in each exchange, assuming that all the trades are executed in one of the five exchanges.

In figure 4, we report the estimated sliding cost curves that the four representative brokers will sustain in the five European stock exchanges. As expected, all the order unit costs faced by all four brokers decrease with the number of executed orders. The negative slopes of the curves are higher for smaller numbers of executions and decrease also with the increase in orders. Both the scale of the figures are logarithmic transformations of the data in order to better represent the strong non-linearity between costs and the number of executed orders.

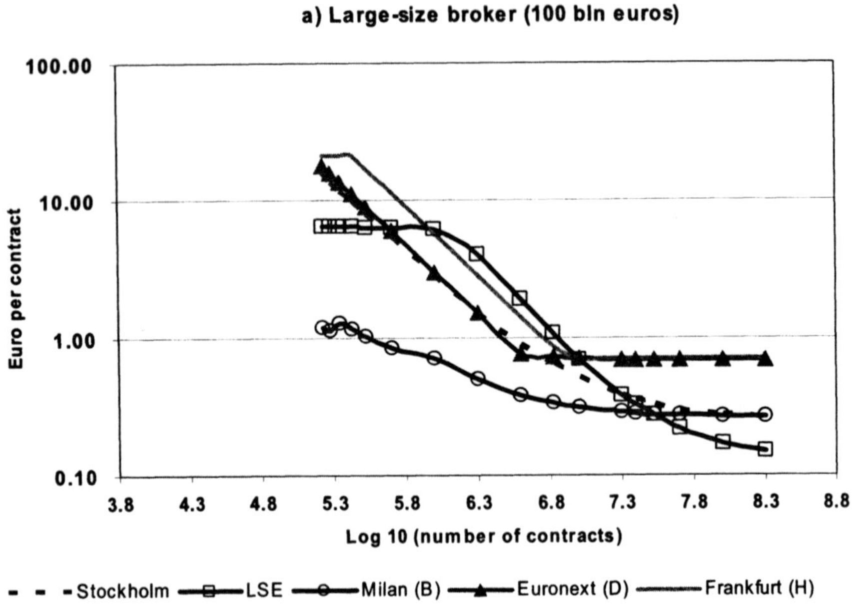

Figure 4.1 - Costs of trading in five European Exchanges - Euro per order executed (large size broker).

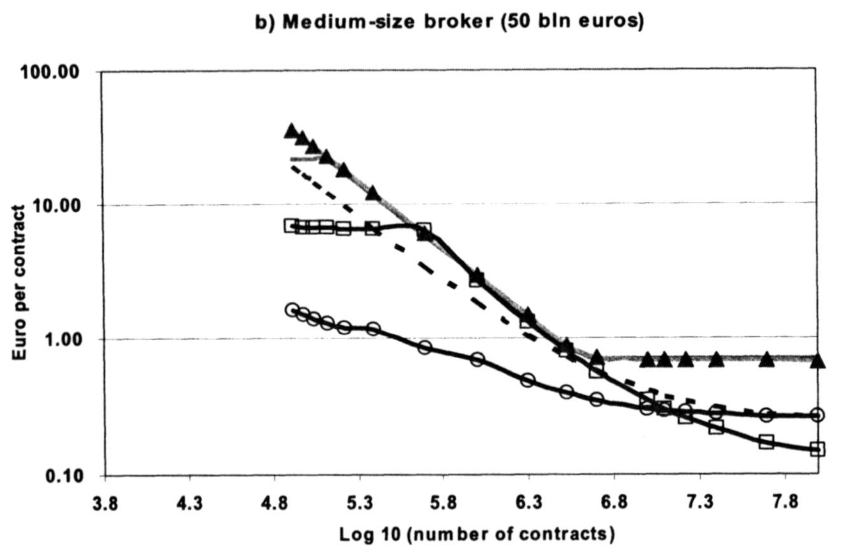

Figure 4.2 - Costs of trading in five European Exchanges (medium size broker).

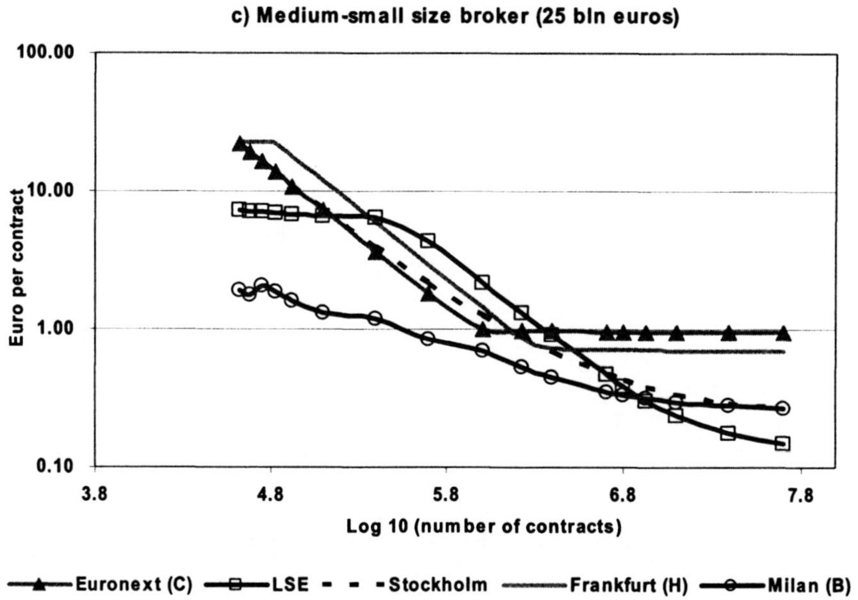

Figure 4.3 - Costs of trading in five European Exchanges (medium-small size broker).

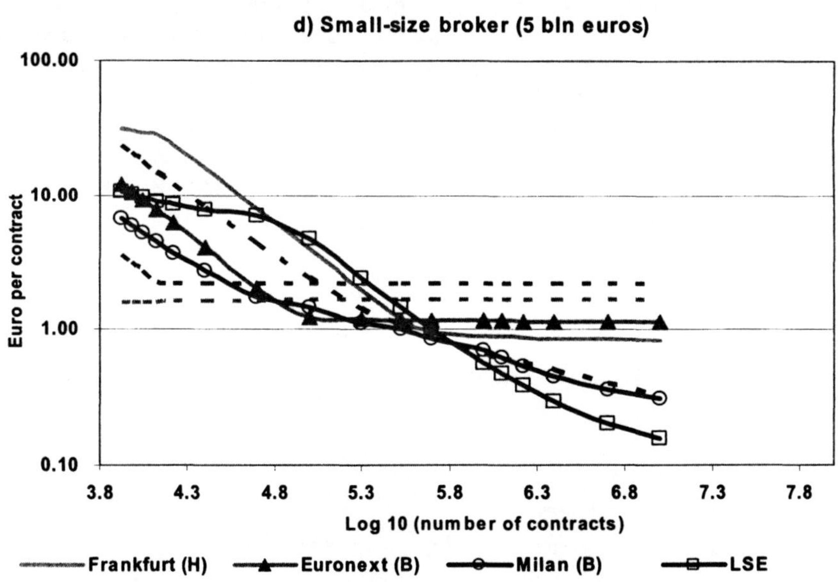

Figure 4.4 - Costs of trading in five European Exchanges (small size broker).

Measured in terms of unit cost of executed order, for all the four type of brokers considered, the London stock exchange has the most competitive prices for high volume trading, while the Milan stock exchange has the less sloped cost curve for the smaller amount of trading. Frankfurt, Euronext and Stockholm exchanges, and to some extent London, despite having very different methods of calculation of trading fees, show very close cost curves by order executed, at least for lower volumes of transactions. For all four exchanges our estimates show a very high negative slope of the cost curve per lower order executed; the Frankfurt and Euronext exchanges have costs that become flat as the orders executed become very high. In figure 4.4 (small brokers) we also report the flat curves per unit cost of executed order that Milan and Euronext offer to small brokers and which become less expensive than the regular program for operators with a very low volume of trading.

The costs of trading among European Exchanges have also been reported with respect to the value of the single transactions. The results, reported in Figure A-1 (appendix), confirm that Milan, overall, is the most competitive exchange; for brokers with medium-small volumes of transactions also Euronext is very competitive. For large and medium size brokers Frankfurt, Stockholm, Euronext and, to some extent, London, show a cost structure that becomes flat as the average value of the single contract increases.

A further analysis regards the changes in trading costs over the last five years. We run the same simulations on the price-list information available in 1999 and used in Lusignani-Onado.[43] The results, reported in figure 5 and A-2 (appendix), show that, from 1999 to 2004, London, Frankfurt and Euronext slightly increased their trading costs (measured by Euro per contracts and by basis point per value of the transaction), while the Milan stock Exchange has reduced its cost curves. The costs of Stockholm remained stable.

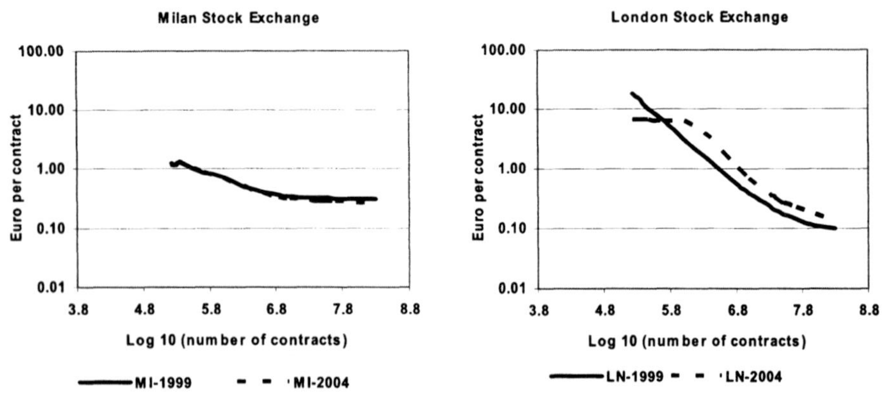

[43] G Lusignani and M Onado (n 35).

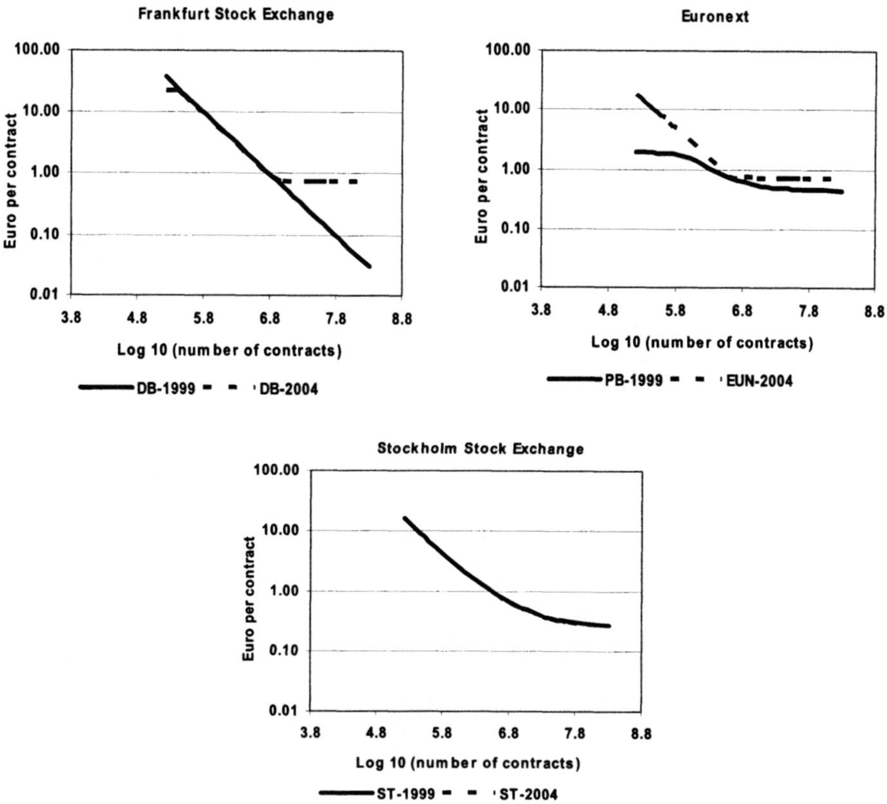

Figure 5 - Change in trading costs - Euro per order executed: 1999-2004 (large broker – 100 bln Euro): Milan, London, Frankfurt, Euronext and Stockholm Stock Exchanges.

In summary, both the trading costs indicators estimated by a bottom-up simulation on price-lists, show the existence of price differences among the five European exchanges.

The bottom-up simulation approach and the estimates of a set of trading costs curves that we obtained in this study can be useful to analyse the competitive scenario of European exchanges with respect to the supply of trading services. In comparison to other studies that evaluate the competitive scenario based upon an estimate on the average cost of trading services, our simulation of the cost curves shows that significant differences among the European exchanges exist, especially for lower amounts of orders executed. Furthermore, since the cost of trading can be reduced by increasing the number of trades for significant amounts, very high costs can arise both for small operators and for cross-border transactions.

As previously described, some of the exchanges offer package conditions of fixed and variable costs to operators that have lower trading activity but, of course, these conditions are less convenient than the average ones. This results in competitive pressures on brokers to increase their scale of business through external consolidation and merger.

The same problem of the high cost of trading services can be faced by large brokers when they need to execute cross-border transactions. In this case, when large brokers execute a cross-border transaction on a non-domestic exchange, they become small operators, and then face higher costs than those sustained in their domestic exchange. In other words, the cross-border transactions become very expensive and reduce the incentive to place a direct order to non-domestic exchanges. On the other hand, cross-border transactions are executed through an indirect broker that is usually a large domestic operator in the same exchange. This limits the increase of direct cross-border transactions and reduces the incentives to trade in non-domestic exchanges.

Price competition for trading services among exchanges should therefore result non only in a convergence in the respective cost curves, but also in the flattening of these curves. Our simulations show that in all exchanges the negative slope of the trading cost curve is very high in correspondence with a lower number of transactions. A possibility to reduce the cross-border costs of transactions is an agreement among exchanges that would allow them to consider brokers that place cross-border orders in the same category of the domestic exchange. In this case, a large broker that faces lower trading fees in the domestic exchange can get similar conditions for cross-border transactions placed on the other non-domestic exchanges. Since the high costs of cross-border transactions are faced by all brokers in Europe, both actions that flatten the cost curves and that allow a 'mutual recognition' of a broker's annual trading volume in all European exchanges would increase the incentives to trade among exchanges in Europe. This will result in closer conditions to the 'implicit merger' among trading European platforms that most studies and practitioner have suggested.

F. Costs of Post-Trading in Europe: A Comparative Analysis

As for trading costs, comparing post trading costs across Europe requires the understanding of the business model adopted by different providers and the selection of the methodological tool which provides the opportunity to frame in the most accurate way such an heterogeneous environment. This said, it does not come as a surprise that so far no firm conclusions about relative post trading costs can be drawn. Firstly, there is relatively little hard information on the cost of clearing and settlement in Europe and in the U.S. and, secondly, there is considerable dispute about the interpretation of existing figures. Methodology-wise, figures can be based either on a survey of settlement charges – a bottom-up approach – or on accounting data revealing the costs incurred by the providers – a top-down approach. In spite of these significant differences, the majority of studies produced to appraise the cost of non European clearing and settlement tend to be based upon a similar assumption. The cost of post trading in Europe is generally compared to the cost of post trading in the U.S.. In general this assumption can be considered acceptable, but it entails some important consequences. Specifically, the U.S. is a domestic market, while an integrated Europe remains a collection of national States. This condition is particularly relevant for the investigation because, as shown in the Giovannini reports, in cross-border transactions direct costs, i.e. fees paid for clearing and settlement, represent a minor component of the overall expenses and a large part of indirect costs does not depend on uncompetitive pricing policies, but are due to legal and tax differences among national states. As a consequence, methodologically, U.S. domestic costs make sense as long as they are used as a benchmark for the cost of domestic clearing and settlement in Europe. In other terms, U.S. costs cannot be considered the reference price (the one to include in a comparison to estimate the degree of completion of the law of one price) for an integration study.[44]

A second, more subtle consequence, relates to the implicit selection of the U.S. business model. A comparison can take place as long as a perfect substitute is examined. In clearing and settlement the perimeters of services are often quite different. Unfortunately, there is no consensus regarding the definition of core vs ancillary services. This entails that only some CSDs, the ones offering a compatible range of services, are directly comparable to U.S. DTCC. In addition, some services along the value chain may be offered, bundled by a single institution at a single all-inclusive tariff or unbundled between several providers, each charging a specific fee. In the U.S.-EU comparison, this is crucially the case for Central Counterparties services (CCP). In the U.S., DTCC is a single point of entry for both CCP and CSD services, whilst in European markets the situation is quite heterogeneous and a comparison can take place only bundling together the services provided by different organisations or it cannot take place at all for those markets where no central counterparty is available, i.e. Denmark.

Lastly, a clear understanding of the implications on cost structure of gross and net settlement must be included in the comparison.[45] In markets where netting is

[44] A more correct U.S.-EU comparison can take place by taking into account three indicators: a cross border transaction originated by a U.S. investor vs a cross-border extra-EU and intra-EU transaction originated by a European investor. This type of exercise is performed in the AFTI (Association Francaises des professionals des titres)/Eurogroup 'Analyses Comparatives du Cout des Operations Titres en Europe et aux USA, et Perspectives d'Evolution' (2002). Findings are that no matter the origin of cross-border transactions (intra-EU or transatlantic) costs tend to be similar for both U.S. and European investors.

[45] A numerical example clarifies this aspect. We might want to compare the cost per delivery (each trade included in the pipeline) of a gross and a net system. Assuming that the number of delivery is 1000 and the number of multilateral balance after netting is 10 and the cost per instruction included in the settlement system is 0.1€ , in the case of gross settlement the cost per

cont. ...

available, the difference in costs resulting from different methodologies is significant. Looking at operating income per transaction, post-netting penalizes markets with a high netting efficiency. Using pre-netting figures, on the other hand, ignores variation in netting efficiency between systems. The main drawback of this is that the benefits of netting are not considered (lower indirect and opportunity costs) while the additional costs of netting to the systems are considered.

Among the different studies comparing EU-U.S. post-trading costs, those based upon a top down approach (for example CEPS (2001) and OXERA/LSE (2002))[46] are more likely to be affected by these problems. Top down studies are subject to other drawbacks: differences in accounting principles and foreign exchange rate treatment. Differences in the accounting standard between jurisdictions can affect the comparability of results and introduce an element of subjectivity into the analysis. Similar problems might appear when a foreign exchange rate must be used to translate financial statements items.

If carefully conducted, traditional static bottom-up studies are likely to be less prone to this type of bias, but they are not immune from other weaknesses, in some cases as severe as the one highlighted for top down approaches. Bottom-up studies require a number of assumptions to generate results that are comparable across institutions, the most important being the model client characteristics. A second crucial aspect in bottom up study is data availability. If financial statement data are always available and 'true', price lists might not be made public and when available might be merely indicative. In addition, several costs components are often bundled together in a single tariff. This creates comparability difficulties because bundling is not consistent across organizations; with different institutions publishing different costs bundles. A related problem refers to heterogeneity in the business models, as discussed. Each market may have a variety of tariff schedules covering the relevant services. For example, in some cases, clearing or CCP costs are bundled with trading costs, while in others, trades matching fees are explicit and segregated from netting fees. For all the reasons listed above, bottom up studies imply a certain degree of subjectivity (definition of model client characteristics, the percentage of netting, size of rebates and volume discounts) and are highly prone to error (unbundling the price lists or including/excluding items).

As different post-trading organizations use differentiated sliding scales based upon volumes, the characteristics of the different model users may affect significantly the comparison. Take as an example findings on the Italian cost structure

delivery is 0.1€, each instruction is a delivery, while for a netting system the cost per delivery will be 0.001€ =(0.1€*10)/1000).

[46] K Lannoo and M Levin 'The Securities Settlement Industry in the EU: Structure, Costs and the Way Forward' (CEPS study) (2001). London Stock Exchange 'Clearing and Settlement in Europe – Response to the First Report of the Giovannini Group' (LSE/OXERA study) (2002).

in the NERA survey.[47] With regards to the clearing and settlement cost for medium, high and low volume users, Italian post-trading costs range as low as 40 b.p for high volume users and as high as around 60 bp for low users. By and large, the gap is due to the different cost of clearing, other sources of cost (matching and settlement) being rather constant. Italian clearing house, CC&G, is charging a tariff equal to 0.18€ per transaction on the initial 40,000 net settlements, moving down to 0.10€ on the next 30,000, and decreasing to 0.05€ for all net settlements above 70,000. Inevitably, the cost of the model users is highly affected if the hurdle size is set above or below each tariff step.

Comparisons in a bottom up study can change dramatically due to the inclusion or exclusion of some items in the tariff structure or their misinterpretation. Using again the NERA survey as an example, we can notice that, imprecisely, they take into consideration matching fees, included in the Montetitoli tariff for OTC transactions, which are not levied for trades taking place on regulated markets and inputs settlement tariff per delivery without taking into consideration that these costs are levied on net settlement.[48]

Aware of the methodological problems highlighted, further less error-prone research, such as the dynamic bottom-up approach used for trading costs comparisons, is required.

G. Conclusions and Policy Implications

The analysis has shown the difficulties of integrating the European securities markets. At the end of the period covered by the FSAP, European legislation has been largely completed (39 measures out of 42), but their practical effects are still to be seen and do not seem to be around the corner. If the final objective, according the Lisbon decisions, was to make Europe (and therefore her securities markets) the most competitive area by 2010, scepticism is more than justified, particularly in the field of the securities industry.

The main points can be summarised as follows:

(i) the identification of each exchange with its home country is still strong: the positive effects of cross-border mergers and alliances have been partially offset by a strong trend towards vertical integration of the various components of the value chain within each country. The myth of the 'national champion' is still solid and now encompasses both the trading and post-trading sector;

(ii) so far, we cannot identify a winning business model for the European exchange: contrary to most expectations, technology and managerial choices have proven that there is no such a thing as the 'best' solution for the exchange industry;

[47] E Linton and M Stark (n 40).

[48] See the previous numerical example (n 45).

(iii) in the trading sector, prices still widely differ across countries (particularly in the comparison between domestic and cross-border trades) and represent a strong barrier to international competition. The privatisation of exchanges has naturally led to price structures aimed at profit maximisation and hinged on different combinations of one-off costs, fixed costs, variable costs. It is therefore very difficult to compare trading costs and identify the most efficient exchange. The main point of our research is that only an estimate of the full cost curve can give the real picture of the problem. Our estimates have shown that the steepness of the curve is much more pronounced than expected. In a given exchange, foreign traders, even if important in their home market, have to face the higher trading costs of small domestic players. This can be seen as a major barrier to competition across European countries;

(iv) in the post-trading sector, comparisons are even more difficult, because different players provide different services and seldom price them separately. Although an estimate of the post-trading cost curves was beyond the scope of this paper, the evidence we analysed suggests that also in this sector the steepness of the curve is a major barrier to European competition;

(v) the net result is that before and during the realisation of the FSAP, most national players have taken measures that in a sense make it more difficult than before to reach the final objectives of the FSAP itself and of the Lisbon conference.

Our analysis shows the flaws of both the European 'legislation first' approach and most theoretical models on integration. From the first point of view, Europe has decided that dictating common rules would end up levelling the playing field. The experience has shown how easily players can still build new obstacles and dig new holes.

From the theoretical point of view, the traditional Di Noia model leads to the identification of a winning exchange via implied mergers, i.e. the emergence of a single trading platform which acts as the hub to national points of access. The real world is different at least for three reasons: (i) different national exchanges (points of access) are not homogeneous because of different national company rules which apply to each issuer; (ii) the model implicitly implies that the cost curves are perfectly comparable, i.e. they are practically flat and differ only by their level; (iii) the model does not distinguish between the listing and trading part of the chain value of the industry. The former is much more segmented than the latter and legislation (both at the European and national level) makes it very difficult to separate them.

The policy implications of our analysis seem far-reaching. First, the 'hands-off' approach (let the market decide) of the European Commission should be abandoned in favour of measures that could help co-operative solutions. The attitude behind the recent European Communication and the ECB document on standards for clearing and settlement systems can be viewed as a step in this direction.

Second, there is a case for intervention on the part of the European competition authority. On the one hand, barriers to competition are already in place; on the other hand, we cannot take for granted that further integration (for instance the merger Euronext-LSE) will be beneficial to the market. Given these economic conditions, the possible emergence of a sole European exchange, in absence of any control on the effects on prices, is not necessarily the best solution.

Third, in the short run the main obstacles to competition are the characteristics of the cost curve in the trading sectors and (presumably) in the post-trading sector on the one hand, and the strict link between listing and trading services on the other hand. In the trading sector it is therefore possible to envisage a sort of 'mutual recognition' of European traders, i.e. a cross membership equal for all European players which would allow each trader to face the same costs wherever the trade is executed. Multiple listings could obviously favour such agreements. Any measure favouring multiple listing (as in the Prospectus Directive) is therefore of the utmost importance. In the post-trading sector, further difficulties arise because of asymmetries of regulation (between players authorised as banks and the others) and because players typically list prices that cover a package of services. This requires a more homogeneous regulation and the unbundling of prices.

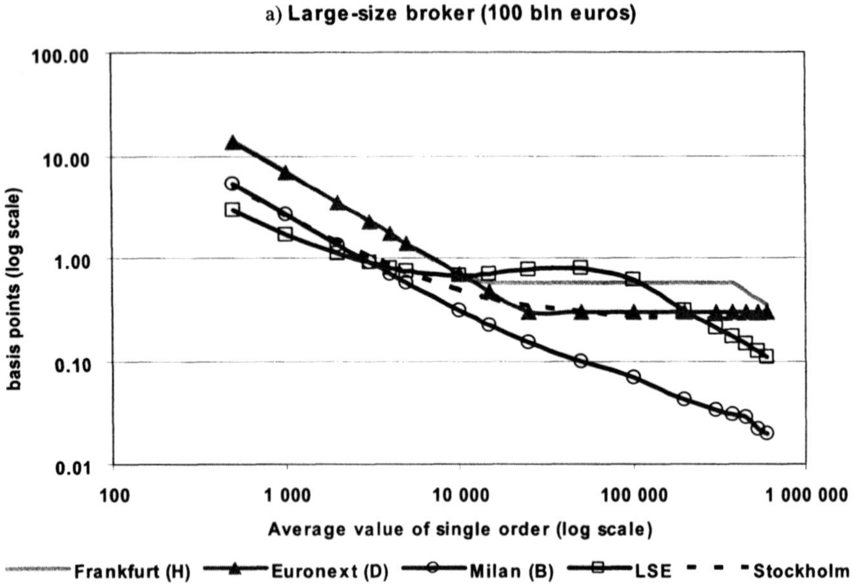

Figure A-1.1 - Costs of trading in five European Exchanges – Basis point for the value of the transaction (large size broker).

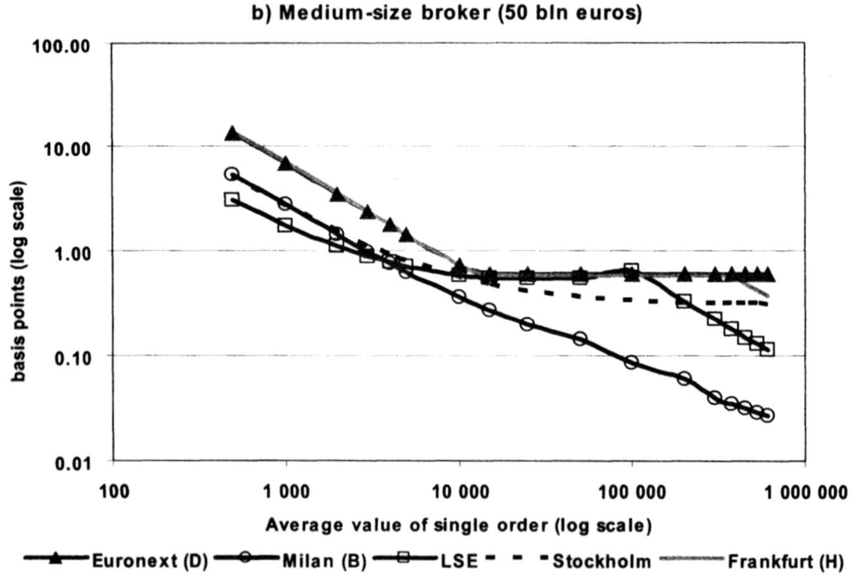

Figure A-1.2 - Costs of trading in five European Exchanges – Basis point for the value of the transaction (medium size broker).

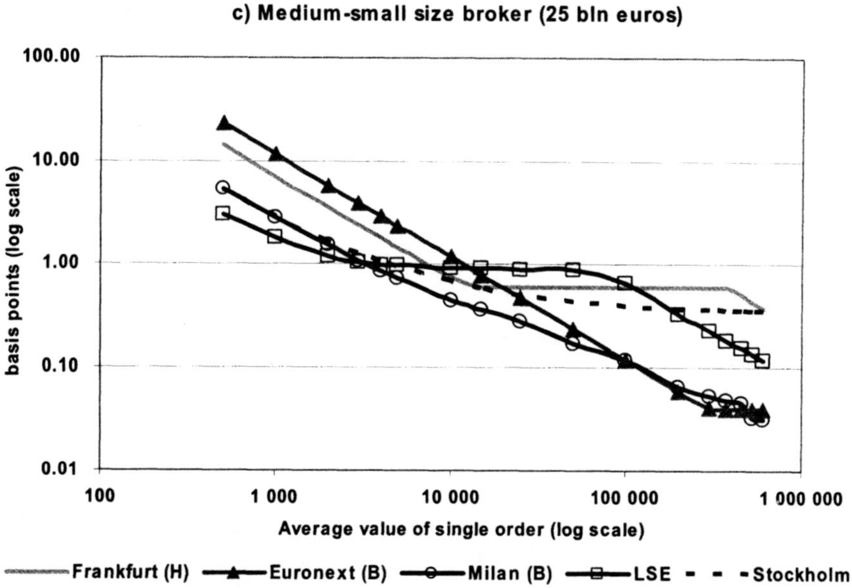

Figure A-1.3 - Costs of trading in five European Exchanges – Basis point for the value of the transaction (medium-small size broker).

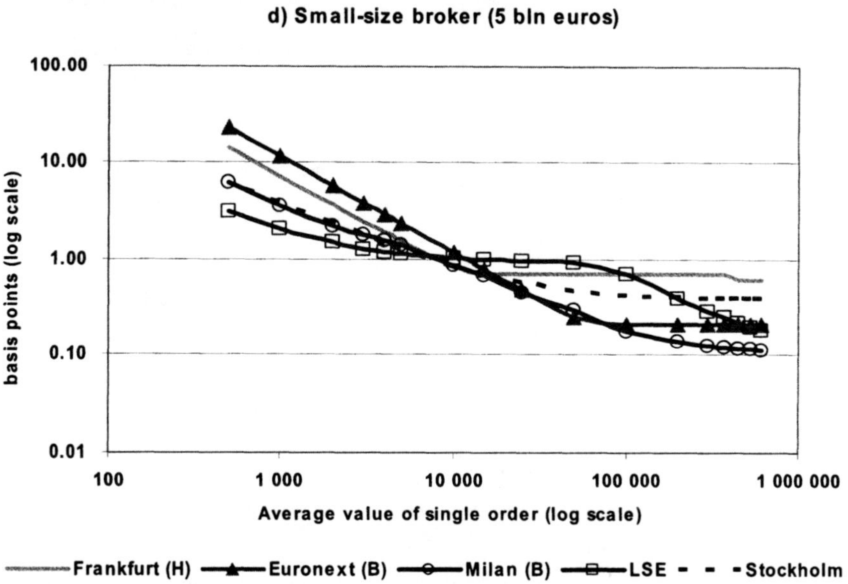

Figure A-1.4 - Costs of trading in five European Exchanges – Basis point for the value of the transaction (small size broker).

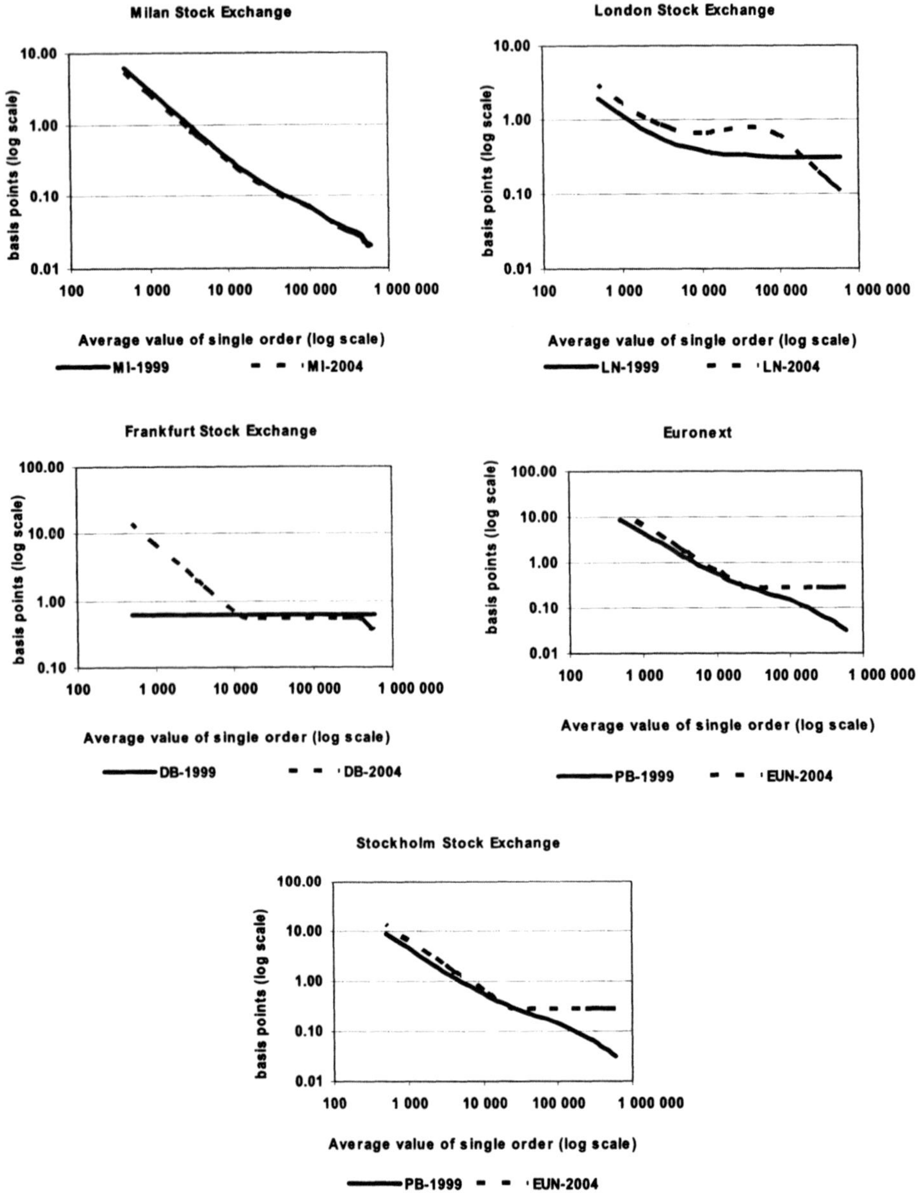

Figure A-2 - Change in trading: 1999-2004 - Basis point for the value of the transaction (large broker – 100 bln Euro): Milan, London, Frankfurt, Euronext and Stockholm Stock Exchanges.

The MiFID and Internalisation

GUIDO FERRARINI and FABIO RECINE*

In this Chapter, we examine the new rules concerning the internalisation of trading orders by investment intermediaries included in the Directive on Markets in Financial Instruments (MiFID). We analyse, first of all, the interplay amongst different interest groups in the legislative process that led to the MiFID. We also try to assess the Lamfalussy regulatory architecture in the light of the MiFID and its formation. We argue, in particular, that the Directive went too far in formulating its core principles in the area of internalisation. For instance, the limit order 'display rule' and the 'quote rule' were specified in the MiFID rather than left to level 2 measures or level 3 actions by CESR. This marks a clear difference from the U.S. system, where similar rules were adopted by the SEC using its regulatory powers under federal legislation. On the whole, the MiFID resulted in substantial re-regulation of securities trading systems, despite the abolition of concentration requirements as to exchange transactions in some countries. In fact, the introduction of detailed provisions was asked for by those constituencies, such as the incumbent exchanges and small-medium sized investment firms, which felt protected by national concentration rules and feared the consequences of further liberalisation of securities trading. By way of conclusion, we argue that the rules examined show that the Lamfalussy structure's main goal, represented by a flexible regulation for European securities markets, has not been reached. We also briefly suggest a new regulatory framework in which implementing rules should be adopted by an independent regulatory agency created at EU level. Along these lines such a body could have solely regulatory powers whilst enforcement should be left to national regulators co-ordinated by CESR.

A. General
B. The ISD Review
C. The MiFID and Internalisation
D. Conclusions

* The views expressed in this Chapter are solely those of the authors and do not necessarily reflect the positions of their respective institutions. Although the paper was jointly drafted and its findings and conclusions are fully shared by the authors, sections A, B (I, II, IV) and C.II are attributed to Fabio Recine while the rest of the paper is attributed to Guido Ferrarini.

A. General

I. Introduction

In this paper, we analyse the new 'rules' concerning the internalisation of trading orders by investment intermediaries included in the Directive on Markets in Financial Instruments (MiFID),[1] which has replaced the Investment Services Directive (ISD).[2] The term 'internalisation' is used to indicate the practice of order matching by investment firms, also called 'in-house matching'. This definition includes both direct executions of clients' orders by broker-dealers for their own account and agency crosses where customer orders are matched against each other.[3] We focus on the treatment of order handling, transparency and best execution, and analyse both the intense political discussion throughout the legislative process and the impact of these rules on European securities markets. Moreover, we consider the regulatory structure that was set-up with respect to EU securities markets following the Lamfalussy Committee's recommendations in 2000.[4] The MiFID was the first Directive to be fully created under this structure, which we try to assess in the light of the Directive and its rules on internalisation. The paper proceeds as follows. In the following paragraph, we introduce the problems created by internalisation of client orders. In section B, we analyse the ISD revision

[1] Directive 2004/39/EC of the European Parliament and of the Council of 21 April 2004 on Markets in Financial Instruments amending Council Directives 85/611/EEC and 93/6/EEC and Directive 2000/12/EC of the European Parliament and of the Council and repealing Council Directive 93/22/EEC (the MiFID), OJ L145 30.4.2004 1-44.

[2] Council Directive 93/22/EEC of 10 May 1993 on investment services in the securities field (the ISD), OJ L141 11.6.1993 27.

[3] See R Davies, A Dufour and B Scott-Quinn 'The MiFID: Competition in a New European Equity Market Regulatory Structure' in this volume 163-197, who note that a narrower definition is also used, referring to a bank or a broker which executes retail orders in-house either by acting as a principal and executing them against its own positions or by sending them to an affiliated market maker.

[4] See Final Report of the Committee of Wise Men on the Regulation of European Securities Markets (the Lamfalussy Report) (15 February 2001) 25. The Lamfalussy Committee was established by ECOFIN on 17 July 2000 with a mandate to assess the current conditions for the implementation of securities markets regulation in the European Union. The Committee was asked 'to assess how the mechanism for regulating those markets can best respond to developments, and, in order to eliminate barriers, to propose scenarios for adapting current practices to ensure greater convergence and cooperation in day-to-day implementation'. As a result, upon adoption of the Committee's recommendations by the Stockholm European Council on 23-24 March 2001, a new structure was set up. New committees were established such as the European Securities Committee (ESC) established in June 2001 with both advisory and regulatory capacities; and the Committee of European Securities Regulators (CESR) also established in June 2001 with various responsibilities including that for advising the European Commission on the detailed implementing rules needed to give effect to framework securities laws. See E Ferran *Building an EU Securities Market* (Cambridge University Press 2004) 75 ff.

process with particular reference to the discussion on internalisation and the regulatory remedies needed to protect investors with respect to internalizing intermediaries. In section C, we critically examine the MiFID's rules on order handling, transparency and best execution. In section D, we draw some conclusions also with respect to the Lamfalussy regulatory architecture and its future developments.

II. The Problem of Internalisation

1. From the ISD to the MiFID

The ISD was adopted in 1993 to introduce a single licence for investment intermediaries and harmonise some aspects of exchange law. In addition to defining regulated markets, the ISD set minimum standards for post-trade transparency in these markets and provided considerable latitude for Member States in the implementation of such standards. Moreover, the Directive allowed Member States to require transactions in equity securities to be carried out on a regulated market.[5] Reference to 'a' regulated market meant that in the case of securities traded in more than one exchange, transactions executed in any regulated market of the European Economic Area would comply with the requirement at issue. As a result, some Member States, such as France, Italy and Spain, maintained 'concentration rules' (i.e. rules mandating exchange execution of share trades) as requirements for the 'best execution' of transactions by investment intermediaries. Other Member States, including the UK, left intermediaries free to execute these transactions off-exchange and also to 'internalise' the same in compliance with general best execution requirements.[6]

The MiFID requires Member States to allow internalisation of orders and, therefore, to eliminate concentration provisions. This is done to promote competition between trading venues and also to offer investors a choice between different trading functionalities, such as regulated markets, MTFs, and internalising intermediaries. At the same time, the Directive regulates internalisation with the provisions that we examine in this paper concerning transparency, order handling and best execution. These provisions were inspired by the intent to create a level playing field between the three types of trading functionalities just indicated and

[5] See G Ferrarini 'The European Regulation of Stock Exchanges: New Perspectives' (1999) 36 Comm Mkt L Rev 569-598; N Moloney *EC Securities Regulation* (Oxford University Press 2002) 663.

[6] For a better description of the national systems mentioned above, see R Davies, A Dufour and B Scott-Quinn (n 3); as to Germany, see J Köndgen and E Theissen 'Internalisation under the MiFID: Regulatory Overreaching or Landmark in Investor Protection?' in this volume 271-296.

also to assure the same level of investor protection with respect to all trading venues. As argued in the 5th recital of the MiFID's Preamble: 'It is necessary to establish a comprehensive regulatory regime governing the execution of transactions in financial instruments irrespective of the trading methods used to conclude those transactions so as to ensure a high quality of execution of investor transactions and to uphold the integrity and overall efficiency of the financial system'. As we argue in this paper, however, the need for levelling the regulatory arena as to the various trading systems is far from clear and may result in over-regulation of new trading venues, reducing their competitive potential with respect to the incumbent exchanges.

2. Pros and Cons of Internalisation

Proponents of internalisation highlight its positive impact on competition in the offer of trading services.[7] Inter-exchange competition is presently not very strong in Europe. First of all, traditional stock exchanges are still the main markets for domestic equities.[8] Moreover, some exchanges have consolidated, even though the process of consolidation has not been as intense as one might have expected.[9] In addition, new regulated markets were created; however, their success has been limited (as in the case of Virt-x) and some had to close down (Jiway and Nasdaq Europe). Also competition from Alternative Trading Systems (ATSs) is not very significant.[10] They are now the principal organised trading venues for bond trading; however, they account for only 1% of equity trading volumes in the

[7] See R Lee 'Capital Markets that Benefit Investors: A Survey of the Evidence on Fragmentation, Internalisation and Market Transparency' (Oxford Finance Group <www.bba.org.uk/content/1/c4/19/92/106813v2.pdf 24>, 2002) noting that two key benefits arise from internalisation: first, it might allow alternative trading venues to compete with a primary or central market; second, it would give market participants a greater diversity of choice as to where to execute their orders. Similarly L Harris *Trading and Exchanges: Market Microstructure for Practitioners* (Oxford University Press 2002) who comments: 'Markets fragment because the trading problems that traders solve, differ. Different market structures serve some traders better than others. Markets fragment when, for enough traders, benefits from differentiation exceed benefits from consolidation'. On the pros and cons of internalisation, see also J Köndgen and E Theissen (n 6).

[8] See SB Ramos 'Competition between Stock Exchanges: A Survey' (FAME Research Paper No. 77, 2003), as to competition in Europe; in general terms, C Pirrong 'A Theory of Financial Exchange Organization' (2000) 43 J L & Econ 437-471, arguing that direct competition between exchanges is limited.

[9] See A Cybo-Ottone, C Di Noia and M Murgia 'Recent Developments in the Structure of Securities Markets' in *Brookings-Wharton Papers on Financial Services* (Brookings Institution Press 2000).

[10] See 'Economics' (Deutsche Bank Research No. 47, January 2005) 8 defining stock exchanges as 'Europe's ECNs' and arguing that 'order-driven ATSs in Europe have little potential for success'.

EU (a much lower share than in the U.S.).[11] The elimination of concentration rules, following to adoption of the MiFID, could enhance ATS's business in some Member States. Furthermore, increased internalisation of client orders by investment firms will offer alternative trading venues to investors and market participants. This might serve investors' divergent needs, as underlined by the main associations of financial intermediaries operating in the City of London (such as IPMA, ISDA, ISMA, LIBA, etc.) in a paper submitted to the European Commission for its second consultation on ISD Revision.[12] The point was raised, in particular, that 'each group [of investors] seeks the most efficient market to meet its needs. No *one* market model has yet been devised which will treat *all* investors "equally"'. Another argument was that stock exchanges are no longer public institutions, but 'for profit' companies whose primary aim is the enhancement of shareholder value: their ability to act in the public interest is 'constrained by the need to increase revenue, cut costs, and maximise profits'.

However, critics of internalisation highlight its negative impact on market quality,[13] also considering the extraordinary development of European stock exchanges over the last twenty years. European bourses operate as electronic market places in continuous time. Liquidity in these markets is provided by limit orders, i.e. orders to buy/sell a given quantity of shares if the price is not above/below a given limit. Limit orders are an important fraction of the order flow in markets such as those operated by Deutsche Börse, Euronext and the London Stock Exchange. Internalisation can reduce the quality of markets because internalisers do not input limit orders in transparent order books, thus reducing the pool of liquidity in the main market. Critics further argue that internalisation leads to a lower degree of price transparency and has a negative impact on the price discovery process. In addition, internalisation may amplify conflicts of interest as retail

[11] See the Proposal for a Directive of the European Parliament and of the Council on Investment Services and Regulated Markets, and amending Council Directive 85/611/EEC, Council Directive 93/6/EEC and European Parliament and Council Directive 2000/12/EC (the MiFID Proposal), 19.11.2002, COM(2002) 625, 8.

[12] See APCIMS, FOA, IPMA, ISMA, ISDA, LIBA, TBMA 'Innovation, Competition, Diversity, Choice, A European Capital Market for the 21st Century' (21 May 2002) (on file with the authors).

[13] See R Lee (n 7) 24 noting that the early theoretical analysis of internalisation stressed two major possible costs: first, it may harm the price discovery function of a market, as orders in a particular security do not compete against each other on a single order book (see K Cohen, S Maier, RA Schwartz, and DK Whitcomb 'An Analysis of the Economic Justification for Consolidation in a Secondary Security Market' (1982) 6 J Banking and Finance 117-136; second, internalisation may divert uninformed traders away from a primary exchange, leaving only informed orders on the latter; as a result, spreads become wider as dealers protect themselves from informed traders (see D Easley, NM Kiefer, and M O'Hara 'Cream-Skimming or Profit Sharing? The Curious Role of Purchased Order Flow' (1996) 51 J Finance 1405-1436).

traders have limited knowledge and cannot effectively monitor internalising firms.[14]

3. The Political Economy of the MiFID

Similar comments help to identify the political economy of legislative reforms such as that attempted by the MiFID with respect to trading systems in general. On the one hand, stock exchanges (particularly those operating in Continental Europe) fight to defend their national franchises, which are in some Member States protected by concentration rules. On the other, investment banks (often belonging to American groups or European financial conglomerates) seek wider territories of action. The business model is that of the City of London, where the Stock Exchange, ATS and internalising firms offer different trading functionalities to institutional and retail investors. On the whole, investment banks defend the rents generated by internalised trades against the stock exchanges protecting their quasi-monopolies in the trade of domestic equities.[15]

As we explain in this paper, several remedies can confront the problems of internalisation once concentration rules have been eliminated.[16] First of all, best execution provisions can take into account the existence of several trading venues to identify the best conditions for a trade. This may also require a transparency regime for off-exchange transactions. In fact, greater transparency enhances price discovery and market efficiency.[17] It also helps investors' monitoring of trade execution by investment intermediaries. Moreover, specific duties can be placed on internalising intermediaries with respect to limit orders that they leave unexecuted and also with respect to the publication of their quotes (see section C below). These duties and other remedies for the consequences of internalisation have been one of the main battle-grounds in the MiFID's formation, as we show in the following section.

[14] See R Davies, A Dufour and B Scott-Quinn (n 3).

[15] Economic studies give some support to both claims. As trading has a natural tendency to concentrate on the main market, consolidation of trading has positive effects on spreads. However, traders' preferences are not homogeneous so that alternative trading systems and fragmentation are justified. In the end, the policy issue is that of balancing consolidation and fragmentation in a given set of circumstances.

[16] See also R Davies, A Dufour and B Scott-Quinn (n 3).

[17] However, a clear-cut solution for all off-exchange transactions is difficult to envisage. As argued by IOSCO in a paper on 'Transparency and Market Fragmentation' (November 2001) 14 'the development of trade execution services outside exchange systems raises the question of whether, and on what basis, regulators need to extend transparency requirements beyond exchanges'; on the whole, regulators 'need to have an approach that will guide them in achieving an appropriate balance given the characteristics of the market in question. This may take account of such factors as the level and nature of the public involvement in trading the asset, the favoured trading method, the weighting of the informational factors determining pricing, the manipulability of the instrument and the available technology'.

B. The ISD Review

We examine, in this section, four stages of the MiFID's formation process: (i) the Commission Communication of 16 November 2000[18] included a preliminary analysis of the relevant issues and was followed by another Commission's document dated 24 July 2001, carrying rather detailed preliminary orientations; (ii) on 25 March 2002 the Commission published for consultation a new document containing 'revised orientations', which differed substantially from the previous ones; (iii) on 19 November 2002, the Commission submitted a formal proposal for a directive on investment services and regulated markets;[19] (iv) this proposal went through intense negotiations in the co-decision procedure which lasted for about two years leading to adoption of the MiFID.

I. Preliminary Orientations

1. The 2000 Communication

In its Communication of 16 November 2000 the Commission noted the existence of 'structural limits' to the ISD deriving both from the generic nature of many of its provisions and from diverging national implementations. The Commission suggested a 'wide-ranging overhaul' of the ISD to overcome these difficulties.[20] With respect to regulated markets,[21] the Commission suggested a review of the following three areas:

(i) *concentration rules*: the Directive allowed Member States to require trading of listed securities to be carried out on a regulated market, provided that certain conditions were met.[22] The anticompetitive effect of similar rules was often

[18] Communication from the Commission to the European Parliament and the Council 'Upgrading the Investment Services Directive (93/22/EEC)'. All the Commission's documents quoted in this article are available at <http://europa.eu.int/comm/internal_market/securities/isd/index_en.htm>.

[19] Proposal for a Directive of the European Parliament and of the Council on Investment Services and Regulated Markets, and amending Council Directive 85/611/EEC, Council Directive 93/6/EEC and European Parliament and Council Directive 2000/12/EC, OJ C71E 25.3.2003 62.

[20] See Communication (n 18) 9.

[21] The Commission also raised the issue of the regulatory treatment of ATSs, as they are authorised as investment firms in some Member States, but have specific features that assimilate them to regulated markets. Therefore, the Commission pointed out that it would be appropriate to apply some of the provisions concerning regulated markets to ATSs as well. Furthermore, the Communication raised the issue of the distinction between admission to trading and admission to listing: see N Moloney (n 5) 694.

[22] Article 14 (3), ISD.

highlighted, despite recognition that concentration rules can also be analysed as best execution principles.[23] However, the Commission suggested that investor protection would be better served by strict enforcement of best execution requirements and proposed to review the provision at issue. At the same time, the Commission recommended revision of the right of Member States to restrict the establishment of new markets on their territory;[24]

(ii) *high-level principles*: the Commission also called for further harmonisation of regulated markets through a common set of principles in respect of orderly trading, transparency, and market integrity. The ISD rules on regulated markets were, in fact, quite narrow and their practical impact had been negligible;

(iii) *transparency*: differences still existed in the level of transparency across EU regulated markets. In particular, the Commission highlighted the existence of divergent transparency requirements for trading with institutional investors and consulted on whether fragmentation of trading across different systems represented a threat to liquid and efficient markets.

The Communication was intensely commented upon by market participants and regulators. The Commission's summary of the replies to the consultation reflected differentiated views.[25] In particular, the proposed repeal of the provision allowing concentration rules provoked mixed reactions. However, the majority of the respondents (14 out of 22) favoured this repeal, while the regulators were split as to the choice to be made.[26] The Commission's document also attracted the attention of the European Parliament. In its final report of 23 March 2001, the Parliament welcomed the Commission's plan to upgrade the ISD,[27] making some recommendations mainly directed to introduce more flexibility in the ISD. In particular, the Parliament expressed a firm view on whether concentration rules should be abolished, by 'demand[ing] the abolition of Article 14 (3) of the ISD, and the equivalent or higher safeguarding of its objective by conduct of business rules'. On the whole, this consultation anticipated some of the main aspects of the debate in the years to follow. While the Commission was just testing the ground and did not make its plans explicit, the various interested parties took position on the central issue of the abolition of concentration rules.

[23] See G Ferrarini 'The European Regulation of Stock Exchanges: New Perspectives' (1999) 3 Comm Mkt L Rev 569, 585; M Tison 'The Investment Services Directive and its Implementation in the EU Member States' (Financial Law Institute wp <http://www.law.ugent.be/fli/WP/WP1999-pdf/wp1999-17.pdf>, 1999) 15.

[24] Article 15 (5), ISD. See Communication (n 18) 15.

[25] European Commission 'ISD Feedback. Synthesis of Responses to COM(2000) 729' (DG Internal Market Working Document, July 2001).

[26] Among the supervisors/regulators, six were in favour of abolition, four against and one suggested further consideration of the issue (see European Commission (n 25) 13 ff).

[27] Report to the Committee on Economic and Monetary Affairs on the Commission communication on upgrading the investment services directive (93/22/EEC) final A5-0106/2001.

2. The 2001 Communication

On 24 July 2001, the Commission published another document including rather detailed preliminary orientations.[28] First of all, the Commission tried to remove any uncertainty about the treatment of ATSs by introducing a new category of 'organised markets'.[29] Within the category of investment firms, the Commission explicitly mentioned, for the first time, firms that internalise orders, suggesting that their impact on price-discovery for individual securities should be addressed by strengthening the obligation to report the relevant transactions to a 'regulated market' immediately after their conclusion.[30] Very detailed rules were also proposed as to the operation of regulated markets, including provisions on the prioritisation and processing of orders and the pre and post-trade transparency of the transactions.

Furthermore, the document in question foresaw an obligation for investment firms that execute orders on behalf of third parties to report quarterly their order-routing practices to competent authorities. This would permit increased transparency as to the choice of venues for executing client orders, thereby allowing more effective monitoring of compliance with 'best execution' obligations. In addition, increased transparency would help to promote investor confidence where there are multiple venues for order execution and a suitable 'reference market' is difficult to identify.[31]

The issue of market fragmentation was addressed by suggesting a rule under which, when securities admitted to trading on a regulated market are negotiated outside the rules and/or systems of a similar market, the investment firm shall immediately submit a transaction report to the relevant market.[32] A critical point

[28] See European Commission 'Overview of Proposed Adjustments: Detailed Presentation' (24 July 2001). For a comment see N Moloney (n 5).

[29] European Commission (n 28) 7. The relevant definition distinguished between client order-matching services provided by investment firms on a discretionary basis and organised single-capacity trading arrangements matching multiple trading interests in financial instruments. The Commission suggested that, if an organised market provided for the trading of instruments admitted to trading on regulated markets, it should be authorised as a regulated market.

[30] European Commission (n 28) 17. This requirement was to be applied to all 'off-market' transactions, including matching of orders on proprietary trading systems. In addition, the Commission proposed a number of provisions addressing the impact of automated order-matching broker or dealer systems on securities trading.

[31] Competent authorities would also have the power to require investment firms to improve their order-routing practices in order to achieve the goal of obtaining 'best execution' for their clients. Moreover, the Commission proposed that the investment firms' duty to safeguard market integrity (previously included in the conduct of business rules) should become a self-standing provision under a revised ISD.

[32] In the Commission's opinion: 'This provision would seek to ensure that the terms under which off-market transactions are concluded are integrated into the overall pricing process for that financial instrument in real-time (or as close as technically feasible). The obligation would

cont. ...

of the Commission's approach was the identification of the regulated market to which off-market trades should be reported. In a trading environment where an instrument may be admitted to trading on several regulated markets in parallel, and where no market necessarily has a contractual relationship with the issuer, there is no straightforward answer to this question. Under the proposal, details of completed off-market transactions were to be transmitted to the 'leading market' or to the 'market of first quotation'.[33]

On the whole, the Commission foresaw a system where all off-market transactions were reported to a regulated market, which was obliged to integrate this information into the information given to the public. For the first time, the Commission pointed out a clear concern about possible shortcomings of market fragmentation, following the deletion of concentration rules. The Commission expressly referred to the U.S. experience and to the work of the FESCO Working Group on Alternative Trading Systems.[34] More specifically, the proposed obligation to disclose order-routing practices sought to address the brokers' practice of routing order flows to dealers or to their in-house trading desk.[35] However, no pre-trade transparency rules were provided for investment firms at this stage.

apply to all completed 'off-market' transactions executed by investment firms involving instruments admitted to trading on a 'regulated market' including both bilateral/OTC transactions and transactions matched on proprietary trading systems/order-books. This proposal is introduced to counter concerns relating to a possible deterioration in the efficiency of the price-discovery mechanism if details on the prices at which an undisclosed part of the market is buying and selling a given security are not made available to the market as a whole.' All investment firms 'which match trades or conclude bilateral transactions' were to be obliged to report price and volume data to a 'regulated market'. The Commission judged this as an essential 'tightening of transparency requirements in respect of 'off-market' trades – both in terms of the *immediacy of reporting* of a completed transaction and *by extending its reach to transactions in all financial instruments* which are admitted to trading on a regulated market'. It then stated: 'These adjustments are proposed to ensure that growing off-market turnover in trading does not operate to the detriment of overall price discovery process by ensuring that completed off-market transactions are made public to other market participants in real-time through their incorporation in an aggregated price feed'.

[33] According to the Commission: 'The 'regulated market' with either greatest turnover or longest tradition of trading in the instrument would seem to be best-placed to assimilate information into a consolidated price feed which is used as a reference by the wider market'. The Commission acknowledged that the proposed solution presented possible drawbacks and noted: 'there is a danger of freezing any historically established role of particular markets as a trading centre for individual instruments and further adding to the 'stickiness' of liquidity'. However, other alternatives such as reporting to competent authorities or simply requiring investment firms to put in place their own arrangements to 'make public' these details were considered incapable of reaching the goal of consolidating price information.

[34] FESCO 'The regulation of ATS in Europe' (September 2000) and 'Proposed standards for ATS' (June 2001).

[35] See for instance on the issue IOSCO 'Transparency and Market Fragmentation' (November 2001).

The market participants' reactions to the document were quite negative. In particular the proposed introduction of a new category of 'organised markets' found little support.[36] The respondents were also divided upon the removal of concentration rules. Whilst there was substantial support for the introduction of effective transparency rules to counter market fragmentation, the mechanism proposed by the Commission to report off-market trades of all instruments admitted to trading on a regulated market met little support.[37] To better understand the different positions, reference can be made to the contributions made public by business associations and market participants. The intermediaries denounced the anti-competitive effect of the duty to report to the 'lead market'. In addition, they highlighted the problems affecting the 'immediate' publication of concluded trades.[38] On the other side, Continental exchanges wanted the Commission to impose more stringent requirements on ATS and internalisers to achieve a level-playing field and balance the abolition of concentration rules. Two of the main exchanges stressed the need for the application of pre-trade transparency rules to off-market trades.[39] Also the London Stock Exchange (LSE) did not support the Commission's proposal. Indeed, under the system in place all trades in UK equities executed by LSE members away from the centralised trading book are reported to the exchange within three minutes and published immediately.[40] However, the LSE submitted that the extension of these reporting requirements to non-member EU investment firms would have been expensive and difficult to achieve, suggesting that the reports should be made to *any* regulated market while the information would be consolidated on a commercial basis by vendors.[41]

[36] See European Commission 'Revision of Investment Services Directive (93/22/EEC), Second Consultation, Annex 2: Summary of Responses to the Preliminary Orientations of Commission Services' (July 2001) 10.

[37] See European Commission (n 36) 14.

[38] See for instance the reply by ISDA (1 November 2001) and TBMA (30 October 2001) (both on file with the authors).

[39] See the reply by Deutsche Börse (31 October 2001) and Euronext (14 November 2001) (both on file with the authors).

[40] Some large trades and the so-called protected trades on the LSE are subject to delays of up to twenty-four hours. This delay has been object of an investigation by the Office of Fair Trading: see the discussion of the reasons for such delay in SM Schaefer 'Competition between Regulated Markets in London' in G Ferrarini (ed) *European Securities markets. The Investment Services Directive and Beyond* (Kluwer law International 1998) 209.

[41] London Stock Exchange 'Response to the Consultation on Proposed Adjustments to the Investment Service Directive' 4 (on file with the authors).

II. Revised Orientations

1. The 2002 Consultation

On 25 March 2002 the Commission published for consultation a new document containing its 'revised orientations', which differed substantially from the previous ones. Firstly, a new category of 'organised markets' was no longer proposed. Rather, the Commission proposed to ensure that 'multilateral order disclosure and execution systems' were properly integrated into the overall market system, thus covering the operation of ATSs.[42] The proposal to oblige investment firms to disclose order-routing practices was withdrawn due to the criticism it attracted.[43] As to the transparency obligations, the revised orientations entailed important changes reflecting the desire to find a workable compromise. Firstly, pre and post-trade transparency obligations were limited to equity instruments. Similar duties could be applied to non-equity instruments in the future.[44] Secondly, the principle was stated that 'comparable transparency obligations should apply to similar trades irrespective of the trading arrangement used to execute the transaction'. Therefore, the revised orientations envisaged pre-trade transparency obligations for regulated markets and ATSs. Thirdly, the Commission introduced a distinction between systematic and incidental internalisation. The former was defined with reference to 'more than 10% of client order flow (calculated as average quarterly flow over last four quarters)' and was subject to heavier post-trade disclosure obligations and more rigorous best execution and conflict of interest management rules. The latter was only subject to best execution requirements. As to pre-trade transparency, the Commission modified its view suggesting that internalised market orders cannot influence price expectations of other clients and therefore should not be reported; furthermore, it questioned whether limit orders should be considered as an expression of potential trading interest and therefore duly reported.[45] Post-trade transparency obligations were referred to off-exchange transactions, however limited to transactions on instruments admitted to trading on a regulated market of which the firm is a direct or indirect member. The

[42] European Commission 'Revision of Investment Services Directive (93/22/EEC), Second Consultation'; European Commission (n 28) 12.

[43] See European Commission (n 28) 23.

[44] According to the Commission, the valuation of non-equity instruments 'does not depend so crucially on timely information regarding the prices at which other (potentially informed) market participants are willing to trade. Often, their value can be established on the basis of fixed reference values, or the value of an underlying (including equity)': European Commission (n 28) 9. However, the Commission provided that the scope of application of transparency rules could be extended to other classes of financial instruments through level 2 measures: European Commission 'Revision of Investment Services Directive (93/22/EEC), Annex I: Revised Orientations' 35.

[45] See European Commission (n 28) 11.

Commission acknowledged that this might imply some off-exchange trades not being reported, however found it justified by the cost that compulsory reporting to the most liquid market (as envisaged in its earlier proposal) would mean for intermediaries. An exception was made for systematic internalisers, who could choose between either setting-up autonomous post-trade publication arrangements (similarly to ATSs) or disclosing information to the most liquid 'regulated market' for trading the instrument at issue (irrespective of whether the firm is a member of that market or not).[46]

On the whole, the revised orientations of March 2002 differed considerably from the preliminary orientations. As to transparency rules, the Commission was under fire both from regulated markets and investment firms. Regulated markets opposed the removal of concentration rules and felt, in any case, that a removal should be balanced by new obligations for internalisers to ensure a level playing field.[47] On the other, financial intermediaries (and national authorities) supported the introduction of new transparency rules for off-exchange trades only with respect to equity instruments.[48] However, from nearly all of the interested parties, 'there was strong opposition to the mechanisms whereby non-exchange order-matching systems would disclose trades to the wider market'.[49] As a result the Commission changed its position considerably by deleting all controversial parts of its original proposal. A lighter regime was introduced for block trades and illiquid securities, while a more cautious approach was adopted as to pre-trade transparency requirements for internalisers.

2. The 'Concentration' Debate

During the consultation period, the proposed removal of concentration rules returned to the front-stage as Euronext publicly advocated the benefits of retaining these rules and highlighted the risks of internalisation for client protection and price formation.[50] Fierce opposition from investment firms followed. In a widely circulated joint document, some of the main intermediaries' associations made the case for internalisation of orders and criticised the concentration rules and

[46] The Commission acknowledged that its approach to transparency 'may not be sufficient to ensure that information on equity trades and quotes ... is effectively consolidated' and therefore suggested that national authorities could request certain parties, public or private bodies, to consolidate information on a reasonable commercial basis.

[47] See European Commission (36) 12.

[48] See European Commission (n 36) 13: 'it was contended that ... extension of a similar level of transparency to other assets markets – fixed income securities and derivatives – would be meaningless (in term of price relevant informational content) and/or counterproductive'.

[49] See European Commission (n 36) 13.

[50] See Lex Column 'Losing concentration' *Fin Times* (7 May 2002).

their anticompetitive effects.[51] However, different views were expressed from within the two interest groups concerned (stock exchanges and investment intermediaries) on the controversial issue of the application of pre-trade transparency rules to internalisers, with opinions more or less divided on national grounds.[52] This can be explained by the fact that the issue at stake was the choice between two different models of markets, existing in UK and continental Europe respectively, and between two different underlying philosophies. In continental Europe, a centralised organisation of trading prevails, in which the price formation is made easier by the obligation to execute orders in a specified trading place.[53] Instead, the Anglo-Saxon model is inspired by a principle of freedom, intermediaries being free to choose the trading place but subject to specific rules of conduct as regards the fiduciary obligation towards the clients. Therefore, as the fundamental issue was deeply rooted in the structure of national markets, interest groups were divided along national lines, despite noteworthy attempts to avoid rigid solutions and find ways to integrate different trading structures in a single market.[54]

III. The Commission's Proposal

1. The Proposed Transplant of U.S. Rules

On 19 November 2002, the Commission published a proposal for a directive on investment services and regulated markets.[55] The explanatory memorandum to the proposal criticised the ISD for not addressing the issues that arise when ex-

[51] See (n 12).

[52] Compare as regards intermediaries the European Banking Federation document 'FBE Statement on the Revised Investment Service Document' 14 June 2002 (which highlights the dissenting views of the French and Italian members), and as regards regulated markets the position of the French-based Euronext, which advocates pre-trade transparency rules for internalisers ('Euronext's Proposals for the ISD in Relation to the EU's Cash Equity Markets' 24 May 2002), in contrast with that of the LSE. See A Sorecki 'LSE Firm on Internalization' *Fin Times* (1 June 2002).

[53] See on the model of Euronext R Davies, A Dufour and B Scott-Quinn (n 3). It has been noted that '… l'organisation privilégiée par la directive semble très proche de l'ancien modèle de marché du Noveau Marché, abandonné par Euronext Paris (…) lors de sa fusion avec les borses belge et hollandaise: G Das Merces 'La refonte de la directive sur les services d'investissement' (2003) Lamy Droit du Financement 138. As regards the structure of the Paris market before the merger see M Pagano 'The Changing Microstructure of European Equity Markets' in G Ferrarini (n 40) 182.

[54] See E Wymeersch 'Revision of the ISD' (Financial Law Institute wp <http://www.law.rug.ac.be/fli>, 2002) 4.

[55] The MiFID Proposal (n 11).

changes compete with each other and with new order-execution platforms. In the Commission's opinion, competition between different methods of trade-execution (exchanges, new trading systems, in-house order execution by investment firms) was the principal regulatory challenge confronting EU securities supervisors. However the ISD, by allowing Member States to keep concentration rules in their legislation, created 'a formidable stumbling-block to the emergence of an integrated and competitive trading infrastructure'. Consequently, the proposal did not envisage the renewal of the 'concentration rule option' and opened the way to off-exchange transactions, including internalisation, in all Member States.[56]

However, through a last-minute *coup de scene*,[57] the Commission accepted the Continental views on pre-trade transparency and included in its proposal rules mimicking the U.S. 'Limit-Order Display Rule' and 'Quote Rule'.[58] The latter (Rule 11Ac1-1) was adopted by the SEC in 1978 and requires broker-dealers who maintain quotes for a security to promptly disseminate these quotations and to honour them.[59] In 1996, the SEC extended this rule to apply to NASDAQ market makers who posted quotes in ECN.[60] Under the 'Display Rule' (Rule 11AC1-4), adopted in 1996 with the Order Handling Rules,[61] dealers who accept limit orders

[56] Article 20 (3) provided that investment firms might execute client orders outside the rules and systems operated by a regulated market or Multilateral Trading Facilities (MTF's) provided that they obtained the express prior consent of clients, to be renewed annually.

[57] According to the press, the change was due to the personal intervention of Mr. Prodi, president of the European Commission: Lex Column 'The Prodi Plot' *Fin Times* (19 November 2002). Indeed a Commission informal draft widely circulated on 3 September 2002 did not envisage any pre-trade transparency obligation for investment firms.

[58] Since 1975, the SEC has increasingly focused on the improvement of order execution: see JC Coffee and J Seligman *Securities Regulation* (Foundation Press 9th ed 2003) 652 ff.

[59] Prior to 1978, the quotes disseminated on Nasdaq by market makers did not specify the number of shares to which the quote applied. In addition, market makers did not always honour their quotes, refusing to trade at the specified price. See JC Coffee and J Seligman (n 58) 652-653.

[60] See KH Chung and RA Van Ness 'Order Handling Rules, Tick Size, and the Intraday Pattern of Bid-Ask Spreads for Nasdaq Stocks' (2001) 4 J Fin Markets 144: 'Under the new rule, if a dealer places a limit order into Instinet or another ECN, the price and quantity are incorporated in the ECN quote displayed on Nasdaq if it represents the best bid or offer in ECN'. JC Coffee and J Seligman (n 58) 653-654, explain the amendment of the Firm Quote Rule with the fact that, under the Limit Order Display Rule, the market maker, who did not want to improve its quotation upon receipt of a customer's superior limit order, could send the quotation to an ECN or a market maker that would comply with the Display Rule (see the text below).

[61] The Order Handling Rules were an important step in the development of the National Market System (NMS), envisioned by the 1975 Securities Acts Amendments (which also contemplated the abolition of fixed commission rates), that would ensure investors competitive markets and best execution of their trades: see JC Coffee and J Seligman (n 58) 650-653. The Amendments fixed five basic goals for the SEC to pursue in implementing the national market system: (i) economically efficient execution of transactions; (ii) fair competition among broker-dealers, among exchanges and between exchanges and other markets; (iii) ready availability of

cont. ...

and specialists must display any customer's limit order, including their full size, when the order is placed at a price superior to the market maker or specialist's own quotation.[62] Therefore, if the prices quoted by market makers left an artificially wide spread, a new source of competition would be introduced by allowing customers to introduce a price quotation that would narrow the bid/asked spread. As a result, brokers holding market orders from their clients would be required by their duty of best execution to execute their trades against these limit orders.[63]

The Order Handling Rules were introduced after a pricing collusion was discovered amongst Nasdaq's market makers, under which they avoided odd-eighths quotes. An empirical study by W. Christie and P. Schultz, which examined an extensive sample of bid-ask spreads for 100 of the most active Nasdaq stocks in 1991, was the first to find that spreads of one-eighth were virtually non-existent for a majority of this sample.[64] In the authors' opinion, the fact that market makers enforced a minimum spread of $0.25 for a majority of large stocks could partially explain why previous research had found trading costs to be higher for Nasdaq than for the New York Stock Exchange.[65] W Christie and P Schultz consequently suggested that the organizational structures of these markets differed in their promotion of competitive spreads. The NYSE specialists, despite enjoying an exclusive franchise in their stocks, faced competition for order flow from floor traders on the exchange, from other exchanges, and from public limit orders. In contrast, Nasdaq market makers competed with each other for order flow, but did not face competition from limit orders (which were executed only if the inside spread reached the limit price).[66]

The publication of the W. Christie and P. Schultz study and the ensuing discussion led to regulatory investigations, class-actions, and numerous academic

quotation and transaction information to broker-dealers and investors; (iv) ability of broker-dealers to execute orders in the best market; (v) opportunity for investors to execute orders without the participation of a dealer (Section 11A).

[62] JC Coffee and J Seligman (n 58) 653 make the following example: if the market maker's quotation were $18 bid and $19 asked, and a customer placed a limit order with him to buy at $18.50, the market maker's bid quotation would become $18.50 bid and $19 asked. If $18.50 were the highest bid price submitted to Nasdaq and $18.75 the lowest asked quotation, then the NBBO (National Best Bid and Offer) would become $18.50 and $18.75, and all transactions would be done at this price until the orders were exhausted or a still superior price were quoted.

[63] JC Coffee and J Seligman (n 58) 653.

[64] See WG Christie and PH Schultz 'Why Do Nasdaq Market Makers Avoid Odd-Eighth Quotes' (1994) 49 J Finance 1813. The two authors also found that either inside bid or inside ask quotes ending in odd-eights (1/8, 3/8, 5/8, 7/8) were absent for 70 of the 100 stocks. They argued that this 'surprising result reflect[ed] an implicit agreement among market makers to avoid using odd-eighths in quoting bid and ask prices and that a large number of market makers per stock is not necessarily synonymous with competition' 1814.

[65] WG Christie and PH Schultz (n 64).

[66] WG Christie and PH Schultz (n 64) 1815.

papers on Nasdaq's trading structures and activities. As a result, several reforms took place.[67] Firstly, market makers agreed to end the convention of avoiding odd-eighth quotes.[68] Secondly, the regulatory responsibilities of the National Association of Securities Dealers (NASD) were separated from the operation of the Nasdaq market through the formation of NASD Regulation Inc. Thirdly, the SEC adopted new Rules applicable to all U.S. markets, but specifically targeted to Nasdaq. Under the Display Rule, dealers have four options when receiving a customer limit order: (i) execute the order against their own inventory; (ii) post the order as their own quote; (iii) forward the order to another market maker who would comply with the Display Rule; (iv) send the order to an ECN.[69] As a result, the general public competes directly with Nasdaq market makers in the quote-setting process.[70]

Economic research made on the impact of the 1996 regulatory reforms confirmed that many of the SEC's objectives had been met. One study showed that quoted and effective spreads on Nasdaq narrowed by approximately 30%, with the largest benefit accruing to investors in stocks with relatively wide spreads prior to the implementation of the SEC rules.[71] Another study analysing the intra-day variation in bid-ask spreads on Nasdaq found that spreads declined significantly after the 1996 reforms and that the magnitude of the decline was largest during midday.[72] This result is consistent with other studies finding that the NYSE spread is narrowest during midday, when competition among limit-order traders is highest.[73] To the extent that the Display Rule makes the role of limit orders on Nasdaq similar to that on NYSE, limit-order traders play an important role in shaping the intraday pattern of spreads for Nasdaq as well.[74]

[67] See JC Coffee and J Seligman (n 58) 653.

[68] WG Christie, JH Harris and PH Schultz 'Why Did NASDAQ Market Makers Stop Avoiding Odd-Eighth Quotes?' (1994) 49 J Finance 1841, found that, immediately after newspapers' reports of the finding of the WG Christie and PH Schultz study, virtually all Nasdaq dealers moved in unison to adopt odd-eighth quotes. As a result, spreads fell nearly 50%.

[69] See MJ Barclay, WG Christie, JH Harris, E Kandel, and P Schultz 'Effects of Market Reform on the Trading Costs and Depths of Nasdaq Stocks' (1999) 54 J Finance 1.

[70] See KH Chung and RA Van Ness 'Order Handling Rules, Tick Size, and the Intraday Pattern of Bid-Ask Spreads for Nasdaq Stocks' (2001) 4 J Fin Markets 143, 144.

[71] MJ Barclay, WG Christie, JH Harris, E Kandel, and P Schultz (n 69) 3, arguing that the significantly higher trading costs among Nasdaq issues previously identified in the literature have largely disappeared. However, approximately 60% of the total decline in trading costs for Nasdaq stocks arose prior to the introduction of the new rules, being largely attributable to the government investigations and negative publicity concerning Nasdaq.

[72] KH Chung and RA Van Ness (n 70) 146.

[73] KH Chung, BF Van Ness and RA Van Ness 'Limit Orders and the Bid-Ask Spread' (1999) 53 J Fin Econ 255.

[74] KH Chung and RA Van Ness (n 70) 146.

2. The Proposed Limit-Order Display and Quote Rules

The Commission proposed, first of all, a transplant of the Limit-Order Display Rule. Article 20 (4) of the proposed Directive provided: 'Member States shall require that, in the case of a client limit order which cannot be immediately executed under prevailing market conditions, investment firms are, unless the client expressly instructs otherwise, to take measures to facilitate the earliest possible execution of that order by making public immediately the terms of that client limit order in a manner which is easily accessible to other market participants'. Therefore, the rule required immediate disclosure of limit orders; however, it would not prevent investment firms from executing the transaction in-house, provided this was done upon receiving the order. In addition, clients could instruct their investment firm not to publish the limit order. This may appear to be in contrast with the public interest inspiring the disclosure duty at issue; however, one should consider that, otherwise, clients could refrain from passing limit orders on to their broker-dealers. In addition, Article 20 (4) permitted non-disclosure of limit orders in respect of large transactions. The mechanisms for disclosure and order execution were not specified, but left to implementing measures.[75]

Moreover, the Commission proposed to introduce a quote disclosure obligation. Article 25 (1) of the proposed Directive provided that investment firms which operated a trading book were to make public a firm bid and offer price for transactions of a size customarily undertaken by retail investors in respect of listed shares in which these firms were dealing. In addition, this Article required investment firms to 'trade with other investment firms and eligible counterparties at the advertised prices, except where justified by legitimate commercial considerations related to the final settlement of the transaction'. The explanatory memorandum defined this provision as a 'quote disclosure rule' and made reference to the U.S. experience, with special regard to the SOES (small order execution system) rules operated by the National Association of Securities Dealers (NASD).[76]

[75] The Commission wrote: 'The client limit order display rule will ensure that investment firms do not withhold price-relevant information – embodied in the terms of a non-executed client limit order – from other market participants. The rule seeks to ensure that this information is made public in a way that the relevant information is immediately and easily visible to other market participants and the marketplace as a whole' (MiFID Proposal (n 11) 21).

[76] See the MiFID Proposal (n 11) 22.

IV. The Political Negotiations during the Co-decision Procedure

1. The Role of Interest Groups

On 20 November 2002, the Commission transmitted its proposal to the European Parliament and the Council. It was the start of one of the most intense political struggles that Europe ever experienced over a single piece of financial regulation. It took nearly two years for the proposal to be finally approved. In the months following the presentation of the proposal by the Commission, the debate intensified and the two opposing camps tried to make their positions clear in view of the beginning of the discussion in the European Parliament and in the Council's working group. This was the climax of the political debate, in which the 'traditional' division between Continental Europe (France and Italy in particular) and the Anglo-Saxon countries re-emerged. As already noted with reference to the Commission's previous consultation, different positions were expressed from within the two interest groups concerned (stock exchanges and investment intermediaries) on the controversial issue of the application of pre-trade transparency rules to internalisers, with opinions divided on national grounds.

The investment intermediaries' associations[77] insisted that the abolition of the concentration rule could be effective only if it was not accompanied by the introduction of other hindrances to the operation of alternative trading venues or to order execution off-exchange. Specifically, they criticised Article 20 (4) (the customer limit order display rule) and Article 25 (the quote disclosure rule) as substantially restricting the possibility of competition for investment firms vis-à-vis regulated markets. Firstly, they criticised the references made by the Commission to the U.S. system, as the European markets lack both the infrastructure to consolidate trade information and an integrated clearing and settlement system. In the absence of a similar infrastructure and system, Article 25 would have no positive effect on fragmentation, as information would be dispersed.[78] The idea that the reporting requirements would lead market forces to create such an infrastructure was labelled as unrealistic.[79] Secondly, intermediaries pointed out that Article 25 would subject dealers executing orders in-house to mandatory market making obligations. This provision was based on the wrong assumption that quotes made by

[77] See the briefing paper by European and International securities and derivatives organisations of 21 March 2003.

[78] The comment echoed the criticism made by the U.S.-based Securities Industry Association (SIA) according to which 'the U.S. SEC rules that serve as the basis for proposed Article 25 are inextricably linked to the information and trading infrastructure in the United States … and cannot simply be transplanted into the very different European markets': see SIA 'Letter to the European Commission, re: Proposed Revision of the Investment Services Directive' (17 March 2003) <http://www.sia.com/international/html/eu_capital_markets.html>.

[79] See European Banking Federation 'Summary of FBE Position on Articles Related to In-house Matching in the Investment Services Directive Proposal' (10 February 2003).

dealers (who put their capital at risk) are in some way equivalent to investors' limit orders on the order book of a regulated market. Thirdly, Article 25 would oblige a dealer to deal with any investment firm or eligible counterparty, with a significant increase of its credit risk. Again, it was pointed out that in the U.S. the situation is significantly different, as the issue is solved through settlement of trades by a central counterparty (the National Securities Clearing Corporation), which guarantees completion of trades and nets deliveries and payments among its participants.[80] However, French and Italian intermediaries did not share these views, defending the imposition of pre-trade transparency obligations on dealers as necessary to create a level playing field.[81] The stock exchanges, hit by the abolition of concentration rules, defended the imposition of pre-trade transparency requirements on internalisers to achieve efficient price-formation in European financial markets.[82]

2. The Role of the European Parliament

As a first reaction, the European Parliament's Committee on Economic and Monetary Affairs rejected the Commission's proposal.[83] The client limit order display rule was to be deleted as it 'would cause limit orders to be routed via regulated markets, since there is no infrastructure in place for publishing and providing access to such orders'.[84] The quote disclosure rule was also to be deleted, because it would not introduce 'a transparency obligation at all. It would actually compel investment firms to buy and sell securities (or 'make a market' in securi-

[80] SIA Letter to the European Commission (n 78) 9.

[81] According to the French Banking Federation (FBF), 'regulated markets must remain a specific category because they offer superior guarantees for investor protection; they must therefore benefit from a presumption of "best execution" … ; order internalising systems must be confined to retail orders, which must be executed at the price recorded simultaneously on the regulated market. In this way, clients will benefit both from the best price and from cost savings generated by automatic straight-through processing (execution, clearing and settlement)'. See FBF 'New Proposal for an ISD: the French Banking Federation calls for a regulatory framework for European markets that fosters orderly competition while protecting investors and enabling companies to raise financing' (7 June 2002) <http://www.fbf.fr/Web/internet/corporatesite.nsf/(PageList)/bankingeurope_home>. The Italian Banking Association (ABI) advocated the creation of an European system of distribution of market information and publication of the best quotation, similar to the U.S. National Market System: see ABI 'La pre-trade transparency come elemento essenziale per la competizione tra mercati europei'(November 2002).

[82] See Federation of European Securities Exchanges (FESE) 'Position Paper by the FESE in Response to the Commission Proposal on the Revision of the Investment Services Directive' (28 February 2003).

[83] See the Draft Report by the British Rapporteur T Villiers, 10 March 2003; see also the article by F Guerrera 'Banks Scent Victory on Share Trades' <http://news.ft.com> (24 February 2003).

[84] Draft Report (n 83) 53.

ties), regardless of the type of customer or size of the order'.[85] This initial report was followed by intense discussion within the Committee on a number of difficult issues. As a result, a compromise solution was found by the British Rapporteur and embodied in her final report of 25 September 2003. Article 20 (4) was restricted to share trading. Article 25 was significantly modified to constrain its impact on market practices. The scope of the quote rule was limited to 'investment firms which practice systematic internalisation in shares' and to 'transactions of a standard market size' (instead of retail investor transactions). In addition, the duty to quote was only to be imposed on the investment firm's 'systematic internalisation clients' (rather than to 'other investment firms and eligible counterparties'). A revised paragraph 3 specified that 'investment firms are permitted to decide … the persons that they accept as clients …', i.e. that the quotation duty is not addressed to the general public. These amendments were accepted by the Parliament in its resolution on the proposal.

The Parliament's compromise solution was generally approved of by various interest groups.[86]

3. The Legislative Process Comes to End

Following the Parliament's resolution, the ECOFIN Council on 7 October 2003 approved a common position with further amendments, notwithstanding the opposition of the UK, Ireland, Finland, Sweden and Luxembourg (not enough to form a blocking minority). As requested by the Parliament, the limit order display rule was restricted to share trading. However, Member States were left free to decide whether the relevant obligation could be complied with by transmitting the client limit order to a regulated market or MTF. Furthermore, the Council permitted firms to publish only one side of the quote and also to publish different prices for different sizes. In addition, the firm quote rule was restricted, as also suggested by the Parliament, to 'systematic internalisers', i.e. investment firms which deal on their own account 'on an organised, regular, and systematic basis' by executing orders outside a regulated market or an MTF. The same rule did not apply to large transactions (as opposed to transactions of a normal market size). Article 25 specified the quotation duty in detail. The orders of retail clients must be executed at the quoted price, whereas those of professional clients can be executed at better prices. While the disclosure duty was directed to market participants in general, the quote obligation was only to be imposed on clients of the investment firm, which was free to choose the same on the basis of considerations such as counterparty risk and settlement risk. Furthermore, the Commission's im-

[85] Draft Report (n 83) 54.

[86] See the article by A Skorecki *Fin Times* (26 September 2003) stating: 'If the banks have been the winners, the exchanges are not admitting it. Euronext, for one, is practically jubilant …. The LSE calls it an "excellent, hard-won compromise"'.

plementing powers were foreseen in detail by the new Article including a reference to the ways in which the disclosure duty should be complied with (e.g. through proprietary arrangements).

The ECOFIN agreement was widely criticised by British MEPs and the relevant interest groups, who attacked the UK Treasury for not accepting compromise proposals brought forward at the last minute.[87] The two texts just considered showed substantial differences, the Council text resulting as more restrictive for investment firms.[88] Some of the points raised by the interest groups were then inserted in a new text, approved at second reading by the Parliament on 30 March 2004 and agreed by the Council on 7 April 2004. However, the final compromise was heavily criticised by the Anglo-Saxon block,[89] feeling that the proposal did not meet their expectations.

C. The MiFID and Internalisation

In this section, we specifically analyse the MiFID's provisions relating to internalisation. In general, they respond to the need to establish a comprehensive regulatory regime governing the execution of transactions in financial instruments irrespective of the trading methods used.[90] This regime includes the rules on post-trade disclosure requiring investment firms 'which, either on own account or on behalf of clients, conclude transactions in shares admitted to trading on a regulated market outside a regulated market or MTF, to make public the volume and price of those transactions and the time at which they were con-

[87] See the article by D Dombey 'UK Criticised after EU Investment Rules Defeat' *Fin Times* (8 October 2003).

[88] For instance, the text approved by the European Parliament included a size threshold, defining systematic internalization as meaning the execution of orders 'up to a standard market size' and using the same criterion for limiting the obligation to deal: such a limit was not present in the Council's text. Furthermore, the Council's text limited the possibility of price improvement by dealers, which was on the contrary allowed by the Parliament.

[89] The UK rapporteur T Villiers stated: 'As European Parliament rapporteur for the directive, I would love to claim that the directive was a UK triumph, but I cannot. While the culmination of two years of hard-fought negotiations in Brussels has undoubtedly brought some progress in freeing the market for share trading in Europe, these advances come at a high price. Those who internalize share trades on a large scale face significant and unnecessary new red tape, requiring them to publish quotes for big trades volumes, with all the extra cost and risk that involves.': see letter to the editor *Fin Times* (6 July 2004).

[90] See the 5th recital of the MiFID's Preamble. See, in general, G Ferrarini 'Contract Standards and the Markets in Financial Instruments Directive (MiFID): An Assessment of the Lamfalussy Regulatory Architecture' (2005) 1 European Review of Contract Law 19.

cluded'.[91] However, in this section we focus on those provisions which appear relatively novel at least from a Continental European perspective, such as those (deriving from U.S. law) on client order handling and the duty to publish firm quotes, and the principle of best execution which the MiFID derived from those countries (like the UK) where internalisation is already practiced on a large scale.[92]

I. Client Order Handling and Display of Client Limit Orders

1. The MiFID Rules

Article 22 MiFID includes clients order handling rules. The framework principle is stated by paragraph 1, asking Member States 'to require that investment firms authorised to execute orders on behalf of clients implement procedures and arrangements which provide for the prompt, fair and expeditious execution of client orders, relative to other client orders or the trading interests of the trading firm'. This provision is complemented by a time priority requirement fixed by the same paragraph.[93] The conditions to be complied with by the order handling procedures and arrangements to be set up by investment firms are laid down by level 2 rules.[94]

[91] See Article 28 (1) MiFID, which also specifies: 'This information shall be made public as close to real-time as possible, on a reasonable commercial basis, and in a manner which is easily accessible to other market participants'.

[92] As the level 2 rules have not been finally adopted at the time of preparing this article, this section refers to CESR's Technical Advice on Possible Implementing Measures of the Directive 2004/39/EC on Markets in Financial Instruments, April 2005 (CESR/05-290b) (hereinafter the CESR Advice). Moreover, the section refers to the two draft Commission proposals for implementing measures published on 6 February 2006: the Draft Commission Regulation implementing Directive 2004/39/EC of the European Parliament and of the Council as regards record-keeping obligations for investment firms, transaction reporting, market transparency, admission of financial instruments to trading and defined terms for the purposes of that Directive (the Draft Commission Regulation); the Draft Commission Directive implementing Directive 2004/39/EC of the European Parliament and of the Council as regards organisational requirements and operational conditions for investment firms, and defined terms for the purposes of that Directive Draft 6/02/06 (the Draft Commission Directive).

[93] See the second sentence of Article 22 (1): 'These procedures or arrangements shall allow for the execution of otherwise comparable client orders in accordance with the time of their reception by the investment firm'.

[94] See the Draft Commission Directive, s. 6, Articles 47- 49. See also CESR Advice (n 92) 42 ff.

Article 22 (2) takes care of limit orders[95] concerning shares admitted to trading on a regulated market, which are not immediately executed under prevailing market conditions. In order to improve market transparency and openness, the rule requires investment firms to make the orders in question public (unless the client expressly instructs otherwise) in a manner which is easily accessible to other market participants. As CESR highlighted 'the purpose of Article 22 (2) (...) is to facilitate and accelerate the execution of client limit orders which firms do not immediately execute under prevailing market conditions. The display of these non-executed limit orders provides the client with additional opportunities for the order to be executed at that price or even to receive price improvement. In addition, limit orders contain price information, which can contribute to price discovery. The display of such unexecuted orders increases the level of pre-trade information available to market participants, facilitates the trading of client orders and contributes to their best execution'.[96] Indeed the fact that these orders are kept secret by intermediaries receiving the same may deprive the market of important information on overall trading interests with respect to a given security and excludes the possibility for other intermediaries to transact against the relevant orders. This provision was inspired by U.S. regulation and, like the latter, intends to allow for price improvements in the client's interest. As already seen (Section B.III.1), the SEC Order Handling Rules include a 'Display Rule' (Rule 11AC1-4) under which dealers who accept limit orders and specialists must display any customer's limit order, including their full size, when the order is placed at a price superior to the market maker or specialist's own quotation. Similarly, Article 22 (2) MiFID is directed to generate price improvements by making public and therefore accessible to other investors those limit orders, which are not immediately executed by the internalisers receiving them. However, the means for making public the orders at issue are not specified by the MiFID.[97]

[95] A limit order is an order to trade 'at the best price available, but only if it is no worse than the limit price specified by the trader', as opposed to a market order that is 'an instruction to trade at the best price currently available in the market': L Harris (n 7) 71 ff.

[96] See CESR Advice (n 92) 72.

[97] The implementing measures would introduce two rules on this issue. Firstly, Article 30 of the Draft Commission Regulation states: 'An investment firm shall be considered to disclose client limit orders that are not immediately executable if it transmits the order to a regulated market or MTF that operates an order book trading system, or ensures that the order is made public and can be easily executed as soon as market conditions allow.' Secondly, at a more general level, Article 31 of the Draft Commission Regulation provides: 'any arrangement to make information public ... must facilitate the consolidation of the data with similar data from other sources'. The underlying regulatory philosophy is explained by the Commission by arguing that 'it is not the task of public authorities to consolidate pre- or post-trade information, and ... this role should be left to the initiative of the markets themselves'. The Commission also recognized, however, that 'the consolidation of information in a fragmented market structure is desirable in view of the general objectives of the level 1 Directive' and specifies that 'the implementing Regulation seeks to facilitate the development of market-led solutions which will achieve

cont. ...

2. Evaluation

The situation is profoundly different in the U.S., where following the 1975 Securities Acts Amendments transaction and quotation information from different markets was consolidated into a single stream of data available to all market participants and investors.[98] Two information systems were created in the U.S. as governmental monopolies: the Consolidated Tape Association (CTA) that provides 'last sale' information for all listed stocks in all markets; and the Consolidated Quotation System (CQS) that provides quotation data for listed securities. The CQS was created after the SEC imposed an obligation on market makers and specialists in exchange-listed securities to report immediately their bid and asked prices and to execute at the quoted prices. In addition, Nasdaq disseminates both transaction and quotation information for Nasdaq securities. Moreover, the SEC extended last-sale transaction reporting to a broad number of over-the-counter stocks, which are known today as the National Market System.[99] In Europe, any such consolidated information system is lacking, while stock exchanges often perform a similar function at the national level. Under the MiFID, also trade information and execution systems other than regulated markets and MTF could be used by internalisers: for example, a bilateral system operated by the same internalising firm or a trade execution system operated by an information provider.[100] In the future, similar fragmented systems could be consolidated in Europe, presumably at the initiative of information providers, provided that a sufficient market for the information required by the MiFID developed. However, Article 22 (2) further specifies that Member States may decide that investment firms comply with the 'display rule' by transmitting the limit orders to a regulated market or MTF. This specification is apparently justified by the aim to assure that the relevant orders are made public and accessible in an effective way.[101] Yet, Member

that consolidation'. See Commission Background Note to the Draft Commission Regulation (n 92) 11.

[98] See JC Coffee and J Seligman (n 58) 651 ff, speaking of an 'informational revolution'.

[99] JC Coffee and J Seligman (n 58) 652: 'these changes brought a wave of sunlight to the over-the-counter market'.

[100] CESR Advice (n 92) 73. At level 2 CESR Advice proposed a 'visibility and accessibility test' and noted that the chosen venue 'should therefore be one that displays the limit order in a way that is visible to other market participants and is widely publicised. The characteristics of that venue, or the information provided in respect of execution options, should provide the greatest possible opportunities for the limit order to be rapidly and easily executed as soon as permitted by market conditions.'

[101] CESR Advice (n 92) 73. According to CESR Advice, '[t]he publication of standard client limit orders where an existing RM and/or MTF offers a public order book, is straightforward, on the grounds that transmission of the client limit order to that venue would make it both "visible" under the pre trade transparency requirements for RMs/MTFs and potentially easily executable, once it becomes executable in terms of market price'. However, CESR noted that the 'visibility test' will not be fulfilled 'where the limit order is sent to a quote driven market

cont. ...

States could be led by protectionism and exploit this option simply to protect their domestic markets.

Article 22 is, therefore, open to criticism on grounds similar to those concerning other MiFID's provisions. While its first paragraph includes a rather uncontroversial framework principle as to order handling in general, its second paragraph tackles an issue which is highly technical and ill-suited for discussion at level 1 of the Lamfalussy procedure. Moreover, the provision adopted, being inspired by U.S. legislation, is unprecedented in Europe. The Member States already allowing for internalisation of share trading by investment intermediaries do not foresee anything like the U.S. Display Rule in their domestic legislations, while the Member States forced by the MiFID to introduce internalisation lobbied for a similar rule also to protect domestic stock exchanges and brokers against the large investment banks' internalising share trades. Under the MiFID's display rule, limit orders by equity investors will either improve the internalisers' quotations or be disclosed to the market. The competition between the internalisers' quotes and their clients limit orders could exercise some pressure on the bid-ask spreads of internalised trades; however, this is a conjecture not yet confirmed by empirical studies concerning the European markets. Moreover, the information systems that will be used to make limit orders public and accessible are fragmented and their effectiveness is untested, while it is totally uncertain, at the present stage, whether Europe-wide information systems will develop as a business following the MiFID's implementation. In addition, Member States deleting concentration rules will likely require that limit orders be sent to regulated markets and MTFs in an effort to protect the same from the domination of mainly Anglo-American investment banks. While the political implications of the display rule are quite clear, its impact on European markets is difficult to predict; also the U.S. precedent may be of limited value given the different structure of U.S. and European securities markets, and the existence of a National Market System in the U.S.. In Europe, equity markets are, to some extent, still fragmented along national borders, while the MiFID's display rule by allowing for national options in its implementation generates doubts about the effectiveness of harmonisation and the regulatory bite of Article 22.

operated by a RM or MTF and is not immediately executable against the quote of any market maker in that share .... Although not a general practice at the moment it is possible that quote driven markets may in future provide an additional facility for disclosing such orders, in which case firms would more easily be able to meet the requirement of Article 22 (2)'.

II. Transparency

The MiFID lays down the rules concerning transparency for intermediaries and multilateral trading facilities (MTF) in its Section 2.[102] As to the debated issue of pre-trade transparency for internalisers, the Directive foresees two main obligations tracking the U.S. Quote Rule.

1. Obligation to Make Public Quotes

Internalisers are required to publish firm quotes only if a number of conditions are met.[103] Firstly, the relevant instruments must be shares admitted to trading on a regulated market and for which there is a liquid market.[104] Secondly, the internalising firm must be a systematic internaliser for these shares, i.e. 'an investment firm which, on an organized, frequent and systematic basis, deals on own account by executing orders outside a regulated market or an MTF'.[105]

[102] The MiFID regulates the pre- and post-trade transparency of transactions concerning only shares admitted to trading on regulated markets. However, Article 65 (1) further provides that, no later than two years after its entry into force, the Commission shall report on the possible extension of pre- and post-trade transparency obligations to transactions in financial instruments other than shares and may submit proposals for related amendments. This reflects the position taken by the European Central Bank, which argued that similar obligations should also apply to debt instruments now accounting for a market capitalisation in Europe exceeding that of listed stocks: see ECB Opinion of 12 June 2003 (CON/2003/9) <http://www.ecb.int>. However, Member States may decide to apply the pre- and post- trade transparency requirements laid down by the Directive to financial instruments other than shares (see recital 46).

[103] See Article 27 (1), MiFID.

[104] The CESR Advice proposed to define liquidity for the purposes of Article 27 with the following thresholds: 'First, all shares should have to meet the common criteria of being traded daily and having a free float market capitalisation of more than €500 million. In addition, the average daily trading activity in the share should exceed 500 trades or €2 million (or the euro equivalent). Each Member State should determine which measure of trading activity it will use and apply only that measure in assessing all its shares' (CESR Advice (n 92) 61). Under the Draft Commission Regulation, a share will be considered to have a liquid market if it has a free float of at least €500 million, and one or (at the election of the Member State) both of the following conditions are fulfilled: average daily number of transactions not less than 500; average daily turnover not less than €2 million (Article 21). Thus the Commission proposes to further restrict the freedom left to Member States by CESR's Advice. According to the Commission, the effect of this regime will be that around 500 shares, representing more than 90% of the overall European markets in terms of turnover, will be covered by the transparency rules which apply to liquid shares: see Commission Background Note to the Draft Commission Regulation (n 92) 9.

[105] See Article 4 (1) (7). CESR defined the concept of 'systematic internaliser' by referring primarily to qualitative criteria related to the organisational aspects of firms. In addition, quantitative criteria are proposed as negative indicators, as they will help to indicate when a firm should be considered as being unlikely to be a systematic internaliser (CESR Advice (n 92) 58).

cont. ...

Thirdly, the transaction size must be up to standard market size.[106] The obligation to publish firm quotes does not apply to systematic internalisers that only deal in sizes above standard market size and in the case of shares for which there is not a liquid market (in this case, internalisers shall disclose quotes to their clients on request).

Article 27 (1) further specifies that 'for a particular share each quote shall include a firm bid and/or offer price or prices', thus allowing an internaliser to publish only one side of the quote; and that 'the price or prices shall also reflect the prevailing market conditions for that share', a requirement which is directed to avoid circumvention of the quote rule through publication of artificial prices. Moreover, systematic internalisers are required to make public their quotes on a regular and continuous basis during normal trading hours, and entitled to update their quotes at any time. Internalisers are also allowed, under exceptional market conditions, to withdraw their quotes. The quote shall be made public in a manner which is easily accessible to other market participants on a reasonable commercial basis (Article 27 (3)). Internalisers, therefore, are not bound to publish their quotes through a regulated market or MTF, but can use other facilities and even organize their own systems to make their quotes public.

2. Obligation to Execute Orders at the Quoted Price

Systematic internalisers are required to execute their clients' orders at the price quoted when receiving the order.[107] However, in the case of orders from professional clients, systematic internalisers may execute those orders at a better price, provided that such a price falls within a range close to market conditions and the orders are of a size bigger than that customarily undertaken by a retail investor.[108] One of the main criticisms of the quote rule was the potential exposure of investment firms to credit risks towards unknown counterparties. Article 27 (5)

However, the Draft Commission Regulation does not endorse the latter indication. Instead, it lays down criteria that are of organisational, commercial and qualitative nature (see Article 20).

106 Article 27 (1) specifies: 'Shares shall be grouped in classes on the basis of the arithmetic average value of the orders executed in the market for that share. The standard market size for each class of shares shall be a size representative of the arithmetic average value of the orders executed in the market for the shares included in each class of shares'. These criteria are further specified at level 2: see CESR Advice (n 92) 63 ff. See now Article 22 of the Draft Commission Regulation.

107 See Article 27 (3), MiFID.

108 Furthermore, 'systematic internalisers may execute orders they receive from their professional clients at prices different than their quoted ones in respect of transactions where execution in several securities is part of one transaction or in respect of orders that are subject to conditions other than the current market price' (Article 27 (3)). The size undertaken by retail investors was fixed by CESR as €7,500 (CESR Advice (n 92) 71): this was endorsed by Article 25 of the Draft Commission Regulation.

aims to avoid this occurrence by allowing systematic internalisers to choose 'on the basis of their commercial policy' which investors should have access to their quotes, provided they proceed 'in an objective non-discriminatory way'.[109] In particular, systematic internalisers may refuse to enter into, or may discontinue business relationships with investors 'on the basis of commercial considerations such as the investor credit status, the counterparty risk and the final settlement of the transaction'. Furthermore, in order to limit the risk of being exposed to multiple transactions from the same client (so called 'multiple hits'), Article 27 (6) allows systematic internalisers to limit, in a non-discriminatory way, the number of transactions with the same client and the total number of transactions with different clients at the same time.

3. Evaluation

In essence, systematic internalisers are charged with a duty to deal with all market participants and can derogate from this duty only for reasons concerning the credit and counterparty risks deriving from their internalisation activities. Therefore, systematic internalisers are placed in a position similar to other 'trading venues' such as regulated markets and MTFs, which are also subject to principles of non-discrimination with respect to investment intermediaries.[110] The reasons for a similar treatment of internalisation are made clear by the formation process of the MiFID: on the one side, the rules just examined (including those on transparency) have satisfied the incumbent exchanges' request for a level playing field; on the other, the internalisers' duty to deal with all investment intermediaries in a non-discriminatory fashion has reduced the fear (typical of small-medium sized intermediaries in Latin countries) that internalisation by large investment banks may subtract liquidity from the stock exchanges forcing local intermediaries out of their traditional markets. However, the limits of the MiFID's response to internalisation are apparent: firstly, the relevant duties are subject to restrictive conditions, such as the requirement for internalisation to be 'systematic' and for shares to be 'liquid'; secondly, the content of these duties has been diluted through the MiFID's negotiation to the point that their regulatory bite is relatively modest (even the 'antidiscrimination' rule admits for exceptions which can be not too difficult to invoke in practice).

[109] However, recital 50 clarifies that systematic internalisers are not allowed to discriminate within the same category of clients, i.e. retail or professional clients.

[110] See Article 42 (1) and (3) for regulated markets; Article 14 (4) for MTFs; Article 34 (1) for central counterparty, clearing and settlement facilities.

III. Best Execution

Article 21 tackles the controversial issue of best execution within the new regulatory framework of trading activities, which allows for 'internalisation' of orders and implicitly forbids 'concentration rules'.

1. The Framework Principle

The best execution principle is formulated by Article 21 (1) in wide terms as follows: 'Member States shall require that investment firms take all reasonable steps to obtain, when executing orders, the best possible result for their clients taking into account prices, costs, speed, likelihood of execution and settlement, size, nature or any other consideration relevant to the execution of the order. Nevertheless, whenever there is a specific instruction from the client the investment firm shall execute the order following the specific instruction'. This provision attracts at least two preliminary comments. Firstly, its ample formulation deserves approval, as it is widely acknowledged that order execution should be assessed not only in terms of price, but also on the basis of different criteria such as size of the order, speed of execution, etc., as foreseen by the provision at issue.[111] Secondly, the best execution principle supplements contract terms and, therefore, the parties are free to regulate order execution differently; in particular, the client can give 'specific instructions' to the investment firm and the latter is bound to comply with them.[112]

The regulatory system concerning the execution of transactions will be profoundly affected in those countries where concentration rules are still in force (like France, Italy and Spain). While concentration of trades in regulated markets offered a relatively easy way to best execution, the freedom granted to intermediaries by the MiFID requires careful analysis of best execution criteria for compliance and enforcement purposes. Article 21 was to some extent inspired by those jurisdictions, like the UK, where the trading of listed securities is already subject to a principle of freedom. Also in the U.S., best execution has always played a central role, deriving from the common law agency duty of loyalty rather than from regulatory fiat; however, the SEC and Congress gave practical implementation to this requirement through the establishment of the National Market System,[113] while self-regulatory organisations have adopted rules guiding their members to obtain best execution of customer orders. In contrast, the absence of an

[111] See J Macey and M O'Hara 'The Law and Economics of Best Execution' (1997) 6 J Finan Intermediation 188, note 26.

[112] See (n 90) and (n 26) and accompanying text.

[113] See SEC 'Market 2000. An Examination of Current Equity Market Developments' (Study V, 2, January 1994).

integrated market in Europe creates further regulatory problems as the same security might be traded in multiple venues based in different jurisdictions.[114]

2. Evaluation

Article 21 (1) defines best execution broadly, by making reference to various aspects of trade execution other than price. This is undoubtedly correct, even though assessing such a broad concept of best execution in individual cases may be difficult. It is not easy, for example, to compare price data with those concerning speed of execution and settlement. Therefore, choosing between best price and high speed of execution may be hard in some cases depending on the type of client, transaction and financial instrument. Yet, a narrow reading of best execution requirements that focuses, for instance, on transaction price and (monetary) cost of execution, would unduly restrain trading freedom and negatively affect competition between trading venues. As a result, legal systems must choose between a broad notion of best execution diluting the same to the point of making it almost meaningless and a narrow concept which would likely benefit the incum-

[114] The Draft Commission Directive further specifies the best execution requirements, in particular as regards three issues. Firstly, an investment firm should select the execution venues that enable it to obtain the best possible result for the client on an order-by-order basis. This specification is justified not only by the protection of the client, but also on competition grounds. See Commission Background Note to the Draft Commission Directive (n 92) 24. Secondly, the Draft Commission Directive departs from CESR's approach and sets a clear benchmark for the execution of retail client orders. According to CESR Advice '(i) it is not appropriate for regulatory requirements to pre-determine the relative importance of the factors under Article 21 (1) of the Directive because each investment firm is best placed and should retain the flexibility to tailor its execution policy to its particular strategies and goals'. More specifically, CESR proposal is as follows: '(i)n determining which execution venues to maintain or include in its order execution policy, an investment firm must review the ability of each relevant venue to offer the best possible result for the execution of its client orders, taking into account the requirements of the investment firm's order execution policy and arrangements. Factors that an investment firm may take into account in considering whether to maintain or include execution venues in its order execution policy, where relevant, include, but are not limited to: execution quality, creditworthiness and ability to avoid market impact. Costs that an investment firm may take into account in considering whether to maintain or include execution venues in its order execution policy where relevant, include, but are not limited to: transaction fees and settlement costs'. (CESR Advice (n 92) 40). Article 44 (3) of the Draft Commission Directive provides that, in respect of retail client orders, the total consideration paid by the client in terms of price and costs should be the most important factor in determining what constitutes the best possible result for the purposes of the best execution obligation. Thirdly, the Draft Commission Directive specifies that dealing on own account with client is also subject to the best execution obligation (see recital 58). Thus, the argument that the best execution obligation would not applicable to dealer-dominated or quote-driven markets, such as bond markets, is rejected. However, some limited derogations from the general rules are allowed to take into account the differences in market structure for particular types of financial instruments (see recital 59 of the Draft Commission Directive).

bent markets limiting the development of new trading venues.[115] Also the concentration rules in force in some Member States, while restraining competition, found support on grounds of best execution and fair trading as they made compliance easier and monitoring less costly.

The MiFID's treatment of best execution is a response to similar difficulties. On the one side, Article 21 (1) enounces a broad concept that is consistent with the Directive's liberalisation goals as to the market for trading venues. On the other, the subsequent paragraphs specify the best execution concept narrowing its scope and making its impact on competition less effective; moreover, the implementing measures will make best execution criteria more specific, at least with respect to retail clients.[116] Article 21 (2) limits the exercise of discretion by intermediaries asking investment firms 'to establish and implement an order execution policy to allow them to obtain, for their client orders, the best possible result in accordance with paragraph 1'. Article 21 (3) requires the order execution policy to include 'information on the different venues where the investment firm executes its client orders and the factors affecting the choice of execution venue'. The same policy 'shall at least include those venues that enable the investment firm to obtain on a consistent basis the best possible result for the execution of client orders'. These provisions might be enforced in the Member States so as to protect regulated markets and MTFs against internalisers. Paragraph 3, in particular, appears as intended to protect the incumbent exchanges which would generally provide the 'consistent basis' needed to assure best execution of client orders. Furthermore, this paragraph requires investment firms which foresee in their order execution policy the possibility that client orders may be executed outside a regulated market or an MTF to inform their clients about it and obtain their express consent before proceeding to execute their orders outside a regulated market or MTF (this consent may be obtained also in the form of a general agreement). Therefore, best execution is regulated in a way that, while leaving intermediaries free to choose (and clients free to give them different instructions), potentially favours the incumbents rather than the new trading venues. This was probably intended as a 'compensation' for countries losing through the MiFiD the possibility to maintain concentration rules. It is also likely that these countries will try to interpret the new provisions in ways that could narrow its scope and limit its impact on competition. After all, Article 21 is loose enough to allow room for manoeuvre in one sense or the other, depending on where its provisions are implemented and enforced. Thus, CESR's role in ensuring that these provisions are effectively implemented will be crucial.

[115] See J Macey and M O'Hara (n 111) arguing that 'well-meaning attempts to mandate best execution as a consumer-protection device run counter to attempts to make markets less centralised and more competitive' and that 'this difficulty makes best execution both un-wieldly and unworkable as a mandated legal duty: pursuing a narrow concept of best execution may make markets less competitive'.

[116] See (n 114) above, referring to Article 44 (3) of the Draft Commission Directive.

D. Conclusions

I. Re-regulation Through the MiFID

This paper has argued that the EU went too far in formulating the Directive's core principles in the area of internalisation. The limit order 'display rule' and the 'quote rule' were specified in the MiFID rather than left to level 2 measures or level 3 actions by CESR. This marks a clear difference from the U.S. system, where similar rules were adopted by the SEC using its regulatory powers under federal legislation. Also the best execution rule was specified in the MiFID to a remarkable level of detail, despite the reference to implementing measures for the adoption of more specific requirements. On the whole, the MiFID resulted in substantial re-regulation of securities trading systems, despite the liberalisation accomplished with respect to the abolition of concentration of exchange transactions in some countries. In fact, liberalisation of trading was accompanied by the introduction of detailed rules with respect to limit order disclosure, quote obligations of internalisers and best execution in general. These rules were asked for by those constituencies, such as the incumbent exchanges and small-medium sized investment firms, which felt protected by national concentration rules and feared the consequences of further liberalisation of securities trading.

The MiFID's re-regulation is further characterised by two sets of circumstances. On the one hand, it is a manifestation of political compromises, such as those described in this paper with reference to internalisation. The display rule and the quote rule included in the Commission's proposal went through a difficult negotiation process that led to a significant reshaping of the original rules. The final provisions are the result of mediation between the UK view (which rejected similar rules as unfit for European/UK markets) and the French-Italian position relying on the U.S. model. Even though the discussion was based on technical arguments, a solution was found on political grounds. It is therefore difficult to predict whether the MiFID's provisions relating to internalisation will generate suitable outcomes from an investor protection perspective, while it is clear that they will increase the costs of internalisation in those countries where this practice already exists under less stringent transparency requirements.[117] On the other hand, the MiFID shows that the various interest groups and political actors prefer to reach their compromises at level 1 of the Lamfalussy architecture, rather than leaving the relevant discussion to level 2 measures or level 3 action. A similar attitude can be easily explained. Firstly, the fundamental regulatory choices are made at level 1: the more contested the relevant issues are, the more detailed the

[117] These costs are emphasized by some commentators: see, for instance, A Caparrós 'Understanding the New Regime for Internalisation of Order Flow in Europe' (2004) 2 Euredia 269, 282.

rules adopted by way of compromise will be.[118] The debate on internalisation confirms it: the rules on pre-trade disclosure were agreed upon at level 1 only after tempering their regulatory bite through detailed prescriptions. Secondly, also level 2 measures are politically determined to the extent that representatives of national governments are involved in the comitology process. Thirdly, level 3 is not immune from political interference; moreover, CESR operates by consensus and is not provided with autonomous regulatory powers.

II. Limits of the Lamfalussy Architecture and Possible Remedies

This paper concludes that the Lamfalussy structure's main goal, represented by a flexible regulation for European securities markets, has not been reached. In fact, level 1 provisions are too detailed and therefore too rigid, while level 2 implementing measures are often confined to residual issues. Consequently, regulatory flexibility at level 2 is not fully exploited, while level 3 actions merely implement levels 1 and 2 provisions.[119] In other words, in the EU, politics shapes securities regulation more than in the U.S., where the interplay between Congress and the SEC, although sometimes difficult, allows for more effective regulatory intervention.[120] In Europe, level 3 action is only ancillary to level 1 and 2 regulation, where the European Commission plays the main role. This may appear to be justified by the need to reconcile, on political grounds, divergent national interests. However, the increased integration of capital markets calls for a greater role of specialised regulators within the general framework set by political institutions. This was also recognized by the Lamfalussy approach, which assigned an

[118] This issue was highlighted also by the third report of the Inter Institutional Monitoring Group (IIMG), which noted that 'the identification of a politically and commercially important issue induces all the stakeholders, in particular market participants, to lobby hard for a detailed technical compromise at level 1. In addition, it is possible that an excessive level of details at level 1 may sometimes demonstrate a residual element of mistrust among political stakeholders'. As regards specifically the MIFID, the report records the opinion of Commission representatives that 'more details on the prominent issue of pre-trade transparency for systematic internalisers should have been left to level 2': see IIMG 'Third Report Monitoring the Lamfalussy Process' (17 November 2004) 19 (available on the Commission's website).

[119] See IIMG (n 118) 42, lamenting that 'quasi-level 3 standards are being created before impending level 1 and level 2 legislation has been passed'.

[120] According to J Seligman, from an historical review of the SEC emerges that 'First (...) resolution of key market structure issues is most likely to occur when Congress adopts laws, rather than through SEC regulation or SRO rules. Second, Congress is most likely to act thoughtfully after a period of serious study by the Commission or Congress. Absent detailed public data, the quality of congressional action tends to be less effective'. See J Seligman 'Cautious Evolution or Perennial Irresolution: Self-Regulation and Market Structure during the First 70 Years of the Securities and Exchange Commission' paper presented at the conference 'Current Issues in Institutional Equity Trading' Palm Beach (11 December 2003) .

important role to the interplay between EU institutions and level 3 committees. Yet, the practical implementation of this approach assigned an excessive role to level 1 legislation and level 2 implementing measures, substantially leaving to the political arena the detailed setting of securities regulation. This was not entirely the fault of the Lamfalussy structure, but of business and political interests wanting to solve the most controversial issues always at level 1 through detailed compromises that often dilute the regulatory bite of the relevant provisions. In addition, the Commission, when adopting implementing rules at level 2, often disregards CESR's Advice, thus raising the question of a political authority (such as the Commission) not taking into account the solutions proposed by a technical body (like CESR). As the rules adopted at level 2 are essentially technical, this shows that political issues also emerge at level 2.

From a theoretical perspective, these problems could be solved if two basic conditions were satisfied. Firstly, the co-decision procedure should always be limited to framework principles, in the narrow sense of core political principles including a broad delegation to implementing measures. This is no doubt difficult to obtain in practice; yet, European institutions and politicians will come to realize that reducing the scope of level 1 legislation is the only practicable way to a consistent and effective EU securities regulation. Secondly, implementing rules should be adopted by an independent regulatory agency created at EU level (along lines which would not be manageable to analyse within the confines of the present paper), operating in lieu of the Commission.[121] This body should have regulatory powers only, whilst enforcement would be left to national regulators co-ordinated by CESR. However, the new agency and CESR should coordinate their work. The former should also comply with strict regulatory standards requiring, amongst others, that market failures be properly identified and rules justified as an appropriate reaction to similar failures. Compliance with these conditions should also assure that harmonisation is limited to cases where national regulators are unfit to deal with cross-border market failures. In the end, these two conditions respond to the core problems identified throughout this paper, such as the political interference with rule setting in highly technical areas and the excessive reach of EU securities regulation determined by political rather than economic considerations. Far from being a panacea, a European independent agency could help to build the EU securities regulation on sounder grounds in areas (like rules of conduct) clearly in need of harmonisation. In other areas, where the need for uniformity is not so apparent or regulatory competition is preferable, a similar agency could curb the development of further regulation if appropriate incentives

[121] In making this suggestion, we are not proposing to create a European SEC, as is sometimes suggested by the authors: see, for different views on this topic the contributions by Y Avgerinos, G Thieffry, R Lastra, G Pozniak and E Pan in M Andenas and Y Avgerinos (eds) 'Financial Markets in Europe: Towards a Single Regulator?' (Kluwer Law International 2003) 145-260; see also RS Karmel 'The Case for A European Securities Commission' (1999) 38 Colum J Transnat'l L 9.

were created in the law to this effect.[122] However, mechanisms of consultation and political accountability would need to be developed to ensure that the interests of market participants and investors are appropriately considered before taking regulatory action.

[122] For similar suggestions, see L Zingales 'The Costs and Benefits of Financial Market Regulation' (ECGI Law wp No. 21/2004 <http://ssrn.com/abstract=536682>, 2004) 54, proposing to create a new Government agency dedicated to estimate the costs and benefits of any new proposed regulation.

Internalisation under the MiFID: Regulatory Overreaching or Landmark in Investor Protection?

JOHANNES KÖNDGEN* and ERIK THEISSEN**

The Chapter sums up the economic fundamentals of internalised stock trading and attempts to make a case for regulation. We then sketch the current practice of internalisation in Germany, with special emphasis on the 'Xetra Best' facility, a trading venue which tries to integrate internalised trading with an organised market. Subsequently we turn to a critique of the relevant parts of the EC Markets in Financial Instruments Directive (MiFID), measuring the latter against the fundamental principles of market efficiency and investor protection. Finally we discuss whether Xetra Best, after some refurbishment, could serve as a blueprint for other European stock exchanges.

A. Breaking New Ground in European Securities Regulation
B. The Case for Regulation: Some Economic Fundamentals
C. The German Version of Internalisation: A View on Current (Pre-MiFID) Market Practice and Regulation
D. A Critical Assessment of the Directive
E. Xetra Best – A Blueprint for Other European Exchanges?
F. Conclusions

A. Breaking New Ground in European Securities Regulation

'Off-market' securities-trading has always been of great concern for securities regulators. Off-market trading might, it was pointed out, result in an erosion of the liquidity of regulated markets by fragmenting the order flow. Furthermore, it may have an adverse impact on the transparency and efficiency of prices. Off-market trading was considered to be inherently undesirable with regard to both investor protection and market efficiency. This is why some European jurisdictions[1] have adopted rules requiring investment firms to execute orders exclusively

* Professor of Law, Rheinische Friedrich-Wilhelms-Universität, Bonn

** Professor of Finance, Rheinische Friedrich-Wilhelms-Universität, Bonn

[1] E.g. Germany as from 1994 (see Stock Exchange Act 2002 Section 22); Switzerland (see SWX Swiss Exchange General Conditions No. 4 (8)); France has adopted a principle of 'concentration des ordres' from the time of foundation of the *Bourse de Paris* (for the current state

cont. ...

by routing them to an exchange or some other regulated market ('duty to trade on the exchange'; 'concentration rule').[2]

Notwithstanding these widely held beliefs, new trading venues where orders could be executed off-market proliferated in the U.S. in the mid-1990s.[3] Put succinctly, American broker-dealers may have a customer order either filled out of their own inventory or traded proprietarily against other customers' orders, in either case acting as the sole counter-party ('internalisation'). Alternatively, brokers may choose to route a customer order, for a minor commission, to some other (often affiliated) 'consolidating broker' or market maker for internal execution ('preferencing', 'payment for order flow').[4] Neither under internalisation nor under payment-for-order-flow practices do broker-dealers expose their internalised orders to competitors.[5] In the years after 2001, those market practices came to be emulated by European investment firms, even in jurisdictions, such as Germany, that subscribe to the 'concentration of orders principle'.[6]

When in the year 2000 the European Commission set out to revise the Investment Services Directive of 1993, the objectives of fostering competition between regulated markets and of improving the transparency of the price discovery process were at the top of the agenda.[7] Obviously, however, what the Commission had in mind at the time was not the practice of executing retail orders through internalised trading. When they thought of competition they meant competition between the traditional exchanges and the blossoming Alternative Trading Systems. And when they referred to off-market trading, they envisaged block-trading by large institutional investors. It was in the early stage of the open consultation process when the business practice of internalisation emerged as a more prominent issue for European regulation.[8] The Proposed Directive of November

of the law see Law No 96-597 Article 45 (1); today Code monétaire et financier, Article L 421-12). The Council Directive 93/22/EEC of May 1993 on Investment Services in the Securities Field (the ISD), OJ L141 11.06.1993, Article 14 (3) had left it to the Member States whether to adopt a rule of 'concentration of orders'.

[2] In Germany, this obligation holds unless the intermediary is explicitly instructed otherwise by his or her customer, see Stock Exchange Act Section 22. For France, see Law 2 July 1996, Article 45, today *Code monétaire et financier* Article L 421-12; see also J Daigre 'La fin des bourses' (2003) Revue de Droit Bancaire et Financier 83.

[3] See already SEC 'Division of Market Regulation, Market 2000: An Examination of Current Equity Developments' (January 1994).

[4] See SEC Release No. 34-34902, Payment for Order Flow (Final Rule, 3 April 1995).

[5] SEC 'Special Study: Payment for Order Flow and Internalization in the Options Markets' (December 2000) <http://www.sec.gov/news/studies/ordpay.htm> E 1.

[6] For Germany, more details will be presented infra, Section C.

[7] Communication from the Commission to the European Parliament and the Council 'Upgrading the Investment Services Directive (93/22/EEC)' COM(2000) 729 final, 4 and 4.3.

[8] For a closer analysis of the legislative process the reader is referred to G Ferrarini and F Recine 'The MiFID and Internalisation' in this volume (2006) 235-270.

2002 already incorporated a set of rules addressing the specific concerns with regard to internalised trading. The focus of these proposed rules was on mitigating conflicts of interests, on ensuring 'best execution' for customers, and on broad transparency requirements, both pre-trade and post-trade, to safeguard the efficiency of price formation.[9] In the ensuing debate over the Proposed Directive, internalisation came to be one of the most controversial issues, with the Commission bravely defending their restrictive regulatory stance. On the other side industry representatives (especially from the U.K.) vociferously argued for a more lenient approach which rested primarily upon three pillars, namely best execution requirements, conflict of interest management, and broad post-trade transparency requirements.[10] The European Parliament yielded to these industry concerns to some extent, and, in a first step, marginally narrowed the investment firm's obligation of pre-trade transparency to the effect that it applies only to so-called 'systematic internalisers'.[11] In the process of the second reading of the proposal, Council and Parliament further eased the restrictions which had been imposed in the Proposed Directive. Pre-trade transparency was limited to transactions of average market size. Investment firms were granted some discretion as to whether to accept multiple orders at the conditions of their published quote. In addition, investment firms were given greater leeway in choosing to which of their customers to give access to their quotes. Not surprisingly, when after all the MiFID[12] came into force on 30 April 2004, Article 27, which specifically deals with the obligations and responsibilities of internalisers, presented itself as one of the longest and bulkiest provisions of the Directive.

The objective of this paper is to discuss the MiFID rules on internalisation against the background of, first, the underlying economic principles and, second, the current practice in Germany. The paper is organized as follows. In section B we provide a brief overview of the economic fundamentals. Section C describes

[9] See Proposal for a Directive of the European Parliament and of the Council on Investment Services and Regulated Markets, and amending Council Directive 85/611/EEC, Council Directive 93/6/EEC and European Parliament and Council Directive 2000/12/EC (the MiFID Proposal), 19.11.2002, COM(2002) 625 final, Explanatory Memorandum II.5.

[10] Confer, as a typical statement, H Davies (chairman, Financial Services Authority) 'Address to The Bond Market Association Annual Meeting' (10 April 2003) <http//:www.fsa.gov.uk/pubs/speeches/sp124.html>. 'We are opposed to a continuation of concentration rules, and we believe that best execution requirements, conflict of interest management and broad post-trade transparency requirements can, and in London do offset any potential risks to investors from internalisation of trades'.

[11] See European Commission 'Investment Services: Commission Welcomes European Parliament Backing for Proposed Directive' (25 September 2003) Press Release IP/03/1291.

[12] Directive 2004/39/EC of the European Parliament and of the Council of 21 April 2004 on Markets in Financial Instruments amending Council Directives 85/611/EEC and 93/6/EEC and Directive 2000/12/EC of the European Parliament and of the Council and repealing Council Directive 93/22/EEC (the MiFID), OJ L145 30.04.2004 1-44.

the current practice in Germany in general and the system Xetra Best in particular. Section D provides a critical assessment of the MiFID rules on internalisation. The concluding section E discusses whether, and to what extent, Xetra Best can serve as a blueprint for other European exchanges.

B. The Case for Regulation: Some Economic Fundamentals

I. Inter-Market Competition vs. Fragmentation of Order Flows

Conventional wisdom in financial economics has it that the concentration of order flow in a single stock market is the prime requisite for achieving optimal market quality. Concentration of orders, it was argued, would improve market liquidity, and high liquidity, in turn, would result in small bid-ask spreads. Sometimes stock markets were indeed considered to constitute a natural monopoly. Today we have become less certain about that. The past decade has witnessed the sprouting up of numerous alternative markets in addition to the traditional exchanges, without any apparent detriment to market quality. To rationalise this seeming paradox it is suggested that inter-market competition may in itself have a benign impact on overall market quality which offsets the undisputed efficiency gains from order flow concentration.[13] Almost certainly, inter-market competition will lower transaction costs. Moreover, the total trading volume on stock markets has multiplied over the last 25 years, making adequate liquidity a lesser issue. Modern low-cost means of communication allow arbitrageurs to profit from, and thereby eliminate, price disparities. They further increase the transparency of bid and ask quotes[14] and they allow to implement order routing techniques pursuant to the principle of best execution. Ideally, the individual market places are not isolated but rather interconnected segments of one large 'virtual' market.[15] As a result, there seems to be no conclusive answer today to the question of whether the fragmentation of order flows impairs or in fact improves overall market quality.

The advantages of inter-market competition referred to above relate to the competition between several stock exchanges, or between stock exchanges and other organized markets. It is much less clear whether these arguments also apply to the competition between organized markets and internalisers.[16] Empirical evi-

[13] HR Stoll (1993) 91.

[14] As, e.g., in the U.S. National Market System.

[15] The notion of segmented markets is adopted from L Harris (1993). A 'virtual' market is a market not constituted as an institution but through systematic interaction of the trading market participants.

[16] See already E Schwark (2004) 729.

dence is rather scant and mostly based on data from the U.S..[17] Furthermore, the findings are rather inconclusive, sometimes indeed contradictory. Hence, any attempts at hypothesising and giving policy recommendations are of tentative character, yielding problem definitions rather than ready solutions.

II. Internalisation and Market Quality: Risks and Benefits[18]

An important potential advantage of internalised trading is no doubt a decrease in transaction costs (execution and/or settlement fees). Execution fees charged by the exchange no longer arise; moreover, clearing and settlement fees may be lower if the internalising broker operates a more efficient system.

The potential implications of internalisation for both market efficiency and investor protection are numerous, however insufficiently explored in their actual consequences.

(1) Like other alternative venues of order execution such as ATS or MTF, internalised trading fragments the client order flow and may reduce the liquidity of regulated exchanges. While it is not established whether and to what extent such fragmentation might impair overall market efficiency, it is a sound guess that it tends to adversely affect market quality on the exchange. Notably internalised trading in less liquid stocks with a large proportion of internalised execution[19] can result in higher bid-ask spreads on the reference market.

(2) Pre-trade transparency will be impaired when, due to systematic internalisation, a sizeable fraction of bids and asks is not disclosed to other market participants. Withholding such trading information will not only severely curtail the basis for price discovery, but also stifle competition between trading venues. Consequently, the overall market liquidity may suffer.

(3) Quote competition may be further impaired if intermediaries are acting at the same time as internalisers and as market makers in the same stocks on a regulated exchange. In this (not uncommon) case the intermediary has no adequate incentive to offer best quotes in the order book of the exchange. This is because the best bid and ask quotes in the order book serve as reference prices for the internalised orders. Thus, improving the quotes in the order book will adversely

[17] Many empirical papers use data from NASDAQ where internalised trading is most common; see, e.g. R Battalio, R Jennings and J Selway (2001); R Huang and H Stoll (1996); C Lee (1993). R Battalio, J Greene and R Jennings (1997), D Easley, N Kiefer and M O'Hara (1996) and M Peterson and E Sirri (2002) use data from the regional exchanges at Boston and Cincinnati. Some conjectures about Germany (Xetra Best system) can be found in E Theissen (2002b) 564.

[18] The following section draws on E Theissen (2002b) 552 ff.

[19] Typically stemming from retail investors preferring internalised trading because of lower transaction costs.

affect the 'internal' quotes and consequently reduce the profit from internalisation.

(4) Typically, retail investors are attracted to internalised order execution by being assured a price which is marginally better than the benchmark price in a given reference market would be.[20] However, this assurance does not guarantee that the investor may not be doing even better trading somewhere else. Further, if a regulated exchange frequently offers execution at prices inside the published bid-ask spread (as is common on the NYSE), execution at the benchmark price (or even at a price marginally better than the benchmark price) is not necessarily 'best' execution.

(5) Another detrimental impact on price quality is premised on a more sophisticated argument.[21] Traders differ with respect to their level of sophistication and to the information they hold. Trades with customers who have access to superior information about the asset value are risky and costly.[22] Retail investors submitting small orders in liquid stocks are unlikely to have privileged access to information. Therefore, the broker-dealer may safely conjecture that these trades are neither risky nor costly to fill. But if broker-dealers systematically internalise these 'easy' trades, it must be the case that the more risky portion of the order flow will be concentrated on the main market (i.e. the reference market). In order to counterbalance the increased risk, market makers on the main market will increase their bid-ask spreads. This, in turn, affects the benchmark prices that determine the prices at which the internalised orders are executed. The crucial question then is whether the internaliser will pass on the cost savings to the customer by offering a sufficient improvement on the benchmark price ('profit sharing hypothesis') or whether he rather executes the order at the benchmark price and reaps the profit ('cream skimming hypothesis').[23] The broker-dealer has an obvious incentive to choose the second alternative, but competition may provide incentives for profit sharing. For the time being, neither theory nor experience from actual practice justify a prediction as to which option a broker-dealer will be inclined to take. But regulators should take precautions against the problem by creating a regulatory framework that minimises internalisers' incentives to engage in cream-skimming.

[20] From an investor's point of view it is irrelevant whether the price improvement results from a better quote or from a lower execution and/or settlement fee charged by his broker-dealer.

[21] We here summarise the more detailed analysis in E Theissen (2002b) 554-557.

[22] The economic literature refers to this cost as the *adverse selection cost*.

[23] See already D Easley, N Kiefer and M O'Hara (1996); R Battalio (1997).

C. The German Version of Internalisation: A View on Current (Pre-MiFID) Market Practice and Regulation

Germany was among the Member States which early on left room for internalised trading under a rather lenient regulatory regime.[24] Three of the systems in place are (or have been) of greater practical importance and therefore deserve closer attention in the light of the pending transformation of the MiFID. All systems have in common that they are open to retail investors only. But each one has some specific characteristics, and each one highlights a particular regulatory issue.

I. The 'Xetra Best' System (Frankfurt Stock Exchange)

1. Market Structure

The 'Xetra Best' System was developed by Deutsche Börse AG and released in September 2002 for use by the Frankfurt Stock Exchange[25] (henceforth: FSE). At first sight it appears paradoxical that one of the big players among the European stock exchanges voluntarily launches a platform allowing internalisation. However, it became apparent early in the decade that some large banks were about to embark on internalisation. The creation of Xetra Best was an attempt to keep the internalised orders on a system operated by (and yielding profits for) the exchange: if you cannot beat them, join them. The plot did not really succeed, however, as the market share of Xetra Best has remained, to say the least, modest.[26]

The aim behind Xetra Best was to create a facility for internalised trading that is under the roof and, to a certain extent, under the control of the exchange. Accordingly, Xetra Best is constructed as a trading facility which is not an organised market itself but is linked to, and technically embedded in, the Xetra electronic trading platform developed and operated by Deutsche Börse AG. Xetra Best is thus closely connected to the Xetra 'open limit order book' and the principles of

[24] A counter-example is France where a statutory unconditional obligation to trade on the exchange (concentration rule) eliminates the option of internalised order execution altogether; see already (n 1).

[25] For the non-German reader it may be appropriate to remark that Frankfurt Stock Exchange is the trading platform (a public law body) whereas Deutsche Börse AG is the exchange's private operator.

[26] J Grammig and E Theissen (2005) 22, found a market share of Xetra Best amounting to 1.5% when considering the number of transactions, and to 0.25% when considering the trading volume.

price and time priority are enforced across both trading venues. The most salient features of Xetra Best are the following:[27]

- It is for the FSE board of management to determine which securities shall qualify for internalised trading under Xetra Best.[28] Trading in Xetra Best is, as is trading in the Xetra open limit order book, subject to supervision by the independent Trading Surveillance Office,[29] and is subject to the standards specified in the Stock Exchange Act (*Börsengesetz*).

- Internalised orders executed in Xetra Best are executed at a price which needs to be at least one cent better than the price at which the order would execute if it were sent to the Xetra limit order book ('reference price').[30] This price setting rule implies that Xetra Best trades need to be executed during the 'main trading phase' of the exchange.[31] The price difference between the execution price in Xetra Best and the reference price taken from the Xetra order book is referred to as the price improvement. The internaliser (in the language of the Xetra Best rules: the 'best executor') enters two parameters into the system: the absolute amount of the price improvement and the maximum order size he is willing to accept for internal execution.[32] Internalised orders are thus executed with a mandatory price improvement relative to a single reference market, namely the electronic market at Frankfurt.[33] This is an implicit promise to investors that not only will they receive a price that has been generated under fair and transparent

[27] For the regulations issued by the FSE see 'Exchange Rules for the Frankfurt Stock Exchange' (1 January 2006) Sections 46-46c. For a more detailed account see J Grammig and E Theissen (2005) 4 ff.

[28] See Exchange Rules (n 27) Section 46 (2).

[29] See Exchange Rules (n 27) Section 12.

[30] See Exchange Rules (n 27) Section 46a (2).

[31] Exchange Rules (n 27) Section 46 (1). The 'main trading phase' is defined by Section 41a (3).

[32] 'Conditions for Transactions on the Frankfurt Stock Exchange' (1 November 2005) Section 37c (2).

[33] The modus operandi being that the 'best executor' reports his improved quote to the Xetra electronic trading system, which then automatically fixes the price charged to the client on the basis of the actual market situation (as documented in the order book); see J Köndgen and E Theissen (2003) 1504. See also Exchange Rules (n 27) Section 46a (2): 'The calculation of the execution price shall be made in accordance with the parameters entered in the system on the basis of such price at which the customer order concerned would have been executed at the same time in the order book of the electronic trading system without considering the Best Executor Quote (potential execution price). In the event that the potential execution of the customer order is carried out in several partial executions in the order book, a corresponding, volume-weighted average price shall be calculated as potential execution price. The execution price in the Best Execution will fall below the potential execution price in the case of a customer buy order and exceed it in the case of a customer sell order, taking into consideration the parameters entered by the Best Executor'.

conditions in Germany's most liquid stock market but also a, however marginal,[34] improvement over that price. Nevertheless and notwithstanding an explicit reference in the Exchange Rules,[35] Xetra Best obviously does not afford investors a 'best execution' guarantee *sensu stricto*. Moreover, it tends to stifle inter-market price competition, because execution linked to a benchmark price generated in Germany's largest exchange screens out the prices existing in the increasing number of alternative execution venues.[36] Finally, empirical evidence suggests that the effective price improvement of a Xetra Best execution is smaller than the minimum one-cent improvement upon the Xetra reference price mandated by the Xetra Best rules. Grammig/Theissen hypothesise that this surprising outcome may at least partially be attributed to the fact that retail customers are less likely to have access to real time quote information than institutional investors, preventing them from optimally timing their orders.[37]

- With Xetra Best, the FSE supplies, for a minor fee, an ancillary service to investment firms (banks and/or broker-dealers) willing to engage in and admitted to internalised trading ('best executors'). However, registration of investment firms as best executors is contingent upon their willingness to act at the same time as liquidity managers ('market maker', 'designated sponsor') in the Xetra order book.[38] This 'dual capacity rule' was designed to curb, if not to prevent, the expected decrease in liquidity on the Xetra trading platform. The rule is, however, a double-edged sword. On the one hand, it may appear to be a valid means of integrating the different trading venues and to mitigate the adverse effects of order flow fragmentation.[39] On the other hand, the investment firm's triple role as internaliser, as commission agent for the customer, and as market maker/liquidity manager in the open order book is a potential source for conflicts of interest. When acting as a market maker the investment firm is under a duty to provide liquidity to the order book and to offer low bid-ask spreads for reasonable trade sizes. By contrast, when acting as an internaliser, it is under a duty to improve upon the price resulting from the open order book. Moreover, as a commission agent, it shall execute the customer order at the best possible price, no matter on what execution venue. It is highly unlikely that an internalising broker will perform each of these obligations with equal loyalty. Empirical results indeed sug-

[34] Given an average price of shares traded within the DAX index of some € 20 a share, the price improvement amounts to a modest 0.05%.

[35] Exchange Rules (n 27) Section 46 (1).

[36] The same observation has been made in the UK, where the price generated through SETS (the electronic trading system of LSE) used to serve as a single benchmark; see Financial Services Authority (2001) para. 5.9.

[37] J Grammig and E Theissen (2005) 23.

[38] Exchange Rules (n 27) Sections 46 (5) and 46b (1).

[39] See already J Grammig and E Theissen (2005) 6.

gest that internalisers realise larger spreads when executing orders via Xetra Best.[40]

- It is not up to the internalising investment firm's unlimited discretion to choose between internalised and on-the-exchange execution. Xetra Best admits only retail client orders in liquid stocks (determined by the management board from case to case) which do not exceed a maximum size of € 50,000, for internalised execution. Furthermore, pursuant to the principle of 'immediacy' (i.e. timely execution), if it is not possible to immediately execute a customer order via Xetra Best, the order is automatically passed on to the Xetra order book. This rule is tantamount to a pre-trade transparency obligation to report limit orders to the open order book.

- Overall market transparency is limited under Xetra Best. Although the Xetra trading system 'knows' the internalisers' quotes, these receive a special electronic mark and do not show up on the trading screens of other market participants. In other words, other market participants are not in the position to react to internalised quotes, leaving the latter without impact on price formation. In addition, neither price nor time priority is enforced between the quotes of different best executors. This would require incoming orders to be routed to the internaliser offering the largest price improvement or, in case of equal price improvements, to the internaliser with the earlier offer.[41] This serves to shelter the Xetra Best price from potential price competition by alternative execution venues. Not surprisingly, Deutsche Börse AG (the operator of FSE) was among the most outspoken critics of pre-trade transparency in the consultation process following the publication of the Proposed Directive.

2. Regulatory Framework

As noted previously, Germany, like some other European jurisdictions, has introduced a rule providing that every client order has to be transmitted to a regulated exchange for execution, unless the client explicitly directs otherwise.[42] If the client is a retail investor, his or her consent is required prior to each transaction (case by case rule). These restrictive conditions for internalisation would be unattractive to internalising banks or brokers, who would obviously prefer to have more leeway when choosing between different trading venues. Indeed, even as a contingent rule, the 'obligation to trade on the exchange' (concentration rule) could have meant an early death for Xetra Best. However, the sponsors of Xetra Best received unexpected support from the supervisory authority. The supervisory authority held that internalised trading using the Xetra Best facility was to be

[40] J Grammig and E Theissen (2005) 9 ff.

[41] J Grammig and E Theissen (2005) 6.

[42] Börsengesetz (Stock Exchange Act) Section 22.

deemed 'trading in the exchange'. The decision, which came as a surprise to most academic commentators, made either party happy: the FSE, because internalising investment firms need no longer ask their clients for their prior consent to internalise which boosted the acceptance of Xetra Best with the brokerage industry; the supervisory authority, because the qualification of Xetra Best as exchange trading by definition gave them supervisory control over internalised trading beyond the general powers over investment firms pursuant to the Investment Services Act 1998.

Section 24 of the Stock Exchange Act introduces the notion of 'exchange price'. Exchange prices are prices that were generated 'on' the exchange under a tightly regulated procedure.[43] The issue is of some relevance, because 'exchange prices' bear, as 'regulated' prices, a special quality mark which may be of advantage in marketing any internalisation system. The supervisory authority in the state of Hessen (where Deutsche Börse AG is incorporated) has decided that prices generated by way of internalised trading in Xetra Best are not exchange prices. This decision is consistent with the view that internalised prices, even if they are based on a price import from a regulated market ('passive pricing'), cannot qualify as exchange prices as long as internalised quotes are not accessible to all market participants.[44]

II. The 'BestEx' System (Berlin-Bremen Stock Exchange)

With the release of the BestEx facility in March 2003, the Berlin-Bremen Stock Exchange[45] and its (then) operator NASDAQ Deutschland made an attempt to emulate, and to compete with, the Xetra Best system. Thus, exactly like Xetra Best, BestEx is an exchange-sponsored internalisation system and is embedded in the electronic trading system of the exchange[46] which mimics an auction market for limit orders but also allows of market making activities. Although BestEx proved a commercial failure and was withdrawn by its sponsors as early as in August 2003, it had some interesting characteristics worth reporting.[47]

Every market participant who is a member of the exchange may register as a 'BestEx Market Maker'. Registration involves a duty of the broker to establish 'BestEx relationships' with other market participants (order flow providers) upon request. This provision is designed to contain the order flow within the system of

[43] See Börsengesetz Section 24.

[44] For a more detailed discussion see J Köndgen and E Theissen (2003).

[45] The Berlin-Bremen Stock Exchange was founded in 2003 through a merger of the regional exchanges based in Bremen and Berlin.

[46] Called 'Super Montage Europe'.

[47] See also J Köndgen and E Theissen (2003) 1504; E Schwark (2004).

the sponsoring exchange. Unlike Xetra Best, price formation under BestEx is based on two reference markets: the first is the order book of (then) NASDAQ Germany; consequently, the procedure of price discovery is largely the same as under Xetra Best.[48] The second reference market is an 'external' venue, defined as the market with the highest liquidity for trading in a given security. In practice, this market will be the FSE's Xetra electronic trading system. The final transaction price is measured by the better quote of either reference market. When there is no quote being supplied by the external market, the management board of the exchange may designate a substitute external market. Again unlike Xetra Best, price improvement is not mandatory but may be individually stipulated between BestEx market makers and order flow providers. As the magnitude of the stipulated improvement remains undisclosed to the client, he or she is not in the position to recognize whether and to what extent the cost advantage is passed on and reflected in the price effectively charged for execution of the order. Like Xetra Best, though for different reasons, BestEx, contrary to the pledge embodied in its trade name, does not and cannot guarantee 'best' execution.

The regulatory issues relating to BestEx were largely the same as with Xetra Best. However, the trading regulations of the Berlin-Bremen exchange publicised, with the approval of the local supervisory authority,[49] the prices generated through internalised trading as 'exchange prices'.

III. Bank/Broker-Sponsored Internalisation Schemes

Among the bank- or broker-sponsored internalisation schemes Deutsche Bank's 'Price Improvement Platform' (PIP), introduced in January 2003, is the best known one. Online-brokerage customers are offered the option to execute their order in certain assets via Deutsche's internal trading platform. The list of eligible assets includes some 50 shares from the most important domestic and international indices.[50] The customer gives his consent to internalised execution for each order individually. Although PIP is designed as a service specifically for retail investors, Deutsche Bank has not put a cap on admissible order volumes. Orders are executed at quotes supplied by a reference market, which, subject to the customer's choice, may be the Xetra electronic trading system or the floor of the FSE, or, for orders in foreign-listed securities, the home exchange of the relevant security. The reference price is defined as the hypothetical price at which the customer order would have executed had it been routed to the reference market.

[48] See (n 33) and accompanying text.

[49] There is no single federal regulator/supervisor for exchanges in Germany, which may result in divergent regulation and enforcement for each market place.

[50] Such as DAX 100, MDAX, TECDAX, EuroSTOXX 50, Dow Jones Stoxx 50, Dow Jones 30, and the Exchange Traded Funds issued by Deutsche's mutual funds subsidiary DWS.

The fact that these hypothetical prices are not generally publicly available limits the pre-trade transparency from the point of view of the individual customer. Deutsche Bank neither guarantees a price improvement nor the passing-on of a cost advantage to the customer.[51] The execution fee is the same regardless of whether the order is executed on the exchange or through internalisation. The improvement for the client consists primarily in lower overall transaction costs, as third-party costs such as exchange fees are not applicable. Moreover, relative to Xetra Best, Deutsche Bank promises superior post-trade transparency as the reference price at the time when the order is executed is disclosed to the customer in the account.

Obviously, even under the liberal construction of the Stock Exchange Act by the German authorities, bank- or broker-sponsored internalisation cannot qualify as 'trading on the exchange'. Consequently such internalisation is not subject to the special supervision of exchange trading by the standards specified in the Stock Exchange Act. While internalisers using the Xetra Best facility are subject to supervision by the exchange's independent Trading Surveillance Office, trading via PIP is supervised by the internal compliance officer only. Of course, investment firms which make internalisation their business have, even before transformation of the MiFID into domestic law, been within the scope of the Investment Services Act (*Wertpapierhandelsgesetz*), thus being subject to its code of conduct.[52] The prevailing reading of this code is that it establishes, at least by implication, a principle of best execution ever since the Act came into force.[53] Therefore it would appear questionable whether the current practice of internalisation conforms to the regulatory standards already in place.

D. A Critical Assessment of the Directive

I. Some General Remarks

Given the paucity of safe empirical evidence on the actual impact of internalisation on price discovery and overall market quality,[54] the ponderous regulation of internalised trading in MiFID Article 27 has indeed been a daring enterprise. At the end of the day, the drafters of the Directive, instead of relying on independent expertise, seem to have chosen to compromise with special-interest group demands from the investment industry on the one hand and the operators of

[51] On its web site, Deutsche Bank, with significant vagueness, declares that customer orders will be executed 'at the reference exchange price or better'.

[52] Wertpapierhandelsgesetz (1994) Sections 31-37a.

[53] HD Assmann and UH Schneider (2003) Section 31 n 2a and Section 35 n 3.3.

[54] See (n 17) and accompanying text.

regulated securities markets on the other.[55] Therefore, and for the time being, a fair assessment of the Directive has to confine itself to measuring the new rules on internalisation against the fundamental policy objectives set by the Commission itself, and to verifying to what extent these rules successfully deal with the challenges to market quality outlined above.

It has to be credited to the drafters of the Directive that, at no time in the drafting process, have they displayed a penchant for extreme or orthodox solutions. Faced with the difficult choice between effectuating inter-market competition and optimising liquidity they did not yield to the demand, voiced by some of the big European exchanges, to confirm and indeed reinforce the concentration rule. Neither did they take the easy way out by removing any hindrance for internalised trading and thereby giving free rein to competition between the different trading venues. Instead, they adopted an approach which might be termed 'controlled liberalisation'. As a result, they did away with the concentration rule in order to reinforce competition for efficient price discovery, yet on a level playing field. Internalisation, they felt, should not be allowed to undermine the traditional market structure altogether.

The Commission has defined as their main regulatory objective 'to preserve overall market quality and efficient price formation'.[56] The objective of investor protection, which in capital market regulation is usually paid equal attention, appears to be of second order. Still, both objectives are easily identifiable in the new Directive, and either one is implemented by a distinctive regulatory device. Market efficiency is to be promoted through pre-trade and post-trade *transparency rules*; protection of investors against unfair treatment by internalising brokers is accomplished through the *principle of best execution*, which is at the core of a broker's professional duties.

Although the fundamental concepts and principles underlying the Directive's provisions on internalisation strike us as clear and plausible, the devil is, as frequently, in the detail. It is to these details that we now turn.

II. Transparency Rules: Is There a Way to Stop Fragmentation?

As noted previously, transparency rules serve the goal of fostering market quality and efficiency. Market participants should be informed about any trading interest in the market, which requires both post-trade and pre-trade transparency. Increased transparency may then countervail the negative implications of abolishing the concentration rule. If internal quotes are immediately reported to a refer-

[55] See the detailed account by G Ferrarini and F Recine (2006).

[56] See 'Revision of Investment Services Directive (93/22/EEC): Second Consultation - Overview Paper' (July 2001) <http://ec.europa.eu/internal_market/securities/isd/index_en.htm> 7.

ence market during normal trading hours, this is likely to broaden the basis for the interaction of orders and eventually creates a larger 'virtual' market. In a certain sense, then, the liquidity which was skimmed off by internalised trading is indirectly 'recycled' into the lead market. Seen that way, it was a defensible solution to restrict the so-called firm-quote disclosure rule to systematic internalisers. This is because only large-scale internalisers have the potential to significantly affect the process of price formation.

To make this recycling of liquidity happen, it is crucial to what market (or markets, for that matter) internalisers have to report (a). Besides, there remains the quest for additional ways and means to either prevent the fragmentation of the order flow or at least to mitigate the erosion of liquidity resulting thereof (b).

(a) In the best of all worlds, trading data should be reported on a consolidated basis, as is the case in the National Market System in the U.S.. This is not going to happen in Europe any time soon, for institutional as well as for technical and commercial reasons. Accordingly, in the debate following the presentation of the Proposed Directive there were pledges to waive or at least to soften the comprehensive transparency requirement, because it would not have any positive impact on fragmentation.[57]

Although this argument may be questionable, the overall transparency requirements for investment firms are indeed far-reaching and burdensome. In their generality the requirements extend to forms of internalisation where transparency, especially pre-trade transparency, does not necessarily improve the data basis for efficient price discovery. Obviously, the Directive presupposes the notion of an 'active' internaliser who considers the current market conditions and then autonomously fixes and reports his quotes. Such quotes would, without doubt, provide important information about overall market conditions. However, the notion of an active internaliser is beside the mark if, as is the predominant practice in the U.S. and Germany, internalisers prefer a mode of passive pricing, either by plain price import from a given reference market or by improving such imported prices by a largely predefined margin. In the first case it is hardly conceivable how the dissemination of such 'passive' quotes would contribute to price discovery. In the second case the relevance varies with the degree to which the internaliser is free to define the magnitude of the improvement margin. If the leeway for discretional improvements is narrow, the relevance of imported quotes for the price discovery process may again be negligible.

Transparency of the internalisers' quotes may, however, serve objectives other than fostering price discovery. If, as is the case in Germany, price priority is not enforced across internalisers, quote dissemination allows customers to compare the prospective execution quality and to choose their bank or broker-dealer accordingly. Thus, mandating transparency may contribute to overall market quality even in cases where it does not contribute to price discovery.

[57] G Ferrarini and F Recine (2006) text following note 55.

The Directive does not specify to which market the internaliser shall report. This may be sensible because the issue does not lend itself to a uniform solution. In the first place, the answer is contingent upon the competitive conditions in national, or maybe in European, securities markets. Currently, regulated markets typically compete for better pricing and leave it to arbitrageurs to smooth out larger price disparities. It would then be consequent to have the internalisers report their quotes only to the reference market (or markets, for that matter) which they have selected as benchmark for their own pricing.

(b) Given the imperfection of any transparency concept with regard to combatting order flow fragmentation as a result of internalisation, it seems worthwhile to think about other devices to mitigate the potential erosion of liquidity. The Xetra Best solution to recruit internalisers as liquidity managers in the reference market is certainly a noteworthy effort in that direction. It remains to be seen whether this solution will stand practical testing.

III. Striking the Balance: Will Investor Protection Be Sacrificed to Market Efficiency?

1. The Duty to Obtain the Customer's Prior Consent (MiFID Article 21 (3) (3))

The duty to obtain the customer's prior consent for internal execution creates an access barrier which neither regulated markets nor MTFs need to overcome, resulting in an apparent 'hierarchy'[58] among the different trading venues and frustrating the basic concept of a level playing field.[59] The Directive leaves it to the discretion of investment firms whether to obtain the customer's consent in the form of a general agreement or separately for each individual transaction. In practice, this is no real alternative, because investment firms will invariably choose the form of general consent for the plain reason that it is less costly. Member States, when transforming the Directive, may consider adopting a more stringent position. According to current German regulation it is sufficient to obtain a general consent from *wholesale* investors.[60] On the other hand, investment firms have to ask *retail* customers for a case by case consent if the order is to be executed

[58] J Daigre (2004) 232.

[59] Which has been reinforced by the Draft Commission Regulation Implementing Directive 2004/39/EC of the European Parliament and of the Council as regards Record-keeping Obligations for Investment Firms, Transaction Reporting, Market Transparency, Admission of Financial Instruments to Trading and Defined Terms for the Purposes of that Directive (the Draft Commission Regulation), 06.02.2006, Recital 5.

[60] Stock Exchange Act Section 22 (1).

off-exchange.[61] Even by stringent criteria of investor protection, this may be a case of over-regulation. The decision to consent to off-exchange execution is not so momentous that a customer has to reconsider the issue prior to each transaction. It is sufficient for him to know on which terms his broker generally handles internalised execution. This, in turn, would require the investment firm to disclose its policy with respect to off-exchange execution prior to obtaining the customer's general consent.

2. The Investment Firm's Duty to Transact at the Quoted Price (MiFID Article 27 (3))

The investment firm's duty to transact at the quoted price is no less than a compulsory contract. It is mitigated through the firm's right to select the customers to whom it grants access to its quotes in the first place (MiFID Article 27 (5)) and through the right to limit the number of multiple hits asked for by the same customer ('multiple hits', Article 27 (6)). With these provisions leaving adequate room for discretion in the conduct of business the Directive strikes a fair balance between the interest of investors in being optimally served and investment firms' freedom to contract. After all, equal treatment is a legal principle primarily imposed on acts of public government and public authorities, furthermore on private contracting with a distinctive 'social' flavour such as employment or residential leases; the principle should not govern doing commercially sound business and transacting in competitive markets. The only problematic provision in that respect is MiFID Article 27 (3) (4), which allows 'price improvements'[62] in transactions with professional clients. This is rather discreet language for a business practice which expressively allows of price discrimination.[63] The rationale behind the provision is difficult to find. A potential, but not very persuasive, justification might be that the Directive presupposes a cost advantage for an investment firm dealing with a professional customer based on economies of scale. There is more to the explanation that the provision is designed to offer professional clients the opportunity to wield their superior bargaining power. Be that as it may, it is an open question to what extent this power of price discrimination is consistent with the principle of 'best execution', to which we turn next.

[61] Remember, though, that trading in Xetra Best is considered to be trading on the exchange; whether this position can be maintained under the MiFID will be discussed infra, E (c).

[62] It is an open question to what extent an internaliser may deteriorate prices by demanding an extra charge as a disincentive to competitors seeking to trade at pre-published quotes; see D Rolland and B Bréhier (2005) 20.

[63] To this point a potential contradiction might be seen between MiFID Article 27 (3) (4) and Recital 50 of the Directive which, for the purpose of giving access to internal quotes, explicitly disallows discriminating between retail clients and professional clients.

3. Is 'Best' Execution Good Enough?

The principle of 'best execution', specified in MiFID Article 21 and its implementing Directive,[64] is by no means a path-breaking invention of the MiFID. In fact, it only specifies the duty of an agent to act in the best interest of his principal, which is a time-honoured principle of general agency law. That having been said, it remains one of the fundamental questions facing the new regime of internalisation, exactly what 'best execution' could mean for off-exchange order execution. First of all, it may be asked, whether and, in the affirmative, to what extent the broker's cost advantage has to be passed on to the client. And that is not all: which duties does the principle of best execution impose when it comes to choosing among various – national or European – reference markets? Asked more provocatively: is internalisation the investor's or the broker's gain?

a) To begin with the language of the Directive: there is at least a latent strain between the general principles of best execution as laid down in MiFID Article 21 and the more detailed standards for internalised execution as provided in MiFID Article 27, some of which may be analysed as specifying what best execution shall entail for systematic internalisers. Recital 58 of the implementing Directive[65] makes clear that an investment firm's dealing on own account with clients is to be considered as the execution of client orders subject to the general requirements of best execution. On the other hand, the standards for executing a customer order at the best possible price clearly differ between the two provisions. MiFID Article 21 (1) requires investment firms to 'take all reasonable steps to obtain, when executing orders, the best possible result for their clients, taking into account price, costs, speed, likelihood of execution (…)'. By contrast, MiFID Article 27 (1) (3) obviously dilutes this duty to obtain the best possible price in that it requires only that 'prices shall reflect the prevailing market conditions for that share'. This soft language begs the question exactly what 'reasonable steps' an investment firm needs to take when choosing to internally execute the customer order. The answer is further obfuscated by Recital 44 of the Directive which provides in rather unambiguous language: 'The obligations for investment firms under this Directive to quote a bid and offer price and to execute an order at the quoted price do not relieve investment firms of the obligation to route an order to another execution venue when such internalisation could prevent the firm from complying with "best execution" obligations'.

[64] At the time of writing, no final version of the implementing Directive had been adopted. See, for an interim version, Draft Commission Directive Implementing Directive 2004/39/EC of the European Parliament and of the Council as regards Organisational Requirements and Operating Conditions for Investment Firms, and Defined Terms for the Purposes of that Directive (the Draft Commission Directive), 06.02.2006, Articles 44-46.

[65] Draft Commission Directive (n 64).

b) The implementing Directive[66] spells out the principle of best execution by establishing a priority order among the various variables constituting best execution: the total consideration (i.e. the price of the financial instrument plus the cost of execution) shall have priority over other variables such as timeliness of execution or settlement. As a corollary rule, the implementing Directive[67] provides that investment firms shall not 'structure or charge their commissions in such a way as to discriminate unfairly between execution venues'. This may be read as an unequivocal clue that internalisers may not choose to offset the customer's gain from a better price with charging a higher execution fee, even if the resulting consideration is still better than when trading at the 'second-best' price of another execution venue.

c) A more difficult task is, given the broad language of the Directive and of Recital 44, to determine the 'reasonable steps' an investment firm has to take to obtain an optimal result for the benefit of the customer. For the purpose of execution via a regulated market or an MTF, the implementing Directive seems to suggest, that even if the investment firm does not deal on own account, i.e. passing on the order to a regulated market or an MTF, it has to be connected to a variety of potential execution venues unless this comes at a 'disproportionate' cost.[68] *A fortiori* it would seem that the search for the best reference price is at the core of an internaliser's obligation to best execution. Taking the principle of best execution seriously, investment firms that internalise customer orders should automatically execute orders at the national best bid or offer (NBBO) irrespective of their own quotations. Indeed they should refer to a European (Euro zone) best bid or offer. From an information technology point of view there is an easy answer: this is technically feasible, and at a reasonable cost.[69]

However, it is no less clear that MiFID Article 27 (1) (3) does not require such best execution proper. The soft obligation to 'reflect the prevailing market conditions' neither requires benchmarking, let alone reference to the best available quote. The notion behind this provision is, again, the 'active' internaliser who, very much like a market-maker, wields some discretion when setting his quotes. For this group one may wonder why, in the first place, for quotes in an open market the Directive provides any constraints to pricing. If, on the other hand, 'passive' internalisers fix their quotes by reference to 'imported' benchmark prices – regardless of whether there is price improvement or not –, they remain free to specify and indeed limit their benchmark quote(s) in their execution policy pursuant to MiFID Article 21 (2) if only the benchmark is within the range of prevailing market conditions. The execution policy thus becomes part of the

[66] Draft Commission Directive (n 64) Article 44 (3) and also Recital 61.

[67] Draft Commission Directive (n 64) Article 44 (4).

[68] Draft Commission Directive (n 64).

[69] See 'Background Note' to the Draft Commission Directive 7.7.1.

basis of the contract between the investment firm and its customer. It affords internalising investment firms some leeway in specifying their undertaking as to best execution of orders at their discretion. The result is far off the target of optimal investor protection. And it is far from clear whether this shortfall may be redressed by a recourse to Recital 44 of the Directive, which suggests that a less than 'best' internal quote could be 'surpassed' by the internaliser's duty to route the order to the execution venue offering the best quote. After all, recitals do not belong to the authoritative part of a Directive. Thus, Recital 44 might at best encourage Member States to enact a domestic rule in accordance with the Recital.

E. Xetra Best – A Blueprint for Other European Exchanges?

It has been submitted that Xetra Best might serve as a blueprint for other European exchanges facing the threat of internalisation once, pursuant to the liberalisation effected by the MiFID, internalisation becomes common market practice across the Member States.[70] As has been shown in the foregoing, Xetra Best indeed has some features attractive both to internalisers and to customers. It is closely connected with and indeed integrated in a regulated reference market, the FSE, thus evading some of the problems typical of internalised trading. It avoids the adverse effects of order flow fragmentation at least to a certain extent. It is subject to a higher level of supervision for the benefit of investors, because internalised trading is not only supervised as an investment service under the MiFID but also as a supplement to trading 'on' the exchange pursuant to the German Stock Exchange Act (*Börsengesetz*). It gives a straightforward answer to the difficult question[71] to what regulated market internalised trades should be reported.[72] Finally, to customers, the mandatory price improvement affords both price and time priority in the execution of their orders. Hence, in our concluding remarks, we consider whether and how much regulatory fine-tuning of the Xetra Best system is needed such as to comply with the requirements of the MiFID and the Draft Commission Regulation, without, on the other hand, having to sacrifice its specific qualities.

a) Some of the problems to solve result from the fact that Xetra Best is of an innovative design which does not neatly fit the Directive's tripartite system of trading venues (i.e. regulated markets, MTFs, and internalisation of orders by intermediaries). It might indeed be termed a 'hybrid' trading system. To be sure, it comes closest to internalised trading, with 'best executors' either trading on own account ('systematic' internalisers pursuant to MiFID Article 4 (1) ((7)) or

[70] J Grammig and E Theissen (2005) 22.

[71] See G Ferrarini and F Recine (2006) text following note 33.

[72] Pursuant to Article 28 (5) of the Draft Commission Regulation (n 59) post-trade information 'shall be made public (...) in the most relevant market in terms of liquidity for that share'.

trading against other customers' orders. Contrary to a first guess, Xetra Best cannot be seen to form an MTF. Even inasmuch the internaliser confines himself to matching customer orders, such matching does not contribute to price formation, because it refers to a quote imported from a regulated lead market.[73] On the other hand, Xetra Best features at least some elements of a regulated market in using the quotes in FSE's open order book as reference quote and with investment firms acting in the dual capacity of internalisers and market makers in the exchange.

b) Arguably, the attempt to integrate a large share of off-market trading into Germany's most liquid regulated market might have *anticompetitive effects*. Other than most systems of internalisation, Xetra Best constitutes a closed system consisting of a regulated market and, by virtue of the 'dual capacity rule',[74] of a connected group of investment firms, with the FSE acting as 'lead market'. Not only does internal execution refer to the FSEs open order book; also, completed trades are being, at least indirectly, fed back into the system. Thus Xetra Best creates a 'compound' of liquidity, enabling the FSE to capture a larger rather than a smaller share of the order flow. To date, no empirical data exist with regard to the question, whether Xetra Best subtracts its (modest) share of the overall order flow from the FSE's trading platform (which would amount to an 'internal' redistribution only) or from some other trading venue. If the second alternative were true this would defy, if not the language, the policy of the MiFID to strengthen competition and to create a level playing field both between regulated markets and between the three execution venues.

c) Given the 'hybrid' construction of Xetra Best, the German regulator consequently applies a dual supervisory regime, imposing not only the standards designed for investment firms as intermediaries but also those for trading in a regulated market.[75] As a matter of principle, there is little doubt that applying this dual regime conforms to European law. As the MiFID does not outright exclude a hybrid trading system, and the dual supervisory standard serves to effectively heighten the level of investor protection, it appears that both the language and the spirit of the Directive are satisfied. What may indeed be questioned is the German regulator's decision to consider trading under Xetra Best as trading in a regulated market with the consequence that using this venue is not contingent upon obtaining the customer's prior consent.[76] It might be argued that MiFID Article 21 (3) applies not to Xetra Best but only to bank/broker-sponsored systems. The better view, however, is that this position cannot be maintained under MiFID, because customers trading via Xetra Best do not fully enjoy the special guarantees which intervene if their orders are transmitted for execution in a regulated market.

[73] This point is generally made by D Rolland and B Bréhier (2005) 19.

[74] As explained above, text accompanying (n 38).

[75] See already supra, C I 2.

[76] See (n 42) and following text.

d) Most conspicuous is the divergence in how the MiFID on the one side and the Xetra Best rules on the other define a '*standard market size order*' (MiFID Article 27 (1) (5)). The definition is crucial for pre-trade transparency, because only dealing for standard market size orders triggers the internaliser's obligation to publish firm quotes (MiFID Article 27 (1) (1) and (2)). Xetra Best, once for all, allows for a maximum order volume of € 50,000. By contrast, MiFID Article 27 (1) (4) has adopted a flexible definition, scaling the 'standard market size' progressively according to the average value of orders executed (AVO),[77] starting from € 6,000 for an AVO larger than € 10,000 and smaller than € 20,000, and with no cap for higher and highest AVOs. This divergent view may be explained in terms of the different policy goals pursued by either ruling. Obviously the MiFID's goal in defining standard size orders as a function of the average turnover in a given security is to combat a fragmentation of the order flow. In other words: the higher the average turnover, the less the impairment of overall liquidity resulting from internal execution. By fencing out large-scale orders it also serves a market function, because it flattens the fluctuation of quotes and makes them immune to abnormal deflections, which in turn improves the efficiency of price formation. On the other hand, constraining the principle of pre-trade transparency to standard market size orders seems at least of an ambivalent nature. It might as well be argued that the rationale of limiting pre-trade transparency to standard market size orders is investor protection: retail customers who typically place only small- or mid-size orders, make a better decision on the basis of quotes published ex ante, whereas professional clients with large-scale orders, by virtue of their superior bargaining power, do not have to rely on pre-trade transparency. The same rationale seems to apply to the policy under Xetra Best rules of putting a cap on admissible orders of € 50,000. Orders of up to € 50,000 cover the lion's share of retail orders.[78] Thus, Xetra Best appears as an execution venue which is primarily targeted on, and designed to serve the needs of, retail customers. That, in turn, begs the question whether Xetra Best execution is governed by the pre-trade transparency principle in the first place.

e) Currently (i.e. pre-MiFID), best executors under Xetra Best need not *make public their quotes*. Accordingly, Xetra Best clearly does not comply with the pre-trade transparency requirement of MiFID Article 27 (3). On a closer look, however, a different argument comes to mind. As discussed previously, Xetra Best uses a passive pricing rule since the reference prices are imported from Xetra, i. e. from a regulated market. Consequently, increased pre-trade transparency would hardly contribute to enhance the quality of price discovery. In other words, the very purpose of imposing ex-ante transparency would not be affected,

[77] As implemented by Draft Commission Regulation (n 59) Annex Table 3.

[78] The provision in Article 25 Draft Commission Regulation (n 59) which defines retail orders as not exceeding € 7.500 is utterly questionable but may be explained by its limited scope of application only for MiFID Article 27 (3) (4).

and the application of MiFID Article 27 (1) would appear to be mere formalism. On the other hand making Xetra Best subject to pre-trade transparency would allow customers to compare between best executors' quotes (or, more precisely, to assess the magnitude of price improvement which each of them grants). Therefore, pre-trade transparency is likely to increase competition among internalisers.

f) MiFID Article 22 (2) provides that orders which are not immediately executed are to be made public. Member States 'may decide that investment firms comply with this obligation by transmitting the client limit order to a regulated market and/or MTF'. Orders which are not immediately executed in Xetra Best are automatically transferred to the Xetra order book. This feature of Xetra Best thus obviously complies with the MiFID rules.

g) It is doubtful whether Xetra Best complies with the *principle of best execution*.

aa) A system of internal execution based on importing reference prices from a single market (or, more generally, from a subset of markets) is consistent with the best execution requirement only if the reference market happens to be the market that yields the best results on a regular basis.

Given that the FSE's Xetra electronic trading system faces not only 'internal' competition by the floor of the FSE but also by several regional exchanges it is far from obvious that Xetra Best meets the above requirement. As a case in point, the floor of the FSE offers 'zero spread trading' in 160 of the most liquid stocks for retail clients.[79] The customer only pays the Courtage, amounting to 0.08% (0.04% for stocks included in the DAX) of the transaction value. Percentage spreads in Xetra (being the sole reference market for Xetra Best prices) thus would have to be low enough to meet this target after the mandatory price improvement is taken into account. This is unlikely to be the case on a regular basis. We thus have to conclude that Xetra Best does not comply with the MiFID's best execution requirement.

bb) We have argued previously that internalised orders tend to be less risky and less costly to execute than the average order on the reference market. The question is whether these cost savings accrue to the customer or to the internaliser. In a competitive market the former should be the case. Regulation therefore should provide incentives for internalisers to pass on their cost advantage to customers. Pre-trade transparency serves that purpose. A more stringent regulatory approach would be to enforce price priority between internalisers.

h) The MiFID rules pertaining to internalisation do not address the question of investment firms acting in 'dual capacity', i.e. as both internalisers and liquidity managers in the Xetra order book. This dual role is not in itself a problem. Even if there were no such requirement, the best executor would be *allowed* to be active in the reference market. The potential conflict of interest is thus not created

[79] The maximum order size is € 10,000 for the constituent stocks of the DAX and € 5,000 and € 3,000, respectively, for specified groups of less liquid stocks.

specifically by the Xetra Best rules. Still, investment firms cannot invariably escape any conflict of interest when acting in the dual role of systematic internaliser dealing on own account and market maker in the regulated lead market.[80] It is difficult to see how an investment firm could at the same time seek to publish 'optimal' quotes as market maker in the lead market, and as a systematic internaliser offer the best possible price for the benefit of its client. Once such conflict of interest situations arise, the MiFID general rules governing conflicts of interest (Articles 13 (3), 18) apply to the effect that the internalising investment firm needs at least to disclose the general nature and/or sources of such conflicts to its customers. However, the investing public would be better served if the two functions were made incompatible as a matter of principle.

F. Conclusions

The MiFID internalisation regime has emerged as the result of long and painstaking political haggling. By and large it has achieved a fair balancing of the conflicting goals of market efficiency (concentration rule vs. fragmentation of order flows), of improving competition between different execution venues (facilitating and upgrading internal execution as a valid alternative to regulated markets and MTFs), without neglect of the needs of (especially) retail investors (enforcement of pre-trade transparency and best execution, requirement of clients' prior consent to internal execution)). It goes without saying that such a daring enterprise could not be perfect in each and any detail. The Directive presupposes the notion of an 'active' internaliser acting like a market maker; it pays too little attention to internalisers trading at 'imported' prices generated in a regulated market. Enabling systematic internalisers to exert price discrimination between retail and professional investors is of questionable wisdom. The principle of best execution, a pillar of the Directive's general code of conduct, has, without apparent technical or commercial need, been relinquished with respect to internal execution.

With the Xetra Best facility supplied by the Frankfurt stock exchange, Germany has developed an innovative variety of internalisation, which avoids some pitfalls of the conventional practice of internalisation and at the same time highlights some deficiencies of the Directive. Whether Xetra Best may serve as a blueprint for other European suppliers of exchange services some day, remains to be seen. In any case, Xetra Best needs to be adapted to the new European regulatory regime.

[80] See already above (n 39) and following text.

References

Assmann, HD and UH Schneider (eds) *Wertpapierhandelsgesetz* (Dr Otto Schmidt 3rd ed 2003).

Battalio, R 'Third Market Broker-Dealers: Cost Competitors or Cream Skimmers?' (1997) 52 J Finance 341-352.

Battalio, R, J Greene and R Jennings 'Do Competing Specialists and Preferencing Dealers Affect Market Quality?' (1997) 10 Rev Finan Stud 969-993.

Battalio, R, B Hatch and R Jennings 'Dimensions of Best Execution for Market Orders: Assessing Differences Between the NYSE and the Nasdaq Third Market' (Indiana University wp <http://www.bus.indiana.edu/Finance/workingpapers/NYSECON5.pdf> 2000).

Battalio, R and C Holden 'A Simple Model of Payment for Order Flow, Internalization, and Total Trading Cost' (2001) 4 J Finan Markets 33-71.

Battalio, R, R Jennings and J Selway 'Will Payment for Order Flow Survive Decimalization?' (Kelley School of Business wp <http://www.kelley.iu.edu/finance/wp3.htm> 2000).

Battalio, R, R Jennings and J Selway 'The Relationship Among Market-Making Revenue, Payment for Order Flow, and Trading Costs for Market Orders' (2001) 19 J Finan Services Res 39-56.

Bloomfield, R and M O'Hara 'Does Order Preferencing Matter?' (1998) 50 J Finan Econ 3-37.

Blume, M and M Goldstein 'Quotes, Order Flow, and Price Discovery' (1997) 52 J Finance 221-244.

Daigre, J 'L'internalisation des orders, une (petite?) revolution en France' (2004) Revue de Droit Bancaire et Financier 231-233.

Easley, D, N Kiefer and M O'Hara 'Cream Skimming or Profit Sharing? The Curious Role of Purchased Order Flow' (1996) 51 J Finance 811-833.

Euronext 'Revision of the Investment Services Directive Euronext's Proposals for the ISD in Relation to the EU's Cash Equity Markets' (2002) <http://www.boursede-paris.fr/en/news7/pdf/Position-paper-internalisation-24052002.pdf>.

Ferrarini, G and F Recine 'The MiFID and Internalisation' in this volume (2006) 235-270.

Ferrell, A 'The Allocation of Investors' Orders and Inefficient Market Competition: A Proposal' (SSRN wp <http://ssrn.com/abstract=224943> 2000).

Financial Services Authority 'Best Execution' (Discussion Paper 2001) <http://www.fsa.gov.uk/pubs/discussion/dp5.pdf>.

Grammig, J, D Schiereck and E Theissen 'Knowing Me, Knowing You: Trader Anonymity and Informed Trading in Parallel Markets' (2001) 4 J Finan Markets 385-412.

Grammig, J and E Theissen 'Is Best Really Better? Internalization in Xetra Best' (University of Tübingen wp http://www.uni-tuebingen.de/ uni/wwo/Grammig/XBest%20RoF%202.pdf> 2005).

Harris, L 'Consolidation, Fragmentation, Segmentation and Regulation' (1993) 2 Finan Markets Inst Instruments 1-27.

Huang, R and H Stoll 'Dealer versus Auction Markets: A Paired Comparison of Execution Costs on NASDAQ and the NYSE' (1996) 41 J Finan Econ 313-357.

Köndgen, J and E Theissen 'Internalisierter Wertpapierhandel zu Börsenpreisen?' (2003) Wertpapiermitteilungen 1497-1509.

Lee, C 'Market Integration and Price Execution for NYSE-Listed Securities' (1993) 48 J Finance 1009-1038.

Macey, J and M O'Hara 'The Law and Economics of Best Execution' (1997) 6 J Finan Intermediation 188-223.

Peterson, M and E Sirri 'Order Preferencing and Market Quality on U.S. Equity Exchanges' (2003) 16 Rev Finan Stud 385-415.

Rolland, D and B Bréhier 'L'internalisation des ordres' (2005) Banque & Droit 17-21.

Rudolph, B and A Röhrl 'Grundfragen der Börsenorganisation aus ökonomischer Sicht' in KJ Hopt and H Baum (eds) *Börsenreform* (1997) 173-285.

Schwark, E 'Internalisierung' in: 'Wirtschafts- und Privatrecht im Spannungsfeld von Privatautonomie, Wettbewerb und Regulierung' (2004) Sections 723-742.

Stoll, HR 'Organization of the Stock Market: Competition or Fragmentation' (1993) 5 J Appl Corporate Finance 89.

Theissen, E 'Trader Anonymity, Price Formation and Liquidity' (SSRN wp <http://ssrn.com/abstract=248706> 2002a).

Theissen, E 'Internalisierung und Marktqualität: Was bringt Xetra Best?' (2002b) 35 Kredit und Kapital 550-571.

Part 3:

Further Issues in Regulatory Harmonization

The Eclipse of Contract Law in the Investment Firm-Client-Relationship: The Impact of the MiFID on the Law of Contract from a German Perspective

PETER O. MÜLBERT

Articles 19 to 24 of the Markets in Financial Instruments Directive (MiFID) establish a new regulatory framework for the legal relationship between an investment firm and its clients. These conduct of business rules supersede the contractual relationship for the provision of investment services that, in turn, is shaped by the terms of the contract, mandatory statutory provisions, and complementary judge-made rules. At first glance, the regulatory framework and the contractual framework are completely independent of each other. In particular, Article 19 (7) only recognizes that investment services are provided on a contractual basis by requiring an investment firm to establish a documentary record regarding the contractual terms but does not mandate any specific contents of such a contract. However, a more detailed analysis shows the MiFID framework to have a profound impact on the structure and contents of the respective contractual relationships. In this respect, Article 20 dealing with the provision of services received through the medium of another investment firm, and Articles 31 and 32 providing for maximum harmonization of the conduct of business rules are of particular importance.

A. Introduction
B. The Present Contractual Approach to Regulating the Firm-Client-Relationship: The German Example
C. The Contents of the Conduct of Business Obligations: Selected Issues
D. Implications for the (German) Law of Contract Relating to Securities Transactions
E. Concluding Remarks

A. Introduction

The conduct of business rules contained in Articles 19-24 of the new Markets in Financial Instruments Directive [1] (MiFID) will revolutionise the field of bank-

[1] Directive 2004/39/EC of the European Parliament and of the Council of 21 April 2004 on Markets in Financial Instruments amending Council Directives 85/611/EEC and 93/6/EEC and Directive 2000/12/EC of the European Parliament and of the Council and repealing Council Directive 93/22/EEC (the MiFID), OJ L145 30.04.2004 1-44. Articles cited in the text are those of the MiFID unless otherwise denoted.

ing law in Germany, and probably in other Continental countries as well.[2] The new regulatory framework for the legal relationship between an investment firm and its client established by the MiFID supersedes the contractual framework for the provision of investment services already in place within Member States, i.e. the framework resulting from a combination of contractual terms, statutory provisions, and complementary rules established by the courts. If provisions or rules that form part of the existing contractual framework are at odds with the new regulatory framework they will have to be abandoned or abolished. In other words, from now on, the investment firm-client relationship will be primarily governed by rules set by regulators. In contrast, contract law and, as a corollary, the courts applying contract law will be relegated to the sidelines when it comes to shaping the legal framework within which an investment firm provides an investment service to a client.

In some Member States at least, this development will have a profound impact on their national legal culture. This is particularly true for Member States such as, for example, Germany and Austria that rely almost exclusively on a contractual framework to deal with the legal relationship between an investment firm and its client in regard to the provision of investment services.

B. The Present Contractual Approach to Regulating the Firm-Client-Relationship: The German Example

Take, for example, the case of securities transactions between an investment firm and its client. Under German law, a customer willing to buy or sell securities through his investment firm enters into a contract with the firm as his commission agent. Sections 383 ff of the German Commercial Code – enacted more than 100 years ago in 1900 – describe the main rights and duties of the parties to a contract concluded on a commission basis ('*Kommissionsvertrag*'), as it is called, albeit in rather general terms. According to Section 384, the investment firm as a commission agent 'is obligated to carry out the transaction being undertaken with the care of a prudent merchant; in so doing it must protect the principal's interests and follow his instructions' (Paragraph (1)) and must give the principal the

[2] For an in-depth analysis of the MiFID see B Maurenbrecher 'Von der Investment Services Directive zur Markets in Financial Services Directive – ein Überblick aus Schweizer Sicht' (2005) Aktuelle Juristische Praxis/Pratique Juridique Actuelle 19; for a brief description of the conduct of business rules see G Ferrarini 'Contract Standards and the Markets in Financial Instruments Directive (MiFID): An Assessment of the Lamfalussy Regulatory Architecture (2005) 1 ERCL 19; for an overview on the Commission Proposal see, inter alia, J Herbst 'Revision of the Investment Services Directive' (2003) 11 J of Financial Regulation and Compliance 211; P Baltzer 'Der Vorschlag der EG-Kommission für eine neue Wertpapierdienstleistungsrichtlinie' (2003) Zeitschrift für Bankrecht und Bankwirtschaft 177; N Hammes 'Die Vorschläge der Europäischen Kommission zur Überarbeitung der Wertpapierdienstleistungsrichtlnie' (2001) Zeitschrift für Bankrecht und Bankwirtschaft 498.

necessary information, especially prompt notice of the conclusion of the transaction; it is obliged 'to account to the principal for the transaction and deliver him anything obtained from the business commissioned' (Paragraph (2)).

The content of these general obligations with respect to the buying or selling of securities is to some degree elaborated by a specific set of standard business conditions used by banks.[3] A long series of decisions by German courts, in particular the Federal High Court of Justice ('*Bundesgerichtshof*'), and an extensive legal literature have provided for clarification and elaboration by interpreting the meaning of the various statutory provisions, by clarifying the (non-)mandatory nature of the provisions in question, by drawing a line between acceptable and unacceptable standard business conditions, and by filling any lacunae in the legal framework resulting from incomplete contracts or incomplete statutory provisions, respectively.[4]

In particular, any new problems arising between investment firms and their clients were mostly discussed and resolved within this contractual setting, i.e. as a question of the contractual rights and duties of the investment firm and its client, respectively. This is even true with respect to an investment firm's obligation to inform the client about the risks of a specific product or service, or to recommend a suitable product or service. Courts either used the notion of pre-contractual obligations to arrive at these obligations, or they held that the parties had tacitly concluded a separate consultancy agreement ('*Beratungsvertrag*') requiring the firm to provide information and even advice on suitable investments to the customer.[5]

The traditional legal environment shaped by contractual concepts and notions only started to change with the implementation of Articles 10 and 11 of the Investment Services Directive. The German legislator refrained from implementing these provisions by amending the provisions in Sections 383 ff of the German Commercial Code dealing with the contract concluded on a commission basis ('*Kommissionsvertrag*'). Instead the legislator opted for implementing these provisions in Sections 31 ff of the Securities Trading Act enacted in 1994. Some of these provisions closely parallel the existing pre-contractual and contractual obligations with respect to buying or selling securities on a customer's behalf.[6] In particular, Section 31 (2) of the Act obliges investment firms to request certain

[3] Sonderbedingungen für Wertpapiergeschäfte; to be found, e.g. in A Baumbach and KJ Hopt *Handelsgesetzbuch* (Beck-Verlag 31st ed 2003) (8) ABG-WPGeschäfte.

[4] For an overview, see, e.g. S Kümpel *Bank- und Kapitalmarktrecht* (Otto Schmidt-Verlag 3rd ed 2004) 10.67 ff; HP Schwintowski and FA Schäfer *Bankrecht* (Carl Heymanns-Verlag 2nd ed 2004) 686 ff; in more detail, e.g. J Ekkenga 'Effektengeschäft' in K Schmidt et al (eds) *Münchener Kommentar zum Handelsgesetzbuch* vol. 5 (Beck-Verlag 2nd ed 2001) note 1 ff.

[5] See text infra and (n 32).

[6] See, e.g. the documentation requirements under Sections 34 (1), 37 (1) Securities Trading Act; as to the parallel between this provisions and contractual obligations see, e.g. HP Schwintowski and FA Schäfer (n 4) 693 note 27.

information from their customers and to provide them with all useful information. After the enactment of the Securities Trading Act, the discussion with respect to banks' duties to furnish information in the field of securities transactions almost immediately focused on the new requirements contained in Section 31 (2) of the Act, whereas the pre-contractual information obligations declined in importance. Courts and commentators still acknowledged their existence, but decisions in clients' favour were mostly based on a violation of Section 31 (2) of the Act, not on any violation of pre-contractual information obligations.

It is possible to identify at least two reasons for this shift in focus, and both of them are of interest in this present context as well. Firstly, in 1997, the precursor to the current Financial Supervisory Authority ('*Bundesanstalt für Finanzdienstleistungsaufsicht*', 'BaFin') issued a guideline detailing its understanding of the information requirements established in Section 31 (2) of the Act.[7] Secondly, in contrast to Article 19 (6) of the MiFID, Article 11 of the Investment Services Directive did not provide for an explicit exception from the general information obligations with respect to execution-only business. Thus, whereas courts could easily tailor the information obligations based on the notion of a pre-contractual relationship to fit the specific requirements of execution-only business, there were some doubts whether Section 31 (2) of the Act – serving to implement Article 11 of the Investment Services Directive – would permit such an adaptation as well.[8]

Given that Articles 19 ff of the MiFID provide for far more detailed conduct of business rules than those contained in Article 11 of the Investment Services Directive, the implementation of the MiFID will intensify the shift in focus that was set in motion by Article 11 of the Directive. Furthermore, to the extent that Articles 19 ff of the MiFID ignore the contractual framework in place at a national level, implementation of the conduct of business obligations will create additional problems for a Member State, and may even require substantial amendments to existing provisions and rules.

In the following, three potential conflicts between the obligations under Articles 19 ff on the one hand, and the national contractual framework, on the other hand, shall be examined against the backdrop of the German legal landscape (Section C). In order to clearly identify the source and nature of these conflicts, some prior clarifications as to the meaning and content of the conduct of business obligations under Articles 19 ff are indispensable (Section D).

[7] As to that, see HMJ Möllers and T Ganten 'Die Wohlverhaltensrichtlinie des BAWe im Lichte der neuen Fassung des WpHG' (1998) 27 Zeitschrift für das gesamte Unternehmens- und Gesellschaftsrecht 773.

[8] For an overview see I Koller in HD Assmann and UH Schneider (eds) *Wertpapierhandelsgesetz* (Otto Schmidt-Verlag 3rd ed 2003) Section 31 notes 134 ff (with references).

C. The Contents of the Conduct of Business Obligations: Selected Issues

I. The Provision of 'Investment Advice' on a Contractual Basis

Advised transactions are probably the rule and not the exception when it comes to retail clients buying or selling securities. Therefore, the interpretation of the term 'investment advice' mentioned, e.g., in Article 19 (4) of the MiFID, is of crucial importance with respect to potential conflicts between the conduct of business obligations and the contractual setting for providing investment services to a client.

According to the definition in Article 4 (1) (4) of the MiFID, investment advice means the provision of personal recommendations to a client, either at the latter's request or at the investment firm's initiative, with regard to one or more transactions relating to financial instruments. CESR,[9] in its Draft Technical Advice, is of the opinion that a contract with the client should not be a prerequisite for the provision of investment advice or, vice versa, investment advice should not only be covered by the Directive if a contractual relationship between the advisor and the client exists. In the words of the CESR Standards on Investor Protection, investment advice can be provided 'either incidentally or under a contract for investment advice'. As CESR points out, the regulatory approach should not depend on unharmonised – and therefore still divergent – principles of private law.

On the other hand, Annex I Section A to the MiFID even lists the provision of investment advice as defined in Article 4 (1) (4) among the core investment services, not the ancillary services. According to Article 19 (1) of the Directive, when providing such core investment services, investment firms shall have to comply in particular with, inter alia, the requirement contained in Article 19 (7) of the Directive 'to establish a record that includes the document or documents agreed between the firm and the client that set out the rights and obligations of the parties, and the other terms on which the firm will provide services. The right and duties of the parties to the contract may be incorporated by reference to other documents or legal texts'.

Obviously, Article 19 (7) of the MiFID implicitly stipulates that investment firms shall provide any core investment service – including investment advice – on a contractual basis. According to the second sentence of Paragraph 7, the right and duties of the firm and the client, respectively, follow from a contract between these two parties, not from any statutory provisions. The opinion of CESR, according to which investment advice can be provided independently of a contract or, put differently, outside a contract, is clearly at odds with the concept underlying Article 19 (7).

[9] As to the following, see CESR 'Draft Technical Advice on Possible Implementing Measures of the Directive 2004/39/EC on Markets in Financial Instruments – Second Set of Mandates' (October 2004) CESR/04-562, 13.

Admittedly, Article 19 (7) does not deal with the formation of a contract that serves as the basis for the provision of investment services.[10] Incidentally, however, Member States are obliged to provide for rules to the effect that the provision of investment advice does lead to the formation of a contract – regardless of the parties' wills. The resulting implications for national contract law will be taken up infra Section C.I..

II. Limitations to the Provision of Information under Article 19 (3) to (5)

Information requirements abound in secondary EC legislation, sometimes even to the extent that consumers are discouraged from absorbing all the information they have to receive. At a first glance, the MiFID does not seem to make any exception to the rule. However, upon closer inspection, the core conduct of business obligations (Article 19 (3) to (5)) investment firms have to comply with whenever they provide any kind of investment service offers a slightly different picture.[11]

Article 19 (3) stipulates that, when a firm provides investment services to a client, it shall provide appropriate information to clients or potential clients on, inter alia, the financial instruments and proposed investment strategies, on execution venues, and on the costs and associated charges. This information requirement aims ultimately at enabling the client 'to take investment decisions on an informed basis'. Therefore, the firm has to include appropriate guidance on and warnings of the risks associated with investments in those instruments or in respect of particular investment strategies so that the clients are reasonably able to understand the nature and the risks of the investment service and of the specific type of financial instrument that is being offered.

By contrast, Article 19 (4) and (5) stipulate that the investment firm shall recommend suitable investment services or financial products (Article 19 (4)) or, at least, issue a warning if the client or potential client is envisaging an inappropriate investment service or financial product (Article 19 (5)). The paternalistic obligation to recommend suitable services and products only applies to the provision of investment advice and portfolio management, though; if the firm provides another service a warning in a standardized format will suffice.

[10] In line therewith, the paper by CESR 'Technical Advice on Possible Implementing Measures of the Directive 2004/39/EC on Markets in Financial Instruments – First Set of Mandates' (January 2005) CESR/05-024b, 61 emphasizes that the advice is not intended to interfere with the way in which contracts are concluded, amended, renewed or terminated under the applicable law of the Member States.

[11] In contrast, the best execution obligation (Article 21) and the obligations with respect to client order handling rules (Article 22) only apply to the execution of orders on behalf of clients in the sense of Annex 1 Section A (1) to the MiFID. See infra Section C.III.3..

1. Article 19 (3) as a Non-Periodical Obligation to Provide Information

The relationship between these conduct of business obligations – Article 19 (3) and (4), and Article 19 (3) and (5) – is neither elaborated in Article 19 nor elsewhere in the MiFID. However, either both obligations are independent of one another or, conversely, both obligations are complementary elements of a more comprehensive obligation. If the second alternative were true, one would expect Article 19 (3) to require the provision of information with each service; if the first alternative were true, the firm may provide information under Article 19 (3) far less often.

CESR's Technical Advice of January 2005 opts for the first solution, albeit without considering the alternative concept. According to the Advice 'an investment firm may be deemed to have complied with the obligation to provide information under Article 19 (3) of the Directive where the client has been given the information on a previous occasion and that information is still up to date'.[12]

If the information given on a previous occasion is deemed sufficient, investment firms will be able to reduce the burdensome information obligations by using standardized information brochures that cover a wider range of investment services and financial instruments. Article 19 (3), as interpreted by CESR, does not require the firm to inform the client anew if the firm provides services in other financial instruments covered in the brochure, and the same holds true for the provision of further services. With respect to the timing, CESR only contemplates a minimum threshold requiring that the information must be provided 'in good time', i.e. the client must still be able to absorb and react to the information.[13] Apart from that, the amount of time that has passed since the firm provided the client with the information brochure is basically irrelevant. The only limitation is that the content of the brochure has to still be valid.

One may question, though, whether CESR's interpretation fully reflects the intention of Article 19 (3). As already mentioned, Article 19 (3) aims at enabling the client to take investment decisions on an informed basis. Regardless of an investment firm's obligation only to recommend suitable investment services and financial instruments (Article 19 (4)) or to warn a client who is envisaging an inappropriate service or instrument (Article 19 (5)), it is still the client who ultimately decides on whether or not to accept the provision of the service offered or the instrument offered. The information provided under Article 19 (3) aims at enabling him to take this decision on an informed basis.

However, if a retail client obtained the relevant information some time ago, one may doubt the empirical validity of the implied presumption that such a client will still be able to take the investment decision on an informed basis.[14] This

[12] See CESR (n 10) 55 Box 9 (2).

[13] See CESR (n 10) 56 Box 8 (3).

[14] For this reason, Section 37d (1) of the German Securities Trading Act requires with respect to a standardised information brochure detailing the specific risks of futures that invest-

cont. ...

is particularly true if the firm furnished the information while providing a different type of investment service or financial instrument. Given this situation, one cannot expect the client to have also absorbed the information that was not relevant for the earlier transaction; one cannot even assume that he still is in possession of the standardized information brochure given to him on the occasion of an earlier transaction.

On the other hand, Article 19 (3) explicitly provides for the possibility of furnishing the information under this Article in a standardized format. The intended effect is to make the information obligation somewhat less onerous for investment firms. However, if firms were required to furnish the information prescribed in Article 19 (3) every time they provide a new service, be it an existing service in relation to a different type of financial instrument or a different service, investment firms would hardly benefit from the option to provide information in a standardized format. Take, for example, a client buying securities and stock on two consecutive days or even on the same day. It would be utterly pointless to require the firm to provide the information under Article 19 (3) including, inter alia, information on the firm, twice a day to the same client.

On balance, then, CESR's understanding of Article 19 (3) seems correct. For the firm to comply with the information obligation it is sufficient for it to have provided the information on a previous occasion, if the information is still valid. In other words, under Article 19 (3) a periodical supply of information – either at regular intervals or with each service provided – is not required.[15]

2. The Limitation to Providing Standardized Information

A further limitation of the conduct of business obligations under Article 19 (3) to (5) results from the fact that these rules do not oblige an investment firm to inform its client about specific risks associated with a particular financial instrument.

(i) Take, for example, the case of the rating of securities. If they have the lowest investment grade and if a rating agency decides to put the securities on the watch list, this is important news for an investor. The same holds true for a client investing in stock if, for example, there are credible rumours that the financial statements of a company or of one its main subsidiaries are not correct. In both cases the information relates to the specific risks associated with an individual financial instrument, not to the specific risks associated with a certain type of financial instruments.

ment firms furnish this brochure at least every two years to their consumer clients. See in more detail PO Mülbert in HD Assmann and UH Schneider (n 8) Section 37d notes 41 ff.

[15] As a consequence, the German legislator will have to revise Section 37d (1) of the German Securities Trading to the effect that a periodical provision of information (see supra (n 14)) will no longer be required since Article 19 (3) aims at maximum harmonization (see infra Section D.II.).

(ii) Whether investment firms are under an obligation to divulge this kind of information to their clients is doubtful, at best. The information obligation under Article 19 (3) does not cover the risks associated with the individual financial instrument. Its scope is limited to the effect that clients, as a consequence of the information provided, should be able to understand 'the nature and risks ... of the specific type of instrument that is being offered'. If Article 19 (3) did not limit the information obligation to the generic risks of a specific class of financial instruments, the second sentence of Article 19 (3) would be pointless and irrelevant because, then, firms would not be able to provide the information under Article 19 (3) in a standardized format.

(iii) Article 19 (4) limits the obligation of a firm providing investment advice or portfolio management to the extent that that firm has to recommend suitable investment services and financial instruments; the furnishing of information is not required. Thus, information related to risks associated with an individual financial instrument might require the firm to omit this instrument from its recommendation. However, if not, the firm is not obliged to pass on this type of information to its client. For example, Article 19 (4) does not always prevent firms from recommending a certain stock only because of credible rumours according to which the company's financial statements might need to be revised. Given this exception, Article 19 (4) does not oblige the firm to inform the client of these rumours. Quite in line with this, CESR's Draft Technical Advice suggests as criteria for assessing the suitability of a recommendation, inter alia, 'the knowledge and experience of the client' with the envisaged transaction. Furthermore, the transaction envisaged may be considered unsuitable for the clients because 'of the risks of the financial instruments involved (e.g. derivatives), the type of transaction (e.g. sale of options)' etc.[16] The specific risks of an individual financial instrument envisaged are not mentioned.

(iv) This is even truer with respect to the obligation under Article 19 (5) to warn the client that the financial instrument envisaged is not appropriate. A warning is only required if the firm considers that, on the basis of the client's 'knowledge and experience in the investment field relevant to the specific type of product or service offered or demanded', the product or service envisaged is not appropriate. Here as well, only generic risk factors associated with a certain type of product are important not, however, those risks associated with the individual product envisaged. Consequently, subparagraph 2 provides for the possibility of providing the warning in a standardized format. If a warning with respect to specific risks associated with an individual product were required, a standardization of the warning to be issued would not be possible. Again, CESR's Draft Technical Advice corroborates this understanding of Article 19 (5). The Advice suggests, with respect to the criteria for assessing the appropriateness, that the firm itself has to define relevant parameters, such as 'types of instruments, types of

[16] CESR (n 9) 44 Box 8 (6 (a)) and (7).

transactions and types of orders in which the retail client has sufficient knowledge or experience'.[17]

3. Article 19 (3) to (5) as an Exhaustive Elaboration of the General Clause in Article 19 (1)

To fill in the lacuna just described resulting from the firm's missing obligation to factor also in the specific risks associated with individual financial instruments, one may consider resorting to Article 19 (1). The wording of this provision is indicative of a general clause. Investment firms have to 'act honestly, fairly and professionally … and comply, in particular, with the principles set out in paragraphs 2 to 8'. For a firm to act fairly and professionally, one might argue, requires that the firm should divulge information to its client on the specific risks associated with an individual financial instrument envisaged.

However, CESR's Draft Technical Advice offers a rather different understanding of Article 19 (1). The Advice states flatly that '[i]nformation owed or addressed to clients, as well as … [other] requirements are dealt with under paragraphs 2 through 8 of Article 19', and that 'CESR is therefore requested to provide technical advice … with respect to issues other than those dealt with in paragraphs 2 through 8 of Article 19'.[18] In other words, CESR is of the opinion that for the purpose of level 2 legislation Paragraphs 2 to 8 bar having any recourse to Paragraph 1. Indeed, if a framework directive already details the scope for possible elaborations of a general clause, any level 2 legislation that introduces additional refinements would be contrary to the principles of the Lamfalussy-approach. Whether the argument could be made that Article 19 (3) to (5) do not at all cover the type of risks in question appears to be doubtful, at least.

III. The Provision of Services Through the Medium of Another Investment Firm (Article 20)

Often, the buying or selling of securities on behalf of a client is not undertaken by the investment firm that receives the instruction to perform the transaction, but by another firm. This is true, for example, for the securities business in Germany. Most public savings banks as well as virtually all of the credit unions are not themselves members of a German stock exchange, but instruct another investment firm – usually a large bank belonging to the same sector – to perform the transaction. Given that the legal relationship between the client and the first firm qualifies as a contract concluded on commission basis in the sense of Sec-

[17] CESR (n 9) 47 Box 9 (7).

[18] CESR (n 9) 38.

tions 383 ff of the German Commercial Code[19] the second bank acts as an Intermediate Commissioner ('*Zwischenkommissionär*') employed by the first firm.[20]

1. A Restatement of Article 20: Provision of the Services upon Instructions Received Through the Medium of Another Investment Firm

The Directive deals with this situation in Article 20 under the heading 'provision of services through the medium of another investment firm'. This heading is thoroughly misleading, though. It implies that the investment firm providing the service referred to in Article 20 is the firm that directly received the instruction from its client. However, upon closer inspection, the concept underlying Article 20 and, more generally, the conduct of business rules opt for the opposite solution. It is the second and not the first firm that provides the investment service referred to in Article 20. Take, for example, the investment service 'execution of orders on behalf of a client'. If a client instructs a firm to buy or sell securities on his behalf, and if the firm does not execute the order, but charges another firm to carry out the transaction, the second firm – and not the first one – provides the investment service 'execution of orders on behalf of clients' to the retail client. This clearly follows from (1) as well as (3) of Article 20. Paragraph 1 addresses investment firms that receive 'an instruction to perform investment or ancillary services on behalf of a client through the medium of another investment firm', and Paragraph 3 holds that an 'investment firm which receives clients' instructions or orders through the medium of another investment firm shall remain responsible for concluding the service or transaction'. Obviously, the heading of Article 20 should actually read as follows: Provision of services upon instructions received through the medium of another investment firm.

2. The Evolution of Article 20

This restatement of Article 20, critics may want to argue, deviates fundamentally from what the Commission had in mind when it first introduced Article 18 (10) – the precursor of Article 20 – in the Proposal for a Directive on Investment Services and Regulated Markets,[21] namely the setting up of a regulatory framework that would be tailored to the specific structure of the asset management business.

[19] See supra Section B.

[20] See No. 8 (1) of the Sonderbedingungen für Wertpapiergeschäfte (n 3); as to the 'Zwischenkommissionär' see, e.g. A Baumbach and KJ Hopt (n 3) Section 384 HGB note 3.

[21] Proposal for a Directive of the European Parliament and of the Council on Investment Services and Regulated Markets, amending Council Directives 85/611/EEC, Council Directive 93/6/EEC and European Parliament and Council Directive 2000/12/EEC, OJ L126 26.05.2000 1-59.

However, even if one accepts that focus as the former starting point, in the tortured process of finding a widely accepted compromise version of the MiFID, the rules originally suggested evolved into a new regulatory concept going far beyond the original intentions. Thus, to understand the meaning of Article 20 in its present form, any recourse to the provisions contained in the Commission Proposal for a Directive on Investment Services and Regulated Markets is of very limited value. It only serves to ascertain that Article 20 must be understood in the systematic context of the Directive in its final form, not by referring to the intentions originally pursued. This clearly follows from analyzing the evolution of Article 20 in some detail.

At a first glance, Article 18 (10), as contained in the Commission Proposal for a Directive on Investment Services and Regulated Markets, very closely resembles the present Article 20. However, a second glance reveals a critical difference. According to subparagraph 3 of the former provision, 'the investment firm which receives client instructions or orders through the medium of another investment firm shall remain responsible for concluding the service or transaction ... in accordance with measures adopted pursuant to paragraph 9', i.e. in accordance with implementing measures adopted by the Commission to ensure that investment firms comply with the general conduct of business obligations prescribed by Article 18 (now: Article 19). With respect to the specific conduct of business rules that apply when an investment firm executes orders on behalf of a client the Commission's Proposal for Article 19 (1) reads as follows: 'Member States shall require that investment firms providing services which entail the execution, whether by the firm itself or another investment firm, of clients' orders ... ensure' the best execution of the said clients' orders. Recital 26 explained the underlying motivation by stating that the best execution obligation 'should apply to the firm which owes contractual or agency obligations to the client – irrespective of whether that firm executes the order itself or relies on another intermediary to do so'. Still, the two provisions were obviously at odds with one another. Article 18 (10) shifted the responsibility for complying with the general conduct of business obligations to the (second) investment firm that receives an instruction, inter alia, to execute clients' orders through the medium of another investment firm, whereas Article 19 (1) placed the best execution obligation with the (first) investment firm that received the order directly from the client. Moreover, as an element of the general conduct of business obligations Article 18 (7) already required the investment firm to establish a documentary record of an agreement between the firm and the client, whereas recital 26 seemed to imply that when it comes to the execution of a client's order a contractual relationship only exists between the client and the first firm.

The final version of the MiFID did away with both inconsistencies. Article 20 (3) has broadened the responsibilities of the (second) investment firm that receives an instruction to execute a client's order by declaring that said firm remains responsible for concluding the service or transaction 'in accordance with the relevant provisions of this Title', i.e. Articles 5 through 35. In line with that, when detailing the best execution requirements, Article 21 (1) now addresses investment firms 'when executing orders', but refrains from also imposing the best execution obligation on an investment firm that provides the execution of clients' orders through another investment firm. Moreover, recital 33 now simply states that the best execution obligation 'should apply to the firm which owes contractual or agency obligations to the client'. The former reference to another intermediary actually carrying out the client's order is missing.

Taken together, the various minor deviations from the Commission's Proposal resulted in a comprehensive new concept for regulating Article 20-situations, i.e. the provision of the services upon instructions received through the medium of another investment firm.

3. Article 20 as a Novel Piercing of the Veil-Approach

The concept underlying Article 20 and, more generally, the conduct of business rules is a securities regulation-kind of piercing of the veil. For the purpose of the conduct of business rules, the investment firm that is deemed to provide the investment service to the client is the one that ultimately concludes the service or transaction. Several important consequences follow from this piercing of the veil-concept:

(i) Firstly, since the second investment firm provides the investment service to the client, the second firm is subject to the obligations under Articles 19 ff. In other words, it is the second firm that, in principle, has to comply with the conduct of business obligations. Consequently, Article 20 (3) holds that the second firm is 'responsible for concluding the service or transaction, ..., in accordance with the relevant provisions of this Title', i.e. with the relevant provisions in Articles 19 to 24.

(ii) Secondly, Article 20 (1) provides for an exception with respect to the obligation under Article 19 (4) to recommend suitable services and/or instruments when providing investment advice or portfolio management, and under Article 19 (5) to issue a warning if the client is envisaging inappropriate services and/or instruments. In order to be able to comply with these obligations, the firm has to obtain the necessary information from the client; a requirement explicitly stipulated in Article 19 (4) and (5). However, in Article 20-situations, the firm does not have to ask the client itself. Instead, because of Article 20 (1) the firm may rely on the pertinent information transmitted by the (first) firm that the client did instruct that the service in question be performed.

(iii) Thirdly, in Article 20-situations the investment firms involved provide not one, but two investment services. The (first) firm directly instructed by the client is receiving and transmitting an order in the sense of Annex 1 Section A (1) of the MiFID, whereas the (second) firm that receives the instruction transmitted by the first firm executes an order on behalf of a client in the sense of Annex 1 Section A (2). Hence, the best execution obligations under Article 21 do not (directly) apply to the first firm and, in particular, to its choice of the second firm, but only to the second firm. Still, groundless differences in the level of investor protection will be avoided if similar requirements to the ones contained in Article 21 are imposed on the first firm as well; Article 19 (1) serves as the pertinent legal basis.

4. CESR's Partial (?) Refutation of the Piercing of the Veil-Approach

The third implication of the piercing of the veil-approach just described, namely the existence of the second investment firm's best execution obligation towards the ultimate client, has very recently been rejected by CESR. Partly in response to the preceding interpretation of Article 20, CESR insists that if a firm executes orders on behalf of a portfolio manager or on behalf of an investment firm receiving and transmitting client orders, that (second) firm is not under a best execution obligation towards the ultimate client.[22] However, in order to protect the ultimate client from being deprived of any protection by a best execution requirement, CESR maintains that, on the basis of the general clause in Article 19 (1), the first firm, e.g. a firm that receives and transmits client orders, is subject to comparable best execution obligations to those provided for by Article 21.[23]

The only argument brought forward by CESR in support of its position is a reference to the Directive's aforementioned Recital 33 according to which the best execution obligation 'should apply to the firm which owes contractual or agency obligations to the client'. Put differently, since as a rule contractual or agency obligations do not exist between the ultimate client and the second firm, best execution obligations do not exist between the two parties either.

However, this argument is not at all convincing. Firstly, according to CESR's interpretation, the best execution obligation is dependent on contractual or agency structures even though the said obligation forms part of regulatory law. Secondly, on a related note, in general, the conduct of business obligations contained in Articles 19 ff are not conceived as a dependent variable with respect to contract law but, quite on the contrary, as rules that determine the minimum content of those contracts to be concluded between a client and an investment firm. Thirdly, CESR's line of reasoning completely ignores the larger setting of the problem, namely the existence of Article 20 and its ramifications. Since the existence of a best execution obligation between the second firm and the ultimate client is a mere consequence of the piercing of the veil-concept enshrined in Article 20, one cannot just confine oneself to denying the existence of such an obligation, but one has to offer an alternative explanation for Article 20 – something, CESR completely fails to do.

[22] CESR 'Technical Advice on Possible Implementing Measures of the Directive 2004/39/EC on Markets in Financial Instruments – First Set of Mandates where the deadline was extended and Second Set of Mandates' (April 2005) CESR/05-290, 36 ff.

[23] CESR (n 22) 36 ff.

5. Problematic Implications of the Piercing of the Veil-Approach

The piercing of the veil-concept underlying Article 19 to 24 is fraught with some problems that are, at best, difficult to solve. To name but three:

(1) The application of Article 19 (3) and (8) to the (second) investment firm.

(i) As already discussed above, Article 19 (3) obliges an investment firm to provide the client with information of a more general nature at least once, namely 'in good time' before the commencement of the provision of an investment service.[24] Article 20 does not exempt the second firm from this obligation. In particular, it does not allow the second firm to rely on information provided under Article 19 (3) to the client by the first firm. This is easily understandable since Article 19 (3) requires, inter alia, the supply of information on the firm and its services.

However, this reading of Article 20 only prevents the second firm from arguing that compliance with the requirements under Article 19 (3) is already achieved by supplying information on the first firm to the client. The second firm is not prohibited from complying with the information requirement by employing the first firm as an agent.

(ii) With respect to the reporting requirements under Article 19 (8), the arguments just described apply *mutatis mutandis*.

(2) The application of Article 19 (7) to the (second) investment firm.

(i) As already also discussed, the obligation under Article 19 (7) of the MiFID to establish a documentary record implicitly stipulates that investment firms are to provide any core investment service on a contractual basis.[25] With respect to Article 20-situations, one may want to question whether such an obligation can also exist with regard to the provision of investment services by the second firm, i.e. the firm that, for example, executes an order to buy or sell securities on behalf of a retail client on the basis of an instruction received through the medium of another investment firm. In particular, the application to these situations would lead to serious problems if for the purpose of introducing level 2 provisions the Commission decided to adopt CESR's Technical Advice regarding the minimum contents of the client records[26] which, in turn, closely follows the CESR investor protection standards published in April 2002.

(ii) In the present context, the following requirements suggested by CESR are of particular importance:

- the retail agreement between the firm and the client must be in a durable medium;
- the client's consent to the terms of the agreement must be evidenced by a signature or an equivalent alternate mechanism;

[24] See supra Section C.II.1..

[25] See supra Section C.I..

[26] See CESR (n 10) 61 ff.

- in good time prior to providing the envisaged investment service the firm must provide the client with the terms of the agreement in a durable medium;
- the firm must obtain the formal evidence of the client's consent to the agreement;
- immediately after the signing, the firm must provide a copy of the agreement to the client.

Exceptions are only available with respect to the 'prior to the provision of services' requirement. The firm may provide the terms of the agreement or obtain evidence of the retail client's consent[27] immediately after starting to provide a relevant service if it is provided on the client's request using a means of communication which does not enable the firm to comply with these obligations in good time prior to the provision of the service.

In Article 20-situations, the second firm could comply with these requirements, at least theoretically, if the exception were to apply. Indeed, receiving the instruction to provide a service on behalf of a retail client through the medium of another firm is probably a prime example for situations in which the firm cannot act in good time prior to the provision of the service. However, even given the applicability of the exception, the second firm will still have to comply with the requirements immediately after starting to provide the service. Having been given an order to buy or sell financial instruments, the firm has to provide the client with an agreement in durable medium, even after the execution of the order. This could either be achieved through the medium of the first firm that would provide the client with the agreement, thereby acting as a two-way medium. The alternative solution, namely sending the agreement in durable medium directly to the client, would only be feasible at all if the second firm were to receive not only the client's name, but his address as well. Even more onerous will be the requirement to obtain the client's signature on the agreement or other client's evidence of consent. One may wonder how many clients will be willing, e.g., to sign an agreement and send it back – either through the first firm or directly to the second firm – once the service has been performed in accordance with their instructions. Finally, the requirement to provide the client with a copy immediately after signing would be as burdensome as senseless, since the client will be already in possession of a signed copy of the agreement.

(iii) There are at least two possible strategies for dealing with these problems. The first one would be to dispute that the legal basis for such level 2 legislation, namely Article 19 (7) and (10) of the MiFID, covers the detailed requirements suggested by CESR. At any rate, one may add, CESR did go beyond the mandate

[27] The firm may lack only evidence of the client's consent not the consent itself before starting to provide the service. Insofar, the wording of paragraph 2 is misleading. Despite the opening reading 'By derogation from paragraph 1, the investment firm may ... obtain the consent of the retail client', the derogation only applies to the situation that the firm cannot obtain evidence of the client's consent in good time as evidenced by the second part of paragraph 2 'if ... a means of communication ... does not enable ... the evidence of consent of the client in accordance with paragraph 1'.

given by the Commission in providing far too detailed level 2 advice.[28] Indeed, the requirement that the retail client agreement must not only be in a durable medium, but also signed (at least?) by the client seems to lack any legal basis in the Directive. The obligation under Article 19 (7) to establish a documentary record cannot be construed as an implicit restriction on the formation of the contract. Article 19 (7) only requires that those documents be put on record that the parties have agreed upon, including the one setting out the respective rights and duties. This is not equivalent to prescribing that a contract has to be in durable medium, and that the client must sign it or provide evidence of consent by an equivalent alternative mechanism. The parties may very well agree on the contents of a document without providing evidence of consent in any tangible form.

The fundamental approach would be to deny that Article 19 (7) also applies to an investment firm that receives an instruction to perform a service through the medium of another investment firm. However, it is rather difficult to substantiate the claim that the provision is not applicable to the second firm that provides the investment service, for example, executing an order on behalf of a retail client.

To begin with, Recital 33, as already mentioned, states that the best execution obligation 'should apply to the firm which owes contractual or agency obligations to the client'. Hence, since the best execution obligation applies to the (second) investment firm[29] there has be a contractual (or agency) relationship between the firm and the client.

Furthermore, the only 'snag' to be found for excluding Article 19 (7) is Article 20 (3). Since the investment firm, which receives the client's instructions or orders through the medium of another investment firm, remains 'responsible for concluding the service or transaction, …, in accordance with the relevant provisions of this Title', the exclusion of Article 19 (7) as a relevant provision seems to offer an easy way out. However, this line of reasoning is fundamentally flawed. Take, for example, the execution of an order transmitted through another firm to buy or sell a financial instrument on a retail client's behalf. The phrase 'shall remain responsible for concluding the service or transaction' refers to the sale that the firm – in order to comply with the retail client's instruction – undertakes, e.g., on the stock market, not the provision of the service to the retail client. Accordingly, the 'relevant provisions of this Title' referred to in Article 20 (3) are only those dealing with the execution of the order, namely Article 21 (best execution) and Article 22 (client order handling rules).

The upshot is that even Article 20 (3) cannot serve as an argument against the application of Article 19 (7) to a firm that receives an instruction to perform a service through the medium of another investment firm.

(3) The application of Article 21 (3) to (5) to the (second) firm.

[28] The Comments of the Zentraler Kreditausschuss (<http://www.zentraler-kreditausschuss.de>) on the CESR 'Advice on Possible Implementing Measures of the Directive 2004/39/EC on Markets in Financial Instruments, Part 1' 34 ff elaborates this criticism.

[29] As to CESR's contrary position, see supra Section C.III.4..

The provision on the best execution of clients' orders just mentioned requires the firm, inter alia, to obtain its clients' prior consent to its execution policy (Article 21 (3)), to notify clients of any material changes to its order execution arrangements or execution policy (Article 21 (4)), and to be able to demonstrate to its clients, at their request, that the firm has executed their orders in accordance with its execution policy (Article 21 (5)).

Now, if the obligation under Article 21 (3) to obtain the prior consent of the client to the firms execution policy were to apply to Article 20-situations, the transmission of clients' orders to a second firm for execution would necessitate complicated structures and additional burdensome paperwork. The firm that executes a client's order could only obtain the prior consent if the first firm receiving and transmitting the order would act as the agent of the second firm in obtaining the prior consent. If the firm, at the time of receiving the order, may transmit the order to one of several other investment firms for execution, the firm would have to act as an agent for each of these firms. As a result, clients will be hit by a deluge of paperwork, i.e. the written execution policies of other investment firms, and, furthermore, firms will not be able to transmit orders received by telephone to another investment firm. Thus, on balance, Article 21 (3) – and, consequently, also (4) – should not be counted among 'the relevant provisions of the Title' under Article 20 (3).

The situation is somewhat different with respect to the firm's obligation to demonstrate that the order has been executed in accordance with its execution policy. Admittedly, the application of Article 21 (5) to Article 20-situation will place an additional burden on investment firms. On the other hand, the burden would be the same if a firm did not receive the orders through the medium of another investment firm, but clients were to place their orders directly with the firm.

D. Implications for the (German) Law of Contract Relating to Securities Transactions

I. The Agreement to Provide Investment Advice

The provision of investment advice is always based on a contract between the firm and its client. This follows from the requirement under Article 19 (7) that the contract be put on record.[30] As a consequence, Member States have to provide for rules according to which the provision of investment advice results in the formation of a contract. However, Paragraph 7 does not require a separate consultancy agreement; the obligations with respect to the provision of investment advice may only be part of a broader agreement.

[30] See supra C.I..

As already mentioned, German law recognises the existence of a contract if an investor approaches an investment firm for advice on how to invest an amount of money, or if, vice versa, an employee of a bank approaches a client to that effect. The Federal High Court of Justice holds that, given these circumstances, the parties tacitly enter into a contract.[31]

In future, courts will have to relax the preconditions for the formation of a consultancy agreement even further. According to Article 4 (1) (4) of the MiFID, investment advice is the provision of personal recommendations to a client, either at the latter's request or on the investment firm's initiative. In turn, a personal recommendation, as defined by CESR's Draft Technical Advice, is the provision of any investment information 'that is held out, either explicitly or implicitly, to the recipient as being suited to, or based on a consideration of, his personal circumstances'.[32] Contrary to the rules established by the Federal High Court, a firm provides investment advice even if, for example, the personal recommendation is not triggered by the fact that the client has invested certain funds with the firm.[33]

II. The Obligation to Provide Information on Specific Risks Associated with the Individual Product

Under Article 19 (3) to (5), firms are free from any obligation to provide information on specific risks associated with an individual product to their customers.[34]

By contrast, German law recognises an obligation to furnish clients with such information. The Federal High Court of Justice developed the pertinent rule in its landmark 'Bond decision', named after the Australian entrepreneur Alan Bond: The Bond decision held that if a firm enters into a (tacitly concluded) consultancy agreement it falls under the dual obligation (i) to select suitable financial instruments; and (ii) to provide the client with information on the financial instrument(s) envisaged, including generic information with respect to this class of instruments (e.g., the state of the economy, and/or the state of the stock market), and specific risks associated with individual instruments.[35]

[31] Bundesgerichtshof, XI ZR 12/93, Wertpapiermitteilungen 1993 1455, 1456.

[32] CESR (n 9) 15 ff Box 1 (1).

[33] One may wonder, though, how firms will comply with the obligation under Article 19 (7) to establish a documentary record including the contract. In particular, if firms provide investment advice not within a personal (one-on-one) relationship, they will not be in a position to know the persons that tacitly accepted to enter into a contract with the bank.

[34] See supra C.II.3..

[35] Bundesgerichtshof (n 31) 1456.

According to a frequently used formula, investment firms have to furnish all the information required to depict a precise earnings-risk-profile of the security in question.[36]

The requirement that in providing investment advice the firm must also cover the specific risks associated with individual financial instruments exceeds the conduct of business obligations under Article 19 (3) and (4). After implementation of the Directive, German courts will have to abandon this particular obligation, at least with respect to investment firms offering cross-border investment advice; i.e. when an investment firm established in another Member State provides investment advice directly to German clients. This follows clearly from Article 31 (1): to secure the freedom of investment firms to provide investment services and activities 'Member States shall not impose any additional requirement on … an investment firm or credit institution with respect to the matters covered by this Directive'. This prohibition would be clearly violated if national rules established stricter requirements for the provision of investment advice; irrespective of whether the stricter requirements follow from contract law or securities regulations.

This result also holds when the German branch of an investment firm in another Member State provides investment advice. Admittedly, Article 32 (1) provides host Member States with some regulatory leeway regarding branches established on their territory. They 'shall not impose any additional requirements save those allowed under Paragraph 7, on the organisation and operation of the branch in respect to the matters covered by the Directive'. But Paragraph 7 tightly restricts the scope of additional requirements. According to it 'the competent authority of the Member State in which the branch is located shall assume responsibility for ensuring that the services provided by the branch within its territory comply with the obligations laid down in Articles 19, 21, 22 … and in measures adopted pursuant thereto', and subparagraph 2 adds that said competent authority shall have the right 'to request such changes as are strictly needed to enable the competent authority to enforce the obligations under Articles 19, 21, 22 … and measures adopted pursuant thereto with respect to the services and/or activities provided by the branch within its territory'. Since Paragraph 7, when mentioning 'measures adopted pursuant to Article 19, 21, 22 …', refers to the implementing measures adopted by the Commission pursuant to Article 19 (10) ff, the only additional requirements that host Member States may impose on branches of foreign investment firms under Paragraph 7 are in the form of a 'request [for] such changes as are strictly needed to enable the competent authority to enforce the obligations under Article 19, 21, 22 …'. In other words, Article 32 provides for maximum harmonization, even with respect to the substantive contents of the conduct of business rules that apply to branches.[37] Recital 32 obviously corrobo-

[36] J Ekkenga (n 4) note 177.

[37] In the same sense B Maurenbrecher (n 2) 24 ff; contrary CESR's first consultation paper, see CESR 'Advice on Possible Implementing Measures of the Directive 2004/39/EC on Mar-

cont. …

rates this understanding of Article 32: 'By way of derogation from the principle of home country authorisation, supervision and enforcement of the operation of branches, it is appropriate for the competent authority of the host Member State to assume responsibility for enforcing certain obligations specified in this Directive in relation to business conducted through a branch within the territory where the branch is located since that authority is closest to the branch, and is better placed to detect and intervene in respect of infringements of rules governing the operations of the branch'. From this recital clearly follows the concept underlying Article 32 (1) and (7). The investment firm's home Member State is solely responsible for the implementation of the conduct of business rules contained in the Directive and in additional implementing measures, whereas the host Member State of a foreign branch is responsible for the supervision of the branch and the enforcement of the conduct of business obligations promulgated by the home Member State.[38] Thus, from the host Member State's point of view, Article 32 (1) and (7) provide for maximum harmonization of the conduct of business rules.

As a consequence, Articles 31 and 32 bar German courts from imposing an obligation on investment firms from other Member States – regardless of whether the firm acts cross-border or through a German branch – to furnish clients with information on specific risks associated with an individual product. German courts are only free to uphold such an obligation with respect to German investment firms if the client specifically asks for this kind of information. One may doubt, however, whether the courts really should establish different levels of investor protection depending on the home country of the investment firm.

III. The Client's Contract with a Firm that Receives Orders Through the Medium of Another Investment Firm

Investment firms that receive clients' orders through the medium of another investment firm shall – as a consequence of Article 19 (7) – provide their (order execution) service to the client on a contractual basis.[39] Member States will have to adapt their laws to the effect that the acceptance of the transmission of a client's instruction – not only the subsequent execution of the client's order – brings about the formation of a contract with the client.

kets in Financial Instruments – Consultation Paper' (June 2004) CESR/04-261b, 55 with respect to Article 19 (3). Note, however, that said sentence is missing in the final document, see CESR (n 10) 55.

[38] However, if a Member State decides to impose additional conduct of business obligations on the investment firms for which he acts as home Member State the competent authority of a host Member State is probably not competent to supervise and to enforce the compliance of a branch with these additional requirements.

[39] Supra C.III.5.(2).

As an aside, this rule could also serve to implement the requirement under Article 21 (5), according to which firms shall 'be able to demonstrate to their clients, at their request, that they have executed their orders in accordance with the firm's execution policy'. It would be utterly pointless to stipulate this requirement if firms were not under a contractual obligation to their clients to furnish the pertinent documents at their clients' request.

Still, while the Member States have to introduce provisions complying with the requirements contained in the Directive, investment firms will probably prefer not to enter into Article 20-situations. Under German law, for example, this is indeed feasible. Investment firms selling or buying financial instruments on behalf of their retail clients will normally proceed on the basis of a contract concluded on a commission basis ('*Kommissionsvertrag*'). At present, a firm that decides not to execute the order itself – mostly because the firm is not admitted to trading on the relevant stock exchange – but to transmit an order to a second firm for execution, will proceed by employing the second firm as a '*Zwischenkommissionär*'.[40] However, Section 400 of the German Commercial Code provides for a second solution. Under Section 400 a commission agent performs the commission in that 'he himself delivers as seller the goods which he is to buy or accepts as buyer the goods which he is to sell' ('*Selbsteintritt des Kommissionärs*'). If a firm proceeds under Section 400 there will be no transmission of clients' orders to a second firm, and, as a consequence, no Article 20-situation, but an Article 21 (3) (3)-situation, i.e. the execution of a client's order outside a regulated market or multilateral trading facility (MTF). If German banks were to opt for this solution they would return to the situation that existed in Germany until the mid-1990s. In 1994, the German banking sector decided to abandon the Section 400-solution – in order to comply with new requirements that resulted from the implementation of the Investment Services Directive.[41]

E. Concluding Remarks

The conduct of business rules contained in Articles 19-24 of the new Directive on markets in financial instruments will lead to a major shift of balance in the field of banking law in Germany and other Continental countries. As the preceding analysis has shown, the provisions of the MiFID determine the contents of the legal relationship between the client and the investment firm to a large degree. To that extent, contract law will be reduced to implement the conduct of business obligation in the contractual relationship between the firm and its client, and, at the same time, be bared to shape that relationship in accordance with its own principles and values. While this development will not result in a total eclipse of contract law at least, we will witness a partial eclipse.

[40] See supra text and (n 19) ff.

[41] As to this, see e.g. HP Schwintowski and FA Schäfer (n 4) 691 ff and notes 22 ff.

Conflicts of Interest in Investment Services: The Price and Uncertain Impact of MiFID's Regulatory Framework

LUCA ENRIQUES

The Markets in Financial Instruments Directive (MiFID) lays down organizational and conduct-of-business rules on conflicts of interest of investment firms and banks providing investment services. It is easy to predict that, as a consequence of the home country control principle (investments firms and banks will have to comply with their own home country rules wherever they conduct their business within the EU), the MiFID will lead to *de facto* complete harmonisation of the rules on conflicts of interest: Member States will refrain from enacting further rules on conflicts of interest so as to avoid to put domestic firms at a competitive disadvantage vis-à-vis EC firms. This chapter inquires into this prospective uniformity, making two points. First, the uniformity will be more apparent than real, because in the absence of rules preventing a firm from acting in the presence of a conflict of interest and/or of rules dispensing it from the general fairness and honesty obligations where certain procedural or disclosure rules are complied with, there will be ample scope for ex post review of the firm's behaviour on the basis of such general obligations. It will be impossible, however, to ensure uniform EU-wide interpretation of such a fuzzy concept as 'fairness'. The second point is that the uniform rules on conflicts of interests will lower the degree of investor protection in at least some Member States (namely, Italy) where regulation would be most needed in light of the lower degree of competition in the financial services industry, the lower level of investor education, and the unimpressive record of the financial services authority. The paper concludes that while the lack of real harmonisation is certainly an unintended result of MiFID, the fact that in some Member States investor protection may decrease due to the harmonisation process is best grasped in light of the objectives of EC securities regulation. Under the EC Treaty, the main purpose of harmonisation of financial services has traditionally been market integration. Investor protection is just an instrumental end, something to be pursued in order to attain market integration. But the two objectives may well conflict, and when they do, market integration easily prevails. Not only is market integration the real purpose of harmonisation under the Treaty, it is also the definite objective of the interest groups that favour EC regulation in this area, i.e. continental players from the main financial centres, whose quest for a single rulebook is easy to understand. Local players, in 'good' as well as in 'bad' jurisdictions, are obviously, if not myopically, happy with the more lenient rules to which the various participants agree at the EC level. Leniency inevitably follows from the fact that investors' needs differ from country to country and that the securities industry is the only effective lobby. The final outcome is a diminution of legal protection for retail investors in 'bad' jurisdictions – who are precisely those who most need such protection.

A. Introduction
B. Why Specific Rules on Conflicts of Interest?
C. The MiFID and Prospective Level 2 Rules on Conflicts of Interest
D. Too Much Scope for 'Honesty and Fair Dealing' to Achieve Uniformity?
E. Same Rules for Different Investor Protection Needs: A Wise Choice?
F. Conclusions

A. Introduction

The Markets in Financial Instruments Directive[1] (MiFID) lays down organizational and conduct of business rules on conflicts of interest of investment firms and banks (hereinafter: firms) (Articles 13 (3) and 18), delegates authority to the Commission to implement them with level 2 measures under the Lamfalussy method[2] (Articles 13 (10) and 18 (3)), and more generally requires firms providing investment services to 'act honestly, fairly and professionally in accordance with the best interests of clients' (Article 19 (1)).

It is unclear whether the MiFID is a maximum or minimum harmonisation directive,[3] but it is easy to see that the Directive will lead to complete harmonisation, whether *de jure* or *de facto*, in that Member States will refrain from enacting further rules on conflicts of interest. In fact, firms and their associations, which have already lobbied CESR against advising the Commission to explicitly grant Member States the power to issue further rules,[4] will find it easy to convince national regulators that imposing further rules on domestic firms would increase their regulatory burden and so put them at a disadvantage with respect to com-

[1] Directive 2004/39/EC of the European Parliament and of the Council of 21 April 2004 on markets in financial instruments amending Council Directives 85/611/EEC and 93/6/EEC and Directive 2000/12/EC of the European Parliament and of the Council and repealing Council Directive 93/22/EEC, OJ L145 04.30.2004 1-44 (the MiFID).

[2] For a detailed description of the Lamfalussy method see e.g. E Ferran *Building an EU Securities Market* (Cambridge University Press 2004) 61-84.

[3] See M Tison 'Financial Market Integration in the Post-FSAP Era. In Search of Overall Conceptual Consistency in the Regulatory Framework' in this volume 445-466. The draft level 2 measure dealing with conflicts of interest contains a provision that, if approved, would greatly restrict Member States' ability to impose additional requirements. See Article 4 of Draft Commission Directive implementing Directive 2004/39/EC of the European Parliament and of the Council as regards organizational requirements and operating conditions for investment firms, and defined terms for the purposes of that Directive (hereinafter: Draft Commission Directive).

[4] See FBE 'Response to Consultation Paper on CESR's Advice on Possible Implementing Measures of the Directive 2004/39/EC on Markets in Financial Instruments' (June 2004) CESR/04-261b, 2 and 16; Italian Banking Association (ABI) 'Comments on CESR's Call for Evidence on the Second Set of Mandates on Level 2 Measures of the Directive in the Markets of Financial Instruments' (July 2004) 1 (both documents are available at <http://www.cesr-eu.org>).

petitors in other countries. All the more so, in light of MiFID's choice to extend mutual recognition to rules on conflicts of interest and conduct of business, which is one of the main innovations of the new Directive:[5] Article 31 provides that 'Member States shall ensure that any investment firm authorised and supervised by the competent authorities of another Member State in accordance with this Directive, and in respect of credit institutions in accordance with Directive 2000/12/EC, may freely perform investment services and/or activities as well as ancillary services within their territories, provided that such services and activities are covered by its authorisation', and, even more to the point, that 'Member States shall not impose any additional requirements on such an investment firm or credit institution in respect of the matters covered by this Directive'.[6] In other words, a Member State imposing stricter rules on conflicts of interest would only be able to enforce them on domestic firms. Clearly, domestic firms and their associations would lobby successfully against any such stricter rules, as putting them at a competitive disadvantage vis-à-vis EC firms.

In short, under the MiFID framework a uniform set of rules on conflicts of interest will apply, if not *de jure* then *de facto*. This chapter inquires into this prospective uniformity, making two points. First, the uniformity will be more apparent than real, because in the absence of rules preventing a firm from acting in the presence of a conflict of interest and/or of rules dispensing it from the general fairness and honesty obligations under Article 19 (1) where certain procedural or disclosure rules are complied with, there will be ample scope for ex post review of the firm's behaviour on the basis of such general obligations. It will be impossible, however, to ensure uniform EU-wide interpretation of such a fuzzy concept as 'fairness'. The second point is that the uniform rules on conflicts of interests will be inadequate to protect investors in at least some Member States – Italy in particular.

The chapter proceeds as follows. Section B briefly outlines the rationale for specific rules dealing with conflicts of interest in the provision of investment services. Section C describes the MiFID regulatory framework. Section D substantiates the first of the two points, showing that the MiFID's 'freedom with disclo-

[5] Compare Article 11 (2), Council Directive 93/22/EEC of 10 May 1993 on investment services in the securities field, OJ L141 06.11.1993 27-46 ('implementation [of rules of conduct] and the supervision of compliance with them shall remain the responsibility of the Member State in which a service is provided') with Article 31 of the MiFID (as reproduced infra, text preceding (n 6)).

[6] See also Article 32 (providing a similar regime with respect to establishment of branches). The only exception to the home country rule is in Article 32 (7), which provides that, in the case of establishment of a branch, '[t]he competent authority of the Member State in which the branch is located shall assume responsibility for ensuring that the services provided by the branch within its territory comply with the obligations laid down in Articles 19, 21, 22, 25, 27 and 28 and in measures adopted pursuant thereto'. Interestingly, this implies that the host country is responsible for the supervision of branches' compliance with the duty of honesty and fair dealing, which, as already hinted, also applies in conflict-of-interest situations.

sure' approach leaves a good deal of scope for ex post evaluation of firms' conduct under the fairness standard, and Section E substantiates the second point, by specifying how the framework may prove inadequate to protect Italian retail investors. Section F concludes.

B. Why Specific Rules on Conflicts of Interest?

To assess the new EC regulatory framework for firms' conflicts of interest, let us first ask why such a framework is needed. The starting point is that under the general contract laws of all EU Member States, a firm that pursues its own interest to the detriment of its clients' interests breaches its contractual or legal obligations and is therefore liable for damages and, in some jurisdictions, to disgorge any profit made in this way. In other words, abuses in conflict-of-interest situations are illegal everywhere. The point is whether ex post judicial reaction is enough to discourage such violations.

From an economic perspective there is an abundant literature to the effect that competition, reputational concerns, self-help by investors, and regulatory oversight combine to make conflicts of interest less of a problem.[7]

The answer to our question thus depends on how effective these market and institutional features are in keeping firms from abusing their power in conflict-of-interest situations. In general terms, however, following Pistor and Xu's incomplete law theory,[8] one may argue that conflict of interest is a good candidate for regulation by specific rules and enforcement not only by the courts but also by a supervisory agency.

First of all, the contract law standards on which a client's suit would be based in the absence of specific rules are too broad and too vague to let a prospective plaintiff feel confident that an abuse will be found to be such by the court. Second, individual claims will often be too small to make it worthwhile to bring suit. Both these factors may lead to underenforcement. Finally, the possible externalities in this area are very substantial indeed: misconduct by firms can undermine investors' trust in financial intermediaries in general.

[7] See, e.g., JAC Santos 'Commercial Banks in the Securities Business: A Review' (BIS wp No. 56/1998 <http://www.bis.org/publ/work56.htm>, June 1998) 10-12.

[8] See K Pistor and C Xu 'Incomplete Law' (2003) 35 NY U J Int'l L & Pol 931; K Pistor and C Xu 'Enforcement Failure under Incomplete Law: Theory and Evidence from Financial Market Regulation' unpublished manuscript (December 2004).

C. The MiFID and Prospective Level 2 Rules on Conflicts of Interest

The MiFID and its implementing measures will introduce a seemingly sweeping set of rules on conflicts of interest in the provision of investment services. As argued above, *de facto*, if not *de jure,* these rules are bound to institute a uniform regulatory framework for EU firms, to which no additional regulation by any Member State is plausible. This Section describes the rules as laid down in the Directive and in the Draft Commission Directive. First, let me remind the reader that the MiFID rules on conflicts of interest apply both to investment firms and banks (Article 1 (2)), although they explicitly refer to investment firms only.

The MiFID level 1 regulatory framework rests on four pillars: (i) organizational duties, (ii) the duty to identify conflicts of interest, (iii) the duty to disclose conflicts, unless organizational duties are sufficient to prevent harm to investors' interests, and (iv) a general duty of honesty and fairness. The content of these duties is to be specified in level 2 measures, by which the Commission may also impose further obligations.

Organization. Article 13 (3) provides that '[a]n investment firm shall maintain and operate effective organisational and administrative arrangements with a view to taking all reasonable steps designed to prevent conflicts of interest as defined in Article 18 from adversely affecting the interests of its clients'. In other words, the Directive requires firms to organize their operations in such a way as to neutralize the possible adverse impact of conflicts of interest on clients.

Identification of conflicts. Article 18 (1) spells out the duty to identify conflicts of interest: 'Member States shall require investment firms to take all reasonable steps to identify conflicts of interest between themselves, including their managers, employees and tied agents, or any person directly or indirectly linked to them by control and their clients or between one client and another that arise in the course of providing any investment and ancillary services, or combinations thereof'. Essentially, the Directive requires firms to have a 'redflag' system that detects conflicts of interest promptly and so ensures that no harm to the clients will follow.

Disclosure. Article 18 (2) provides that '[w]here organisational or administrative arrangements made by the investment firm in accordance with Article 13 (3) to manage conflicts of interest are not sufficient to ensure, with reasonable confidence, that risks of damage to client interests will be prevented, the investment firm shall *clearly* disclose the *general* nature and/or *sources* of conflicts of interest to the client *before undertaking business on its behalf*'.[9]

As this wording makes clear, the disclosure obligation is conditional upon the firm's judgment that the organisational and administrative arrangements in place cannot ensure the prevention of damage to clients. A bona fide judgment that those arrangements can prevent such risks, in turn, will imply no violation of the

[9] Emphasis added.

disclosure requirement, even if it turns out ex post that a client's interests actually have been damaged.

The disclosure must be 'clear' and include information about the 'general' nature and/or about the sources of the conflict. Yet, it is far from clear what is meant by disclosing the general nature 'and/or' the sources of a conflict of interest. The wording would seem to suggest *a contrariis* that there is no need to disclose the specific nature (i.e. content) and the extent of the conflict of interest.

Finally, disclosure has to be made before undertaking any business on behalf of the client. Clearly, this provision does not preclude 'once-and-for-all' disclosure of a given conflict of interest at the outset of the relationship with the client, especially considering that it is sufficient to disclose a conflict's 'general nature' and sources.

Honesty and fair dealing. Article 19 (1) imposes a broad and open-ended obligation upon firms: 'Member States shall require that, when providing investment services and/or, where appropriate, ancillary services to clients, an investment firm act *honestly*, *fairly* and professionally in accordance with the best interests of its clients'.[10]

Arguably, the requirement of honesty and fair dealing *always* applies, i.e. both where there is no conflict of interest situation and, *a fortiori*, where there is one. In other words, in this framework, it will never be enough for firms to comply with the specific conflict-of-interest rules of Articles 13 and 18 and their implementing measures. To fulfil their duties to their clients and to comply with existing rules, firms will always have to ensure that their clients are treated honestly, fairly, and professionally in accordance with their best interests. This implies that the greater the freedom to act granted by specific conflict-of-interest rules, the broader the relevance of general duties under Article 19 (1) as a guide to their behaviour whenever a conflict arises. Only once level 2 measures are implemented, of course, will it become clear how central these general duties will be for the treatment of conflicts of interest. We now therefore turn to level 2.

The level 2 measures. Article 13 (10) provides that '[i]n order to take account of technical developments on financial markets and to ensure the uniform application of paragraphs 2 to 9, the Commission shall adopt, in accordance with the procedure referred to in Article 64 (2), implementing measures which specify the concrete organisational requirements to be imposed on investment firms performing different investment services and/or activities and ancillary services or combinations thereof.' That is, the Directive delegates the Commission to adopt level 2 measures specifying the organizational requirements on firms also in order to 'prevent conflicts of interest ... from adversely affecting the interests of its clients'.

[10] Emphasis added.

Again '[i]n order to take account of technical developments on financial markets and to ensure uniform application of [Article 18,] paragraphs 1 and 2,' the Directive further mandates the Commission to issue level 2 measures to:

'(a) define the steps that investment firms might reasonably be expected to take to identify, *prevent*, *manage* and/or disclose conflicts of interest when providing various investment and ancillary services and combinations thereof;

(b) establish appropriate criteria for determining the types of conflict of interest whose existence may damage the interests of the clients or potential clients of the investment firm'.[11] (Article 18 (3)).

This mandate is very broad. The Commission may introduce further obligations in addition to those imposed at level 1, i.e., organizational, identification, and disclosure duties. The power to define steps to 'prevent' and 'manage' conflicts of interest, for instance, would allow the Commission to impose a duty to abstain should disclosure alone be insufficient, in the Directive's words, 'to ensure, with reasonable confidence, that risks of damage to client interests will be prevented.' As the British regulations of conflicts of interest recognize,[12] there can in fact be cases in which there is no way to manage a conflict of interest other than by declining to act on a client's behalf. However, as we shall see below, the Commission did not go so far as to suggest level 2 adoption of the duty to abstain as a last resort.

More generally, the Commission may impose whatever requirement it deems necessary to prevent and manage conflicts of interest, provided that it does not contradict specific level 1 rules.

With respect to disclosure, the Commission may clarify what the content must be and, depending also on the level of detail required, whether disclosure can be once-and-for-all or must be made for each given transaction. The Commission may also clarify which conflicts of interest may damage clients.

Finally, Article 19 (10), provides that, '[i]n order to ensure the necessary protection of investors and the uniform application of paragraphs 1 to 8, the Commission shall adopt, in accordance with the procedure referred to in Article 64 (2), implementing measures to ensure that investment firms comply with the principles set out therein when providing investment or ancillary services to their clients'. The Commission thus also has a general power to establish more specific content for the general duty to 'act honestly, fairly and professionally in accordance with the best interests of its clients'. Arguably, therefore, even if the regulatory powers under Article 18 (3) (a) were not as open-ended as they appear to be, there are no bounds to the Commission's discretionary power to make additional rules on conflicts of interest in order to enforce the principles of Article 19 (1).

[11] Emphasis added.

[12] FSA Handbook (2004) 'Conduct of Business' Ch. 7, 7.1.4E and 7.1.9G.

To conclude, the Commission's level 2 legislative power with respect to conflicts of interest is the broadest and could easily result in additional obligations for firms. It is impossible, therefore, to assess the new regulatory framework until the level 2 implementing measures have been finally adopted.

The Draft Commission Directive. Thus far, after two consultation papers[13] and one technical advice[14] from CESR, the Commission has issued one Proposal for a Commission Directive dealing with conflicts of interest.[15] Its contents may be described as follows.[16]

(i) *Organizational duties.* Article 22 of the Draft Commission Directive provides that Member States have to require 'investment firms to establish, implement and maintain an effective conflicts of interest policy set out in writing and appropriate to the size and organisation of the firm and the nature, scale and complexity of its business'. It also specifies that where 'the firm is a member of a group, the policy must also take into account any circumstances, of which the firm is or should be aware, which may give rise to a conflict of interest arising as a result of the structure and business activities of other members of the group'. The content of the conflicts policy is twofold: first, 'it must identify, with reference to the specific investment services and activities and ancillary services carried out by or on behalf of the investment firm, the circumstances which constitute or may give rise to a conflict of interest entailing a material risk of damage to the interests of one or more clients'. Second, 'it must specify procedures to be followed and measures to be adopted in order to manage such conflicts' (Article 22 (2)).

Further, the Draft Commission Directive identifies the purpose of the organizational policies adopted in order to manage conflicts of interests: they must be 'designed to ensure that relevant persons engaged in different business activities involving a conflict of interest ... carry on those activities at a level of independence appropriate to the size and activities of the investment firm, and to the degree of risk entailed to clients' (Article 22 (3)). It then lists five possible measures and procedures that investment firms are required to adopt *so long as* they are 'necessary and appropriate for the firm to ensure the requisite level of independence' (Article 22 (3)). These measures and procedures include Chinese walls (i.e. barriers preventing the exchange of information among different areas), the sepa-

[13] CESR 'Advice on Possible Implementing Measures of the Directive 2004/39/EC on Markets in Financial Instruments' (Consultation Paper June 2004); CESR 'Draft Technical Advice on Possible Implementing Measures of the Directive 2004/39/EC on Markets in Financial Instruments, 1st Set of Mandates' (Second Consultation Paper November 2004).

[14] CESR 'Technical Advice on Possible Implementing Measures of the Directive 2004/39/EC on Markets in Financial Instruments, 1st Set of Mandates' (January 2005) (hereinafter Technical Advice).

[15] See supra (n 3).

[16] Since this paper focuses on investment services, investment recommendations are beyond its scope and CESR's proposed rules regarding them will here not be dealt with.

ration of supervisory functions, measures relating to the remuneration of persons in areas whose profitability is linked to that of another area, measures against 'inappropriate influence' and procedures ensuring that the same person does not wear two hats in the same transaction or in separate transactions involving a conflict of interest. Article 22 (3), also specifies that '[i]f the adoption or the practice of one or more of those measures and procedures does not ensure the requisite level of independence, Member States shall require investment firms to adopt such alternative or additional measures and procedures as are necessary and appropriate for those purposes'.

The conflicts policy is to be disclosed to retail clients or potential retail clients in the form of 'a description, which may be provided in summary form'. Where the client so requests, further details of that policy should be provided to him or her in a durable medium.[17]

(ii) *Identification of conflicts.* In its Technical Advice CESR had proposed rules that would require firms to have a written conflicts policy in place and to ensure that the policy 'includes all reasonable steps to identify at least conflicts of interests arising' in certain situations and that 'these steps are effectively implemented'.[18] The relevant situations were described in general terms (e.g. situations in which the firm has incentives to favour one client over others or in which it stands to gain from 'volumes of business transacted').[19] CESR also proposed to require firms to pay 'special attention to at least' three areas of business, 'particularly where the firm or a person directly or indirectly linked by control to the firm performs a combination of two or more of them': proprietary trading, portfolio management, and 'corporate finance business, including underwriting and/or selling in an offering of securities and advising on mergers and acquisitions'.[20] Noticeably absent from this 'short list' were commercial banking activities.

The Draft Commission Directive follows CESR's advice with regard to the description of general situations involving conflicts of interest, but fails to require firms to pay any special attention to specific areas of business.[21]

[17] Article 30 (1) (h). 'Durable medium' means 'any instrument which enables a client to store information addressed personally to that client in a way accessible for future reference for a period of time adequate for the purposes of the information and which allows the unchanged reproduction of the information stored' (Article 2 (2), Draft Commission Directive). As the Technical Advice specified, '[d]urable media include in particular floppy discs, CD-ROMs, DVDs and the hard drive of the client's computer on which the communication is stored, but they do not include websites unless they fulfil the criteria contained in the definition of a durable medium'. Technical Advice (n 14) 9. Article 3 of the Draft Commission Directive specifies the conditions under which a website can be regarded as a durable medium.

[18] Technical Advice (n 14) 43.

[19] Technical Advice (n 14) 43-44.

[20] Technical Advice (n 14) 44.

[21] Article 21, Draft Commission Directive.

As already seen before, the conflicts of interest policy has to devise measures and procedures that allow the investment firm to identify the relevant conflicts of interest.

(iii) *Inducements.* According to CESR's Technical Advice, inducements should be permitted 'only if they can reasonably assist the investment firm in the provision of services to its clients and do not, and are not likely to, impair compliance with the duty [...] to act in the best interests of the client'.[22] Firms should 'take all reasonable steps to ensure that relevant persons do not offer or accept [prohibited] inducements'.[23]

The Draft Commission Directive regulates inducements in greater detailed.[24] It only allows for: (a) fees, commissions and non-monetary benefits paid or provided to or by the client or a person acting on his or her behalf; (b) fees, commissions and non-monetary benefits paid or provided to or by a third party or a person acting on behalf of a third party, where two conditions are satisfied: (i) 'the existence, nature and amount of the fee, commission or benefit, or, where the amount cannot be ascertained, the method of calculating that amount, must be clearly disclosed to the client, in a manner that is comprehensive, accurate and understandable, prior to the provision of the relevant investment or ancillary service;[25] (ii) the payment of the fee or commission, or the provision of the non-monetary benefit must enhance the quality of the relevant service to the client and not impair compliance with the firm's duty to act in the best interests of the client'.[26]

(iv) *Disclosure.* The Draft Commission Proposal adds very little to the level 1 framework with regard to disclosure. It just states that '[w]here, in case of a specific conflict of interest, an investment firm is not reasonably confident that the measures adopted under its general conflicts policy could prevent the risk of damage to its clients it shall, in accordance with the Directive, disclose the general nature or source of the conflict of interest'.[27] Disclosure has to be made 'in a durable medium and includes sufficient detail, taking into account the nature of the client, to enable that client to take an informed decision *with respect to the investment or ancillary service* in the context of which the conflict of interest arises'.[28]

[22] Technical Advice (n 14) 45.

[23] Technical Advice (n 14) 45.

[24] Article 26, Draft Commission Directive.

[25] For the purposes of point (b) (i), investment firms are to be allowed 'to disclose the essential terms of the commission arrangements in summary form', provided that they undertake 'to disclose further details at the request of the client' and provided that they honour that undertaking (Article 26, Draft Commission Directive).

[26] Article 26 (b) (ii).

[27] Article 22 (4), Draft Commission Directive.

[28] Article 22 (5), Draft Commission Directive (emphasis added).

No clear answer is given as to whether conflicts of interest may be disclosed once and for all at the outset of the contractual relationship (or, later on, when the conflict situation arises, again once and for all), or whether each single conflict of interest relating to any individual transaction or recommendation will require disclosure in writing. In general, one might argue that, in order to judge compliance with the MiFID's requirements on disclosure, a core issue will be the nature of the client, so there could be a requirement for more frequent disclosure to unsophisticated retail investors. However, more 'standard' conflicts of interest may well be disclosed once and for all even to retail clients, as is suggested by the reference to the *investment or ancillary service* rather than *transaction*. In any event, there is no bright-line rule on this point, so that compliance will have to be judged case-by-case ex post, depending on the nature of the recipient and the circumstances.

Where disclosure is once and for all, its content is necessarily generic and standardized. This means the stock of documents the client receives and signs when entering into an investment services contract will include one describing 'the general nature and/or sources' of all the conflicts of interest in which the firm finds or can find itself.

Finally, with respect to the general duty of honesty and fair dealing, the Draft Commission Directive provides no meaningful guideline on its contents with respect to conflict of interest situations.

D. Too Much Scope for 'Honesty and Fair Dealing' to Achieve Uniformity?

In sum, the regulation of conflicts of interest under the MiFID will rely on organizational arrangements to prevent, manage, and identify them, coupled, when necessary, with a disclosure obligation plausibly to be complied with once and for all for each conflicts situation, and on a very general duty of fairness and honesty under which supervisors and, at least in the majority of the Member States,[29] judges in liability suits brought by clients can conduct quite a broad review of the firm's behaviour with respect to conflicts of interest. Such light-touch ex ante regulation may lead to a much lower degree of uniformity than envisaged. The greater the freedom to act, the greater the scope for the operation of ex post fairness review by supervisory authorities and courts; and such a substantive review appears impossible to harmonise.

Clearly, this set of rules will leave firms with a good deal of freedom to act in conflict-of-interest situations. For one thing, information barriers, even when adopted, can be ineffective. The empirical evidence shows that Chinese walls do

[29] See M Tison (n 3) also for the argument that under the MiFID itself conduct of business rules should be enforceable in courts by clients or potential clients.

not prevent leaks of confidential information between the various units of an investment firm.[30] Second, Chinese walls only bar the flow of *confidential* information between departments. They serve no purpose with respect to conflicts of interest pertaining to facts already available to the public. In itself, however, public availability of information is no guarantee that the firm will not exploit the situation. It may well do so, counting on the client's ignorance or trust in the firm's integrity, which may well be misplaced.

In practice, even arrangements designed to ensure the independence of the various departments may turn out to be of little use to clients, if the firm's culture is conflict-prone. For example, it may be public knowledge that an investment bank is assisting a company in an IPO; and no matter how independent the people in the brokerage arm can be 'on paper', they may be tempted to stuff their clients' portfolios with those shares, if they think that this will be appreciated by the firm's top management.

Further, studies in behavioural economics have shown that freedom to act in conflict-of-interest situations, with or without disclosure, may damage the principal even where there is no bad faith on the part of the agent. One study shows that agents tend to be affected unconsciously, i.e. that they pursue their own interest in perfect good faith.[31]

Disclosure, which in any event the MiFID only requires when it is needed according to the discretionary judgement of the firm itself, may not be enough to prevent abuses. Another study shows that disclosure of conflicts of interest can lead to more aggressive and conflicted behaviour on the part of the self-interested agent and to enhanced (but misplaced) trust by principals, especially the less sophisticated ones.[32] Hence, disclosure in itself may even prove to be counterproductive for clients' interests.

To conclude, the rules aimed at preventing and managing conflicts of interest are drafted in such a way as to leave plenty of room for action by the conflicted firm, and hence, alas, for unfair and dishonest behaviour. As a consequence, there is also ample scope for ex post fairness review of firms' behaviour by supervisory authorities and judges.[33]

[30] See HN Seyhun 'Conflicts of Interests in Securities Firms and Chinese Walls' mimeo, (December 2002) (providing empirical evidence of the ineffectiveness of Chinese walls in the U.S.); A Lehar and O Randl 'Chinese Walls in German Banks' (SSRN wp <http://www.ssrn.com/abstract_id=424010>, 2003) (same with respect to Germany).

[31] See DA Moore et al 'Conflict of Interest and the Unconscious Intrusion of Bias' (Harvard NOM wp No. 02-40 <http://www.ssrn.com/abstract_id=324261>, 2002).

[32] See DM Cain et al 'The Dirt on Coming Clean: Perverse Effects of Disclosing Conflicts of Interest' (2005) 34 J Legal Stud 1.

[33] Note that with respect to branches established by other EU Member States firms, the host country competent authority oversees honesty and fair dealing (see supra (n 6)). Therefore, firms operating cross-border through branches will achieve very little uniformity of rules on conflicts of interest.

In this case, though, it is easy to see that the legal treatment of conflicted transactions will hardly be uniform across the EU. There is simply no way to ensure convergence of fairness reviews by judges. And it is equally easy to predict that there will be no successful co-ordination of securities regulators' enforcement policies at level 3 under the Lamfalussy approach. In fact, 'fairness,' insofar as it can even be called a concept, is a fuzzy one,[34] that, intuitively, is deeply imbued with local or national culture. Furthermore, as is argued in Section B, conflict-of-interest regulation facilitates enforcement by clarifying in advance what may and what may not be done, as opposed to judging it after the fact according to broad standards. If this is the case, not only will the MiFID achieve less harmonisation than envisaged, because much may turn on the fairness concept, but in the end it will also *regulate* very little. What it certainly does is to grant supervisory authorities the power to second-guess firms' behaviour under the very broad standards of fairness and honesty, a task some of them may well be ill-equipped to perform,[35] and which may well lead to unprincipled and unpredictable regulatory reactions.

One may counter that this outcome is inevitable, i.e. that no matter how strict and specific the rules are, there is no way to prevent supervisory agencies and courts from reviewing firms' behaviour for fairness. First of all, this is not true, because at least in theory, the Directive might have established that, when the procedural or substantial rules have been complied with, no ex post fairness review can be conducted.[36] Second, if rules on conflicts of interest are any help, it is thanks to their albeit imperfect ability to screen unfair behaviour, so that, up to a point, more rules should mean less unfair behaviour and thus less ex post fairness review. Let us imagine, in this context, that in the absence of regulation a firm could possibly take 20 self-interested actions, of which 10 are fair and 10 are unfair. A lenient specific rule on conflicts of interest might cut the number of self-interested actions to 14, of which 8 are fair and 6 are unfair.[37] More restrictive rules could lower the number to 10, of which 6 are fair and 4 unfair. In the last case, then, regulation halves the scope for ex post fairness review. Of course, a regime that allows 20 self-interested actions to be taken could well be better than one allowing only 10, because the latter also prevents some value-increasing transactions. The point here, however, is simply that there will be less harmonisa-

[34] Cfr CM Yablon 'On the Allocation of Burdens of Proof in Corporate Law: An Essay on Fairness and Fuzzy Sets' (1991) 13 Cardozo L Rev 497.

[35] See Section E.

[36] Such is the case with rules on corporate directors' self-dealing in some jurisdictions. See, e.g., L Enriques 'The Law on Company Directors' Self-Dealing: A Comparative Analysis' (2000) 2 Int'l & Comp Corp L J 321-324.

[37] Since these rules are imperfect in screening fair and unfair behaviour, not only will unfair behaviour not be ruled out altogether, but some fair actions will be ruled out because, it being difficult for a judge to identify them as fair, the legal risk may be too high.

tion under the former regime than under the latter, because there is more scope for ex post review which is impossible to harmonise.

E. Same Rules for Different Investor Protection Needs: A Wise Choice?

In Section C we saw that MiFID's rules on conflicts of interest are quite lenient and that level 2 measures are likely to be no less so. Here, I argue that such a regulatory framework may be appropriate to Member States where markets and non-legal institutions work reasonably well and thus there is no need for stricter rules, but that it is ill-suited to regulate conflicts of interests in other Member States – Italy in particular, where they will diminish the already low level of investor protection.

Section B referred to the economic literature arguing that competition, firms' concern for reputation, self-help by investors, and supervision make conflicts of interest a less severe problem. If Member States' financial services markets differ in those respects, therefore, uniform rules will have a different impact on them. Where competition among financial services providers is strong, concern for reputation is high, investors can protect themselves, and supervisory authorities effectively police behaviour, MiFID's rules on conflicts of interest may well be enough to protect investors. In countries with weak competition, little concern for reputation, financially illiterate investors, and ineffective supervisory authorities, they will probably not suffice. Italy is a good example of a country where MiFID will be inadequate.

Competition. In Italy, perhaps as in other European countries but certainly much more than, say, in the UK, regulatory barriers to entry into the market for investment services are high. This is because (until very recently at least) the Italian market for corporate control in banking has been foreclosed to foreign banks by the Bank of Italy's long-standing policy of protecting national banks.[38] In a market for investment services that is dominated everywhere by banks, preventing foreigners from taking over Italian banks means shutting them out, because mergers and acquisitions are virtually the only means of entry into the banking market. This, in turn, adversely affects competition in the Italian market for investment services, because intuitively outsiders (foreigners) would be more aggressive competitors than incumbents.

Investor self-help. Italian retail investors are less sophisticated than their counterparts in many European countries.[39] Arguably, this means that they are less able than others to defend themselves against intermediaries' abuses.

[38] See, e.g., T Buck and A Michaels 'Brussels Seeks Bank Bids Pledge from Italy' *Fin Times* (European ed) (9 February 2005) 1.

[39] See L Guiso, M Haliassos and T Jappelli 'Household Stockholding in Europe: Where Do We Stand and Where Do We Go?' (2003) Econ Pol'y 123, especially 157 (providing data on

cont. ...

Concern for reputation. In Italy ethical standards are lower than in some other Member States, according to measures of trust in different countries. In Italy the level of trust is lower than in Ireland, the UK, the Netherlands and the Scandinavian countries,[40] suggesting that Italians tend more than others to expect opportunistic behaviour. This expectation, in turn, implies that people in general will be less indignant over the opportunistic behaviour of others: they may discount it or at least find it 'less' wrong.[41] So social sanctions for opportunistic behaviour are less severe, and arguably market sanctions as well.[42]

Supervision. In Italy, the supervisory authority in charge of protecting investors in securities (Consob) is understaffed, has a very old-fashioned, ministry-like form of internal governance, and must work with a system of sanctions for conflict-of-interest abuses that are usually either laughable (fines up to around €100,000) or so draconian they are never applied (removal of all the directors and appointment of an administrator). As a result, Consob is seldom proactive, and when it does punish wrongdoing (long after the fact), the fines that it levies are tiny compared to the gravity of the offence.[43]

Further, when asked for guidance on the interpretation of securities laws, Consob has a tendency to stick to their letter and to refrain from construing them so as to avoid loopholes. For instance, in 1997 Consob issued an opinion in which it allowed banks to underwrite securities and then to resell them to retail investors without a prospectus.[44] Consob did hold on that occasion that conflict-of-interest

economic literacy in various European countries that show that Italy has the lowest score in a panel comprising also France, Germany, the Netherlands, Sweden, the UK, and the U.S.).

[40] See R La Porta et al 'Trust in Large Organizations' (1997) 87 Am Econ Rev 333, 337.

[41] Cfr L Enriques 'Bad Apples, Bad Oranges: A Comment from Old Europe on Post-Enron Corporate Governance Reforms' (2003) 38 Wk Forest L Rev 911, 915 (arguing that 'in some European countries, and certainly [in Italy] ... most people have feelings of admired envy rather than of outrage in the face of a CEO who cashes in a pile of stock options before the market price of her company's shares collapses, or even in the face of insider trading violations').

[42] Market sanctions are also less severe in a context of low ethical standards, because it is particularly hard to signal one's superior ethical standards and because, with a low degree of competition in banking and financial services in general, people have no reason to expect that other firms will behave better.

[43] In the Cirio case (see infra text accompanying (nn 47-49)), the banks' officers and directors whom Consob found to have violated conflicts of interest rules (having shifted the bankruptcy risk to retail investors by selling them bonds and using the proceeds in part to repay their loans) were held liable to pay fines averaging approximately € 12,500. See 'Cirio, multata l'alta finanza' *Il Sole 24 Ore* (18 March 2005) 34. More precisely, the officers and directors of six primary banks were sanctioned for violations of conflicts of interest rules. See Consob 'Bollettino Quindicinale No. 3.1' (2005) 39-60.

[44] Consob Communication No. 97006042 of 9 July 1997 (<http://www.consob.it/main/documen-ti/bollettino_normativa_ante_98/c97006042.htm?hkeywords=97006042&docid=6&page=0&hits=7>).

rules would apply, but it gave a very restrictive answer to the question of when a conflict-of-interest situation arises.[45]

Even worse for investors, Italian law prevents Consob from providing information on its investigations to civil law judges deciding liability suits by investors against banks.[46]

It is hardly surprising, in a framework like this, that some banks have been keen to exploit investors' lack of sophistication and inability to assess financial risk, by either actively marketing, or at least failing to warn against the implied risk of the bonds of now infamous issuers such as Cirio and Parmalat.[47] In some instances, they shifted part of the default risk from their own balance sheets to their clients' portfolios.[48] This is the prototypical conflict-of-interest abuse perpetrated by a commercial bank.[49]

What is worth emphasising here is that such abuses have taken place despite conduct-of-business rules that, on the books at least, are arguably more stringent than the MiFID's. Under Consob's rules, before a self-interested firm can act it must disclose the nature and extent of its conflict of interest and obtain the client's authorization.[50] Although this provision was not enough to prevent abuses, it is now proving useful to investors suing banks[51] and to Consob in applying the (small) monetary sanctions on banks' directors and managers.[52]

To conclude, due to regulatory barriers to competition in the market for investment services, less financial literacy, lower ethical standards, and less than perfectly effective oversight, Italian investors would seem to be in special need of specific rules addressing firms' conflicts of interest. The MiFID will introduce a laxer regime than that now in place, increasing the scope for self-interested action subject to ex post review for honesty and fair dealing. It may well be that the compromise reached in Brussels between the need for protection and the need for flexibility is the best possible for countries like Britain, the Netherlands, or Den-

[45] Consob Communication (n 44). For a critique, see R Costi and L Enriques *Il mercato mobiliare* (Cedam 2004) 343 and note 70.

[46] See Article 4 (10), Legislative Decree 58/1998.

[47] See M Onado 'I risparmiatori e la Cirio: ovvero, pelati alla meta. Storie di ordinaria spoliazione di azionisti e obbligazionisti' (2003) 5 Mercato concorrenza regole 517-523; R Pardolesi, AMP and A Portolano 'Latte, lacrime (da coccodrillo) e sangue (dei risparmiatori). Note minime sul caso Parmalat' (2004) 1 Mercato concorrenza regole 211-212.

[48] See M Onado (n 47) 518.

[49] See e.g. JAC Santos (n 7) 11-12.

[50] Consob Regulation No. 11152 of 1 July 1998 (<http://www.consob.it/main/documenti/Regolamentazione/normativa/reg11522.htm>) Article 27. To be sure, the Regulation provides for special, more lenient rules for the portfolio management service. See Article 45.

[51] See e.g. Tribunale di Venezia (22 November 2004) *Pitteri v. Deutsche Bank s.p.a.*, (2005) I Contratti 5.

[52] See Consob (n 43).

mark. But in light of the recent experience with Cirio and Parmalat, one doubts that the same is true for Italy.

Of course, one may counter that this is Italy's problem, and that it would be even worse for the EU as a whole to impose stricter rules on all Member States just because those rules are needed in one of them. But that is exactly the point: why adopt maximum harmonisation, whether *de jure* or *de facto*,[53] when investor protection needs are different across the EU?

A counter-rebuttal might be that a single rulebook on conflicts of interest and investment services in general would lower firms' compliance costs in providing services cross-border, and thus lead to greater market integration and competition. Increased competition, in turn, it can be argued, would make conflicts of interest less of a problem for investors.

The problem with this reasoning is that, first, as Section C has argued, the MiFID has achieved little effective harmonization in the regulation of conflicts of interest. Second, there may be other barriers to integration that the Directive does not address, like those in the market for corporate control we discussed above. Third, as argued by Hertig, the costs of complying with host Member States' rules of conduct under the first Investment Services Directive are simply not a significant entry barrier.[54] Fourth, competition alone may be insufficient to prevent opportunistic behaviour, the likelihood of which also depends on factors such as investors' sophistication, reputational concerns, and the effectiveness of oversight. A more integrated market for investment services will likely leave investors' financial literacy unchanged, and it is far from certain that foreign firms will bring their higher ethical standards to bear on their employees rather than themselves adapt to the laxer local environment: after all, it may be hard for foreign entrants to signal their superior ethical standards to customers.[55] Finally, the home country competent authorities can be expected to be somewhat less keen to enforce conflict-of-interest rules on firms' cross-border operations: for mainly political reasons, they will tend to concentrate on abuses that harm domestic investors.[56] As a result, adapting to local ethical standards when operating abroad will not significantly increase the risk of enforcement actions at home.

[53] See supra (n 6) and accompanying text.

[54] See G Hertig 'Imperfect Mutual Recognition for EU Financial Services' in R Buxbaum et al (eds) *European Economic and Business Law* (de Gruyter 1996) 218, 227.

[55] Consider also that a firm with a higher degree of integrity will have to charge higher fees than a lower integrity firm, because the latter may be profitable thanks to conflict-of-interest abuses even if it charges lower fees.

[56] See DC Langevoort 'Structuring Securities Regulation in the European Union: Lessons from the U.S. Experience' in this volume 487-508.

F. Conclusions

To conclude, the specific conflict-of-interest rules in the MiFID and in prospective level 2 measures are quite lenient all in all, and leave ample scope for honesty and fairness obligations in conflicts of interest situations, thus ensuring little real or 'effective' harmonisation.[57] In the countries where such rules are most needed, the new regime will actually decrease investor protection, unless of course level 2 rules are designed differently from the Draft Commission Directive.

Why is this the outcome? While the lack of real harmonisation is certainly an unintended result, the fact that in some Member States investor protection may decrease due to the harmonisation process is best grasped in light of the objectives of EC securities regulation. Under the EC Treaty, as Niamh Moloney has observed,[58] the main purpose of harmonisation of financial services has traditionally been market integration. Investor protection is just an instrumental end, something to be pursued in order to attain market integration. But the two objectives may well conflict, and when they do, market integration is bound to prevail.

Not only is market integration the real purpose of harmonisation under the Treaty, it is also the definite objective of the interest groups that favour EC regulation in this area, namely continental players from the main financial centres, whose quest for a single rulebook is easy to understand. Local players, in 'good' as well as in 'bad' jurisdictions, are obviously, if not myopically, happy with the more lenient rules to which the various participants agree at the EC level. Leniency inevitably follows from the fact that investors' needs differ from country to country and that the securities industry is the only effective lobby.[59] The consequence is a diminution of legal protection for retail investors in 'bad' jurisdictions – who are precisely those who most need such protection.

[57] See M Tison (n 3).

[58] See N Moloney *EC Securities Regulation* (Oxford University Press 2002) 5-9; N Moloney 'Investor Protection and the Treaty: An Uneasy Relationship' in G Ferrarini, KJ Hopt and E Wymeersch (eds) (n 33) 17, especially 48.

[59] Cfr Second Consultation Paper (n 13) 5 (in the consultation process for the technical advice on MiFID level 2 measures, 'few responses were received [from retail consumers and retail clients]'). During MiFID's legislative work, the financial industry succeeded in watering down the Commission's proposed regime on conflicts of interest, which 'would have required firms to refrain from acting for the client in the event that they could not, with reasonable confidence, organise themselves in such a way as to prevent any risk of prejudice through conflicts of interest'. J Herbst 'Revision of the Investment Services Directive' (2003) 11 J Fin Reg & Compliance 215.

The 'Public Offering of Securities' Concept in the New Prospectus Directive

ALAIN PIETRANCOSTA*

An important method of financing corporations, the 'public offering of securities' has for some time also been a key concept in capital markets law. However, rather curiously, the European capital markets regulation did not dignify the concept with a substantive definition. The gap has been closed by Prospectus Directive 2003/71/EC of 4 November 2003, with important practical and theoretical implications in terms of financial markets harmonization, investors' protection and corporate law. Unfortunately, a number of questions remain with respect to the precise contours of the definition of 'public offering of securities'.

A. An Innovative but Evasive Definition of the 'Offer of Securities to the Public'
B. The Clarifications Brought on by an A Contrario Interpretation of the Exemptions

Directive 2003/71/EC of 4 November 2003 (the Prospectus Directive),[1] and implementing Regulation 809/2004 of 29 April 2004,[2] have rebuilt the community architecture of any prospectus to be published when securities are offered to the public or admitted to trading. Long awaited, its adoption incontestably constitutes an important step toward the goal of integrating European capital markets.[3]

* The author would like to thank Carol A.F. Umhoefer, partner at Piper Rudnick LLP in Paris, France, for her valuable contribution to the writing of this article.

[1] Directive 2003/71/EC of the European Parliament and of the Council of 4 November 2003 on the prospectus to be published when securities are offered to the public or admitted to trading and amending Directive 2001/34/EC, OJ L345 31.12.2003 64-89 (the Prospectus Directive). The Directive was to be transposed by 1 July 2005 at the latest.

[2] Commission Regulation 809/2004 of 29 April 2004 implementing Directive 2003/71/EC of the European Parliament and of the Council as regards information contained in prospectuses as well as the format, incorporation by reference and publication of such prospectuses and dissemination of advertisements, OJ L149 30.04.2004 1-134. Adde, CESR 'Recommendations for the Consistent Implementation of the European Commission's Regulation on Prospectuses No. 809/2004' (February 2005) CESR/05-054b.

[3] See European Commission 'Release IP/03/1018' (15 July 2003); European Commission 'Release IP/04/563' (29 April 2004); A Pietrancosta 'Directive prospectus et mesures d'application' (2004) Rev de Droit Bancaire et Financier 265 and in M Baizard and P Raimbourg (eds) *Ingénierie financière, fiscale et juridique* (Dalloz Action 2006); Cleary, Gottlieb, Steen & Hamilton memorandum 'The EU Prospectus Directive – Impact on European Capital Markets' (2004) 1009 PLI/Corp 1428; B François 'Vers une nouvelle définition de l'appel pu-

cont. ...

Indeed, the role of disclosure of information, and its regulation, are fundamental in determining efficiency in the financial markets. It goes without saying that the volume and quality of information available with respect to issuers is critical to the proper functioning of financial markets. The credo is by now well established. The traditional concept of caveat emptor has ceded, under a system conceived and developed in the United States, to the philosophy of full disclosure, whose fundamental purpose is to force the disclosure of information that is specific, reliable, honest and complete and which the markets depend on to operate under optimal conditions. Information requirements thus have a regulating effect on the behaviors of market participants (principle of 'disclosure regulation'), and substantive regulation only plays a secondary role. This philosophy adorns the institutional approach with the democratic virtues of liberty (authorities are less susceptible to accusations of unnecessary interventionism because the system assumes a certain intelligence of the participants and the market's capacity to self-regulate) and equality (transparency operates for the benefit of everyone, in law if not in fact).[4] The Prospectus Directive, which completes the Transparency Directive[5] was therefore one of the natural goals of the Financial Services Action Plan (FSAP).[6]

The Prospectus Directive is not entirely innovative. Its subject matter was already addressed by Council Directive 80/390/EEC (the 'Listing Particulars Directive')[7] (last modified by Directive 94/18/EC,[8] then integrated in the Directive

blic à l'épargne' (2004) Recueil Dalloz 1652; I Le Gris and M-L Ossa-Daza 'Objectifs et enjeux de la directive No. 2003/71/CE du 4 novembre 2003 concernant le prospectus à publier en cas d'offre au public de valeurs mobilières ou en vue de l'admission de valeurs mobilières aux négociations' (2005) Bull Joly Bourse 5; R Pretorius and J Ferreira 'The Implementation of the New Prospectus Directive in the United Kingdom' (2005) 20 J Int'l Banking L & Reg 56-64.

[4] See A Pietrancosta *The Influence of Financial Imperatives and Market Forces on French Corporate Law* (Transactive 2000) and on <http://www.droit21.com>; A Pietrancosta 'La modernisation des voies de l'harmonisation européenne du droit boursier' (2004) 200 Pet Aff 3.

[5] Directive 2004/109/EC of the European Parliament and of the Council of 15 December 2004 on the harmonisation of transparency requirements in relation to information about issuers whose securities are admitted to trading on a regulated market and amending Directive 2001/34/EC, OJ L390 31.12.2004 38-57. See A Pietrancosta 'La directive transparence des sociétés cotées' (2005) Rev de droit bancaire et financier 41.

[6] See A Pietrancosta 'L'avancement du plan d'action pour les services financiers (PASF)' (2002) Rev de droit bancaire and financier 205 and A Pietrancosta 'Dernière ligne droite pour le plan d'action pour les services financiers' (2004) Rev de droit bancaire and financier 44.

[7] Council Directive 80/390/CEE of 17 March 1980, coordinating the requirements for the drawing up, scrutiny and distribution of the listing particulars to be published for the admission of securities to official stock exchange listing, OJ L100 17.04.1980 1-26.

[8] Directive 94/18/EC of the European Parliament and of the Council of 30 May 1994 amending Directive 80/390/EEC coordinating the requirements for the drawing up, scrutiny and distribution of the listing particulars to be published for the admission of securities to official

cont. ...

2001/34/EC)[9] and Directive 89/298/EEC[10] (the 'Public Offer Prospectus Directive').[11]

However, in aiming for minimal harmonization in order to leave room for national preferences (which generate additional costs, delays and uncertainties) the Listing Particulars and Public Offers Directives did not fully satisfy the requirements of mutual recognition. This principle was therefore intrinsically limited, to the extent that Member States were authorized to require a translation of the information document and the inclusion of additional information, whether tax-related or related to methods of giving notice to investors.[12]

As a matter of fact, few cross-border offers were implemented. Deutsche Telekom's June 1999 retail share offering across all eleven Euro-area countries was the exception, perhaps the sole exception,[13] understandably: due to regulation disparities among the Member States, Deutsche Telekom had to negotiate several months with the authorities to determine how information would be disclosed. The language requirements for prospectuses were in themselves a significant problem: in certain Member States, only the prospectus summary was to be translated, whereas in other countries (Italy and Spain, notably), the entire prospectus had to be translated (145 pages for Deutsche Telekom). In France, the translation problem gave rise to legal issues because of the Law of 4 August 1994 (also known as 'Toubon Law', named after the minister who sponsored the bill) protecting the French language. In a 20 December 2000 decision, the French Supreme Administrative Court ('Conseil d'État') annulled rules promulgated by the French regulatory authority,[14] citing the 'Toubon Law'. The possibility of draft-

stock-exchange listing, with regard to the obligation to publish listing particulars, OJ L135 31.05.1994 1-4.

[9] Directive 2001/34/EC of the European Parliament and of the Council of 28 May 2001 on the admission of securities to official stock exchange listing and on information to be published on those securities, OJ L184 6.07.2001 1-66.

[10] Council Directive 89/298/EEC of 17 April 1989 coordinating the requirements for the drawing up, scrutiny and distribution of the prospectus to be published when transferable securities are offered to the public, OJ L124 5.05.1989 8-15.

[11] See generally HS Bloomenthal and S Wolff *International Capital Markets and Securities Regulation* (Sweet & Maxwell 2001) 10E s. 9A.01 (1).

[12] See AB St John 'Regulation Of Cross-Border Public Offerings Of Securities in the European Union: Present and Future' (2001) 29 Denv J Int'l L & Pol'y 239; FESCO 'A "European Passport" for Issuers – A Report for the EU Commission' (Summer/Fall 2001).

[13] See, e.g. S Ascarelli 'Calling Small Investors, Everywhere'; 'Deutsche Telekom's Massive Simultaneous Offering Sets a Precedent'; 'In Global Market for Stocks, Geography Isn't Destiny' *Wall St J* (European ed) (16 June 2000) 13; W Wright 'Deutsche Telekom Plans First Global Retail Offer' *Fin News* (8 May 2000); 'Deals of the Year, Equity, European Retail Loves DT' *Euromoney* (10 February 2000) 88; International Equity 'Deutsche Telekom's Bumpy Ride' *Euromoney* (10 August 1999) 26.

[14] Conseil d'État, 20.12.2000, obs Lienhard (2001) D aff 383; note Ruet (2001) Bull Joly Bourse 145 para. 30; Raynouard (2001) Recueil Dalloz 1713; obs Molfessis (2001) RTD civ

cont. ...

ing an offering prospectus in a foreign language customarily used in financial markets was therefore legislated by Law 2001-1168 of 11 December 2001[15] (the 'Murcef Law', French acronym for 'Urgent Economic and Financial Reform Measures'),[16] implemented by a financial authority rule ('Règlement COB 2002-03') approved by Ministerial Decree on 12 March 2002.[17] There were other difficulties, related to informational requirements for launching an offer, such as the possibility of marketing shares before publication of a prospectus, authorized in certain countries and forbidden in others. Advertisements – when authorized – were subject to different rules: in France, for example, a television ad for the Deutsche Telekom shares was prohibited because it featured a man in a car who was not wearing a seat belt.

This legal context was evidently disadvantageous, to the extent that the economic benefits of effective cross-border offering regulations appear obvious, both for buyers (greater variety of issuers and therefore easier diversification of risks) and for issuers (reaching a larger market at lower cost). These benefits explain the international efforts to harmonize the rules governing prospectus disclosure.[18] In short, ambitious reform was necessary to implement a modern and functional regulatory system, capable of encouraging issuer access to pan-European capital markets while assuring adequate information for investors in the context of public offerings. It is to this end that the Prospectus Directive aspires.

Formally, the entire regulatory scheme for prospectuses is redrawn: in one common framework we find all provisions regarding prospectuses, whether circu-

234. Adde, L Ruet 'Commentaire de l'article 14 du projet de loi dite Murcef' (2001) Bull Joly Bourse 339; obs Libchaber (2001) Revue Trimestrielle de droit civil 709; JC Vecchiatto 'Les vicissitudes de l'utilisation de la langue française dans l'appel public à l'épargne en France' (2001) 152 Gazette du Palais 37.

[15] Journal Officiel de la République Française No. 288 12.12.2001, 19703.

[16] Article L 412-1 a. 1er mod Code monétaire et financier.

[17] Journal Officiel de la République Française No. 81 6.04.2002, 6084. See A Pietrancosta 'Réglementation – panorama des modifications' (2002) Rev de droit bancaire et financier 142.

[18] Re: efforts in particular at the IOSCO 'International Disclosure Standards for Cross-Border Offerings and Initial Listings by Foreign Issuers' Report of the Technical Committee (1998); IOSCO 'The Report on Implementation of International Disclosure Standards' (2000); the response of the FESCO 'A "European Passport" for Issuers – A Report for the EU Commission' (2000) Fesco/00-138b and 'A European Passport for Issuers – A Report to the EU Commission' (2001). For a general appreciation of the problem, see HS Scott 'Internationalization of Primary Public Securities Markets' (2000) 63 Law & Contemp Probs 71; DW Arner 'Globalisation of Financial Markets: An International Passport for Securities Offerings?' Symposium International Monetary and Financial Law in the New Millennium (2001) 35 Int'l Law 1543; JW Hicks 'Harmonization of Disclosure Standards for Cross-Border Share Offerings: Approaching an "International Passport" to Capital Markets?' *The Earl A. Snyder Lecture in International Law* (2002) 9 Ind J Global Legal Stud 361; TG Siew 'Regulatory Challenges in the Development of a Global Securities Market – Harmonisation of Mandatory Disclosure Rules' (2004) Sing J Legal Stud 173.

lated in the context of a simple public offering of securities or a listing on a regulated market.[19] This broad coverage of the Directive requires particular attention from the reader.

Fundamentally, the goal of integrating European capital markets modifies the original spirit of 'minimum harmonization-mutual recognition', which is now a more ambitious 'maximum harmonization[20]-single European passport'. Setting common standards for information disclosure in Europe creates the conditions for using one document in all national markets and eliminates grounds for national interference. This ambition and the means of its realization are not without inconveniences, which were highly criticized during the drafting stage by market practitioners, who underscored[21] in hearings the costs and rigidities resulting from greater exigencies with respect to the information to be provided in the prospectus[22] and from the designation of an originating Member State delivering the European 'passport'. These factors, it is argued, combine to dissuade issuers in the Member States as well as issuers from third-party countries. The preference for home state control, requiring intervention of the authority of the Member State where the issuer is incorporated, raised fears relating to the expertise of the

[19] Recall that in the United States, the integration of two distinct disclosure systems – one applicable to the 1933 Act and the other to the 1934 Act – was carried out in 1982.

[20] This principle is not without its nuances, Whereas 15 having in the end been introduced in the Directive following a parliamentary amendment to the effect that 'the disclosure requirements of the present Directive do not prevent a Member State or a competent authority or an exchange through its rule book to impose other particular requirements in the context of admission to trading of securities on a regulated market (notably regarding corporate governance)', as long as these requirements do 'not directly or indirectly restrict the drawing up, the content or the dissemination of a prospectus approved by a competent authority'. See C Huhne (Committee on Economic and Monetary Affairs) 'Recommendation for second reading on the Council common position for adopting a European Parliament and Council directive on the prospectus to be published when securities are offered to the public or admitted to trading – Final' (13 June 2003) A5-0218/2003 (5390/4/2003 – C5-0143/2003 – 2001/0117(COD))).

[21] A consultation that they considered insufficient, see, e.g., Opinion of the Economic and Social Committee (EESC) on the Proposal for a Directive of the European Parliament and of the Council on the prospectus to be published when securities are offered to the public or admitted to trading, OJ C80 3.04.2002 52-60; this was quite a paradox for the first text drafted in accordance with the Lamfalussy procedure.

[22] See, e.g., observations in the responses from the International Primary Market Association (IPMA) during the public debates; see V Boland 'Call to Scrap Share Reform' *Fin Times* (5 September 2001) and 'Opposition Mounts to EU Securities Directive' *Fin Times* (7 September 2001); A Crooke 'Securities Markets Attack EU Prospectus Reforms' *Legal Media Group* (9 September 2001); P Freeman 'Letters to the Editor – Clearly More Work is Needed on the Prospectus Directive' *Fin Times* (14 September 2001); M Evans 'Prospectus Directive Could Triple Legal Bills for International Offerings' (October 2002) Int'l Fin L Rev; and the responses from J Todd 'Letter to the Editor: Prospectus Proposal Would Lower Cost of Raising Capital' *Fin Times* (9 September 2001) and 'Letters to the Editor – Misconceptions on the Single European Prospectus' *Fin Times* (10 September 2001).

national authorities and intra-European regulatory competition.[23] While the new system does have its drawbacks, home country control is not without logic, to the extent that national authorities, due to their knowledge of local issuers, can regulate more effectively.[24] Furthermore, the home seat criterion introduces a competitive aspect, because of recent European company law initiatives encouraging freedom of election of the home seat by companies incorporated in any of the Member States. Finally, the home seat criterion is only one of several criteria set by the Directive, important amendments having been made in order to free the choice of the competent authority for wholesale markets.

One means of reaching the desired level of 'equi-efficiency' was naturally to define common terms for the two types of transactions triggering prospectus requirements: listing on a regulated market and public offering of securities.

The delimitation of the first type of transaction – listing on a regulated market – requires limited commentary. Compared with the Listing Particulars Directive of 1980, one simply observes that the new Directive does not distinguish between 'regulated markets',[25] refusing demands of the smallest of them.[26]

The delimitation of the second type of transaction – public offering of securities – includes important changes and merits closer scrutiny. Indeed, unlike the formal procedure of listing on a regulated market, a public offering is a key substantial concept, the salient transaction on financial markets, justifying the application of regulations protecting the investor. It is the lower limit, the threshold and the trigger for these regulations. Its determination thus allows better appreciation of the Directive's goals, the philosophy of the system and its priorities. This eases interpretation of the Community rules and an evaluation of their underlying imperatives and the means of attaining them.

The Community legislator was aware of the stakes and undertook a real effort concerning the definitions. Previously, the absence of a single definition of 'public offering' was roundly criticized. The first report of the Committee of Wise

[23] See supra; see also, inter alia, HE Jackson and EJ Pan 'Regulatory Competition in International Securities Markets: Evidence from Europe in 1999' (2001) 56 Bus Law 653; M Evans 'Commission Drops Choice of Competent Authority from Prospectus Directive' (July 2002) Int'l Fin L Rev; 'European Securities Regulation, Spoilt Choice' *The Economist* (7 November 2002); Opinion of the Economic and Social Committee (EESC) on the Proposal for a Directive of the European Parliament and of the Council on the prospectus to be published when securities are offered to the public or admitted to trading, Brussels, 17.02.2002, and infra; compare advantages of international harmonization in TG Siew (n 18).

[24] See on the investors' 'home bias', Commission Staff Working Document 'Financial Integration Monitor' (6 May 2004) SEC(2004) 559, 30. See, as to U.S. law, MB Fox 'Retaining Mandatory Securities Disclosure: Why Issuer Choice Is Not Investor Empowerment' (1999) 85 Va L Rev 1335.

[25] See Prospectus Directive (n 1) Whereas 12.

[26] See e.g., Commentaries of the London Stock Exchange on the proposal, www.europa.eu.int. The Investment Market asked to be excluded from the regulated markets.

Men on the regulation of European securities markets, dated 9 November 2000, took cognizance of the situation, which could result in one transaction's treatment as a private placement in certain – but not all – of the Member States. Such a system could only discourage 'firms from raising capital on a Community-wide basis and therefore from having real access to a large, liquid and integrated financial market',[27] and impede the development of wholesale markets as well as private placements and institutional investor operations. Since the adoption of the Prospectus Directive, there is a veritable Community definition of public offering of securities, in and of itself an innovation, even if the definition is not fully instructive (A); and a reconfigured system of exclusions and exemptions, from which one can deduce most of the guidelines for interpretation (B). Here I will examine how the new Directive changes the contours of the definition of public offering as compared with its predecessor, and its position vis-à-vis other systems, in particular in France and the United States. I conclude with observations on the possible use of those new criteria for public offerings, in view of distinguishing the legal status of issuers.

A. An Innovative but Evasive Definition of the 'Offer of Securities to the Public'

'Member States shall not allow any offer of securities to be made to the public within their territories without prior publication of a prospectus'. This fundamental principle, laid out in Article 3 (1) of the Prospectus Directive, assumes that its principal distinctive elements are specified in a manner compatible with the goal of maximum harmonization. Such specifications can be found in the definitions set forth in Article 2 of the Directive.

I. A Comprehensive Definition of 'Securities', Borrowed from the Investment Services Directive

The Prospectus Directive, in Article 2 (1) (a), states that the term 'securities' means 'transferable securities as defined by Article 1 (4) of Directive 93/22/EEC with the exception of money market instruments as defined by Article 1 (5) of Directive 93/22/EEC, having a maturity of less than 12 months', it being specified that 'for these instruments national legislation may be applicable'.

In this context it is helpful to recall Article 1 (4) of Directive 93/22, relating to investment services, which indicated that 'securities' meant:

- 'shares in companies and other securities equivalent to shares in companies;

[27] See Prospectus Directive (n 1) Whereas 5.

- bonds and other forms of securitised debt which are negotiable on the capital market;

- and any other securities normally dealt in giving the right to acquire any such transferable securities by subscription or exchange or giving rise to a cash settlement excluding instruments of payment';

and Article 1 (5) of the same Directive which referred, with respect to money market instruments, to 'classes of instruments which are normally dealt in on the money market'.[28]

The intention of the Prospectus Directive consists of setting out an extensive definition of securities (in actuality difficult to grasp),[29] 'which includes warrants and covered warrants and certificates', but not commercial paper.[30]

The goal of the directive has not been negatively affected by the replacement of Directive 93/22/EEC relating to investment services by Directive 2004/39/EC on markets in financial instrument (MiFID).[31] The risk of definition by cross-reference is avoided, because the definition now implicitly refers to the provisions of the latter text, which confirms this will for comprehensiveness. Pursuant to Article 4 (1) (18) and (19) of the MiFID, 'transferable securities' means :

'those classes of securities which are negotiable on the capital market, with the exception of instruments of payment, such as:

a) shares in companies and other securities equivalent to shares in companies, partnerships or other entities, and depositary receipts in respect of shares;

b) bonds or other forms of securitised debt, including depositary receipts in respect of such securities;

c) any other securities giving the right to acquire or sell any such transferable securities or giving rise to a cash settlement determined by reference to transfer-

[28] Comp. Directive 89/298/EEC (n 10) Article 3 e), which defined securities as: 'shares in companies and other transferable securities equivalent to shares in companies, debt securities having a maturity of at least one year and other transferable securities equivalent to debt securities, and any other transferable security giving the right to acquire any such transferable securities by subscription or exchange'. Comp. Article 2 (1) (a) of the proposal, dated 9 August 2002: 'securities as defined by Article 1 (4) of Directive 93/22/EEC with the exception of bonds or other debt securities, having a maturity of less than one year, and which are not subordinated, convertible or exchangeable and do not give a right to subscribe to or acquire other types of securities and that are not linked to a derivative'.

[29] See Prospectus Directive (n 1) Whereas 12.

[30] The condition relating to one year's maturity was introduced at the suggestion of the European Parliament (amendment 13). See C Huhne (Committee on Economic and Monetary Affairs) 'Report on the proposal for a European Parliament and Council Directive on the prospectus to be published when securities are offered to the public or admitted to trading – Final' (27 February 2002) A5-0072/2002 (COM(2001) 280 – C5-0263/2001 – 2001/0117(COD)) 14.

[31] Directive 2004/39/EC of the European Parliament and of the Council of 21 April 2004 on Markets in Financial Instruments amending Council Directives 85/611/EEC and 93/6/EEC and Directive 2000/12/EC of the European Parliament and of the Council and repealing Council Directive 93/22/EEC, (the MiFID) OJ L145 30.04.2004 1-44.

able securities, currencies, interest rates or yields, commodities or other indices or measures';

and 'money-market instruments': 'those classes of instruments which are normally dealt in on the money market, such as treasury bills, certificates of deposit and commercial papers and excluding instruments of payment'.

One nonetheless notices that the broad scope of the Prospectus Directive, which keeps alive the difficulties of characterizing operations in light of ever-evolving financial and market techniques,[32] does not extend to all monetary and financial instruments, contrary to (for example) French law.[33] The Prospectus Directive thus shows how, at the Community level, the concept of 'securities' stands up against more recently established categories.

II. A New and Extensive Definition of 'Offer to the Public'

The Prospectus Directive includes for the first time a definition of 'offer to the public'. The notion covers, pursuant to Article 2 (1) (d), 'a communication to persons in any form and by any means, presenting sufficient information on the terms of the offer and the securities to be offered, so as to enable an investor to decide to purchase or subscribe to these securities', it being specified that 'this definition shall also be applicable to the placing of securities through financial intermediaries'.

The inclusion of a direct and positive definition constitutes 'a major innovation'[34] at the Community level which in itself is to be applauded. This new solution can be contrasted with the cautious position adopted by the 1989 Directive, which failed to set forth such a definition, alluding to the difficulty of reaching a common position on the issue.[35] The goals of the reform required that this obstacle be overcome, 'to ensure a common approach to this subject in order to avoid disparities in investor protection in an era when, through electronic communication networks, investors can be reached throughout Europe (and elsewhere). Dif-

[32] See A Pietrancosta 'Le droit des sociétés sous l'effet des impératifs financiers et boursiers' (Transactive 2000) 313 ff.

[33] Monetary and Financial Code, Articles L 411-1 and L 411-2. See A Pietrancosta 'Appel public à l'épargne' (2002) 19 Dict Joly Sociétés and A Pietrancosta (n 32) 313 ff; T Bonneau and F Drummond *Droit des marchés financiers* (Économica 2001) 79; Y Paclot 'Qu'est-ce qu'un instrument financier?' (2003) 79 Lexbase Hebdo N8062AAT and Y Paclot 'Vers une définition de la notion d'instrument financier? (A propos du Livre Blanc du Comité de droit financier Paris Europlace)' (2003) 100 Lexbase Hebdo N9896AAR.

[34] Amended proposal for a Directive of the European Parliament and of the Council on the prospectus to be published when securities are offered to the public or admitted to trading and amending Directive 2001/34/EC, Brussels, 9.08.2002, COM(2002) 460, 12.

[35] See Directive 89/298/EEC (n 10) Whereas 7: 'Whereas, so far, it has proved impossible to furnish a common definition of the term "public offer" and all its constituent parts'.

ferent interpretations of the 'public offer' requirement in the Member States may have the effect that in certain cases securities can be sold without any disclosure requirement (and this behaviour can affect the entire European capital market)',[36] as recognized in the Wise Men's Report of 9 November 2000.

Here again, the Directive aims to provide an extensive formulation, which naturally gave rise to long discussions within the different European forums. Evidently, the supporters for an open approach outflanked those who wished for greater definitional precision. Article 2 (1) (d) is in fact a type of catch-all provision.

Thus, the channels through which the offer is made appear to be irrelevant, which is doubly underscored by the text: 'in any form and by any means'. The requirement that the offer be in writing, proposed at one point in the debates,[37] having been strongly rejected, one must take into account all forms of communication – written, oral or visual – regardless of the media: from the traditional newspapers, prospectuses, brochures, posters, letters and reviews to the more modern telex, radio, electronic networks and in particular the Internet.[38] *Ubi lex non distinguit non distinguere debemus.*

Likewise, no restriction is given with respect to the offeror. We learn, from a special provision, Article 2 (1) (i), that offeror 'means a legal entity or individual which offers securities to the public'; and we learn indirectly from Article 3 (2), that the obligation to circulate a prospectus applies to initial offerings as well as *resales* of securities, and to both total and partial offers, the new text leaving off the literal restrictions of the 1989 Directive.[39]

[36] Amended Directive Proposal (n 34) 12.

[37] See C Huhne (n 30).

[38] For the position of the IOSCO, see 'Securities Activity on the Internet – A Report of the Technical Committee of the IOSCO' (September 1998, June 2001 and October 2003). For reactions of foreign regulators, see e.g., Interpretative Release of the SEC 'Use of Internet Web Sites To Offer Securities, Solicit Securities Transactions, or Advertise Investment Services Offshore' (23 March 1998) 17 CFR Parts 231, 241, 271, 276 (Releases No. 33-7516, No. 34-39779 No. IA-1710 and No. IC-23071); recommendation published on 28 May 1998 by the British Financial Services Authority on Unauthorised Investment advertising over the Internet; in Germany, the position of the *Bundesaufsichtsamt für den Wertpapierhandel* (BAWe) 'Public Offerings over the Internet – Annual Report for 1997' 14 ff; or in France, Bull COB No. 329 (November 1998) 92.

[39] Comp. Article 1 Directive 89/298/EEC (n 10): 'This Directive shall apply to transferable securities which are offered to the public for the first time in a Member State provided that these securities are not already listed on a stock exchange situated or operating in that Member State. 2. Where an offer to the public is for part only of the transferable securities from a single issue, the Member States need not require that another prospectus be published if the other part is subsequently offered to the public'.

In fact, two elements suffice to make the offer. *Primo*, there is a communication, a term preferred over invitation,[40] solicitation[41] or promotional message,[42] and which assumes an intention to transmit a message, to establish a relationship with someone. *Secundo*, this communication must have a determined content, presenting 'sufficient information on the terms of the offer and the securities to be offered, so as to enable an investor to decide to purchase or subscribe to these securities'. This requirement should exclude, inter alia, general promotional communications, vague allusions to current or future offerings, etc.

The final draft, contrary to earlier versions, does not refer to the objectives of the offeror. The only criterion is the content of the information transmitted. This information must be related to an offering of securities for 'purchase' or 'subscription'. This alternative formula begs the question of the qualification of certain transactions made for consideration but consummated by other means (exchanges, etc.), or the treatment of offerings without consideration, which have appeared in the past few years on certain Internet sites and have led the Securities and Exchange Commission to take action following complaints by investors.[43]

The communication must also include a minimum of precise information, taking into consideration the addressees of the communication: this minimum content must allow the investor to make a decision whether to purchase or subscribe. This is, in fact, the single most distinctive element of the definition. Yet many questions arise with the interpretation of this requirement: How does one determine what prompts an investor to buy or subscribe? Is the investor to be considered subjectively? Should we refer to an average or ideal investor, considered *in abstracto*? Does this archetype exist? Or should distinctions be made among categories of investors?

With the view of providing a modicum of legal certainty, it was suggested that this 'offer to the public' be aligned with the notion of 'offer' as defined in contracts law, so that a communication does not constitute an offer unless its acceptance would form a contract.[44] Only offers 'that create a contractual obligation' would have triggered 'the obligation to publish a prospectus'.[45] However, this conception – legalistic as it is – was abandoned, certain Member States observing

[40] See Proposal for a Directive of the European Parliament and of the Council on the prospectus to be published when securities are offered to the public or admitted to trading, Brussels, 30.05.2001, COM(2001) 280; and C Huhne (n 30).

[41] See Council of the European Union 'Interinstitutional File: 2001/0117 (COD)' (19 October 2001) 13004/01.

[42] See Directive Proposal (n 40).

[43] As to these transactions that are often free only in name, see 'SEC Brings First Actions To Halt Unregistered Online Offerings of So-Called "Free Stock"' (1999) Release 99-83 <http:// www.sec.gov./news/presindx.htm>.

[44] Council of the European Union, Brussels, 16.05.2002 (29.05); C Huhne (n 30).

[45] C Huhne (n 30).

'that such an approach would introduce the prospectus requirement at too late a stage, arguing that investors need the protection of the prospectus when the issuer is raising money by means of, for instance, an advertising campaign'.[46] From this preventative measure came definitions that are inevitably and deliberately evasive, which translate into considerable room for interpretation by the national authorities.

In this regard, it is rather revealing that, as concerns the addressees of an offer, no definition, attempt at definition or even reference to the 'public' appears in the text,[47] which only evokes 'persons' and 'an investor'. Such it is that these fundamental characteristics of the public offer must be found elsewhere than in its positive definition.

The same observation can be made at national levels. French law is exemplary in this regard. Law 98-546 of 2 July 1998 relating to various economic and financial provisions (DDOEF),[48] which has repealed the pertinent provisions of the Commercial Law of 24 July 1966, introduced a unitary definition, both objective and synthetic of 'appel public à l'épargne' ('public offering') (now found at Article L 411-1 (2) of the Monetary and Financial Code). The definition states that, with respect to non-listed securities, an offer to the public 'consists of ... the issuance or transfer of financial instruments to the public by means of either advertising or solicitation, or to credit establishments or investment services providers'.

In reading the text, it appears that three elements are necessary:[49]

(i) A specific transaction in financial instruments: either an issuance (newly issued securities), by definition organized by the issuer; or a sale (securities not newly issued), initiated by the issuer or by a third party, the law of 1998 having recognized the notion of 'dissident sales'.

(ii) Recourse to certain means: 'advertising, solicitation, credit institutions or investment firms'. The enumeration of these procedures is exhaustive, but in its broadest sense, the term advertising appears sufficiently large to encompass them all. In reality, advertising, understood as such, is the essence of all 'public offerings', so that this requirement appears pleonastic.

(iii) A transaction with the public. No matter which method is used, a public offer does not exist if the transaction is not targeting the public. The 1998 law set this element as an autonomous, fundamental condition. However, the law does not give any positive definition of the term public. The notion should be understood in consideration of 'public offering', understood as a solicitation of the unanimous crowd of investors. This hypothesis is, however, by nature non-controversial. In practice, the debate relates to borderline situations, such as to

[46] Council of the European Union (n 44).

[47] The disappearance of all references to the public was in the Amended Directive Proposal (n 34).

[48] Journal Officiel de la République Française No. 152 3.07.1998, 10127.

[49] A Pietrancosta (n 33) 23 ff.

shareholders or employees of the issuer, or other particular categories of offerees. Under the old regulations, the authorities were led to take a position on this type of situation. The general approach, then, notably at the 'Commission des opérations de bourse', was that the numerical element was critical.[50] Accordingly, if a public offering exists every time that the transaction is aimed at persons without personal relationships among them or with the issuer,[51] proof of such a relationship no longer suffices to exclude the presumption of a public offer when several hundreds or even thousands of persons are concerned.[52] But the law of 2 July 1998 forces a revision of this approach due to the legislator's deliberate choice in favor of a principally qualitative definition of 'public offer', taking into consideration the categories of solicited investors: investment professionals, employees of the issuer or a group company, current shareholders or unidentified investors, etc. The uncertainties caused by this imprecision of the notion are, however, expected to be attenuated through the laying out of exemptions relating to limited investments. These exemptions reveal, by deduction, the contours of public offering.

U.S. law, model in the field, is even more illustrative. The federal laws governing securities do not contain any positive definition of 'public offering'.[53] The elaboration of the concept was many years in the making and developed exclusively and implicitly from the various exemptions, as discussed below.

B. The Clarifications Brought on by an A Contrario Interpretation of the Exemptions

The Prospectus Directive was, paradoxically, awaited for the enumeration of the exemptions from the disclosure obligations it would impose. The boundaries of this field of inaction were one of the critical issues arising under the reform. In fact, the heterogeneity of national laws removing certain securities offerings from prospectus requirements was universally seen as one of the principal obstacles to developing European private and institutional placement markets,[54] because in

[50] Adde, Rép min Justice No. 7405, JO Sénat Q, 7.05.1968, 220; CA Paris (4 February 1981) Bull COB (3 March 1981).

[51] See e.g. distribution of catalogues with subscription bulletins to numerous persons unrelated to the persons distributing the catalogues, COB Report for 1981, 29.

[52] For organizations of alumni of elite French schools, see COB Report for 1984, 29.

[53] For a (rare) definition in the jurisprudence, see AD Orrick 'Non-Public Offerings of Corporate Securities – Limitations on the Exemption Under the Federal securities Act' (1959) 21 U Pitt L Rev 1: 'The term "public offering" must refer to all offerings of securities where the public interest is not remote and the relationship between the issuer and offeree does not create special advantages in the offerees substantially different from the status of members of the public at large to be able to obtain all necessary information about the issuer and its securities'.

[54] See Opinion of the Economic and Social Committee (n 23).

such a context companies could not easily conduct cross-border offerings. Consequently, the new text was expected to assure the legal certainty necessary to develop these capital market segments, while guaranteeing uniform treatment and protection of investors throughout the European Union by way of more precise definitions of the exemptions.

The Prospectus Directive, due in particular to the successive amendments that enriched the initial proposal, attempts to avoid disappointment, though one could regret (in light of its importance) the scattering of the provisions which are occasionally difficult to interpret as a whole. For example, it is not always easy, on a first reading, to navigate between the cases where the Directive does not apply (Article 1), the cases where the obligation to publish a prospectus does not apply (Article 3), and the exemptions, *stricto sensu*, from the prospectus requirements (Article 4). Distinguishing between these cases is nonetheless a necessity, given the legal consequences, especially for the Member States, which depending on the circumstances, have the possibility of customizing application of the Directive.

However, with the focus on the clarifications brought to the concept of public offering, another distinction between exemptions becomes more important. Indeed, not all of the exemptions are significant in this regard. All depends on each exemption's respective purpose.

For some, the purpose is to avoid redundancy with guarantees existing elsewhere. Such is the case for the mandatory exemptions,[55] based on the characteristics of the issuer (Member State, regional or local authority, international organization, central bank, credit institution),[56] legal nature of the securities (units issued by collective investment undertakings other than the closed-end type, which are regulated by other laws),[57] related guarantees (securities guaranteed by a Member State or a regional or local authority),[58] or the type of transaction (securities offered in connection with a tender offer or merger).[59]

The purpose of other exemptions is to set a threshold, under which it is considered inefficient, for economic reasons, to apply costly protection measures. The best example is contained in Article 1 (2) (h), which states that the Directive does not apply to 'securities included in an offer where the total consideration of the offer is less than Euro 2.500.000, which limit shall be calculated over a period of 12 months'. This provision was not contained in the original draft, and manifests the legislator's desire to exclude modest transactions from Community regulation. As a technical matter, one can nonetheless question what the consequences

[55] Directive 89/298/EEC (n 10) distinguished mandatory exemptions and voluntary exemptions, partial or total. See Articles 2 and 5.

[56] Prospectus Directive (n 1) Article 1 (2).

[57] Prospectus Directive (n 1) Article 1 (2) (a).

[58] Prospectus Directive (n 1) Article 1 (d).

[59] Prospectus Directive (n 1) Article 4 (1) (b) and (c).

would be of exceeding this threshold. As for regulatory authority, one can deduct from this provision that each Member State is free to require a prospectus – no doubt simplified – in connection with such transactions. Harmonization is at risk in this market segment and the single passport system is therefore more difficult to implement, even though the issuer can spontaneously submit the offer to the requirements of the Directive.[60] Another case should be mentioned: the obligation to publish a prospectus shall not apply to 'an offer of securities with a total consideration of less than Euro 100,000', a limit that is also calculated 'over a period of 12 months'.[61] This exemption can appear surprising to the extent that, as we have seen, the Directive states that it is not applicable to security offerings in a total amount of less than Euro 2,500,000. *A coherentia*, it should be deduced that the Member States are prohibited, notwithstanding the freedom of initiative left to them under the Euro 2,500,000 threshold, from requiring a prospectus for offers less than Euro 100,000.[62] The question on what the exact consequences are of exceeding the yearly limit is raised in the same terms.

From this first series of hypotheses, one understands that little can be inferred from an *a contrario* reading of the exemptions, at least on a conceptual level. Besides, the letter of the Directive prohibits such inferences, specifically providing that most exemptions do not rule out the possibility that the issue is in fact a public offer.[63]

Other exemptions, however, based on the number of persons targeted by the offer or on their characteristics, are by nature more instructive. By way of an *a contrario* interpretation, they help to better uncover the hidden concept of public offer. Since they cannot be analyzed as simple exceptions reflecting extraneous motivations, their definitions are substantive in scope. In this light, these exemptions become negative – and obviously significant – illustrations of what a public offer is, defined in opposition to the specificities relating to private placements (I). However, the likely non-exhaustive character of these negative illustrations, to the extent that they undoubtedly do not represent all types of private or limited offers, raises the question of whether the text is coherent, or is missing a conceptual link (II).

[60] Prospectus Directive (n 1) Article 1 (3). The Amended Directive Proposal (n 34), with respect to offers of less than Euro 2,500,000, to exclude the prospectus obligation; following the position of the Council, it was decided to exclude them entirely from the Directive, Council of the European Union 'Interinstitutional File: 2001/0117 (COD)' (24 March 2003) 5390/4/03 REV 4 ADD 1. For its part, France has chosen to exclude a prospectus requirement in such a case, see the transposition Law 2005-842 of 26 July 2005 'pour la confiance et la modernisation de l'économie' Journal Officiel de la République Française 27.07.2005, 12160.

[61] Prospectus Directive (n 1) Article 3 (2) (e).

[62] In this sense, Council of the European Union (n 60); 'Financial Services Policy and Financial Markets – Securities Markets' 3rd Informal Meeting on Prospectus Transposition – Summary Record (26 January 2005) MARKT/G3/WG D(2005).

[63] Prospectus Directive (n 1) Article 1 (3).

I. Exemptions Revealing the Contours of the 'Public'

Certain exclusions from the obligation to establish a prospectus hold an undeniable definitional component.[64] A careful reading of the pertinent provisions allows one to move closer to the critical contours of a concept that cannot be reduced to an anonymous crowd of investors, representing only an extreme, and easy, case. This reading reveals that the limits of the 'public' are met well before reaching the anonymous crowd, at a stage determined by both quantitative and qualitative elements. The essential provision is Article 3 (2) of the Directive, which excludes from mandatory prospectus requirements an offer of securities 'addressed solely to qualified investors' and/or 'addressed to fewer than 100 natural or legal persons per Member State, other than qualified investors'. From this one can logically[65] conclude that the public to which the Directive refers must be composed of a minimum number of persons, who if not novices, at the very least are without sufficient sophistication or qualifications, whether proven or legally presumed.

This feature of the Directive borrows from solutions found elsewhere. For example, in the United States, the Securities and Exchange Commission has long taken the initiative, through special rules, of exempting from registration certain categories of securities offers, defined from quantitative and qualitative considerations. Among the better known are:

- Rule 506 adopted in 1982 in the context of Regulation D, successor to Rule 146 of 1974,[66] which considers an offer private if the purchasers are all 'accredited investors', and therefore belong to one of the eight categories set forth in Rule 501 (a) (1): banks, savings and loan associations, insurance companies, brokers and dealers, investment companies, business development companies, public or ERISA pension funds with assets exceeding USD 5 million, directors and managers of the issuer, natural persons having a net worth greater than USD 1 million or personal yearly income greater than USD 200,000, trusts with assets greater than USD 5 million and any group composed of the foregoing. The offer will be considered private even if extended to 35 non-accredited investors, as

[64] This was all the more evident in the Amended Directive Proposal (n 34) which expressly linked these exemptions to the definition of public offering of securities. See Article 2 (2).

[65] Even if some officials still wonder, rather surprisingly, whether or not the kinds of offer mentioned in Article 3 (2) are 'public offers' for the purposes of other provisions of the directive (such as the definition of 'home Member State' in Article 2 (1) (m) and the regulation of advertisements in Article 15), see 'Financial Services Policy and Financial Markets – Securities Markets' (n 62).

[66] See L Loss *Fundamentals of Securities Regulation* (Aspen Publishers 2003) 317 ff; TL Hazen *The Law of Securities Regulation* (West Publishing 1996) 234 ff; MET Beach 'Unregistered Offerings of Corporate Securities' <http://d2d.ali-aba.org 90>; L Walton and LB Morgan *Exempt Transactions: Practical Ways To Sell Securities* (Practising Law Institute Corporate, Law and Practice Course Handbook Series 1998) 245.

long as they are 'sophisticated' or have a sophisticated 'purchaser representative',[67] 'sophisticated' meaning that they have sufficient knowledge and experience in financial and business matters to be capable of evaluating the merits and risks of the prospective investments.[68]

- Section 4 (6) of the Securities Act, from the 'Small Business Investment Incentive Act' of 1980, exempts offers of less than USD 5 million, if exclusively targeting accredited investors.[69]

- Rule 505, based on Section 3 (b), exempts offers equal to or less than USD 5 million placed with no more than 35 purchasers, without any sophistication condition,[70] but provided that the issuer complies with certain disclosure obligations.[71]

- Famous Rule 144A, known by all large institutional investors, which covers the resale of securities purchased in a private offering. These securities are known as 'restricted securities',[72] because the resale conditions are such as to avoid, in the absence of adequate information, the creation of a public secondary market.[73] Purchasers of restricted securities cannot sell them to the public without being considered 'underwriters'[74] and therefore subject to registration requirements.[75] Rule 144A on Private Resales of Securities to Institutions provides purchasers with a safe harbor, a bright-line rule allowing them to avoid this qualification.[76] Resale is unregulated if undertaken consciously and without a public offer, within a circle of 'qualified institutional buyers', including large institutions: banks and savings and loan associations, insurance companies, investment companies, ER-

[67] Rule 501(h).

[68] Rule 506 (b) (2) (ii). Certain disclosure obligations are nonetheless borne by the issuer in this case. See Rule 502 (b) (1).

[69] 'The provisions of section 5 of this title shall not apply to: [...] transactions involving offers or sales by an issuer solely to one or more accredited investors, if the aggregate offering price of an issue of securities offered in reliance on this paragraph does not exceed the amount allowed under section 3 (b) of this title, if there is no advertising or public solicitation in connection with the transaction by the issuer or anyone acting on the issuer's behalf, and if the issuer files such notice with the Commission as the Commission shall prescribe'. See T Hazen (n 66) 221; MET Beach (n 66) 62; L Walton and LB Morgan (n 66) 252.

[70] See MET Beach (n 66) 89; T Hazen (n 66) 217; L Walton and LB Morgan (n 66) 245.

[71] See Rule 502 (b) (1).

[72] Rule 144 (a) (3).

[73] See Rule 502 (d). These limitations do not apply to the exemption provided by Rule 504 for offers of less than USD 1 million.

[74] Securities Act, Section 2 (11).

[75] Securities Act, Section 4 (1).

[76] Adde T Hazen (n 66) 266; JS Hoffman 'Rules 144 and 144A' in *PLI's Understanding the Securities Laws 2004* (Practising Law Institute 2004) 243; TK Edmonson, MA Stegemoeller, MA Pfeiffer and HR Phillips *Exemptions from Securities Act Registration: Section 4(2), Regulation D, Rule 144a, And Regulation 'S' Offerings* (Practising Law Institute 1998) 171.

ISA or public pension funds, business development companies, dealers and groups composed of the foregoing.[77]

[77] Rule 144A (a) (1): 'For purposes of this section, qualified institutional buyer shall mean:

i. Any of the following entities, acting for its own account or the accounts of other qualified institutional buyers, that in the aggregate owns and invests on a discretionary basis at least USD 100 million in securities of issuers that are not affiliated with the entity:

A. Any insurance company as defined in section 2 (13) of the Act;

B. Any investment company registered under the Investment Company Act or any business development company as defined in section 2 (a) (48) of that Act;

C. Any Small Business Investment Company licensed by the U.S. Small Business Administration under section 301 (c) or (d) of the Small Business Investment Act of 1958;

D. Any plan established and maintained by a state, its political subdivisions, or any agency or instrumentality of a state or its political subdivisions, for the benefit of its employees;

E. Any employee benefit plan within the meaning of title I of the Employee Retirement Income Security Act of 1974;

F. Any trust fund whose trustee is a bank or trust company and whose participants are exclusively plans of the types identified in paragraph (a) (1) (i) (D) or (E) of this section, except trust funds that include as participants individual retirement accounts or H.R. 10 plans.

G. Any business development company as defined in section 202 (a) 22 of the Investment Advisers Act of 1940;

H. Any organization described in section 501 (c) (3) of the Internal Revenue Code, corporation (other than a bank as defined in section 3 (a) (2) of the Act or a savings and loan association or other institution referenced in section 3 (a) (5) (A) of the Act or a foreign bank or savings and loan association or equivalent institution), partnership, or Massachusetts or similar business trust; and

I. Any investment adviser registered under the Investment Advisers Act.

ii. Any dealer registered pursuant to section 15 of the Exchange Act, acting for its own account or the accounts of other qualified institutional buyers, that in the aggregate owns and invests on a discretionary basis at least USD 10 million of securities of issuers that are not affiliated with the dealer, Provided, that securities constituting the whole or a part of an unsold allotment to or subscription by a dealer as a participant in a public offering shall not be deemed to be owned by such dealer;

iii. Any dealer registered pursuant to section 15 of the Exchange Act acting in a riskless principal transaction on behalf of a qualified institutional buyer;

iv. Any investment company registered under the Investment Company Act, acting for its own account or for the accounts of other qualified institutional buyers, that is part of a family of investment companies which own in the aggregate at least USD 100 million in securities of issuers, other than issuers that are affiliated with the investment company or are part of such family of investment companies. Family of investment companies means any two or more investment companies registered under the Investment Company Act, except for a unit investment trust whose assets consist solely of shares of one or more registered investment companies, that have the same investment adviser (or, in the case of unit investment trusts, the same depositor), Provided That, for purposes of this section:

[...]

v. Any entity, all of the equity owners of which are qualified institutional buyers, acting for its own account or the accounts of other qualified institutional buyers; and

vi. Any bank as defined in section 3 (a) (2) of the Act, any savings and loan association or other institution as referenced in section 3 (a) (5) (A) of the Act, or any foreign bank or savings and loan association or equivalent institution, acting for its own account or the accounts of other

cont. ...

In France, before the transposition of the Directive,[78] the 2 July 1998 law also espoused these principles, excluding from the definition of public offer the issuance or sale of financial instruments to 'qualified investors' or a 'limited circle of investors'.[79]

A 'qualified investor' was defined as a legal person having the competence and means necessary to evaluate the risks inherent to financial instrument transactions.[80] In application of this legal definition, Article 1 of Decree 98-880 of 1 October 1998[81] listed the categories of these investors, presented under a tripartite classification:

(i) *de jure* qualified investors, so called because of their legal status, as long as they acted on their own account (credit institutions, financial companies, investment firms, insurance companies, savings institutions regulated by the Social Security Code, etc);

(ii) qualified investors by choice, a group that included quasi-professional investors who, although not licensed to provide investment services, had sufficient expertise (capital-risk companies, stock corporations with total consolidated balance sheet exceeding Euro 150 million, national government-controlled companies engaged in industrial or commercial activities having shares listed on a regulated EEA market, certain mutual companies, etc) and companies held (99% or more) by qualified investors;

(iii) qualified investors acting as agents on behalf of a collective investment undertaking or on behalf of a qualified investor falling into one of the aforementioned categories.

qualified institutional buyers, that in the aggregate owns and invests on a discretionary basis at least USD 100 million in securities of issuers that are not affiliated with it and that has an audited net worth of at least USD 25 million as demonstrated in its latest annual financial statements, as of a date not more than 16 months preceding the date of sale under the Rule in the case of a U.S. bank or savings and loan association, and not more than 18 months preceding such date of sale for a foreign bank or savings and loan association or equivalent institution'.

[78] See Article L 411-2 of the Monetary and Financial Code, modified by the Law 2005-842 (n 60) implemented by AMF General Regulation, Article 211-1 ff.

[79] Monetary and Financial Code, Article L 411-2 para 1. See A Pietrancosta (n 33) 39 ff; E Cafritz and O Tene 'La réglementation des placements privés en France' (2003) 2 Bull Joly Bourse et Produits Financiers 126.

[80] Monetary and Financial Code, Article L 411-2 para 2. See A Pietrancosta (n 33); E Bernard and F Peltier 'Investisseur qualifié: la frontière de l'ordre public de protection en droit des marchés financiers' (1998) 69 RD bancaire et bourse 156; H Hovasse 'Investisseurs qualifiés et cercle restreint d'investisseurs' (1998) 70 Revue de droit bancaire et de la bourse 191; MJ Experton 'L'investisseur qualifié' (1999) Bull Joly Bourse 140.

[81] Decree 98-880 of 1 October 1998 applying dispositions of Article 6 of Ordinance No. 67-833 of 28 September 1967, modified, creating the 'Commission des opérations de bourse' and relating to disclosure to securities holders and disclosure of certain market transactions, Journal Officiel de la République Française No. 228, 2.10.1998, 14938.

The 'limited circle of investors' referred to a group of persons, other than qualified investors, having a personal relationship with the issuer's managers, whether professional or family in nature.[82] Such a circle was presumed to exist where the number of persons concerned was less than 100 (Decree of 1 October 1998).

Accordingly, those familiar with French law do not feel lost in *terra incognita* when discovering the terms of the Prospectus Directive.[83] In fact, possible influence between French and EU regimes would be reciprocal, since Directive 89/298/EC was already inapplicable to securities 'offered to persons in the context of their trades, professions or occupations' and/or 'to a restricted circle of persons'.[84] One could say, in this respect, that the new Community text simply adds specificity there where it was missing from the predecessor Directive, if this specificity were not so essential in terms of harmonization.

With respect to the quantitative exemption, one can observe that the Prospectus Directive abandoned the generic expression 'limited circle of persons',[85] and instituted a bright-line limit on the number of offerees of a private offer, which is henceforth the quantitative limit of the notion of 'public'.[86]

The threshold was to evolve during the debates. The 30 May 2001 draft set the limit at 149 persons. Several months later, it was specified that qualified investors should not be included when counting the number of offerees.[87] Later, as a precautionary measure, it was indicated that these persons could be either natural or legal persons.[88] The limit was then lowered to 99 in the 9 August 2002 proposed directive and subsequently maintained, despite a parliamentary proposal which was justified by the reasoning that if too low, in particular for larger Member States, the threshold exemption would have limited practical effect.[89] This appears excessively pessimistic, considering that the Directive, like in French law, contains a generous solution compared to that in effect in the United States.[90]

[82] Monetary and Financial Code, Article L 411-2 para 3. See A Pietrancosta (n 33) 43 ff.

[83] See B François 'Vers une nouvelle définition de l'appel public à l'épargne' (2004) 23 Recueil Dalloz, Cahier droit des affaires 1652. Comp. for Germany, where 'there was no precise numerical threshold delimiting private placements and public offers'; C Schmies 'The Implementation of the EU Prospectus Directive in Germany' (2005) 20 J Int'l Banking L & R 585-589.

[84] Directive 89/298/EEC (n 10) Article 2 (1).

[85] An analogous expression was still contained in the proposal dated 30 May 2001.

[86] Prospectus Directive (n 1) Article 3 (2) (b).

[87] See Council of the European Union (n 41).

[88] C Huhne (n 30) amendment 20, 19.

[89] See C Huhne (n 20) amendment 13.

[90] See e.g. J Bartos 'Offering Rules: What the US and Europe Can Teach Each Other' (October 2003) Int'l Fin L Rev 16; adde, BD Speck and J Tanega 'Private Equity Placements: Com-

cont. ...

This observation is all the more accurate in light of the fact that the limit of 99 persons applied 'per Member State'. The limit is accordingly multiplied by the number of Member States concerned, which potentially represents, throughout the Union, a fairly sizable group of investors.

With respect to the qualitative exemption, the notion of 'qualified investors' is an additional manifestation of the trend in modern financial regulation – nonetheless compatible with the principle of equality –, to differentiate among categories of investors based on their qualifications.[91]

Again, the scope of the exemption changed significantly with the passage of time, as the definition of qualified investors was successively expanded. The 30 May 2001 proposal only included 'credit institutions, investment firms, other authorised or regulated financial institutions, insurance companies, collective investment schemes and their management companies, pension funds and retirement funds, supranational institutions, government and central administrative authorities'. Article 2 (1) (e) of the final text lists: '(i) legal entities which are authorised or regulated to operate in the financial markets, including: credit institutions, investment firms, other authorised or regulated financial institutions, insurance companies, collective investment schemes and their management companies, pension funds and their management companies, commodity dealers, as well as entities not so authorised or regulated whose corporate purpose is solely to invest in securities; (ii) national and regional governments, central banks, international and supranational institutions such as the International Monetary Fund, the European Central Bank, the European Investment Bank and other similar international organisations'. One can especially remark the presence of persons other than market professionals, so as to favor the development of private placements and to guarantee coherence with the revision of the Investment Services Directive.[92] Some are automatically included: 'iii) other legal entities which do not meet two of the three criteria' set out to define small and medium-sized enterprises (SMEs) (i.e. 'an average number of employees during the financial year of less than 250, a total balance sheet not exceeding Euro 43,000,000 and an annual net turnover not exceeding Euro 50,000,000').[93] Others are admitted only upon

paring the Laws in Switzerland, the European Union, the United Kingdom and the United States' (2006) 21 J Int'l Banking L & R 213-226.

[91] See Council Directive 93/22/EEC of 10 May 1993 on Investment Services in the Securities Field, (the ISD) OJ L141 11.06.1993 27-46 Articles 11 (1), 11 (3), 14 (4) in particular Whereas 23 explaining that 'to protect investors …, it is therefore appropriate to take account of the different requirements for protection of various categories of investors and of their levels of professional expertise'. Adde, Directive 97/9/EC of the European Parliament and of the Council of 3 March 1997 on Investor-Compensation Schemes, OJ L084 26.03.1997 22-31 Annex I; and especially the MiFID (n 31) Annex II.

[92] See C Huhne (n 30) amendment 15; Opinion of the Economic and Social Committee (EESC) (n 21).

[93] Prospectus Directive (n 1) Article 2 (1) (f).

authorization requested and obtained from the Member State where the person is incorporated or resident. This is the case of SMEs (v) and certain natural persons (iv), if the latter meet at least two of the three following criteria: a) having 'carried out transactions of a significant size on securities markets at an average frequency of, at least, 10 per quarter over the previous four quarters'; b) possess a securities portfolio whose value exceeds Euro 500,000; c) currently or formerly work 'for at least one year in the financial sector in a professional position which requires knowledge of securities investment'.[94] To this end, a register listing the SMEs and natural persons meeting these criteria will be made available to all issuers.[95] Registered investors will be able to decide at any time to renounce their qualified investor status.

The circle of qualified investors thus defined, the Directive posits the principle that a securities offering addressed to them[96] need not be accompanied by a prospectus within the Member State concerned,[97] without any limit in number of the targeted investors. The threshold for 'public' here again appears higher in Community law than in U.S.[98] or French law. This generosity can also be found in the regime of private offers because unlike in U.S. law, the offeror can resort to advertising or general solicitation. Likewise, even though the text does lack some clarity, it is logical for the resale of securities which were not part of a public offering to benefit from the exemptions set in Article 3, without a minimum holding period, as long as the offering does not conceal a public placement.[99]

The configuration of these exemptions is, as we see, highly instructive with respect to the elements of a public offering. Other indications can be found to give a more complete and accurate picture of 'public offering', such as the exemptions from the obligation to publish a prospectus for share offerings addressed to existing shareholders,[100] or securities offerings targeting directors or employees;[101] these exemptions, which are conditional, indicate that these persons are not by nature excluded from the public. In brief, members of the 'hard core' public, which would fully reveal itself in the extreme case where all those who

[94] Prospectus Directive (n 1) Article 2 (2).

[95] Prospectus Directive (n 1) Article 2 (3).

[96] The restriction, in the proposal of 30 May 2001 that qualified investors must act on their own behalf, had disappeared, certain persons fearing that as written the restriction 'would seem to exclude a fund manager buying such securities on behalf of one of the funds it manages', see C Huhne (n 30) 53.

[97] Prospectus Directive (n 1) Article 3 (2) (a).

[98] See e.g. J Bartos (n 90).

[99] See Prospectus Directive (n 1) Article 3 (2) last paragraph. Interestingly, the new French disclosure regime, as the previous one, does not contain any special provision applying to the resale of securities.

[100] Prospectus Directive (n 1) Article 4 (1) (d).

[101] Prospectus Directive (n 1) Article 4 (1) (e).

could register as qualified investors would do so, appear to be natural persons without specific competence with respect to securities or without significant financial resources. This delimitation unveils the *ratio legis* of the protection enshrined by the Directive, designed primarily for those who have neither knowledge ('*savoir*') nor wealth ('*avoir*').[102]

II. The Missing Link to a Coherent Whole

The definition of private offering implicitly reveals the notion of public and as a correlation the reasons justifying regulations governing public offers, which regulations should not apply where it is not necessary to protect investors. This superfluousness can be deduced from an investor's ability to evaluate for him or herself the risks inherent to a transaction due to his/her financial acumen, and/or to financially bear such risks. The underlying idea, determined by economic efficiency, is to refrain from imposing additional and costly disclosure requirements without a corresponding significant benefit for investors and the markets.[103]

In U.S. law, this principle has long existed. In a famous 1953 decision, the only interpretation of the concept of private placement, the U.S. Supreme Court stated that the registration (and thus disclosure) exemption under federal law[104] in favor of private offerings must rely on the offerees' actual need for protection.[105] Therefore, an offering is not public if it targets persons able to '*fend for themselves*'.

The quality of the offerees trumps their quantity, for the decisive factor depends on their capacity to evaluate, understand or bear the inherent risks of the offer.[106] Even so, ruled the Court, nothing would prohibit the Securities and Ex-

[102] The wealth factor, deemed '*censitaire*' in France but '*courue*' in the United States, is reinforced by the exclusions in Article 3 paragraphs c) and d) for securities offerings 'addressed to investors who acquire securities for a total consideration of at least Euro 50,000 per investor, for each separate offer' and/or offers of securities 'whose denomination per unit amounts to at least Euro 50,000'. This type of exclusion was also expanded from the original 30 May 2001 proposal, which was limited to securities offerings requiring an investment of at least Euro 150,000 per investor.

[103] As to this fear, see C Dammers 'How EU Rules Will Deny Access to Retail Markets' (December 2002) Int'l Fin L Rev.

[104] Section 4 (2) of Securities Act of 1933.

[105] *S.E.C. v. Ralston Purina Co.*, 346 U.S. 119 (1953). RW Jennings, H Marsh and JC Coffee *Securities Regulation, Cases and Materials* (University Casebook Series, 7th ed 1992) 328; TL Hazen (n 66) 224 ff; HS Bloomenthal *Securities and Federal Corporate Law* (Clark Boardman Company, Ltd. and Sage Hill Publishers 1997) ch. 4 s. 14; SA O'Dowd and K Guse *Non-public Offerings: The Offering Process Under Regulation D* (Practising Law Institute Corporate Law and Practice Course Handbook Series 1997) 113; MET Beach (n 66) 59.

[106] See L Walton and LB Morgan (n 66) 243; MET Beach (n 66) 61; SA O'Dowd and K Guse (n 105) 116; T Hazen (n 66) 230 ff. See for later additions by the caselaw, *Lively v.*

cont. ...

change Commission from implementing numerical tests to ease application of the law.[107]

French law, since its 1998 reform, largely adopts this logic, the 2 July 1998 law representing for most a transition from a quantitative concept to a qualitative concept of the public offering.[108] Henceforth, determining whether an offering is public or private depends essentially on the characteristics of the persons who are solicited, that is, their professional competence (qualified investors) or their personal knowledge of the issuer (limited circle of investors). The numerical threshold is only a secondary definition, a presumption intended to reduce uncertainty in defining a limited circle of investors.

One can regret that the Directive did not embrace this logic more fully, and limited itself to this kind of secondary level of definitions, listing cases for exemption without linking them to broader notions. One will look in vain for a conceptual definition of qualified investor or limited circle of investors. This deficiency would be without consequence if the listed exemptions covered all possible cases of the private offer. Nonetheless, it is reasonable to take the position that, as in national laws, the exemptions should be examined as negative, non-exhaustive illustrations of the public offer. They should be construed as safe harbors, setting specific conditions in order to avoid the legal requirement, without excluding the possibility for an offeror to prove the private nature of an offer made in other circumstances. Therefore, between the positive definition of public offer and the list of transactions that are not considered public offers, there seems to be a missing link, which, if present, would give the entire regime true coherence. This link is obviously a general definition of the private offer, which should itself take into consideration any link between the offeror and the offerees that presumably allows them access to the type of information contained in a prospectus and consequently rendering the prospectus requirement superfluous. It is not sure, however, that all EU countries will adopt such an approach.

This same concern for coherence leads to reflections on the possibility of another missing link (albeit not from the Prospectus Directive) between public offers and the legal status of their issuer. The Prospectus Directive is nearly silent on this point, setting no condition prior, nor obligation subsequent, to the offer, with respect to the issuer. Generally speaking, it is remarkable that such requirements, triggered by a simple public offer, are relatively rare in Community company law, which prefers to divide companies according to whether their shares

Hirschfeld, 440 F.2d 631, 633 (10th Cir. 1971); *SEC v. Continental Tobacco*, 463 F.2d 137 (5th Cir. 1972); *Doran v. Petroleum Management Corp.*, 545 F.2d 893 (5th Cir. 1977); *Sorrell v. SEC*, 679 F.2d 1323 (9th Cir. 1982).

[107] See A Pietrancosta (n 32) note 1695.

[108] See P Marini 'Report No. 413 prepared for the Commission for the Finance, Budget Control and Economic Statements of the Nation' (vol 2) Annex to minutes of the session held 29 April 1998; A Pietrancosta (n 33) note 38.

are listed on a regulated market.[109] The Community solution is quite different from that of French law, which, with the law of 2 July 1998, created an automatic reciprocal relation between the public offering of securities, even unlisted, and the special status of publicly-held issuer ('*émetteur faisant appel public à l'épargne*'), from which numerous legal consequences flow.[110] Accordingly, the public offering of securities always leads to a change in the legal status of their issuer and this status exclusively results from the realization of such an offering. Whether it is appropriate to build a relationship of such intensity is debatable, however, given the confusion introduced between an act (public offering) and a state of being (status of the issuer).[111] If the dispersion of shareholders undoubtedly creates specific problems, well-described by agency theorists, that the legislator must tackle, distinctions made between the causes of this dispersion leave the observer confused. It would surely be more satisfying and rational, like in certain U.S. law solutions, to set rules that are specially triggered once the link between the issuer and the shareholders becomes too tenuous. These observations merit at least to be taken into account, as reflection on the difficult subject of legal classification of companies is under way at the EU level.[112]

[109] The Prospectus Directive follows this rule, obliging issuers whose securities are admitted to trading on a regulated market to provide, at least annually, 'a document that contains or refers to all information that they have published or made available to the public over the preceding 12 months in one or more Member States and in third countries in compliance with their obligations under Community and national laws and rules dealing with the regulation of securities, issuers of securities and securities markets' (Article 10 (1)).

[110] See A Pietrancosta (n 32) note 1698 ff and (n 33) note 60 ff; M Germain 'Les sociétés qui font appel public à l'épargne' in JJ Daigre (ed) *La modernisation du droit des sociétés* (GLN-Joly 1997) 31; B François 'L'appel public à l'épargne, critère de distinction des sociétés de capitaux' thesis Paris II (September 2003).

[111] See A Pietrancosta (n 33) note 61.

[112] See Report of the High Level Group of Company Law Experts on a Modern Regulatory Framework for Company Law in Europe (November 2002) <http://europa.eu.int/comm/internal_ market/company/modern/index_en.htm> 34 ff; Communication from the Commission to the Council and the European Parliament 'Modernising Company Law and Enhancing Corporate Governance in the European Union – A Plan to Move Forward' COM(2003) 284.

Nonfinancial Disclosure between 'Shareholder Value' and 'Socially Responsible Investing'

FRANCESCO DENOZZA

Under European law, issuers of financial instruments must disclose as soon as possible information which would be likely to have a significant effect on the prices of those financial instruments. When a sufficient number of investors decide whether or not to carry out stock investments in a specific company after having taken into account nonfinancial information, information of this kind can have a significant effect on the prices. It follows that the disclosure of socially relevant data may be mandatory even when those data are financially immaterial and their disclosure may harm the company and its actual shareholders. Thus we become aware of the existence of a conflict between investors interested in nonfinancial information and other investors. The European law's choice of imposing the disclosure of nonfinancial information even when it could harm the company and its shareholders, puts the interest of investors concerned only with the maximisation of the value of their shares after the interests of other investors.

A. Financial and Nonfinancial Disclosure
B. The Notion of Nonfinancial Information
C. The Interpretation of the Transparency Directive and its Relationship with the Market Abuse Directive
D. The Notion of 'Inside Information'
E. From the Interpretation of Law to the Analysis of Conflicts Amongst the Different Interests of the Individuals Involved: The 'Shareholder Value' Model
F. Disclosure Duties: Not a Matter of Increasing Overall Welfare, but of Favouring One Out of Different, Conflicting, Interests

A. Financial and Nonfinancial Disclosure

This paper evaluates whether listed companies should be required to provide not only financial, but also social disclosure. The issue to be discussed is that of a possible mandatory disclosure of socially relevant data, even when they are financially immaterial, and especially when their disclosure may harm the company and its actual shareholders. The matter will be examined from the viewpoint of the rules that govern the general disclosure duties of listed companies. We shall ignore the possible interests of other stakeholders and shall only focus on the shareholders' and investors' interests. We shall not take into consideration the fact that certain countries promulgated new rules, or planned legislative reforms, requiring the disclosure of considerably more social or environmental information.[1] This legislation is inspired by the aim of protecting social interests that are different from, and perhaps, in conflict with shareholders' and investors' interests. It usually represents a set of special rules which are not integrated in the general framework of the rules (especially embodied – in EU law – in the Transparency, Prospectus and Market Abuse Directives) governing general disclosure duties.

We shall also ignore the fact that many companies are already voluntarily reporting in terms of sustainable development as well as with regards to the related social and environmental issues. Even though voluntary social disclosure is purported to be improving – both in quality and quantity – the mandatory option remains an issue deserving adequate attention as it could well be relevant from a practical and theoretical point of view. From a *practical* point of view, the main concern – with regards to a system of voluntary disclosure – is related to the precision of those standards that establish exactly what ought to be disclosed, and to the appropriate verification of what actually is disclosed. In the case of fraud, a mandatory rule implies a more rigorous definition of what may be included in social reports and appropriate sanctions. From a *theoretical* point of view, the main issue concerns the identification of the interests protected by the disclosure. At present, for various reasons, pressure is being put on companies to report on social and ethical matters, but there is no accepted hierarchy in the classification of goals pursued by such 'social disclosure'. The application of mandatory rules necessitates, instead, a more precise identification of the interests protected by the rules.

To summarise, this paper focuses on two issues: a) whether the general rules imposing mandatory disclosure in the interest of investors, ought to be interpreted in the sense that listed companies may be obliged to disclose (in appropriate cases) even nonfinancial information; b) which interests we can suppose to be protected by the duty to disclose even nonfinancial information.

The first issue implies an interpretation problem relating to the rule establishing that listed companies must disclose all information which, 'if it were made public, would be likely to have a significant effect on the prices of… financial instruments or on the prices of related derivative financial instruments' (Article 1 (1) and Article 6 (1), Market Abuse Directive).

The second issue is a more substantial one. It evokes the problem pertaining to conflicts existing amongst different shareholders and different investors. What is at stake is the critique of a conception of shareholders and investors as '*a single*

[1] C Williams and JM Conley 'An Emerging Third Way? The Erosion of the Anglo-American Shareholder Value Construct' (SSRN wp <http://ssrn.com/abstract_id=632347>, 2004).

economic abstraction',[2] which originates from the American literature and now seems to inspire even European law as well as a large part of European doctrine.[3] I shall argue that this conception is over-simplistic and that through the use of notions such as 'shareholder value' or 'reasonable investor', it tends to hide the fact that shareholders, as well as investors, may have different goals, different interests and different conceptions on what should be considered as rational. They have in fact different needs, different attitudes toward risk and different beliefs. Thus, corporation and financial market laws cannot be viewed as a set of rules whose only aim is that of maximising a single, definite goal (shareholder value or investors' overall welfare). The idea that corporation and financial market laws may be interpreted as simple tools for furthering a given purpose (i.e. for protecting only one identified interest) is an illusion. On the contrary, corporate and financial market laws decide about conflicts of interests that exist amongst shareholders and amongst investors. Bearing in mind this fact (which the notions of shareholder value and of reasonable investor are inclined to hide) the interpretation of the rules becomes more complicated, though a lot closer to reality.

B. The Notion of Nonfinancial Information

Nonfinancial information is a residuary class and inevitably contains heterogeneous elements. Therefore a preliminary analysis of this category is necessary in order to better clarify the exact type of nonfinancial information relevant for this paper's purpose.

At first glance, we may identify nonfinancial information with the information pertaining to those facts that do not affect a company's financial performance. Some margins of ambiguity however remain. As is well-known, there are many situations in which socially relevant events may affect a company's financial results; for example, the case in which *substantial* fines are attached to the socially unwanted activity of a company.

I would not consider this kind of information as nonfinancial. I believe that information concerning facts exposing a company to the risk of being fined is financially relevant and therefore must be disclosed just like any other financial fact. In fact, in this case, what must be disclosed is not so much the event as such,

[2] 'Note: Should the SEC Expand Nonfinancial Disclosure Requirements?' (2002) 115 Harv L Rev 1433.

[3] H Hansmann and R Kraakman 'The End of History for Corporate Law' (2000) 89 Geo L J 439-468; G Ferrarini 'Shareholder Value and the Modernisation of European Corporate Law', in KJ Hopt and E Wymeersch (eds) *Capital Markets and Company Law* (Oxford University Press 2003) 223-260; R Kraakman et al (eds) *The Anatomy of Corporate Law: A Comparative and Functional Approach* (Oxford University Press 2004); P Joerg, C Loderer, L Roth and U Waelchli 'The Purpose of the Corporation: Shareholder-value Maximization?' (ECGI Finance wp No. 95/2005 <http//ssrn.com/abstract_id=690044>, 2006).

but the expected sanction, when its imposition becomes sufficiently certain. Therefore, we define nonfinancial information as information pertaining to those facts that do not affect directly (as such considered) the company's financial performance. According to this definition, we may distinguish between facts that do not have financial relevance (which are therefore included in the class of nonfinancial information), and financially relevant information such as that relating to events which may expose the company to possible pecuniary losses.

However, it is necessary to make other qualifications within the concept of nonfinancial information. Certain facts, as for example, corporate governance rules adopted by a company, do not affect how much profit a company may make and from this point of view, cannot be considered as 'financial facts'. They are, however, facts that can affect the way profits are administered and distributed. Therefore the information concerning those facts is different from the information regarding facts which affect neither the sum of the profits generated, nor the way in which they are distributed. For the purpose of this paper, this kind of information will not be considered as nonfinancial information.

To conclude, as well as in order to have an intuitive idea of exactly what information will be considered in this paper, we may distinguish information depending whether it affects: *how much* profit is generated; *how* it is generated[4] and *how* it is administered and distributed. From now on we shall concentrate on the second category.

Having fixed an albeit rough definition, we can put forward a few examples. Let us imagine a hypothetical case in which a company decides to re-locate the import of a fundamental input from an 'ordinary' State to a State that does not respect human rights, or the case in which the Board of a company discovers that profits made by a foreign subsidiary originate from a policy of intolerable exploitation of the local workforce. In both cases, we presume that no rule violation exists and therefore that there is no prospect of punishment. However, we ask ourselves whether or not those facts should be disclosed.

C. The Interpretation of the Transparency Directive and its Relationship with the Market Abuse Directive

We shall commence with interpretation problems. The Transparency Directive usually adopts the '*financial*' qualification in order to characterise the information that issuers are required to disclose. Article 4 is devoted to the 'annual *financial* reports'. Article 5 to 'half-yearly *financial* reports'. According to Article 6, the management statement shall provide 'an explanation of material events and transactions that have taken place during the relevant period and their impact on the

[4] C Williams 'The Securities and Exchange Commission and Corporate Social Transparency' (1999) 112 Harv L Rev 1197-1312, 1210.

financial position' and 'a general description of the financial position and performance'. However, these provisions must be coordinated with the general principle established in Article 6 of the Market Abuse Directive, which requests Member States to ensure that issuers of financial instruments inform the public as soon as possible of inside information, defined as 'information of a precise nature which has not been made public' and 'which if it were made public, would be likely to have a significant effect on the prices of those financial instruments'. I believe that above all we must establish whether nonfinancial information (in the sense above defined) can be included in the set of 'inside information' whose disclosure is mandatory, or whether nonfinancial information is excluded from the class of 'inside information' by definition, i.e. because it cannot affect a company's financial performance and therefore is presumed not to affect the prices of 'those financial instruments'.

If the issue were to be solved in favour of the first alternative, I would argue that the reference to the financial character of the periodic disclosure should not be considered as conclusive. It would make little sense that disclosure of nonfinancial information was mandatory in the hypothesis of ad-hoc disclosure and optional in the hypothesis of periodic disclosure. The proper solution would be to consider the description of periodic reports provided by the Transparency Directive as an indication of the minimum contents those reports must have, and without prejudice, of those cases in which further information is required, according to the rule established by Article 6 (1) of the Market Abuse Directive. In other words, I maintain that the relationship between Article 6 (1) of the Market Abuse Directive and the relevant rules of the Transparency Directive must be conceived as the relationship between a general principle and specific regulations of specific cases.

D. The Notion of 'Inside Information'

The interpretation of the notion of inside information faces certain difficulties, which have been worsened (rather than removed) by the implementing Directive 2003/124/EC, which (Article 1 (2)) provides that 'information which if it were made public would be likely to have a significant effect on the price of financial instruments... shall mean information a reasonable investor would be likely to use as part of the basis of his investment decision'.

Reference to the reasonable investor tends to make European law more akin to American law in which the main reference is the concept of 'materiality', defined by the Supreme Court through stating that information is material if 'there is a substantial likelihood that a reasonable shareholder would consider it important in making an investment decision'.[5] Problems however arise from the fact that the 'reasonable investor' (or 'reasonable shareholder') test is ambiguous. Is the 'reasonable investor' an abstract concept (whose contents anyone may speculate), or should the ways in which the actual investors make their investment decisions be taken into account?

It is obvious[6] that the assessment of the possibility of a price moving effect is an *ex ante* evaluation ('...the question whether, in making an investment decision, a reasonable investor would be likely to take into account a particular piece of information should be appraised on the basis of the ex ante available information...', Commission Directive 2003/124/EC). This premise cannot however imply that we are permitted to ignore the behavior of actual investors. The 'reasonable investor' cannot be conceived as an 'ideal type'. That of a reasonable investor is an empirical notion which must be defined in accordance with the observation of the actual investors' behaviour.

Therefore, if we refuse the alternative of considering the reasonable investor as an abstract concept (which would mean leaving the definition of the reasonable investor to the unconstrained discretion of the courts) we will be faced with a second problem.

We can easily imagine cases in which different groups of investors take into account – for their investment decisions – facts of a different nature. This may well be the case of nonfinancial information. It is a well-known fact that the rapid growth of the so-called socially responsible investment has been one of the key trends in the financial world over the past few years. According to a recent report, nearly one out of nine dollars under professional management in the United States was involved in socially responsible investing in 2003, accounting for roughly USD 2.16 trillion, equivalent to 11.3% of investment assets under professional management in the U.S..[7]

In cases where different groups of investors take into account facts of a different nature, the alternative would be between the interpretation of the reasonable investor standard, which takes into account only information considered as relevant by the average investor (at least 50% of investors?) and the interpretation according to which even information considered important only by a qualified minority of investors may be material and 'price sensitive'. I would argue that the first alternative cannot be embraced not only because the 'average person' test, used in the working document ESC 12/2003, and widely criticised[8] has been

[5] *TSC Industries, Inc. v. Northway, Inc.*, 426 U.S. 438 (1976); G Ferrarini 'La nuova disciplina europea dell'abuso di mercato' (2004) Riv Soc 54.

[6] See e.g. CESR 'Advice on Level 2 Implementing Measures for the proposed Market Abuse Directive' (December 2002) 22 ff.

[7] Social Investment Forum '2003 Report on Socially Responsible Investment Trends in the United States' (December 2003) <www.socialinvest.org>.

[8] Comments on the EC Working Documents ESC 12/2003, 13/2003 and 14/2003 <http://europa.eu.int/comm/internal_market/securities/abuse/index_en.htm>.

abandoned and substituted by the reasonable investor test, but in particular as the reasonable investor test, interpreted as equivalent to the average investor test, may conflict with the main rule that all information likely to have a significant effect on prices must be disclosed.

We know that in order to have an effect on prices, the size of a group of investors considering specific information as relevant need not necessarily reach fifty per cent of all investors or thereabouts. On the contrary, it is obvious that a percentage of eleven per cent of the total investor community and – according to case circumstances – even a lower percentage, may have an impact on the market (i.e. may influence prices with its investment decisions). At this point, we may choose between two alternative solutions: the first solution, where information relevant to a small percentage of investors – but immaterial to the average reasonable investor – is not classified as inside information, even though the decisions of the investors who take this information into account, are able to influence the prices; the second solution, where the possible effect on prices is conclusive and thus the obligation to disclose includes all information considered by a number of investors whose investment decisions are able to affect the prices. I maintain that we must embrace the latter alternative.

The reasonable investor's standard cannot be interpreted in a way that may entail a conflict with the main criterion, that is – and remains – the criterion of the incidence on prices. Reference to the average investor's behaviour could be useful in order to establish a prima facie presumption concerning the type of information that must be disclosed. However, when there is evidence that there exists a sufficient number of investors who decide whether or not to carry out stock investments in a specific company after having taken into account a specific kind of information, information of this kind must then be disclosed, even if it concerns a fact that the average investor considers completely irrelevant.

I believe that this solution can also be motivated from another point of view. In European law, the duty to disclose is strictly connected to the prevention of insider trading (there is a coincidence between the notion of insider information and of information to be disclosed). Let us now imagine that an insider becomes acquainted with the fact that a company has re-located the import of an important input from an 'ordinary' State to a State in which human rights are not respected. We may presume that the decision has no financial consequences (the input price remains the same). Are we in the position to establish that there is no disclosure obligation, thus accepting the risk that before the information becomes public the insiders will sell the stock in the hope of making a profit by means of variations in their prices, caused by the decision to sell by those investors offended by the indirect support the company in question gives to a 'rogue' State? I believe that the answer should be negative and therefore we should opt for a solution which compels insiders to make public, all information regarding facts that even a small – though not irrelevant – fraction of investors may consider when making investment decisions.

This interpretation has the obvious fault of widening the set of information that must be disclosed, as well as making its borders some what uncertain. I believe that the reasonable investor's standard may come to our aid when interpreted (as we proposed before) as a mere presumption of irrelevance of information that is not considered by the average investor. The disclosure obligation (in the interpretation that I support) would in fact include all facts the average investor takes into consideration, together with those facts which specific evidence suggests are taken into account by a noninsignificant portion of the investors community.

E. From the Interpretation of Law to the Analysis of Conflicts Amongst the Different Interests of the Individuals Involved: The 'Shareholder Value' Model.

At this point, I would move from the interpretation of the rules and focus on evaluating the interests of the individuals involved. At a first glance, the interests protected by mandatory disclosure obligations can be easily identified with the investors' interest of being informed of any relevant fact concerning securities offered for sale so that 'competing judgements of buyers and sellers as to the fair price of a security, brings about a situation where the market price reflects as nearly as possible a just price'.[9] As I said before, I intend to follow this line of reasoning, and therefore I shall not consider any other possible interests, as, for example, the general public interest concerning information of the community in general, or the interests of other specific 'stakeholders' (e.g. employees).

Having established that only investors' interests will be taken into account, the question as to whether all investors are equally interested in having unlimited disclosure of any relevant fact still remains. Generally, it is easily conceivable that people who consider their stock in a company as a long-term investment may have scant interest in the disclosure of facts that do not affect the performance of the company in the long run. They may even prefer certain facts not to be disclosed, when the costs of their disclosure for the company outweigh the benefits long-term investors may obtain from such disclosure.[10] With specific reference to the present issue (that of the duty to disclose nonfinancial information) one might easily imagine facts, considered by the majority of the investors as immaterial, whose diffusion may have negative consequences for a company. The usual example of trading with a rogue State may help to illustrate the point. The disclo-

[9] C Williams (n 4) 1210, notes 58 and 59. See also T Baums 'Changing Patterns of Corporate Disclosure in Continental Europe: the Example of Germany' (ECGI Law wp No. 4/2002 <http://ssrn.com/abstract_id=345020>, 2002).

[10] C Angelici 'Note in tema di informazione societaria' in AA.VV. (eds) *La riforma delle società quotate* (Giuffrè 1998) 264 ff.

sure of this information could have negative effects not only on stock prices (as we have already seen), but also on a company's commercial reputation, at least when groups of consumers exist who take into consideration the overall behaviour of firms, whilst deciding on which company they will buy the necessary products from.

The peculiarity of this situation arises from the fact that the negative consequences are not an indirect effect of an event which is already negative as such (as is the case of disclosure of financial difficulties that can have negative consequences on a company's credit). Trading with a rogue State is – from an economic point of view – an absolutely neutral fact that, according to the circumstances, could even be profitable. Negative economic effects arise only with – and as a consequence of – disclosure. Therefore, the problem is whether or not the shareholders must suffer a reduction in profit opportunities of a company as a consequence of the imposition concerning the obligation to disclose even those facts that are of no interest to the vast majority of shareholders and investors. If we opt for a positive answer, as in my opinion we ought to, the consequence is that the shareholders' interest relating to the maximisation of a company's profit and of 'shareholder value', turns out to be sacrificed not to external interests of other stakeholders, but to the interest of (a minority of) other investors and shareholders.

The long and rich debate on 'optimal' disclosure and on the efficiency of mandatory rules has usually ignored problems connected with possible conflicts between the interests of different groups of investors.[11] The only interest considered as legitimate seems to be the interest of the short-term investor who decides at all times exactly what stock to sell, what stock to buy and what stock to keep in his portfolio. The protection of other, less prompt and painstaking investors, is entirely committed to the diversification of the investments amongst different companies.

The analysis of the disclosure costs has therefore been focused on the material costs of collecting and releasing information, and on some external effect of disclosure that could be detrimental for the firm (as may be the case when information concerns facts that competitors are interested to know). However, none of those costs are considered as a possible reason for permitting managers to maintain confidential information investors believe to be relevant for their investment decisions. Disagreement exists regarding the respective ability of the legislator and the market to accomplish the task of providing investors with the exact information they need. There is no doubt whatsoever though about the fact that investors are entitled to have complete information about all relevant facts, no matter how much it costs to provide it. In this perspective the difference between the text of Article 68 (1) of the 2001/34/EC Directive (repealed by Article 20 of the

[11] See e.g. L Zingales 'The Costs and Benefits of Financial Market Regulation' (ECGI Law wp No. 21/2004 <http://ssrn.com/abstract_id=536682>, 2004).

Market Abuse Directive) – according to which 'the competent authorities may ... exempt the company from this requirement, if the disclosure of particular information is such as to prejudice the legitimate interests of the company' – and the rules now in force, may appear very significant.

The point is that the possible conflict between shareholders interested in maintaining certain information (e.g. the fact that the company is dealing with rogue states) confidential, in order to preserve their investments' value, and those investors wishing to obtain any and all information which may have an effect on the stock's price, rather than having being effectively resolved in favour of the latter, has been simply ignored. The most widespread model in the international literature appears to be inspired by a conception in which there is no place for conflicts between the interests of different groups of shareholders and investors. What has been described here as a conflict amongst different subjects (namely, different groups of investors with completely different beliefs and preferences) is instead conceived of as a conflict between different interests of the very same subject (the ideal investor, presented as an economic abstraction supposedly having only one well identified interest). In this perspective the conflict between the present shareholders – possibly interested in maintaining certain information confidential – and other investors interested in total disclosure – is akin to the 'conflict' between my wanting to spend an afternoon walking, on one hand, and my desire to go on the same afternoon to the cinema. This is presented not as a conflict *amongst* different subjects, but as a 'conflict' *within* the same subject.

The reason being, that in this perspective, a shareholder, meaning a partner participating in an enterprise together with other partners to divide the success, disappears. This picture is substituted with another, that of the investor who has purchased shares in a certain company, though has not yet decided to sell them.

In this perspective, an investor takes on the temporary guise of shareholder in the period between the decision to purchase and the decision to sell certain shares. This explains why the interest in keeping certain information confidential (information that could damage the company and its present shareholders) is not thought of as a potential source for significant conflict. In this conception, *the terms of the hypothetical conflict would not belong to two different groups of individuals, but would belong to the one and same individual (investor) caught at different moments of her activity* (the moment in which she sells shares – and is therefore interested insofar that information regarding true and negative facts is not revealed – and the moment in which she buys other shares – and is therefore interested insofar that all information corresponding to true facts of all kinds be disclosed). It is quite clear that within a similar group of 'persons', conflicts of interest (in the sense of conflicts among different individuals having different interests) cannot be conceived. One can solely imagine 'conflicts' between different ways of providing the greatest degree of satisfaction to the same common interest. It is not a matter of favouring one interest over another, but of identifying the solution that maximises the only relevant interest.

F. Disclosure Duties: Not a Matter of Increasing Overall Welfare, but of Favouring One Out of Different, Conflicting, Interests.

The case of nonfinancial information can put the model described at the previous paragraph under pressure. The model functions on the premise that no conflict exists between the various groups of investors concerning information to be disclosed. The model considers the possibility that certain investors may be indifferent to the disclosure of certain information that other investors are interested to know. The possibility that *groups of investors may also have a legitimate interest in the non-disclosure of certain information* seems instead to be beyond the horizons of this theoretical model. As we saw, this possibility may instead become reality in the case of nonfinancial information.

To analyse this conflict, and its possible solutions, we can imagine the existence of two groups of investors: one group of investors interested in companies not being obliged to disclose certain information (and should be – on the contrary – allowed to treat it as legitimate company secrets), and another group of investors having the exact opposite interests. Given the context in which we are moving, we will call the first group the 'selfish' investors and the second group the 'altruistic' investors. The existence of these two groups contradicts – as we shall see – the presumed absence of conflicts amongst the different groups of investors concerning the information that must be made public. Therefore, the issue cannot be conceived as a mere matter of optimisation of the fulfilment of one given interest (whether described as a protection for investors or whether described as a maximisation of so-called shareholder value). I shall argue that the choice of imposing a disclosure duty even of nonfinancial information (as is the case in European law, at least according to my interpretation of the definition of inside information provided by the Market Abuse Directive) cannot be justified in terms of efficiency (identified with the maximisation of overall welfare), but only as the consequence of a (political) choice to favour the altruistic against the selfish investors.

The usual example of business with rogue States may help to illustrate the point. As we have already underlined, the peculiarity of this case derives from the fact that here the negative consequences are not the indirect effect of the revelation of an event that is in itself negative. Here, it is disclosure itself that harms the company, in that it can produce negative effects on shares and at times create the risk of boycott by those consumers who, whilst choosing the companies from which they buy the products, are accustomed to evaluating the companies' overall behaviour.

Let us now observe how the choices upon mandating the disclosure of information of this kind may affect the well-being of the two groups of investors we have singled out. We can imagine two different regimes, one in which the disclosure of nonfinancial information is mandatory, and another one in which companies are allowed not to disclose information about facts having as such no direct effect on the economic conditions of the company.

First of all, let us consider a system that imposes disclosure. In this system the well-being of the altruist investors is (concerning the profile of interest here) maximised and there is no doubt whatsoever that they would prefer this system to that of legitimate confidentiality. We may now ask ourselves if the same preference may be attributed to the selfish investors. At this point it must be taken into consideration that in a system in which the duty to disclose does not exist, the company may compare the profit margins deriving from the conclusion of a certain transaction (socially open to criticism), with the probability of suffering losses, as far as its reputation may be damaged, should the transaction ever be discovered. The managers must decide whether the possible gains outweigh the possible losses (obviously discounted by the probabilities of being discovered). In a system of mandatory disclosure, instead, the company is officially deprived of the possibility of hiding the fact that its profits derive from social misconducts. Even if we consider not what the company ought to do, but what it can do in fact, it is equally evident that the possibilities of taking advantage of profits stemming from social misconducts are worsened. The gains stemming from this conduct can no longer be compared with the *probability* that the transaction becomes public domain, but shall be compared, either with the *sureness* of negative consequences – in the case the company decides to comply with the rule – or – in the case in which the company decides not to fulfil its obligation – with the *probability* of the same consequences *together with* the penalty foreseen for infringement. It is therefore obvious that in a system in which nonfinancial information is subjected to a regime of mandatory disclosure, companies have less possibilities to exploit the opportunities of gains offered by possible social misconducts.

Considering now a regime of legitimate confidentiality, we can observe in the first place the situation of the selfish investors. There is no doubt that in this system they could suffer losses from the occasional and sudden diffusion of information damaging the company's reputation (information that they could not take into account due to the absence of any obligation to disclose the information in question). It is also certain, however, that they can cope with this problem by means of a simple diversification of their investments; diversification that usually allows them to compensate the eventual losses suffered for lack of information, with the major profits earned by companies who succeed in keeping secret their social misconducts. Given that the opportunities for profiting that the company may take advantage of under a regime of legitimate confidentiality, are – by definition – more ample and numerous than those present in the other system, the result is that a bigger pie can be made available and that – thanks to the diversification of the investments – all investors can share the gains.

We therefore may reasonably presume that this system maximises – in comparison to the other system – the well-being of the selfish investors, whilst minimising the well-being of the altruist investors (by reducing their possibility of carrying out investments that – from their point of view – would be appropriate).

Given the fact that the mandatory disclosure regime increases the well being of the altruistic investors, whilst the legitimate confidentiality regime increases that of the selfish investors, the choice in favour of the first system cannot be presented as the imposition of a duty to disclose facts that every investor is equally interested to know (even though some investors – the shareholders of the company involved in social misconducts – can occasionally suffer losses from the disclosure). Facts, therefore, which all could, *ex ante* (meaning when each one ignores in how many cases it shall benefit, and in how many cases it shall be disadvantaged by the rule of obligatory disclosure), agree to submit to a regime of mandatory disclosure.

On the contrary, it can well be imagined that the majority of the selfish shareholders and investors might prefer the opposite regime of legitimate confidentiality, in which the opportunities for profiting and the value of the shares are not negatively influenced by the duty to disclose information that for most shareholders and investors is of absolutely no interest at all.

To summarise: what is at stake here is neither a conflict between shareholders and other stakeholders, nor a simple problem of maximisation of the (*ex ante*) common interest of all investors. What we are facing is a real conflict among the interests of different groups of investors, and the European law's choice of imposing the disclosure of nonfinancial information even when it could harm the company and its shareholders, puts the shareholders' interest in the maximisation of the value of the shares in which they have invested (the so-called shareholder value) after, not the external interests of other stakeholders, but the interests of other investors. Therefore, there are reasons to doubt the consistency and usefulness of a notion such as that of maximisation of 'shareholder value' as it ignores the conflicts which may exist amongst the various groups of investors and shareholders, and proves to be useless in solving the most delicate problems that arise from these possible conflicts.

Part 4:

After the Financial Services Action Plan

Effective Policy Design for the Retail Investment Services Market: Challenges and Choices Post FSAP

NIAMH MOLONEY

This essay considers the choices and risks faced by the EU in designing policy for the retail investment services market in the wake of the large-scale regulatory reforms introduced by the FSAP. It argues that a multi-stranded, evidence-based strategy, which incorporates nuanced, non-regulatory policy design initiatives, is essential for the achievement of the EU's objective of promoting an effective retail investment services market through the support of rational and informed investor choice.

A. The EU Investment Services Market and Retail Investor Policy
B. The Delivery of Retail Policy Through a Regulatory Strategy
C. The Regulatory Strategy as Expressed Through the MiFID Conduct of Business Regime
D. The Risks of a Regulatory Strategy
E. A Multi-Stranded Strategy for the Retail Markets
F. Conclusion

A. The EU Investment Services Market and Retail Investor Policy

I. Introduction

Since the adoption of the FSAP in 1999,[1] the EU has been engaged in a massive reform of capital market regulation in order to construct an efficient and liquid pan-EU capital market. One of the most striking features of the post-FSAP regime is the extent to which the EU now regulates, rather than supports the construction of, the single capital and investment services market. The new intensity of EU capital market regulation also reflects the dramatic influence of Lamfalussy legislative model for delegated lawmaking. Capital market rules are now adopted in the form of principles-based 'level 1' measures, adopted under normal EU inter-institutional procedures, and detailed 'level 2' rules adopted by the

[1] Communication from the Commission 'Implementing the Framework for Financial Markets: Action Plan' COM(1999) 232 (the FSAP).

Commission, advised by the Committee of European Securities Regulators (CESR) and supervised by the European Securities Committee (ESC).[2]

As part of its re-characterization of EU capital market regulation as a full-blown regulatory system, rather than simply a device for supporting market integration which produces regulation as a by-product, the FSAP identified the retail investor, the unlocking of household savings, and the development of retail markets as key components of its agenda for regulatory reform and capital market construction. The new regulatory regime for investment services contained in the cornerstone Markets in Financial Instruments Directive 2004 (MiFID)[3] sits at the heart of the FSAP and of this new retail investor agenda. In particular, the MiFID conduct of business regime (Articles 19, 21 and 22), represents the first attempt to address the key investor/investment firm relationship, in all its characterizations, from execution-only to discretionary portfolio management, from marketing to pre-contract disclosure and contractual protections, from initial advice and suitability assessment to order execution, and across on- and off-line sectors. It has been described by the Commission as one of the 'the mainstays of investor protection'.[4] As such, it reveals the dominance of regulation as a strategy for managing the retail markets.

II. Promoting Retail Activity

This new focus by the EU on the retail markets is directed towards unlocking the largely untapped pool of retail capital and channel it to the markets. The Commission has noted that '[p]rivate sector savings in Europe amount to some 20% of GDP – a valuable asset, if efficiently used, to stimulate growth and job-creation'.[5] The original ISD Communication, on which MiFID is based, refers to the importance of '[a]ccess to the widest possible pool of potential investors' in strengthening price discovery and lowering the cost of capital and of 'mobilising

[2] Proposed in the Final Report of the Committee of Wise Men on the Regulation of European Securities Markets (15 February 2001) (the Lamfalussy Report). See E Ferran *Building an EU Securities Market* (Cambridge University Press 2004) 77-111.

[3] Directive 2004/39/EC of the European Parliament and of the Council of 21 April 2004 on Markets in Financial Instruments amending Council Directives 85/611/EEC and 93/6/EEC and Directive 2000/12/EC of the European Parliament and of the Council and repealing Council Directive 93/22/EEC (the MiFID), OJ L145 30.04.2004 1-44.

[4] Proposal for a Directive of the European Parliament and of the Council on Investment Services and Regulated Markets, and amending Council Directive 85/611/EEC, Council Directive 93/6/EEC and European Parliament and Council Directive 2000/12/EC (the MiFID Proposal), 19.11.2002, COM(2002) 625, 26.

[5] Second FSAP Report, 31.05.2000, COM(2000) 336, 3.

household savings'.[6] The benefits of retail market integration and greater retail participation have been catalogued as including: lower transaction costs; higher rates of return with greater possibilities for diversification; greater availability of financial products; more efficient price formation following on greater trading volumes; and wider economy-based benefits following from an increased supply of investment capital.[7] The funding needs of the post-accession Member States are also emerging as a strong impetus for developing the EU market across retail (and wholesale) sectors.[8] Reflecting wider social and demographic trends, the EU has also recently recognized the importance of the individual becoming financially independent and saving for retirement through a diversified range of market investments which provide flexibility and choice as to levels of risk and return.[9] The 2004 Asset Management Expert Group Report, for example, pointed to European demographic dynamics and the need for private retirement provision planning.[10] The promotion of retail market activity has also emerged as a strong theme of the post-FSAP policy agenda. In its important 2005 Green Paper on Financial Services 2005-2010, for example, the Commission called for more efficient, long-term financial services products to complement state welfare provision and argued that a 'cost-efficient fund industry, where gains are passed on to end-investors, can be part of the solution to Europe's pension deficit'.[11]

This policy focus also reflects an international policy concern with individual financial literacy and independence, with promoting greater diversity in personal saving mechanisms to support personal pension provision, and with seeking to

[6] Communication from the Commission to the European Parliament and the Council – Upgrading the Investment Services Directive (93/22/EEC), 15.11.2000, COM(2000) 729 (the ISD Communication), 5-6. See also 7th FSAP Report, 02.12.2002, 9.

[7] London Economics (in association with PricewaterhouseCoopers and Oxford Economic Forecasting) 'Quantification of the Macro-Economic Impact of Integration of EU Financial Markets' (November 2002) 9.

[8] 10th FSAP Report, 02.06.2004, 1.

[9] See the Lisbon Council 'Presidency Conclusions' (23-24 March 2000) para. 21. The importance of a strong retail market given demographic trends and the transfer of pension provision from the state and from employers to individuals is a major concern in the UK. Financial Services Authority (FSA) 'The Treasury Committee – Inquiry Into Restoring Confidence in Long Term Savings' (17 June 2004) (the FSA Treasury Evidence) <http://www.fsa.gov.uk> para. 3.

[10] Asset Management Expert Group Report on the FSAP (May 2004) <http://europa.eu.int/comm/internal_market/finances/actionplan> 24. See also F Bolkestein Speech on 'Reviving European Growth' to the European Parliament (8 January 2004) <http://europa.eu.int/rapid>.

[11] Green Paper on Financial Services Policy 2005-2010, COM(2005) 177 (the Green Paper) Annex 16 and 17. A similar theme emerges from the White Paper on Financial Services Policy 2005-2010 (December 2005) 7 where the Commission noted that '[a]s the public sector gradually withdraws from financing some aspects of social systems, there is a need for increased awareness and direct involvement of citizens in financial issues'.

understand how retail investors behave.[12] The UK Financial Services Authority, for example, has recently expressed concern as to the exit of savers from the market, the deferring of re-entry to the market, and over-reliance on property investments.[13]

Examples of the expression of these policy objectives for the retail markets through regulatory strategies abound across the FSAP. The 2003 Prospectus Directive, for example, is designed, in part, to build the confidence of 'small investors' in the EU capital market and provide them with a wide range of competing investment opportunities.[14] The 2004 Recommendation on the simplified UCITS prospectus is designed to ensure that UCITS disclosure is easily understood by the 'average retail investor' and that the risk profile of the fund is understood by the 'average investor'.[15] The retail investor has also emerged as a key focus for post-Parmalat policy-making.[16]

In practice, however, retail investor activity in the investment services market is patchy, limited, and generally confined to local markets. There is strong evidence of an entrenched home bias in the small number of savers who do access the markets.[17] Telling evidence of the lack of pan-EU integration in the retail investment services market comes from the June 2004 Financial Integration Moni-

[12] See e.g. C Camerer 'Regulation for Conservatives: Behavioural Economics and the Case for "Asymmetric Paternalism"' (2003) 151 U Pa L Rev 1211, 1228 and J Fanto 'Regulatory Implications of Individual Management of Pension Funds: Comparative Investor Education' (1998) 64 Brooklyn L Rev 1083. In its first major policy document on financial education, the UK FSA has also stressed the impact of the ageing population and the need for individuals to take control of their finances, including through market investments. FSA 'Towards a National Strategy for Financial Capability' (the FSA 2003 Education Report) 7. The 'savings gap' and the need for consumers to make long-term savings for retirement and to understand the risks involved in complex financial products have been identified as 'priority risks' to the FSA's regulatory objectives. FSA 'Financial Risk Outlook' (2005) <http://www.fsa.gov.uk/pages/library> (FSA 2005 Financial Risk Outlook) 9-10.

[13] FSA 'Financial Risk Outlook' (2004) <http://www.fsa.gov.uk/pages/library> (FSA 2004 Financial Risk Outlook) 61 and FSA 2005 Financial Risk Outlook (n 12) 45.

[14] Directive 2003/71/EC of the European Parliament and of the Council of 4 November 2003 on the Prospectus to be Published when Securities are Offered to the Public or Admitted to Trading and amending Directive 2001/34/EC (the Prospectus Directive), OJ L345 31.12.2003 64-89, Preamble Recital 41.

[15] Commission Recommendation on the UCITS Summary Prospectus 2004/384, OJ L144 30.04.2004 44-58.

[16] Certain ESC delegations tied the scandal to retail investor protection against conflicts of interests, particular in the bond market. Summary Record of the Eighteenth Meeting of the European Securities Committee/Alternates (17 February 2004) ESC 8/2004, 6.

[17] See further N Moloney 'Building a Retail Investment Culture Through Law: The Markets in Financial Instruments Directive' (2005) 6 Eur Bus Org L R 341.

tor which examined headline trends in EU financial market integration.[18] It reported marked differences in the investment vehicles used to manage long-term savings and pensions of households and employees.[19] Direct cross-border offers of retail financial products generally remain the exception.[20] The follow-up Monitor in 2005 reported little change: 'the degree of fragmentation in retail markets is still considerable'.[21] The 2004 Securities Expert Group also found that outside the sophisticated investor sphere, activities were generally locally-organized when targeted to SMEs and retail investors.[22] CESR similarly reported in 2004 that: 'Retail markets are not integrated ... retail investors do not as a general rule operate cross-border, relying on national markets, and on collective investment schemes where they seek exposure to non-domestic markets'.[23]

The mismatch between the scale of the EU's ambitions in the retail investment services market and the reality of pan-EU retail investor activity means that designing an effective strategy demands nuanced policy choices. The dangers and limitations of regulation as a strategy for managing capital market risk are exacerbated in the post-FSAP retail market context, which is characterized by liberalization on the supply-side, an inexperienced retail investor base, untested regulatory strategies and disclosure formats, and a likely rapid increase in the supply of investment products. These features will place considerable strain on MiFID's generic regulatory disciplines unless the supporting ancillary strategies are robust. This essay argues, therefore, that the EU's strategy for the retail investment services markets, which is based almost exclusively on regulatory mechanisms (sections B and C) carries significant risks (section D). More creative, holistic, and joined-up policy-making which integrates a range of non-regulatory strategies (section E) is required. Although some signs are emerging that post-FSAP policy design will be more sophisticated and will see heavier reliance on non-regulatory strategies, this momentum must be sustained.

[18] Commission Staff Working Document 'Financial Integration Monitor' (6 May 2004) SEC(2004) 559 (the Financial Integration Monitor 2004).

[19] Financial Integration Monitor 2004 (n 18) 3.

[20] Financial Integration Monitor 2004 (n 18) 5.

[21] Commission Staff Working Document 'Financial Integration Monitor' (7 July 2005) SEC(2005) 927 (the Financial Integration Monitor 2005), 11.

[22] Securities Expert Group Report on the FSAP (May 2004) <http://europa.eu.int/comm/internal_market/finances/actionplan>) 10.

[23] CESR Preliminary Progress Report 'Which Supervisory Tools for the EU Securities Market' (October 2004) (the Himalaya Report) CESR 04-333f, 7.

B. The Delivery of Retail Policy Through a Regulatory Strategy

I. A Regulatory Strategy

From the investment firm perspective, the MiFID conduct of business regime can, by easing market access for investment firms through harmonized rules, generate choice and competition in services and products and, thereby, potentially provoke retail investor activity. Given the entrenched home bias among investors and resistance to new entrants,[24] harmonized rules and ease of access can also allow new entrants to 'camouflage' their differences from domestic participants. Firm and investor market access is thereby promoted. But the investor-facing, regulatory function of the MiFID regime with respect to the retail markets is more ambitious.

The EU's regulatory strategy for the retail investment services markets, as expressed through MiFID, is based on the assumption that a connection exists between regulation and investor activity. The Commission placed the MiFID proposal in the context of 'investors turn[ing] to market-based investments as a means of bolstering risk-adjusted returns on savings and for provisioning for retirement'[25] and described MiFID in terms of its constructing an 'investor friendly market'.[26] A similar approach was followed by the European Parliament's influential ECON Committee during the MiFID negotiations: 'One of our most important objectives must be to produce an ISD framework which encourages savings. It is crucial to ensure proper protection for retail investors and to help build investor confidence'.[27] This assumption as to a link between regulation and retail activity has also been reflected in market reaction to the FSAP.[28]

[24] The Banking Expert Group Report on the FSAP (May 2004) <http://europa.eu.int/comm/internal_market/finances/actionplan>) 10 referred to the bias for 'local and familiar institutions' in financial services delivery.

[25] MiFID Proposal (n 4) 4.

[26] MiFID Proposal (n 4) 15.

[27] Report to the Committee on Economic and Monetary Affairs on the First Reading of the MiFID Proposal A50287/2003 (the First ECON Report) 92. The Committee's Recommendation for the Second Reading on the Council MiFID Common Position A5-0114/2004 (the Second ECON Report) 42 similarly refers to the dangers of making execution-only more costly and deterring retail savings. ECON fought throughout the MiFID negotiations to keep execution-only services free of suitability requirements which could 'deprive consumers of a low cost simple method of saving'.

[28] The Banking Expert Group Report (n 24) 3 and 21 noted that pan-EU differences in consumer protection in financial services have a 'dampening effect' on market integration and that resistance to new entrants on domestic markets could be overcome by developing confidence in levels of protection. See also the Asset Management Expert Group Report (n 10) 15 in support of the notion that investor protection can enhance products and services in the eyes of the investing public.

This regulatory strategy, as expressed in MiFID, has two strands: (i) regulation as means for delivering investor protection, investor confidence, and increased retail activity and (ii) regulation as a device for generating investor choice and empowering investors.

II. Investor Protection and the MiFID Regulatory Strategy

Senior Commission officials have described MiFID as an investor protection measure using a regulatory rhetoric, and reflecting an institutional culture of investor protection, which was practically unknown prior to the FSAP when market access perspectives dominated.[29] The Proposal was expressly designed to 'strengthen the investor protection provisions which are contained in embryonic form in the existing Directive'.[30] The recitals refer regularly to investor protection: recital 31, for example, makes clear that '[o]ne of the objectives of this Directive is to protect investors'. The Lamfalussy clause for the conduct of business regime, Article 19 (10), is to 'ensure the necessary protection of investors, and the uniform application' of the new regime. Similarly, the Final CESR Mandate from the Commission for level 2 conduct of business rules included the protection of

[29] E.g. 'Reputational disciplines and the self-interest of market participants in sustaining investor confidence cannot be relied upon to guarantee market integrity .... There is a need for enlightened regulation to define the rules of the game and for strong policemen to enforce these rules .... [MiFID] should equip regulators with a comprehensive set of regulatory disciplines to tackle the risks to which the modern retail investor is exposed .... A high level of protection is crucial *in its own right* [emphasis added]. It is also a pre-condition for the effective operation of the ISD passport'. Speech by Director General Schaub of the Internal Market Directorate General on 'Economic and Regulatory Background to the Commission Proposal for Revision of the ISD' to the Danish EU Presidency Conference on 'European Regulation of Investment Services' (15 October 2002) <http://www.europa.eu.int/comm/internal_market/speeches> 8 and 10.

[30] MiFID Proposal (n 4) 8 and 29. See also the Communication from the Commission to the European Parliament pursuant to the second subparagraph of Article 251 (2) of the EC Treaty concerning the common position of the Council on the adoption of a Directive of the European Parliament and of the Council on Markets in Financial Instruments, amending Council Directives 85/611/EEC and 93/6/EEC and Directive 2000/12/EC of the European Parliament and of the Council and repealing Council Directive 93/22/EEC, 12.01.2004, COM(2004) 15, 2.

The Council's Common Position similarly stated that the overall objective of MiFID was the 'creation of an integrated financial market in which investors are effectively protected and the efficiency and integrity of the overall market are safeguarded .... [MiFID] will ensure that investors enjoy a high level of protection when making use of investment firms, wherever they are located in the EU. Common Position. Statement of the Council's Reasons (8 December 2003) 2.

investors among the three key objectives to be followed in developing the conduct of business level 2 rules.[31]

But investor protection (together with its outcomes and its delivery) is complex and controversial. In the EU context, investor protection through regulation carries additional risks as a policy objective given the vulnerability of investor protection to being hijacked for protectionist motives, the tensions between market-access driven harmonization and domestic regulatory policies and choices, and the limits of EU competence, although this last has rarely seemed to trouble the institutions.

Reflecting the link made in EU investment services policy between law and investor activity, the promotion of investor confidence through regulation appears to be at the heart of the investor protection strategy. The Explanatory Memorandum to the MiFID Proposal, for example, provided that the new investor protection regime would allow investors to be confident that investment firms would act diligently and in their best interests.[32] The European Parliament also took the view during the MiFID negotiations that protection was linked to confidence.[33] Investor confidence in the pan-EU market and its dependence on appropriate regulatory protection has been raised by the 2004 Expert Groups[34] and features heavily in the retail interests-driven 2004 FIN-USE Report.[35] Although investor confidence confers a virtually limitless power on regulators, while being, at the same time, almost incapable of definition or empirical testing,[36] and notwithstanding the post-FSAP focus on evidence-based lawmaking and cost-benefit analysis, the Commission remains committed to its new-found regulatory rhetoric and culture. It argued in the 2004 10th FSAP Report that, while it accepted the need for evidence-based policy-making, analytical metrics were not sufficiently

[31] Formal Request for Technical Advice on Possible Implementing Measures on the Directive on Markets in Financial Instruments 2004/39/EC (the Final CESR MiFID Mandate) (June 2004) 5.

[32] MiFID Proposal (n 4) 8 and 29.

[33] First ECON Report (n 27) 92.

[34] The Banking Expert Group Report (n 24) 3. It also appears in market discussions. See, e.g., the London Stock Exchange's Response to CESR's First Call for Evidence on MiFID (19 February 2004) <http://www.cesr.org>.

[35] 'Consumer protection rules can be a tool to enhance the confidence of investors as they venture into the large, multinational sector that is on the horizon'. FIN-USE Forum 'Financial Services, Consumers and Small Businesses. A User Perspective' (October 2004) (the FIN-USE Report) 4.

[36] For example, the SEC's adoption of Regulation FD prohibiting selective disclosure to, inter alia, analysts (Final Adopting Release No. 33-7881) has been criticized for being justified on grounds of investor confidence without empirical evidence of how the change to disclosure practices would impact on confidence. S Choi and A Pritchard 'Behavioural Economics and the SEC' (SSRN wp <http://ssrn.com/abstract=500203>, 2003) 17 and 35.

developed to allow regulators to quantify with precision the costs and benefits of proposals, particularly with respect to intangibles such as investor confidence.[37]

Confidence might, however, be linked to investor trust in regulation, on which is built trust in the market and in market institutions.[38] The broad consensus on the need for pan-EU conduct of business rules, harmonized at a high level, which held during the MiFID negotiations, may, in addition to reflecting market access benefits, also suggest the support regulation gives to firms in gaining investor trust, and to investors in identifying 'lemons' among investment firms. Establishing trust is otherwise very costly for firms.[39] The need for firms to generate trust (and the associated benefits of regulation) acquires particular resonance in the EU retail investment service market where there is only a limited tradition of market investment. Specific threats to trust include confusion as to the protections available across the market and variations in the level of protection.[40] Other threats to trust include confusion as to how to navigate a widening range of products and firms and the risks posed by aggressive marketing. Recent evidence has suggested that the home bias is linked in part to a lack of investor confidence as to the interpretation of non-local disclosure.[41] This might be overcome by MiFID's standardized marketing and disclosure protections, particularly where they are based on the evidence-based needs of an appropriately modeled EU retail investor.

III. Investor Choice and the MiFID Regulatory Strategy

The EU's regulatory strategy for the retail markets is also based on supporting investor empowerment and investor choice.[42] Informed choice by an active retail

[37] 10th FSAP Report (n 8) 15.

[38] L Stout 'The Investor Confidence Game' (SSRN wp <http://ssrn.com/abstract=322301>, 2002) 3.

[39] T Frankel 'Regulation and Investors' Trust in the Securities Markets' (2002) 68 Brooklyn L Rev 439, 441 and DC Langevoort 'Structuring Securities Regulation in the European Union: Lessons from the U.S. Experience' in this volume 487-508.

[40] The risks posed to internal market construction by investor confusion as to the protections available is often raised in EU policy. See e.g. Communication from the Commission to the Council and the European Parliament – E Commerce and Financial Services (the 2001 E Commerce Communication), COM(2001) 66, 7 and 10; and FESCO 'Standards and Rules for Harmonizing Core Conduct of Business Rules for Investor Protection' (2001) FESCO/00-124b, 6.

[41] A Kumar 'Is the Local Bias of Individual Investors Induced by Familiarity or Information Asymmetry?' (SSRN wp <http://ssrn.com/abstract=572642>, 2004).

[42] In its report on 'Building Financial Capability in the UK: The Role of Advice' (2004) (FSA 2004 Education Report) the FSA stressed empowerment and choice: 'If people know what they want and how to get it, the market for financial services becomes less one-sided and a lot more efficient. Consumers will be able to demand better, cheaper and more appropriate products and services' 1.

community could serve as a powerful driver for optimum product and services and greater levels of retail activity.[43] Facilitating fair access to the trading process can build a cohort of investors more likely to access the markets.

Choice has featured strongly in the recent development of the EU's retail investment services regime. The 2001 E Commerce Communication, for example, which made the initial case for conduct of business harmonization, argued that diverging national rules would lead to fragmented markets and deprive investors of choice, more competitive prices, and economies of scale.[44]

Investor autonomy and choice are central themes of the MiFID conduct of business regime, as discussed in section C below. In particular, choice was strongly supported by the European Parliament as a model for constructing the new retail investor regime.[45] Taking a generally robust view of investor competence and of the importance of individual autonomy, the European Parliament's ECON Committee strove to minimize protective regulation, with its related associations of cost and paternalism. The importance of choice (and the related reduction of regulatory costs) has also, perhaps unsurprisingly, been embraced by the market.[46] A discordant voice has emerged, however, in the shape of the October 2004 FIN-USE Report. It warned generally that '[i]ncreased competition ... does not necessarily work to the benefit of consumers [of financial services]. There is no automatic link, for example, between wider choice sets and widespread consumer gains'.[47]

While the empirical evidence on how pan-EU choice may work is patchy (section D below), the new emphasis on choice and empowerment does sit uneasily with certain realities, particularly in the absence of more holistic retail policy

[43] See the Asset Management Expert Group Report (n 10) 12 on the need for the EU asset management industry to respond to an increasingly broad range of investor preferences and L Cunningham 'Behavioural Finance and Investor Governance' (2002) 59 Washington & Lee L Rev 767, 789 on the impact of the baby boom generation on the supply of financial products and services.

[44] The 2001 E Commerce Communication (n 40) 4.

[45] The characterization of the investor as rational, autonomous, and exercising choice was also taken up by ECOSOC (the European Economic and Social Committee) during the MiFID negotiations. It called for level 2 to be based on a 'model of a far-sighted well-informed customer who is a position to take independent economic decisions on his own authority' in its Opinion on the Proposal for a Directive of the European Parliament and of the Council on Investment Services and Regulated Markets, and amending Council Directives 85/611/EEC and 93/6/EEC and European Parliament and Council Directive 2000/12/EC, COM(2002) 625, OJ C220 2003 1, para. 4.10.

[46] See, in response to CESR's 'Advice on Possible Implementing Measures of the Directive 2004/39/EC on Markets in Financial Instruments – Consultation Paper' (June 2004) CESR/04-261b (First CESR Draft Level 2 Advice), the views of APCIMS (Association of Private Client Investment Managers and Stockbrokers) (10 September 2004) 9 and of the London Stock Exchange (17 September 2004) 2 <http://www.cesr.org>.

[47] FIN-USE Report (n 35) I and, more generally, 4.

development. Investment services and products are risky and investor decision-making is faulty. Increasing choice across the EU and attempting to change investor behaviour may cause the investor to fall prey to opportunistic investment advisers and inappropriate products, even where disclosure is made available to support good decisions. Efficient retail markets, based on choice, need demand-side policy intervention which builds effective and informed investors. The UK FSA, for example, has expressly placed 'capable and confident' consumers, using understandable disclosure of rewards, risks, and commitments, at the heart of its recently adopted programme for efficient and fair retail investment services markets.[48] As discussed in section E, effective investor education and close attention to the development of a range of appropriate investment products should form part of EU retail policy development for the investment services markets, if investor choice is to be effectively realized.

C. The Regulatory Strategy as Expressed Through the MiFID Conduct of Business Regime

I. Scope of the Regime

The EU's regulatory strategy for the retail investment services market, as expressed in the cornerstone MiFID conduct of business regime, is designed to produce a cohort of robust, informed, and active investors, exercising autonomous choice. The conduct of business regime covers: the obligation to act fairly, honestly, and in the best interests of investors (Article 19 (1)); information and marketing disclosure to be fair, clear, and not misleading (Article 19 (2)); the information to be provided prior to contract conclusion (Article 19 (3)); suitability rules (Article 19 (4)-(6)); the customer agreement (Article 19 (7)); reporting requirements (Article 19 (8)); best execution (Article 21); and order handling (Article 22).

The conduct of business regime is subject to the level 2 process. The negotiation and development of the level 2 rules, which has been a controversial and highly resource-intensive process, suggests that an unprecedented level of rule harmonization is bearing down on the retail markets. This carries significant risks given the untried nature of the rules, the risks attaching to regulation as an exclusive strategy for the retail markets, and the immature pan-EU investor base (section D below).

[48] See FSA Treasury Evidence (n 9) para. 8 and 9, and C McCarthy Speech to FSA Annual Public Meeting (July 2004) <http://www.fsa.org.uk/pubs>. See also C Camerer (n 12) 1232-1234 on the role of disclosure in a competitive marketplace in 'encouraging a better informed consumer' and moving consumers closer to 'educated consumer status'.

Following the Commission's first informal MiFID mandate (January 2004),[49] CESR placed a first call for evidence on MiFID, following which, in June 2004, it produced its First Draft Level 2 Advice.[50] This draft advice, and the first informal mandate, covered, in detail: Articles 19 (2), 19 (3), 19 (7) and 19 (8); Article 21 (in outline); and Article 22. A formal Final Mandate was issued following the adoption of MiFID in June 2004. It confirmed the initial January mandate and added mandates for Article 19 (1) and Articles 19 (4)-(6).[51] Similarly detailed Draft Advice followed on Article 19 (4)-(6) (Second Draft Level 2 Advice)[52] and on Article 19 (1) and (in more detail) the best execution regime (Third Draft Level 2 Advice).[53] The Final First Mandate Advice was communicated to the Commission in January 2005 and the Final Second Mandate Advice (including the best execution regime from the First Mandate) in April 2005.[54] After this lengthy consultation process, February 2006 saw the publication (and formal transmission to the European Parliament) of the Commission's ground-breaking draft level 2 Directive on MiFID, which includes the conduct of business regime.[55] It is now clear that the Commission, while relying extensively on the CESR advice, has generally adopted a more cost-conscious, calibrated, and light touch approach than CESR to the conduct of business regime and to regulation as a strategy for managing the retail market.

[49] 'The Provisional Mandate to CESR for Technical Advice on Possible Implementing Measures concerning the Future Directive in Financial Instruments Markets' (22 January 2004) (the CESR Provisional Mandate).

[50] First CESR Draft Level 2 Advice (n 46).

[51] CESR Final MiFID Mandate (n 31). A Second Call for Evidence was issued on the new elements of the mandate.

[52] CESR 'Draft Technical Advice on Possible Implementing Measures of the Directive 2004/39/EC on Markets in Financial Instruments – Second Set of Mandates – Consultation Paper' (October 2004) CESR/04-52 (the Second CESR Draft Level 2 Advice).

[53] CESR 'Draft Technical Advice on Possible Implementing Measures of the Directive 2004/39/EC on Markets in Financial Instruments, Aspects of A19 (1) Best Execution, and Market Transparency' (March 2005) (the Third CESR Draft Level 2 Advice).

[54] CESR 'Technical Advice on Possible Implementing Measures of Directive 2004/39/EC on Markets in Financial Instruments – First Set of Mandate' (January 2005) CESR/05-024c (the Final CESR First Mandate Advice) and CESR 'Technical Advice on Possible Implementing Measures of Directive 2004/39/EC on Markets in Financial Instruments – First Set of Mandates (Best Execution) and Second Set of Mandates' (April 2005) CESR/05-290b (Final CESR Second Mandate Advice).

[55] Draft Commission Directive implementing Directive 2004/39/EC of the European Parliament and of the Council as regards organisational requirements and operational conditions for investment firms, and defined terms for the purposes of that Directive Draft (the Draft Level 2 Directive). A draft Regulation has also been published which sets out the MiFID level 2 rules concerning record-keeping, transaction reporting, market transparency, and admission to trading.

The conduct of business regime applies when investment firms provide investment services and/or ancillary investment services to investors (Article 19 (1)). The wide range of services included within 'services' and 'ancillary services' (Annex I, Sections A and B, respectively) catches those investor/investment firm relationships which are of particular relevance to the retail community, including: reception and transmission of orders; execution of orders (including execution-only services); portfolio/asset management; and investment advice. The Article 19 regime (and the draft level 2 rules) are, however, generic and are not designed to cover the full range of investment services. The resilience of the generic rules applicable to investment advice and portfolio management, in particular, now look set to be severely tested given the increasingly complex and risky universe of investments now available for advice and asset management, particularly with respect to investments in sophisticated alternative investment vehicles.

Advice operates as the gateway for the conduct of business strategy, determining, for example, the nature of the new suitability regime. It is defined in MiFID Article 4 (4) as the provision of 'personal recommendations' to an investor, either upon her request or at the initiative of the investment firm, in respect of one or more transactions relating to financial instruments. The evolution of this key definition of 'investment advice' at level 2 is revealing as one of the first major illustrations of how the traditional drivers of retail policy (investor choice, cost reduction, investor dependence, and so on) are addressed in this new EU policy context and from a regulatory perspective. CESR's initial approach to investment advice was set out in its Final Second Mandate Advice.[56] General recommendations and marketing communications which were not based on a consideration of personal circumstances fell outside the regime under this approach. Personal recommendations, those which, 'taking into consideration all of the relevant circumstances,' involved a recommendation to carry out a transaction relating to financial instruments, suited to or based on a consideration of the personal circumstances of the recipient, came within it. Considerable controversy arose with respect to CESR's proposal that general financial planning and asset allocation advice not linked to a specific investment recommendation, would come within 'investment advice' and, accordingly, the related suitability disciplines. Market reaction was generally hostile: a common theme of the consultation was that the costs in terms of the allied suitability requirements could discourage firms from providing this service. Nonetheless, CESR's Final Advice included generic advice on financial instruments within 'investment advice'. While potentially costly, CESR's approach might be argued to reflect a practical view of the emerging retail market. The new cohort of investors, if it emerges, is likely to place considerable reliance on gen-

[56] Final CESR Second Mandate Advice (n 54) 7-11. For the lively consultation see the Second CESR Draft Level 2 Advice (n 52) 8-16 and the Third CESR Draft Level 2 Advice (n 53) 9-12.

eral investment advice on the basics of financial planning and asset allocation, particularly given current limited levels of investor education. By contrast, the Commission's approach is more robust and, in effect, excludes generic advice, reflecting a more cost-driven (and, therefore, choice-conscious) regulatory perspective on the retail markets. The current rules (Draft Level 2 Directive, Article 52) define investment advice in terms of a personal recommendation, made to a person in that person's capacity as an investor or potential investor, which is presented as suitable for, or based on a consideration of the circumstances of that person, and which constitutes a recommendation to make an investment decision with respect to a particular financial instrument. The Background Note refers expressly to generic advice as being excluded from the Directive but contains an unusually nuanced reference to the features of the retail market in justification: 'the exclusion of generic advice ... avoids the danger of regulating financial planning entities that, in many cases, operate as charities providing valuable financial advice free of charge'.[57]

This section outlines the main features of MiFID's regulatory strategy for the retail investment services markets, as expressed through the conduct of business regime.

II. Disclosure

1. The Disclosure Regime

The two objectives of the EU's regulatory strategy for the retail investment services market, investor protection and investor choice, meet in the extensive disclosure rules. Article 19 addresses marketing, pre-contract, and contract disclosure, while Articles 21 and 22 cover disclosure in order execution. The reliance on disclosure as a major plank of the conduct of business regime suggests a strong characterization of the investor as rational and reflects the regulatory strategy's emphasis on informed investors and on limited intervention in the investor decision.[58] The Article 19 (3) marketing information requirements, for example, are designed to ensure investors are: 'reasonably able to understand the nature and risks of the investment service and of the specific type of financial instrument that is being offered and consequently to take investment decisions on an informed basis'.

[57] Commission 'Background Note' 31.

[58] On disclosure controls as emphasizing investor autonomy and freedom to make high risk investments see H Jackson 'Regulation in a Multisectored Financial Services Industry' (1999) 77 Wash U L Q 319, 333.

2. Article 19 (2)

As is clear from the 2002 Distance Marketing Services Directive (DMD),[59] marketing disclosure is a major concern for EU retail policy given potential investor vulnerability.[60] Under Article 19 (2), all information, including marketing communications, which is addressed by an investment firm to clients or potential clients, must be fair, clear and not misleading.

CESR's advice (Final First Mandate Advice) was detailed and specifically targeted to retail investors, given their greater vulnerability and limited ability to bargain for disclosure, the material effect marketing communications have on investor decisions, and the disproportionate impact of marketing disclosure as compared to disclosure provided later in the investment process.[61] CESR's main focus was on requiring key disclosures and risk warnings rather than on prohibiting particular forms of disclosure: investor autonomy was a dominant theme. But the advice also revealed considerable evidence of a more managerial approach to disclosure and of control over particular information which is vulnerable to misinterpretation. CESR advised that investment firms must avoid accentuating the potential benefits of an investment without giving a fair indication of risk. Key items must be given due prominence, important risk warnings must not be obscured, and claims must be capable of substantiation. Competent authorities can require investment firms to provide evidence as to the accuracy of factual claims. The specific content requirements for Article 19 (2) disclosure which CESR proposed are extensive and suggest considerable control over how investment firms approach the new retail market. Firms must take all reasonable steps to ensure the purpose and content of communications are likely to be understood by the 'average member' of the investor group addressed. Although this requirement is likely to generate some challenges in a cross-border, pan-EU context, given the different capabilities of investors, it is an attempt to ensure that pan-EU disclosure is related to investor profiles and that marketing of complex and risky products is not inappropriately targeted to vulnerable investors. There is also striking evidence of a concern to promote rational decision-making. CESR sought to manage the use of disclosure which is prone to investor over-reaction, such as suggestions of endorsement by a regulatory authority (prohibited), tax information, simulated historic returns (prohibited), past performance indicators, estimates, forecasts, and

[59] Directive 2002/65/EC of the European Parliament and of the Council of 23 September 2002 concerning the Distance Marketing of Consumer Financial Services and amending Council Directive 90/619/EEC and Directives 97/7/EC and 98/27/EC, OJ L 271 09.10.2002 16-24.

[60] 'It [is not] enough to place our faith in the commercial self-interests of market participants … a single case of cross-border mis-selling could compromise the entire project'. Results of Commission Conference on Financial Integration, (23-24 June 2004) MEMO/04/160 (the Conference Conclusions) <http://www.europa.eu.int/rapid>.

[61] Final CESR First Mandate Advice (n 54) 45.

comparative information. The ban on simulated returns, in particular, suggests a managerial and paternalistic approach from CESR.[62] There is also a high degree of prescription in how past performance material is used.[63] Overall, CESR's approach suggests a degree of micro-management of what disclosure reaches investors.

While the Commission's approach in the Draft Level 2 Directive (Article 27) is broadly similar to CESR's (and includes the innovation concerning targeting an 'average' investor), there are important differences with respect to simulated returns and past performance disclosure, where the Commission has taken a significantly more robust, and less managerial, view of investor competence. Simulated historic returns are permitted, subject to risk warnings and the construction of the returns on the basis of recognized indices, and the restrictions on past performance information are more limited.

3. Article 19 (3)

Article 19 (3) is the core disclosure provision. It requires firms to provide appropriate information 'in a comprehensible form' to clients and potential clients about the investment firm and the services provided, the financial instruments involved, the proposed investment strategies (including risk warnings and execution venues), and the related costs and associated charges. Investors must be 'reasonably able to understand the nature and risks of the investment services and of the type of instrument being offered and, consequently, to take investment decisions on an informed basis'. The objective, as with Article 19 (2), appears to be to build an informed and empowered investor base, using relevant and comprehensible information.

Based on CESR's advice and the Commission's current draft rules (Draft Level 2 Directive, Articles 29-31, level 2 will require a formidable range of information to be provided to investors 'in good time' and in a 'durable medium' before the provision of new services (exceptions apply to contracts concluded through distance methods). The disclosure required includes information on the firm, the nature of the services, the financial instruments involved and their risks, commissions and fees, guarantors, and the arrangements for safeguarding client assets. Risk warnings, particularly with respect to financial instruments, form a key part of the disclosure strategy. The Commission's risk disclosure require-

[62] The response to this requirement was hostile, with a number of industry respondents finding this an overly prescriptive and unjustified restriction on a useful disclosure and marketing tool.

[63] The information must, inter alia, be relevant, a risk warning must be provided, the reference period must not be less than one year, and any benchmarks used must be clear and balanced. Concern as to the correct use of past performance also appears in the UCITS regime. The 2004 UCITS Prospectus Recommendation (n 15) contains detailed information on how past performance information should be presented in UCITS summary prospectuses, para. 1.5.

ments (Article 31) are drafted in more generic terms than CESR's instrument-specific approach. Article 31 requires that a general description of the nature and risks of the financial instruments in question must be provided and must be sufficiently detailed to enable the client to understand the nature and specific risks of the instrument. Particular care is taken to calibrate the disclosure to the capacity of the investor. The risk disclosures (as to instrument risk, volatility risk, financial commitments and contingent liabilities, and margin requirements), are to be relevant to the instrument, and the status and level of knowledge of the client. The requirement to disclose costs (Article 33) is also particularly important for the retail community, given increasing concern as to the inability of investors to assess the impact of costs and commission on returns.[64] Notably, given recent concerns as to flawed gatekeeper incentives, the investment firm disclosure required includes disclosure on the firm's conflicts of interest management policy (Article 30 (1) (h). It is also significant, given the critical importance of enforcement for investors (section D), that specific disclosure on redress is required with respect to the availability of compensation funds, although CESR's approach was more extensive, requiring disclosure of non-EU compensation funds and out-of-court redress mechanisms.

Asset/portfolio management services are subject to extensive disclosure requirements. These requirements are set, however, in generic terms. The recent growth of alternative investments, an increase in retail appetite for these investments,[65] and the increased risk of asset managers feeding riskier investments into investor portfolios, particularly where managers form part of multi-service investment firms holding own account portfolios of hedge fund units and other riskier investments, may place considerable strain on the effectiveness of the Article 19 (3) disclosure regime in protecting investors. Under the Commission's draft rules (Draft Level 2 Directive, Article 30 (3)), the disclosure must include a summary of key contractual information, including the types of financial instrument which may be included in the portfolio, the management objectives, the level of risk to be reflected in the manager's exercise of investment discretion, and specific restrictions on that discretion. The asset manager must also provide the investor with details as to the method and frequency of portfolio evaluation and of any authorized delegation of the portfolio management service.

4. Article 19 (7) and Article 19 (8)

Article 19 (7) requires the investment firm to establish a documentary record of the firm/investor relationship, including the client agreement. CESR's advice

[64] Investors do not appear to interpret fees and charges rationally, often linking high fees to firm reliability: FSA 'Price of Retail Investing in the UK' (FSA Occasional Paper 6) (2000).

[65] See generally PriceWaterhouseCoopers 'The Regulation and Distribution of Hedge Funds in Europe' (2005).

on the content of this record focused in particular on the portfolio management contract where the investor may not be in a position to ask for particular information to be specified contractually. Its advice included a controversial requirement for a contractual benchmark against which manager performance could be measured. The Commission has adopted a lighter touch, not specifying particular elements of the documentary record (other than requiring that a summary of the key contractual limits on investment discretion be provided, as outlined above) and making the benchmark reporting requirement only one of the possible 'appropriate method[s] of evaluation and comparison' to be established by investment firms to allow the investor to assess the firm's performance (Draft Level 2 Directive, Article 30 (2)).

Under Article 19 (8), clients must receive adequate reports from firms on the services provided, including on the costs associated with transactions and services. Key reports required under the Commission's draft rules (Draft Level 2 Directive, Articles 40-43) include contract notes in respect of order execution and periodic reports for portfolio management services, covering, inter alia the (market or fair) value and performance of the portfolio and total amount of fees and charges incurred, and required at six monthly intervals (reduced from the three month period initially proposed by the Commission).

5. Articles 21 and 22: Best Execution and Trading Disclosure

Under Article 21 (3) firms must have a best execution policy in respect of each class of instrument. Article 21 (3) also, and controversially, requires firms to provide appropriate information to clients on this policy prior to the provision of the service, to obtain client consent to the policy, and, where the policy provides for ex-regulated market/multilateral trading facility execution (essentially, execution through internalization), to inform them of this possibility and obtain their prior express consent before proceeding to execute. Consent can be obtained in a general agreement, or in individual transactions.

CESR's level 2 advice suggested that the information provided on the policy include: a description of how the firm seeks best execution, including the relative importance of the factors feeding into best execution decisions; a warning where a client's instruction on execution conflicts with firm policy; each execution venue on which the firm places significant reliance in meeting best execution; and a statement that the investor could request a complete list of all venues in the execution policy. CESR also advised that the policy include the process for communicating changes to the policy, whether the firm could execute client orders through internalization or carry out other potentially conflicted execution transactions (and the applicable conflicts policy), and a description of the firm's process for selecting, monitoring and reviewing its execution arrangements. These requirements, while relatively onerous, are considerably lighter than those originally proposed by CESR, which suggested that mandatory lists of venues and empirical information, such as the percentage of firm orders directed to each venue, might be required. The market response to the original CESR proposals was hostile and argued that detailed execution disclosure would not be meaningful to investors, likely to overwhelm them, not relevant in that investors only care about the net result, and costly to compile.[66]

In its draft rules, the Commission has further limited the execution policy disclosure required of firms. It has required that the information provided contain only an account of the relative importance the investment firm assigns to the different factors feeding into best execution, a list of the venues on which the firm places 'significant reliance', and a statement that client instructions can prejudice the achievement of best execution in accordance with the firm's policy (Draft Level 2 Directive, Article 46). One conclusion that can be drawn from the development of this disclosure regime is the willingness of CESR and the Commission to reflect market opinion on the costs of disclosure, which suggests a concern to ensure regulatory costs are not passed on to investors and choice prejudiced as a result.

The Commission's light-touch approach seems appropriate, although the need, in principle, for this disclosure remains questionable. The objective of this disclosure is to inform clients about execution, help them to compare execution services, and foster competition on a quality of service basis. It also operates as a control on conflicts of interests where a firm seeks to internalize trades. Disclosure of this nature places an enormous burden on the retail investor. The obligation here should be on the firm to make the execution decision according to the Article 21 requirements, subject not to consent by the investor, but to enforcement procedures where best execution standards are not met. Placing a positive consent obligation on the investor transfers part of the best execution obligation to the retail investor, who is unlikely to fulfill it effectively. An additional decision-making point, which is only likely to confuse investors, is created. The disclosure is all the more disconnected given that it not, as discussed in section E, partnered with parallel policy strategies, such as an investor education policy which could address the trading process. There is some heartening evidence, however, of a concern in the Draft Level 2 Directive to connect the different policy choices. As discussed below, one of the innovations of MiFiD is to establish a clear benchmark for best execution for retail orders (linked to price). This is justified in part in the Background Note on the grounds that retail investors 'are unlikely to have the time or specialist knowledge to understand or evaluate detailed disclosures related to best execution [or have] the resources to make an effective comparative evaluation of the execution policy of the firm'. Nonetheless, the philosophical attachment to some degree of disclosure remains.

The general Article 22 requirement that execution of investor orders be prompt, fair, and expeditious has been interpreted by CESR and the Commission as demanding disclosure (and again, investor interpretation of complex informa-

[66] Third CESR Draft Level 2 Advice (n 53) 31.

tion) concerning aggregation of orders. In particular, where aggregation of orders occurs, it must be disclosed to clients who must also be informed that aggregation can disadvantage them.

6. Disclosure as a Regulatory Strategy

The large disclosure component of the conduct of business regime suggests a regulatory strategy based on supporting autonomy and choice. Rational decision-making is supported through information. Informed choice is supported by the likelihood of greater comparability through the standardization of information.[67]

The disclosure regime does not, however, make many concessions to limited ability. But conduct of business-based disclosure addresses individual decision-making. It should, therefore, take particular account of the decision-making process, the relevance, comprehensibility, and timeliness of disclosure, and the ability of individuals to use the information, not least as information provides the foundation for the regulatory strategy's support of investor choice. The potentially helpful notion of the 'average investor' is, however, increasingly appearing across EU securities regulation, usually tied to simplifying the form in which disclosure is delivered.[68] The 'average investor' also appears throughout the conduct of business disclosure regime, with the regime reflecting some key weaknesses in decision-making, particularly with respect to risk assessment, the impact of costs, and the effective interpretation of financial data. Overall, however, the regulatory strategy assumes an informed retail community with high levels of competence in decoding information. Even allowing for the exaggerated claims behavioural finance can make for irrational investor behaviour, this is rather at variance with the well-documented evidence of poor investor decision-making (section D). These difficulties are likely to be deepened in the pan-EU context, unless disclosure is buttressed with ancillary education, enforcement, governance, and product development strategies, as discussed in section E.

III. Execution-Only

The focus on choice is also reflected in the lack of any real attempt through the regulatory strategy to limit potentially prejudicial investment choices or behaviour, such as speculative or excessive trading. Promoting choice means accepting that investors will make their own calculations as to the risk/return rela-

[67] The UCITS Prospectus Recommendation (n 15), e.g., makes a connection between harmonized disclosure, comparability, and choice (Recital 2).

[68] It has been used in the Prospectus Directive (n 14). The 2004 UCITS Prospectus Recommendation (n 15), e.g., is designed to ensure the prospectus is 'easily understood by the average retail investor' (Recital 1).

tionship, that they make 'bad' choices, and that they may choose to prioritize low-cost, low-support services. It also assumes a degree of risk tolerance with respect to retail investor funds. The Banking Expert Group Report reflected this view, suggesting that securities and investment products attract discretionary income and generate a higher tolerance of risk.[69]

The Article 19 (4)-(6) suitability regime is revealing in this regard. Execution-only services, and services involving direct offers of products, have been subject to a minimal suitability regime. As a result, the investor's freedom to choose to sacrifice the benefits of full-service advice for low costs is accommodated. Article 19 (6) reflects the popularity of execution-only services with investors[70] and a policy assumption that investor choice of a low-cost, low-protection service should be supported. The need to keep the execution-only regime free of regulation in order to support investor choice was a running and frequently controversial theme of the MiFID negotiations.[71] A light touch execution-only regime was also strongly supported by the market.[72]

But execution-only is an inherently riskier service for retail investors. They will not be protected from potentially faulty decision-making. Choice of a low-cost regime trumps a more interventionist, paternalistic response. The regime does, however, control choice by controlling the level of risk which can be assumed by the investor in suitability-free, execution-only trading. First, the service is buttressed by background regulatory protections such as the best execution and orderly trading requirements of Articles 21 and 22. Second, the suitability requirement only falls away if the investor has been 'clearly informed' as to the limited nature of the service, although investor competence and capability as to

[69] The FIN-USE Report (n 35) 16 similarly referred to the distinction between financial services used to facilitate the investment of surplus income/capital (such as broking and asset management services) and those needed to carry on the activities of daily life.

[70] There are approximately 1.2 million execution-only customers in France, 3.5 million in the UK, and over 2 million in Germany. Several million retail investors across the EU also buy UCITS without advice through direct offers and fund supermarkets. Second ECON Report (n 27) 42.

[71] The European Parliament championed suitability-free execution-only services following the Commission's initial proposal which imposed light suitability requirements on execution-only (n 4) 26. The Council ultimately followed the Parliament's position. In the Second ECON Report (n 27) 42 the importance of choice was stated by the ECON committee in strong terms: 'These basic "no frills" services – fast, low cost and value for money – are a vital part of the range of choices which should be available to investors .... Investors should not be compelled to pay for advice which they neither need nor want. This would deter saving and be an unreasonable restriction on investor choice'.

[72] See generally Proshare 'Evidence to the European Parliament MiFID Hearings Appendix 1' <http://www.proshare.org/Press> (ProShare Parliament Evidence) para. 10-14. See also the London Stock Exchange noting that it 'is vital to investors, as to impose unnecessary costs on firms would remove a low cost dealing option for their clients'. Response by London Stock Exchange to CESR's Second Call for Evidence (29 July 2004) 1.

the implications of this warning is assumed. Third, execution-only services may only be provided at the initiative of the client, although the general advertising of such services will not attach the suitability rules.[73] Fourth, the investment firm must comply with the Article 18 (conflict of interest) obligations. Finally, and most paternalistically, only certain investments qualify as being eligible for execution-only treatment: shares admitted to trading on a regulated market or equivalent third country market, bonds or other securitized debt (excluding debt instruments which embed a derivative), UCITS, money market instruments, and other 'non-complex' instruments.[74] The relatively wide range of investments (including third country securities) eligible under execution-only services should allow more effective investor diversification, which should be a key concern of any effective retail investor strategy. As discussed in section E, however, the list may be too porous and may not adequately reflect the potential risk posed by UCITS or shares in highly structured products traded on regulated markets (such as shares in companies which are, in effect, wrappers for hedge fund products).

CESR's approach (Final Second Mandate Advice) to 'non-complex instruments' emphasized the importance of flexibility and of protecting the ability of the markets to develop new products to meet consumer demand. In effect, CESR supported investor choice. It characterized non-complex instruments in broad terms as non-derivative financial instruments, that are easily realizable, and that do not involve any liability in excess of the initial contribution. It also advised that information on the product (structure, costs and other factors having a material effect on its performance) should be easily accessible and likely to be understood by the 'average retail client'. The Commission's approach follows this advice (Draft Level 2 Directive, Article 39). It remains to be seen whether this approach, based on indicators linked to disclosure and liquidity, is sufficiently robust in practice to ensure that execution-only service are confined to less risky products. The effectiveness of supervisory convergence and of 'regulatory learning' at level 3 of the Lamfalussy process is likely to be key to the effectiveness of the 'non-complex' instrument device as a filter for suitability requirements given continual market and product innovation.

[73] MiFID, Recital 30 provides that a service is, by default, provided at 'the initiative of a client', unless it is demanded in response to a personalized communication from the firm which contains an invitation or is intended to influence the client in respect of a specific financial instrument or transaction. But where the service is prompted by a communication containing a promotion or offer of financial instrument, made by any means, which by its very nature is general, and which is addressed to the public or a larger group or category of clients or potential clients, it remains provided at the initiative of the client.

[74] Article 19 (6). The restricted list of investments was added at the Common Position stage when the suitability test was removed from execution-only services. This revision was rejected by the European Parliament in its Second Reading. It ultimately agreed to the restricted list once it had been expanded to include third country securities.

But choice must go hand in hand with capability. As with much of the conduct of business regime, the execution-only regime should be placed within an education framework, given, in particular, the evidence of persistent diversification failures and of over-trading by investors.

IV. Trading Requirements

1. Trading Rules

This combination of extensive disclosure and the promotion of investor choice suggests a regulatory strategy which promotes an essentially positive view of the markets and of trading. This is reinforced by the trading rules (Article 22 on order handling and, in particular, Article 21 on best execution).

The trading rules are designed to generate competition in execution services, bring down costs, improve price formation, and remove conflicts of interests from the execution process.[75] But they are also connected to MiFID's retail strategy and to participation in the markets as they are designed to ensure that competition in the order execution market ultimately benefits the end investor: the regime 'compel[s] firms acting on behalf of end-investors to make active use of new trading opportunities to get the best deal .... This will ensure [that] competition between different types of order-execution venue works to the advantage of the end-investor'.[76]

2. Best Execution: Article 21

Best execution rules seek to address the information imbalance between the investor and firm as to price formation and ensure that an investor's trade is executed on the most favourable terms.[77] Best execution becomes a core investor protection measure where trading is fragmented across competitive order execution markets and transparency is potentially muddied, as in the EU where structural changes have occurred to the pan-EU order execution market with the growth of off-exchange execution. Retail investors, facing considerable handicaps in navigating the transparency and execution risks of a competitive order execution market, should benefit from a best execution requirement that firms consider trading conditions across a variety of venues. Under Article 21 (1) investment

[75] MiFID Preamble, Recital 5 states that the Articles 21 and 22 execution rules are necessary to ensure a high quality of execution and uphold the integrity and efficiency of the financial system, while the Article 21 (6) Lamfalussy clause for best execution links best execution to investor protection and the fair and orderly functioning of markets.

[76] MiFID Proposal (n 4) 6.

[77] MiFID Preamble Recital 5.

firms must take all reasonable steps when executing orders to obtain the best possible result for their clients, taking into account price, costs, speed, likelihood of execution and settlement, size, nature, and another relevant considerations. Article 21 (2) requires investment firms to establish and implement effective arrangements, including establishing and implementing an order execution policy, to allow them obtain the best possible result. Finally, under Article 21 (4) firms are to monitor the effectiveness of their execution arrangements and policy and identify and correct any deficiencies.

The more elaborate and complex best execution policy at level 2, however, and the more onerous the monitoring and reporting requirements, the greater the likelihood of costs being passed on to investors. CESR has emphasized the importance of flexibility in execution design and the need to ensure firms have broad discretion as to how they organize their business models, stating that 'it is not appropriate for regulatory requirements to pre-determine the relative importance of the factors' set out in Article 21 (1) for execution decisions. The Commission's draft rules (Draft Level 2 Directive, Article 44) follow this approach and set out in general terms the criteria according to which firms should assess the relative importance of the best execution factors (including the status of the client as retail or professional).

Unusually, but in a reflection of the increasingly sophisticated approach to the retail markets, specific reference is made to the position of retail investors and the costs of execution, given that retail investors are largely concerned with price. The search costs involved if speed, market impact, and other factors were also considered would increase the costs of best execution while not reflecting retail investor needs. Article 44 (3) therefore establishes a benchmark for best execution in the retail markets. Firms are to take the necessary steps to ensure that the best possible result is achieved for retail investors in terms of the total consideration, representing the price of the instrument and the execution costs. Other factors (speed, likelihood of execution and settlement, size and nature of the order, market impact, and other implicit transactions costs) are to be given precedence over immediate price and cost considerations only where they are instrumental in delivering the best possible result for the retail client.

V. The Suitability Regime

Disclosure, choice, and more effective execution all suggest a regulatory strategy for the retail markets based on limited intervention in the investor/investment firm relationship. This strategy reflects an essentially positive view of the markets and of investor decision-making abilities and the paramount importance of investor choice. The MiFID regulatory strategy does, however, adopt a more protective approach under the new suitability regime.

Suitability/know-your-client requirements are traditionally associated with regulatory strategies based on a paternalistic approach to the retail investor. They reflect the information asymmetry in the firm/investor relationship and the reliance of the investor in the investment firm's expertise and judgment. Increasingly, they are associated with minimizing the behavioural defects under which investors operate.[78] Suitability and 'know your client' controls are most often associated with portfolio management but they also apply to investment advice services. Their introduction represents a major change to the EU's retail investor protection regime and the high-water mark of the extent to which the new regulatory strategy for the retail markets intervenes paternalistically in the investor's decision.

The Article 19 suitability regime takes two forms, the assessment of 'suitability' and of 'appropriateness', depending on the level of reliance on the investment firm.

Under Article 19 (4), where the firm provides general investment advice or portfolio management, an extensive 'suitability' check is required. The firm must obtain the necessary information regarding the investor's knowledge and experience in the investment field relevant to the specific type of product or service, financial situation, and investment objectives. The suitability check should enable the firm to recommend the investment services and financial instruments 'suitable' for the investor. At level 2, CESR avoided prescriptive lists of the information to be obtained from investors, given the potential costs of unnecessary questions, in favour of guidelines and examples which illustrate the criteria for assessing the minimum level of information required. Similarly, CESR's criteria for assessing suitability were flexible and included the investor's investment objectives and knowledge and experience and the level of risk involved.

The Commission's approach (Draft Level 2 Directive, Articles 36 and 38) is similar, requiring the firm to obtain such information as is necessary for it to understand essential facts about the client and for the firm to have a reasonable belief that the transaction meets the client's investment objectives, that the client is able financially to bear the investment risks involved, and that the client has the necessary experience and knowledge in order to understand the risks involved. Information concerning the investor's financial situation is directly addressed: relevant information includes information on the source and extent of regular income, assets, investments and real property, and regular financial commitments. Similarly, information as to investment objectives is set out in Article 36 and can include the relevant time horizon, risk-taking preferences, risk profile, and the purposes of the investment. Article 38 sets out the generic requirements as to how suitability is assessed, including with reference to: the type of service, transaction and instrument involved; the nature, volume and frequency of the investor's transactions; and the level of education, profession or former profession of the investor. In an important protection for the investor, and in example of MiFID's

[78] L Cunningham (n 43) 798-799.

degree of prescription, where information is not provided the investment firm must not recommend investment services or instruments.

Under Article 19 (5), a lighter touch 'appropriateness' regime is imposed. It applies where services 'other than Article 19 (4)' services are provided. These would involve more limited, non-tailored, advice services, typically linked to general recommendations concerning a particular product, which do not come within the Article 1 (5) definition of investment advice, and which are not based on a close assessment of the investor's circumstances. The firm is to ask the investor to provide information regarding her knowledge and experience in the investment field relevant to the specific type of product or service demanded, so as to enable the firm to assess whether the service or product is 'appropriate'. The appropriateness assessment is directed towards a 'one-off' transaction by the investor, and not on the appropriateness of an overall portfolio of investments. A more limited test was certainly envisaged by the European Parliament, which, in line with its investor-choice-led philosophy, wanted Article 19 (5) to be cast in terms of the firm only 'assist[ing] the client or potential client to decide whether the specific type of product or services is appropriate for him'.[79] It also stressed the importance of investor autonomy under the lighter touch regime: 'the impetus behind a light touch sales regime is to simplify current sales practices, to reduce costs to the consumer and to encourage them to make active choices about the products or services offered'. CESR's approach has been light touch, emphasizing the linkage between the information obtained and the product in question, and suggesting that the information reflect the investor's familiarity with investment services and products and trading history. It has also stressed that risk warnings be as short and concise as possible. The Commission's approach (Draft Level 2 Directive, Articles 37 and 38) is similar, with the bulk of its suitability requirements directed to the Article 19 (4) advice regime.

The suitability regime does, therefore, intervene in the investor/investment relationship by imposing suitability obligations on firms which go considerably beyond the broadly standardized disclosure elsewhere in Article 19. But investor choice, and the related need to manage costs and regulatory burdens, is a recurring theme of the suitability regime. Where the investor opts for higher levels of advice, is choosing from a wide range of possibly complex options, and cedes greater control over the investment decision, progressively heavier obligations are imposed on the firm. But in the absence of ancillary strategies, if a retail investor cohort does emerge execution-only investors in particular may operate under unnecessary disadvantages.

[79] Second ECON Report (n 27) Amendment 19. Similarly, it sought to dilute the assessment obligation placed on the firm to warn the investor where the firm considers the service 'is not appropriate' (the formula adopted) to 'may not be appropriate'.

D. The Risks of a Regulatory Strategy

Whether this exclusively regulation-based strategy, designed to produce a competent, risk aware, and active EU retail investor, is a secure foundation for EU retail policy for the liberalized investment services market depends on a number of risk factors considered in this section.

I. The Risks of Greater Retail Engagement

A threshold question arises as to whether MiFID's core assumption as to the benefits of an active retail community is well-founded given the evidence on how retail investors behave.

How retail investors behave in the post-FSAP market matters. Capital allocation based on sentiment and irrationality will not deliver capital to those sources most in need of it, will generate greater risk, and, ultimately, cause wider economic damage.[80] If retail investors systematically sustain losses, this will also amount to a wider welfare loss and may, ultimately, deter investors from the emerging EU retail market place. Governments, and the EU, promote investment by retail investors for a range of reasons, but increasingly in order to support long-term savings, particularly pensions, and to promote the flow of savings to investment. Rational investors supposedly invest to smooth income to match consumption levels.[81] In practice, investors invest to increase the value of their investments and to make money.[82] For whatever reason retail investors access the market, however, the evidence suggests that they operate under a series of resource, information, and behavioural handicaps which prejudice them and which might suggest a more nuanced retail investor policy, as discussed in section E below.

While it is axiomatic that investors are not well-informed about the fundamentals of investing and risk,[83] behavioural finance argues that investor decision-making is systematically psychologically-driven and unrelated to fundamental information about asset values:[84] 'Individual traders are often regarded as at best

[80] M Kahan 'Securities Laws and the Social Costs of "Inaccurate" Stock Prices' (1991) 41 Duke L J 977.

[81] S Choi and A Pritchard (n 36) 13-14.

[82] S Choi 'Law, Finance, and Path Dependence: Developing Strong Securities Markets' (SSRN wp <http://ssrn.com/abstract_id=299386>, 2002) 1: 'Investors part with their money in the expectation that they will receive even more money from their investments'.

[83] One UK fund manager recently noted that private investors 'always pile in when it's too late'. A Joliffe 'Investors Remain Wary of Equities Amid Rising Prices' *Fin Times* (22 February 2005) 3.

[84] One commentator has observed with respect to behavioural finance that: '[The] old paradigm of an efficient market is crumbling … the outlines of a new paradigm are dimly visible in

cont. ...

uninformed, at worst fools'.[85] The classic troika of errors concerns failure to diversify, holding stocks for too long due to loss aversion, and trading too frequently, incurring heavy trading costs.[86] The often-cited Barber and Odean series of studies, which examine investor returns as compared to market returns, suggest that individuals continually sustain losses as compared to the market average.[87] After allowance for risk-adjustment, Barber and Odean have linked this underperformance to over-confidence, over-trading, and the loss-aversion-driven tendency of investors to hold losing shares and sell strong performers. It is also now clear that retail investors do not follow good diversification practices and regularly underestimate the impact of trading costs. The 2003 Jackson study, for example, shows wide dispersion in brokerage trading accounts, with the worst performing accounts showing returns considerably below the median return.[88] It suggests that equity trading accounts do not necessarily follow market-adjusted returns and that individual investments tend to be more risky, with investors facing much greater dispersion of returns, than market indices would suggests.[89] Jackson links this underperformance to incomplete diversification and higher transaction costs (as compared to the market).[90] The Enron collapse has provided one of the starkest examples of the frequency and dangers of inadequate retail investor diversification. Under US law, the 401k pension plan, sponsored by employers, can include employee shares and be subject to employee investment decisions, which can in-

resulting cloud of intellectual dust': L Stout 'The Mechanisms of Market Inefficiency: An Introduction to the New Finance' (2003) 28 J Corp L 635, 639. For analyses making more limited claims for behavioural finance see D Langevoort 'Taming the Animal Spirits of the Stock Markets: A Behavioural Approach to Securities Regulation' (2002) 57 Nw U L Rev 135 and R Gilson and R Kraakmann 'The Mechanisms of Market Efficiency Twenty Years Later: The Hindsight Bias' (2003) 28 J Corp L 715, 717-731. For a more sympathetic perspective see L Cunningham (n 43) 769-786.

85 J Coval, D Hirshleifer and T Shumway 'Can Individuals Investors Beat the Market' (SSRN wp <http://ssrn.com/abstract_id=364000>, 2002) 2.

86 See e.g. B Barber and T Odean 'Does Online Trading Change Investor Behaviour' (2002) 3 Eur Bus Org L R 83.

87 See e.g.: B Barber and T Odean (n 86) and 'The Courage of Misguided Convictions' (1999) 5 Fin Analysts J 41. See also: T Odean 'Are Investors Reluctant to Realise Their Losses' (1998) 53 J Finance 1775; H Jackson 'To What Extent Should Individual Investors Rely on the Mechanisms of Market Efficiency: A Preliminary Investigation of Dispersion in Investor Returns' (2003) 28 J Corporation L 671; J Coval et al (n 85); and A Poteshman and V Serbin 'Clearly Irrational Financial Market Behaviour: Evidence from the Early Exercise of Exchange Traded Stock Options' (2003) 58 J Finance 37.

88 For this analysis, based on the B Barber and T Odean 2000 sample (discussed in B Barber and T Odean (n 86)) see H Jackson (n 87) 677-678.

89 H Jackson (n 87) 676-679. He acknowledges that this does not reflect the extent to which investors have diversifiable risk, which they are not rewarded for, or what the returns look like when placed in the investor's overall market portfolio.

90 H Jackson (n 87) 687.

clude investing 100% of retirement savings in employer securities. One of the more egregious outcomes of the Enron collapse was the scale of the losses sustained by employees who had invested all their retirement savings in Enron shares.[91]

But the recent equity market correction suggests, if anecdotally, that investors do learn and should not be restricted through overly-protective securities policy.[92] UK investors, for example, are now increasingly seeking downside protection through growth-products which typically offer some form of capital guarantee in return for the investor foregoing returns if investments do well.[93] It also appears that retail investors, as a group, are becoming more aware of financial regulation and more interested in the market and the regulatory environment generally.[94] A formal challenge to the received wisdom as to irrational investor behaviour comes from the 2002 Coval study[95] which showed that the top performing quartile of brokerage accounts monitored outperformed the market by an average of 0.5 percent per month, suggesting that some investors are better than others at picking shares (after risk adjustment). The authors argue that skillful individuals learn through trading to exploit market inefficiencies to earn abnormal profits, beyond those available from established strategies linked to size, value, or momentum. Retail investors may not, therefore, be uniformly disruptive or irrational in the market and they may, in fact, support efficiency: 'Individual investors have been much maligned in the finance literature in recent years. This paper shows that not all individual investors are foolish'.[96] Similar evidence comes from the 2003 Jackson study.[97] It found that over the period 1991-2002, the net trades of full-service retail and execution-only brokerage clients in Australia, trading on the Australian Stock Exchange, positively forecasted future short-term market and cross-sectional returns. The study concluded that while retail investors do act in a highly systematic fashion they are not, at least in the short term, irrational.

[91] 57% of total Enron 401k assets were invested in Enron stock. This situation was not atypical in the U.S. with employees in one in five companies suffering real losses through assuming high levels of diversifiable risk. H Jackson (n 87) 680-683.

[92] See K Burgess 'Sales Surge Suggests Renewed confidence' *Fin Times* (27 August 2003) 3, reporting industry opinion that investors had 'learned Hard lessons' during the prolonged market fall, become more realistic about stock market rises, were taking a wider view of asset allocation by investing in bonds more widely, and that: 'investors' psychology has changed. Investors are calculating risk and reward differently'.

[93] FSA 2004 Financial Risk Outlook (n 13) 64.

[94] FSA 'What Consumers Know about Financial Regulation' (FSA Consumer Research Paper 29) (2004) 7 which found that the most informed consumers of financial services were those owning equity savings products, unit trusts, and personal equity plans.

[95] J Coval et al (n 85).

[96] J Coval et al (n 85) 18.

[97] A Jackson 'The Aggregate Behaviour of Individual Investors' (SSRN wp <http://ssrn.com/abstract=536942>, 2003).

Retail investors also seem to be enjoying something of a rebirth internationally as a source for good, rather than of irrational, market-damaging volatility. The Google initial public offer, and its direct retail involvement via an auction mechanism, for example, has been commended for allowing retail investors to impact more heavily on price formation and to counter more volatile, profit-taking institutional trading.[98] The more traditional characterization of the erratic and undesirable retail investor,[99] vividly described as the 'weak animal that must sadly but necessarily be culled out of the investing herd to improve the species,'[100] or, at best, corralled into tracker investment funds,[101] is on the wane. Increasingly, the retail investor is being regarded by some commentators as informed, central to the capital markets and, given the pressure on public pension provision, to economic stability more generally.[102] Wider demographic and pension trends also suggest that retail investors will be an increasingly important constituency. They are already a statistically significant group: 42% of all outstanding equity, for example, is directly held by retail investors in the U.S., 16% in the UK, 17% in Germany, 17% in France, and 24% in Australia.[103]

The evidence is therefore equivocal. It is clear that retail investors are handicapped by biases and that they regularly make errors concerning market mechanics, particularly with respect to diversification and the impact of trading costs. They also, however, show a capacity to learn and may, tentatively, act as an important source for market efficiency. The EU's regulatory strategy, based on encouraging investor access and with its emphasis on choice and autonomy, may, therefore, be justified in light of the empirical evidence.

[98] Lex 'Google IPO' *Fin Times* (4 May 2004) 22 noting that 'There is much that is novel about the Google auction. One less anticipated consequence could be the rehabilitation of retail investors as desirable shareholders'.

[99] J Coval et al (n 85) 2.

[100] L Stout (n 38) 35.

[101] S Choi 'Regulating Issuers not Investors: A Market-Based Proposal' (2000) 88 Cal L Rev 279.

[102] For some recent examples from the U.S., which must also be seen through the lens of the long U.S. tradition of market investment and the long-standing political and regulatory concern for the small investor, see L Stout (n 38) arguing that the 'trusting' retail investor, holding a small portfolio, is at the heart and soul of the huge U.S. market and should be supported; C Hurt 'Moral Hazard and the Initial Public Offering' (2005) 26 Cardozo L Rev 711, criticizing the modern IPO process as a mechanism for extracting wealth from the core retail community; and J Fanto (n 12) 1093 arguing that small investors are as 'critical to the survival of capitalism as are the elites and, without their support and participation, institutional investors and capital markets would not exist'.

[103] A Jackson (n 97) 3, 7 and 41. The Jackson study also shows evidence of substantial individual participation rates of, e.g., approximately 25% in the U.S. and UK, a very high 41% in Australia, and a lower rate of 13% in France.

Nonetheless, the weight of evidence as to the risks of retail engagement suggests that investment services policy should be more balanced and nuanced. At the least, an EU regulatory regime which facilitates trading by investors should also introduce some devices to counter common investor errors through, for example, education (section E below). [104] The regulatory strategy also requires more nuance. As outlined in section C, the range of information provided under the conduct of business regime places considerable demands on an investor's capacity to understand sophisticated financial information and may simply generate confusion. Firms might, for example, have been required to prioritize certain risk disclosures. The embryonic state of the EU market might also have suggested a requirement for basic disclosure concerning diversification, which is a well-known pitfall for retail investors.[105]

II. The Risks and Costs of Regulation

The EU's strategy for the retail investment services markets is heavily based on regulation. This raises a number of risks

1. Capture Risks

The association between investor protection and regulation makes the EU's regulatory strategy particularly vulnerable to public choice and protectionist pressures at all stages of the Lamfalussy process.[106] Investor protection and investor confidence, with their strong political resonances, provide regulators with a powerful rhetoric for expanding their own power through an ever-increasing rule and disclosure-based matrix.[107] The ease with which the Commission has taken up the

[104] The evidence that investors are irrational and engage in repeat speculative, losing trades has led to some calls for regulation to dampen enthusiasm for market investment and obstruct trading. L Stout 'Technology, Transaction Costs, and Investor Welfare: Is a Motley Fool Born Every Minute' (1997) 75 Washington U L Q 791.

[105] H Jackson (n 87) 687. Some evidence as to a concern to promote diversification emerged during MiFID's development. The last revisions to Article 19 (6) (the execution-only regime) included the European Parliament's amendment that the scope of the 'securities' subject to the execution-only regime be expanded to include non-EU securities. This was supported by the market as increasing choice and diversification opportunities. See FBE Memorandum to Members of the ECON Committee of the European Parliament (19 February 2004).

[106] On the extent to which the Lamfalussy process allows for balancing of different interest groups and controls institutional capture see E Ferran (n 2) loc. cit.

[107] On the need for caution in capital market lawmaking given rent-seeking, see L Ribstein 'Bubble Laws' (2003) 40 Houston L Rev 77, 79. On the dangers of regulatory capture generally see J Macey 'Corporate Law and Corporate Governance: A Contractual Perspective' (1998) 18 J of Corp L 185.

investor protection rhetoric, which may represent regulatory empire-building, combined with the potential for detailed rule-making at level 2, may lock EU policy-making for the retail markets into a regulatory straitjacket which associates regulatory investor protection with retail engagement. Policy may not, as a result, look closely enough at what, beyond regulation-based protection, drives retail investor engagement and decision-making.[108] Regulation-based retail policy can also be a dangerous tool, given problems of over-reaction after scandal and crisis[109] and, particularly in the EU context, the danger that protection becomes politically-motivated cover for national interests. The difficult passage of the MiFID internalization and pre-trade transparency rules saw the otherwise dominant theme of investor choice fall away, particularly with respect to the price improvement ban with respect to retail trades, and concepts of investor protection more closely based on restricting choice and autonomy arise, suggesting that investor protection was being used to cover protectionist interests.[110]

2. Expectation Risks

A retail policy based on extensive investor protection of the kind envisaged in the conduct of business regime also carries expectation risks, particularly where the effect of regulation is to convey certain signals as to the safety of the developing retail investment services market. Regulation can do little to prevent fraud when market exuberance disables healthy investor distrust.[111]

In many respects markets are inherently unfair, and attempts to suggest that retail investors are anything but handicapped as compared to their professional counterparts may be irresponsible. The split between retail and wholesale sectors means that markets are inherently discriminatory[112] and, arguably, must be, given the different profiles of both sectors. Markets also discriminate in terms of investor characteristics such as competence, skill and resources, and in terms of inves-

[108] The SEC, e.g., has been characterized as being locked into a self-perpetuating 'groupthink' on investor protection and regulation. See S Choi and A Pritchard (n 36) 36 citing a speech by ex-SEC Chairman A Levitt: 'Investor protection is our legal mandate. Investor protection is our moral responsibility. Investor protection is my top personal priority'.

[109] For a counter-argument, showing how the SEC has acted as a bulwark against overreaction to crises see J Coates 'Private vs. Political Choice of Securities Regulation: A Political Cost/Benefit Analysis' (2001) 41 Va J Int'l L 531.

[110] See, e.g., Report 'Could Brussels Drive Share Trading out of Europe' (2003) Int'l Fin Law Rev 17, 20.

[111] L Ribstein (n 107) 79-80. On the disabling effects of investor exuberance on gatekeeper discipline see also J Coffee 'Gatekeeper Failure and Reform: The Challenge of Fashioning Relevant Reforms' in G Ferrarini, KJ Hopt, J Winter and E Wymeersch (eds) *Reforming Company and Takeover Law in Europe* (Oxford University Press 2004) 454.

[112] See J Markham 'Protecting the Institutional Investor – Jungle Predator or Shorn Lamb' (1995) 12 Yale J of Reg 345.

tor access to information and to trading. It is well-established that retail investors face higher costs and diversification problems as compared to professional investors.[113] The trading process is shot through with unfairness, with the law only able to manage the risks of insider dealing and market abuse sporadically.[114] Investors are generally best advised to devolve decision-making to market professionals and passive investment funds. The wrong signals may, therefore, be sent by the new regulatory regime as to the reality of market investment and the limitations of the power of choice.

The rhetorical and practical effect of regulation can, therefore, become counterproductive unless expectations are carefully managed. Rules cannot provide a complete bulwark against losses provoked by investment firm failure, or wider market problems, and the danger arises that trust and confidence in marketing, services, and investing can quickly evaporate. Retail policy may best serve investors by promoting a healthy degree of informed investor scepticism, although the EU needs to tread a very fine line between caution and encouraging trust in the new market and the concept of market investing. This may be best achieved by balancing regulation and the signals it conveys with ancillary policies including education as to the limits of regulation and effective enforcement (section E below).

3. Regulatory Costs and Damage to Market Innovation

Regulation carries costs for market participants. Investor protection rules, in particular, tend to increase exponentially and to be based on high levels of protection tied to the needs of the most vulnerable investor group.[115] But the effective promotion of investor choice, which is central to EU retail policy, requires retail market strategies beyond regulation. It assumes a degree of de-regulation and the support of retail investor activity through market forces rather than government intervention. Compliance costs can, however, damage market forces and reduce the range of services and products provided by firms and their willingness to engage with the retail sector.[116] Cross-border retail investment services provision is costly and can be made more so with burdensome regulation.[117] Concerns as to

[113] H Jackson (n 87).

[114] C Bradley 'Disorderly Conduct and the Ideology of "Fair and Orderly Markets"' (2000) 26 J of Corp L 63; E Otness 'Balancing the Interests of Retail and Institutional Investors: The Continuing Quest for Transparency in Today's Fragmented Equity Markets' (2002) 96 Nw U L Rev 1607.

[115] See S Choi and A Pritchard (n 36) 37 noting the tendency of regulators to focus on 'widows and orphans' when constructing protection systems.

[116] FSA Treasury Evidence (n 9) para 7.

[117] CEPS (Centre for European Policy Studies) have argued that following the tightening of best execution and disclosure requirements by MiFID, and with operating conditions becoming more demanding, smaller brokers may opt to stay out of retail business. CEPS 'EU Financial

cont. ...

the regulatory burden represented by the FSAP emerged very strongly from the 2004 Expert Groups Reports.[118]

Harmonization should ease market access for firms and promote investor choice by, taking the least ambitious of the claims made for harmonization, removing regulatory obstacles to market access by firms already planning to engage in cross-border retail investment services. But when harmonization becomes re-regulation and detailed regulation, it runs the risk of imposing burdensome costs and of damaging market innovation and investor choice. Investor protection harmonization can, given the market integration and political context of the EU, result in unhappy compromises and confused objectives, which can, in certain Member States, prejudice levels of investor protection.[119]

This is particularly the case where regulatory competition as a driver of choice and innovation is largely removed, as is implicit in the MiFID regime.[120] The removal of regulatory competition becomes sharply apparent at level 2: not only is the depth of the intervention in Member States' regimes clear from the new rules, but the Draft Level 2 Directive is expressed as 'exhaustive harmonization'.[121] Even though Article 19 is not expressly based on maximum harmonization, the level of intervention at level 2 leaves very little room for Member State discretion or investment firm innovation, particularly with respect to disclosure. Elsewhere there is greater flexibility, although much will depend on the extent to which Member States 'gold plate' the level 2 rules on implementation. The best execution regime, for example, allows firms considerable discretion in designing execution systems, while the suitability regime is designed to provide firms with benchmarks as to how suitability is assessed and does not impose detailed information-gathering requirements on firms. Nonetheless, some degree of scepticism is suggested in relation to the Commission's argument in the Background Note that the Draft Level 2 Directive takes a 'principles-based' approach. It is reveal-

Regulation and Supervision Beyond 2005' (CEPS Task Force Report No. 54) (January 2005) 9. In a similar vein, warning of the dangers of onerous suitability requirements and of the risk of firms leaving the marketplace and reducing consumer choice, see the BBA Response, Commission's Autumn 2004 Consultation on the Expert Group Reports <http://forum.europa.eu.int/Public> 4.

118 See the Securities Expert Group Report (n 22) 10-13.

119 See the analysis by L Enriques of MiFID's new conflict of interest regime (Articles 13 and 18) which, he argues, will lower levels of investor protection in Italy given the prevailing regulatory, market, and cultural context. L Enriques 'Conflicts of Interest in Investment Services: The Price and Uncertain Impact of MiFID's Regulatory Framework' in this volume 323-340.

120 While this essay reflects the FSAP's basis in harmonization as a means of market integration rather than in regulatory competition, the debate still rages on the merits of the two techniques. For a wide-ranging critique in the context of the primary markets see E Ferran (n 2) 50-57.

121 Commission 'Background Note' 7.

ing, however, that the language of incentives has crept into the Draft Directive: the 'principles-based' rules are designed to create 'strong incentives for the firm to monitor its own activities and determine whether its activities comply with the principles set out in the Directive'.[122]

Regulatory cost reduction in the EU context, and a coherent approach to the retail markets, also demands that the wider universe of EU regulation is considered in developing new rules to avoid costly duplications and overlaps.[123] The relationship between the MiFID marketing regime and the 2002 Distance Marketing Directive and 2000 E Commerce Directive,[124] for example, and between the MiFID portfolio management regime and the UCITS regime must be clear. CESR made some efforts to ensure consistency in preparing its advice for the Commission,[125] but has also frequently referred to the practical difficulties which may arise on implementation. The implementation process should also consider the risks of unnecessary disruption to, and the imposition of costs on, existing investor/investment firm relationships. The re-categorization of investors and the re-running of suitability tests may, for example, generate excessive costs. Some grandfathering provisions have, however, been included. MiFID Article 71 (6) allows firms to continue treating existing professional clients as such, as long as the categorization had been granted on the basis of an adequate assessment of the expertise, experience and knowledge of the client which gives reasonable assurance that the client is capable of making his own investment decisions and understands the risks involved.[126]

The message on the prejudicial effects of costs on investor choice appears to be impacting on policy development. MiFID makes some attempts to ensure that undue costs are not imposed on the core investment advice regime, which is central to the retail strategy. Under Article 5 (5) Member States have the option to

[122] Commission 'Background Note' 6.

[123] The Securities Expert Group Report (n 22) 8 noted that care was needed to 'ensure coherence across all regulation impacting on financial markets'. During the MiFID negotiations, the ECON Committee regularly toned down the degree of protection offered in the MiFID regime, often by referring to the wider matrix of contract, product, disclosure, and marketing rules in existence (First ECON Report (n 27) 92).

[124] Directive 2000/31/EC of the European Parliament and of the Council of 8 June 2000 on certain Legal Aspects of Information Society Services, in particular Electronic Commerce, in the Internal Market ('E Commerce Directive') OJ L178 17.07.2000 1-16.

[125] The Article 19 (2) and (3) level 2 disclosure regime is stated to apply without prejudice to related measures including the Prospectus Directive, the UCITS regime, and the E Commerce Directive regime (Final CESR First Mandate Advice (n 54) 46).

[126] Reflecting a concern that millions of contracts, particularly in Germany where 36 million contracts were thought to be affected, might have to examined and revised. Second ECON Report (n 27) 43. Similarly, MiFID, Annex II which sets out when professional investors can be categorised as such does not apply where firms have previously used similar parameters and procedures.

permit competent authorities to delegate authorization and monitoring of advisers to self-regulatory bodies, although firms remain subject to the Article 19 conduct regime.[127] The disclosure regime has also been streamlined in places. Article 19 provides for disclosure to be produced in standardized formats (Article 19 (3)), while the risk warnings required under Article 19 (5) and (6) may be made available in standardized formats. The Commission placed restraints on the level 2 regime in its mandate to CESR. It was to avoid excessive and costly intervention in investment firm business and avoid formulations which would 'lead to over-prescriptive, excessively detailed legislation, adding undue burdens and unnecessary costs to the firms and hampering innovation in the field of financial services'.[128] The level 2 advice from CESR contained a number of indicators on the importance of reducing costs, while it is clear that the level 2 rules have been curtailed and relaxed through the different CESR drafts, in the Commission's draft rules, and following market reaction to the Commission's draft rules.

More generally, the Commission in its 2005 Financial Services Green Paper has cautioned the EU institutions against 'Commission proposals being mushroomed into unnecessary, sapping complexity' and warned the Member States of the risks of 'gold-plating' EU obligation during national implementation.[129]

Overall, and particularly where regulation is the major policy strategy for the retail markets, innovation and competition should be recognized as accompanying drivers for effective retail markets,[130] and should be diluted, where possible, by non-prescriptive measures, such as education and product development, which can limit the need for prescriptive rules (see section E below).[131]

4. Wholesale and Retail Partitioning

Effective containment of costs and the protection of innovation and choice demands appropriate management of the retail and wholesale investment services sectors. Careful management of both sectors allows the burden of regulation to be appropriately spread. In principle, tailored regulation, which benefits those in

[127] Reflecting concerns that inclusion of investment advice under MiFID would require significant investment in authorization and supervision, but limited benefits, given the current domestic-orientation of advice services. MiFID Proposal (n 4) 30. They have also been subject to a customised capital adequacy regime to avoid 'unjustified or over-onerous regulatory demands'.

[128] Final CESR MiFID Mandate (n 31) 5. This was added to ensure that level 2 'should not intervene in any micromanagement of investment firms'. Summary Record of the Sixteenth Meeting of the ESC (8 December 2003) ESC/46/2003, 4.

[129] Green Paper (n 11) 6.

[130] The FSA is opposed to imposing prescriptive regulation as the sole element of its retail market strategy, given the expense and risk of reducing investor choice. FSA Treasury Evidence (n 9) para. 7.

[131] For a contrary perspective see FIN-USE Report (n 35) 27 on the need to balance innovation with protection.

need of assistance but does not restrict the freedom of action of more robust actors, can be regarded as 'asymmetrically' paternalistic, and as bridging the gap between market forces and more paternalistic views of regulation.[132] Appropriate tailoring is all the more essential given the exponential character of investor protection and the risk of retail standards leaking across to effective wholesale markets and becoming the norm, as seems to have happened with the Prospectus Directive. The wholesale market should be kept clear of retail standards of regulation as innovations on the wholesale side can filter back to the retail markets. Retail investors in packaged products, for example, ultimately benefit from the ability of institutional investors, such as collective investment funds, to operate in low-cost, low-regulation environments. Developments in the wholesale sector, particularly where competition is strong, also often precede retail market benefits, as reported by the Securities Expert Group.[133]

MiFID appears to have taken the need for tailoring to heart, at least in principle. In its First Reading on MiFID, ECON's concern with the costs of regulation led it to emphasize the importance of distinguishing between professionals and others, given the risk of 'severely disrupting markets'.[134] Article 19 is expressly declared to be applied having regard to the different needs of the retail and wholesale sectors: the Article 19 (10) Lamfalussy clause provides that level 2 rules must take into account the retail or professional nature of the investor. MiFID Annex II contains detailed guidelines on when 'professional' clients are to be categorized as such.[135] Article 24 also exempts transactions between firms and 'eligible counterparties' from the conduct of business regime. At level 2, effective partitioning has emerged as a major theme of the Commission's draft rules, with key disclosure obligations (particularly Article 19 (2) and (3)) expressly limited to retail investors and with particular requirements applying to best execution for retail investors given that retail investors are largely concerned with price and the costs of execution (section C).

[132] C Camerer (n 12) 1212. See also S Choi and A Pritchard (n 36) 66-68 on the need to 'partition' investors in regulating.

[133] See (n 22).

[134] 'Applying protections to professionals which have been designed for retail markets drives up costs and damages the millions of retail clients who save via institutional investors such as UCITS, fund managers and pension funds' (First ECON Report (n 27) 41).

[135] Detailed consideration of these rules is outside the scope of this essay. In essence they categorize professional investors in terms of those automatically treated as professional (although they may request higher levels of protection) and those who may be treated as professional, but this latter group must choose not to benefit from detailed conduct of business protection. The former category includes authorised entities (such as UCITS and investment firms), large undertakings based on balance sheet, turnover, and own fund thresholds, institutional investors, and government bodies. The latter category is more fluid and is based on considerations of investment experience (based on transaction frequency), portfolio size, and whether the investor has worked in the investment/markets sphere.

III. The Limits of Law in Promoting Retail Activity

One of the most striking features of MiFID, and implicit in the EU's regulatory strategy for the retail markets, is the link made between the regulation of investment services and retail activity. The FSAP generally is based on the controversial premise that law is a, if not the, crucible within which the integrated capital market will be forged. MiFID builds on this assumption, reflecting a belief that retail market access may remain subdued in the absence of an appropriate regulatory framework. This raises the difficult question as to the relationship between regulation and pan-EU investor behaviour, described by one leading regulator as a 'chicken and egg scenario'.[136]

There are limits to what law can achieve in promoting retail investor activity. The extent to which law drives economic outcomes is much disputed. A wealth of empirical material, driven by the research of economists La Porta, Lopez de Silanes, Shleifer, and Vishny, models the relationship between capital market rules and indicators of economic development and financial sector growth, such as the value of stock markets, numbers of listed firms, and levels of dividend payouts.[137] The wider positive relationship between financial sector/financial intermediary growth and economic growth has also been examined.[138] This research focuses, for the most part, on the informational and agency problems in the primary, public securities markets. It addresses the connection between indicators of capital market growth and the rules governing, and impacting on, capital-raising, typically offer-disclosure, insider dealing, company law/corporate governance, and minority protection rules,[139] rather than the secondary retail investment services market. It is difficult to extrapolate from this research, which has been questioned,[140] any firm conclusions about the relationship between retail investor be-

[136] J Tiner Speech on 'The Future of EU Financial Services Regulation. A UK Perspective' (19 May 2004) (discussing the potential but difficult link between developing a retail market and appropriate regulation) <http://www.fsa.gov.uk/pubs/speeches>.

[137] See, in particular, R La Porta, F Lopez de Silanes, A Shleifer and R Vishny 'Legal Determinants of External Finance' (1997) 52 J of Finance 1131. For a review of the literature see S Choi (n 82).

[138] R King and R Levine 'Finance and Growth: Schumpeter Might be Right' (1993) 108 Quart J Econ 681; R Rajan and L Zingales 'Financial Dependence and Growth' (1998) 88 Amer Econ R 559; and R Levine 'Law, Finance and Economic Growth' (1999) 8 J Finan Intermediation 8.

[139] See, e.g., R La Porta, F Lopez de Silanes, and A Shleifer 'What Works in Securities Laws' (SSRN wp <http://ssrn.com/abstractid=425880>, 2003), suggesting that mandatory disclosure requirements, combined with ease of private enforcement, are strongly correlated with larger stock markets.

[140] F Partnoy 'Why Markets Crash and What Law Can Do about It' (2001) 61 U Pitt L Rev 741; J Coffee 'The Rise of Dispersed Ownership: The Roles of Law and the State in the Separation of Ownership and Control' (2001) 111 Yale L J 1; and J Franks, C Mayer and S Rossi 'The

cont. ...

haviour in the secondary markets and regulation. The relationship between law and the investment markets is, at best, an uncertain one,[141] albeit that a positive one is an article of faith for regulators.

Little is known as to what drives retail investor activity, much less pan-EU activity. It is by no means certain that increased product and service supply (assuming that investment firms will react to MiFID's liberalization) will generate pan-EU activity and dispel the home bias. Strong cultural and local factors may impede the development of pan-EU retail activity, independently of any regulatory measures to increase investor choice and confidence.[142] Many of the divergences in Member State retail investment markets are not, ultimately, susceptible to regulation, particularly where they concern cultural differences with respect to savings and finance.[143] Investors are also subject to a number of handicaps which limit their enthusiasm for the markets including loss aversion, a preference for easy access to savings, poor understanding of investment products, and the legacy effect of past losses. While regulation can attempt to deal with understanding and disclosure problems, biases and preferences for liquid savings are less easily dealt with through regulatory measures.

Given that investors have strong preferences for local providers,[144] the growth of the pan-EU retail market may depend on the extent to which firms can disguise themselves, particularly through online service provision (or branches), as home firms, by operating in investors' languages and selling services and products which are closely linked to the domestic market. Detailed harmonization of investor protection may therefore work, but only insofar as it is supply-side driven and allows seamless operation of on-line passporting activity.

Origination and Evolution of Ownership and Control' (ECGI Finance wp No. 09/2003 <http://ssrn.com/abstract=354381>, 2003).

[141] See J Lawrence 'The Economics of Market Confidence: (Ac)Costing Securities Market Regulation' (SSRN wp <http://ssrn.com/abstract=2046432>), relying on data from the New Zealand stock exchange, its economy, and recent law reforms to argue that investor confidence is linked to macroeconomics conditions and not regulation.

[142] '[T]he jury is still out on the extent to which increased cross-border product offer [in the asset management sector] would be matched by demand': Asset Management Expert Group (n 10) 9. The Banking Expert Group Report (n 24) 21 also cautioned that it was 'difficult to gauge whether harmonization of retail financial markets [would] unleash real demand-driven benefits for consumers'. Similarly, see FSA, HM Treasury, Bank of England 'The EU Financial Services Action Plan: A Guide' (July 2003) 18.

[143] These barriers include 'cultural and linguistic barriers, different approaches to consumer savings habits and tax regimes. In these areas there is virtually nothing that EU legislation can do. It should therefore not attempt to try' (J Tiner (n 134)). The Banking Expert Group Report (n 24) 18 included among the structural barriers to retail integration the 'complexity … and long term perspective of certain products which lead consumers to favour locally established entities with whom they can develop a 'relationship'. Trust in the reliability of the supplier is essential'.

[144] Financial Integration Monitor 2005 (n 21) 11.

A realization appears to be growing that the adoption of pan-EU regulatory solutions in the retail markets will not deliver the same benefits as in the wholesale markets. Commissioner Bolkestein noted in January 2004 that regulators should be humble, and recognized that regulation cannot force regulation.[145] This theme continued in the June 2004 FSAP Report with the Commission noting that the extent to which legislation drives integration was difficult to judge given the impact of the euro, technology, and cyclical economic factors.[146] The Commission also admitted that, contrary to the FSAP's distinct institutional and legislative legacy, it was difficult to assess whether it was improving cross-border opportunities for investors and investment firms.[147]

This loss of faith in the ability of law to deliver retail market activity chimes with a more general nervousness about the direction of the retail project. The Securities Expert Group has suggested that there might be some merit 'in starting a debate on whether and how retail markets should be further integrated'.[148] This is in marked contrast to the wholesale project, the success of which might be linked to the widespread shared conviction that integration of these markets was a worthy and achievable goal.[149] A nervousness as to integration in the retail financial services markets more generally was also evident at the Commission's landmark June 2004 high level conference for regulators and market participants considering the status of the FSAP and how to take it forward.[150] The major concern is, undoubtedly with the future development of the retail financial services market more generally, particularly with respect to banking and insurance products. MiFID brings a considerable degree of convergence in the retail investment services regime, although it does not address the investment products issue or difficult service delivery questions. The 2005 post-FSAP Green Paper has, however, targeted asset management and retail financial services (particularly with respect to savings products) for further reform, but takes a soft line, emphasizing consultation and 'working with the grain of the market'.[151]

The growing awareness at policy levels as to the limitations of law in retail market integration reinforces the need for more creative strategies, in addition to regulation, to support the retail investment services market, such as education-

[145] Speech by F Bolkestein on 'Learning the Lessons of the Financial Services Action Plan' to Edinburgh Finance and Investment Seminar (29 January 2004) <http://www.europa.eu.int/rapid> 1.

[146] 10th FSAP Report (n 8) 14.

[147] 10th FSAP Report (n 8) 14.

[148] The Securities Expert Group Report (n 22) 7.

[149] Speech by Commissioner Bolkestein on 'Future Directions for European Financial Integration' Commission Conference on European Financial Integration: Progress and Prospects (22 June 2004) <http://www.europa.eu.int/rapid>.

[150] Conference Conclusions (n 60).

[151] Green Paper (n 11) 11-13.

based, governance, and product development measures. The relationship between retail activity in the secondary markets and regulation is, at the very least problematic, and an exclusive reliance on law to manage the retail market may be counter-productive.

IV. The Need for Evidence

The MiFID conduct of business regime, and the EU's reliance on a regulatory, disclosure-based strategy for the retail market, is based on assumptions as to the nature of investor confidence, the features of the average EU investor, and the effectiveness of particular regulatory mechanisms, such as disclosure, that are not tested in the EU marketplace. When combined with the wider uncertainties of the impact of law on investor behaviour, this suggests that considerable care is needed in system design. An effective regulatory regime which acts as the cornerstone of EU retail investment services policy, will need considerably greater real-life information on how the EU retail investment services market will work, what provokes rational retail investor activity, and which types of public intervention, regulatory and otherwise, are most effective. While this research can be led by industry to a certain extent, the information required for overall policy development is unlikely to be produced by firms acting in their own interests. Proprietary data sets from investment firms on trading behaviour and investor returns, while rich in data from trading accounts, are unlikely to be made available where they suggest that particular types of investor trading, while rich in fees, are low in returns.[152]

EU intervention on the retail investment service market must therefore also include EU-sponsored detailed and large-scale investigations into the nature of the EU retail investment services market as it develops. A more detailed assessment of investor trading, for example, should yield important information as to the extent to which investors diversify, whether they trade too frequently and if this damages returns, their average returns, and how they allocate funds. This evidence could inform disclosure policy, suitability controls and the advice process, and investor education.[153] Evidence is also needed on how investor behaviour and financial capability varies across the EU, the risks and difficulties faced by investors, how investors are likely to exercise choice in an integrated market, and what disclosure, products, and services are most likely to promote effective and

[152] H Jackson (n 87) 670 and 688.

[153] See, H Jackson (n 87) 679 and 687 noting that surprisingly little good information is available on how investors perform and calling for the SEC to carry out more analysis of investor returns and, in particular, investor portfolios which would allow fuller analysis and support investor education policies. He suggests that the SEC could produce a disclosure document, as part of its education strategy, showing how investors, in general, perform in the markets. For a similar call see also A Jackson (n 97) 25.

informed pan-EU investor activity.[154] It is notable that FIN-USE, whose views are revealing as the only retail-focused actor on the policy stage at present, has called for studies into how retail investors react to disclosure, specifically UCITS summary prospectus disclosure – particularly as 'no market testing was carried out with consumers'.[155] The December 2005 White Paper suggests a closer focus by the Commission, albeit *ex-post facto* which limits its effectiveness, on cost benefit analysis of FSAP measures more generally, but specific initiatives are required with respect to the retail markets and retail investor behaviour.[156]

E. A Multi-Stranded Strategy for the Retail Markets

The uncertain outcomes of a regulation-driven retail strategy, combined with the risks and costs involved, suggest that appropriate flanking policies concerning enforcement, product development, and education are necessary to minimize the risks of ineffective laws and inefficient investor reaction. In addition, and to minimize the risk of costly and ineffective lawmaking in particular,[157] the lawmaking process should represent retail investor interests effectively. Overall, more creative thinking is needed as to the key components of retail investment services policy if the currently dominant policy objective of a pro-active capital supplier, competently navigating the integrated EU investment services market, is to be realized in practice.

I. Enforcement

1. Enforcement and Supervision

Effective enforcement of breaches of the MiFID conduct of business regime is central to developing retail investor confidence in the pan-EU investment services market. Public enforcement of investment firm breaches of the MiFID rules as

[154] The FSA has called for research into pan-EU consumer behaviour, buying experience, financial capability, and the extent to which consumers are treated fairly across all Member States. See Speech by J Tiner on 'European Financial Integration: Progress and Prospects' Commission Conference (22 June 2004) <http://www.fsa.gov.uk.pubs/speeches>.

[155] FIN-USE Report (n 35) 25.

[156] White Paper (n 11) 6. In the White Paper the Commission committed to a full legal and economic assessment of all FSAP measures by 2009. The Commission's approach to FSAP cost benefit analysis is set out in 'FSAP Evaluation, Part I: Process and Implementation' (November 2005).

[157] For an extensive application of this risk analysis to the EU's primary markets see E Ferran (n 2).

implemented, and EU enforcement of Member State breaches concerning the implementation of MiFID, will be critical for the overall success of the regime.

Enforcement has emerged as a striking theme of the ongoing post-FSAP analysis.[158] In its November 2005 consultation on FSAP Evaluation, for example, the Commission isolated enforcement of Member State breaches as critical for FSAP success and noted that 'there is considerable work to be done in the area of transposition,' given the evidence that Member States are consistently missing implementation deadlines.[159] The Lamfalussy structures have introduced a new dimension to effective enforcement, with CESR playing a key role in supporting peer group reviews, monitoring consistent implementation, and encouraging mediation between supervisors where problems arise on implementation and enforcement.[160]

At Member State supervisory level, MiFID establishes a considerably more sophisticated regime (as compared to the precursor Investment Services Directive) for the supervisory and enforcement powers which must be available to competent authorities in policing MiFID (Article 50). Article 51 also requires that appropriate administrative measures can be taken, or administrative sanctions made available, without prejudice to the right of Member States to impose criminal sanctions. Supervisory responsibility for enforcement of the conduct of business regime is located in the firm's home Member State. The competent authority of the branch Member State, however, is responsible for ensuring that investment services provided by the branch comply with Articles 19, 21 and 22 (Article 32 (7)). Issues of co-ordination and co-operation, and of consistency in supervision across the Member States arise, as a result, particularly where investors receive services through a passporting firm on a services basis, although MiFID does introduce formal co-operation and communication requirements under Articles 56-62. Questions as to the effectiveness and experience of supervisors also arise, particularly for those Member States where, so far, there is an immature and inexperienced retail investor market. Important practical questions also arise as to the resources (staff, financial, etc) available to home Member State supervisors where they are responsible for multi-host State activities. The policing of retail investor activity from the home Member State can be highly resource-intensive given the potential numbers involved, the range of products, differing investor capabilities and profiles across the Member States calling for nuanced supervision (particularly with respect to suitability requirements), and the range of investment firms potentially involved.

[158] See, e.g., the 10th FSAP Report (n 8) 1 in which the Commission noted that 'regulation alone does not deliver an integrated single market' and that effective enforcement was also needed and the Green Paper (n 11) Annexes 6-8.

[159] See (n 156) 34-35.

[160] Himalaya Report (n 23) 11 and 15.

The key to the effectiveness of pan-EU supervision of the retail market, if it emerges, lies in CESR. In its important 2004 Himalaya Report, it discussed supervision in considerable detail, particularly with respect to the challenges raised by the home/host relationship. It noted, in particular, the need for 'confidence in the capability to act of the Home competent authority'.[161] Imbalances can arise in the interests, incentives, and resources of the home Member State as supervisory anchor for pan-EU, multi-jurisdictional investment services activity. CESR has already noted differences across the Member States with respect to supervisory intensity and the deployment of resources to supervision.[162] It is particularly concerned as to the adequacy of resourcing in the home Member State where an investment firms has significant host activities, and as to the effectiveness of pan-EU supervision of conduct of business regulation, where an investment firm has branches in a number of Member States.[163] The effectiveness of branch supervision, in particular, and communication between supervisors will be critical. Recent evidence suggests that physical establishment presents the best opportunities for capturing local business. The 2005 Financial Integration Monitor reported that consumers do not appear to distinguish between buying products from domestic or foreign providers, as long as they are established in the local market – only 5% of EU citizens have bought financial products in another Member State.[164]

CESR has identified convergence in supervisory, investigative, sanctioning, and information exchange powers as essential for 'any credible Home/Host relationship or Network arrangement'.[165] More ambitious tools which CESR has proposed include its acting as a 'supervisor of supervisors' through peer pressure mechanisms, the adoption of a mission statement on supervision, and better access by supervisors to regulatory information. On a practical level, effective 'supervisory learning' through CESR will be of key importance given the immature nature of the pan-EU retail market, and the likelihood of new challenges emerging if investment firm and investor behaviour changes under liberalization. Although there are currently considerable cultural differences towards market investment and differing degrees of investor activity across the Member States,[166] nonetheless, common challenges exist in terms of the emerging retail cohort with respect to education, the management of disclosure, and the consistency of core disciplines such as suitability requirements. References to the European supervisory mindset, and a European reflex are increasingly appearing in policy pro-

161 Himalaya Report (n 23) 18.

162 Himalaya Report (n 23) 12.

163 Himalaya Report (n 23) 19.

164 Financial Integration Monitor 2005 (n 21) 10.

165 Himalaya Report (n 23) 2.

166 Debt securities, e.g., are very popular investments in Italy (as the impact of Parmalat scandal on retail investors made clear) but are rare investments among retail investors in the UK.

nouncements and documents.[167] CESR has, however, noted the lack of convergence in core supervisory approaches and objectives with respect to, for example, the acceptable level of risk which investors should carry.[168] Although CESR's tentative suggestion that 'all significant [market] innovations be subject to pan-EU assessment at an early stage' is ambitious,[169] it will be critical that the different pockets of retail expertise which are likely to develop across the EU supervisory chain are shared as the market develops. The UK FSA, for example, is building considerable expertise in managing retail access to sophisticated alternative investment vehicles.[170] CESR's proposals in the Himalaya Report for staff exchanges, joint training programmes, and data bases will be essential for an effective EU supervisory approach to the retail market.

2. Investment Firm Liability and Investor Enforcement

But market discipline plays a key role here as well. Market mechanisms which promote good behaviour by investment firms depend, in part, on the active policing by investors of firm failures, particularly with respect to investment advice.[171] The development of an effective retail investor constituency includes, therefore, the development of a cohort of investors empowered, and sufficiently informed, to monitor investment firms under the new regime and to exercise liability rights, whether contractual or otherwise. Civil liability regimes continue to represent a major sensitivity for the Member State/EC separation of powers, however, and continue to differ, notwithstanding tentative movements in, for example, the Prospectus Directive.[172] Procedural mechanisms supporting litigation, such as class actions, are also significantly weaker in the EU as compared to the U.S..[173]

[167] See, e.g., Speech by C McCreevy on 'Regulatory and Supervisory Challenges of Financial Integration' (Lamfalussy London Summer Dinner) (27 June 2005) <http://www.europa.eu.int/rapid> ('European supervisors … need to develop this 'European reflex' and think and act in pan-European dimensions').

[168] Himalaya Report (n 23) 12.

[169] Himalaya Report (n 23) 13.

[170] See FSA 'Wider Range Retail Investment Products. Consumer Protection in a Rapidly Changing World' (FSA Discussion Paper 05/03) (June 2005).

[171] On the link between liability structures and healthy gatekeeper incentives see, e.g., B Black 'The Legal and Institutional Preconditions for Strong Securities Markets' (2001) 48 UCLA L Rev 781 and J Coffee (n 111).

[172] Article 6 requires Member States to ensure liability regimes are in place to ensure liability is imposed on those responsible for a prospectus.

[173] On the difference between U.S. and EU liability structures and cultures in the context of the Parmalat scandal, see G Ferrarini and P Giudici 'Financial Scandals and the Role of Private Enforcement: the Parmalat Case' (ECGI Law wp No. 40/2005 <http://ssrn.com/abstract_id=730403>, 2005).

Some moves are being made towards improving and standardizing contractual rights under investment services contracts. Intervening with respect to contractual protections is a relatively recent strategy for the EU retail investment services regime, following the cooling-off or withdrawal rights contained in the 2002 DMD. Article 6 (1) of the DMD grants consumers a fourteen day withdrawal right with respect to financial services (subject to exceptions which include time- and market-sensitive investments) which are concluded through distance methods. These DMD rights represent a much higher degree of intervention in the investor/investment firm relationship than previously in EU investment services regulation.[174] Standard form contract disclosure on redress mechanisms (required under DMD Article 3 (4)), should also support active policing by investors of their rights.[175]

Given the barriers retail investors face in mounting legal actions, easy access to complaint and recompense systems, both domestically and on a cross-border basis, is essential to the development of an active retail market.[176] Low-cost and accessible out-of-court settlement procedures have a particular role to play here. In the 2005 Financial Services Green Paper, the Commission argued that '[r]edress systems could help to increase consumer confidence in the market so that the full benefits of integration can be realized'.[177] Calls have also come from the market for the improvement of investor protection through pan-EU enforcement structures and, in particular, for a universal ombudsman service.[178] While centralized dispute resolution systems are some way off, attempts are being made to establish pan-EU dispute resolution systems with network-based measures such as FIN-NET. Established in 2001, it provides a redress network for financial-services disputes by linking together national out-of-court settlement bodies. It is supported by a Memorandum of Understanding on a Cross-Border Out-of-

[174] The 2001 E Commerce Communication (n 40) 13 noted that financial services are heavily contract-based and that contractual terms and conditions determine the attractiveness of financial products, but that contractual rules for the protection of consumers diverged across the Member States, inhibiting the establishment of an internal market in retail financial services. While it called for greater convergence which would balance the need to maintain product innovation and choice with the need for greater uniformity, limited progress has been made.

[175] Standard form contract disclosure on how to complain has been supported by APCIMS on the grounds that 'if consumers are to feel that they can safely invest in the market, then not only do they have to have the security that firms are well regulated but also that there is reasonable redress available to them should something go wrong' (APCIMS Response to CESR's First Call for Evidence (February 2004) 5). See also FIN-USE Report (n 35) 13.

[176] Lack of access to dispute resolution systems was highlighted as a potential structural obstacle to market integration by the Banking Expert Group Report (n 10) 21.

[177] Green Paper (n 11) Annex 18.

[178] APCIMS 'Making the Financial Single Market Work. Priorities after the Financial Services Action Plan' (September 2003) 1.

Court Complaints Network for Financial Services.[179] The Commission has recently acknowledged that '[m]ediation and alternative dispute resolution schemes, such as ... the SOLVIT [designed for resolving Member State/Commission disputes with respect to Member State breaches] and FIN-NET networks, offer considerable potential'.[180] But FIN-NET does not yet cover the investment services industry fully on a pan-EU basis.[181] The building blocks of pan-EU dispute resolution are in place, however, with MiFID Article 53 encouraging Member States to develop out-of-court settlement procedures.[182] This seems to be an area ripe for potential development through level 3 of the Lamfalussy process, in that CESR could promote, advise on, and co-ordinate pan-EU movements towards dispute resolution systems.

II. Education and Investor Capability

MiFID's regulatory strategy for the retail markets suggests the development of an informed and rational EU investor, equipped to choose between competing products and services in the integrated market and to make rational investment choices. But the conduct of business regime is not based on a firm foundation of pan-EU investor education.

The promotion of higher levels of financial literacy and capability has recently catapulted to the top of regulatory agendas worldwide given the move towards self-supported pensions and the need for savers to take control over their financial futures.[183] Investor education must also play a central role in the EU's nascent retail investor strategy. The markets hold dangers for ill-informed investors, operating under a series of resource and competence handicaps, which are exacerbated in the context of the developing pan-EU market. Education can promote the development of an informed and effective retail investor cohort which can contrib-

[179] Commission Recommendation 98/257/EC of 30 March 1998 on the Principles Applicable to the Bodies Responsible for out-of-court Settlement of Consumer Disputes, OJ L115 17.04.1998 31-34.

[180] Green Paper (n 11) 7.

[181] The Austrian and Italian limbs of FIN-NET, e.g., do not cover securities. The Asset Management Expert Group Report (n 10) 24 also reported that while the Commission had made considerable efforts to establish and publicize FIN-NET, not all retail investors were familiar with it and it needed greater publicity.

[182] See also Distance Marketing Directive (n 59) Article 14 and E Commerce Directive (n 124) Article 15.

[183] J Fanto (n 12) 1083: 'Investor education is of worldwide concern simply because of demographics'. The FSA has recently prioritized education policy, stressing the ageing population and the parallel need for investors to take control of their finances. See the FSA 2003 Education Report (n 12), the FSA 2004 Education Report (n 42), and FSA 2005 Financial Risk Outlook (n 12).

ute effectively to the EU capital market. It can also actively promote investor engagement with the markets,[184] given that gaps in understanding deter investors.[185] Formal education policies can help support investor choice by reducing the burden of protective regulation and enhancing the effectiveness of disclosure. As investors become more informed and better able to interpret disclosure and make appropriate choices they become less in need of costly, interventionist regulation. In the absence of a coherent and sustained education regime, the costly and sophisticated new disclosure regime is not only unlikely to be accessible to investors, but is unlikely to address fundamental misunderstandings as to the nature and risk of market investing.

Now is the appropriate time for formal education measures to be taken, both in the interests of developing an informed investor constituency and as a critical element of a retail strategy based on choice and the reduction of regulatory costs. Worldwide, the focus, as never before, is on developing investor capability and investor education systems. Education is also increasingly appearing as an essential element of an integrated strategy for the retail markets and as a less aggressive and risky way of influencing investor decisions.[186]

The question arises, however, as whether the EU has a role in delivering investor education as part of an overall retail investor strategy. While many education initiatives are best run at domestic level,[187] there is an argument for a discrete EU education policy supporting EU harmonization. Investor education could address practices which may emerge, such as day-trading, which while not necessarily a subject for regulatory intervention, might warrant softer but EU-consistent intervention, given the unsophisticated nature of the EU retail investor base.[188] Education on how to manage disclosure, particularly with respect to comparability and the risks of pan-EU investing,[189] seems appropriate for a dis-

[184] J Fanto (n 12) 1086 notes the dual function of education in assisting the decision-making process and in introducing investors to the markets in cultures where popular market investing is not common.

[185] '[W]hile some consumers may have made a rational decision not to engage in the market, our concern is that others may not be engaged due to their lack of understanding and confidence' (FSA 2003 Education Report (n 12) 6).

[186] S Choi and A Pritchard (n 36) 76-77. In the post-Enron reform context, see L Cunningham 'The Sarbanes Oxley Yawn: Heavy Rhetoric, Light Reform (And it Just Might Work)' (2003) 35 Conn L Rev 915, 922, regretting that the Sarbanes Oxley Act-centred reform process did not include encouraging stronger markets through education.

[187] On different cultural responses to education initiatives see J Fanto (n 12) 1103, noting how in heavily centralised states credible education needs to come from a government source.

[188] L Cunningham (n 43) 802: 'Day trading represents precisely the kind of force in the marketplace that investor-education programs emphasizing biases such as overconfidence would serve to counteract'.

[189] The move to country-of-origin control for on-line financial services by the Distance Marketing Directive (n 59) and E Commerce Directive (n 124) has been linked to education and consumer awareness initiatives. See the FSA 'Implementation of the E Commerce Directive'

cont. ...

crete EU initiative. As the basic elements of sound financial planning are not country-specific, an EU response, tracking the construction of an integrated retail investment services markets, seems warranted. A policy which addressed the essentials of effective market investment, such as the importance of diversification,[190] the potential consequences of over-trading, and the impact of trading and other transactions costs (which are the subject of extensive disclosure under the MiFID conduct regime), could form the core of an EU education strategy. Although the EU has constitutional competence with respect to consumer education initiatives,[191] level 3 of the Lamfalussy process, involving co-operation between national authorities co-ordinated through CESR, seems an appropriate forum for developing an education policy, based on solid evidence as to investor needs in the pan-EU market.

Effective education delivery is, however, multi-stranded. The EU investment services industry, in particular, should play a major role in delivering education as it has the opportunities to link education to product and service development and to marketing, and is arguably incentivized to promote investor awareness.[192] Public authorities may also face conflict of interests and capture risks in highlighting particular investment strategies and risks. But there is a need for some public involvement, particularly as educated investors deliver efficient markets which impact more widely on society.[193] There is also a risk of education becoming a mar-

(FSA Consultation Paper 129) 34-36 which builds in the promotion of consumer risk awareness of the EU on-line financial services market as part of the FSA's implementation strategy.

[190] The importance of diversification and of education as to how to and why to diversify is increasingly appearing in the literature and in regulatory policy. Jackson argues that rather than deploring the ill-advised lack of diversification by investors, it is important to make efforts to ensure that where regulatory policy pushes the notion of market efficiency, investors are not just aware of the value of information, but also that risk-adjusted returns will only be delivered given adequate diversification and reasonable transaction costs. H Jackson (n 87) 684. Moves are also afoot in the U.S. to require the sponsor of employer pension funds (the 401k) to advise plan holders on the importance of diversifying beyond employer securities (C Camerer (n 12) 1236).

[191] Article 153 (1) EC provides that in order to promote the interests of consumers and ensure a high level of consumer protection, the Community is to, inter alia, promote their right to education.

[192] For an example from the securities exchanges, see the Euronext 'education centre' site which contains a Q and A section, advice for investment clubs, and a section on 'how to start trading' (<http://www.fese.be>). In June 2004, the London Stock Exchange re-launched its investor education website 'as part of its drive to enable private investors to make informed investment decisions' (LSE Press Release) (28 June 2004) <http://www.londonstock exchange.com>. Firms are similarly engaging in education. In the UK major high street banks have offered financial awareness classes in local schools, for example: J Felix 'Girls Learn to Dodge Debt Time Bomb' *Observer* Cash Supplement (18 January 2004) 3.

[193] L Cunningham (n 43) 790 noting that better informed investors will make superior capital allocations, leading to wider social advantages, which calls for a public input into investor education policy.

ket commodity and reflecting the biases and business needs of investment services providers, particularly if a competitive market does develop in investment advice. Regulators can deliver core messages which investment firms may be less inclined to (for example, with respect to the impact of trading costs).[194]

A striking movement towards investor education at pan-EU level has, however, recently developed, suggesting the emergence of a more rounded retail market strategy. The 2004 Asset Management Expert Group called for concrete investor education initiatives, particularly given the pressure to improve levels of retirement saving, which would be essentially industry-based but developed in consultation with national regulatory authorities and all other concerned parties. It also supported an EU-wide approach, noting that while national initiatives were being taken in the Member States: 'considering that the challenges, specifically those on retirement provisioning are not country specific, the group debated whether an EU wide approach is actually needed to achieve further advancement in this regard'.[195] The Forum Group on Analysts also noted the importance of retail investor awareness of the fund management industry, including with respect to how research is paid for and commissioned.[196] Given MiFID's support of a low-protection execution-only regime, it is significant that the Group called for education on how to interpret research and tips and on the inherent risks and conflicts involved.[197] FIN-USE has supported financial education as part of a wider securities market strategy, particularly with respect to pan-EU activity, given that 'encouraging users to take advantage of more choice and better prices in other Member States is not a priority for most national governments'.[198] Education initiatives were also called for in the European Parliament's van den Burg Report on the Current State of Integration of EU Financial Markets (2005).[199] Most significantly, perhaps, in its 2005 post-FSAP Green Paper, the Commission called for education measures, stating that while the EU regime emphasizes disclosure, 'unless consumers themselves develop the skills and knowledge needed to understand increasingly complex financial products, consumers cannot make well-informed investment decisions on the basis of this information'.[200] This theme reappeared in the December 2005 White Paper, but was anchored this time to spe-

[194] Similarly execution-only firms are unlikely to provide education on the benefits of passive investing.

[195] Asset Management Expert Group Report (n 10) 24.

[196] Forum Group on Financial Analysts 'Financial Analysts: Best Practices in an Integrated European Financial Market' (2003) 43.

[197] Forum Group on Financial Analysts (n 196).

[198] FIN-USE Report (n 35) 11-12. It warned, however, of the 'severe financial and personnel constraints' education delivery would place on the Commission.

[199] Committee on Economic and Monetary Affairs 'Report on the Current State of Integration of EU Markets' (van den Burg Report) (April 2005) A6-0087/2005.

[200] Green Paper (n 11) 18.

cific initiatives. Although the Commission argued that the prime responsibility for consumer education lay with the Member States, it made a commitment to promoting a 'pan-EU exchange of views on financial education, consumer literacy and best practice' and to 'facilitate common projects'.[201]

Following this momentum, a more nuanced approach now appears to be informing new retail market initiatives. The recent moves over 2004/2005 towards developing an EU response towards the retailization of hedge funds, and to managing retail access to packaged sophisticated alternative investments, for example, are building in investor education as a key component of any reforms designed to support retail access to these investments.[202]

III. Aggressive Intervention and Product Development

1. Intervention in Decision-making

Enforcement and education strategies do not intervene aggressively in investor decision-making nor disturb the essentially choice- and autonomy-driven nature of the EU's regulatory strategy as expressed in the MiFID retail investor regime. It may be that more intrusive intervention in product development and in management of the investor decision is needed if the retail market is to develop rationally and effectively.

Rational, value-maximizing investors are best advised to access the markets through low cost, diversified, passive index funds. The evidence suggests that they do not.[203] If EU retail investment services policy seeks to ensure the most rational outcome from investor decision-making, it can shape the decision-making process in a number of increasingly interventionist ways. Light intervention suggests disclosure, supported by investor education. Heavier intervention supports the investment advice process and regulates the investor/investment firm

[201] See (n 11) 7. Specific initiatives include a Commission conference on financial literacy and education in 2007 – an unusual development given the previously wholesale-market-focus of Commission 'outreach' activities.

[202] See, e.g., the European Parliament's initiative on hedge funds (Committee on Economic and Monetary Affairs 'The Future of Hedge Funds and Derivatives' (Purvis Report) (January 2004) A5-0476/2003, which called for education measures with respect to high risk investments, sponsored by the industry and national regulators.

[203] This point is being made with increasing frequency by commentators. See, e.g., H Jackson (n 87). L Ribstein (n 107) 97 similarly argues that: 'Ordinary investors should be investing in balanced portfolios through index mutual funds rather than betting on individual stocks. If they must try to beat the market, they should rely on fund managers and other advisors rather than their own imperfect judgment and stale information. They certainly should not be actively trading, or worse yet day trading, buying on the margin, or voluntarily sinking all of their retirement funds into their employers' stock'.

relationship. The most intrusive forms of intervention mould the investment decision directly by restricting the range of products available to retail investors or promoting particular products through government-labelling, tailored delivery and regulatory systems, taxation, or low-cost incentives.

The EU has, so far, based its retail regime on the less interventionist options, as required, of course, by constitutional competence restrictions. The MiFID regime does not promote particular services or the benefits of passive investing. The execution-only regime and the support of easy and low-cost access to trading, without any attempt to insert trading blocks, also suggest support for investor autonomy. But more direct management of investor behaviour is not unknown to EU securities regulation: the public offer regime restricts the sale of particular classes of securities to sophisticated investors. More generally, the MiFID split between retail and wholesale regulation manages how the retail investor accesses the marketplace.

Support for more direct management of retail investor behaviour is now appearing more frequently as the retail investor attracts more attention and the evidence of how retail investors behave accumulates.[204] It is difficult to make the case for swingeing regulatory intervention, through, for example, taxation policy or rules which prevent retail investors from accessing particular services and products. Any such policies run the risk of not differentiating between vulnerable investors and those who wish to speculate and can safely navigate the markets. They disrupt the policy of informed investor choice which lies at the heart of the EU regime. Important threshold questions also arise: which products and services are 'safe' in a rapidly evolving marketplace and can regulators/policy-makers, subject to bias and public choice pressures, be entrusted with this judgment? Merit regulation of this sort has been out of fashion since the early 20th century:[205] markets have become infinitely more varied and innovative since then. Direct intervention also carries the taint of excessive paternalism and is likely to provoke

[204] P Mahoney 'Is There a Cure for Excessive Trading' (1995) 81 Va L Rev 713, 740, e.g., has called for greater policy emphasis on the benefits of diversification and of limited trading and for less emphasis on issuer disclosure which tends to promote investor activity. Similarly, H Jackson (n 87) 674 asks whether regulatory policy should discourage investors from direct trading, which may be prompted by the illusion of power given by extensive issuer disclosure, given the evidence of underperformance and diversification errors. S Choi (n 101) has controversially argued that retail investors should be limited to investing in passive funds managed by major investment firms. S Choi and A Pritchard (n 36) 65-66 canvass the possibility of restructuring investor choice by, e.g., preventing investors from trading in shares of (pre-re-organization) bankrupt companies and requiring investors to invest through market intermediaries. R Gilson and R Kraakman (n 84) 738-739 have argued, in the context of the diversification errors made in employee 401k pensions, that 'we would be wise to limit the investment discretion of these employee-investors, precisely in order to prevent them from harming themselves'.

[205] For a classic merit argument see WO Douglas 'Protecting the Investor' (1934) 23 Yale L J 521.

hostile public and political reactions.[206] In the EU it would sit very uneasily with FSAP objectives, the free movement of capital, a MiFID regime based on choice, and growing political sympathy with the retail community. It is also extremely unlikely that highly interventionist regulation, which moves well beyond harmonization, would be within the EU's constitutional competence.

It may be that the EU's regulatory strategy for the retail market should simply acknowledge, and accommodate the reality, that there are 'safer' ways in which retail investors can access the markets, while not restricting investor choice. While neutral education has a key role to play here, the development by the Member States of investment and savings products which embed protections and diversification strategies carries the dual benefits of managing rational investor access to the market and of reducing regulatory costs.[207] Member State initiatives of this kind should be accommodated within the MiFID structure and encouraged through regulatory learning and the sharing of expertise through CESR at level 3 of the Lamfalussy process.

2. Choice and Investment Products

Market innovation concerning retail investment products should also be supported. If MiFID's regulatory strategy of promoting investor choice is to be fully realized, the pan-EU liberalization of products which increase investor choice and promote diversification must form part of the EU's retail investor strategy. There are signs, however, that the Commission is considering how to increase the range of investment products and, importantly, strengthen the parallel advice and distribution channels. Commissioner McCreevy recently called on the EU fund industry in uncompromising terms: '[i]f the EU fund industry is serious about being the investment vehicle of choice for the European retail investor ... it will need to help retail investors find the right product for their needs in a more diverse marketplace [and] give them confidence that they are accessing these products under

[206] There was a hostile reaction in the U.S., e.g., to attempts to change the U.S. ERISA to prevent employees from investing 100% of their 401k employee pension plans in employer stock post Enron. Critics regarded such a ban as paternalistic, based on 'government-knows-best', and contrary to the best interests of employees who could benefit from a large ownership stake (H Jackson (n 87) 680).

[207] The UK has developed a suite of 'Sandler products' which are designed to embed diversification and risk control, to be subject to a cost cap, and to have a tailored, lighter advice and marketing regime. HM Treasury 'Consultation on Stakeholder Savings and Investment Products' (June 2004) and FSA 'A Basic Advice Regime for the Sale of Stakeholder Products' (November 2004). They have been supported as a means of winning back retail investors by allowing firms to market products which have, in effect, a government imprimatur. See, e.g., Editorial 'Restoring Trust in Financial Services' *Fin Times* (16 June 2004) 18.

appropriate conditions … fee disclosures and clear information on risks and investment policies are crucial'.[208]

There are some interesting and tentative signs that CESR sees a role for itself at Lamfalussy level 3 in supporting product development. It has recently raised the possibility of promoters of certain pan-EU products seeking CESR pre-clearance.[209] At the very least, the MiFID regime should not obstruct the development of packaged, diversified products (by the markets or by the Member States) which seek to promote and support diversified, low-cost retail investor access to the market. The graduated suitability regime, and, in particular, the lighter Article 19 (5) product-related regime will be of particular importance here.

The resilience of MiFID's generic conduct of business requirements in a rapidly evolving investment product environment will also be essential if MiFID is to deliver investor choice effectively. Chief among the current product initiatives are the current and controversial moves to manage the alleged retailization of the hedge fund industry, as retail investors seek access to hedge funds and riskier sophisticated alternative investment vehicles.[210] Considerable care will be needed in designed a pan-EU vehicle for these investments, if this approach is adopted, but the initial first step is to ensure that MiFID's advice and distribution/marketing disciplines, contained in the conduct of business regime, are sufficiently robust to ensure appropriate disclosure, advice, and suitability assessment in respect of these investments. The MiFID regime has already been identified as serving as a guide to clarifying the boundaries between product producers, distributors, and advisers in the evolving investment product chain.[211] CESR will have a key role to play in calibrating the generic MiFID regime, at level 2 and 3, as the investment services market evolves.

Education remains a softer, less costly, less prone to capture, and less complex way of influencing pan-EU investor decisions. In particular, education policies could provide potentially controversial disclosure on average relative investment performance, according to services and products, and by different groups of investors, relative to each other. Neutral education on the merits of passive investing and diversification, at least, is essential, if unattractive to market interests. But here we are the sharp end of the conflict between business-driven supply side and demand side interests. It is not yet clear whether the EU's enthusiasm for the re-

[208] Speech by C McCreevy on Investment Funds to Commission Hearing (13 October 2005) <http://europa.eu.int/rapid>.

[209] CESR 'The Role of CESR at Level 3 under the Lamfalussy Process' (October 2004) CESR 04-527b, 17.

[210] See, e.g., PriceWaterhouseCoopers (n 65); Green Paper on the Enhancement of the EU Framework for Investment Funds (the Investment Funds Green Paper), COM(2005) 314; Purvis Report (n 202); and van den Burg Report (n 199).

[211] Speech by C McCreevy on 'Pension Funds and Asset Management: A European Perspective' (Irish Association of Pension Funds Conference) (22 September 2005) <http://europa.eu.int/rapid>.

tail investor will embrace even this form of soft intervention in influencing how investors choose to access the market.

3. The UCITS Regime

One of the earliest forays by the EU into securities and investment services regulation involved product regulation with the introduction of the UCITS regime in 1985.[212] The UCITS – undertaking for collective investment in transferable securities – is heavily regulated in terms of disclosure, governance and structural requirements, and investment limits, and benefits from an EU-wide passport once authorized in accordance with the UCITS regime. Given the importance of the UCITS product in the retail markets, an effective EU retail strategy demands that close attention is given to the UCITS product and to its interaction with the new MiFID advice and distribution system.

Considerable progress has been made in developing the UCITS product as a retail-focused, pan-EU investment product, subject to strict investment limits and governance controls, which can deliver diversified exposure to EU-wide investments.[213] It has enjoyed a strong reputation: '[f]rom an investor protection perspective, there have not been notable financial scandals involving UCITS. UCITS has provided a solid underpinning for a well-regulated fund industry'.[214] The Commission has identified the UCITS as forming part of the solution to the EU's pension deficit.[215] Investment fund/UCITS activity is generally strong across the EU, with 16% of UCITS funds operating cross-border. Over 28,000 UCITS funds manage € 4 trillion of assets and enjoy pan-EU and international recognition.[216]

Recent revisions (UCITS III) which came into force in 2004 have, however, loosened the UCITS investment restrictions and, in particular, allow UCITS to leverage through the use of derivatives up to 100% of net asset value and, in effect, use hedge-fund-like, and considerably riskier, investment strategies.[217] At

[212] Council Directive 85/611/EEC of 20 December 1985 on the Coordination of Laws, Regulations and Administrative Provisions relating to Undertakings for Collective Investment in Transferable Securities (UCITS), OJ L375 31.12.1985 3-18.

[213] It has been described as a 'recognised global label of quality and investor protection' and as a hub of inflows from non-EU investors. Asset Management Expert Group Report (n 10) 8. Commissioner McCreevy (n 208) has highlighted the potential of investment funds generally as the 'vehicle of choice for private retirement provisioning'.

[214] Investment Funds Green Paper (n 210) 3.

[215] Green Paper (n 11) 16.

[216] Green Paper (n 11) 3.

[217] Directive 2001/108/EC of the European Parliament and of the Council of 21 January 2002 amending Council Directive 85/611/EEC on the Coordination of Laws, Regulations and Administrative Provisions relating to Undertakings for Collective Investment in Transferable Securities (UCITS), with regard to investments of UCITS, OJ L41 13.02.2002 35-42 and UCITS Prospectus Recommendation (n 15).

level 2, CESR's Asset Management Group has considered the scope of the 'eligible assets' for UCITS III funds. Its advice includes when structured financial instruments, non-UCITS collective investment schemes, and financial derivatives are eligible for investment, and the techniques allowed for efficient portfolio management.[218]

With the UCITS III regime, the traditional UCITS fund now has the potential to change character considerably, but without being embedded in a tailored regulatory regime. UCITS III products may now represent very different risks to the traditional UCITS investment, but are still treated as conservative, retail investor-friendly, savings products under the UCITS umbrella. This approach has consequences across the investment services regime with the MiFID conduct of business regime and the UCITS framework likely to be placed under some strain.

UCITS are still, for example, 'non-complex products' and available for execution-only services, free of suitability checks, under MiFID (Article 19 (6)). In terms of UCITS-product requirements, CESR's UCITS III advice, if adopted as level 2 rules, would impose detailed valuation requirements on UCITS III as well as require that the UCITS has the organization and means to carry out valuations, supporting the general risk measurement and management procedures required under Article 21 of the UCITS Directive.[219] The Commission's 2004 UCITS Recommendation on Derivative Use[220] also recommends risk management procedures concerning, for example, maximum exposure and measurement of market risk, leverage, and counterparty risk. But it remains to be seen whether the UCITS regime will meet the internal control and risk management demands of the highly leveraged and speculative investments which are now possible under UCITS III. It also remains to be seen whether the MiFID advice and suitability regime, and its disclosure requirements, will support investor access to these riskier products. Expectation risks may be considerable as retail investors may associate the UCITS III product with the traditional, conservative product originally developed under the UCITS regime. Much will depend on the effectiveness of the generic disclosure, advice, and suitability requirements imposed on the distribution of UCITS units by investment firms under the MiFID conduct of business regime. The Commission has acknowledged that the levels of disclosure and investor protections which attach to the UCITS may be called into question by the UCITS III reforms.[221]

[218] CESR 'Advice on Clarification of Definitions concerning Eligible Assets for Investments of UCITS' (CESR UCITS Consultation Paper) (March 2005) CESR/05-064b and CESR 'Advice to the European Commission on Clarification of Definitions concerning Eligible Assets for Investments of UCITS' (CESR UCITS Advice) (January 2006) CESR/06-005/.

[219] See (n 218).

[220] See (n 15).

[221] Green Paper (n 11) 14.

Retail policy must, accordingly, be developed holistically across the different market sectors and across the different EU entities involved in investment services policy-making.

IV. Retail Investor Governance

Finally, an effective retail policy, and particularly one which is heavily based on regulation, must include the promotion of the organization of investors such that they can impact on lawmaking and on the market and generate choices, protections, practices, and products tailored to their needs.[222]

One of the more striking features of the current assessments of the FSAP and Lamfalussy process is the extent to which concern has arisen, for the first time, that retail interests have not been adequately represented in the development of the EU's retail strategy through the lawmaking process. The MiFID negotiations provide stark indications as to the imbalance in representation. During the European Parliament's open consultations on MiFID, the UK-based ProShare[223] appears to have been the only recorded participant representing retail interests. At level 2, the problem is exacerbated. CESR is to 'consult extensively and at an early stage with market participants, consumers and end-users in an open and transparent manner',[224] and is widely regarded as striving for transparency and consulting widely. CESR's First Draft Level 2 Advice called directly for retail investor involvement, drawing the attention of retail investors to questions 'of direct interest to them', such as the best execution rules.[225] Nonetheless, only two of fifteen members represent retail interests on the Market Participants Consultative Group, which advises CESR generally.[226] In practice, the consultation process is entirely dominated by industry interests. Of the seventy seven responses to

[222] For an example of retail investor political weight feeding into regulation see the adoption by the SEC of the controversial Regulation FD which was heavily criticized by the market as endangering the free flow of high quality corporate information. But, designed to redress the perceived unfairness of selective disclosure and level the playing field in information between professional and retail investors, it is seen as a victory for the small investor and 'closely related to the recent increase in individual investing in public markets'. J Duggan 'Regulation FD: SEC Tells Corporate Insiders to "Chill Out"' (2001) 7 Wash U J L Pol'y 159, 162 and 170.

[223] ProShare states on its website (<http://www.proshare.org>) that is, increasingly, the 'voice of the retail investor' and actively seeks feedback from retail investors to allow it to promote retail interests in London and Brussels.

[224] Commission Decision 2001/527/EC establishing CESR, OJ L191 2001 Article 5.

[225] First CESR Draft Level 2 Advice (n 46) 2.

[226] Euroshareholders, which represents, through national shareholder associations, the interests of individual shareholders, and the Swedish Shareholders Association. At the time of writing, there is no retail representative among the 21 members of the specific CESR Consultative Panel on MiFID.

CESR's First Draft Level 2 Advice, only one formally represented the interests of private investors.[227] Similarly, of the seventy eight responses to the Second Draft Level 2 Advice, which addressed suitability, a matter of particular concern for retail investors, only four represented retail interests.[228] By contrast, industry is becoming increasingly organized and vocal, with the City of London, for example, recently opening an office in Brussels.

In its First Interim Report in May 2003, the Lamfalussy Inter-Institutional Monitoring Group noted that it was important for all stakeholders, including the 'wider public' to understand how the Lamfalussy process works.[229] In its Second Report, the Group went further and expressed concern as to the evidence of a lack of retail investor involvement in the new lawmaking process.[230] Concern at the limited impact of the retail community is also evident from the ESC, which was concerned that there was 'poor capacity from the end-users side to follow all consultations and provide sufficient input'.[231] The problem may be structural and linked to the multi-layered and consultation-intensive level 2 process. In its 2005 review of the FSAP, CEPS argued that the time-consuming and resource incentive consultation process prejudices consumer and less-powerful interest group involvement,[232] allowing the procedure to be dominated by market interests.

In a major change to the previous dynamics of investment services policy-making, evidence is now emerging, however, of a striking move towards promoting fuller EU retail investor involvement. The Commission has called for greater strategic input into the FSAP assessment process from a full range of stakeholders, including consumers and investors.[233] Attempts have been made to match the rhetoric with action to address the resource and organizational difficulties faced by the retail sector. FIN-USE was set up in July 2003 by the Commission as an Expert Forum to examine financial services policies from the user/demand side perspective.[234] Its recommendations have included 'effective involvement

[227] Response of the Danish Shareholders Association to CESR's Draft Level 2 Advice (17 September 2004). Their response concentrates on 'questions of importance to the private investor'.

[228] The Danish Shareholders Association (which represents 'citizens in their capacity as investors'); the Swedish Shareholders Association (which represents 'private individuals who invest in stocks, mutual funds, and other stock-related securities'); the Federation of German Consumer Organisations; and the UK Financial Services Consumer Panel.

[229] Inter-Institutional Monitoring Group 'First Interim Report Monitoring the New Process for Regulating Securities Markets in Europe' (May 2003) 6.

[230] Inter-Institutional Monitoring Group 'Second Interim Report Monitoring the Lamfalussy Process' (December 2003) 29, referring to a 'considerable problem' relating to the representation of retail investors and consumers.

[231] ESC Minutes 28/2004 (5 July 2004) para. 8.

[232] CEPS 2005 FSAP Report (n 117) 7.

[233] Green Paper (n 11) Annex 18.

[234] Commission Press Release IP/03/1119 (25 July 2003).

and representation of the user perspective at all levels of policy-making. FIN-USE would wish to see regulators and policy makers in the EU having in place mechanisms for consumer interests to be effectively represented'.[235] The importance of FIN-USE as a new, robust, and vocal participant in the financial services policy debate (aside from any assessment as to the merits of its views), is also clear from its recent report on consumer voice.[236] Pointing to the very poor levels of consumer/retail involvement and to the difficulties in promoting consumer interests, which require expert and market-specific knowledge, through national groups, it called for much greater attention to be paid to retail participation in policy-making and for FIN-USE to be maximized as a forum for channeling retail interests through to policy-making. More generally, the 10th FSAP Report refers to the need to take full account of the views of the public in integrating financial markets.[237]

Concerns as to poor levels of retail input into policy-making span the institutions. The ECOFIN Council's conclusions on the current status of the integration in June 2004 supported greater input by retail investors,[238] while the European Parliament's 2005 van den Burg Report on financial integration regretted the lack of input from consumers and users and called for measures to promote and support retail awareness. Internal Market Commissioner McCreevy, in one of his first major speeches on the FSAP in December 2004 included consumers among those he would be consulting with in building the post FSAP strategy.[239]

More specifically, March 2005 saw CESR hold a Consumer Day on the MiFID mandates, supported by a user-friendly discussion paper which highlighted questions of particular interest to retail investors. This is a striking and revealing development, albeit one that occurred after the major consultations had closed.[240] The discussions reveal a very different dynamic on controversial CESR rules.[241] Importantly, confirming the remarkable sea-change currently underway in retail

[235] FIN-USE Report (n 35) I and 5. It went on to note that 'there has not been a broad and systematic consultation with consumers and end-users in relation to securities regulation' ((n 35) 28).

[236] FIN-USE 'The Consumers' Voice in the European Financial Services Sector' (2006).

[237] 10th FSAP Report (n 8) 10.

[238] 2587th Meeting of the Council Press Release, Council Conclusions (Economic and Monetary Affairs) (2 June 2004) 12.

[239] Speech by C McCreevy on 'Assessment of the Integration of the Single Market for Financial Services by the Commission' (CESR Conference) (6 December 2004) <http://europa.eu.int/rapid>.

[240] CESR 'Summary of the Main Conclusions – MiFID Consumer Day' (May 2005) CESR/05-350.

[241] In striking contrast with the formal consultation process, support emerged for including generic investment advice, subjecting margin loans to suitability, the applicability of best execution obligations to portfolio management, and a prohibition on providing services where sufficient information was not provided for a full suitability assessment.

investor governance, CESR expressed its concern at the lack of retail involvement throughout the MiFID consultation process and announced that it would organize similar meeting to develop the retail dialogue.

The momentum appears to be sustained. Beyond the establishment of FIN-USE, the Commission has committed to introducing practical steps to improve retail representation,[242] a commitment which it reinforced in the important November 2005 consultation on FSAP Evaluation.[243] The Commission acknowledged the range of criticism on poor retail and consumer involvement in financial services policy making and the need for concrete measures. Its specific response was to maximize FIN-USE and to encourage participation from user groups in consultations.[244]

Considerable obstacles remain in terms of formal retail investor organization and representation, given their fragmented presence on the EU market and generally home-facing profile. The MiFID Consumer Day saw consumer organizations point to the lack of financial knowledge and resources in consumer associations and their inability to engage effectively with the CESR consultation process. This seems to call for EU-led support for the organization of retail interests. The Commission's targeting of FIN-USE could be significant in this regard. FIN-USE could be used more formally through the Lamfalussy process, perhaps sitting on the CESR Market Participants' Consultative Group CESR could also continue to target its consultations directly to consumer interest groups, taking practical steps in terms of summaries, examples, and user-friendly language. Investor education may lie at the heart of this dilemma: more informed and educated investors are more likely to push for collective action and promote the development of lobby groups. The pressure coming from so many quarters for investor education, and its linkage to the effectiveness of so many elements of the new regulatory regime, suggests that careful consideration of how such a policy might proceed, its coverage, and its delivery mechanisms, is now a policy priority for the retail programme.

F. Conclusion

The prize is potentially great: an informed and active retail community which re-balances the policy dialogue, supports market efficiency by improving the flow of capital to investment, and provides a bulwark against the looming pension crisis. The risks are likewise considerable, given the immature state of the retail investor base and unpredictable changes in market behaviour following liberaliza-

[242] Commission 'Working Document on Application of the Lamfalussy Process to EU Securities Market Legislation' (November 2004).

[243] FSAP Evaluation (n 156).

[244] FSAP Evaluation (n 156) 17.

tion. Traditionally, the EU has operated through regulatory strategies, not least because of constitutional constraints and the regulatory demands of market integration and home Member State control. The very recent signs from the post-FSAP policy debate are heartening, particularly with respect to education and retail governance. But close attention must continue to be paid to the ancillary, non-regulatory strategies which are necessary to support an effective retail investment services market and if the EU, in the calmer post-FSAP environment, is to develop as a sophisticated and nuanced capital market regulator.

Financial Market Integration in the Post FSAP Era. In Search of Overall Conceptual Consistency in the Regulatory Framework

MICHEL TISON

This Article looks into the concepts underpinning the current generation of capital market integration directives, that follow the 'Lamfalussy-approach'. In particular, we examine whether the level 1-directives are based on minimum or maximum harmonisation. We submit that the European lawmakers have failed to clarify this issue, thereby reducing legal certainty for the various stakeholders (suppliers, investors and supervisors alike). In addition, the adoption of yet a new harmonisation technique runs the risk of creating inconsistencies with the previous generation of financial market integration directives, adopted under the 1992 Internal market program. Finally, we look at how the Prospectus Directive and MiFID divide regulatory and supervisory powers between home and host state.

A. Introduction
B. The Underlying Regulatory Concepts: From Minimum to Maximum Harmonisation or Something in Between?
C. Division of Regulatory Powers Between Home and Host State
D. Conclusions

A. Introduction

Rarely has one seen such a high pace of adoption of financial regulation at EU level as during the final stage of the Financial Services Action Plan (FSAP). The result is impressive, both in terms of quantity and as concerns the ability to stick to the time-schedule set forth in the FSAP. Though much regulation is still to come under the form of 'level 2'-rules, to be adopted by the European Commission, it is clear that the FSAP, backed by the Lamfalussy-process, has given a serious boost to the regulatory efforts aimed at the integration of capital markets in the EU.

Time has come to overlook the progress achieved over the last few years, and to examine whether all this new regulation actually will produce what it intended to: to create a truly integrated EU-wide financial market. From a legal point of view, an important precondition to analyse this question is to look at whether the legal foundations and principles on which the integration efforts rest, satisfy the requirements of consistency. Consistency in this respect relates to whether the different, interrelated directives adopt similar rules and principles, such as to create a level playing field between competing market actors and activities, and therefore to eliminate competitive distortions between Member States. The need to achieve consistency has often severely impaired the chances to have EU directives adopted, as was illustrated by the discussions on the regulation of trading venues in the Draft Directive on Financial Markets (MiFID), where the technicalities on pre-bid and post-bid transparency threatened to paralyse the adoption of the Directive.

The need to ensure consistency also appears at a more general level. When carefully looking both at Directive 2004/39/EC on Markets in Financial Instruments (MiFID) and at the Prospectus Directive, on which we will focus our analysis, we can see some important modifications in the underlying legal principles, compared to the previous financial integration directives, adopted under the 1992 Single Market Programme. This was not only the case as concerns the predecessors of the mentioned directives, which at present have been abolished, namely the 1993 Investment Services Directive, the 1989 Public Offers Directive and the 1980 Listing Prospectus Directive. The same principles still underpin the regulatory framework for credit institutions under the 2001 Codified Banking Directive, as well as the 1985 UCITS-Directive. While these directives clearly were based on the paradigm of minimum harmonisation and mutual recognition, the present Prospectus and MiFID directives no longer express the idea of minimum harmonisation. The latter directives also modify the home-host country allocation of powers, inter alia by introducing new residual powers for the host state supervisory authorities, which did and do not exist under the Internal Market Directives of the previous generation.

In the first part of this paper, we will examine to which extent the 'silent' modification of the underlying concepts in MiFID and the Prospectus Directive may affect the overall structure and consistency of the legal framework for financial market integration. We will in particular focus on the issue of minimum versus maximum harmonisation.

In a second part, we will analyse how modifications in the division of powers between home and host state in the new directives are likely to have an impact on market integration. Attention will not only be paid to cross-border activities of investment firms and (regulated) markets, but also to transactional regulation (in particular conduct of business rules) under the new directives, highlighting the main modifications compared to the ISD. A particular question in this regard is whether the allocation of powers in MiFID will stand the scrutiny of primary EC law, taking into account recent case-law of the ECJ. As for the Prospectus Directive, a critical issue is how the Directive influences prospectus liability regimes, and whether additional regulation is needed in this area.

B. The Underlying Regulatory Concepts: From Minimum to Maximum Harmonisation or Something in Between?

It is well known that the regulatory paradigm underpinning the directives adopted under the 1992 Internal Market Programme consisted of, in line with the subsidiarity principle, regulating only at EU level what was necessary to create a climate of mutual confidence amongst Member States in the quality of each others' regulatory standards. The preambles to the main financial integration directives of the 1992 generation highlighted this approach by referring to 'necessary but sufficient harmonisation'.[1] This concept of so-called minimum harmonisation allowed Member States to maintain or introduce more stringent regulatory requirements towards domestic financial institutions, within the area covered by harmonisation. However, a degree of regulatory competition was introduced through the accompanying principle of mutual recognition: a Member State would have to balance its own regulatory interests against the risk of adverse competitive effects for its domestic financial industry by exceeding the common minimum standards. The potential for unwanted downsizing of regulatory standards was counterweighed by the fact that, in practice, the 'minimum' investor protection offered by the EU directives already reached a high level, particularly compared to pre-existing rules in many Member States. Moreover, maintaining high standards in regulation, either in prudential or in transactional regulation, was perceived in some jurisdictions as a factor of attractiveness of the financial system, more than as a deterrent. This 'competition for excellence' explained why the adoption of the first generation of financial market directives under the 1992 Internal Market Programme did not lead to a substantial decrease of regulatory standards in those Member States with strict regulation (e.g. United Kingdom).

The directives adopted under the Lamfalussy process seem to have departed from the 'minimum harmonisation' approach, but it is unclear which concept – if any – has replaced it, as both the preambles and the provisions of the Directives remain largely silent on this issue. Part of the answer may reside in the Lamfalussy approach itself, with the use of level 1 'framework principles' and level 2 'technical implementation' rules. In particular within the scope of the rules harmonised at level 1, the mandate to further specify and implement the general standards through level 2-rules, suggests that level 2 rules are likely to be exhaus-

[1] See, for instance, paragraph 6 of the preamble to the 2000 Codified Banking Directive (Directive 2000/12/EC of the European Parliament and of the Council of 20 March 2000 relating to the taking up and pursuit of the business of credit institutions, OJ L126 26.05.2000 1-59; paragraph 52 of the preamble to the UCITS Directive (Council Directive 85/611/EEC of 20 December 1985 on the coordination of laws, regulations and administrative provisions relating to undertakings for collective investment in transferable securities (UCITS), OJ L375 31.12.1985 3-18); paragraph 3 of the Preamble to the Investment Services Directive (Council Directive 93/22/EEC of 10 May 1993 on investment services in the securities field, OJ L141 11.06.1993 27-46).

tive in substance. This could be even more the case when use is made not of a directive but of a regulation as legal instrument for level 2 rules, the latter being directly applicable in the legal order of the Member States without further implementation.

However, we submit that the Lamfalussy approach is not, in itself, incompatible with the idea of minimum harmonisation. First, the Lamfalussy procedure does not automatically empower the Commission to adopt level 2 measures, but only to the extent it has received a mandate to do so in the framework directive. Consequently, the Lamfalussy procedure does not automatically result in detailed, exhaustive regulation at EU level, limiting or in fact even eliminating altogether the powers of Member States to regulate. Second, where a level 2 mandate has been given to the Commission in the framework directive, the terms of the mandate are often phrased as to empower the Commission to give 'minimum' execution to a general provision. This suggests that the mandate, even if it can result in a high level of detail, does not in itself preclude Member States from maintaining stricter requirements domestically. This conclusion also seems consistent with the philosophy of the Lamfalussy procedure. The multi-level approach in rule-setting did not intend to eliminate Member States' powers in the matters covered by substantive EU harmonisation, as they existed under the 'minimum harmonisation' directives. It was mainly devised as an answer to the rigidity of the institutional dimension in the law-making process at EU level, in view of the pace of developments in the securities industry. Speeding up the rulemaking process therefore can perfectly co-exist with keeping regulatory standards at EU level on a 'minimum but sufficient' level, where the level 2 rules would do no more than provide a more advanced level of detail of the 'minimum' principles laid down in the framework directives.

A further major concern voiced in the Lamfalussy-report, however, related to the perceived absence of clear EU-wide regulation on a large number of issues (such as prospectuses, conduct of business rules, etc.), which prevented the implementation of the mutual recognition regime.[2] This criticism seemed more closely related to the concept itself of minimum harmonisation, as one of its implications was to maintain fairly general, and often vague rules in the financial integration directives, which subsequently suffered from uneven implementation and divergent interpretations in the Member States. The remedy under the form of multi-level regulation clearly results, as the practice of MiFID and the Prospectus Directive demonstrates, in highly detailed and extremely technical rules, not only at level 2, but even at level 1, at least for politically more sensitive issues.[3] Once again, this approach is not in itself incompatible with the concept of minimum

[2] Final Report of the Committee of Wise Men on the Regulation of European Securities Markets (15 February 2001) (the Lamfalussy Report) 10.

[3] The regulation of pre-trade transparency for internalisation of orders amply illustrates this phenomenon: one can hardly consider these rules as merely 'high level principles'.

harmonisation, which would allow Member States to maintain more stringent domestic regimes for the actors and transactions under their jurisdiction, though it is true that its scope will in fact probably be substantially reduced by the detailed level 2-rules.

The issue outlined above obviously is not merely an academic one. It raises the issue to which extent Member States, when implementing the new generation of directives, will be obliged to loosen regulatory requirements in their domestic laws that are more severe than the directive. For instance, could a Member State maintain a more severe definition of what constitutes a 'public' offer of securities, under the form of a quantitative threshold of 50 solicited persons, instead of 100 under the Prospectus Directive?[4] Could a Member State impose more stringent prudential requirements for its domestic investment firms than those contained in MiFID? Could the home Member State impose more severe reporting requirements than those imposed by Article 25 MiFID and its implementing rules at level 2?[5]

Different approaches could be adopted with respect to this issue, bearing in mind that no clear answer is provided by the directives or by the Lamfalussy-system itself.

I. Maximum Harmonisation?

A first approach would entail that, in the absence of any enabling clause in the 'Lamfalussy generation' directives, comparable to the 'minimum harmonisation' clauses in the 'generation 1992' directives, the harmonisation should be considered to have a maximum character.[6] This approach would not completely eliminate all flexibility at national level, as often level 2 mandates are formulated in the level 1 framework directives as 'minimum requirements'. Consequently, a Member State would still be enabled, within the confines of level 2 regulation, to be more severe than the EU rules. As a result, the former concept of minimum harmonisation would be substituted by a more restricted concept of minimum

[4] See Directive 2003/71/EC of the European Parliament and of the Council of 4 November 2003 on the prospectus to be published when securities are offered to the public or admitted to trading and amending Directive 2001/34/EC (the Prospectus Directive), OJ L345 31.12.2003 64-89 Article 3 (2) (b), according to which the obligation to publish a prospectus does not apply to an offer of securities addressed to fewer than 100 natural or legal persons per Member State, other than qualified investors.

[5] At present, some Member States do indeed impose such stricter requirements onto their investment firms. Loosening these requirements would entail costly modifications to be made to the existing IT systems for the sake of reporting obligations.

[6] In its technical meaning, maximum harmonisation thus means that Member States are no longer empowered to impose 'superequivalent' standards: see J Herbst 'Revision of the Investment Services Directive' (2003) 11 J Fin Regulation & Compliance 211, 213.

regulation at level 2, only applicable when expressly provided for in the mandate under the framework directive.[7] This would substantially reduce regulatory diversity amongst Member States, without altogether eliminating it.

If the harmonisation is deemed 'maximum', MiFID radically departs from the approach to harmonisation followed by its predecessor, the 1993 Investment Services Directive. It would also result in inconsistencies between the prudential regimes applicable to investment firms and to credit institutions. For the latter, the Codified Banking Directive would still allow for stricter rules at national level as regards prudential regulation, while this would not be the case for the authorisation requirements applicable to investment firms under MiFID. This is all the more surprising since the prudential requirements for both categories of financial institutions are largely similar in substance, in particular when it comes to assessing the quality of the internal organisation, the internal structure and the group environment of the supervised institutions. Finally, the divergent approaches under MiFID and the Codified Banking Directive present the risk of disrupting the level playing field between both categories of financial institutions. A similar situation arises within the prudential regulatory framework for investment firms, as the provisions on regulatory capital are still based, at least in part, on 'minimum harmonisation'. This was not only true for the regime of solvency and other ratios which are still in force at present.[8] The 'minimum harmonisation' approach will also continue with the entry into force of the Directive on Regulatory Capital, which incorporates the Basel II-accord into EU law.[9] There does not seem to be a rational justification for allowing Member States to impose stricter capital requirements, while precluding them from exceeding the EU standards in other prudential matters as regards regulation of investment firms.

[7] Sometimes, this qualification could be less explicit. See, for instance, the heading of Article 7 Prospectus Directive, which refers to 'minimum information'. Article 7 itself contains the mandate to the Commission to determine at level 2 the specific information which must be included in a prospectus, without, however, mentioning that this would be 'minimum' information. As the heading preceding an article is not legally binding, it remains unclear whether the information at level 2 would be a 'minimum', to be possibly completed by national regulation, or whether it would contain an exhaustive catalogue of information requirements, precluding a Member State from imposing a more extensive 'minimum scheme' in national law.

[8] See, e.g. Article 113 (1) of Proposal for Directives of the European Parliament and of the Council, Re-casting Directive 2000/12/EC of the European Parliament and of the Council of 20 March 2000 relating to the taking up and pursuit of the business of credit institutions and Council Directive 93/6/EEC of 15 March 1993 on the capital adequacy of investment firms and credit institutions (18 October 2005) 12890/05 (the Recast Codified Banking Directive), as regards limits on large exposures. No similar 'enabling clause' has however been maintained for the 8% solvency ratio when use is made of the standardised approach to contain credit risks.

[9] See Article 9 (1) of the Recast Codified Banking Directive (n 8).

II. Minimum Harmonisation?

The opposite view holds that, in the absence of a clear provision in the new directives as to the 'maximum' character of the harmonisation, Member States remain free to enact more severe requirements into their domestic systems, as long as they do not conflict with the mutual recognition regime. Under this approach, Member States could exceed the level of EU regulation either at level 1 or level 2, even if the level 2 mandate would not be worded as a minimum mandate. As, in the Lamfalussy system, level 2 regulation is to be regarded as the further implementation of the framework principles adopted at level 1, the mandate given to the Commission to regulate at level 2 can never be wider than to further specify the rule under level 1. This specification at level 2 can, depending on the wording of the mandate, be either exhaustive or not. In both occurrences however, Member States would remain competent to add (technical) requirements to the standards set at level 2, assuming that they have the residual competence to exceed the level of harmonisation at level 1.

III. Between Minimum and Maximum Harmonisation: 'Effective Harmonisation'?

In recent discussions, the European Commission seems to have adopted a 'third way' to the underlying concept of harmonisation, namely a paradigm of 'adequate' or 'effective' harmonisation.[10] Though it is not yet clear what its precise significance is, the notion would refer to the *effet utile* or effectiveness-doctrine, as developed by the Court of Justice in the context of the implementation of directives into national law. According to this theory, the choice of means and methods left to Member States when implementing a directive should be such as to ensure the effectiveness of the result prescribed by the directive. This approach could possibly lead to reducing the powers of Member States to exceed the level of harmonisation, to those cases where additional regulation does not hamper the effective application of the directive. This seems to imply that the issue has to be decided on a case-by-case basis, depending on the matter subject to harmonisation. It is clear that such an approach, though pragmatic, is not likely to promote legal certainty, lacking transparency as to the areas where harmonisation

[10] For instance, the Background Note to the Draft Commission Directive implementing Directive 2004/39/EC of the European Parliament and of the Council as regards record-keeping obligations for investment firms, transaction reporting, market transparency, admission of financial instruments to trading, and defined terms for the purposes of that Directive (the Draft level 2-Directive) s. 2.2, uses the notion of 'adequate' harmonisation without, however, providing more guidance as to its significance. See <http://europa.eu.int/comm/internal_market/securities/docs/isd/dir-2004-39-implement/dir-backgroundnote_en.pdf>.

has reached a 'maximum' character and those where Member States are still allowed to impose 'superequivalent' rules in national law.

As regards 'level 2' measures, the goal of achieving uniform application of certain standards across Europe, would make a stronger case for considering these rules as 'maximum' harmonisation. In the context of the draft level 2 directive under MiFID, the European Commission stresses that the level 2 directive establishes a 'highly harmonised' legal regime, designed to ensure the uniform application of the level 1 standards. It is therefore 'not intended that Member States and competent authorities should add supplementary rules to those strictly needed for the transposition of the implementing Directive, as this would be contrary to the goal of achieving uniform application'.[11] Some ambiguity remains, however, to the extent that the Commission does not refer to 'maximum' harmonisation; nor does the Commission formulate a strict prohibition for Member States or competent authorities to maintain additional rules compared to the level 2 standards.

IV. Conclusion

We can conclude from the above developments that different arguments suggest that MiFID and the Prospectus Directive do not embrace the principle of 'maximum harmonisation', although its actual impact may be mitigated in fact by the high level of detail in standards set at level 2. This approach seems more consistent with the general system of the Treaty, and the division of regulatory powers between the EU institutions and Member States. To the extent that a directive prescribes a specific result to be attained, it will generally not be contrary to the directive for a Member State to maintain or introduce more stringent regulatory standards. Provided that a Member State duly applies the mutual recognition regimes by not applying its stricter standards to incoming services, the mere existence of a framework directive does not in itself preclude that Member State from maintaining such stricter rules, and, consequently, does not hamper the effectiveness of the directive. This conclusion can be supported by the legal foundation of the financial integration directives in Article 48 EC: harmonisation of national laws, whether through framework directives or through detailed level 2 regulation, is not an objective in itself, but only serves as a means to effectively realise the economic freedoms of the Treaty.[12] Therefore, it can be submitted in line with the general principle of subsidiarity that maximum harmonisation could only be imposed at EU level when it is necessary to achieve the aim of market integra-

[11] See the Background Note (n 10) s. 2.2 *in fine.*

[12] Compare ECJ, *Peter Paul and others v Bundesrepublik Deutschland* Case C-222/02 (2004) ECR I-9425 para 36, where the Court held that the harmonisation directives primarily served the objective of market integration.

tion. Absent a clear demonstration of this necessity being absent in the directives (or their preamble), Member States should therefore retain competence to adopt stricter rules in the purely domestic confines of their national laws, as long as this does not conflict with the Treaty freedoms. Only when stricter rules at national level amount to a restriction to the (outbound) cross-border free movement of a domestic enterprise, they would have to satisfy the general good-test in order to be permitted under the Treaty. The Court's approach in *Alpine Investments*[13] showed some leniency to Member States in this regard, in the sense that maintaining the confidence in domestic financial markets could justify possible restrictions, *in casu* a prohibition to cold call potential clients in other Member States, on outgoing financial transactions. It remains unclear, however, whether the Court would maintain a similar flexibility in the presence of detailed harmonised rules.

The impact of the 'minimum harmonisation' paradigm will most probably be mitigated in practice by different elements. First, it is clear that the level 2 implementation rules are devised at a high level of investor protection and of technical detail, which will concurrently reduce the likelihood of more strict regulation at national level.[14] This is amplified by the fact that 20 out of the 67 provisions of MiFID are caught by mandates for further refinement at level 2.[15] Second, though labelled 'high level principles', many provisions in the framework directives also reach a high level of detail and technicality, which reduces flexibility for Member States in the implementation of these objectives into their national laws. Nevertheless, it may still be expected that numerous practical problems will arise in the stage of implementation of the directives at national level. In any case, the mere submission by commentators that the present generation of financial integration directives adopts the paradigm of 'maximum' harmonisation[16], is not supported by the provisions of the directives, the characteristics of the Lamfalussy regulatory structure or the general system of division of powers between the EU and the Member States.

[13] ECJ, *Alpine Investments v Ministerie van Financiën* Case C-384/93 (1995) ECR I-1167 para 42-44.

[14] See also J Herbst (n 6) 213, who points in this respect to 'maximum harmonisation' in substance, i.e. reaching a high level of substantive convergence, if not identity between the Member States.

[15] See B Sousi 'La procédure Lamfalussy à l'épreuve de la directive concernant les marchés d'instruments financiers' (2004) 2 Euredia 209, 214.

[16] See, for instance, PM Boury and R Panasar 'The Prospectus Directive: Creating a Single European Passport' *PLC Global Counsel Equity Capital Markets Handbook 2004/05* 17.

C. Division of Regulatory Powers Between Home and Host State

Contrary to the uncertainty surrounding the level of harmonisation under the Lamfalussy-generation directives, the mutual recognition regime that prevailed under the directives of the 1992 Internal Market Program has been maintained and further consolidated. Indeed, the Lamfalussy report stressed the need to strengthen the mutual recognition regime, in order to avoid duplication of regulation and controls in cross-border activities. MiFID and the Prospectus Directive widen the scope of mutual recognition and of the home country control rule in different respects. However, several areas still remain outside the ambit of the rule, while both directives also appear to widen the residual powers of the host state supervisory authority in emergency situations. We will examine this more in detail for MiFID and the Prospectus Directive separately.

I. Home-Host Country Regulation and Supervision under MiFID

1. Prudential Regulation of Investment Firms

The extension of the mutual recognition regime under MiFID compared to the former regime of ISD, has taken place mainly through widening the scope of the notion of 'investment services' and 'financial instruments'. As regards investment services, the upgrade of investment advice from non-core to core investment service, means that all specialised investment advisers will need an authorisation as investment firm. On the other hand, they will also benefit from the European passport regime. The inclusion of the operation of an MTF in the list of investment services, means that an investment firm will be able to use its European passport to extend its activities as a MTF-operator in other Member States.[17]

The extension of 'financial instruments' mainly covers commodities derivatives, including weather or climate derivatives and emission trading rights. The extension will not only cover the brokerage activities in these instruments, but also portfolio management or investment advice relating to it.

The prudential regime applicable to investment firms has not undergone other substantial modifications, except for the residual supervisory powers of the host state, which did not receive any particular attention during the negotiations and discussions on the draft directive. Under the ISD regime, prudential supervision was of the exclusive competence of the home country supervisor. The rule was

[17] See also F Buisson 'La directive sur les marchés d'instruments financiers: quels enjeux pour la protection des investisseurs et le maintien de l'intégrité du marché?' (2004) 2 Euredia 237, 243.

considered to be fundamental for promoting market integration, by eliminating the costs and burdens of duplication in supervision.

Under the ISD regime, Article 19 provided for a possible exception to the home country rule in cases of (possible) threat to the protection of investors in the host country by an investment firm authorised and supervised in another Member State. However, a detailed analysis of the provision made it clear that the drafters of ISD had mainly effected a 'cut and paste' operation from the Second Banking Directive, which in the end proved to be ineffective in the context of ISD. Indeed, Article 19 provided for a residual power of intervention by the host state competent authority, to be exercised after consultation of the home state authority, in cases where the investment firm did not comply with the provisions in the host state adopted 'pursuant to those provisions of [the ISD] which confer powers on the host Member State's competent authorities'. The latter condition could not refer to any competence in the area of prudential supervision, since the ISD had not conferred any power to the host state in that respect, contrary to the Second Banking directive, where the host state prudential authority remained in charge of the supervision of branch liquidity.[18] The reference to a competent authority in Article 19 ISD could also refer to the authorities in charge of supervising conduct of business rules or of regulated markets, to which the investment firm could seek admission in the host Member State. However, it was doubtful whether ISD had to be interpreted in such a way as to reducing the discretion of the host state authorities in exercising these supervisory powers to an incoming investment firms, by subjecting it to prior consultation with the home state prudential authorities. We submitted that Article 19 ISD eventually proved to be meaningless, given the absence of residual prudential powers in ISD, by contrast with the situation under the Second Banking Directive.[19]

The drafters of MiFID seem to have been conscious of this problem, as Article 62 of MiFID obviously widens the scope of the host state's competent (i.e. prudential) authority. The procedure to follow before the host state authority can take 'precautionary measures' has remained unchanged compared to ISD: before intervening, the host state competent authority should refer to its home state homologue for adequate measures to be taken. Only when this referral does not produce satisfactory results (either because the investment firm fails to comply with the measures ordered by the home state authority, or because the home state

[18] Article 27 Codified Banking Directive. See also C Biancheri 'The Co-operation amongst Supervisory Authorities under the Investment Services Directive' in G Ferrarini (ed) *European Securities Markets. The Investment Services Directive and Beyond* (Kluwer Law International 1998) 367.

[19] See for more details M Tison 'The Investment Services Directive and its Implementation in the EU Member States' in J Stuyck, F Abraham, and E Terryn (eds) *Financial Services and Financial Markets in Europe. Changes and Adjustments* (Leuven University Press 2000) 125, 148-149.

authority has failed to intervene), the host state authority is empowered to take the 'precautionary measures' necessary to protect its domestic investors.

Contrary to Article 19 ISD however, Article 62 of MiFID now clearly indicates in which circumstances the above procedure will apply, namely in case of 'clear and demonstrable grounds for believing that an investment firm ...is in breach of the obligations arising from the provisions adopted pursuant to this Directive ...'. When the investment firm is active under the freedom to provide services, the provisions referred to are all of the competence of the home state, and include both authorisation requirements, prudential regulation and conduct of business rules. As far as branch activities in the host state are concerned, Article 62 (1) further specifies that the procedure applies for those provisions 'which do not confer powers on the competent authority of the host Member State'.

The provision consequently allows the host state supervisory authority to take up residual intervention powers, after consultation with the home state, within the – normally exclusive – sphere of competence of the home state in the matters for which it has received competence under MiFID, i.e. prudential supervision and compliance with conduct of business rules when acting under free provision of services. It will also apply to credit institutions providing investment services.[20]

As far as the host state is competent to exercise supervision under MiFID, e.g. for conduct of business through a branch in the host state, Article 62 (2) confirms the possibility for the host state supervisor to take all adequate measures to halt infringements of the rules, without any prior consultation of the home state supervisor. This competence does not suffer any restriction pursuant to Article 62 (1).

As a result, Article 62 (1) MiFID allows the host state to actually break through the home country control principle in cases where host state investor protection is under threat.[21] The procedure may prove to be adequate in situations where the home state supervisor fails to properly discharge its functions, and urgent intervention is needed to avoid major market disturbances or systemic crises. At present, the host state authorities did not have any legal basis for intervening in such situations, neither under ISD or under the general system of the Treaty, which indeed does not allow a Member State to intervene unilaterally against another Member State which is allegedly in breach of its (supervisory) obligations under EC law.[22]

[20] See Article 1 (2), fourth indent MiFID.

[21] A similar provision is contained in Article 61 (3) as regards activities of a (regulated) market in the host state through remote access.

[22] See, in the context of the Television Directive: *Commission v Belgium* Case C-11/95 (1996) ECR I-4115; *Denuit* Case C-14/96 (1997) ECR I-2785. Compare, with respect to the UCITS Directive, the Belgian *Fleming Flagship*-case: Conseil d'Etat (4 June 1997) (1997) Rev Banque 588; M Tison (n 19) 149-150.

Article 62 MiFID is not, however, without raising serious concerns. Even though the use of this competence is surrounded by different safeguards, such as a proportionality requirement (only 'the appropriate measures needed to protect investors' can be taken by the host country supervisor) and the prior consultation of the home state, it is not excluded that this provision will effectively weaken the home country rule, and to a certain extent reinstall duplication of supervision in a cross-border context. In order to avoid possible abuse of this residual clause, it will be up to the European Commission to closely scrutinise the use of this procedure. It may therefore be welcomed that the directive provides for immediate notification to the European Commission of all measures taken by the host state under this provision. In order to maintain a long-standing climate of mutual confidence amongst supervisory authorities, it may be preferable for a Member State to have recourse only to its residual intervention power as an ultimate remedy, and to foster as much as possible close co-operation with the home state.[23]

Finally, Article 62 MiFID highlights a further source of disparity between the supervisory systems created under the 1992 Internal Market Program directives, and the Lamfalussy-directives. This leads to the inconsistent result that, pursuant to MiFID, the host state supervisor is empowered to take precautionary measures against a credit institution authorised in another Member State solely as regards investment services provided in its territory, since the Codified Banking Directive does not allow to do so with respect to other banking services. Similarly, the UCITS directive still is, as far as the structure and investment rules of an investment firm are concerned, based on an exclusive competence of the home state, without any residual power for the host state. The lack of overall uniformity obviously is not likely to promote (legal) certainty.

2. Cross-border Activity of Markets

While the ISD still to a large extent granted legal privileges to 'regulated markets' under the form of the concentration rule and the possibility to organise remote access on a cross-border basis, MiFID aims at paving the way for competitive equality between different trading venues (either regulated markets, MTFs or internalisation by investment firms). The possibility for these markets to operate on a cross-border basis is essential both for enhancing market liquidity and for reducing transaction costs through economies of scale. However, cross-border expansion is not unlimited, and supervision may still be fragmented between home and host state. The operating conditions moreover vary according to the type of market venue.

A *regulated market* will always be organised and operated by a market operator that is supervised by its home state authority. The legal structure of a regu-

[23] See also F Recine 'The New Framework for Cooperation between Supervisory Authorities in the Markets in Financial Instruments Directive' (2004) 2 Euredia 335, 361-362.

lated market, in particular the question whether or not it has legal personality, remains a matter of national law. When legal personality has been attributed to a regulated market under national law, the (home) Member State will decide how the obligations imposed by MiFID as regards organisation and operation of the market are to be allocated between the market operator and the regulated market entity. Though not specified in the Directive, the regime of regulated markets seems to be based on the assumption that the market operator and the regulated market have the same home Member State, i.e. the state in which the market has its head office or registered office (in case it has legal personality). Indeed, the Directive never contemplates the possibility of both being situated in a different Member State, nor does it refer to the possibility for the market operator to expand its activities across borders, for instance by setting up a regulated market in another Member State. By contrast, regulated markets have been given the possibility to grant access to their trading platforms in other Member States through remote access, providing them a 'European passport' for their trading services. This single passport regime, which already existed under ISD, has been further elaborated in Article 42 (6) MiFID. This provision obliges host Member States to offer appropriate arrangements to regulated markets of other Member States so as to facilitate access to and trading on these markets by remote members or participants established in the host country.

It is striking that MiFID does not label the cross-border activity of regulated markets as 'provision of services' in the sense of the EC Treaty, but merely stipulates an obligation incumbent on the host Member States to provide for 'appropriate arrangements'. This approach can probably be explained by the circumstance that regulated markets do not necessarily qualify as a (legal) 'person' to whom the Treaty freedoms apply. Nonetheless, the situation is in fact close to an actual single passport: the foreign regulated market can offer its trading services to local market participants without having to obtain any additional authorisation, and normally under the exclusive supervision of the home country. The cross-border activity of the regulated market that is not a separate legal entity could also legally be approached as a cross-border provision of services by the market operator.[24] In this perspective, MiFID actually provides for a European passport for market operators, allowing them to expand their services relating to the operation of regulated markets across borders.

The 'appropriate arrangements' regime for regulated markets is markedly less developed than for investment firms, which have been the subject of detailed harmonisation. First, MiFID does not provide for any branch establishment regime for regulated markets or, as the case may be, the market operators. Thus, if a regulated market was to be operated by the branch of a foreign market operator, the supervision of the regulated market would clearly fall under the branch Mem-

[24] See also CESR 'Preliminary Progress Report: Which Supervisory Tools for the EU Securities Markets?' (October 2004) <http://www.cesr-eu.org>.

ber State. This situation would call for close co-operation between the supervisors of the home state of the market operator, responsible for supervising the latter, and the branch state, responsible for market regulation and supervision, as the latter would be considered the home state of the regulated market.

Second, even the situation in which the market operator is only active under provision of services by seeking for cross-border remote access to the regulated market(s) it operates, will lead to shared supervision by home and host state. Article 56 (2) applies some form of 'economic substance test' in deciding who should supervise the operation of the regulated market which has set up 'arrangements' in another Member State: when the importance of these operations in the host state, taking into account the situation of its securities markets, has become of substantial importance for the functioning of the securities markets and the protection of the investors in that state, the home and host country supervisors will establish 'proportionate cooperation arrangements'. This seems to point to a joint responsibility for supervision, although the Directive is not very clear on the issue. The economic substance test has to be assessed taking into account the relative situation of the remote regulated market, compared to the domestic hostcountry securities markets, and not in relation to the relative size of the market operations in the home and host country. It is clear that, in the present stage of market integration, Member States apparently are not yet willing to lose control over the supervision of locally active securities markets.

The possibilities for cross-border activity of a *Multilateral Trading Facility* (MTF) under MiFID have been modelled on the principles applicable to regulated markets, to such an extent as to create a high degree of competitive equality amongst both categories of trading venues. The operational structure of an MTF is, however, somewhat different: while a regulated market will by definition be managed or operated by a 'market operator', MiFID provides for two possibilities in respect of MTF's: the MTF can be operated by a 'market operator', that by definition also manages or operates a regulated market.[25] Alternatively, the operation of an MTF may be entrusted to an investment firm.[26] To that end, the list of investment services in the annex to MiFID has been extended so as to include the operation of MTF's into the list of core investment services.[27] The latter situation offers facilities for cross-border expansion in the operation of MTF's that do not exist under the regime of regulated markets. To the extent that an MTF is operated by an investment firm, the latter will enjoy the full benefits of the European passport: it will be able to operate an out-of state-MTF through direct provision of services from another Member State or by setting up a branch office. Likewise, an investment firm will be able to use its European passport to allow clients situated in other Member States to execute transactions on its home state operated

[25] See the definition of 'market operator' in Article 4 (13) MiFID.

[26] Article 4 (15) MiFID, that refers to both possibilities in the definition of a MTF.

[27] See Annex I, A, (8) MiFID.

MTF, and to grant remote access to the MTF to financial institutions established in other Member States. Like for regulated markets, MiFID obliges Member States to provide appropriate arrangements so as to facilitate the access to and the use of their systems by remote users or participants.[28]

As far as supervision of the operator of an MTF is concerned, the supervisory regime will follow the home country control paradigm when the operator is an investment firm, as the cross-border expansion of the business as operator of an MTF is covered by the European passport. Similarly, the 'market operator', when providing 'appropriate arrangements' for remote access to an MTF in other Member States, will be subject to supervision in its state of origin. Contrary to the situation of regulated markets, where some joint responsibility for supervising the market operation follows from Article 56 (2) MiFID, the Directive does not refer to a 'substance' test in deciding to allocate supervisory powers between home and host state, when an MTF is accessible in different Member States through 'appropriate arrangements'. Irrespective of the general obligation for the supervisory authorities to co-operate and to offer mutual assistance[29], the supervision of the operating conditions of an MTF will be of the competence of the home state of the market operator.

3. Transactional Regulation: Conduct of Business Rules

One of the areas in which MiFID has made substantial progress in attaining regulatory convergence amongst Member States, is the area of conduct of business. The adoption of detailed level 2 rules will result in real European rulebooks for investment activities.[30] Beside the convergence in substance, the shift to home country control as regards cross border provision of services is an important step forward in making the single passport a powerful tool for truly integrated markets.

At the same time, MiFID has not clearly resolved the discussions that existed under the ISD regime as to the legal nature of the conduct of business rules and their enforceability in contract or in tort by investors.[31] In the present situation, no uniform picture emerges from the situation in the different Member States: in the absence of clear provisions in the laws of most Member States as to the action-

[28] Article 31 (5) MiFID.

[29] See Article 56 (1) MiFID.

[30] See the proposal for a directive cited *supra*, n 10. This leaves aside the question whether integration through law is likely to produce the most optimal results. See for a critical approach: N Moloney 'Building a Retail Investment Culture through Law: the 2004 Markets in Financial Instruments Directive' (2005) 6 Eur Bus Org L Rev 341-422.

[31] See, on this issue, M Tison 'Conduct of Business Rules and their Implementation in the EU Member States' in G Ferrarini, KJ Hopt and E Wymeersch (eds) *Capital Markets in the Age of the Euro* (Kluwer Law International 2002) 65, 78-80.

ability in court of conduct of business rules, the prevailing opinion in a minority of Member States holds that conduct of business rules are of a purely supervisory nature and cannot, therefore, be relied upon in court by an investor (e.g. Germany). In most Member States, however, the opposite opinion would prevail, even though case law seems to be rare, if not inexistent.[32] The 'objectives' to be attained through conduct of business rules, as Article 11 ISD had phrased it, have been replaced by 'high level principles' in Article 20 MiFID, which altogether attain a substantially higher degree of precision. The main innovation compared to ISD lies in the circumstance that the further refinement of the 'principles' is no longer left to the Member States, but to the Commission through a level 2 mandate. It still remains unclear, however, to which extent the conduct of business rules should be considered as mere supervisory rules, or whether they will also be actionable in court by investors. It goes without saying that the conduct of business rules have at least a supervisory nature. This appears clearly from Article 17 (1), according to which Member States should ensure that their competent authorities monitor the activities of investment firms, so as to assess compliance with the operating conditions (including conduct of business rules) provided for in MiFID. This does not in itself exclude a possible private enforceability of the conduct of business rules. The underlying general objectives of MiFID plead in favour of private enforceability: even stronger than under ISD, the preamble to MiFID stresses investor protection as a primary objective of the Directive.[33] Likewise, the conduct of business rules (and related client handling rules) are part of the section entitled 'Provisions to ensure investor protection'. Although this does not provide a conclusive argument, as investor protection could also be promoted through supervisory rules, an analysis of the substance of the 'high level principles' shows that precise obligations are imposed on investment firms towards investors (e.g. keeping of records of rights and duties of parties, obligation to hand over reports to the investor, ...). In conclusion, it seems fair to assert that the conduct of business rules, even more strongly than under ISD, are likely to be relied upon by investors against investment firms, and will create legally enforceable rights.

[32] See, for instance, the situation in Belgium, where the same scholarly debate took place when implementing Article 11 ISD into the Belgian Law of 6 April 1995. It should be noted that Belgian courts have in recent years been surprisingly cautious in holding investment firms liable on the basis of the conduct of business rules. In most cases, liability was founded on general rules of contract law (duty of diligence in contract, ...) instead of referring to the (often more detailed) conduct of business rules. This may indicate that the detailed conduct of business rules can, at least in part, be construed through interpretation of the general standards of contractual duties or tort liability.

[33] This situation contrasts with the sectorial directives of the 1992 Internal Market Programme, for which the ECJ held in *Peter Paul and others* (n 12) that the protection of depositors only constituted a side-effect of the primary aim of the directives, i.e. achieving market integration.

Finally, it should be noted that MiFID has split up the supervisory competence between cross-border provision of services and branch establishment, by allocating regulatory and supervisory competence for the latter to the host country. By shifting to home country control for cross-border services, a major criticism against the compatibility of Article 11 ISD with the EC Treaty has been wiped away. However, it remains to be seen to which extent the automatic submission of branches to the host state conduct of business rules will resist scrutiny with Article 43 EC on freedom of establishment. The ECJ's decision of 5 October 2004 in the *Caixa-Bank France* case,[34] may cast some doubts in this respect. In this case, the French subsidiary of Caixa-Bank had taken up a deposit-taking activity in France through the offer of interest bearing sight accounts, which contravened French regulations. After being ordered to halt the offer of these accounts by the Banque de France, Caixa-Bank challenged this decision in court, which referred the case to the ECJ. The Court decided that the prohibition under French law to offer interest bearing accounts did constitute a restriction to freedom of establishment for Caixa-Bank, as it deprived the latter of an important means of gaining market access in the French market, taking into account in particular the competitive advantage that local banks with an extensive network of branches enjoyed. The Court considered that the general good could not justify the restriction.

The judgment in *Caixa-Bank France* is important, as the ECJ for the first time examined the compatibility of rules on financial products, which relate to the exercise of an economic activity, with the freedom of establishment. The Court acknowledges that such rules could in some circumstances restrict effective market access through an establishment. It remains to be seen whether or not this case will provoke a plethora of new cases, where host state rules governing the exercise of an economic activity will be challenged under the Treaty provisions on freedom of establishment. The argument could be transposed as well to conduct of business rules under MiFID: if a disparity of conduct of business rules between home and host state could result in restricting an effective access to the host state market by the branch of a foreign investment firm, this may amount to a prohibited restriction to the freedom of establishment. The allocation of powers to the branch state under MiFID should therefore continue to be interpreted in line with the Treaty freedoms, which could limit the actual exercise of this competence.

We further submit that even *Caixa-Bank* will not fully put host state conduct of business rules under pressure in the name of freedom of establishment: in *Caixa-Bank*, the ECJ concluded to the existence of a restriction to freedom of establishment only after having pointed at the cardinal importance for the foreign competitor to use the remuneration of bank deposits as an effective tool to penetrate the market. Implicitly, the Court applied a 'contestable market' approach in

[34] *CaixaBank France v Ministère de l'Économie, des Finances et de l'Industrie*, Case C-442/02 judgment of 5 October 2004, not yet reported in ECR.

identifying the restriction to market access: foreign competitors should be granted the necessary means to effectively enter into competition with locally established financial institutions.[35] It is doubtful whether the conduct of business rules can play the same pivotal role in allowing foreign competitors to challenge host state established enterprises as was the case in *Caixa-Bank France*. First, the conduct of business rules do not, in general, shape the essential characteristics of a financial service, but mostly impair on the conditions under which a financial product will be offered (information as to the products offered, disclosure of conflicts of interest, disclosure of client handling rules, inquiry as to the situation of customers – KYC, …). Disparities in these conduct of business rules will only exceptionally be such as to form an essential element in realising effective market penetration for a new market entrant. Furthermore, the nature of the financial products will in many cases enable to 'exploit' a competitive disadvantage between foreign investment firms that do not have an extensive branch network, and firmly established local competitors in the host Member States, as was the case in *Caixa-Bank France*. Although, for some investment services, the proximity between the supplier and the client may provide a competitive advantage to the locally established firms (e.g. private banking activities), this will not be so for many other investment services (e.g. execution-only services). For the latter, it will be largely indifferent whether or not the supplier has a wide-spread branch network, as other means of communication can act as a suitable substitute (e.g. on line trading). In conclusion, it may well be that the ECJ's move in *Caixa-Bank France* will remain exceptional, and does not threaten the allocation of regulatory and supervisory competence with respect to conduct of business rules to the host state.

II. The Home-Host Country Division in the Prospectus Directive

1. Consolidation of the Home Country Rule

The elaboration of a single legal regime for prospectuses encompassing all public offers of securities, and the extension of the regime of mutual recognition of prospectus approvals make the 2004 Prospectus Directive a landmark instrument in promoting the legal framework for capital market integration. Notwithstanding the uncertainty surrounding the nature of the Directive with respect to the residual powers of Member States (see above), it is clear that market participants are likely to make increasing use of the possibilities to raise capital across

[35] According to Spaventa, however, the Court failed to clearly delimit the concept of market access in *Caixa-Bank*, thus potentially allowing the scrutiny of any measure regulating economic life (E Spaventa 'Note under Case C-442/02 *Caixa-Bank France*' (2005) 42 Comm Mkt L Rev 1151, 1156).

national borders. The detailed harmonisation of the contents and presentation of the prospectus and its ancillary documents realise a high degree of regulatory convergence in the EU. In comparison to its predecessors, the Prospectus Directive substantially extends the scope of mutual recognition, both as regards the scope of public offers caught by the directive, and with respect to the form and contents of the prospectus to be made available to investors. Finally, Article 15 of the Prospectus Directive contains general standards concerning advertisements in connection with a public offer of securities, and entrusts the home Member State with supervisory powers in this respect.

In all the abovementioned areas, the principle of mutual recognition, and the (exclusive) allocation of supervisory powers to the home state competent authority, concurrently deprives the host state to impose additional requirements or to take up supervisory competence. As regards advertisement, the Prospectus Directive thus attains a degree of convergence which is still largely absent in the other financial industry directives, where the host state generally retains residual powers in the interest of the general good.[36] The mutual recognition regime will, however, only apply for advertising made by or on behalf of the issuer or the offeror.

The issue of prospectus liability, on the contrary, has hardly been touched upon by the Prospectus Directive, and therefore remains mainly an area to be regulated in national law. Article 6 of the Prospectus Directive only contains a minimum obligation as to the indication of the persons who bear responsibility for the contents of or omissions in the prospectus, subjecting them to the normal regime of liability law. This seems at least to indicate that Member States may not allow these persons who bear responsibility to waive their liability. The directive also does not contain any indication as to the law applicable to liability claims in a cross-border offer. National conflict of laws rules will often enable aggrieved investors to sue the issuer (or other person deemed responsible) according to their local host state laws, as the place where the damage has produced its effects. From the point of view of the issuer, this risk of application of foreign liability laws will have to be taken into account in structuring the transaction, in view of the disparities existing amongst Member States as to the legal foundations of and conditions attached to prospectus liability.[37]

[36] This if, for instance, still the case for banking and investment services – leaving aside the limited impact of conduct of business rules, and in the context of the distribution of parts of investment funds under the UCITS Directive.

[37] Compare C Sandberger 'Die EU-Prospektrichtlinie – 'Europäischer Pass für Emittenten' (2004) 7 EWS 297, 303.

2. Derogation from Mutual Recognition: The 'Precautionary Measures' Regime

Paradoxically, the extension of the scope of mutual recognition in substance goes along with increased powers for the host Member State to set aside the mutual recognition regime in situations of threat to (host state) investors. Article 23 of the Prospectus Directive enables the host state, in the event of irregularities, to take 'precautionary measures', after prior referral of its findings to the home state authority, and where the intervention of the latter has proved unsuccessful or unsatisfactory. The directive foresees this residual competence in two situations: (1) the issuer or the financial institution in charge of the public offer have committed irregularities, or (2) the obligations attached to admission of the offered securities to a regulated market, have not been observed. The latter situation finds a reasonable explanation in the circumstance that admission to a host state's regulated market is still of the competence of that state. The residual host state power in case of 'irregularities', on the contrary, may have a more disturbing impact on the system of mutual recognition. The 'irregularities' that can enable the host state to take precautionary measures are not further specified in the Directive, and could therefore result in duplication of prospectus scrutiny for multinational issues. As Article 23 constitutes an exception to the principle of mutual recognition, which forms a cornerstone for the promotion of capital market integration, it must, in our view, receive a strict interpretation. This means first that the nature of measures to be possibly taken by the host state must be strictly necessary to safeguard investors' interests, and not may unduly impair on the cross-border capital raising activity of issuers. More importantly, the proportionality requirement does not enable the host state competent authorities to proceed to systematic scrutiny of prospectuses that have been approved by the competent home state authority. Excessive intervention by the host state can be considered contrary to the objective of the Prospectus Directive and to the EC Treaty provisions on capital movements.

D. Conclusions

The above general developments illustrate the conceptual ambiguities surrounding the legal patterns for capital market integration in the Lamfalussy-generation directives. Although the multi-level approach to regulation should in principle be welcomed as a powerful mechanism to promote market integration through appropriate legal instruments, new questions arise as to the (residual) powers of the Member States when implementing the Lamfalussy-style directives. The various assessment exercises made in recent years with respect to the financial integration directives have revealed that the lack of legal certainty constitutes a serious deterrent for financial services suppliers to expand their business internationally, notably in the retail segment. Although the EU regulatory framework in the 'Lamfalussy era' will result in a high degree of regulatory detail,

Member States may still have an interest in maintaining more stringent rules in specific areas, for a multitude of reasons (specificities of the domestic market, regulatory tradition, ...). The absence of clear identification as to the level of harmonisation does not allow for conclusiveness regarding the form of harmonisation (minimum, maximum or intermediate) presently used.

More importantly, the sequence of integration directives in various segments of the financial industry, based on different underlying concepts, amplifies the risk of internal inconsistencies. This paper has highlighted this risk inter alia by analysing the powers of the competent authorities to intervene in situations of deficient home state control under MiFID and the Prospectus Directive, as compared to the1992 Internal Market directives in the fields of banking and collective investment. It is clear that the dynamics of the regulatory process in market integration may not come at the price of diminished legal certainty and regulatory loopholes. The 'silent' modification of the host state residual powers to take 'precautionary measures' in some directives is likely to create confusion due to its lack of uniformity. This will be all the more inconsistent when taking into account the move to more integrated cross-border supervisory structures within the Member States, as the same supervisor will have differentiated supervisory tools at hand depending on the financial institution under supervision. It goes without saying that the credibility of the regulatory process in the markets will increase if the EU institutions manage to maintain a dynamic integration process while minimising internal inconsistencies.

Securities Clearing and Settlement: Regulatory Developments in Europe

EDDY WYMEERSCH*

The subject of clearing and settlement has recently become one of the most controversial issues in the creation of a European securities market. The cost and rigidities flowing from the present state of integration in these post trading services have been identified as significant restrictions, especially in the cross-border trading. In the absence of a European harmonization directive, restrictions remain numerous. The paper gives an overview of the different activities that are undertaken in Europe and outside and aiming at removing the barriers on intra-European trading or regulating this activity with a view of protecting the interest of investors. Most important in this field are the removal of the Giovannini barriers, the standards of the ESCB-CESR and finally the expected directive proposals of the European Commission. In the meantime the market structure may be changing in the near future, due to consolidation at the level of securities trading.

A. A Short Introduction to Securities Clearing and Settlement
B. The Legal and Regulatory Environment of Securities Clearing and Settlement
C. Conclusion
D. Later Developments

A. Short Introduction to Securities Clearing and Settlement

When securities have been traded, whether on a regulated market, through an MTF,[1] or OTC,[2] the transaction has to be executed. The following overview gives

* Professor at the University of Ghent, Chairman of the Banking, Finance and Insurance Commission. The paper reflects solely personal opinions.

[1] 'Multilateral Trading Facility' (MTF) means a multilateral system, operated by an investment firm or a market operator, which brings together multiple third-party buying and selling interests in financial instruments – in the system and in accordance with non-discretionary rules – in a way that results in a contract in accordance with the provisions of Title II of Directive 2004/39/EC of the European Parliament and of the Council of 21 April 2004 on Markets in Financial Instruments amending Council Directives 85/611/EEC and 93/6/EEC and Directive 2000/12/EC of the European Parliament and of the Council and repealing Council Directive 93/22/EEC, OJ L 145 30.04.2004 1-44. See Article 4 (1) (15) of Directive 2004/39/EC (hereafter referred to as 'MiFID').

[2] 'Over-the-counter' (OTC) trading is a method of trading that does not involve a multilateral system. In over-the-counter markets, participants trade directly with each other, typically

cont. ...

only a short schematic presentation of the process. In practice there are numerous alternatives that may lead to different technical and legal solutions.

This quite complicated process takes place in several steps: first the position of the respective parties has to be confirmed and settlement instructions matched, to make sure that there is agreement about the respective position of the buyer and the seller.[3] This process should be undertaken immediately after the trade has taken place to ensure that parties would be able to check what they have traded and can introduce changes immediately after having discovered possible discrepancies. After this first stage, as parties will be confronted with clearly determined rights and obligations, one may consider that from a legal point of view they will not be entitled to change their position being bound to their agreement. To the extent that this agreement is binding, it will also facilitate the later stages in the processing of the transaction, and therefore contributes to the safety of the overall process. Automation and as much as possible Straight Through Processing (or STP)[4] will enhance the overall process.

The next stage in the process relates to clearing. According to the standard terminology, this consists of calculating the different rights and obligations of the different parties that have been acting on the market. In most cases, orders will not be dealt with order by order, but will be pooled in order to offset the maximum amount in terms of securities to be transferred and moneys to be settled. The procedure then aims at minimising the volume of the funds, or securities that finally have to be transferred. It is essentially based on multilateral netting, and aims at reducing the final positions of the involved parties, thereby reducing their respective risk positions.

Clearing may take at least two forms. According to the first scheme, the respective rights and obligations are pooled and the resulting net positions are calculated. This system amounts to netting the respective positions.

According to another procedure, the respective rights and obligations are transferred to a central entity which substitutes itself to the contracting parties. This is done by the entity becoming counterparty to every buyer and to every seller, substituting itself to all market parties. This Central Counterparty (CCP) offers a ready execution for all obligations, while it will setoff internally all transactions, sending only the net positions for further execution.

The third stage in the process concerns settlement. It consists of transferring the securities in the books, by debiting the position of the seller and crediting that

through telephone or computer links. See ECB-CESR 'Standards for Securities Clearing and Settlement in the European Union' (September 2004) 88, glossary <http://www.ecb.int/pub/pdf/other/escb-cesr-standardssecurities2004en.pdf>.

[3] See ECB-CESR Standards (n 2) 11, Standard 2.

[4] Straight-through processing is the completion of pre-settlement and settlement processes based on trade data that are manually entered only once into an automated system. See ECB-CESR Standards (n 2) 91, glossary.

of the buyer. This takes place on the basis of the purchase price having been paid. The process of transferring the securities calls for some further explanation.

In the traditional technique, whereby securities were represented by certificates of title, transfer implied physical transmission of the documents. This still is the case for bearer certificates that are held by the investor, or by his bank.

In practice, many bearer certificates do not circulate, but are deposited with an intermediary, a central securities depository (CSD) or a bank. The bank may redeposit the securities with the CSD, or keep it in its own vaults: depending on the applicable law, the legal position may be the same. In exchange for the documents so deposited, the intermediary books the securities in the account of the depositors. They obtain a credit in their securities account that corresponds to their part of the securities in the bank's safe. To simplify the paperwork, securities deposited often take the form of 'global certificates' whereby one document stands for the whole, or a large part of the entire issue. The securities that have been credited to the investor's account will be considered to be subject to the same rules as the underlying bearer security as far as their circulation is concerned. Legally, they will be considered 'bearer' securities, although obviously this is not the case.[5]

Technically registered securities or nominative securities could also be dealt with in the same way. In these cases, the legal regime is that of the underlying security. If the securities exist in dematerialised form, i.e. are only represented by bookkeeping registrations, the circulation regime would be entirely based on the bookkeeping entries. The applicable law will decide what the circulation regime looks like.

Settlement is the procedure whereby the securities are booked from one account to the other. If the securities are deposited with the CSD, transfer will lead to a debiting and crediting in the accounts of the investor, or his bank, with the CSD. In some jurisdictions individual investors have direct accounts at CSDs and, therefore, movements in these accounts will be rather frequent, and occur each time one of the investors buys or sells. CSDs have then to open thousands, even millions of accounts.

In most systems however, securities are held indirectly, through banks taking care of the custody. The CSD opens accounts to the intermediate bank, usually two, one for the bank's own securities, one for its clients' securities. If both buyer and seller have their accounts at the same bank, the transfer may take place on the books of that bank, without passing to the CSD (internalised settlement). This procedure will also be followed if both banks hold the securities through another, an agent bank. The percentage of securities that pass through the CSD varies from state to state: if the securities are held indirectly, they may either be transferred

[5] See Unidroit 'Explanatory Notes to the Preliminary Draft Convention on Harmonised Substantive Rules Regarding Securities Held With an Intermediary' (Study LXXVIII, doc. 19) <http://www.unidroit.org/english/workprogramme/study078/item1/archive/s-78-19-e.pdf>.

within the bank, or among the banks. The first happens when the banks internalise trading, a procedure to be increasingly followed after the implementation of the MiFID.

The transfer of the securities normally implies that the purchase price is paid. This process takes place depending on the procedure followed, whether by debiting or crediting the account at the bank where the securities accounts have been held. Here payment will intervene against securities: this notion is usually called 'delivery versus payment'. It is defined as 'the link between securities transfers and funds transfers that ensures that a delivery occurs if, and only if, payment takes place'.[6] The fact that no title is transferred until payment has been obtained is an important safeguard for investors, on both sides of the transaction. The seller is not dispossessed of his securities until his cash account is credited; the buyer holds his money up to the very moment that the securities are credited to his securities account. The notion of DVP is crucial to the proper functioning of the settlement process. Conceptually it can be considered as elimination of a central part of the risk from the settlement process, at least as far as the intermediate parties are concerned. However, upon looking closely at the technicalities of the procedure, one sees that often some time lapses between the securities and the cash side of the transaction, thereby putting the parties at risk. The investor then supports a twofold risk: normally, as a depositor, he takes a risk on the seller, from which he has not yet received the securities although his cash account would already be debited. By being deprived of the securities without having obtained the cash, he can not fall back on its securities position, in case no payment is made, and the cash has already been debited from his account. Legally however, the conditions will be stipulated in a sense that both legs become effective simultaneously.

Cash payment may be effected within the bank where buyer and seller hold accounts. This is called payment in 'commercial bank money'. It may also take place between banks, which then leads to a movement in their accounts held at the central bank. The CSD where the securities movement has to be registered is then informed about the cash movement, and both are registered on a technically simultaneous basis. However, central banks do not open accounts to all financial intermediaries, and are even less willing to grant credit to all banks: if a bank has no direct access to the central bank account, it will use a cash settlement agent that has such access. If credit is needed, it will be fully collateralised, limiting the risks supported by the central bank, but also limiting the credit risk in the system. In several European states, only the latter procedure is accepted.

[6] See ECB-CESR Standards (n 2) 84, glossary.

B. The Legal and Regulatory Environment of Securities Clearing and Settlement

The purpose of this paper is to attempt to give a short overview of the numerous initiatives that have been undertaken over the last few years for dealing with the issue of clearing and settlement in Europe. From a rather technical, backward subject, it has recently moved to the forefront of public attention and calls for regulation have come from all sides.

The legal regime under which securities are cleared and settled is a highly complicated matter. Numerous hard and soft legal provisions may be applicable and, at the same time, authorities at different levels of the legal structure have been producing recommendations, standards, policy papers and statements dealing with securities settlement. This paper will attempt to take stock of these different layers of action, and put them in an historical and legislative perspective.

I. Private Law

Private law rules – contract law and conflicts of law rules – coexist more or less harmoniously with public law and organisational provisions. Prudential rules indirectly influence the way transactions are dealt with. Also, soft law rules such as the standards imposed by the Central banks, and more recently so-called level 3 standards would also contribute to shape the transactions. There are only very few EU rules applicable. All this takes place in an eminently multinational context, whereby different legal regimes may conflict. This involves not only the EU and its 25 Member States, but the U.S., Switzerland and Japan legal systems as well. It is clear that this overview will remain scant, and that only part of the legal and regulatory environment can be developed here.

Firstly, the relationships of securities holders with their depositories, mainly banks, are of a contractual nature. The standard contract terms of a client with its bank have to be supplemented by the rules that govern the functioning of the settlement system, and which will usually be laid down in the legislation or in secondary rules. However, as several parties intervene in the final processing of a transaction, each will have its own contract terms, not necessarily harmoniously adapted to those of the other parties. In each case, different public law provisions may have an influence. In many cases, these relationships will have foreign elements and hence conflict of law rules will have to be taken account of, both in terms of contract law, and of rules applicable to securities as movable property.

The Hague Convention[7] aims at designating the law applicable to securities held with an intermediary, but does not as such deal with substantive law.[8] It firstly introduces a system of choice of law in the account agreements: parties may choose for the law governing the account agreement provided that in that jurisdiction the relevant intermediary – being the intermediary that maintains the securities account for the holder – has an office that has sufficient connections – as defined – with that jurisdiction. If no such choice has been made, different successive fall-back rules apply: the office where the account agreement has been entered into, the place where the intermediary has been incorporated, or finally where his principal place of business is located.[9]

II. National Legislations on Securities Settlement

National legislations on securities settlement systems or on central depositories will determine central parts of the applicable legal regime. So for example Belgian law is applicable to transactions affecting securities deposited within a Belgian CSD and registered in the accounts of a Belgian bank. As one of the important international CSDs is recognised as a Belgian CSD, being also a bank, the ambit of the Belgian rules is quite important.

The regulation applicable to CSDs is in most states focused on the rules governing the status of the securities held in its accounts and the modes of transfer of the securities. Indirectly the legislation pays little attention to the risks represented by the CSD and by the consequences of its failure. Most CSDs have relatively low own funds, on the basis that their operations are rather low risk. Whether that is true will be taken up later.

Another layer of regulation addresses the parties intervening in the process. Most of these participants have the status of a bank or of an investment firm (not all: the majority of CSDs are not banks) and hence are subject to traditional prudential regulation. Several of these banks are specialised in securities business, and could be designated as 'special purpose banks'. Under the Basel I framework, this means that they have to meet the capital requirements aimed at protecting the creditors of the bank in case of its failure. However, there are no specific rules addressing the risks flowing from the securities business, especially from the credit risk linked to the clearing and settlement of securities transactions. The present rules take into account credit risk in general terms, although only in an imperfect way, i.e. on the basis of end of day positions, where settlement risk

7 'The Hague Convention on the Law Applicable to Certain Rights in respect of Securities held with an Intermediary' <http://hcch.e-vision.nl/index_en.php?act=conventions.text&cid=72>. The convention has not been yet signed nor ratified.

8 See Article 2 Section 3 of the The Hague Convention (n 7).

9 See Article 5 of the The Hague Convention (n 7).

most of the time arises during the day and is offset before the end of the day. If risk piles up during the day, the supervisor might not be timely informed. Furthermore a crucial risk factor is that operational risk is presently not taken into account: needless to say that settlement organisations are very reliant on the safety and efficiency of their IT procedures for transferring the securities. Hence business continuity schemes require special attention. In the future Basel II framework, there will be capital requirements determined in function of operational risk, and supervisors will be able to impose additional requirements if the overall position of the bank does not offer sufficient supervisory 'comfort', intraday risks included. However, these rules will enter into force only by 2007, and still require considerable legislative and regulatory preparation, both at the EU (i.e. through a directive)[10] and at the Member State level.

III. International Recommendations

There are several studies and recommendations that have been prepared dealing with securities clearing and settlement in recent years. The present short overview merely serves to situate these, and indicate the link with the European activities, without any detailed analysis.

1. The CPSS-IOSCO Recommendations

The diversity of legal regimes applicable to the securities settlement systems has called for a worldwide harmonisation effort. This has resulted in a set of international standards, called the CPSS-IOSCO[11] standards on clearing and settlement, laying down the guidelines for a supervisory regime affecting both the reliability and safety of the systems, and the efficiency of their operations. This worldwide initiative was supported on the one hand by the central banks,[12] and on

[10] See Proposal for Directives of the European Parliament and of the Council Re-casting Directive 2000/12/EC of the European Parliament and of the Council of 20 March 2000 relating to the Taking up and Pursuit of the Business of Credit Institutions and Council Directive 93/6/EEC of 15 March 1993 on the Capital Adequacy of Investment Firms and Credit Institutions – Annexes techniques, 14.07.2004, COM(2004)486 <http://europa.eu.int/eur-lex/en/com/pdf/2004/com2004_0486en.html>. The Directive has since been agreed by Council and Parliament.

[11] Published by the Bank for International Settlement (BIS) and drawn up by the Committee on Payment and Settlement Systems (CPSS) and by the International Organization of Securities Commissions (IOSCO) 'Recommendations for Securities Settlement Systems' (November 2001) <http://www.bis.org/publ/cpss46.htm>; and the 'Assessment Methodology "Recommendations for Securities Settlement Systems"' (November 2002) <http://www.bis.org/publ/cpss51.htm>.

[12] For further details on the CPSS see <http://www.bis.org/cpss/cpsspubl.htm>.

the other by the securities commissions.[13] Indeed, in the original approach these are the two principal poles of interest dealing with the regulation of clearing and settlement business. As banks were only marginally involved, the prudential regulators were not directly concerned. The international standards are addressed to securities settlement operations worldwide: therefore they have been formulated at a relatively high level of generality. Also they reflect the systems as are in existence in most of the states to which they are addressed. The role of banks, including custodian banks has remained largely unmentioned, and banking supervisors were not involved in drafting the recommendations.

The CPSS-IOSCO standards have no binding force on their own: Member States and their supervisory authorities are expected to abide by them. However, the binding value of the standard may in part be derived from the markets, in the sense that risk adverse operators are likely to leave aside markets that would clearly not conform to them. More important however is the fact that these standards are being used by the International Monetary Fund, as the basis on which its assessment of national securities settlement systems is based. In the Financial Stability Assessment Programmes (FSAPs) that the IMF is undertaking, said standards are regularly put on the agenda, and their implementation is verified on the basis of a very detailed questionnaire called the 'assessment methodology'.[14]

2. The Group of Thirty

The Group of Thirty is a group of leading bankers, central bankers and academics that acts as a think tank in international financial affairs. They have published reports on numerous financial matters, several of which have dealt with 'Clearance and Settlement in Securities Markets'. Their 1988 document has drawn attention to the need for DVP, a central aspect in the safe functioning of the systems.

Their most recent report, published in 2003,[15] formulates a series of twenty recommendations, standing for the 'best practices' to be promoted in international markets, thereby essentially addressing cross border clearing and settlement, in this case on a worldwide scale. Although their recommendations run to a certain extent parallel to the CPSS-IOSCO Standards, they take a more outspoken industry point of view, and therefore pay attention to issues like efficiency and the removal of transcontinental cross border barriers.

The three main headings under which the recommendations have been grouped are: strengthening an interoperable global network, mitigating risk, and improving governance.

[13] For further details on the IOSCO see <http://www.iosco.org/about/>.

[14] See (n 11).

[15] The Group of Thirty's (G30) 'Global Clearing and Settlement: A Plan of Action' (2003) (for an executive summary <http://www.group30.org/docs/executive_summary.pdf>).

These recommendations serve as guidance for operators in the markets, professional associations and for regulators worldwide.

3. Unidroit[16]

The Unidroit proposed convention deals with substantive issues relating to securities held with intermediaries. As legal systems present some significant differences, it follows a neutral formulation, and attempts to adhere to a functional approach. A wide range of substantive subjects are tackled: rights resulting from a credit to an account; legal consequences of acquisitions or dispositions ('sale or purchases' in a non neutral formulation); creation of security interests; bona fide holder status (referred to under 'effectiveness of debits or credits'); prohibition of upper tier attachments, etc. The convention is proposed for discussion and approval by the Unidroit Member States.

IV. Initiatives at the European Level

1. Directives Adopted

In the European Union, few rules have been enacted that relate to the securities settlement business. On the one hand settlement has not been qualified as a banking service, excluding settlement services – but not custody – from the ambit of the harmonisation and mutual recognition directives. Securities clearing and settlement are almost exclusively national subjects: national regulations offer a wide variety of legal regimes, with substantial differences as to the prudential safeguards. Only the recently adopted MiFID contains a provision relating to settlement, as it deals with free access to settlement systems, and this from the angle of allowing investors to settle their trades on the system of their choice.

The MiFID provisions[17] require Member States to grant foreign market participants access to national clearing and settlement service providers subject to the same non-discriminatory, transparent and objective criteria which apply to local participants. Markets participants shall have the right to designate the system on which they want to have their transactions settled, provided necessary links are in place.

[16] For the Unidroit publications see <http://www.unidroit.org/english/workprogramme/study078/item1/archive/s-78-18.pdf> and <http://www.unidroit.org/english/workprogramme/study078/item1/archive/s-78-19-e.pdf>.

[17] Article 34 of the MiFID.

2. The Giovannini Reports on Clearing and Settlement

In 1996, the Commission installed an advisory group under the direction of Alberto Giovannini to advise on different subjects of financial regulation. The fourth[18] and fifth[19] of these reports (the latter entitled 'Cross border Clearing and Settlement Arrangements in the European Union') are currently receiving ample attention and deal with barriers to cross border securities settlement. From a perspective of integration of the markets, the reports have identified a number of barriers that either prevent cross border settlement or at any case make it less efficient. Therefore these barriers should be removed. Removal of these barriers is not only the task of regulatory action: several are due to divergent market practices and therefore should be removed by having market practitioners agree on common practices and standards. ECSDA, the associations of European CSDs, is making progress in removing the first group of hurdles identified by Giovannini.

For integration purposes, the starting point for triggering more efficient cross border settlement, aims at rendering free choice between execution venues effective and non discriminatory. To that end it was considered that first priority should be given to the harmonisation of the opening hours and of settlement deadlines (barrier 7), subjects that would call for coordination among the market practitioners, without regulatory action. Simultaneously, in order to guarantee efficient and reliable communication between participants, a common communication protocol is called for: the use of a Swift protocol will allow an efficient interface between the different service providers (barrier 1) and should be introduced and adopted for the Eurosystem, inciting all market operators to follow suit. Once these objectives are achieved, progress can be made in other fields, such as removing barriers in the fields of settlement periods,[20] in the matter of corporate actions, in issuance practices,[21] and in achieving intraday finality on a cross border basis.

The report also addresses some issues of taxation, especially calling for coordination with respect to the provisions of Member States requiring the collection of taxes within their jurisdiction, thereby creating a bias as to the place of settlement. Other proposals require quite fundamental rethinking of the securities sys-

[18] The Giovannini Group 'Cross-border Clearing and Settlement Arrangements in the European Union – First Report' (November 2001) <http://europa.eu.int/comm/economy_finance/publications/giovannini/clearing1101_en.pdf>.

[19] The Giovannini Group 'Second Report on EU Cross-border Clearing and Settlement Arrangements' (April 2003) <http://europa.eu.int/comm/economy_finance/publications/giovannini/clearing_settlement_arrangements140403.pdf>.

[20] In most Member States based on T+3, at least for equity, except for Germany (T+2). It seems rather unlikely that an intermediate step to T+2 would be introduced, as T+1 rules are probably beyond reach, both in terms of reliability and of cost.

[21] Progress has been made e.g. in the techniques of allocation of an ISIN code in a timely and consistent way.

tem in Europe: this relates to redefining the status of rights flowing from securities ownership in the different European jurisdictions.[22] Uneven application of conflicts of law rules is directly linked to the previous item.[23] One could designate this as the creation of a European securities code, dealing with questions of ownership, transfer of title through book entry, ownership and legal position in multi-tiered systems and so on. Harmonisation of these private law subjects may look ambitious, but should actively be pursued.

Within the purview of this short and incomplete summary, it is useful to note that several of these objectives could be achieved by voluntary action from the industry, or by relatively minor changes in the regulatory provisions. Others however have to be taken up at the level of political action, for which the Commission is responsible. The importance of the Commission's Communication thereby becomes evident.

3. The Commission's Communication

The Giovannini barriers are a prerequisite for further progress in making overall securities settlement more efficient. It seems clear that more has to be done, on the one hand to ensure that the existing facilities fully interact, on the other that an efficient supervisory system – based on robust regulations – is put in place. These issues are addressed in the Commission Communication, published on April 28, 2004, under the title 'Clearing and Settlement in the European Union – The way forward' and inviting for wide public comments.[24] The latter have been summarized and are available at the Commission dedicated website (see under 'CESAME', the consultative group constituted by the Commission).[25]

In the Commission's analysis, integration of the European market for clearing and settlement services has to be driven on the one hand by removing a certain number of existing significant barriers (see the Giovannini proposals), on the other by pursuing an active competition policy (not only to avoid anti-competitive positions, denial of access or discriminatory pricing, but also to let market forces shape the overall scheme according to which post-trade securities transactions will be dealt with) while introducing an efficient supervisory regime. In these matters the Commission intends to follow a 'functional' approach that takes account of the diversity of situations in Europe and addresses the same transactions in the same way, irrespective of the type of institution that engages in the transac-

[22] Giovannini Report (n 18) 55, barrier 13.

[23] Giovannini Report (n 18) 57, barrier 15.

[24] Communication from the Commission to the Council and the European Parliament – Clearing and Settlement in the European Union – The Way Forward, COM(2004) 312 <http://europa.eu.int/comm/internal_market/financial-markets/clearing/index_en.htm>.

[25] See for further information <http://europa.eu.int/comm/internal_market/financial-markets/clearing/cesame_en.htm#overview>.

tion. The latter point is of significant importance due to the sharp competitive tension that exists in the European markets between several types of operators and in the face of which regulators and supervisors – including the Commission – should take a neutral stand. In a highly divided market as is the case in Europe, the regulator should not act as an arbitrator of economic behaviour, thereby structuring the market and curtailing competition, but rather let competition fully play its role. In that sense the Commission aptly underlined that it would remain neutral, and that the process should remain market-led.[26]

The Commission's proposals are structured along policy lines, only some of which will be mentioned here: (i) open up access to all operators to securities settlement facilities; (ii) introduce a safe common regulatory and supervisory framework; (iii) right of access and choice; (iv) address governance issues; (v) address legal and taxation discrepancies; (vi) competition issues.

Liberalisation of Access. Under the MiFID, market participants will be granted the facility to access clearing and settlement systems in other states and hence to choose the place where the transactions will be settled. However, access has been opened up for market participants, not for settlement systems, nor for Central Counterparties. If access had not been liberalised for all operators, it might have resulted in multiple direct or indirect links of market participants with settlement locations without the main operators – the CSDs and CCP – being able to connect to each other. It is as if passengers could take all trains, but the different railway systems remain unconnected. Therefore the mandatory connection rule should be extended to settlement systems and to CCPS to get connected to the other systems, allowing market participants to effectively choose to clear or settle in the system of their choice. The competition effects of the rule would be significant: operators would have to offer the most efficient service to be able to outcompete other settlement venues. Over time, this may lead to concentration, as market participants will have an advantage of concentrating their business in one or two operators. Structurally, consolidation should result, thereby eliminating the offer of 25 or more settlement venues, not the most efficient structure.

Liberalisation applies to market participants and clearing and settlement operators, but does it extend to securities issuers? At present, securities are most of the time deposited with the CSD located in the state where the issuer is located. In some systems, this situation may be due to tradition, in others rooted in legal provisions. Once that choice has been made, it is irreversible: if another CSD offered better conditions, the securities could not be relocated to the more efficient CSD. There is therefore no market for CSD services. The situation may be different for bonds – especially for Eurobonds –, where the location has usually been the CSDs that are internationally active, the so called International CSDs (i.e. Euroclear and Clearstream). The Commission's communication announces that it

[26] See Communication (n 24) 10 and 11.

'wants to consider in more detail' this matter.[27] Apart from the direct competitive advantage, for instance on the cost of CSD services, it seems clear that effective competition for CSD services could substantially contribute to the consolidation process and to rendering the overall apparatus for settlement more efficient to the benefit of issuers, markets and investors. A further thought could be given to the provision whereby CSD services can only be offered by CSDs: it is argued that due to the specific risks that are incurred by CSDs, these services can only be offered by an organisation that has a very low risk profile, or even as some present it, is 'risk free'. This transforms CSDs into de facto monopolists, whose pricing power is limited by their ownership and governance structure. Is there any convincing reason why, provided the well identified risks are adequately addressed, these services could not be offered by any other operator in the market e.g. a custodian? The question deserves further detailed analysis.

A Common Regulatory Framework. At present, clearing and settlement services, not being qualified as banking services, fall outside the scope of the harmonisation directives. Hence the rules on mutual recognition do not apply, which leads to allowing for free establishment but only according to the general conditions of the Treaty and, due to the sometimes significant stability concerns at stakes, fully subject therefore to local supervision. National supervisors are not bound by the directives to allocate supervisory responsibility to one of them, e.g. to the home supervisor, nor can they effectively delegate competences to a colleague supervisor. Cross border services can be offered, but only within the limits of the treaty freedoms. Custody services are qualified banking services and hence enjoy the European passport. As banks often offer not only custody but allow securities to be transferred within the accounts they keep for their customers, part of the settlement activity only enjoys the benefit of the European passport.

The subject of supervision is a rather complex one, and raises delicate issues of home and host supervision.[28] It involves, as mentioned above, three lines of supervision: central banks' oversight, securities supervision insuring the smooth functioning of the markets, and prudential supervision, to the extent that institutions – whether or not with banking status – play an important role both in the CSD function, and as custodians. Also, for cross border transactions, the degree of cooperation between these three lines of supervision is quite different: standard schemes have been developed in securities and banking, based on the home country principles, while central banks, due to the specific nature of their intervention and the responsibility attached to it, have refrained from allocating oversight responsibilities among themselves. As a consequence, in cross border matters, each

[27] See Communication (n 24) 25.

[28] See for further details M Tison 'Financial Market Integration in the Post FSAP Era. In Search of Overall Conceptual Consistency in the Regulatory Framework' in this volume 445-466.

of the supervisors involved claim full competency for all matters, leading to rather complicated coordination exercises.

The Commission document proposes to deal with the matter within a Lamfalussy type of procedure, whereby authorisation, regulation and supervision would be delegated to level 2 regulation. It refers to the ESCB-CESR standards as the basis for level 2 implementing measures. This approach can be satisfactory on condition that sufficient guidance has been laid down at level 1, i.e. in the directive itself. The functional approach is thereby the only workable way: otherwise considerable distortions would result, leading to structural changes in the markets.

To deal more specifically with the supervisory cooperation, the Commission's document considers taking the home country model as a starting point.[29] Mutual recognition and the European passport necessarily result. This should be supported: it is of great importance that in these matters, many of which may have systemic relevance, a clear line of command be established, and that especially in case of emergency, decision making, and hence responsibility not be diluted over numerous participants, committees and unclear command lines. However, the Commission's proposal is limited to branches and cross border services: subsidiaries would remain under the supervision of the 'host' Member State, i.e. the state where the registered office of the subsidiary is located. There are solid economic reasons to deal with subsidiaries and branches on the same footing, provided that the consequences of this choice are clearly spelled out.[30] Indeed, from a management point of view, both are identical and the group is managed on an integrated basis.

The attribution of exclusive supervisory responsibility to the home supervisor is likely to raise important issues in the case operations of a securities clearing or settlement operator reaches a size that is likely to create considerable risk in a host state. In this case, information flows would have to be agreed on to ensure that the host supervisor is able to remain sufficiently informed of the evolution of the business affecting directly its territory also in order to evaluate the degree of risk generated. If the volume further increases and reaches a systemic level in the host state, cooperation should be intensified, allowing the host state to be able to follow the decision making process by the home supervisor. Where multiple hosts are involved, a committee structure will be necessary: this can be useful for exchanging information and for reaching common views. However, in order to allow effectiveness of final decision making, the home supervisor should remain empowered to ultimately take the necessary decisions. Procedures such as those presented by the Commission in the proposed directive on capital adequacy could further serve as the basis for discussions in this field.[31]

[29] See Communication (n 24) 19.

[30] See also Case C-442/02 *CaixaBank France v Ministère de l'Économie, des Finances et de l'Industrie* [2004] ECR I-8961.

[31] See Article 129 of the Proposal (n 10).

Another point in the Commission's Consultative paper relates to the need to investigate and if possible harmonise the rules governing the legal status of the securities held and traded with intermediaries. This ambitious project is known as 'legal certainty', almost a contradiction in terms! The Communication rightly recalls those private law rules already introduced in the existing directives, such as the Finality Directive (zero-hour rule, netting, finality) and the Collateral Directive.

However, many further issues remain to be investigated both at the national and – considerably more complex – cross border level, within the EU or outside. Different rules probably lead to a different legal outcome depending on whether the securities are held in physical form, by way of book entry or in dematerialised form; directly and indirectly held securities should further be distinguished. The legal status of the rights of investors to their securities may vary considerably from state to state: full ownership, co-ownership, and entitlement are three oft referred to types of claims on securities deposited, but it is not sure whether the three terms used cover the same legal reality in each jurisdiction. In any case, full protection of securities holders against all adverse claims should be achieved, whether by conferring property rights, or by refusing any claim that may take precedence over the rights of the investor. A well known controversy relates to the date of transfer: is the book entry decisive, or should the agreement to transfer be considered the cut off point at which risk passes? The communication also mentions the upper tier attachment issue i.e. in which a creditor attaches the deposited securities of the bank where his debtor's bank holds its account, thereby in fact seizing the securities of all depositors with that bank. In addition to the private law questions, further clarification is needed regarding corporate actions, i.e. decisions made by issuers with respect to their securities and which affect the settlement as such: payment of dividends, issuance of new securities, takeovers etc. Here, precise rules on the dating of the transaction, but also on recourse on the debtor or issuer, are needed.

To answer these questions the Commission has installed a group of legal experts. Reference is made to Unidroit's work that has to be adapted to the EU context. The matter is considered of considerable importance but due to the diversity of legal regimes, agreements are unlikely to be reached in the short term.

V. The European ESCB-CESR Standards[32]

The CPSS-IOSCO international standards can be considered too general and not particularly appropriate to the specific situation that exists in the European markets. Indeed European markets are characterised by a high degree of fragmentation, calling for special attention for cross border transactions. Some of the

[32] See for the full text <http://www.cesr-eu.org/>

market segments present characteristics that have not been addressed in the international standards. Therefore, it was considered necessary to adapt the international standards to the European scene. This has been done in the Standards for Securities Clearing and Settlement, proposed for adoption in October 2004 by the ESCB, pursuant to a decision by the Governing Council of the ECB and by the Committee of European Securities Regulators. The purpose of the European standards has been to strengthen and deepen the requirements flowing from the international level, and adapt them to the specific market situation in Europe. This process will be examined subsequently.

It is important to clarify what the legal nature of these standards is. A double track analysis has to be followed. On the one hand the Standards answer the needs of the central banks. European central banks require a certain number of legal provisions to be met by banks to allow access to their facilities, especially lending. These are the 'User Standards', which contain the conditions correspondents must meet. At law, the user standards can be analysed as 'contractual conditions', which the banks put forward to offer access to their funds and to operations with the bank. Banks have little choice but to subscribe to these conditions. Central banks however have a wider interest in these standards: as guardians of financial stability they want to safeguard the banking system against systemic disturbances.

From the CESR side, the standards can be designated as belonging to Level Three Rulemaking, according to the now well established Lamfalussy terminology, being the rules agreed on amongst the securities supervisors as the yardstick to be used in developing their policies or upon which their individual decisions will be based in the fields of clearing and settlement. These rules are not binding on the market participants, but on the signatories, viz. the CESR members. It can be expected that signatories will either implement the standards if they have sufficient powers, or if not apply to their legislators to adapt the law.

The European standards are based on the same subdivision of the subject matters as the CPSS-IOSCO recommendations: therefore one finds the same 19 topics, with almost identical headings. Some of the standards have not been adapted, although others have been substantially changed. This approach has been followed to underline that there can be no contradiction between the two sets of standards, so that institutions that meet the European standards necessarily meet the international ones. This feature is not without importance for the assessment procedures.

In many respects the European standards are more detailed and more demanding. This is due to the fact that they apply to developed securities markets, for which the primary need is to upgrade existing practices while preparing the field for intense integration. On other points the European standards reflect the rapidly changing challenges facing the industry: the need for detailed provisions on business continuity and disaster recovery has become more poignant after the events of 9/11 in the U.S..

Differently from the international standards is the provision for each standard of 'key elements'. While the standard itself should be met by the addressee of the standard, the 'key elements' contain more detailed provisions that will be the subject of a specific assessment within the assessment methodology, taking into account the differentiated scope of application of each standard, as indicated in the key element. Each standard is further commented on in a detailed 'explanatory memorandum' which offers a useful description of the field in which the standard is expected to operate.

A major point of difference and of controversy is the scope of application. The European standards apply not only to CSDs, but also to custodian banks and to service providers active for the settlement industry as well. Some standards even call on supervisors and legislators to enact legislation that can support the necessary changes in the system. The question arises how supervisors will enforce standards that are addressed to operators not under their direct supervision, for example in Standard 2 to 'operators of systems for trade confirmation, affirmation, and matching of settlement instructions'. Indirectly, however, the banks, CSDs and other operators that are subject could be urged to call only on service providers that are willing to adhere to the standards and their objectives.

One of the important differences between European and American markets is, for instance, the existence of multiple CSDs, and the fact that some CSDs have banking status.

CSDs play a significant role in securities settlement in many states: each state has at least one CSD, and often more than one for different types of securities (bonds v. equity).

Not only their legal status, but also their factual role differs from state to state. Previously, many of these were state owned, or closely associated to the central banks, and hence enjoyed a strong public interest protection. However, as their function is being better perceived in today's competitive markets, and as the perception of the risks they are exposed to goes beyond mere credit risk – which many CSDs do not incur as they do not engage in lending – the question of their adequate prudential framing is receiving increasing attention. Indeed, most CSDs allegedly do not incur explicit credit risk arising from lending, but they may be exposed to implicit credit risk as a consequence of their normal way of doing business, while their operational risk is not to be underestimated. As a consequence, supervisors are looking closely – and in any case should do so – into the prudential regime applicable to their national CSDs. The supervisory regime applicable to CSDs appears to be rather unclear in many jurisdictions: apart from original registration – sometimes by the law itself – there does not always seem to be a follow up of prudential requirements, if any.

Another feature in which European market structure is specific is the presence of CSDs with banking status. This applies to a limited number of national CSDs (Austria, Hungary) but essentially relates to the two systemically significant international CSDs, the so-called ICSDs. While traditional European CSDs do not manipulate the cash used for settling securities transitions – this takes place at the central bank – the ICSDs as banks receive deposits from their clients, other banks, and give credit in connection with the settlement of the securities transactions, essentially when these take place on their books. Historically this way of proceeding stems from the origins of the Eurobond market, for which these banks acted as CSDs, hence holding the securities on their books, and settling both the cash and the securities legs on their books. As a large part of this market relates to foreign currency, mainly in U.S. dollar, payment could only occur at the ICSD or through the banking sector. The efficiency of the procedure is beyond doubt: both legs can be settled simultaneously, and credit is available when needed. But at the same time, clients of the bank might fear incurring a higher risk, as a failure of the bank might endanger not only their cash holdings, but also their securities deposited with that bank. Depending on the legal rules applicable to that bank, the securities are not in danger: clients should have a claim to revindicate 'in rem' their securities, of which they remained the owners. Nevertheless the failure of the bank may paralyse the settlement operations, and if the system operated by the bank is sufficiently important, this might rock financial markets. In order to prevent this type of systemic risk the proposed European Standards contain detailed provisions with respect to the safeguards that have to be built into the system both at the level of the CSD and of the custodian. This feature was strongly objected to: the industry is of the opinion that the Basel II framework adequately addresses all risks incurred by the banks, and hence no additional requirements can be justified. However, Basel II does not address securities business in particular, and especially does not contain rules on settlement risk. Moreover, as mentioned previously settlement is most of the time intraday, and up to now prudential risks are measured only end of day. Therefore the Standards contain clear language to the effect that on the one hand they will not constitute double use with the Basel II rules, but on the other that the specific risks should be addressed in an adequate way. This is the subject of further investigations.

For ICSD, Standard 9 contains a series of detailed provisions on the way these banks have to mitigate their risks. These provisions focus on collateralisation, but not exclusively. Although collateral is an easy technique of securing transactions, it is inflexible, hence expensive, and may not always be justified. Therefore some flexibility was allowed in the Memorandum, explaining that standard.

Once it was accepted that the risks of ICSDs have to be covered, the same principle should apply to other entities that play a significant role in the overall settlement system. As mentioned, the risks incurred by these banks are taken into account according to the general Basel II rules. In some cases, if the volume of their risk so incurred might reach systemic dimensions, a further analysis should be made of this type of risks. This task will be undertaken within the assessment methodology.

C. Conclusion

The subject of securities clearing and settlement is one of the central points of attention in the Post FSAP Commission action. Is has been dealt with in several international and European working parties. The ultimate goal consists of creating a performing, efficient but safe system for post trade services. There is still a considerable amount of work to be done before that objective is fully reached. But the stepping stones are in place ....

D. Later Developments

The present paper outlines the state of development of this subject about one and a half year ago. It still describes the present status. The ESCB-CESR standards await final adoption probably after the Commission will have published its position about a future directive. Work has been progressing on the Giovannini barriers, on 'legal certainty', on the Hague Convention and at Unidroit. However, in none of the fields a final decision has been reached.

Developments in the markets may change the way the subject will be dealt with in the future, as a consequence of the consolidation of the trading platforms, leading to a repositioning in the post-trade activities. To be followed ....

Structuring Securities Regulation in the European Union: Lessons from the U.S. Experience

DONALD C. LANGEVOORT

Politics aside, the question of whether the EU should create an SEC is about the trade-offs between scale and accountability. This paper considers that trade-off in the U.S. context, with specific attention the SEC's apparent role as a 'global' securities regulator on matters relating to issuer disclosure. The principal claim is that in making enforcement decisions, there will likely be a 'home bias' toward domestic enforcement actions that makes extraterritorial actions less likely, thus reducing the incentives to comply. To the extent that this is typical of regulatory behavior, then there may be lessons for Europeans considering the question of institutional design. More broadly, the paper also considers some of the institutional features that make SEC enforcement policy what it is, which may or may not be exportable (or which policy makers in Europe may not want to import) to the European context.

A. The Primacy of Enforcement
B. The Influences on SEC Enforcement Discretion
C. The Potential for Home Bias in SEC Enforcement
D. Lessons for the EU
E. Conclusion

Much of the rich policy debate in Europe over the appropriate structure of securities regulation focuses on whether there should be a 'European SEC'[1] and is largely about the trade-offs between scale and accountability. Scale has to do with the regulatory authority needed to respond coherently to the needs of issuers and

[1] E.g., G Hertig and R Lee 'Four Predictions About the Future of EU Securities Regulation' (2003) 3 J Corp L Stud 359; Y Avgerinos 'The Need and the Rationale for a European Securities Regulator' in M Andenas and Y Avgerinos (eds) *Financial Markets in Europe: Towards a Single Regulator* (Kluwer Law International 2003); G Thieffry 'The Case for a European Securities Commission' in E Ferran and C Goodhart (eds) *Regulating Financial Services and Markets in the 21st Century* (Hart Publishing 2001); E Wymeersch 'Regulating European Markets: The Harmonisation of Securities Regulation in Europe in the New Trading Environment' in E Ferran and C Goodhart (supra) 189. From a U.S. perspective, see E Pan 'Harmonization of U.S.-EU Securities Regulation: The Case for a European Securities Regulator' (2003) 34 Law & Pol'y Int'l Bus 499; R Karmel 'The Case for a European Securities Commission' (1999) 38 Colum J Trans L 9.

investors in an integrated European capital market and facilitate the building of globally competitive market mechanisms. Here, the argument favors a large-scale regulator because investment and capital market activity in Europe long ago moved beyond the national level and the regulatory issues clearly cross all European borders.

The natural fear, however, is that as regulatory authority scales upward, regulatory accountability diminishes. Part of this is purely political – member countries lose control over securities law policy by ceding it to a centralized authority, and hence the ability to favor or protect particular interests or constituencies. This has fed lengthy debates over sovereignty and subsidiarity in the context of EU economic integration, perhaps mainly by countries that sense more to lose than gain from true integration.[2] But there is a serious normative concern. The choice of a single 'monopolist' regulator raises the risk that the regulatory choices will diverge from the objectives that by most accounts should drive securities regulation: efficiency and (to many, at least) fairness. Hence the interest in systems promoting issuer choice and regulatory competition so as to discourage and limit the effects of inefficient regulation.

None of this is unique to Europe, of course. Academics in the U.S. have for some time explored alternative structures to the scope of securities regulation that would shift authority away from the SEC back to the states, to other countries or to private (or semi-private) structures such as stock exchanges and alternative trading systems.[3] The common assumption of the critics is that the SEC behaves inefficiently too much of the time because of its imperialistic jurisdiction. Their proposals are serious and powerful, although they have gained little political traction even among the likely beneficiaries.[4]

My paper is an exploration of both scale and accountability in U.S. securities regulation, with the hope that some of the lessons may translate well for purposes of European policy-making. It does not try to resolve the ultimate comparative

[2] Although the Lamfalussy procedure moves the coordination process toward greater speed and efficiency, it did not recommend a centralized regulator. N Moloney 'The Lamfalussy Legislative Model: A New Era for the EC Securities and Investment Services Regime' (2003) 52 Int'l & Comp L Q 509. The tone in much of the literature on the appropriate structure of EU securities regulation is pessimistic about whether the politics make such discussion even realistic, though G Hertig and R Lee (n 1) predict some progress. My aim is simply to contribute to the normative discussion, without any reference to political realism.

[3] E.g., S Choi and A Guzman 'Portable Reciprocity: Rethinking the International Reach of Securities Regulation' (1998) 71 S Cal L Rev 903; R Romano 'Empowering Investors: A Market Approach to Securities Regulation' (1998) 107 Yale L J 2359; P Mahoney 'The Exchange as Regulator' (1997) 83 Va L Rev 1453.

[4] See J Coates IV 'Private vs. Political Choice in Securities Regulation: A Political Cost/Benefit Analysis' (2001) 41 Va J Int'l L 531; see also F Tung 'From Monopolists to Markets?: A Political Economy of Issuer Choice in International Securities Regulation' (2002) Wisc L Rev 1363. On the relevance to the European question, see H Jackson 'Centralization, Competition and Privatization in Financial Regulation' (2001) 2 Theoret Inq L 649.

question of the desirability of regulatory consolidation versus competitive fragmentation: that ultimately involves the empirical question of how well market mechanisms can substitute for the loss of regulatory control through either efficient pricing of risk or the development of private institutions for investor self-protection, and there is insufficient consensus about that.[5] My focus instead is an exploration of the status quo – how the SEC deals with the scale it has, and what institutional forces make it more or less accountable for how it performs.

The specific issue addressed here, which has interesting implications for Europeans along a number of dimensions, involves the SEC's credibility as a 'global' securities regulator. Much as been made in both the law and finance literature about the so-called 'bonding hypothesis' – that firms in countries with insufficient investor protection choose to cross-list their securities in U.S. markets so as to submit voluntarily to SEC jurisdiction and hence commit to investors that they will obey a higher legal standard.[6] The implicit assumption (though not a necessary one) is that the SEC enforces its regulation proportionately with respect to both domestic and foreign issuers. Recent high-visibility actions by the Commission in Parmalat and other European scandals would seem to bolster that credibility, which the SEC surely wants to encourage.[7]

My hypothesis, however, is that there is a significant 'home bias' in securities regulation, just as there appears to be in the portfolios of most investors.[8] That is to say, scarce regulatory resources are expended in a discriminatory way, with disproportionately less being devoted to extraterritorial enforcement. A limited body of empirical evidence supports such a bias toward domestic enforcement; one aim for this paper is to explain, within a broader exploration of agency accountability, why it is likely to be a robust phenomenon that says something important about international securities law.

[5] E.g., JD Cox 'Regulatory Duopoly in U.S. Securities Markets' (1999) 99 Colum L Rev 1200.

[6] See JC Coffee 'Racing Toward the Top?: The Impact of Cross Listings and Stock Market Competition on International Corporate Governance' (2002) 102 Colum L Rev 1757; GC Doidge, GA Karolyi, and RM Stulz 'Why are Foreign Firms that are Listed in the U.S. Worth More?' (2004) 71 J Fin Econ 205; GA Karolyi 'The World of Cross Listings and Cross Listings of the World: Challenging Conventional Wisdom' (Ohio St U wp, 2004). The question of whether or to what extent the bonding hypothesis is the best description of the data is contested. For a thoughtful speculation on the feasibility of 'piggybacking' on another regulatory regime, see B Black 'The Legal and Institutional Preconditions for Strong Securities Markets' (2001) 48 UCLA L Rev 781, 816-19.

[7] See M Schroeder and S Ascarelli 'Global Cop – New Role for SEC: Policing Companies Beyond U.S. Borders' *Wall St J* (30 July 2004) A1.

[8] E.g., J Coval and T Moskowitz 'Home Bias at Home: Local Equity Preferences in Domestic Portfolios' (1999) 54 J Finance 2045; G Huberman 'Familiarity Breeds Investment' (2001) 14 Rev Fin Stud 659; K Lewis 'Trying to Explain Home Bias in Equities and Consumption' (1999) 37 J Econ Lit 571. Explanations abound for the home bias, some rational, others behavioral.

If the bias is robust, there are lessons for European policy-makers. First, any temptation to justify a lesser-scale European securities regulator because assertive U.S. regulation compensates for any lingering European gaps would be misguided. Second, my suspicion would be that a home bias would not be unique to the U.S. but rather a common feature of comparative securities regulation. If that is so, then the exercise shows the risk for the EU in relying on a system of country-by-country regulation that is not fully integrated. In the face of a home bias, regulation is unlikely to be applied efficiently to cases where the impact is diffusely multi-national, a phenomenon likely to become more and more common as international securities markets evolve.

I also have a more general aim in this study, whether or not the home bias claim succeeds. Those who either favor or reject the idea of a European SEC sometimes use the U.S. SEC as an archetype for what they want or don't want. The implicit assumption is that the performance of the SEC would be replicated in its European counterpart. But that is likely only if the many institutional features that make the Commission what it is are successfully transplanted. A study of how the Commission makes enforcement decisions can shed light on the agency as an institution, showing just how much transplantation would be required for those who admire the SEC enough to want replication, and what might be altered in the institutional context of a European SEC for those wanting different outcomes.

A. The Primacy of Enforcement

Like all forms of regulation, securities law involves a combination of standard-setting and enforcement.[9] In much of the academic literature on international securities regulation, the former is highlighted and the latter almost relegated to status as a given – it simply presumes that countries enforce what their laws say. This, however, is unrealistic because it ignores the role of limited resources and enforcement discretion (and hence potential bias) in policy implementation, especially when the prevailing standards tend toward ambiguity. On a global scale, a well-known example is in the area of insider trading.[10] In the last decade or so, more than a hundred countries have adopted laws that largely mimic those found in the EU or the U.S., with local variations. As written, many are quite impressive, often far more coherent than the patchwork found in the U.S.. A study by Bhattacharya and Daouk, however, demonstrated that there is little or no positive market reaction to the adoption of these laws measured by changes to the cost of

[9] On the enforcement process, see R Ferrara and P Khinda 'SEC Enforcement Proceedings: Strategic Considerations for When the Agency Comes Calling' (1999) 51 Admin L Rev 1143.

[10] A forceful exploration of this is B Rider 'Policing the International Financial Markets: An English Perspective' (1990) 16 Brook J Int'l L 179.

capital in domestic markets.[11] Only when the country in question begins to demonstrate a credible enforcement commitment (which is fairly rare) does the market begin discounting the risk of insider trading opportunism.

Public securities law enforcement is an intriguing phenomenon, in part because it occurs as seldom as it does. In the U.S., the seemingly aggressive SEC brings only 500-600 enforcement proceedings each year, of which roughly 25% deal with financial reporting and general issuer disclosure.[12] This in a universe of some 17,000 reporting companies, not to mention the thousands of broker-dealers, investment advisers and others within the Commission's jurisdiction. In turn, the vast majority of these enforcement proceedings are settled, meaning that the sanctions imposed are often diluted (if not eliminated nearly entirely, as in many cease and desist proceedings) to strike a deal that obviates the need for costly litigation. Historically, this paucity of enforcement has been seen as the product of severely limited resources. Although the SEC's budget has been increased recently, the amount of the increase still pales compared to the scale of the regulatory task unless one assumes that some other high-powered institutional forces are also strongly at work.

As a result, the Commission staff needs to leverage its resources.[13] For example, it chooses cases carefully for their publicity value, because a front page story creates more salience for the enforcement program than a score of cases that get minor coverage or none at all, even though the severity of the harms may well be the same. The staff's inclination to settle nearly all its cases reflects the view that the publicity associated with numerous settlements, in which the defendants at least cannot deny the wrongdoing and agree to some sanction, is worth far more than one or two hard fought victories in court – not to mention the risk of a well-publicized defeat instead of victory.

Of course direct enforcement is not the only mechanism that exists to induce compliance. Private lawsuits outnumber SEC enforcement actions, though cases are limited to those settings where there is sufficient economic incentive to sue. Compliance is also accomplished by enlisting 'gatekeepers' such as bankers, lawyers and accountants.[14] The standard idea here is that these repeat players have liability and reputational incentives to thwart impropriety by their clients,

[11] U Bhattacharya and H Daouk 'The World Price of Insider Trading' (2002) 57 J Finance 75; U Bhattacharya and H Daouk 'When No Law is Better than a Good Law' (SSRN wp <http://ssrn.com/abstract=558021>, 2005).

[12] See JD Cox, RS Thomas and D Kiku 'SEC Enforcement Heuristics: An Empirical Inquiry' (2003) 53 Duke L J 737.

[13] See Major Human Capital Challenges at SEC and Key Trade Agencies: Hearing Before the Subcommittee on Oversight of Government Management, Restructuring and the District of Columbia, Committee on Governmental Affairs, U.S. Senate, 107th Cong. (2003).

[14] JC Coffee 'Understanding Enron: It's About the Gatekeepers, Stupid' (2002) 57 Bus Law 1403; R Kraakman 'Gatekeepers: The Anatomy of a Third Party Enforcement Strategy' (1986) 2 J L Econ & Org 53.

though some of the impact probably comes simply because when the number and diversity of decision-makers forced to become involved in a particular setting increases, a fraudulent conspiracy becomes that much harder to launch.[15] Moreover, the SEC is adept at harnessing the self-interest of professionals: lawyers, for example, benefit considerably from the perception of substantial enforcement risk and can be expected, on average, to inflate that threat to their clients.[16] In this way, enforcement risk may be amplified.

My point here is only that the Commission allocates its scarce enforcement resources very carefully, and in the next section we will consider how it makes those decisions. For now, what is important is the consequence, which is there will be something of an acoustic separation between the standards that are set and the way those standards are actually enforced. The recent financial reporting scandals and the Sarbanes-Oxley Act offer a good example on the domestic side. As many have pointed out, most all of the substance of the Act (and resulting SEC rules) relating to corporate disclosure practices is an elaboration of standards that were latent in existing law but simply not enforced.[17] The CEO/CFO certification requirement probably imposes little greater liability risk than had been present for a long time in light of the signature requirements for 10-K's and 10-Q's, but the SEC did very little to impose supervisory responsibility on senior officers prior to the scandals.[18] Similarly, the open-ended narrative required by the Management Discussion & Analysis could always have been read to require disclosure of nearly any 'likely' material event necessary to understand why the current financials might not be a good predictor of future performance – a disclosure obligation well beyond how the requirement was actually enforced, at least until Enron and Worldcom.

Even the most controversial of the Sarbanes-Oxley standards, the internal reporting controls provision,[19] is an extension of an under-enforced predecessor with its own statutory origins. In the aftermath of corporate and political corruption scandals in the 1970's, Congress enacted the Foreign Corrupt Practices Act of 1978, which in part requires public companies to keep 'accurate' books and records and have a system of internal accounting controls necessary to assure that corporate assets are properly overseen. Potentially – and probably as intended – it

[15] See N Katyal 'Conspiracy Theory' (2003) 112 Yale L J 1307.

[16] See DC Langevoort and R Rasmussen 'Skewing the Results: The Role of Lawyers in Transmitting Legal Rules' (1997) 5 S Cal Interdiscip L J 375.

[17] E.g., L Cunningham 'The Sarbanes-Oxley Yawn: Heavy Rhetoric, Light Reform (and it Just Might Work)' (2003) 35 Conn L Rev 915.

[18] See L Fairfax 'Form Over Substance?: Officer Certification and the Promise of Enhanced Personal Accountability Under the Sarbanes Oxley Act' (2002) 55 Rutgers L Rev 1.

[19] See M Alles and S Datar 'How Do You Stop the Books from Being Cooked? A Management-control Perspective on Financial Accounting Standard Setting and the Section 404 Requirement of the Sarbanes-Oxley Act' (2004) 1 Int'l J Discl & Governance 119.

was a major statutory incursion into corporate governance. But within a few years, the Commission signaled that it had no intention of enforcing the law to the letter, and relegated internal controls to a lesser subject of regulatory attention until the recent scandals.[20]

The point, then, is that 'regulation by enforcement' is the norm in the U.S. and should be a focus of any analysis of regulatory strategy. That is not in the spirit of former SEC Commissioner Roberta Karmel's criticism of the Commission for subtly *expanding* its jurisdiction through enforcement instead of rulemaking,[21] but rather with respect to the many ways in which the Commission has more or less consciously chosen *not* to be as aggressive as it might.

B. The Influences on SEC Enforcement Discretion

A theory of how the SEC exercises its discretion is helpful not just to predict the likelihood of a home bias in enforcement but more generally for those (as in Europe) who are contemplating the trade-offs between scale and accountability involved in the creation of a pan-European regulatory agency. Unfortunately, while political science offers some tools of interest – e.g., capture theory, public choice models[22] – none is well accepted enough empirically or nuanced enough to offer robust predictions about the SEC in its particularized institutional context. Indeed, differences of opinion about what constitutes 'the public interest' in securities regulation means that there is no agreed-upon baseline against which even to test for systematic departures.

What does seem clear is that securities regulation has a fairly stable base of political support in the U.S., weakening only during strong bull markets. This is not necessarily the product of widespread public influence, at least directly. Except in times of serious perceived scandal – of which the U.S. has probably had only two, once in the 1930's and again briefly in 2002 – retail investors have demonstrated relatively little political clout. Commonly, the external influences on regulation have been more organized: lawyers, the securities industry, the business community, etc. More recently, organized labor, state officials, and state and private pension fund managers have emerged as additional forces with which the SEC must reckon (or with which it can ally).

Within this disparate group of organized interests, there has developed some consensus on the desirability of securities regulation at its core: mandating some

[20] Exchange Act Rel. No. 17500 (29 January 1981).

[21] R Karmel *Regulation by Prosecution: The Securities and Exchange Commission Versus Corporate America* (Simon and Schuster 1981).

[22] See SM Phillips and JR Zecher *The SEC and the Public Interest* (MIT Press 1981); D Haddock and J Macey 'Regulation on Demand: A Private Interest Model With an Application to Insider Trading' (1987) 30 J L & Econ 311; J Coates IV (n 4).

basic disclosure, and sanctioning clear-cut instances of fraud.[23] After all, most securities regulation is just a solution to the economists' lemons problem, and firms (both issuers and those in the securities industry) on the more legitimate end of the scale appreciate a mechanism that helps separates out the lemons from the rest of the fruit. Investor confidence generates wealth for those who supply the relevant goods.[24] The support wanes mainly when the subject of regulation or enforcement is more ambiguous in its utility. The history of U.S. securities regulation suggests that aggressive enforcement has often *increased* during more conservative administrations – perhaps to mask deregulation that is occurring in the regulatory arena.[25] But it is almost always enforcement against behavior that can be portrayed as horribly sour. For example, the SEC received much credit in the 1980's, during the Reagan and Bush administrations, for its aggressive insider trading campaign against the likes of Ivan Boesky, Michael Milken, Dennis Levine and so on. Whatever ones views of the merits, this was a group that could easily be marginalized as 'bad apples' – something which many in the business community were especially happy to see in light of the close connections between the people and firms involved and the facilitating of aggressive corporate control transactions.[26]

It is tempting to describe a form of 'regulatory capture' here, though I do not find the concept particularly helpful as applied to the SEC. It is a familiar problem of pluralism: there are too many well organized interests with conflicting agendas for any one to securely effectuate a capture – the business community shares some goals with Wall Street but is completely antagonistic on others, while the states, unions and pension funds have very different interests. The better image is one of an SEC that regularly bargains with all these groups in the way it chooses to exercise discretion, sometimes conferring favors on one or another to gain something in return. As John Coates has pointed out, for example, the Commission has demonstrated a remarkable willingness to accommodate industry interests in such areas as the adoption of private offerings under Regulation D, the shelf registration process, and Rule 144A (thereby creating a large sphere of deregulated or unregulated capital raising transactions).[27] But at the same time each

[23] See A Khademian *The SEC and Capital Marketplace Regulation: The Politics of Expertise* (University of Pittsburgh Press 1992) 174 (examining the politics of support for the SEC enforcement mission).

[24] Whether an excess of confidence can be a bad thing for investors is the subject of HTC Hu 'Faith and Magic: Investor Beliefs and Government Neutrality' (2000) 78 Tex L Rev 777.

[25] See DC Langevoort 'Managing the Expectations Gap in Investor Protection: The SEC and the Post-Enron Reform Agenda' (2003) 48 Vill L Rev 1139.

[26] For a criticism of the aggressiveness, see D Fischel *Payback: The Conspiracy to Destroy Michael Milken and His Financial Revolution* (HarperCollins Publishers 1995).

[27] See J Coates IV (n 4).

of those concessions is marked by limitations that would not exist were industry demand the only explanation behind them.[28] Much more is going on.

The capture idea is further muddled in light of the extraordinary influence of the legal profession on the Commission.[29] Lawyers dominate the SEC staff, with most senior staff (and commissioners) having a relatively short tenure. This has led some to speculate that there is an agency cost problem here: senior officials will trade concessions to private interests in return for future job or client prospects. Two problems, however, make this problematic. First, the broad consensus among officials needed for significant action makes it hard for one or a handful of officials to push policy in the direction of a particular interest. Second, the dominating strategy for opportunistic officials would instead be to create some new body of regulation that is dense and difficult to interpret or apply, and upon departure claim the rents associated with expert informational advantage. That may lead to more regulation rather than less. The same can be true in the enforcement area: the most feared enforcers are in high demand to shift sides because of their external reputations and credibility with members of the Commission staff who remain behind. To the extent that there is lawyer capture, in other words, it will have a diffuse pro-regulatory bias difficult to square with a simple theory of industry capture.[30]

Lawyers aside, a public choice model is somewhat more plausible, especially in light of the support among the organized interests for a significant baseline of securities enforcement – the amount necessary to signal a credible commitment to exposing and removing the lemons. It is entirely possible that decisions dealing with matters beyond this baseline are largely the products of bargaining with affected interest groups, the outcomes of which will vary with the shifting political landscape and resource needs at any given moment. However, the assumption behind this is an anthropomorphic conception of the SEC as unified rational actor, rather than a bureaucracy. Shift the focus to the bureaucratic nature of the Com-

[28] For example, as much a benefit as Rule 144A has turned out to be, especially in the international sphere, it was heavily criticized initially as too restrictive to do much good. In all these deregulatory initiatives, the Commission has made an effort to retain bureaucratic control over the public markets – and designed the initiatives so as not to threaten the public franchise the Commission has gained.

[29] See H Kripke *The SEC and Corporate Disclosure: Regulation in Search of a Purpose* (Law and Business 1979).

[30] Perhaps the one place where lawyer capture does seem to have diminished the Commission's fervor is in enforcement actions against lawyers. After a period of saber-rattling in the 1970's, the Commission nearly ceased its enforcement activity against lawyers, depriving it of a mechanism for leveraging enforcement resources via a gatekeeper strategy. The Sarbanes-Oxley Act has created the appearance of a step-up in the threat against the profession, though it would probably be premature to predict long-lasting aggressiveness in Commission enforcement in this area.

mission and staff (something beyond the mere fact that five commissioners are involved in formal agency decisions)[31] and the inquiry changes considerably.

The SEC as a bureaucracy is something of a 'black box' that has not yet been opened and systematically explored.[32] To me, an interesting project would be to borrow from an increasingly rich body of work in institutional economics that emphasizes the adaptive role that internal culture plays in organizations[33] to try to predict what features we might expect in a bureaucracy like the SEC. One idea on which this work builds is that cultures operate as a coordination device. In any setting in which coordinated action is necessary among large number of individuals, the 'cognitive environment' must be simplified lest there be endless disagreement among agency actors, which leads to paralysis. By contrast, when there is a shared cultural understanding on key issues, the possibility of productive activity increases. In turn, there is also a motivational element here: to the extent that productive activity consonant with shared beliefs does occur, it legitimates and reinforces the belief system in a way that strengthens the commitment of the actors involved. (Lack of productive activity consistent with these beliefs, on the other hand, is demoralizing – something that the SEC has faced from time to time).

To say that cultures play an adaptive role does not give us any clue as to the content of that cultural understanding, and it is important not to romanticize something like the SEC role as 'the investor's champion' (its motto) as a cultural imperative. But I do think that such a self-image can have traction, especially in the hands of SEC chairmen sensitive enough to tend to it. My prediction is that one would find within the Commission staff a belief system that (a) overestimates the amount of venality and opportunism among business people; (b) underestimates the sophistication of retail investors and the checks on overreaching created by markets and institutions; and therefore – importantly – (c) overestimates the importance of law (and hence the role of the Commission) in creating marketplace integrity.[34] (To be clear, I think there is ample venality in the business community, insufficient investor sophistication, and that law is important – it's simply that those impressions are over-amplified within the SEC culture). A cor-

[31] All formal actions of the SEC are by majority vote at a meeting at which a quorum of commissioners is present. However, the Chairman has executive control over the agency's budget and staffing, and thus has a higher level of working control over the agency.

[32] See DC Langevoort 'The SEC as a Bureaucracy: Public Choice, Institutional Rhetoric and the Process of Policy Formation' (1990) 47 Wash & Lee L Rev 527; Khademian (n 23) 1-5.

[33] E.g., B Hermalin 'Economics and Corporate Culture' in CL Cooper, S Cartwright and PC Earley (eds) *The International Handbook of Organizational Culture and Climate* (John Wiley & Sons, Ltd. 2001); R Cooter and M Eisenberg 'Fairness, Character and Efficiency in Firms' (2001) 149 U Pa L Rev 1719; D Miller 'The Architecture of Simplicity' (1993) 18 Acad Mgt Rev 116.

[34] Certain of these are extensions of predictable psychological biases, a point emphasized in S Choi and A Pritchard 'Behavioral Economics and the SEC' (2003) 56 Stan L Rev 1.

ollary of (c), in turn, is an inflated sense of the contribution that SEC enforcement makes in marketplace integrity. While Commission staff members are well aware of the size and resources of market participants (indeed, take some 'David versus Goliath' pride in the inequity) they believe that they are at least holding their own, and making progress. Maintaining such a belief system to the greatest extent possible is what makes coordination and motivation possible. When doubts creep in – as happened in the 1980's when faith in market efficiency rose in a way that called the SEC's mission seriously into question – the culture turns fragile and matters are opened for renegotiation in ways that diminish productivity.

How might this admittedly abstract portrayal of agency culture affect SEC enforcement choices? Again, I will assume the commitment to the core objective of combating abject securities fraud (significant investment scams, market manipulations, corrupt deceit) when discovered. Beyond that, however, my prediction would be that enforcement choices reflect a balance of attentiveness to the often conflicting demands of the influential constituencies noted earlier and the need to signal a continued commitment to the mythology. Elsewhere, for example, I have argued that the SEC's long standing crusade against insider trading – to which it has devoted time and attention that is probably disproportionate to the economics of the phenomenon – is as much symbolic as substantive.[35] Insider trading cases (especially those involving high status actors) are highly salient, evoking emotional responses from the public that increase the visibility and legitimacy of the SEC's mission. It is an effective form of 'branding' U.S. style securities regulation. To that I would add an internal dimension as well: it is an equally effective way of demonstrating a consistent commitment to the mythology that enables productive activity. Here again the 1980's crusade against M&A based insider trading on Wall Street is a perfect illustration. It came at a time of serious doubt within the agency about the legitimacy of other aspects of securities regulation (especially mandatory disclosure mechanisms), which were at the time the subject of significant deregulation. In many ways, the stepped-up aggressiveness was compensatory, and not just for public consumption.

The foregoing has emphasized a strategic dimension to the choice of enforcement cases, with special attention to the need to leverage scarce enforcement resources. A separate problem is the identification of cases in the first place.[36] The SEC staff and their counterparts at the self regulatory organizations do some real-time surveillance with respect to market manipulation and insider trading, and inspections in the form of both periodic visits of securities firms and 'sweeps' do occur and can lead to enforcement. But the most serious cases of abuse are typically hidden from plain view and come to the attention of the staff only after the

[35] DC Langevoort 'Rereading *Cady, Roberts*: The Ideology and Practice of Insider Trading Regulation' (1999) 99 Colum L Rev 1319.

[36] See DM Nagy, RW Painter and MW Sacs *Securities Litigation and Enforcement: Cases and Materials* (West Publishing Company 2003) 624.

fact, when someone 'blows the whistle'. Actual whistle-blower reports are possible, though the Commission's responsiveness to unverified complaints has been questioned. Short-sellers are also common sources of information of potential wrongdoing, though again the motives here are mixed. In fact, a surprisingly large number of SEC enforcement actions come about simply because the staff reads the financial press: journalists' report on some evidence of fraud or impropriety, and the staff is interested enough to follow up with at least an informal inquiry. To the best of my knowledge, for example, Enron was a story in the press before it was a subject of SEC investigation, as were many of the other recent scandals.[37]

C. The Potential for Home Bias in SEC Enforcement

Based on the foregoing, my prediction is that there would be a systemic bias in favor of SEC enforcement actions directed at subjects with a strong presence in the U.S., as opposed to subjects who operate extraterritorially. Some evidence along those lines already exists: a study by Siegel found only a very small number of actions against foreign issuers over a multi-year period.[38] A close look at the costs and benefits associated with allocating scarce enforcement resources along a number of dimensions suggests that the difference is likely to persist.

I. Costs

The simplest point should be fairly clear: on average, investigating and pursuing a securities claim is likely to cost more when subjects are located in foreign countries. Travel costs will be higher, and the possibility that testimony and documents will be in a foreign language will make the investigation slower and more difficult. Even were the SEC to open branch offices in other countries (as it no doubt someday will), the additional costs will still be considerable. And, of course, to the extent that subpoena enforcement or litigation requires the involvement and cooperation of regulators from another country or the local judici-

[37] For a criticism of the SEC's handling of Enron, see *Financial Oversight of Enron: The SEC and the Private Sector Watchdogs – Report of the Staff to the Senate Committee on Governmental Affairs* (8 October 2002).

[38] J Siegel 'Can Foreign Firms Bond Themselves Effectively by Submitting to U.S. Law?' (MIT wp 2001), discussed in J Coffee (n 6). Interesting, and amply consistent with my analysis, is the fact that more than 40% of the foreign firms in the Siegel sample were Canadian. See MR King and D Segal 'International Cross-Listing and the Bonding Hypothesis' (Bank of Canada wp No. 2004-17 <http://ssrn.com/abstract=555953>, 2004).

ary, there will be another layer of expense.[39] Expense also has a temporal dimension: foreign investigations are likely to take longer, meaning that the opportunity costs associated with committing to a foreign case will be higher. Just from these points, we might predict that given two possible investigations of roughly equal probability of benefit, the domestic matter would likely have the higher expected value.

II. Discovering Evidence of Possible Wrongdoing

In the literature on home bias among investors, one explanation is that in an environment of high information costs, investors will take note of stocks that generate salient news, which is more likely closer to home.[40] The same point, presumably, relates to regulators. Recall that SEC investigations are often prompted by news reports or other salient events. Commission staff members will observe more domestic news than foreign.

We should not overstate this, because there are some simple remedies to overcome an informational bias alone. Some enforcement staff could be detailed to look only for foreign matters worthy of investigation. However, for reasons discussed below, I doubt that the SEC would want to commit to anything that would counter a home bias completely.

III. Benefits: The Diffusion of Interests in a Multinational Setting

Another fairly basic point has particularly interesting implications in a globalized capital marketplace. Consider an issuer with 33% U.S.-based investors. Any benefit from a successful enforcement action goes mostly to non-U.S. investors, even thought the costs will be predominately borne by the SEC. On average, the choice between investment in foreign versus domestic investigations will favor the latter. We have emphasized, however, that investor interests are but part of the story. Perhaps the stock exchanges and the securities industry would pressure the SEC to bring a larger number of foreign cases to assure the credibility of the U.S. 'bond' and so generate more cross-listing and transactional business in the U.S. by foreign issuers.

One response to this is that the diffusion of organized interests in the U.S. is such that these alone would not be enough to offset the economics otherwise favoring a home bias. Moreover, the incentives of the exchanges and securities

[39] And perhaps roadblocks, notwithstanding formal commitments toward cooperation. See A Licht 'Games Commissions Play: 2x2 Games of International Securities Regulation' (1999) 24 Yale J Int'l L 61.

[40] E.g., G Huberman (n 8).

firms is somewhat muddled. The internationalization of the investment banking business makes it so that business is likely to be captured by a small number of multinational firms regardless of location. The exchanges and trading systems have a stronger incentive, because cross-listings do generate listing and transaction-based income. My suspicion, however, is that the technology-driven fragmentation of global trading is severely eroding the economic value associated with 'listings'. As we move toward a point where no single exchange will have a dominating position in the trading of any given stock, the incentives of the exchange begins to look much like that of the regulator. It will have more of an interest in those issuers for which it has the largest market share, less where there is more fragmentation. And if fragmentation comes to be the order of the day generally, then no trading site will have enough incentive to invest heavily in monitoring or enforcement, and the concept of listing as a bonding device will begin to disappear.

The more important point, however, is that stock exchanges have little need to pressure the SEC toward a system of proportionate enforcement in order to gain listing fees. As Jack Coffee has pointed out, even a discriminatory system favoring domestic enforcement can still support a healthy cross-listing environment[41] – the U.S. commitment to enforcement simply has to be better than what is offered elsewhere to make cross-listing worthwhile to issuers from countries with weak investor protection regimes. If what I said above is right that the long-run returns associated with competing for listings are diminishing, then just offering a little bit of enforcement internationally would be a politically stable strategy – strong potential competitors are unlikely to emerge (especially as long as European securities regulation remains fragmented).

My point so far has related solely to the exchanges and their incentives to enlist the SEC on their behalf. In theory, at least, the problems associated with trading fragmentation become less important when we shift our focus away from the exchanges to the SEC itself – why couldn't it rent out its enforcement capacity by creating a fee-funded international division, with fees set high enough to offset the higher costs associated with cross-border work? If the value of SEC enforcement is indeed great enough from a cost-of-capital perspective, enough issuers desiring greater international exposure would presumably choose to commit.

Were the SEC structured differently (and certain other conditions satisfied), there might be something to this. The existing structure, however, creates a different set of incentives, along the lines described earlier. Though it easily could be, the SEC is not a self-funded agency: all fees go to the U.S. Treasury, and the entire budget of the Commission comes via the appropriations process. This is a carefully chosen political solution, one that gives both Congress and the White House more control over the SEC than would otherwise be the case. With that choice made, the SEC's incentives are necessarily political rather than economic.

41 See J Coffee (n 6).

Furthermore, we return to a point just made about stock exchange incentives. The SEC need only offer a little more than other regulators to make the U.S. the cross-listing site of choice for foreign issuers in need of bonding assistance, and in a fragmented but integrated capital market, the likelihood that other regulators will invest heavily enough to compete with respect to issuers beyond their home region is small. Like Delaware in state corporation law, the U.S. may have a lead that is not worthwhile for other to try to erode.[42] If so, then the U.S. is unlikely to incur the costs to implement a more comprehensive system of extraterritorial regulation.

IV. Political and Internal Incentives

At first glance, it might seem that domestic politics would favor the opposite of a home bias. The subjects of extraterritorial enforcement presumably have less political clout than those domestically, so that focusing the SEC's attention abroad would lower the heat here. The answer to this again goes back to our earlier discussion about politics – there is little evidence of the kind of consensus among the organized interests to effectively cause such a result. Indeed, if there is anything to the notion that the SEC adds economic value by allowing good companies to more credibly distinguish themselves from the bad, then the good companies in the U.S. would likely insist on more careful policing domestically, against those with whom the good most clearly compete for capital. Good regulation begins at home, and in the face of scarce resources, may stay there. The securities industry and the exchanges also have good reason to insist on a strong domestic focus – the greatest threat to their reputation (and the portion of their economic rents derived from investor confidence) is the sense that the U.S. cannot even keep its own house in order.

A home bias is also consistent with the SEC's internal incentives. To some extent this overlaps points already made: domestic issues are more visible and easier to address than foreign ones, and more cases can be done domestically than internationally. Because the SEC is anxious to leverage by creating the impression of productivity, volume counts. There are also more subtle points. The internal culture of the agency feeds on salient accomplishments, which are more likely (all other things being equal) when both the impact and the publicity are closer to home. The Commission staff will happily take on a Parmalat-type case – though probably not do enough to expose it in the first place – because it is on a worldwide stage. The less visible foreign issuers are the ones more likely to be ignored.

Finally, there is a disincentive that comes from the demands of cooperation. As is familiar in most all inter-agency turf battles, cooperation requires giving up

[42] E.g., M Kahan and E Kamar 'The Myth of State Competition in Corporate Law' (2002) 55 Stan L Rev 679; M Roe 'Delaware's Competition' (2003) 117 Harv L Rev 588.

control and credit, and bureaucracies do that poorly. Given a choice of an enforcement action over which the SEC can maintain control and one where it will, in addition to incurring significant costs, be forced to act diplomatically and perhaps even dim its own lights to induce continued cooperation, the former is more attractive. All other things being equal, that preference, too, ripens into a home bias.

V. Evaluating the Consequences

All of these points come together to suggest that the SEC's exercise of enforcement discretion – a central tool of policy formulation – will be biased in the direction of more attention to domestic matters. The Commission will continue to police extraterritorially but on a limited basis, with most of the emphasis on 'world class' fraud. In some sense, this prediction is simply that SEC enforcement will mirror what we see on the regulatory side, where foreign actors explicitly face less regulation than their U.S. counterparts.[43]

By hypothesis, this will reduce the deterrence associated with regulation compared to that for domestic actors (which itself is probably suboptimal) unless foreign actors misperceive and overestimate the threat because they are unfamiliar with the enforcement probabilities or something makes up for the deficiency. The former is a possibility, at least early on.[44] The SEC cultivates its role as a tough enforcer through publicity and other means, and lawyers and accountants – who gain from the work generated by a fear of liability – may well over-amplify the message. Over time, however, this misimpression is unlikely to persist. There is substantial evidence in the U.S. that fear of SEC liability rises and falls based on available feedback, such that there will be times when the threat appears extremely remote and noncompliance rates rise. It is hard to believe that foreign issuers will not gradually learn of the differential treatment and adjust their behavior accordingly.

As to the possibility of substitutes, let us assume for the moment that home country enforcement varies significantly and is often inefficient. One other possibility is that private securities litigation can make up the deficiency. U.S. courts have indicated a willingness to apply a fairly liberal extraterritorial scope to Rule 10b-5, though the record is somewhat uneven.[45] Other countries are at least giv-

[43] Though that has changed somewhat after Sarbanes-Oxley. See R Karmel 'The Securities Exchange Commission Goes Abroad to Regulate Corporate Governance' (2004) 33 Stet L Rev 849; M Perino 'American Corporate Reform Abroad: Sarbanes-Oxley and the Private Foreign Issuer' (2003) 4 Eur Bus Org L Rev 213. My prediction would be that the foreign application of these new provisions will be significantly under-enforced.

[44] See J Coffee (n 6).

[45] See generally JD Cox, RW Hillman and DC Langevoort *Securities Regulation: Cases and Materials* ch. 19 (Aspen Publishers 4th ed. 2004).

ing serious thought to liberalizing their class action procedures in the investor protection area, so that the real fear will be of private rather than governmental action. There is at least anecdotal evidence that this is so in the U.S.. My sense, however, is that many of the same biases that affect public enforcement will also affect private litigation, and that it will require a fairly substantial evolution in foreign civil procedure (and the legal profession in many countries) to create an efficient environment for the resolution of multinational frauds. Even in the U.S. – with its very active plaintiffs' bar – the incidence of class actions is limited to larger issuers who suffer big enough price drops to create a credible inference of loss causation.[46] I suspect that given the cost effects, the segment of international issuers that will attract private litigants will be even narrower.

How troublesome this is depends on perspective. If world-wide financial markets efficiently price the risk of opportunism, then a double standard might actually have a virtue, along the lines that Merritt Fox and some others have claimed.[47] Fox argues that countries *should* have a home bias in securities regulation, because pricing efficiencies make investor concerns less pressing. The more important objective is to aid domestic issuers in the capital marketplace by reducing the risk of opportunism, which translates into more efficient allocation of productive inputs. The domestic economy gains to the extent that it does this job of separating lemons from the sweeter fruit.

If one has less faith in pricing efficiency, on the other hand, then the situation is more complicated. The risk is greatest with respect to issuers of ambiguous nationality – an increasingly large class as the world economy integrates. When neither the U.S. nor any other country has enough interest to take lead responsibility for monitoring and enforcement, then it is likely that these firms will fall through the cracks so that gaps in regulatory coverage appear.

D. Lessons for the EU

I. Home Bias

For Europe, the main lessons from this bring us back to both scale and accountability. First, there is no reason to assume that the U.S. is the world's de facto enforcer simply because of the way it has articulated its jurisdiction. Second, so far as the design of a European regulatory regime is concerned, standard

[46] For some data on the selection bias fraud on the market litigation, see S Choi and J Bohn 'Fraud in the New Issues Market: Empirical Evidence on Securities Class Actions' (1996) 144 U Pa L Rev 903.

[47] M Fox 'The Political Economy of Statutory Reach: U.S. Disclosure Rules in a Globalizing Market for Securities' (1998) 97 Mich L Rev 749; M Fox 'Retaining Mandatory Securities Disclosure: Why Issuer Choice is not Investor Empowerment' (1999) 85 Va L Rev 1335.

setting and enforcement cannot be separated without a severe loss of regulatory quality: enforcement discretion is a key standard setting mechanism. And if enforcement discretion has a local bias, then a fragmented system of enforcement will create a series of gaps. As to the EU, if we assume that national regulators will exhibit similar biases, then the absence of a centralized enforcement authority will lead to a great deal of regulatory unevenness – even if there is a high degree of harmonization of the particular standards to be applied. Unless one believes that a newly created agency would over-enforce in a way that is worse than fragmented under-enforcement, the argument would seem to cut considerably in favor of a European SEC.

The same would be true if one accepts Merritt Fox's argument. To the extent that Europe is seriously interested in economic integration, then it becomes important to have a system in place that allocates productive resources efficiently, and does not let one country's firms gain an unfair advantage over others. Lax enforcement in some countries hinders efficient integration. And, of course, there is a risk of enforcement protectionism. Choices either not to pursue a domestic issuer or to deliberately pursue a foreign competitor raise a serious risk, especially in countries with a more concentrated financial services or industrial sector so that the possibility of regulatory capture is greater.

So it seems to me that the normative case for a European SEC is compelling if one assumes the objective of capital market integration, so long as there is a reasonable expectation of accountability from the centralized regulator. I am well aware that such an assumption is questionable, and that practical politics stand in the way of the sense of vision expressed by the Treaty of Rome. Gerard Hertig and Reuben Lee even suggest that though a European SEC is likely to emerge, it will lack serious enforcement powers, at least initially, because those powers are too threatening to particular countries. Based on the analysis here, that would significantly compromise the regulatory apparatus.

II. Transplanting the SEC

Putting aside the specific question of likely home bias, our inquiry into the SEC's enforcement incentives also suggests some lessons with respect to the design of a European counterpart. It is not necessary that we pass judgment on whether the SEC on average delivers high quality regulation, something over which people quarrel.[48] A close look at the Commission points out many of the institutional features that make it what it is. Should it move in the direction of an

[48] A study by Howell Jackson and Eric Pan found a fairly high degree of respect for the SEC's regulation by lawyers and others involved in European capital raising transactions. H Jackson and E Pan 'Regulatory Competition in International Securities Markets: Evidence from Europe in 1999 – Part I' (2001) 56 Bus Law 653.

EU securities regulator, Europe will have to decide how many of these institutional features should be incorporated, and think hard about what it will get if key features are altered. And because of inevitable cultural and political differences, there is a risk that some features may not be transplantable at all. My aim here is simply to review some of those institutional features, leaving to others the question of inter-continental compatibility.

Politics. The SEC's status as a mildly bipartisan, 'independent' regulatory agency is significant. The presence of at least two commissioners from the outside political party creates points of entry and influence for the constituencies that might otherwise be disenfranchised at the time. There is far more transparency in the agency's operations as a result. In this setting, compromise is also more likely – no interest group wants dissenters who will send alarms to their strongest constituents, or generate publicity that risks arousing the investing public. This is a substantial moderating influence.

Drilling down a bit deeper, that moderating influence is in turn the product of interest groups that offset each other. To repeat, retail investors are not influential except in rare political crises. But the fear that they could become aroused in the face of a substantial decline in stock market prices or broad scandals is serious,[49] and no interest group wants to be caught on the wrong side of investor anger. In that sense, broad public participation in the stock markets is very much part of the SEC's institutional landscape. So is the emergence of strong political voices on the investor side, largely associated with labor unions, pension plans and other large institutions. While these cannot dominate and may well have agendas different from the interests of retail investors, they do operate defensively and can bargain for certain policy shifts. Even the business community is far from monolithic – as noted earlier, the securities industry and the issuer community often conflict in their interests, and key members of each group recognize the importance of a solid baseline of regulation to protect against unfair competition by dishonest actors (or to protect against too-easy entry by start-ups). The securities industry, in particular, seems to recognize that investors must be encouraged to invest and feel safe in so doing, and wants the Commission to play an expressive role in creating the right impressions.

My sense is that the SEC would be a very different institution were it not for this diversity of special interests, with substantially less autonomy. Nor would it be anything like it is without the latent presence of broad public shareholdings. On the other hand, the political dynamic is an accountability device, preventing too much of a shift in any one direction. For example, this explains the SEC's willingness to deregulate substantially in 'institutional' markets even though it maintains fairly tight control over access to the public markets.

Economics. Another important institutional feature is that the SEC cannot directly internalize the costs and benefits that it generates; its budget is under Con-

[49] See J Coates IV (n 4).

gressional (and executive branch) control. It must regularly bargain for resources – which are kept fairly scarce – thus making the agency more politically accountable.

Attention to resource needs explains much. The other political branches have only an indirect interest in the substance of regulation, and regularly permit interest groups to intervene. Again, this points in conflicting directions. Members of Congress may well threaten intrusive regulation (even over the Commission's objections) in order to induce political contributions or other forms of support. The SEC then often plays the role of broker, forming alliances and offering more moderate treatment – with large amounts of enforcement discretion built in – by way of alternative. The result can be an enhancement of its own resources plus closer cooperation with the interest groups. Europe would get a very different agency performance if resources were made less subject to these political pressures, or if the political power were more concentrated, as is the case with financial institutions in some countries.

Culture. The SEC has some autonomy because of the conflicting external interests just described, and has developed an internal culture in adaptation to the agency's political and economic environment. The culture – which promotes certain myths about the Commission's function and history – makes the agency more functional because it helps coordinate and motivate behavior that might otherwise devolve into simple bureaucratic slack.

It would be naïve to think that this kind of culture would spring up easily. The SEC's roots were planted in the crisis of the 1930's, with a resulting ideology reflecting the politics of the times. The curiosity is how it transformed once that first generation was gone. Because they play a crucial coordinating role, cultures are 'sticky' – constant change is disorienting rather than stabilizing. But they become routine and less potent unless cultivated. At some times in the Commission's history, strong motivation was provided by a continuing identity of opposition to elite political and economic interests. Some of this was a legacy of talented senior officials whose ethnicity was not as welcome in corporations and law firms as it is today. (Put bluntly, a strong Jewish subculture was a crucial part of SEC history, especially from the period after World War II through the early 1970's)[50]. But precisely because of welcome social change, that oppositional culture diminished, too, although it is not gone entirely.

The question today is what, if anything, still feeds the culture. To some extent, suggested earlier, the cultivation is deliberate: the campaign against insider trading was a way of generating symbolically rich victories for both internal and ex-

[50] Louis Loss tells of having little choice but to seek a government job in the 1930's because of this – leading to one of the most important careers in the history of securities regulation. L Loss *Anecdotes of a Securities Lawyer* (Little Brown & Co Law & Business 1995) 28-29. The legacy of discrimination within legal institutions is a story hardly unique to the SEC, of course. See, e.g., L Caplan *Skadden: Power, Money and the Rise of a Legal Empire* (Farrar Straus Giroux 1993).

ternal audiences. Another possibility, albeit risky, is to harness the fact of staff turnover by creating an internal tournament that rewards short-term loyalty to the Commission's mission by conferring credentials that are readily marketable once the person decides to leave. Once again, aggressiveness and willingness to regulate are adaptive behaviors for lawyers in particular, even if they ultimately expect to be on the other side.

My suspicion is that none of this would be sustainable, however, absent the political conditions noted earlier. A functional SEC is in the interest of many groups, who have to be willing to tolerate the cultural conditions necessary to its productivity. An important mediating role here is played by the legal profession, which has a particularly strong self-interest in SEC productivity – and indeed benefits from SEC aggressiveness. SEC alumni play key roles in working out compromises among interest groups and the Commission, and are the prime facilitators of the transfer of human capital back and forth between the SEC and the private sector. That, too, is an institutional feature without which we would observe very different kinds of behaviors.

Because culture is so multi-factored and path dependent, this is a particularly hard matter to think through in terms of European transplantability. Suffice it to say, however, that institutional design must seek to produce accountability notwithstanding some bureaucratic autonomy from political forces. If culture does not do this, something else must.

The Role of the States. One important institutional feature is something we have not yet addressed. In 1934, Congress created the SEC without taking power away from the states. They continued to have a role with respect to both mandatory disclosure in capital raising transaction (the traditional focus of 'blue sky law') and antifraud enforcement. Over time, that role has diminished. But as New York Attorney General Elliot Spitzer and others have shown recently, it remains potent, and if the states continue to see economic opportunity in securities enforcement, may grow. The political rise of the states' influence in investor protection because of the massive size of their public pension funds is one of the most important stories in the evolution of contemporary securities regulation.

There is an element of accountability here that should not be lost on a European audience.[51] The substantially blurred border between federal and state jurisdiction in securities regulation means that – if the political conditions are right – the states can challenge and compensate for SEC deficiencies. More routinely, the presence of the states also responds to what might be a spillover of home bias. For many of the same reasons, the SEC also exhibits a size bias: except with respect to symbolic areas like insider trading, SEC enforcement cases tend to focus on sizable misconduct appropriate to the Commission's national scale. Many state officials express frustration at the SEC's unwillingness to devote resources to

[51] See R Karmel 'Reconciling Federal and State Interests in Securities Regulation in the United States and Europe' (2003) 28 Brook J Int'l L 495.

smaller-level investment scams, even though the aggregate harm from their persistence is often considerable. Through their own organization (NAASA) state securities regulators have banded together in the last two decades to fill gaps left by the Commission, and it is this pattern of cooperation that has strengthened the willingness to challenge the SEC more aggressively.

Private litigation. One of the surprising features of SEC enforcement is how infrequent it is given the scale of the regulatory task. Constrained resources are an important institutional feature of American securities regulation. Indeed, especially before Sarbanes-Oxley, it is hard to see how there was much of any sense of deterrence from infrequent actions that were typically settled on terms the defendants were willing to live with. In this light, the role played by private actions is important; the number of such actions is greater than the number of public enforcement actions, and the potential exposure greater (putting aside criminal penalties).

As is well known in the U.S., a robust system of private securities litigation is a mixed blessing: some, perhaps substantial, level of speculative litigation results, which costs investors and others a considerable amount while benefiting lawyers on both sides considerably. The right balance of incentives is hard to achieve. However, there is a distinct possibility that without the supplement of easily-invoked private actions, public securities enforcement in the U.S. would require much greater resources to be anything near effective. For Europe, that would mean a choice between adopting the complex set of institutions required for private litigation or substantially more resources for the regulatory agency.

E. Conclusion

Whether Europe should adopt an SEC is a hard question, even apart from the politics. As a matter of scale, it surely should. Indeed, if my point about home bias is generalizable, then even a pan-European scale is too small – and so is the U.S. scale. We should be talking about the need for a world-wide securities regulator, or at least contemplating the costs and gaps associated with not having one.

The issue is accountability, recognizing the ability of bureaucracies to stifle innovation. Unlike some, I do not presume that public agencies governing the capital markets necessarily do more harm than good to economic efficiency unless strongly prodded by powerful incentives. Like all institutions, bureaucracies are complicated and they can, under the right circumstances, be productive compared to other options. Looking at the U.S. SEC, one is struck by the complexity of influences that make it what it is. Whether one admires the SEC or not, we should admit that its replication in Europe would not be particularly easy. For better or worse, a European SEC would be a markedly different creature.

Index

30 (Group of) 474

accountancy profession 79
agency problems 4, 9, 418
Alternative Trading Systems (ATSs) see MTFs
asset management services 397
    investment funds 70, 410 ff
auditor 18, 20 ff
    independence 70

Banking Directive
    Second 453
Basel I 470
Basel II 448, 471
BestEx 281-282
best execution see conduct of business rule
Blue Sky Laws 505

Caixa Bank 460-461, 478
capture risk 411
Centros 61, 104, 112, 124
CESR 187-188, 202-208, 258 ff, 305, 328-330, 339, 370, 382 ff, 456, 478-484
Chinese walls 328, 331
civil law systems 5
clearing and settlement see securities clearing and settlement
conduct of business rules 242, 243, 287, 299, 304, 322 ff, 381 ff, 454, 458
    best execution 165 ff, 202-203, 237, 264, 272 ff, 312 ff, 391 ff
    concentration rule 164 ff, 201 ff, 235 ff, 271, 455
    conflicts of interest 322 ff, 397
        disclosure 325, 330
        identification of 325, 329
        inducements 330
        organization 325, 328
    contract law 300 ff
    eligible counterparties 417
    execution-only 169, 400, 430
    know-your-client 404
    sophisticated investors 432
    suitability rules 307, 391
companies acts 144
comply or explain 122, 131, 143, 148
concentration rule see conduct of business rule
corporate governance
    codes 12, 71 ff, 126, 131, 143 ff
    convergence 4, 21
    economic growth 9
    enforcement of 143, 151
    internal controls 158
    regulation of 143 ff
    risk management systems 158
    statement 150, 158
    voluntary codes 79
corporate law 59, 66
    scandals 70, 85

Daily Mail 112, 126-127
default rules see rules
Delaware 82, 89
dematerialization 467
derivative (and class) actions 71
directors
    board of 150, 159
    election of 79
    executive compensation 78
    stock option compensation 70, 108
    managerial entrenchment 69
disclosure 365 ff
    corporate 76-78, 132, 148
    risk 397 ff
    quote 235 ff, 271 ff
    US regime 354
Distance Marketing Directive 395, 415

E Commerce Directive 415
Enron 75, 86, 409
European Securities Committee (ESC) 187, 236, 395
European Court of Justice (ECJ) 106, 111, 138
executive compensation see directors

FESCO 202-203, 244, 341-342, 389

FESE 216, 254-255
financial services
home and host state supervisory authority 454
fragmentation 164 ff, 202, 242 ff, 274 ff
freedom of establishment 138
FSAP 187-188, 201, 228-229, 340, 381 ff, 443 ff

gatekeepers 489
Giovannini Reports see securities clearing and settlement

harmonization 32, 34, 86, 122 ff, 187 ff, 237, 242, 270, 299, 322-326, 341-345, 388 ff, 446, 471 ff, 504
Hague Convention 469

incomplete contracts 128-129
information
confidential 332, 373-377
disclosure 70-76, 169 ff, 253-257, 269, 321 ff, 365 ff, 391
financial 365 ff
nonfinancial 365 ff
inside 369-372
insider trading 70-76
Inspire Art 61, 93, 104, 112, 125
institutional investors 417
integration
benefits of 200 ff
economic integration 64 ff,
European markets 37, 40-61, 199 ff, 339, 343, 347, 382-385, 444 ff
retail market 383
post trading organizations 213
interest groups 68 ff
internalisation 166 ff, 203 ff, 235 ff, 272 ff, 398-399, 455
client prior consent 286
payment for order flow 272 ff
preferencing 167, 272
systematic internalisers 188, 247 ff, 273 ff
investment
firm-client relationship 300 ff, 382
services 239 ff, 299 ff, 381 ff
investor
choice 389 ff
education 428
enforcement 425
protection 70, 165, 284 ff, 387 ff, 455 ff
retail 286 ff, 382
IOSCO 202, 471-472
ISD 163 ff, 201, 237 ff, 272 ff, 301

Lamfalussy Report 234, 456
Lamfalussy structure 234, 268, 272, 308, 322, 381, 423, 443
legal options (opt-in/opt-out) 119 ff
level 2 measures 268-270, 314-317, 322-328, 381 ff, 444 ff, 478
liquidity 171, 202 ff, 284 ff

mandatory rules see rules
Market Abuse Directive 368 ff
market for corporate law
competition for investments 64 ff
competition for incorporations 81 ff
market manipulation 71
mergers and acquisitions 108
MiFID 163 ff, 205 ff, 235 ff, 272 ff, 299, 382 ff, 444 ff
Multilateral Trading Facilities (MTFs) 204, 237 ff, 272 ff, 321 ff, 455
mutual recognition 326, 346, 452

NASDAQ 172-178, 190, 250-252, 260, 281-282, 294-295
National Best Bid Offer (NBBO) 176-177, 250, 289
National Market System 181, 259-264, 285
NYSE 172-176, 249-251, 269, 276

one-share one-vote 135
equal voting rights 70
order
limit orders 167 ff, 239 ff, 277-280, 295
standard market size orders 291
order handling rules 165, 249, 257, 391 ff
display rule 175 ff, 249 ff
quote rule 175 ff, 249 ff
ownership structure 9-10

pan-European markets 342, 381, 419
Parmalat 75, 85, 336, 425
price
  discovery 164 ff
  improvement 287
  volatility 168
privatization 72-76
professional clients 418
prospectus 339 ff
  Directive 339 ff, 400, 444 ff
  language requirements 341
proxy
  voting 74
  organization 151, 160
prudential supervision 454
public offering 347 ff
  prospectus 70, 339 ff

regulated market 164, 202 ff, 237 ff, 273 ff, 398-402, 457
regulatory
  competition 32 ff, 59, 63, 112, 121 ff, 344, 414
  costs 414, 418
rules
  default 119 ff
  mandatory 119 ff

Sarbanes-Oxley Act 79, 85, 147, 428, 491
SEC 175, 249, 485 ff
securities clearing and settlement 206 ff, 275, 465 ff
  Giovannini Reports 206, 473
  central counterparties 206 ff, 466
  costs of post-trading 226 ff
  delivery versus payment 468
  integration 209
shareholder
  activism 151
  litigation 76
  minority shareholders 160
  protection 77, 92, 101
  rights 74, 99
  value 371-373
Stock Exchanges
  Borsa Italiana 180, 211
  Deutsche Börse 181, 212, 239, 277 ff
  Euronext 182, 212
  Frankfurt Exchange 181, 277 ff
  London Stock Exchange 180, 212, 239
  Stockholm Stock Exchange 219 ff
stock options see directors

takeover 71, 76
  Directive 109, 124-125
  anti-takeover laws 96
  statutes 117
The City Code on Takeover and Mergers 93
Tobin's q 7
trading 70, 163 ff, 398 ff, 456 ff
  costs 217 ff
    explicit and implicit 218
  rules 239 ff, 271 ff, 403
  off-market 271
transparency
  Directive 368 ff
  pre- and post-trade 165, 168, 203 ff, 262, 273 ff

Überseering 112, 124
UCITS Regime 435 ff, 444, 455

Xetra Best 277 ff

yardstick competition 32 ff

Printed in the United Kingdom by
Lightning Source UK Ltd., Milton Keynes
138189UK00005B/142/A